MANAGING NONPROFIT ORGANIZATIONS

Join Us at Josseybass.com

JOSSEY-BASS™
An Imprint of
WILEY

Register at **www.josseybass.com/email** for more information on our publications, authors, and to receive special offers.

Managing Nonprofit Organizations is accompanied by an Instructor's Guide, which is available free online. If you would like to download and print a copy of the guide, please visit: www.wiley.com/college/tschirhart

Essential Texts for Nonprofit and Public Leadership and Management

The Handbook of Nonprofit Governance, by BoardSource

Strategic Planning for Public and Nonprofit Organizations, 4th Edition, by John M. Bryson

The Effective Public Manager, 4th Edition, by Steven Cohen et al.

Handbook of Human Resources Management in Government, 3rd Edition, by Stephen E. Condrey (Ed.)

The Responsible Administrator, 6th Edition, by Terry L. Cooper

The Jossey-Bass Handbook of Nonprofit Leadership and Management, 3rd Edition, by David O. Renz, Robert D. Herman & Associates (Eds.)

Benchmarking in the Public and Nonprofit Sectors, 2nd Edition, by Patricia Keehley et al.

Museum Marketing and Strategy, 2nd Edition, by Neil Kotler et al.

The Ethics Challenge in Public Service, 3rd Edition, by Carol W. Lewis et al.

Measuring Performance in Public and Nonprofit Organizations, by Theodore H. Poister

Human Resources Management for Public and Nonprofit Organizations: A Strategic Approach, 3rd Edition, by Joan E. Pynes

Understanding and Managing Public Organizations, 4th Edition, by Hal G. Rainey

Fundraising Principles and Practice, by Adrian Sargeant, Jen Shang, and Associates

Making Critical Decisions, by Roberta M. Snow et al.

Achieving Excellence in Fundraising, 3rd Edition, by Eugene R. Tempel, Timothy L. Seiler, and Eva E. Aldrich (Eds.)

Handbook of Practical Program Evaluation, 3rd Edition, by Joseph S. Wholey et al. (Eds.)

MANAGING NONPROFIT ORGANIZATIONS

Mary Tschirhart and Wolfgang Bielefeld

JOSSEY-BASS
A Wiley Imprint
www.josseybass.com

Copyright © 2012 by John Wiley & Sons, Inc. All rights reserved.

Published by Jossey-Bass
A Wiley Imprint
One Montgomery Street, Suite 1200, San Francisco, CA 94104-4594
www.josseybass.com

Cover image by Getty. Copyright © by Ashim Mittler, Frankfurt am Main.

No part of this publication may be reproduced, stored in a retrieval system, or transmitted in any form or by any means, electronic, mechanical, photocopying, recording, scanning, or otherwise, except as permitted under Section 107 or 108 of the 1976 United States Copyright Act, without either the prior written permission of the publisher, or authorization through payment of the appropriate per-copy fee to the Copyright Clearance Center, Inc., 222 Rosewood Drive, Danvers, MA 01923, 978-750-8400, fax 978-646-8600, or on the Web at www.copyright.com. Requests to the publisher for permission should be addressed to the Permissions Department, John Wiley & Sons, Inc., 111 River Street, Hoboken, NJ 07030, 201-748-6011, fax 201-748-6008, or online at www.wiley.com/go/permissions.

Limit of Liability/Disclaimer of Warranty: While the publisher and author have used their best efforts in preparing this book, they make no representations or warranties with respect to the accuracy or completeness of the contents of this book and specifically disclaim any implied warranties of merchantability or fitness for a particular purpose. No warranty may be created or extended by sales representatives or written sales materials. The advice and strategies contained herein may not be suitable for your situation. You should consult with a professional where appropriate. Neither the publisher nor author shall be liable for any loss of profit or any other commercial damages, including but not limited to special, incidental, consequential, or other damages. Readers should be aware that Internet Web sites offered as citations and/or sources for further information may have changed or disappeared between the time this was written and when it is read.

Jossey-Bass books and products are available through most bookstores. To contact Jossey-Bass directly call our Customer Care Department within the U.S. at 800-956-7739, outside the U.S. at 317-572-3986, or fax 317-572-4002.

Wiley publishes in a variety of print and electronic formats and by print-on-demand. Some material included with standard print versions of this book may not be included in e-books or in print-on-demand. If this book refers to media such as a CD or DVD that is not included in the version you purchased, you may download this material at http://booksupport.wiley.com. For more information about Wiley products, visit www.wiley.com.

Library of Congress Cataloging-in-Publication Data

Tschirhart, Mary.
    Managing nonprofit organizations / Mary Tschirhart, Wolfgang Bielefeld. —1st ed.
      p. cm.
    Includes bibliographical references and index.
    ISBN: 978-0-470-40299-3 (hardback); ISBN: 978-1-118-25864-4 (ebk);
    ISBN: 978-1-118-23388-7 (ebk); ISBN: 978-1-118-22017-7 (ebk)
    1. Nonprofit organizations—Management. I. Bielefeld, Wolfgang. II. Title.
HD62.6.T785 2012
658'.048—dc23

2012015525

CONTENTS

Acknowledgments ix

The Authors xiii

PART ONE: UNDERSTANDING, ENVISIONING, AND CREATING 1

1 Understanding Nonprofit Organizations 3

2 Effective and Ethical Organizations 11

3 Founding Nonprofits and the Business Case 33

4 Organizational Structure 60

PART TWO: STRATEGIZING, RESOURCING, AND ALIGNING 83

5 Formulation of Strategy 85

6 Resource Acquisition 111

7 Financial Stewardship and Management 140

8 Marketing 168

PART THREE: LEADING, MANAGING, AND DELIVERING 199

9 Boards and Governance   201

10 Executive Directors and Leadership   228

11 Strategic Human Resource Management   255

12 Motivation and Performance   280

PART FOUR: EVALUATING, CONNECTING, AND ADAPTING 299

13 Program Evaluation   301

14 Public and Government Relations   327

15 Partnerships, Alliances, and Affiliations   356

16 Organizational Change and Innovation   384

17 The Future of Nonprofit Leadership and Management   418

Appendix: Mapping of Chapter Content to NACC Guidelines for Study in Nonprofit Leadership, the Nonprofit Sector, and Philanthropy   425

Notes   429

Index   469

ACKNOWLEDGMENTS

We would like to thank the Jossey-Bass/Wiley team for their support and encouragement. This book would not have been possible without the patience and gentle guidance of Allison Brunner, Nathinee Chen, Alison Hankey, Rebecca Heider, Nina Kreiden, Elspeth MacHattie, and Dani Scoville.

Our sincere gratitude extends to Charles Coe and Lynda S. Clair. Charlie expertly drafted the financial management chapter and was a cheerleader during our efforts to finish the book manuscript. Lynda was instrumental in helping us distill complex financial and human resource management topics into material suitable for our audiences.

This book has benefited greatly from the thoughtful comments of reviewers. Their suggestions on content and presentation have helped to improve the chapters and the supplementary teaching materials. We sincerely thank them for joining us on this journey as we worked to meld our individual writing styles and perspectives. We list the reviewers here, along with their institutional affiliations at the time of the review process.

Alan Abramson, director, Center for Nonprofit Management, Philanthropy, and Policy, George Mason University

Rikki Abzug, associate professor, Anisfield School of Business, Ramapo College of New Jersey

Richard Brewster, executive director, National Center on Nonprofit Enterprise

William A. Brown, associate professor, Bush School of Government and Public Service, Texas A&M University

Jeffrey L. Brudney, Albert A. Levin Chair of Urban Studies and Public Service, Cleveland State University

David Campbell, associate professor, Department of Public Administration, Binghamton University, State University of New York

Russell A. Cargo, senior fellow, Midwest Center for Nonprofit Leadership, University of Missouri-Kansas City; principal, Third Sector Services, LLC

Celine Chew, senior lecturer, Cardiff Business School, Cardiff University

Monica Dignam, chief of research, ASAE: The Center for Association Leadership

Mark Hager, associate professor, School of Community Resources and Development, Arizona State University

Margaret E. Harris, emeritus professor, Voluntary Sector Organisation, Aston University, England

Margaret Henderson, director, Public Intersection Project, School of Government, University of North Carolina

Thomas Jeavons, executive director, Association for Research on Nonprofit Organizations and Voluntary Action (ARNOVA)

Kevin P. Kearns, professor, Graduate School of Public and International Affairs, University of Pittsburgh

Jane S. Kornblut, principal, Third Sector Services, LLC

Jack Krauskopf, distinguished lecturer and director, Center for Nonprofit Strategy and Management, School of Public Affairs, Baruch College, City University of New York

Roger A. Lohmann, emeritus professor, Division of Social Work, West Virginia University

Roseanne Mirabella, professor, Department of Political Science and Public Affairs, Seton Hall University

Vic Murray, adjunct professor, School of Public Administration, University of Victoria

Michael O'Neill, professor, School of Management, University of San Francisco

John Palmer Smith, former director, Helen Bader Institute for Nonprofit Management, University of Wisconsin-Milwaukee

Stefan Toepler, assistant professor, Department of Public and International Affairs, George Mason University

Dennis R. Young, Bernard B. and Eugenia A. Ramsey Chair of Private Enterprise, Andrew Young School of Policy Studies, Georgia State University

THE AUTHORS

Mary Tschirhart is a professor in the School of Public and International Affairs at North Carolina State University, and she also directs the university's Institute for Nonprofit Research, Education and Engagement. She formerly taught nonprofit management as a faculty member at Indiana and Syracuse Universities. She is the president of Pi Alpha Alpha, the national honor society for students of public administration. She has served as a vice president on the boards of ARNOVA (Association for Research on Nonprofit Organizations and Voluntary Action) and IRSPM (International Research Society for Public Management), and as Nonprofit Management Section chair for the National Association of Schools of Public Affairs and Administration and chair of the Public and Nonprofit Division of the Academy of Management. She is on the editorial boards of the *Nonprofit and Voluntary Sector Quarterly, Public Administration Review, Public Management Review,* and *Journal of Public and Nonprofit Sector Marketing*. She has also served on the boards of nonprofit organizations and a community library. Her experience includes being the executive director of a statewide nonprofit arts organization and consulting to nonprofit organizations in the United States and other countries. She holds a PhD degree in organizational behavior and human resource management from the University of Michigan, an MBA degree in arts administration, and a BA degree in philosophy.

Wolfgang Bielefeld is professor emeritus at the School of Public and Environmental Affairs and the Center on Philanthropy at Indiana University-Purdue University Indianapolis. He has taught at the University of Texas at Dallas, the University of Minnesota, and Stanford University. He is a former coeditor of the *Nonprofit and Voluntary Sector Quarterly* (from 2005 to 2010) and has served on the editorial board of *VOLUNTAS: International Journal of Voluntary and Nonprofit Organizations*. He has served on the board of ARNOVA and was the program chair for an annual conference of that organization. His professional experiences include serving on the board of Lutheran Child and Family Services of Indiana/Kentucky and consulting for a variety of nonprofit organizations. Bielefeld earned his PhD degree in sociology from the University of Minnesota. He also holds an MA degree in marketing, an MA degree in sociology, and a BS degree in engineering. He has authored numerous articles and coauthored a number of books, including *Nonprofit Organizations in an Age of Uncertainty: A Study of Organizational Change,* which won the 2001 ARNOVA Best Book Award, the 1999 Independent Sector Virginia A. Hodgkinson Research Prize, and the 1999 Academy of Management, Public and Nonprofit Division, Book of the Year Award.

PART ONE
UNDERSTANDING, ENVISIONING, AND CREATING

CHAPTER ONE

UNDERSTANDING NONPROFIT ORGANIZATIONS

It all starts with the mission. Nonprofit organizations have a distinct mandate to be good stewards of the resources they receive toward the pursuit of their mission, whether those resources come in as philanthropic dollars, government contracts and grants, membership dues, or earned income through revenue-generating activities. In this book we focus primarily on how nonprofits pursue their missions in the general social, cultural, legal, historical, and economic context of American life. We offer some examples from other countries and believe much of what we offer is applicable to international contexts. Still, this is a book about leadership and management and thus needs to be embedded in a particular place and time.

The importance of context becomes clear when we look at the competencies proposed in November 2011 for nonprofit managers and leaders by the Non-Profit Management Education Section of NASPAA (National Association of Schools of Public Affairs and Administration). Members of this NASPAA section suggest that students pursuing nonprofit careers should be able to apply knowledge and understanding of

1. The history, values, ethics, and philosophies of nonprofit organizations, and the need for transparency in nonprofit management practices to maintain the public trust
2. The current legal frameworks for operating a nonprofit organization, and the process of forming an incorporated nonprofit organization

3. The fundamental principles and concepts of fiscal management, revenue generation, and fundraising, and the ethical imperative to be a good steward of the financial resources of the nonprofit sector
4. The leadership challenges of the sector as they relate to the strategic management of nonprofit organizations, which requires integrating the roles, responsibilities, and relationships of the board of directors, the executive director, the employees, the volunteers, and all stakeholders in meeting the mission of the organization
5. The human resource and volunteer management principles necessary to manage a nonprofit organization's core services and functions
6. The standards for accountability, performance measurement, and program evaluation, and the appropriate techniques for using both quantitative and qualitative methods to measure the performance of nonprofit organizations

The contents of this book can serve as a foundation for these six competency areas. We go beyond building knowledge and understanding in each area and add additional topics to enhance leadership and management capacity. To orient readers and provide a roadmap of what is to come, we offer a quick overview of each part and chapter.

A Roadmap Through the Chapters

Our comprehensive approach to excelling at managing and leading nonprofits is built around competency and curriculum guidelines developed by NASPAA and by NACC (Nonprofit Academic Centers Council). A summary of the NACC guidelines appears in the Appendix, where they are mapped to the chapters in this book. The six NASPAA competency guidelines have been given earlier in this chapter. Both NASPAA and NACC recognize the importance of understanding the historical development of the nonprofit sector and its values base. These issues are touchstones for our chapters. We discuss how ideas about specific management and leadership topics evolved over time and whether or not they are backed up by theory and empirical evidence. We repeatedly return to the ways in which values influence management and leadership decisions as well as the behaviors of board members, donors, staff, volunteers, and others, and how all this affects the effectiveness of a nonprofit.

As a social psychologist and a sociologist, we are steeped in our respective disciplinary traditions. However, we draw from additional disciplines as well to introduce readers to source documents and thought leaders for the ideas in the book. All our topics and recommendations for practice are grounded in the academic literature. In choosing our main examples we made sure that readers would have enough background information and in some cases even videos for a further exploration of these cases. We also provide additional learning tools in the form of questions for discussion and exercises at the end of each of the main content chapters.

In Part One, we discuss understanding, envisioning, and creating nonprofit organizations. In Chapter One, after this introduction to the book, we give a general overview of the nonprofit sector. In Chapter Two we explore ways to consider the effectiveness of nonprofits and encourage ethical behavior among those working within them. We look at multiple dimensions of organizational effectiveness: goal achievement, resource acquisition, health and efficiency of internal processes, stakeholder satisfaction, and ability to learn and adapt. In Chapter Three we examine topics important to those interested in establishing a nonprofit organization and laying an effective groundwork for future action. We show the many different origins of nonprofits. Drawing on the entrepreneurship literature, we consider how people, capital, and opportunity come together in nonprofits to deliver social value. We also discuss how to make the case for a new nonprofit, including writing the business plan. Chapter Four covers options for organizational structure. We look at formalization, complexity, and other structural elements that influence information processing, and we consider possible structural deficiencies.

In Part Two we turn to strategizing, resourcing, and aligning, because throughout their existence nonprofits should have a mission and a vision and should acquire and manage resources to pursue them. Chapter Five covers the formulation of strategy. Topics include the general strategic orientations that nonprofits adopt and the strategic planning process. We also consider the emergence of strategies in nonprofits. Chapter Six covers resource acquisition. In this chapter we examine the variety of revenue sources employed by nonprofits, including grants, gifts, and earned income. We discuss philanthropy, addressing types of gifts and donors, as well as fund development and grant proposal writing. Chapter Seven reviews financial stewardship and management. We outline best practices for policies, accounting, budgeting, banking, borrowing, financial risk management, auditing, and financial analysis. Chapter Eight provides knowledge and tools for effective marketing. We cover the philosophy of and orientations to marketing, marketing planning, and branding. In addition we explore options for the pricing, promotion, and distribution of goods and services.

In Part Three we focus on human resources and discuss leading, managing, and delivering the mission. Chapter Nine covers boards and the broader topic of governance. We discuss the responsibilities of boards, roles of executive directors in relation to boards, determinants of board effectiveness, options for board configurations and composition, and tools for facilitating governance and managing conflict. Chapter Ten adds leadership and executive directors to the mix. We explore the basis of leadership and the responsibilities of executive directors. We also consider nonprofit founders, leadership transition, and leadership development. In Chapter Eleven we turn our attention to strategic human resource management. We look at ways to measure and build human resource capacity. We then look at human resource management through the stages of initial involvement, development, maintenance, and separation. As a follow-up to Chapter Eleven, in Chapter Twelve we explore performance as determined by ability and motivation. We offer tools to increase ability and to enhance motivation to perform.

Our final section, Part Four, covers evaluating, connecting, and adapting the nonprofit. We begin with program evaluation in Chapter Thirteen. We see an effective program evaluation process as key to accountability management. We review how to prepare for evaluation, choose an evaluation approach, apply theories of change and logic models, clarify program goals, and collect data, all with an eye to meeting the practical challenges to effective evaluation. Chapter Fourteen covers public and government relations. In this chapter we look at image and reputation, strategic communication, and the public relations process. We also cover risk assessment and crisis management. Focusing on government relations, we discuss lobbying and advocacy. Chapter Fifteen covers partnerships, alliances, and affiliations. We examine reasons for collaboration, types of relationships, the collaboration process, and ways to promote successful collaborations. Chapter Sixteen introduces readers to models of organizational change and innovation in nonprofits, external and internal drivers of change, and resistance to change. We lay out strategies for managing change and innovation processes and include ideas on how to generate innovations. In Chapter Seventeen, our final chapter, we consider the future of nonprofit management. We share both our own and others' thoughts on trends in the nonprofit sector and how they may change nonprofit management practices. Our goal is to leave readers with ideas on how they may develop their leadership skills for an ever-changing world.

The Nature of Nonprofit Organizations

This book is not about management and leadership in general; it is about management and leadership in the *nonprofit* sector. Yet it may not be clear what we mean by *nonprofit*, given the many different types of nonprofits in the United States and the alternative terms used to describe the sector.

Although none of these terms describe the nonprofit sector completely, each emphasizes an important aspect of it. The term *voluntary sector* emphasizes that the sector benefits greatly from the work of volunteers. The sector has always been rooted in voluntarism and although the degree of voluntary participation in service delivery and management varies across the organizational types in the sector, all have boards of directors and most do not offer any form of monetary compensation or reimbursement for expenses to board members. *Independent sector,* or *third sector,* emphasizes that the sector is part of neither government nor the business sector, although it may have close relations with both. *Not-for-profit sector* emphasizes the distinction from profit-focused enterprises. *Charitable sector* underscores the sector's role in providing direct relief to those in need. *Philanthropic sector* highlights the fact that many organizations in the sector receive charitable donations. *Civil society sector* emphasizes that many organizations in the sector are the embodiment of an engaged group of citizens with a shared interest in improving their communities. *Tax-exempt sector* points out that these organizations are eligible for exemptions from most taxes. These exemptions are granted to promote activities benefiting the public. *Social sector* captures the role of the sector in enhancing the social fabric. Other countries use yet other terms to describe the organizations that people in the United States call nonprofits. Popular names include *nongovernmental organizations* (NGOs) and *civil society organizations.*

Throughout this book, we use the term most commonly used in the United States, the *nonprofit sector.* It does not mean that the organizations in the sector cannot make a profit. Organizational growth may rely on obtaining more resources than are needed to cover current expenses. What the term *nonprofit* stresses here is that these organizations do not exist to make a profit to enrich private owners, as businesses do. In fact, nonprofits do not have owners or stockholders who are legally entitled to a share of the organization's profits. Any profits made should be allocated toward the accomplishment of the organization's mission.

Diversity in the Nonprofit Sector

In the United States the common feature of all nonprofit organizations is that they qualify for tax-exempt status under the U.S. Internal Revenue Code.[1] Of the close to 1.6 million registered nonprofits in the United States, the majority are *public charities,* about 1 million. This group, exempt under Section 501(c)(3) of the tax code, includes but is not limited to churches, hospitals, clinics, schools, day-care centers, all manner of human service organizations, museums and theaters, and a variety of neighborhood organizations.

Members of this group have broad public support, rather than funding from a single source, and are considered *public-serving* organizations. In Chapter Three we go into more detail on the qualifications an organization must meet to be classified as a public charity. Public charities employ over 7 percent of the country's paid workforce.

The U.S. tax code recognizes twenty-five types of nonprofits, including public charities, the most common type. About 100,000 nonprofits are classified as *private foundations*. These nonprofits make grants to support worthy causes and may operate their own programs using funding from a single source or a small number of sources. Over 500,000 tax-exempt organizations are classified as other types of nonprofits, such as chambers of commerce, fraternal organizations, social and recreational clubs, and business leagues. These nonprofits provide valued services and attract resources as mutual benefit (*member-serving*) organizations. Overall in 2009, registered nonprofits in all Internal Revenue Service (IRS) categories accounted for 9 percent of the wages and salaries paid in the United States.

There is no precise, accurate count of the number of organizations making up the U.S. nonprofit sector. The U.S. government does not require churches and other religious places of worship to register as nonprofits, so it is difficult to get a handle on how many exist. One estimate is that there are close to 280,000 religious congregations in the country, all eligible for the benefits given to 501(c)(3) nonprofits.[2] There are also many grassroots organizations that are not legally incorporated and thus left uncounted. These may be local, volunteer organizations that have a political change agenda or that rely on volunteer workers to care for and help others using little financial capital or physical infrastructure. David Horton Smith suggests that the nonprofit sector also contains what he refers to as deviant nonprofits, such as gangs, cults, covens, and quasi-underground organizations such as the Ku Klux Klan. These organizations operate outside normal conventions and are not legally recognized or tax exempt, but they are like nonprofits in not being organized to make a profit.[3]

A variety of factors account for the existence of this diverse set of organizations.[4] In the early history of the United States, voluntary action was the primary way things got done in communities. Lacking an extensive government and with limited private wealth, citizens voluntarily banded together to deal with social problems. Some nonprofits were established to provide services that neither government nor businesses would or could effectively provide. Nonprofits often function in areas where markets are lacking, such as the provision of food and shelter to those without money to pay for them. In addition, nonprofits provide services that government, with its reliance on voter mandates, cannot. For example, nonprofits provide public health services and education that government is unable to fund with public dollars.

Nonprofits serve a number of other functions. They are an important feature of the U.S. political landscape, providing vehicles for combining people's individual voices and pushing their desires for action. Advocacy nonprofits can be found on all sides of political issues. In this way they contribute to pluralism in the U.S. political system. Nonprofits may also provide people with places to meet and to relate to others who share their interests and values. This gives individuals ways to have fun and to enjoy activities such as sports competitions or cultural festivals. In this way nonprofits contribute to the establishment of social capital and the solidarity of American society, helping individuals to form bonds of trust and reciprocity with others. These bonds make it easier for community members to jointly address matters of common concern. When community members trust each other and can rely on each other to help when needed, joint actions such as community watch programs are more effective. Nonprofits also help with personal development needs. They allow individuals to express their spirituality, creativity, and altruistic impulses and to develop social and leadership skills. At their core, nonprofits nurture and sustain the values and identities of their participants.

Between September of 2009 and September of 2010, 26.3 percent of Americans over sixteen years of age volunteered through or for a nonprofit. In 2010, nonprofit organizations received $290.9 billion in charitable contributions (of which $211.8 billion came from individuals). These figures attest to the importance of nonprofits to the social fabric of American life. Couple this with the financial scope of the nonprofit sector and nonprofits' importance increases. In 2009, the nonprofit sector's share of the gross domestic product (GDP) was 5.4 percent. In that year, public charities reported over $1.41 trillion in revenues. They also held $2.56 trillion in total assets.

Leading and Managing in the Nonprofit Sector

Leaders and managers of nonprofits face a variety of challenges. One of the most important is to keep the mission in mind in all decision making. Nonprofits must operate to fulfill their mission and are limited in their engagement in activities far afield from it. In addition they must keep in mind that the real owner of a nonprofit is the public.[5] It is the public to whom they are ultimately accountable. There are no designated shareholders or owners to please. Nonprofits are subject to the claims, and possible control, of many stakeholders, including donors, clients, board members, staff, volunteers, government at all levels, and community members. The expectations of these stakeholders can vary widely and leaders must balance competing demands.

Lester Salamon and others describe a number of additional challenges.[6] Many nonprofits face fiscal difficulties, some starting with government cutbacks in the 1980s in areas where nonprofits were active. Government assistance has became more targeted and tied to stricter requirements. Not all nonprofits experiencing losses in government funding have been able to offset those losses with growth in private giving or earned income. There is growing competition as more for-profits move into areas traditionally served by nonprofits, such as health care, higher education, and employment training. The rise of B corporations, which are required to make decisions good for society, not just their shareholders, adds to the continuing erosion of sector boundaries.[7] In addition nonprofits are under pressure from funders who are demanding more evidence that the nonprofits they fund are making a measurable positive impact, with some funders seeing themselves as investors with rights to influence strategic decisions.

The legitimacy of the nonprofit sector has been challenged on a number of fronts. One challenge is presented by those who feel this sector is part of an expanding government welfare state and is serving as an instrument of government. Another comes from those who feel it is too professionalized and out of touch with those it serves. These criticisms, coupled with a number of high-profile scandals, have raised public concerns about the nonprofit sector. This confronts nonprofits with a *distinctiveness* imperative.[8] Nonprofits need to reinforce their identity and their worthiness for the benefits and discretion afforded them.

As this short summary of challenges illustrates, today's nonprofit leaders must navigate turbulent waters in the pursuit of their organization's mission. As part of a larger network of actors, some with contradictory views and approaches to pressing social problems, nonprofits are shaping our current reality and our future. Innovations that emerge and are tested in nonprofits will contribute to fundamental debates about what is possible and how to achieve it or avoid it.

We wrote this book with the sincere hope that it will not only provide information and tools to enhance the capacity of nonprofit managers and leaders but also inspire individuals to consider careers in the nonprofit sector. Whether serving in a paid position, as a board member, or as a volunteer, individuals working in the nonprofit sector have the opportunity to act on their values and promote their vision for a better world.

CHAPTER TWO

EFFECTIVE AND ETHICAL ORGANIZATIONS

The Chicago Association of Neighborhood Development Organizations (CANDO) closed its doors in 2002 after suffering disagreement about its mission, difficulty gaining financial support, and disengagement by its members.[1] *Even its leaders questioned the need for CANDO by the end of its last strategic planning process. What happened to this organization after almost twenty-three years of serving neighborhood development agencies and advancing policy benefiting them? On some dimensions the organization was effective. It membership had grown from 20 agencies to over 220. However, this growth may partially explain its downfall as it tried to serve more and more diverse interests. Also, individual member agencies were becoming more powerful, partly due to the successful efforts of CANDO to get them legitimacy and resources. As they became more self-reliant, they had less need for CANDO. Many CANDO members pursued contracts from the City of Chicago, making them reluctant to support CANDO's efforts to aggressively lobby the city for resources and changes. Over time a new generation of leaders, with less fire in their bellies for advocacy and community organizing, took charge of CANDO. Expectations for quantifiable results grew, both for CANDO and its member agencies. In the end, CANDO's lack of focus and expansive, noncontroversial programming left it with apathetic board members, staff, and external stakeholders who lacked the desire to fight for its survival.*

The Baptist Foundation of Arizona (BFA) closed after over fifty years in existence, but not due to the apathy of those associated with it. In this case, fraudulent behavior led to fines and jail sentences for top leaders. When it filed for bankruptcy in 1999, BFA had $530 million in liabilities despite its claims of $70 million in assets.

The BFA had been founded as a financial institution that promised market returns to participants entrusting their assets to the nonprofit to manage. The idea was that BFA would help worthy ministries with resources and expertise while investing participants' funds. However, to maintain an attractive facade for participants, it hid its bad loans and debts; misrepresented its certificates of deposit, thus harming the financial status of elderly clients purchasing the CDs; used a Ponzi scheme, which allowed early investors to make a profit but required a continual influx of new investors to pay earlier ones; sold only the right to occupy property to elderly clients who thought they were buying the property itself; and inappropriately inflated the value of properties. At least one inappropriate transaction personally benefited specific BFA leaders engaged in the activity. Leaders' unethical efforts to keep the nonprofit afloat resulted in losses for many BFA investors.[2]

◆ ◆ ◆

This chapter addresses the question of what makes a good nonprofit. Our opening cases illustrate the difficulty of ensuring that nonprofit organizations are effective and ethical. Multiple stakeholders can pull a nonprofit in different directions and lead to compromises that keep it from excelling. Questions can arise concerning which stakeholders' interests should have the greatest priority and how to handle conflicts of interest. A nonprofit can experience mission drift. In this chapter we explore how to evaluate nonprofits and avoid these difficulties.

Nonprofit organizations directly or indirectly influence many aspects of our lives, including our education, health, spirituality, recreation, security, news and information, safety, consumer behavior, and housing. Nonprofits make significant contributions to the economic well-being of neighborhoods through employment and other activities. The tax and other government benefits they may receive are drawn from public resources. Many nonprofits attract philanthropic dollars from individuals and institutions. Some compete with for-profit businesses for contracts and clients.

Because of the central role of nonprofits in people's lives and communities, as well as the government and philanthropic funds they receive, nonprofits have a heightened responsibility to operate in an effective and ethical manner. Nonprofits that are seen by stakeholders as acting inappropriately or ineffectively are unlikely to be able to attract support. Scandals can raise concerns about the nonprofit sector as a whole, not just the individual nonprofits involved in them.

Given the importance of effective and ethical behavior for nonprofit organizations, we use this chapter to set some foundational ideas for later chapters of the book. First, we examine the multiple dimensions of organizational effectiveness, and then we look at the context for ethical decision making at the personal, professional, organizational, and societal levels. These overarching views lead to implications for leaders who wish to ensure that their nonprofit is perceived as being good as well as doing good. In later chapters we elaborate on the basic concepts presented here. For example, in Chapter Thirteen we go into detail on the technical process for evaluating programs and in Chapter Seven we offer guidance for financial management to avoid fraud and other unethical behaviors.

Multiple Dimensions for Evaluating Effectiveness

In the simplest terms, effective organizations are the ones that accomplish their missions. However, there are numerous reasons why this calculation is often not feasible in evaluating the effectiveness of nonprofits. It may be hard to quantify the achievement of a mission, especially if the nonprofit's purpose relates to intangible quality issues or addresses complex social problems. It is difficult to judge the effectiveness of some nonprofits in the short term. Are nonprofits that are attempting to alleviate poverty or find a cure for cancer ineffective because poverty and cancer have not been eradicated? Can we determine if a nonprofit whose mission is to develop youths for productive roles in society is effective before these youths become adults? We may even disagree on what it means to be a productive member of society. Assessment of nonprofit organizational effectiveness requires multifaceted approaches that acknowledge the challenges of achieving complex, difficult, long-term missions. We also need to recognize that effectiveness assessments may come from multiple stakeholders with different perspectives and potentially competing interests. What looks like an effective nonprofit to one stakeholder may not look nearly as effective to another stakeholder.

We draw from the academic literature to focus on five general and complementary approaches to judging effectiveness that can help nonprofit leaders identify their organization's strengths and weaknesses.[3] The first, the goal accomplishment approach, examines organizational outputs. The second, the resource acquisition approach (sometimes called the system resource approach) focuses on inputs needed by the organization. The third, the internal processes approach, assesses the health and efficiency of internal dynamics as inputs are transformed into outputs. The fourth, the stakeholder approach, looks at the satisfaction of stakeholders inside and outside the organization. The fifth approach examines how well the organization adapts over time.

Goal Accomplishment

One approach to evaluating a nonprofit is to consider how well it meets or exceeds its goals. Goals may be set to encourage a certain level of outputs, such as number of clients served, programs delivered, or service sites added. Unlike the business sector, which can comfortably use profit as a metric for success, the nonprofit sector should be careful to treat the amount of revenue generated or donations received as an input, not a goal.[4]

In the case of CANDO, the nonprofit was a victim of its own success in reaching its early goals to bring more resources for neighborhood development activities to its member organizations and to increase its number of members. As the members became more diverse and less dependent on CANDO, their motivation to support the nonprofit diminished. CANDO struggled to set new goals and find ways to measure its success in reaching them. Members disagreed on CANDO advocacy goals, given their desire to avoid offending the City of Chicago in order to preserve the city's goodwill toward their own organizations. In the end CANDO was unable to demonstrate that it should be kept alive.

Achievement of goals may not indicate achievement of mission. If goals are set and rewards tied to them, staff may change their behavior to achieve the goals and even compete against one another, ignoring the more fundamental mission, and ultimately resulting in the folly of achieving one outcome while hoping for another.[5] For example, a nursing home's goals to build a new facility and expand its number of beds may be met, but the emphasis placed on expansion may undermine the home's mission of providing high-quality care to its current patients. Teachers' desire to meet goals set for student satisfaction ratings may result in teachers who are popular but students who are not well educated.

A nonprofit should set goals that are highly likely to align with its mission. Chapter Thirteen offers a logic model approach that can be helpful in linking goal-related outputs to mission-related outcomes. We recommend that goals be

- **Measurable**. There should be clear evidence available to show whether or not a goal has been met. A goal to provide households with educational materials on nutritious diets is easily measureable, but a goal to change eating behaviors of members of those households is not measureable without extensive research.
- **Time bounded**. It should be clear how long the nonprofit has to achieve the goal. For example, a goal to reduce obesity among young adults cannot be accomplished in a day or even a week. The timeline should be realistic.

Effective and Ethical Organizations

- **Accepted**. Goals need to be clearly understood and accepted by those held accountable for their achievement as well as by those who will be using goal achievement to judge a nonprofit's effectiveness. Consensus on goals can be achieved through strategic planning and performance review processes, as discussed in Chapters Five and Thirteen.
- **Challenging but feasible**. When goals are too easy or impossible, they are unlikely to be taken seriously by stakeholders. A classic goal statement is President John F. Kennedy's address to Congress announcing the goal of sending a man to the moon and back before the end of the decade. Another example of the power of challenging but feasible goals is found in the achievements of the March of Dimes, an organization that started with a mission to eradicate polio and that then, when that goal was reached, set a less concrete but more ambitious goal of preventing birth defects.
- **Prioritized**. Setting parameters on how to pursue multiple goals helps to make clear the policies and codes of conduct that are not to be violated and the resources that will be available for the pursuit of certain goals versus others. For example, a foundation may set a goal to build the capacity of youth-serving nonprofits through its grantmaking but may also limit its reach to a specific geographical area or to what can be funded after other program priorities are addressed.

Resource Acquisition

In addition to looking at goal-related outputs, a nonprofit can evaluate effectiveness in terms of the extent to which it has acquired the inputs needed to accomplish its mission. Following are examples of types of inputs that nonprofit leaders may wish to use as partial indicators of effectiveness:

- **Human resources**: number and quality of staff, volunteers, and board members
- **Financial resources**: number and size of donations, grants, contracts, and sponsorships
- **Capital resources**: facilities, equipment, and materials
- **Knowledge resources**: expertise, information from needs assessments and evaluations, and consulting services
- **Program resources**: participants, waiting lists, referrals, collaborators, partners, technology, programs, and products
- **Community-based resources**: positive media attention, endorsements, and public goodwill toward nonprofit

Counts of resources attracted say little about how those resources are used once they are obtained or what it cost to attract them. Therefore this type of evaluation is best used when the level of a resource brought into an organization can be linked to its actual results. For example, the effectiveness of a health clinic may be judged by its ability to attract top doctors. The quality of the doctors is an indicator of the quality of care received by the patients. A federated funder like the United Way may be evaluated on the amount of gifts it attracts from private donors, because the input of donations directly translates into how much financial support the United Way can provide to other nonprofit agencies.

We can see from the case of the Baptist Foundation of Arizona that a nonprofit's ability to attract inputs is insufficient evidence to demonstrate that it is an effective organization. In the pursuit of inputs, BFA violated sound banking and investment practices. Its inputs were insufficient to cover its outputs, as shown by its liabilities exceeding its assets. It gave out loans that were not repaid or were repaid below the level BFA needed to stay afloat. In the interest of attracting more investments and deposits, this nonprofit misrepresented its products, putting the buyers in financial jeopardy.

It is often easy and expected for a nonprofit to count and report inputs. The inputs may serve as an indicator that those providing the inputs see the nonprofit as legitimate and that the nonprofit has sufficient means to perform well. Annual reports may include number of volunteer hours, amount of donations, length of client waiting lists, and other input measures to show effectiveness. Some nonprofits offer comparative data, reporting how their inputs stack up against those of similar organizations or benchmark standards. Tracking inputs can reveal trends that leaders may want to investigate further. For example, a decline in donations may be examined to see if it is due to fewer new donors than in the past, smaller donations than in the past, or the dissatisfaction of donors with how past gifts were used, or is due to other reasons. Therefore we conclude that inputs provide a useful but limited perspective that can be complemented with other approaches to evaluating effectiveness.

Internal Processes

In addition to evaluations of outputs and inputs, nonprofits may be judged on the efficiency, harmony, and ethics of their internal operations. Does the nonprofit have any bottlenecks that interfere with its delivery of services or production of goods? Are there dysfunctional conflicts? Is there a high undesired turnover of workers due to frustration with assignments, poor morale, or concerns about ethics? Criteria related to this aspect of effectiveness deal with how well the organizational systems are working.

Evaluation using internal process criteria may be especially useful when a nonprofit relies heavily on teamwork or has complicated technology. In these cases, disruptions to the flow of work can have especially large negative effects on the pursuit of the organization's mission.

The case of BFA shows the importance of having checks in organizational systems to catch ineffective and unethical policies and practices. A few BFA board and staff members were able to engage in bad asset management activities for many years without being stopped. Not all BFA leaders agreed with the strategies being used to hide the nonprofit's financial status, but they were unable or unwilling to push for changes. Even Arthur Andersen, the accounting firm auditing BFA, did nothing to reveal or stop the practices and ended up offering $217 million to investors hurt by BFA, to spare itself from further court proceedings.[6] The internal processes of BFA led to its eventual bankruptcy.

A close look at the internal operations of a nonprofit can uncover areas for improvement as well as opportunities for praise. Audits are one means to get a picture of financial operations but, as in the case of BFA, they may be insufficient. Organizational development consultants can provide more comprehensive diagnostics for examining the internal functioning of nonprofits. For nonprofits that cannot justify using external reviewers, toolkits for self-assessment are available online and in print. In addition to revealing ethical concerns, internal reviews can reveal opportunities for improving efficiency—in other words, reducing the inputs needed to generate outputs. However, it is important to see efficiency not as an end in itself but rather as something that should be pursued to carefully steward resources to better achieve the nonprofit's mission. For example, a hospital may be efficient in performing surgeries in that it uses operating rooms and physicians at low cost, but at some point, too much of this efficiency can undermine patients' recovery, which is the outcome of more interest in judging effectiveness.

Nonprofit leaders who wish to demonstrate their nonprofit's effectiveness on this dimension should focus on highlighting good internal management practices. Some nonprofits, such as hospitals and universities, may be eligible to go through certification or accreditation reviews to show that their organization, program, or product meets industry standards or codes. Nonprofits can also compete for awards such as the Malcolm Baldrige National Quality Award, given to U.S. organizations for performance excellence. Evaluation scores, such as cleanliness ratings for restaurants, or formal recognitions, such as a declaration that a nonprofit is a role model for best practices, may also be available to show effectiveness in internal operations. Nonprofits may also offer tours or demonstrations to show off how well they function.

Stakeholder Satisfaction

Numerous parties, such as client groups, employees, volunteers, board members, unions, government regulators, the press, suppliers, customers, donors, contractors, collaboration partners, and competitors may influence or be influenced by a nonprofit organization. These stakeholders have varying degrees of legitimate claims and power to influence the organization's behavior. The relative level of satisfaction of these stakeholders is an additional gauge of an organization's effectiveness.

When we look at CANDO and BFA we see problems with important stakeholders. Without members willing to invest in the nonprofit, CANDO was unable to survive. BFA got into trouble with the government and its investors, who lost an estimated $570 million. Both these nonprofits were able to satisfy key stakeholders in their early years. For example, CANDO helped to improve the economic condition of residents of Chicago neighborhoods, and BFA helped Baptist ministries with funds and expertise. But in the end, the appreciation of what they did for these stakeholders was inadequate for their continued existence.

Some nonprofits' primary function is to provide an outlet for participants' ideas and beliefs. The nonprofit allows volunteers, staff, and donors to express their values, commitments, or faith through their involvement in the nonprofit. For these nonprofits, having high internal efficiency may undermine this part of their purpose. It is less important for a Habitat for Humanity volunteer to use only the number of nails required than for the volunteer to be hammering and thus serving others. Far fewer nails would be used if only experienced construction crews were used on house-building projects. Similarly, community theaters may find a job for all who wish to participate, even if the quality of a production suffers. Advocacy and religious organizations may ask all to join in song at events, even those who sing out of key. The benefit is in the act of joining a community and sharing a common purpose. For these types of nonprofits, stakeholders' satisfaction with their involvement in the nonprofit can be a highly relevant effectiveness criterion.

Using a stakeholder satisfaction approach for evaluating effectiveness becomes more complex as the number and diversity of stakeholders that need to be considered grows. Stakeholders can have conflicting interests and make competing demands on an organization. For example, employees may want higher wages and a nicer work environment, whereas donors may want more of the budget to go to direct program services rather than to administrative overhead and labor and facilities costs.

Effective and Ethical Organizations

Stakeholder mapping is a technique nonprofit leaders can use to identify and strategize about stakeholders.[7] Each stakeholder can be profiled to summarize the nature and strength of its interests or stake in a nonprofit, the legal and ethical claims it can make on the nonprofit, and its relative power. In addition a map can help in exploring what the nonprofit needs from a particular stakeholder that it can or cannot get from other stakeholders. The map also can be used to show relationships among stakeholders in order to better develop strategies for managing groups that share interests and perspectives. Figure 2.1 is a simple stakeholder map with examples of possible priorities for communicating with different stakeholder groups.

FIGURE 2.1. EXAMPLE OF A SIMPLE STAKEHOLDER MAP

Stakeholder Influence on Nonprofit's Policy and Resources ↑	**Keep Satisfied** Housing minister National media Partner organizations	**Key Players** Service users Major funders Local authority Local MP [Member of Parliament] Trustees Local media Staff
	Monitor Wider general public	**Keep Informed** Other funders Local community

Stakeholder Interest in Nonprofit →

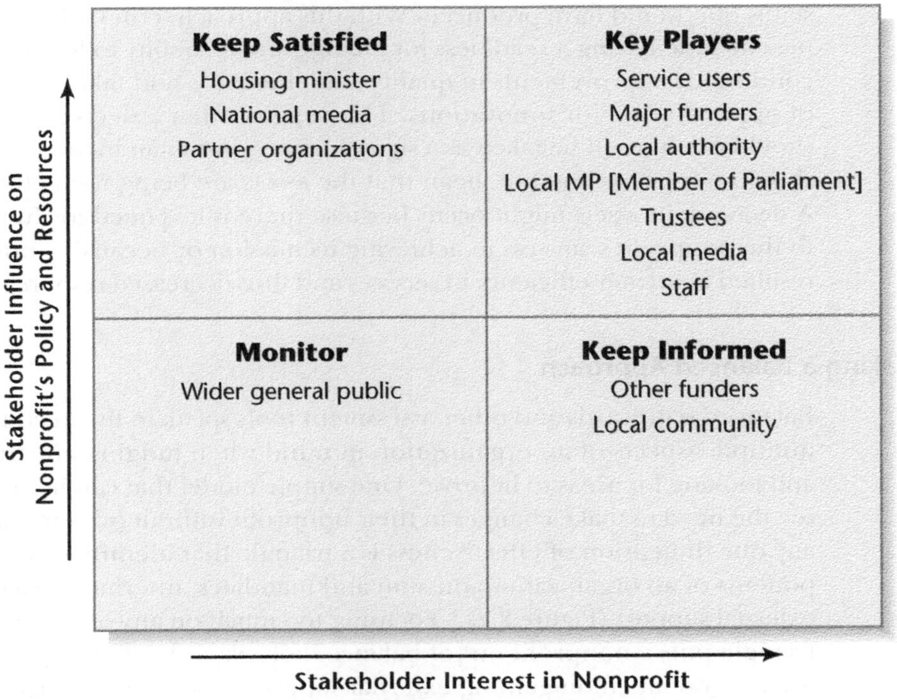

Source: KnowHow NonProfit, "Example Stakeholder Map," http://www.knowhownonprofit.org/campaigns/communications/effective-communications-1/stakeholdermap.jpg/view. Reprinted by permission of KnowHow NonProfit.

Growth, Learning, and Adaptation

As a complement to the other approaches, evaluation can also focus on a nonprofit's ability to respond to internal and external changes as well as its ability to grow and continuously improve. Survival is a crude measure of effectiveness, as is growth in size of staff, budget, and services. Certainly a nonprofit's failure to remain relevant to stakeholders, as in the case of CANDO, may result in closure, but there may be other reasons. For example, a family foundation may decide to spend down its assets rather than use smaller payouts that would prolong its existence. If a nonprofit successfully completes its mission, as the March of Dimes did in its fight against polio, its leaders may choose to change the nonprofit's mission or perhaps, just as appropriately, choose to close.

The ability to adapt in order to capture new opportunities and reduce vulnerabilities and inefficiencies is a better indicator of effectiveness than mere survival but is more challenging to measure. It may be difficult to evaluate whether a change resulted in better outcomes than maintaining the status quo would have produced. With this approach, criteria for effectiveness include having a readiness for change and an ability to learn, making continuous improvements in quality and efficiency, and taking advantage of opportunities for innovations. This suggests that a decrease in assets should not by itself be taken as a sign of failure, just as an increase in assets should not be assumed to mean that the assets are being used effectively. A decrease in assets might occur because there is less need for funds due to the nonprofit's success in achieving its mission or because innovations resulted in greater efficiency in services and thus decreased resource needs.

Taking a Balanced Approach

Balanced scorecards and other assessment tools speak to the need to keep multiple aspects of an organization in mind when judging effectiveness and looking for areas to improve. One simple model that can help leaders see the need to make changes in their nonprofit without overemphasizing any one dimension of effectiveness is a triangle that identifies three components of an organization: mission and mandates, internal capacity, and external support (Figure 2.2).[8] Focusing too much on any one point of the triangle puts a nonprofit out of balance. For example, if an organization focuses too much on gaining external support, it may experience *mission drift*, chasing money or other forms of external support like public accolades rather than pursuing its true purpose. If it emphasizes its mission and mandates without having the needed internal capacity, it may overpromise what it can deliver. If it focuses on building internal capacity beyond what the community needs, it is wasting resources. Preceding its closure,

FIGURE 2.2. TRIANGLE OF ORGANIZATIONAL FOCI FOR BALANCING

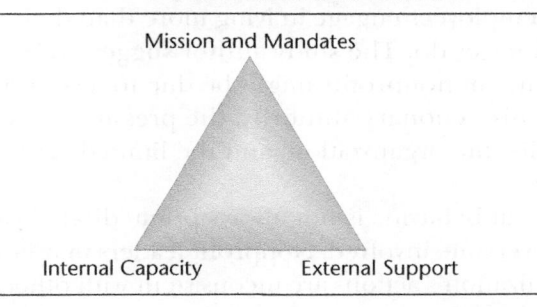

```
                    Mission and Mandates
                            /\
                           /  \
                          /    \
                         /      \
                        /_____\
            Internal Capacity    External Support
```

CANDO was weak on all three corners of the triangle, but its mission was arguably its weakest point. It failed to find a purpose that had adequate meaning for its members, resulting in their withdrawal of support and reducing the organization's capacity.

There are many tools to help nonprofits keep the triangle in balance. For example, perhaps a careful needs assessment would have helped CANDO better align its mission with the interests of potential supporters. The BFA struggled to gain the external support and internal capacity to handle the demands of its asset management services, but if it had had better internal financial controls, and a more feasible strategic approach to growth, perhaps it could have avoided its financial losses.

♦ ♦ ♦

Nonprofit leaders need to manage inputs, processes, outputs, and stakeholders' satisfaction as the organization grows, learns, and adapts to changing internal and external conditions. Use of the various approaches to judging effectiveness helps nonprofit leaders to uncover aspects of a nonprofit that need improvement, such as internal capacity, mission focus, and external support. Choices related to methods of understanding, pursuing, evaluating, and advertising effectiveness may involve ethical dilemmas. Therefore we turn our attention next to ethics for the nonprofit sector.

Ethics for Nonprofits

The news media are full of stories of unethical behavior in nonprofit organizations. The public hears about embezzlement, influence buying, exploitation of vulnerable clients, and other abuses. Rates of misconduct by nonprofit staff were reported to be higher in 2007 than in the previous six years, approaching but not quite matching the frequency reported for the government and for-profit sectors.[9] A 2008 study suggested that nonprofit employees engage in lying more than their counterparts in for-profit businesses do. The study author suggested that the higher prevalence of lying in nonprofits might be due to less bureaucracy combined with more discretionary authority, the pressure to accumulate financial resources for the organization, and the limited career mobility found in nonprofits.[10]

Unethical behavior is not always premeditated or understood to be wrong by everyone involved. Nonprofit leaders may fail to see that their or their organization's actions are inconsistent with others' values and norms or even the law. Ethical dilemmas abound: Is growth for growth's sake OK when the inputs needed for growth could go to other nonprofits? Should nonprofits take donations from institutions that do not express the same values or are working at counter-purposes? How much transparency is appropriate in revealing client or donor information? How should conflicts of interests of board members and staff be handled? What is appropriate compensation for work performed? When is it OK to fire a volunteer or end a program? Should a nonprofit accept funding for a program that is in danger of closing or that is less efficient or effective than one offered by another provider? These are just some of the ethical judgments that nonprofit leaders may face.

Ethical minefields within the nonprofit sector have led to calls for greater accountability, government regulation, protection of whistle-blowers, and codes of conduct, all in the interest of ensuring that nonprofits act appropriately and according to established standards or accepted values. What, then, are the duties and obligations of nonprofits? What, from an ethical standpoint, should take precedence as a guide for organizational action? To begin to address these questions, we look at four levels of ethics: personal, professional, organizational, and societal. At each level there are actors that serve as standard setters, moral guides, and watchdogs. As we proceed through the chapters, we will present resources available to keep nonprofits on an ethical path and to identify ethical dilemmas.

Personal Ethics

Everyone has a personal sense of right and wrong that he or she brings to the workplace. Individuals' values and beliefs about appropriate and desired behaviors are developed through interactions with caregivers, teachers, entertainers, media, family, religious institutions, peers, and others.[11]

Ethical behavior tends to be linked to an individual's demographic and personality characteristics.[12] Youths tend to have less well-developed personal morality systems than adults do and tend to be more influenced by their peers. Researchers have long examined how personality affects ethical decision making. For example, they have found that individuals with an internal locus of control are more likely than those with an external locus of control to consciously make ethical decisions and to resist societal and authority pressures to harm another person. *Locus of control* refers to how much control and responsibility individuals believe they have over what happens to them. Those with a stronger internal locus of control believe they personally have more control and take greater personal responsibility for the consequences of their actions. Individuals with Machiavellian character traits believe that the ends justify the means and are more likely to do whatever it takes to achieve desired results, even if it involves deception and manipulation of others for personal gain. A lesson from the research on what predicts personal morality is that leaders should not assume that because someone is involved with a nonprofit he or she is trustworthy and will know and follow what the nonprofit leader accepts as ethical guidelines. The moral codes of the organization should be made clear to all to whom they apply, and organizational systems should be put in place to prevent and catch unethical behavior.

In some cases, moral codes may be controversial. For example, the Boy Scouts of America makes all Scouts memorize the organization's oath and repeat this oath at Scout events:

> On my honor I will do my best
> To do my duty to God and my country
> and to obey the Scout law;
> To help other people at all times;
> To keep myself physically strong,
> Mentally awake, and morally straight.

The Boy Scouts of America has come under fire for its statements requiring belief in God and its position against homosexuality and its policy of expelling Scouts and troop leaders for lack of conformance. In *Boy Scouts of America et al. v. Dale*, the U.S. Supreme Court, pointing to the right of freedom of association, held that the organization could exclude homosexuals as adult leaders, a reversal of a lower court decision. The nonprofit's decision to interpret its code to allow exclusion of some individuals, despite public and legal protests, highlights how nonprofits may exercise their right to adhere to moral codes within the limits of the law, even if this means excluding individuals who are unwilling to accept the established interpretations of the organization's code.

The work context can affect individual ethical conduct, so it is important for nonprofit leaders to explain and reinforce what is and is not acceptable behavior. Even when individuals are exposed to the organizational leaders' value systems, their greatest allegiance tends to be to their personal values. For example, even if everyone else in a workplace is getting benefits from being dishonest, an individual's personal belief that dishonesty is wrong can be enough to override any temptation to lie.[13] Given the likely variation in personal morality among individuals in an organization, nonprofit leaders should evaluate the work setting to see if unethical behavior is being encouraged by overly high demands on workers that lead them to take inappropriate shortcuts, poor role models for ethical decision making, or compensation systems that make them feel it is OK to take resources from the organization because the pay is too low or because others do so without being sanctioned. The likelihood that employees will behave unethically increases when they perceive that the reward system is unfair, they are under excessive pressure to meet performance objectives, they are part of a group that is benefiting from acting unethically, or they think their leaders do not have a commitment to ethical standards.[14] When some individuals are seen to suffer no consequences from acting unethically, it may also influence others to be unethical, particularly if they do not have a strong internal value system.

Some nonprofits provide tools and training to shape ethical thinking and provide guidance for ethical dilemmas. Reminding workers and board members of professional, organizational, and societal standards and codes can help keep unethical behaviors in check. Though individuals have predispositions to evaluate the ethics of a situation in a certain way, they are open to being influenced by company guidelines, value statements, and codes of conduct.[15] The goals of training should be to

- **Build moral awareness**. Help workers recognize situations involving ethical issues.
- **Frame moral decision making**. Give workers tools to use in making decisions about whether or not actions are ethically sound.
- **Clarify moral intent**. Promote the values that should take priority in making decisions.
- **Encourage moral action**. Explain the consequences of compliance and noncompliance with ethical codes.[16]

Kenneth Blanchard and Norman Vincent Peale offer a simple way to encourage ethical behavior.[17] Adapting their ideas, nonprofit workers should ask themselves three general questions about a proposed action:

1. Is it legal? (Am I violating any laws or organizational policies?)
2. Is it balanced and fair to all concerned? (Will my action create a win-win situation?)
3. How will it make me feel about myself? (Will I be proud of what I have done and willing to tell others what I did?)

If an employee can give positive answers to these questions, the action has passed a very basic ethics test. Nonprofits can further help workers judge whether an action will be acceptable by providing them with more detail on what issues to look at and how to look at them. For example, the World Wildlife Fund (WWF) guides workers' ethical conduct in relation to its various stakeholders by elaborating on its code of conduct for employees in order to address behaviors toward other employees, the public at large, governments and organizations, the media and opinion influencers, corporate partners, suppliers and consultants, and the WWF institution.[18] Focusing on specific behaviors—similar to the ones discussed in this book—the WWF code makes it clear that it is wrong to accept bribes, favor personal connections in awarding contracts, be dishonest in working with corporations, fail to share credit with partners, discriminate against or prejudge others, or be disrespectful.

Professional Ethics

Some nonprofit employees and volunteers are professionals, with a set of norms and rules that obligate them to act in certain ways as members of their specific professions. In the case of certified professionals, breaking professional codes may cause them to lose their credentials and ability to legitimately practice their professions. In the United States, for example, doctors, lawyers, and certified public accountants must adhere to codes for professional practice or risk losing their licenses. Membership in some professional associations is voluntary, and nonprofit workers who join these groups may have a choice of whether or not to be certified by them. For example, not all members of the Association of Fundraising Professionals have earned a CFRE designation (certified fundraising executive). Members with that designation agree to follow the Donor Bill of Rights (see Exhibit 2.1) and the CFRE program accountability standards.

EXHIBIT 2.1. THE DONOR BILL OF RIGHTS

Philanthropy is based on voluntary action for the common good. It is a tradition of giving and sharing that is primary to the quality of life. To ensure that philanthropy merits the respect and trust of the general public, and that donors and prospective donors can have full confidence in the nonprofit organizations and causes they are asked to support, we declare that all donors have these rights:

I. To be informed of the organization's mission, of the way the organization intends to use donated resources, and of its capacity to use donations effectively for their intended purposes.
II. To be informed of the identity of those serving on the organization's governing board, and to expect the board to exercise prudent judgment in its stewardship responsibilities.
III. To have access to the organization's most recent financial statements.
IV. To be assured their gifts will be used for the purposes for which they were given.
V. To receive appropriate acknowledgement and recognition.
VI. To be assured that information about their donation is handled with respect and with confidentiality to the extent provided by law.
VII. To expect that all relationships with individuals representing organizations of interest to the donor will be professional in nature.
VIII. To be informed whether those seeking donations are volunteers, employees of the organization or hired solicitors.
IX. To have the opportunity for their names to be deleted from mailing lists that an organization may intend to share.
X. To feel free to ask questions when making a donation and to receive prompt, truthful and forthright answers.

Source: Association of Fundraising Professionals, "Donor Bill of Rights" (n.d.), www.afpnet.org/ethics. Copyright © 2011, Association of Fundraising Professionals (AFP), all rights reserved. Reprinted with permission from the Association of Fundraising Professionals.

This means that they agree to resign from any organization that attempts to force them to violate codes of conduct for the fundraising profession.

As more certified professionals trained in ethical conduct for their professions enter the nonprofit sector, we may see professional norms and standards spilling over to other job functions. Nonprofit leaders can benefit from identifying the sets of professional ethics that are applicable to their nonprofit's operations. By integrating professional standards for ethical conduct into their organization's behavioral codes, they can avoid conflicts across standards and deepen the guidance they provide to workers.

Organizational Ethics

Nonprofit leaders can foster organizational cultures that reinforce ethical behavior. One of the most influential methods may be to use values-based leadership. Top leaders can be role models for ethical behaviors and ensure that key values are infused into organizational policies and practices. Thomas Jeavons suggests that there are five core attributes of ethical nonprofit managers: integrity, openness, accountability, service, and charity.[19] By personally demonstrating these attributes, leaders set the tone for the rest of the organization.

- **Integrity**: honesty writ large; full and accurate representation in all matters; adherence to professed principles
- **Openness**: transparency about rationales, approaches, actions, and outcomes
- **Accountability**: readiness to explain choices and answer for behaviors
- **Service**: commitment to serve the public good and to the fulfillment of the organizational mission over personal interests
- **Charity**: actualized concern for the welfare of others; treatment of others with love and respect

If leaders reflect these values, and encourage others in their organizations to do the same, they can build and maintain trust in their nonprofits and demonstrate a strong commitment to ethics. Consider the example of the Detroit Zoo. When the zoo director was found to have lied about having a doctoral degree in zoology, the zoo's board decided to let him keep his job if he apologized on the zoo's Web site and accepted the board's decision to dock him for a month's pay of a little over $16,000. The zoo director wrote, "I accept the board's sanctions with the seriousness with which they were given, and hope that my performance going forward will justify that they made the right decision."[20] What message about values and ethical expectations did this send to the rest of the organization?

A variety of organizational structures and systems can be used to encourage ethical behavior and signal accountability. Large nonprofits may benefit from having an ethics committee or ethics ombudsperson to serve as the point of contact and to open an avenue for reflection and debate on possible ethical dilemmas or violations. Job application materials can be screened to weed out candidates with tendencies toward misrepresentation and fraud. Formal policies to support and protect whistle-blowers may help workers feel comfortable with raising concerns and challenging what they view as unethical policies or practices. Reward and punishment systems that are aligned with desired ethical behaviors may help to constrain bad behaviors and motivate good ones. Training programs and orientation manuals along with ethical codes can give guidance on how to handle situations and decisions with ethical implications. Paid employees, volunteers, and board members can be asked to sign conflict-of-interest statements, revealing those areas where their personal interests may conflict with organizational interests. Internal controls can be used to check for compliance with ethical codes: for example, supervisors can occasionally review how and to whom services are provided to make sure that all those who are eligible and able to be served receive appropriate attention from workers.

Societal Ethics

Nonprofits, especially public charities, bear heavy expectations for ethical behavior. These organizations exist because the public and the government expect them to contribute to the public good. Self-serving behavior is antithetical to their roots as counterbalances to for-profit corporations. Societal pressures encourage nonprofits, and those working within them, to go beyond the letter of the law in the ethical level of their governance and operations.

Watchdog groups set standards for the nonprofit sector and monitor behavior. By posting reports on how well nonprofits are meeting these standards, the watchdogs can encourage practices they believe to be good behavior. These groups exist with a focus on particular fields as well as on the sector as a whole. The National Charities Information Bureau, Charity Navigator, the American Institute of Philanthropy, insideGOOD, and the Better Business Bureau Wise Giving Alliance are just a few of the organizations that try to keep nonprofits in check by informing potential donors, volunteers, employees, and others about nonprofits' inputs, processes, and outcomes.

The legal environment for nonprofits also serves as a check on unethical behavior. Nonprofits are subject to many of the same laws that restrict for-profit businesses and have additional rules that address their charitable, tax-related, and lobbying activities. At the federal level, the government attempts to control nonprofits through a range of mechanisms including disclosure and reporting requirements, registration of lobbyists, employment-related laws, tax structures, and federal funding and contracting rules. States may also use tax structures, registration and reporting requirements, contracting rules, employment and lobbying laws, as well as insurance requirements, licensing, fundraising laws, and accounting and audit rules. At the local level, nonprofits may need to be in compliance by obtaining permits, such as parade or gaming permits, and honoring zoning and other codes. They may be subject to local probate court rulings regarding charitable bequests, *cy pres* petitions to change the giving mandates of a grantmaking foundation, and other matters. Lack of compliance with laws and court rulings at the federal, state, and local levels can result in fines and revocation of benefits.

There is continued debate about the need for more regulation to encourage nonprofit accountability. Demonstrating this concern, in 2004 the Finance Committee of the U.S. Senate began holding hearings and asked for proposals for stricter regulation. In 2005, the Panel on the Nonprofit Sector presented a report to Congress promoting the idea of enhanced self-regulation by the sector over increased government regulation and oversight, and in 2007, the panel produced a report with principles for good nonprofit governance and ethical conduct.[21] The topics covered in the report fit four main categories: legal compliance and public disclosure, effective governance, strong financial oversight, and responsible fundraising.

The enthusiasm and capacity for self-regulation by members of the nonprofit sector is mixed. Principles of practice developed by organizations serving as a voice for the sector, such as the INDEPENDENT SECTOR, have not been widely adopted. State-level efforts have seen more success. For example, the *Standards for Excellence: An Ethics and Accountability Code for the Nonprofit Sector,* established by the Maryland Association of Nonprofit Organizations, has many adherents.[22] It has served as a model for other states' efforts to promote ethical practices and accountability. Some trade associations offer accreditation and certification programs for nonprofits.[23] Although they may produce codes of conduct and ask their nonprofit members to adhere to them, monitoring and enforcement mechanisms are usually weak. Though nonprofits may prefer to be responsible for keeping their houses clean, studies showing erosion of public confidence in the nonprofit sector[24] may be the forbearer of increased government scrutiny and legislation.

Countries vary in the extensiveness of their regulatory landscape for nonprofits. The scope and composition of the nonprofit sector in each country varies widely, as do the rules under which that country's government asks nonprofits to operate. In some countries, nonprofits are under a heavy government hand, as in Egypt where government employees are often assigned to work at nonprofits.[25] The requirements for establishment and operations tend to be more rigorous in developed countries and countries where nonprofits get more advantages from government. Some countries, such as the Netherlands, have taken on the task of accrediting nonprofits and encouraging donors to give only to the accredited ones.

Their hope is that nonprofit accountability will be improved when there is a threat of lost donations from lack of compliance with accreditation standards.[26] In some regions the nonprofit sector is being reborn, and with it the legal structures that encourage and constrain it. Eastern Europe, for example, is seeing a revival of interest in nonprofits, as organizations once discouraged in the communist regime acquire renewed legitimacy. The country setting does not affect just the legal environment for nonprofits, it also influences values, norms, and expectations. For example, gift exchange among business partners is considered good manners in Asia but may be interpreted as a bribe in the American context.[27] Nonprofit leaders operating in diverse cultural contexts are likely to find a variety of interpretations of the ethics of situations and should be sensitive to cross-cultural differences.

Concluding Thoughts

This chapter has reviewed effectiveness and ethics for nonprofit organizations. We have argued for a multidimensional approach to judging nonprofits. By looking at nonprofit effectiveness from multiple angles, we gain complementary insights to guide practice and policies. Also, by identifying multiple levels of influence on ethics, we can see how ethical decision making may be shaped by nonprofit leaders. Personal, professional, organizational, and societal values and norms should all be considered in establishing codes of conduct and compliance systems within a nonprofit.

The next chapter explores the founding of nonprofits and the business case. Effective and ethical behaviors are shaped from the first day that a nonprofit is envisioned, and as the organization operates, value systems may become more and more ingrained. Understanding the complexity of judgments of effectiveness and ethics can help nonprofit founders and their successors to identify and address organizational weaknesses and to celebrate achievements.

Questions for Consideration

1. Nonprofits are increasingly being called on to be accountable for the resources and discretion they receive in order to operate. Given the multiple dimensions of effectiveness and the long-term, hard-to-quantify missions of many nonprofits, when should we feel confident that a nonprofit is doing enough good to justify the resources and discretion given it?

2. What basic ethical standards do you think employees should uphold? Are these standards different for people who are working in a nonprofit compared with people in a for-profit organization? Why or why not?
3. What types of information do you think nonprofits should provide to the public in annual reports? What information should watchdog agencies provide on the nonprofits they are monitoring? Can any of this information be misleading in judging a nonprofit's effectiveness?

Exercises

Exercise 2.1: Rough Stakeholder Map

One approach to evaluating effectiveness is to look at the satisfaction of stakeholders. To get a sense of how a particular nonprofit is likely to be viewed by its stakeholders

1. Pick a nonprofit organization and review its mission. List five stakeholders (individuals, organizations, or institutions) that are likely to influence or be influenced by the nonprofit. Be sure to include at least one internal and one external stakeholder.
2. Create a table with the columns shown in Table 2.1 and as many rows as you need, and fill it out for each stakeholder on your list of stakeholders.
3. Now, place each stakeholder into a simple stakeholder map like the one shown in Figure 2.1, showing your designation for that stakeholder (keep satisfied, monitor, keep informed, or key player).
4. Discuss the weaknesses of your analysis and the potential value of a more comprehensive stakeholder audit for a nonprofit.

TABLE 2.1. STAKEHOLDER'S VIEW OF THE NONPROFIT

Stakeholder	What Might This Stakeholder Want from the Nonprofit?	What Does the Nonprofit Want from This Stakeholder?	Type and Degree of Influence This Stakeholder Has over the Nonprofit?	What Effectiveness Criteria Is This Stakeholder Likely to Use to Evaluate the Nonprofit?

Exercise 2.2: Annual Report Analysis

Find an annual report of a nonprofit.

1. What dimensions of effectiveness are covered in the report?
2. What measures are used to demonstrate effectiveness on each of these dimensions?
3. Are these good measures?
4. Does the annual report convince you that the nonprofit is effective? Why or why not?

Exercise 2.3: Situations for Ethical Analysis

Thomas Jeavons argues that nonprofit leaders should demonstrate integrity, openness, accountability, service, and charity. For each of the following situations, consider which of these five values, if any, might be an issue, and describe how the potential issue should be addressed.

1. A nonprofit signs a business contract with the firm owned by one of its board members. The contract was given without competitive bidding, and it is unclear whether the nonprofit could have received the same services with the same quality at a better price from another firm. It is not illegal in the state where this nonprofit is incorporated for board members to have self-dealings (for example, to make a contract with a board member's firm).
2. Volunteers for a nonprofit have access to personal information on donors and are sharing this with individuals outside the organization. They have revealed that a major donor listed as anonymous in the annual report is actually a well-known philanthropist in the area.
3. The annual report for a nonprofit includes photos of individuals who have no association with the organization, but the placement of these photos makes it appear that these individuals were served by the nonprofit.

Exercise 2.4: Multilevel Ethical Influences

Find an article about a nonprofit scandal or controversy, or interview a nonprofit leader about an ethical issue the leader faced. How did the ethical standards and values of each of the levels discussed in this chapter—personal, professional, organizational, and societal—come into play in the situation?

CHAPTER THREE

FOUNDING NONPROFITS AND THE BUSINESS CASE

Featured as one of twelve high-impact nonprofits in a best-selling business book,[1] Teach For America is a poster child for a successful nonprofit. What may be surprising is that the idea for the organization was developed in 1989 by a student at Princeton University for her undergraduate thesis. Founder Wendy Kopp didn't treat her thesis just as an academic exercise. She raised $2.5 million in start-up funding, filled out the paperwork to legally establish the nonprofit, and in 1990, began the organization's work with a small staff. Today, Teach For America reaches more than 400,000 students across the country. Kopp's idea that top college students would choose to teach in public schools if they thought they could make a real difference had resonance with a wide range of supporters and with the college students she succeeded in recruiting and developing into leaders for education reform. Kopp put in long hours to grow the organization, wondering at times if it would survive and adapting it to meet a series of challenges. It is now the largest source of teachers for low-income communities. She has written two books that help tell the story of Teach For America and its founding impulse to eliminate educational inequity in the United States.[2] As a well-known social entrepreneur, Wendy Kopp has been a speaker at numerous seminars where she has encouraged others to pursue their ideas for new nonprofits. In a YouTube video she gives advice to entrepreneurs including "embrace your inexperience" and "search for allies."[3]

◆ ◆ ◆

Many nonprofits are started every year, a small percentage of them by college students who, like Wendy Kopp, develop their ideas in courses or through service-learning experiences. In the United States the nonprofit sector is growing faster than the government or business sector.[4] Data from other countries also indicate the popularity of the nonprofit form of organization.[5]

How do nonprofit organizations get started? What is the business case for them? What factors support or hinder social entrepreneurs? What steps need to be taken to successfully launch a new nonprofit organization? This chapter will address these and related questions. More details on the entrepreneurial process and social entrepreneurship in relationship to program and process innovations are covered in Chapter Sixteen, on organizational change and innovation. Here we focus on the entrepreneurial move to create a new nonprofit organization.

Organizational Founding

Nonprofits, unlike biological entities, do not always have a clear birth date. An organization may receive legal recognition years after it began to serve the public. Legal recognition might also come before a nonprofit has carried out any mission-related activities, held its first board retreat, or opened a bank account. In this chapter we explore organizational founding, that is, birth, as one of the key stages of a nonprofit's existence.[6]

What happens when an organization is first established can shape its nature for its entire existence. A founder may imprint norms and values that are hard to change, even after that founder leaves.[7] Founders may determine how and to what extent the original mission can be altered. The governing board, initially chosen by the founder, may be more committed to the founder than to the organization and unwilling to challenge the founder's wishes. The identity of the organization may become tied to the founder, making it difficult for a successor to be accepted or to change the ways in which the founder managed or led the nonprofit. Over time the founder may actually harm the long-term health of the organization because of his or her central role and inability to give up control, a problem sometimes called *founder's syndrome.*

Also, new nonprofits shape the collaborative and competitive environment around them. Other organizations may need to adapt in response to this new entrant in their field of activity. The entrant may be an *innovator organization,* introducing new ideas to the field, or a *reproducer,* replicating what others are already doing.[8] Teach For America was an innovator, changing the way college students got involved in teaching, and pushing a school reform agenda. As a consequence of its presence as a source of teachers, schools changed their practices in order to capture and leverage this new resource. Reproducers are new nonprofits that follow an established model, such as new additions to the Habitat for Humanity chapter network, private schools that are part of a national chain, and nonprofits that are similar in missions and approaches to other nonprofits that already exist in their communities.

Organizations can be founded in a number of ways. For example, organizations may be created by an individual entrepreneur with a new idea acting outside any existing organization, as in the case of Teach For America. They may be established through legislative action, as in the case of the American Red Cross, which was founded in 1881 by Clara Barton and a circle of her acquaintances and modeled after the International Red Cross. One of the oldest nonprofits in the United States, Harvard University, was established in 1636 by a vote of the Great and General Court of the Massachusetts Bay Colony. Nonprofits may be spun off from a larger, parent nonprofit, as in the case of churches that spring from a parent congregation, or federated associations that set up chapters or affiliates. The American Cancer Society, for example, established local chapters and then, years later, transformed these local chapters into regional organizations.[9]

Some organizational transformations are so profound and radical that it can appear that one organization died and a fundamentally new one was born, though the original name and legal status may be retained. For example, Anthony Filipovitch describes the transformation of a volunteer-run community crisis care center into a community medical clinic.[10] The organization moved from crisis care to chronic care, volunteers to paid staff, paper records to an integrated management information system, and per-visit medical care to an integrated case management system. Very little of the old organization was retained.

A number of environmental and individual factors are necessary for organizational founding and initial survival.[11] Supportive environments offer resources, technology, rules, norms, and beliefs that allow a nonprofit's establishment.[12] Research that examines the founding process through an entrepreneurship lens highlights helpful personal dispositions, traits, or attributes of entrepreneurs (founders) as well as what makes a nurturing context for the entrepreneurial process.[13] In general this research reveals that founders are most successful in creating and keeping their organizations alive in infancy when they can access needed resources, operate under supportive government policies, and employ the discretion that comes with having a purpose and approach perceived by the public as legitimate. It is also helpful if they recognize and adopt strategies appropriate for the nonprofit's environmental conditions.[14]

Entrepreneurship for Social Benefit

Although the term *entrepreneurship* was first defined in the 1700s, to date there is no single widely accepted definition of the term. The economist Richard Cantillon (circa 1730) defined *entrepreneurship* as self-employment. Following this orientation, Jean Baptiste Say, in 1816, defined the *entrepreneur* as one who uses all means of production to create profit through the value of the products thereby produced. The focus of these and related definitions is on the savvy businessperson seeking to exploit an opportunity to make a profit.

An alternative orientation to entrepreneurship was put forth by Joseph Schumpeter in the 1930s. Schumpeter's focus was on the entrepreneur as an innovator, on the creative drive itself, and on the impacts of entrepreneurship on industry and the economy, particularly on the "creative destruction" of industries and their replacement by new ones. This macro interpretation is especially important in that the goal of many social entrepreneurs is to address and correct major social problems by means of innovations that have large-scale, transformative social impacts.

In 1986, Dennis Young helped turn attention to entrepreneurship in the nonprofit sector. He distinguished nonprofit entrepreneurs from other nonprofit managers by the entrepreneurs' engagement in breaking new ground and going beyond customary managerial practices or ordinary decision making.[15] Thus, entrepreneurs are those innovators who found an organization, develop or expand programs and services, create new methods, or redirect the mission of a nonprofit. Consistent with Young's conceptual treatment, entrepreneurship can occur within organizations (sometimes referred to as *intrapreneurship*), through the creation of partnerships among existing organizations, or through the founding of a new organization. Our focus in this chapter is on organizational creation. More specifically, we are interested in nonprofits emerging through social entrepreneurship.

Social Entrepreneurship

The term *social entrepreneurship* became popular in the 1980s. It refers to the creation of products, organizations, and practices that yield and sustain social benefits, and it captures the simultaneous pursuit of social and financial returns on investment. Social entrepreneurs are change agents who pursue social objectives with innovative methods. In 2006, Paul Light noted the limitations of definitions that focused narrowly on social entrepreneurs as individuals and social entrepreneurship as a reliance on business methods in a nonprofit context. As Light explains, a social entrepreneur can be any individual, group, network, organization, or alliance of organizations that seeks large-scale change through pattern-breaking ideas about the ways in which governments, nonprofits, and businesses can address significant social processes.[16]

Social trends and developments in the nonprofit sector during the 1980s and 1990s provided the impetus for a growing interest in social entrepreneurship. Attention was spurred by

- Concerns that traditional approaches to basic social needs were ineffective
- An interest in innovative solutions bringing sustainable improvements
- An openness to market-based and businesslike approaches to social problems
- The privatization of public services and government contracting
- Outcomes-based rather than needs-based approaches to grantmaking and contracting
- Engaged, strategic approaches to corporate involvement in social and community issues[17]

Social entrepreneurs can learn from their purely profit-seeking business counterparts (*commercial entrepreneurs*)[18] by adapting Sahlman's PCDO model[19] showing the importance of integrating *people, context, deal,* and *opportunity* in entrepreneurial ventures. Drawing from the PCDO model, Austin, Stevenson, and Wei-Skillern offer a social entrepreneurship framework (Figure 3.1) that shows the overlap of *people and capital* with *opportunity* to create a *social value proposition* in an environmental *context* of tax, regulatory, sociocultural, demographic, political, and macroeconomic influences.

People and Capital

The social entrepreneurship model emphasizes the people who actively participate in the venture. The motivations of the people involved in commercial entrepreneurship on the one hand and in social entrepreneurship on the other are likely to be significantly different. Economic self-interest is likely to play less of a role in social entrepreneurship than in commercial entrepreneurship. For example, Wendy Kopp was not motivated to create Teach For America to increase her personal wealth nor was personal gain a motive for her original investors. The people component is critical to Teach For America's unique approach to a social problem. This nonprofit selects "promising future leaders" from a range of educational backgrounds, rather than experienced and certified teachers. This choice of whom to involve reflects a long-term social reform agenda that is as important, if not more important, than a short-term focus on classroom effectiveness. Also, as mentioned in this chapter's opening scenario, Kopp sees the work of finding allies as critical to the success of a venture.

One of Kopp's greatest challenges was finding the financial resources to persevere. Early in her efforts to build the organization she wondered if she

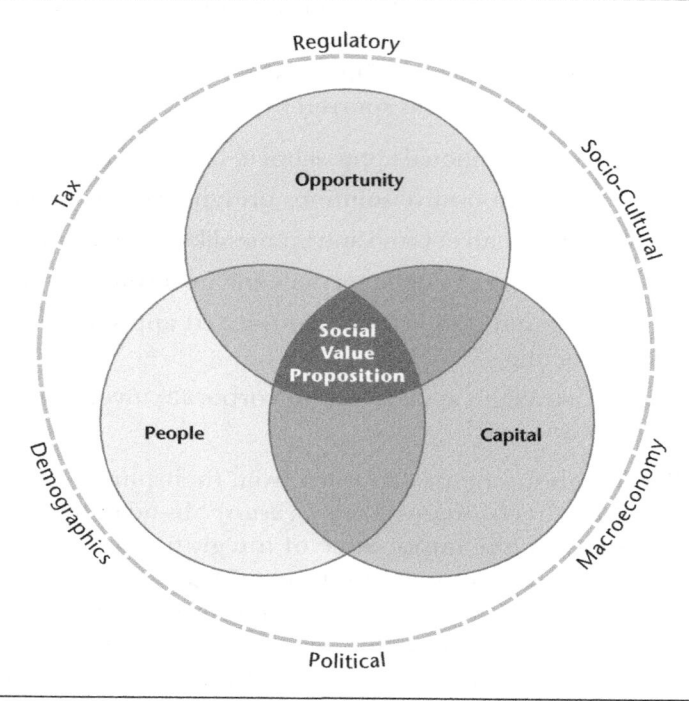

FIGURE 3.1. SOCIAL ENTREPRENEURSHIP FRAMEWORK

Source: From James Austin, Howard Stevenson, and Jane Wei-Skillern, "Social and Commercial Entrepreneurship: Same, Different, or Both?" in *Entrepreneurship Theory & Practice*, vol. 30, issue 1, 1–22. Copyright © 2006 John Wiley & Sons, Inc. Reprinted with permission.

would be able to pay the monthly payroll. Capital is a critical component of entrepreneurial ventures. One of the newest options for capital for some social entrepreneurs is social impact bonds. Started in the United Kingdom and now gaining interest in the United States, this financing mechanism is built on the idea of paying for performance. The government makes payments to private and philanthropic investors for projects that demonstrate measurable success. The goal is to save the taxpayers money and attract new financing to address social problems.[20]

Context

Contextual elements outside the control of the entrepreneur influence success or failure. Commercial and social entrepreneurship ventures may be subject to different regulatory, financing, tax, sociopolitical, and other influences. The nonprofit Teach For America, for example, has to rely on its alumni base to accomplish its school reform agenda. It also has to rely on schools to accept its teachers and allow them to be effective. Unlike for-profit firms, it can accept donations that qualify the givers for tax deductions. Once Teach For America teachers get to the classroom, and especially once their term of service ends, there is little the nonprofit can do to manage their activities. As the Teach For America Web site states: "Armed with the experience, conviction, and insight that come from leading children to fulfill their potential, our alumni are working from all sectors to shape our schools, policies, and investments in low-income communities."[21] The alumni and philanthropic contexts, among others, are critical to the achievement of the Teach For America mission. Other nonprofits as well have unique contextual factors that affect their ability to achieve their mission.

Social Value Proposition

A project's or organization's social value proposition addresses the reasons why individuals will choose to be involved in a particular effort over other alternatives. For Teach For America, it explains why college students are willing to forgo larger salaries to devote time to teaching in schools serving low-income neighborhoods when teaching is not their long-term career objective, why schools will accept Teach For America teachers over more experienced and certified instructors, and why donors are willing to share their resources in exchange for a promise that the nonprofit will work to close students' achievement gap. The social value proposition typically speaks to fundamental values that the people involved in an enterprise's transactions hold dear, such as the importance of social equity, justice, spiritual well-being, honesty, self-respect, freedom, and integrity.

Opportunity

For a social entrepreneurship enterprise to be successful, enough individuals need to believe that it has a chance to achieve a desired future state. This creates the opportunity for the enterprise to have the needed market for the venture. Social entrepreneurs identify something they can do that others are not doing because it is not viable within existing commercial markets. Teach For America, for example, took advantage of the opportunity to put people with its agenda into low-resourced schools needing teachers. By doing so, it could encourage greater passion for school reform and create future leaders to drive change. It also could help schools that otherwise might not be able to afford to increase capacity to improve students' educational experiences. A deficit of teachers combined with individuals' latent interest in short-term teaching experiences created the opportunity for an organization such as Teach For America.

◆ ◆ ◆

If any of the major elements in Austin, Stevenson, and Wei-Skillern's model are not adequately aligned, the entrepreneurial venture is likely to fail. For example, if a new law were to be passed requiring that all high school teachers have an education degree (context), the types of individuals selected by Teach For America would need to change (people), requiring more financial resources for hiring (capital), eventually affecting the nonprofit's chance to nurture future leaders for education reform through firsthand classroom experience in low-income schools (opportunity), and ultimately making it more challenging to close the achievement gap (social value proposition).

Consideration of the differences between social entrepreneurship and commercial entrepreneurship involves a number of implications for practice. Social entrepreneurs, more than commercial entrepreneurs, need to pay attention to

- **Centrality of social value.** This must be the first and foremost consideration.
- **Organizational and environmental alignment.** Alignment with the social interests of external supporters may be needed to deliver social value. For example, social entrepreneurs operating under nonprofit status cannot tap into the same capital markets as commercial entrepreneurs, given that they cannot distribute surpluses to investors.
- **Organizational boundaries.** Boundaries may need to be more flexible. For example, Ashoka Fellows pursue their social entrepreneurship visions while receiving support both financially and professionally from Ashoka. They may even join together to leverage the impact of their individual organizations. Their entrepreneurial efforts cross organizational boundaries.
- **Cooperation.** Social value may be enhanced by cooperation instead of competition. Decisions may be made to allow another organization to have more commercial profit in order to maximize the overall social benefit. Social entrepreneurs may recognize that they can have a greater social impact if they work as part of a coalition rather than as independent actors.

Entrepreneurial Process

The entrepreneurial process involves all the functions, activities, and actions that are associated with perceiving and pursuing opportunities. It has the following components:[22]

- Formation of an idea that is recognized as an opportunity
- Decision to start a new organization to pursue the opportunity
- Development of plans

- Determination of resource needs and acquisition of initial capital
- Development and implementation of strategies for market entry
- Acquisition of resources for growth and development of growth strategies
- Launch and growth
- Harvest (that is, achievement of benefits)

Entrepreneurial success is influenced by a combination of individual, social, organizational, and environmental factors.[23] Personal attributes interact with environmental opportunities and role models to influence the innovation (idea creation) stage. These and other personal factors, such as job dissatisfaction or commitment, social factors, such as networks and family, and environmental factors, such as resources and competition, may influence the decision to launch the venture. Market, resource, and other environmental factors; personal managerial talent; and organizational capabilities will likely influence the planning, initial implementation, growth, and end stages. Recent research has concluded that there is no set of psychological or behavioral attributes that can definitively differentiate entrepreneurs from other individuals.[24] Although not conclusive, studies have, however, found high levels of locus of control and risk taking and a need for independence and achievement to be related to entrepreneurship.[25]

Recognition of an Entrepreneurship Opportunity

Where do ideas for entrepreneurship come from? Arthur Brooks suggests that changes in technology, public policy, public opinion, tastes, or society and demographics can inspire entrepreneurial activity.[26] Peter Drucker lists seven spurs for innovative idea creation:[27]

- The unexpected in an organization, including success, failure, or some other event
- An incongruity between reality as it actually is and reality as it is assumed to be or as it "ought to be"
- The changing needs of internal organizational processes
- Surprising changes in industry or market structure
- Demographic changes
- Changes in perception, mood, or meaning
- New knowledge (both scientific and nonscientific)

Each nonprofit's founding story is unique. For example, the founders of Alcoholics Anonymous rejected the prevalent idea that alcoholism was a personal moral failing and wanted to create an organization that would help alcoholics find a greater power to overcome their problem. One of the founders had a spiritual awakening that led him to work the rest of his life to bring freedom and peace to other alcoholics.

The World Wildlife Fund was created by sixteen of the world's leading conservationists out of a shared understanding that the expertise to protect the world environment existed but financial resources were inadequate to support the conservation movement on a worldwide scale. They determined that a new organization was needed to fundraise internationally and collaborate with existing organizations.

The March of Dimes was created by President Franklin Roosevelt, who struggled with polio during a time when that disease was on the rise. He wanted to use the organization to raise money to fight polio and deliver aid to those suffering from it.

Share Our Strength began in response to the 1984 to 1985 famine in Ethiopia, with the idea that everyone can contribute to the global fight against hunger and poverty and that sustainable solutions lie in sharing everyone's strengths. The founders were correct in thinking that they could create an organization to mobilize industries and individuals to use community wealth for lasting change.

Jerry Kitzi offers some advice for those wishing to identify new opportunities.[28] He suggests looking at a service or product through a different lens to see what value could be added. For example, do users view and experience a service differently from the way volunteers or staff do? He also suggests challenging old assumptions. For example, do new technologies change what can be offered and how? And he recommends brainstorming with current colleagues, competitors, and customers to develop new ideas. Rather than operating under the adage "If it isn't broken, don't fix it," an entrepreneur searching for an opportunity may wish to pursue the question "How can we make it better?"

Making a Business Case for a New Nonprofit

New ideas for providing social benefits or making social improvements need to be evaluated before these ideas are judged to be opportunities. Once they are so judged, the entrepreneurship process moves into the organization-creating stage. Jerry Kitzi presents an opportunity assessment framework for social entrepreneurship.[29] The idea for a new organization can be assessed on three dimensions:

- **Social value potential.** Does it have strategic alignment, achievable outcomes, partnership or alliance potential, and organizational benefit?
- **Market potential.** Does it tap user needs and desires, generate funder interest, and have the ability to capture market share?
- **Sustainability potential.** Can the idea be developed and implemented to have more benefits than costs, as well as adequate income potential, organizational capacity, and funder interest?

Figuring out the social value, market, and sustainability potential of a new nonprofit is critical to the development of a written business plan. A business plan can help the idea originator and potential supporters evaluate the feasibility and needs of a new nonprofit. The plan includes an assessment of the environment and lays out the business concept, helping to justify investments in the organization's development. The business plan should include financial projections, program objectives, and operational goals, along with a timeline to help leaders define and measure progress.

The business plan differs from the strategic plan in its purpose and content. The strategic plan explains how an organization will achieve its objectives over a specified period of time. It provides an internal roadmap for obtaining and using resources to achieve the mission. Typical elements of the strategic plan are a vision statement, mission statement, goals, objectives, action plans, risk analysis and contingency plans, competitive analysis, and financial outline.[30] Strategic plans change over time in order to give timely guidance for running the organization so as to pursue agreed-upon goals. The use and development of strategic plans will be discussed in more detail in Chapter Five, on formulation of strategy.

In contrast the business plan is written for an external audience, rather than as guidance for internal workers (employees, volunteers, and board members). It explains to outsiders the fundamentals of the nonprofit organization, showing why those involved think that it is viable and serves a useful purpose. The business plan positions the nonprofit in the larger environment. It may be shared with an outsider to raise money, find a partner, get a loan, attract new leaders, and check assumptions about the viability and value of the nonprofit.

The following is a generic outline of the topic headings for a business plan:

- **Title page.** Gives the title of the document, the name of the organization, the names of the board members and the executive director, and contact information.
- **Table of contents.** Lists the topics covered in the plan.
- **Executive summary.** Summarizes the content of the plan.

- **Mission and organizational description.** Gives an overview of the organization, answering basic questions about its purpose, history, form, size, accomplishments if any, and capacity.
- **Market analysis and environmental assessment.** Shows the reader that there is sufficient demand and willingness to cover costs for the product or service, and describes the competitive and collaborative environment.
- **Services or products to be offered.** Explains what will be offered and why; goes into depth on the mission and vision of the organization and on its objectives.
- **Operations.** Describes how the service or product will be produced and delivered.
- **Marketing plan.** Explains how the product or service will be positioned in the market and promoted to attract clients and consumers.
- **Board of trustees.** Explains who has governing authority in the organization and describes the board structure and bylaws; may include résumés.
- **Membership.** Explains qualifications for membership (if the organization has members) and any dues structure; describes benefits and rights given to members based on their membership classification.
- **Management and personnel.** Describes the executive team and the other personnel who will be running the day-to-day operations of the organization; includes a discussion of the volunteer program, if applicable; includes résumés of key staff members.
- **Funds required and their expected use.** Explains what is needed for the organization to be set up and to thrive; shows donors and investors how their contributions fit into the organization and how contributions will be solicited and stewarded.
- **Financial statements and projections.** Gives detailed financial statements, budgets, cost estimates, and revenue projections.
- **Appendices and exhibits.** Provides supporting documents and supplementary information.

Business plans do not need to be long, elaborate documents. They should concisely and clearly state what business the nonprofit is in and the social value proposition. It should be clear who is being served and how, avoiding jargon specific to the industry. The reader should be able to clearly ascertain what the organization is providing to the target market and why the market would find this product or service desirable. The financial statements should be realistic and consistent with other sections of the business plan. Sample business plans can be found on the Internet as well as in some texts on nonprofit entrepreneurship.[31]

Exhibit 3.1 displays the table of contents and executive summary for NPower Basic's business plan submitted in 2005 to the Yale School of Management, Goldman Sachs Foundation, and Partnership on Nonprofit Ventures.[32] NP-Basic is a workforce development program involving disenfranchised youth from underserved communities who have received training in delivering computers and technical support to resource-strapped nonprofits. The business plan lays out how every dollar invested in NP-Basic returns sixteen dollars to the community in the form of jobs and nonprofits that are more productive after receiving computing equipment and technical assistance.

Nonprofit Vision and Mission Statements

Perhaps the most important elements of the business plan are the vision and mission statements. The vision statement expresses a nonprofit's ultimate goal, and the mission statement guides the actions of the organization and inspires employees and investors. The mission statement should convey the nonprofit's essential purpose, approach, and values, distinguishing it from other organizations. Its words are often the ones most repeated to explain why the nonprofit exists. It should be concise and jargon-free so that it is easy to understand for those who are not familiar with the nonprofit and easy to use as a touchstone for those most connected to the nonprofit. Following are a few one-sentence mission statements that address purpose, approach, and values:

> United Way improves lives by mobilizing the caring power of communities around the world to advance the common good.
>
> St. Vincent Hospital is a medical institution dedicated to providing quality patient care with unrelenting attention to clinical excellence, patient safety, and an unparalleled passion and commitment to assure the very best healthcare for those we serve.
>
> The National Trust for Historic Preservation provides leadership, education, and advocacy to save America's diverse historic places and revitalize our communities.
>
> The mission of the Urban League movement is to enable African Americans to secure economic self-reliance, parity, power and civil rights.

EXHIBIT 3.1. NPOWER BASIC BUSINESS PLAN, APRIL 2005

Table of Contents

1.	Executive Summary	1
2.	Description of Social Business Venture	3
	2.1 Rationale	3
	2.2 Mission	4
	2.3 Target Market	4
	2.4 Business Model	4
	2.5 Value Proposition	6
	2.6 Social Return on Investment	7
	2.7 Business Objectives	9
	2.8 Track Record	9
	2.9 Leadership Team	10
	2.10 Critical Success Factors	10
3.	Industry and Market Analysis	11
	3.1 The Target Market for NP-BASIC	11
	3.2 Segment Analysis	12
	3.3 Market Acceptance	13
	3.4 Competitive Analysis	14
	3.5 Summary of Major Competitors	15
	3.6 Competitive Advantages	16
	3.7 Summary of Competitive Advantages	17
4.	Marketing Plan	17
	4.1 Marketing Objectives	17
	4.2 Product	18
	4.3 Placement and Distribution	19
	4.4 Pricing	20
	4.5 Promotions Plan	22
	4.6 Performance Milestones	22
5.	Management Plan	22
	5.1 NP-BASIC Team (Year One)	23
	5.2 Commitment and Coordination with Parent Nonprofit (NPower NY)	24

6.	Operations Plan	25
	6.1 Staffing	25
	6.2 Implementation	25
	6.3 Ongoing Services	26
	6.4 Internal Operations and Continuous Improvement	27
	6.5 Sales Management and Oversight	27
7.	Financial Plan	28
	7.1 Pro Forma Statement of Activities	28
	7.2 Pro Forma Statement of Financial Position	30
	7.3 Pro Forma Statement of Cash Flows	31
8.	Risk Assessment, Sensitivity Scenarios, and Contingency Plan	31
9.	Appendices	36

Executive Summary

NPower Basic ("NP-Basic") combines a successful workforce development program for disenfranchised youth with an all-in-one technology service that uses a "hub and spoke" model to meet the basic technology needs of nonprofits. Staffed in part with graduates of NPower's workforce development program, the service offers a network of preconfigured and software-loaded desktop computers and provides installation, monitoring, maintenance, remote support, a help desk, and onsite technical assistance visits. NP-Basic offers critical products and state-of-the-art support at low prices by achieving economies of scale and receiving direct donations of expensive software and hardware from Microsoft and Cisco.

The service's social value is reinforced by its commitment to hire staff from New York City's underserved communities. NP-Basic recruits entry-level staff from a workforce development program known as the Technology Service Corps (TSC), which is run by its parent organization NPower NY. TSC is a twelve-week intensive training program that teaches urban young adults aged eighteen to twenty-four a unique combination of technical and professional skills, and provides mentoring by NPower NY's senior consulting staff and hands-on service to the nonprofit community. Since 2002, TSC has graduated and found jobs for nearly one hundred out-of-school youth who were previously in low-wage, dead-end jobs or who were unemployed, incarcerated, or even homeless. TSC has been the ticket to a meaningful future for these individuals and a path to a lifelong career. Typically wages rise approximately 133 percent to over $26,000 post-program and on an hourly basis, post-TSC wages ($12.75/hour) are 113 percent higher than minimum wage ($6/hour) in New York City.

NP-Basic's social return on investment is 16. This means that for every dollar invested in NP-Basic, more than $16 is returned to the community in the form of more productive nonprofits and more jobs for previously disenfranchised youth.

(continued)

Earned income for this venture is generated by charging low setup and maintenance fees for each installation. NP-Basic's target customers are the decision makers at the nearly 3,500 small New York City nonprofits that have fewer than ten staff and operating budgets of less than $1 million. Organizations ranging from small community-based social service organizations to local performing arts groups will be the initial target audience for NP-Basic.

Key Objectives

- To help resource-strapped nonprofits obtain the technology support they need while saving money that can be applied to further their organizational missions.
- To gain a 3 percent market penetration of the initial target market for NP-Basic by Year Three (approximately one hundred New York City nonprofits). The total spending power of these one hundred nonprofits is $50 million to $100 million, and together they employ three hundred to five hundred people.
- To provide a supportive work environment for graduates of NPower NY's workforce development program, TSC. NPower Basic will provide 221 six-month rotations through its help desk for TSC graduates.

By leveraging potential underwriting, corporate affiliations, and TSC, NP-Basic delivers a critical high-quality service at an affordable cost with important community benefits.

Potential competitors include Dell, value-added resellers (VARs), other management service providers, consultants, small organizations offering information technology (IT) services ancillary to their primary missions, and savvy internal staff who by default, or in rare cases by design, have taken on an IT management responsibility.

NP-Basic enjoys key competitive advantages over these alternatives including: (1) access to broader resources available through NPower NY such as software and product donations, foundation support for technology capacity building, and a steady labor pool of entry-level technicians from its TSC program; (2) proven experience and strong relationships with small nonprofits through NPower NY's four years of successful and well-regarded service to these customers; (3) the lowest pricing available to this segment; (4) a comprehensive service offering that includes hardware, software, and services; (5) technologically advanced information protection through state-of-the-art server backups; (6) a strong history of customer service that focuses exclusively on nonprofit organizations; and (7) a compelling social value through its incorporation of TSC and provision of affordable technology services to nonprofit organizations.

The marketing plan for NP-Basic is designed to acquire new customers through a combination of print and electronic media, including advertising, sponsorship of technology events, and promotion through its Web site. NP-Basic also will target the NPower NY client base, its foundation supporters, additional foundations that support small nonprofits, umbrella nonprofits, and nonprofit incubator groups to market the service.

NP-Basic is run by the Director of Services and Strategy who has more than thirteen years of managerial, service, and operational experience. In addition, the Senior Manager of Service Delivery has nineteen years of technical and business expertise, having worked at prominent private sector technology companies including Microsoft, EDS, and Razorfish. NP-Basic also benefits from a strong commitment from NPower NY's board of directors and senior management, who bring a successful fundraising track record, sales expertise, workforce development skills, and technical leadership, as well as critical shared resources for marketing, finance, and human resources that keep operating costs at a minimum.

NP-Basic operations take place in three places: shared space at NPower NY headquarters, its client sites, and most significantly, cyberspace. Typically the process is as follows: nonprofits place orders with an NP-Basic salesperson, an on-site assessment is done, computers and other hardware are ordered and configured with software, the system is installed at the client site, and services start immediately with constant monitoring, maintenance, and customer support through a help desk and via remote support. From start to finish this process can take as little as seven days, although the processing of the donations may lengthen it somewhat. The team meets on a weekly basis to review key metrics and goals.

NP-Basic projects a three-year Pro Forma Statement of Activities indicating earned revenue growth of 61 percent in its second year and 103 percent in Year Three reaching revenues of $500 thousand in Year Three. Major risks include not being able to reach sales targets, higher-than-anticipated costs, being unable to sustain the service at a price that small nonprofits can afford, providing inconsistent quality of service, and being unable to retain a high-performing management team. Careful growth, management, and cost control will mitigate each of these risks and allow the venture to remain sustainable and successful even while managing multiple and, oftentimes, unpredictable risks.

Source: Adapted from *NPower Basic Business Plan April 2005*, http://faculty.maxwell.syr.edu/acbrooks/pages/Courses/Documents/Soc%20Ent/NPowerNY.pdf. Reprinted with permission.

Establishment Process

Entrepreneurs have a range of options for proceeding with their idea of creating a new nonprofit. This section outlines the choices and steps that move this idea into reality in the legal environment of the United States. In other countries with other laws and regulations, options for form and process may vary.

There are many reasons to formally establish a nonprofit. Once formalized, it takes on an identity beyond that of its founders. This is helpful in limiting the liability of individuals associated with the nonprofit and helping to ensure that the organization continues after the founders leave. Once it has gained legal recognition, the nonprofit has the ability to take out loans, make contracts, and keep property and other assets in the organization's name. It also acquires added credibility, making it more likely to be able to attract donations and other support. In addition, the nonprofit can get benefits that are specific to its chosen legal form.

One of the first options is whether to set up the nonprofit as an *unincorporated association, charitable trust,* or *nonprofit corporation.* Unincorporated associations are the simplest legal form; they can have a bank account in their name and contributions to them are tax deductible. They have few other benefits but also minimal record-keeping requirements. The charitable trust is a common legal form in many other countries but has relatively limited use in the United States. In the United States, this form tends to be used by organizations whose purpose is to make grants. The most common type of legally recognized nonprofit in the United States is the nonprofit corporation.

Nonprofit corporations may be either *public benefit* organizations or *mutual benefit* organizations. Public benefit organizations are primarily public serving. They fit into the IRS (Internal Revenue Service) classification system as 501(c)(3) and some of the 501(c)(4) organizations. Mutual benefit organizations are primarily member serving and consist of some of the 501(c)(4) organizations and the other nonprofit tax classifications, except for the (c)(3)s. See Exhibit 3.2 for a listing of all the IRS classifications used for organizations that may qualify for tax exemptions.

When we think of nonprofits, most individuals think of 501(c)(3) organizations. These nonprofits are defined by the IRS as "religious, educational, charitable, scientific, literary, testing for public safety, to foster certain national or international amateur sports competition, or prevention of cruelty to children or animals organizations." The appeal of becoming a 501(c)(3) organization is that the nonprofit gains increased receptivity to appeals for support, tax deductibility for donors, eligibility for low-cost mailing permits, exemption from some taxes, ability to apply for gambling permits in some states, eligibility for government and foundation contracts and grants, and discounts from some businesses. However, once established as a 501(c)(3) organization, the nonprofit is not allowed to engage in political campaigning, is subject to limits on lobbying and unrelated business activity, must ensure that social activities for participants are insubstantial if they are unrelated to its mission, and must also ensure that no excess benefits or inurements go to staff or board members or to their relations. More information on restrictions is provided in Chapter Fourteen, on public and government relations.

The (c)(3) classification is not available to all nonprofits. Some entrepreneurs who wish their organizations to engage heavily in advocacy choose to pursue a 501(c)(4) rather than a 501(c)(3) classification. As a (c)(4) the

EXHIBIT 3.2. ORGANIZATIONS THAT MAY QUALIFY FOR TAX EXEMPTIONS UNDER IRA RULES

501(c)(1)	Corporations Organized Under Act of Congress (including Federal Credit Unions)
501(c)(2)	Title Holding Corporation for Exempt Organization
501(c)(3)	Religious, Educational, Charitable, Scientific, Literary, Testing for Public Safety, to Foster National or International Amateur Sports Competition, or Prevention of Cruelty to Children or Animals Organizations
501(c)(4)	Civic Leagues, Social Welfare Organizations, and Local Associations of Employees
501(c)(5)	Labor, Agricultural, and Horticultural Organizations
501(c)(6)	Business Leagues, Chambers of Commerce, Real Estate Boards, etc.
501(c)(7)	Social and Recreational Clubs
501(c)(8)	Fraternal Beneficiary Societies and Associations
501(c)(9)	Voluntary Employee Beneficiary Associations
501(c)(10)	Domestic Fraternal Societies and Associations
501(c)(11)	Teachers' Retirement Fund Associations
501(c)(12)	Benevolent Life Insurance Associations, Mutual Ditch or Irrigation Companies, Mutual or Cooperative Telephone Companies, etc.
501(c)(13)	Cemetery Companies
501(c)(14)	State-Chartered Credit Unions, Mutual Reserve Funds
501(c)(15)	Mutual Insurance Companies or Associations
501(c)(16)	Cooperative Organizations to Finance Crop Operations
501(c)(17)	Supplemental Unemployment Benefit Trusts
501(c)(18)	Employee Funded Pension Trust (created before June 25, 1959)
501(c)(19)	Post or Organization of Past or Present Members of the Armed Forces
501(c)(21)	Black Lung Benefit Trusts
501(c)(22)	Withdrawal Liability Payment Fund
501(c)(23)	Veterans Organization (created before 1880)
501(c)(25)	Title Holding Corporations or Trusts with Multiple Parents
501(c)(26)	State-Sponsored Organization Providing Health Coverage for High-Risk Individuals
501(c)(27)	State-Sponsored Workers' Compensation Reinsurance Organization
501(c)(28)	National Railroad Retirement Investment Trust
501(d)	Religious and Apostolic Associations
501(e)	Cooperative Hospital Service Organizations
501(f)	Cooperative Service Organizations of Operating Educational Organizations

Note: Other organizations that may qualify for exemption, such as 501(c)(24)s and farmers' cooperative associations that fall under section 521, are not included in this IRS organization reference chart.
Source: Derived from Internal Revenue Service, *Tax-Exempt Status for Your Organization*, IRS Publication 557 (October 2010).

nonprofit can do more lobbying. Other classification choices are well suited to associations that primarily work to serve their members, such as labor unions(c)(5), recreational clubs (c)(7), and industry and trade groups(c)(6).

In establishing a 501(c)(3) it is necessary to determine whether the organization is a private foundation or a public charity. The organization will be deemed a private foundation unless it fits one of the exception areas or can meet the tests to be a public charity under Section 509(a) of the Internal Revenue Code. There are two types of private foundations: operating and nonoperating. Nonoperating foundations do not administer substantial programs or services other than their grantmaking operations. Private foundations must not self-deal (contract with staff or board members' businesses) and must meet minimal requirements for distributing their assets, abstain from excess business holdings, and refrain from certain expenditures. Public charities get more tax exemptions, less burdensome reporting requirements, and additional fundraising opportunities.

A nonprofit is considered a public charity if it is any of the following:

- A church, or convention or association of churches
- A school
- A hospital, cooperative hospital service organization, or medical research organization operated in conjunction with a hospital
- A government unit as described in section 170(c)(1) of the Internal Revenue Code
- An organization operated solely for the benefit of a government-owned college or university
- A recipient of substantial support in the form of contributions from a publically supported organization, a government unit, or the general public
- An organization that normally receives not more than a third of its support from gross investment income and more than a third from contributions, membership fees, and gross receipts from activities related to its exempt functions (subject to exceptions)

Once the founder decides what legal form to pursue, an application can be made to the federal government for a *definitive ruling*, based on support the organization has received to date, or an *advance ruling*, based on support the organization will receive during its first five tax years.

However, instead of pursuing an IRS designation for a new nonprofit, a founder may pursue fiscal sponsorship for his or her product or service, establishing it as a program under an existing nonprofit, or the founder may have the new venture's finances and donations administered through a donor-advised fund of a community foundation, thus negating the need for a more advanced form of legal recognition as an unincorporated corporation, independent charitable trust, or nonprofit corporation.

A founder may take other steps to formalize a nonprofit besides applying for recognition of tax exemption from the IRS and obtaining a definitive or advance ruling. One of the first steps is to obtain an *employee identification number*. This number is particularly important if the nonprofit will be hiring employees. Some nonprofits, such as hospitals and universities, may need to obtain consents to operate from state and local authorities. Consents may be required if a government is trying to restrict the number of nonprofits of a certain type in a geographical area.

At the state level it is necessary to prepare and submit articles of incorporation. The articles of incorporation tend to be a very simple document that describes basic facts about the organization—the founders, contact information, and basic purpose. Bylaws that describe the rules under which the board of the nonprofit will function are also needed and should be filed with the state. Bylaws are described in greater depth in Chapter Nine, on boards and governance. In some states it is necessary to register to fund raise and lobby, and to apply for exemption from state income and property taxes.

After their nonprofit's formal incorporation, founders need to have the mind-set that the nonprofit is no longer their organization. It exists to serve a public purpose. The founder cannot deduct business-related expenses on his or her personal taxes. It is also important that the founder set up a system of checks and balances so that no one person can gain too much power and control in the organization. For this reason a founder should not serve as both the executive director and a member of the board of directors. Board members should be chosen for their ability to govern the organization and should show loyalty to the organization, not the founder.

Starting a Nonprofit from an Existing Organization

As mentioned at the beginning of this chapter, in addition to being started from scratch, new nonprofits can arise from existing organizations. We briefly describe some of the possibilities in the following sections.

Spin-Offs

The term *spin-off* refers to the creation of a new organization from an existing organization. A nonprofit may spin off another nonprofit or a for-profit operation. Depending on the motivations behind them, we can distinguish between restructuring-driven, entrepreneurial, and mission-driven spin-offs.[33]

Restructuring-driven spin-offs are initiated by the parent company for strategic or operational motives, often arising from a restructuring or refocusing of the parent. These motives may involve financial issues (equity and debt considerations), regulatory relief (the requirement of a government agency), or the fit and focus of various internal business activities or units.[34] The less strategically important and connected to core operations an activity is, the more likely it is to be spun off by a parent.[35]

The diversity of motivations for spin-offs is suggested by these examples. The Ludwig Institute for Cancer Research (LICR) is a nonprofit that conducts laboratory and clinical research to improve the control of cancer. It has spun off commercial enterprises so that these enterprises can hold the licenses for technologies developed by LICR and potentially turn them into diagnostic or therapeutic applications. LICR does not have the capability to turn its discoveries into commercially viable products, and it can retain its research focus by turning market development activities over to these spin-off companies. The Nature Conservancy spun off NatureServe, which collects and manages data on species and ecosystems. After more than twenty years of providing professional staff, databases, and scientific and technical support to a network of partners for this work, the Nature Conservancy decided it was best to have an independent nonprofit serve as a membership organization for the network, rather than for the conservancy to continue to host it as a tangential activity. Leaders Thru Literacy is another example of a nonprofit that emerged from an existing nonprofit. Board members of the parent nonprofit, the Quaqua Society, did not want to dilute the society's focus and thus felt a spin-off was appropriate.[36]

Entrepreneurial corporate spin-offs are driven by one or more individuals in existing organizations who are frustrated when their ideas are not endorsed by top management or who want to exploit an unused potential related to their experience and knowledge built within the parent company.[37] Entrepreneurial spin-offs are bottom-up processes, where the entrepreneur is both the originator of the spin-off decision and the driver of the process. In the case of nonprofits, this spin-off could also involve a dissenting faction of a nonprofit, such as a sect of a cult or church. One study found that people who were very satisfied with their jobs were 75 percent less likely to become entrepreneurs than those who were unsatisfied and that the propensity to leave and start a new organization decreased the more the employee was paid.[38]

There are numerous examples of nonprofits that were started by those who developed their ideas while affiliated with an existing nonprofit. Yale

University, originally called the Collegiate School, was started by a group of religious conservatives who were unhappy with Harvard University's break from the influence of the church.[39] Millard Fuller started the Fuller Center for Housing in 2005 after being ousted by the board from Habitat for Humanity International, the nonprofit he cofounded in 1976. A former Church of Scientology member started FACTNet and was eventually stopped from illegally sharing unpublished and copyrighted documents taken from the church.[40]

Mission-driven spin-offs are created as means to help fulfill the core purpose of a nonprofit. For example, the parent nonprofit's mission may be to create new enterprises for economic development, job training, empowerment of a disadvantaged group, increased diffusion of green technologies, or facilitation of sustainable demonstration projects.

One instance of this type is Smart Roofs. This limited liability for-profit company was created by a nonprofit group, Sustainable South Bronx, that teaches job skills—in this case, how to install and maintain vegetative gardens on rooftops. Another nonprofit, Women's Action to Gain Economic Security, helps low-income women create housecleaning cooperatives that use environmentally safe cleaning products.[41] The Vera Institute of Justice has spun off more than sixteen nonprofit organizations that started as demonstration projects, such as the Police Assessment Resource Center, Center for Alternative Sentencing and Employment Services, Legal Action Center, Esperanza, Job Path, and New York City Criminal Justice Agency. The institute now offers a toolkit for spin-offs.[42]

Companion Organizations

Nonprofits sometimes facilitate the creation of new *companion organizations*, with which they plan to closely associate. For example, a group of organizations might create a trade association that allows them to work together to obtain bulk discounts and support their shared lobbying interests. An independent 501(c)(3) organization might set up a foundation to fund raise for a museum or school. Given that tax deductibility of donations is not a benefit for all categories of nonprofits, it might make sense for a nonprofit lacking this benefit to create a separate nonprofit that will be attractive to donors seeking tax deductions. The NAACP, one of the country's oldest civil rights organizations, has made use of a variety of companion organizations, including a for-profit organization that produces its magazine; branch chapters that are 501(c)(4) organizations; its national headquarters, which is a 501(c)(3); and a special contributions fund organization that is also a 501(c)(3).

Subsidiaries

As found in the case of the NAACP, there are situations where one organization (the parent) can exercise operational control over another (the *subsidiary*). This relationship is generally established by the parent so that it can receive benefits from the subsidiary. A subsidiary of a nonprofit is a corporation owned or controlled in whole or in part by the nonprofit.[43] The subsidiary may be a nonprofit or a for-profit. Other terms for a subsidiary include *affiliate, support corporation,* and *title holding company.* Each of these terms refers to a specific type of subsidiary. Subsidiaries can be formed for a variety of reasons, including protecting the parent's tax-exempt status; protecting the parent from debts and liabilities from certain activities; attracting grants, contributions, or equity and debt financing; or helping the parent overcome organizational capacity deficiencies, enhance community image, offer incentive compensation, or transfer ownership of activities to employees or other parties.[44]

Parent nonprofits exercise control over subsidiaries via a subsidiary's articles of incorporation, bylaws, and board of directors. For example:

- The parent may prepare the articles of incorporation and bylaws. The articles may provide that the parent has the right to approve any amendments. The bylaws may provide that the parent has the right to appoint the board of directors and to remove directors without cause and the right to approve any amendments.
- The governing document of the subsidiary may require it to be bound by the decisions of the parent.
- Representatives of the parent may be board members, officers, or executive staff of the subsidiary and may have voting power to cause or prevent action by the subsidiary.
- The subsidiary may be a membership organization, with the parent as the only member.

Although the subsidiary can be controlled by its parent, it is important to note that the subsidiary needs to be established and recognized by the parent, and also recognized by third parties, as an independently incorporated organization managed by a board of directors. The parent should not manage the day-to-day affairs of the subsidiary. Even though the boards of the parent and subsidiary may overlap, it is recommended that the subsidiary board also include outside directors. The parent and the subsidiary should maintain separate books and records, bank accounts, meetings and minutes, stationery, and tax returns, and each should sign documents in its own corporate name.

Franchise Relationships

According to Sharon Oster, "The franchise relationship is a kind of halfway house between the freestanding entrepreneurial enterprise and the branch office."[45] It is characterized by four traits, which are established by contractual agreement (as opposed to ownership control):

- The franchiser gives the franchisee the right to use the franchiser's trademark or sell its products.
- The franchisee pays the franchiser for this right.
- The franchiser gives some assistance and maintains some control over the way the business is operated.
- Any residual profits or losses go to the franchisee.

Franchises are restricted to certain industries in the corporate world (for example, fast-food outlets and automobile dealers); however, franchises are relatively prevalent in the nonprofit world. They include well-known organizations such as Goodwill, the United Way, the Red Cross, the Boy Scouts of America, and the American Cancer Society. When a nonprofit sets up a franchise, its franchisees may be either for-profits or nonprofits. For example, the National Football League is a 501(c)(6) unincorporated nonprofit association. The Green Bay Packers team is a nonprofit corporation and part of the NFL system. In contrast, the Detroit Lions team is a for-profit NFL franchise owned by William Clay Ford Sr. In 1990, over half of the top one hundred charitable nonprofits were franchise organizations.[46]

Should a nonprofit establish a subsidiary or a franchise? Oster compares the advantages and disadvantages of having a branch office (wholly owned satellite) and having a franchise. She concludes that a satellite is good whereas a franchise is only fair at protecting the nonprofit's reputation or brand and at coordinating fundraising efforts. A franchise is good whereas the satellite is poor at improving access to capital, reducing managerial shirking, and encouraging volunteer efforts.[47] We can extend these conclusions by considering where subsidiaries would fall in Oster's framework. In situations where a parent exercises a great deal of control over a subsidiary, the subsidiary would have the same benefits and drawbacks as the branch office. Subsidiaries characterized by lesser control would fall somewhere in between the branch office and the franchise in terms of their pros and cons.

Relationships with affiliate organizations may not always proceed smoothly. The affiliate may resist control by its parent or act in ways that harm the larger network due to conflicts of interest. For example, the San

Antonio chapter sued Habitat for Humanity International after HFHI asked its chapters to sign a new membership agreement. The San Antonio chapter wanted to continue to use the Habitat name without signing the agreement.[48] The national Girl Scout organization, Girl Scouts of the USA, wanted to consolidate, effectively eliminating local councils including the Manitou Girl Scout Council, which went to court. The councils are organized as separate legal entities, though the national organization charters them to sell cookies and other merchandise under the Girl Scout trademark. A Wisconsin circuit judge ruled that the national organization could not eliminate the council as part of a reorganization.[49] It is important for nonprofit leaders considering affiliate agreements to consider which levels and types of control will be held by the affiliate and which by the parent.

Concluding Thoughts

The entrepreneurial impulse helped to shape the nonprofit sector as we experience it today. Due to the efforts of social entrepreneurs, innovative approaches are continually being tested to address social problems that cannot viably be addressed by commercial markets. With the support of well-conceived missions and well-thought-out business plans, founders who have identified an opportunity and the people and capital to pursue it may create a nonprofit that can thrive. Whether a nonprofit emerges as a spin-off, subsidiary, or franchise or is established outside of an existing organization, its social value proposition will likely frame its fundamental approach and the types of supporters it can attract.

In the next chapter we elaborate on structure and design choices for nonprofit organizations. These choices may change in the different stages of a nonprofit's existence. Still, what a founder establishes as operating principles and values may limit what choices are considered. Knowing the founding story of a nonprofit may help to explain how it appears years later.

Questions for Consideration

1. What ideas do you have for a new nonprofit? How would you go about finding out if your idea is worth pursuing? Are there sources of support for social entrepreneurship ventures in your community that might be helpful in exploring your idea?

2. What factors do you think explain the growth of the nonprofit sector in the United States over the past decade? Do you expect more or less growth in the next ten years? Why or why not?

Exercises

Exercise 3.1: Social Entrepreneurship Model

Analyze a nonprofit business plan, and apply the social entrepreneurship model to it. Who are the key people, and what are the capital, opportunity, social value proposition, and context outlined in the plan? You may use the online NPower business plan that is the source for Exhibit 3.1 or another nonprofit's business plan.

Exercise 3.2: The Founder's Story

Select three nonprofit organizations, and read the organizational history provided on each one's Web site. The history is often provided in an "About Us" section of the site. What importance is given to the founder in each history? Compare and contrast the three histories. In what ways are they similar, and in what ways are they dissimilar?

Exercise 3.3: Mission Analysis

Find a nonprofit's mission statement. Identify the words in the statement that indicate the nonprofit's purpose, approach, or values. What are the strengths and weaknesses of the mission statement? What recommendations do you have for improving it?

CHAPTER FOUR

ORGANIZATIONAL STRUCTURE

Southend Community Services (SCS) was founded in 1974 to serve the residents of one of the most disadvantaged neighborhoods in Hartford, Connecticut, and developed a strong track record as a provider of quality programs for clients of all ages.[1] In 2000, the city obtained a multimillion dollar, five-year Youth Opportunities grant from the U.S. Department of Labor and chose SCS as the key contractor to provide services. The program was designed to keep in-school youth on track, lead out-of-school youth back to school or alternative ways to earn a diploma, and help older youth make transitions to college or full-time employment.[2] The contract allowed SCS to expand its work with at-risk youth, and by 2004, the organization was running multiple programs for young children, youth, and the elderly throughout the city. In 2005, however, it faced the expiration of the Youth Opportunities money, with no possibility of renewal. This would eliminate 40 percent of the organization's budget. After an analysis of community needs and the organization's internal strengths, it was determined that the organization would be most effective if it focused only on youth job training programs and eliminated services to young children and the elderly. Services for youth were reorganized into five separate tracks, created to meet the circumstances and needs of discrete participant groups, and the organization was renamed Our Piece of the Pie. It was also determined that more and better performance data were needed to expand reach and results, and consequently a new information technology system was acquired. Three of the programs not focused on youth were moved to other organizations or spun off. A fourth program, child care, was refocused to support the youth job program. After the reorganization, an extensive public information and education campaign was launched to secure new funding, and by 2008, the organization had replaced the lost contract dollars as well as the money previously brought in by its other three programs.[3] Figure 4.1 shows the reorganization of the programs.

Organizational Structure

FIGURE 4.1. REORGANIZATION OF SOUTHEND COMMUNITY SERVICES

SCS decided to adapt one of its non-youth programs to support the new mission and to exit the remaining three.

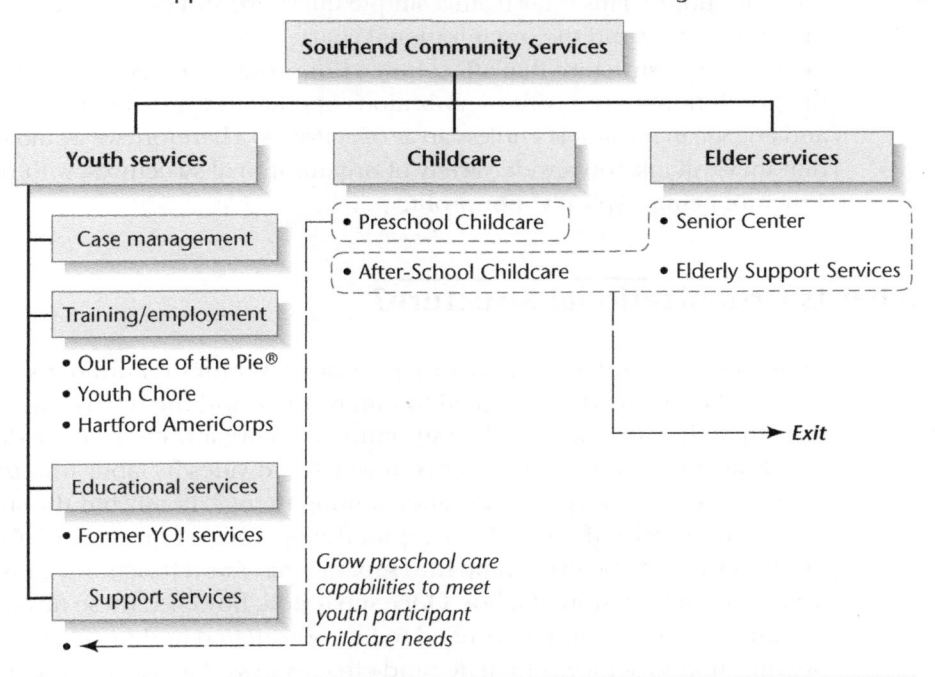

```
                    Southend Community Services
          ┌──────────────────┬──────────────────┐
     Youth services       Childcare         Elder services
          │                  │                   │
    Case management    • Preschool Childcare   • Senior Center
                       • After-School Childcare • Elderly Support Services
    Training/employment
    • Our Piece of the Pie®
    • Youth Chore
    • Hartford AmeriCorps                       ──→ Exit

    Educational services
    • Former YO! services
                         Grow preschool care
    Support services     capabilities to meet
    •  ←─────────────    youth participant
                         childcare needs
```

Source: "Our Piece of the Pie (formerly Southend Community Services): Making the Biggest Difference in Hartford," April 2006. Reprinted by permission of The Bridgespan Group.

As the experience of Southend Community Services and Our Piece of the Pie shows, nonprofit organizations need to figure out how best to deliver their programs and services. These decisions will have effects on the arrangement and operations of the various units and other elements that make up the organization. A nonprofit's structure is designed and created during the founding of the organization and then evolves, or is reorganized, continuously from that point on. At times, in fact, reorganization may be critical for a nonprofit's success or survival. As a result, nonprofit managers must understand the structure of their organizations, the consequences of this structure for their organizations, and the structural alternatives available should the need for reorganization arise.

In this chapter we examine an important aspect of nonprofits, the configuration and design of their structures. Many nonprofit organizations have an organizational chart, such as the one shown for Southend Community Services in Figure 4.1. These charts show the various units or departments that make up the organization and indicate how they are related to each other. We can think of this as a simple visual representation of the organization's structure that helps to answer the question, How should we organize ourselves to get our work done? This is far from a simple question, and organizational structure goes far beyond the organizational chart. This chapter reviews the many dimensions of structure that affect how a nonprofit's work gets done. We take the position that nonprofit organizations operate in many different contexts and engage in an almost endless array of activities. Therefore we would expect that they will take on a wide variety of organizational structures, with no one structure being "typically" nonprofit.

What Is Organizational Structure?

In the most general sense, structure provides a way for organizations to meet two conflicting needs—the need to differentiate and the need to integrate. As Henry Mintzberg states: "The structure of an organization can be defined simply as the sum total of the ways in which it divides its labor into distinct tasks and then achieves coordination among them."[4] In any but the smallest organizations with the simplest output, the operation and work of an organization needs to be broken up into separate tasks and functions. This is the organization's division of labor. Once separated, however, these diverse and disparate tasks and functions need to be coordinated and integrated for an organization to achieve efficiency and effectiveness. The greater the division of labor, the more need there may be for mechanisms for integration.

Organizational structure designates formal reporting relationships, including the number of levels in the hierarchy and the span of control of managers and supervisors.[5] It also identifies the grouping together of individuals into departments, and departments into the total organization. Finally, it includes the design of systems to ensure effective communication, coordination, and integration of effort across departments. By doing so, the organizational structure supports the production of outputs and achievement of organizational goals, minimizes or at least regulates the influence of individual variation on the organization, and provides the setting within which power is exercised and decisions are made.[6]

Nonprofit structure does not exist in a vacuum of course, and it is important to understand its relationship to other aspects of the organization. Most of the writing about organizations, by both practitioners and academics, is organized around the essential elements of all organizations,

FIGURE 4.2. ELEMENTS OF ORGANIZATIONS

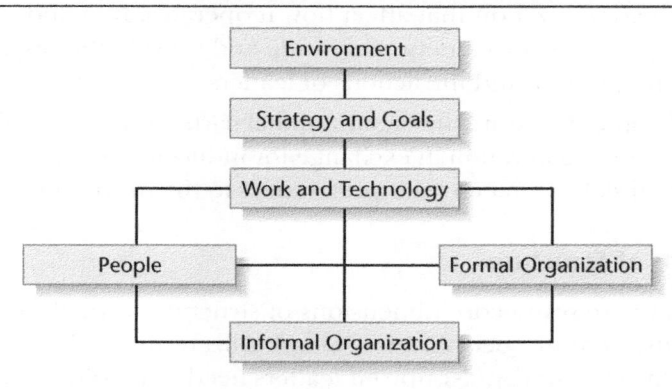

```
                    Environment
                         │
                  Strategy and Goals
                         │
          ┌──── Work and Technology ────┐
          │              │              │
       People            │       Formal Organization
          │              │              │
          └──── Informal Organization ──┘
```

Source: Adapted from W. Richard Scott and Gerald Davis, *Organizations and Organizing: Rational, Natural, and Open System Perspectives* (Upper Saddle River, NJ: Pearson Prentice Hall, 2007).

including structure. As Figure 4.2 shows, structure (formal and informal) connects to goals and strategy, work and technology, and people. Each element has reciprocal influences on the others and on the structural design, and the environment influences all of the elements, demonstrating the complexity of the management and analysis of nonprofit organizations.

These elements can be described as follows:[7]

- **Environment**. This encompasses all the significant elements outside the organization that influence its ability to survive and achieve its ends. These include physical, technological, cultural, financial, and social factors.
- **Strategy**. This term describes the choices an organization makes about which markets or clients it intends to serve. It includes the specific tactics the organization employs and the output goals it sets for itself.
- **Work and technology**. Work involves the tasks the organization needs to accomplish given the goals it has set for itself. Technology is the way in which work is accomplished and the techniques and process used to transform inputs into outputs.
- **Formal organization**. This is the more or less explicit codification of how the work of the organization is done and how its parts relate to each other. It includes elements such as human resource practices, the design of jobs, and the overall organizational structure.

- **Informal organization.** This describes the emergent characteristics of the organization that affect how it operates. It includes culture, norms and values, social networks inside and outside the organization, power and politics, and the actions of leaders.
- **People.** These are the organizational participants who make contributions to the organization in exchange for inducements, using their knowledge and skills to match their preferences to the needs of the organization.

Dimensions of Structure

There are seven core dimensions of structure: formalization, complexity, centralization, specialization, standardization, professionalism, and hierarchy of authority.[8] Nonprofit leaders need to consider how much of each dimension is needed for an effective and ethical organization.

- **Formalization** is the amount of written documentation in an organization. This could include job descriptions, procedures, regulations, codes of conduct, employment contracts, board bylaws, and policies. The more formalized a nonprofit, the less workers need to invent new procedures to get work done and the less uncertainty they have in their daily tasks. The price is that they also have less flexibility.
- **Complexity** is determined by the number of different activities or subsystems in an organization. *Vertical complexity* refers to the number of hierarchical levels of the organization. The Wikimedia Foundation organizational chart displayed in Exhibit 4.1 shows four levels, differentiated by the intensity of the shading of the boxes. *Horizontal complexity* refers to the number of units at similar levels. Wikimedia has five units at the chief officer level. *Geographical complexity* describes the spatial distribution of the organization. For example, Amnesty International in the Unites States is divided into five regions, each with its own staff: Southern, Mid-Atlantic, Northeast, Midwestern, and Western. Some nonprofits have complex parallel structures with two executive directors. For example, arts organizations sometimes have an artistic director and an administrative director, with distinct structures beneath each of them.
- **Centralization** is determined by the hierarchical level that has the authority to make decisions. In centralized organizations decisions are made primarily at the top level of the organization. Organizations are decentralized when decisions affecting the whole organization are also made at lower levels of the organization. In nonprofits, centralization issues can come into play in deciding what decision-making discretion to give the board versus the staff, and staff versus volunteers. Nonprofit membership associations often give legal rights to make certain decisions to their members, helping to decentralize the organization.

- **Specialization** is the degree to which organizational tasks are subdivided into separate jobs. If specialization is extensive, each employee performs only a narrow range of tasks. If specialization is low, employees perform a wide range of tasks in their jobs. Specialization is sometimes referred to as the division of labor. In organizing a nonprofit the designer needs to ask whether the workforce should be made up of specialists, generalists, or a combination of both.
- **Standardization** is the extent to which similar work activities are performed in a uniform manner. In highly standardized organizations, such as prisons, work content is described in detail, and similar work is performed the same way at all locations. Some standardization may be needed to comply with government regulations and contracts.
- **Professionalism** relates to the level of formal education and training of employees. Professionalism is considered high when employees require long or specialized periods of training to hold jobs in the organization or need certification or accreditation. Having professional workers—for example, certified social workers—is often a requirement to obtain government funding. Volunteer-based organizations or those that use mutual support models often consider sharing similar experiences with clients to be more important than professional training. The use of professionals in a nonprofit can be threatening or off-putting to those who have been working in nonprofits in similar roles without the professional training.
- **Hierarchy of authority** describes who reports to whom and the span of control for each manager, as covered previously in our discussion of organizational charts.

Types of Structure: Two Ideal Types

In the development of thinking about organizational structure, several ideas and formulations have been particularly important and useful. One of the most influential formulations about organizational structure was Max Weber's description of *bureaucracy*.[9] A bureaucratic organization has features such as a hierarchy of authority, limited authority, a relatively high level of specialization and division of labor, technically qualified personnel, positions separated from position holders, procedures for work, rules for incumbents, and differential rewards. These features were seen by Weber as enhancing organizational rationality and efficiency, especially as compared with organizations run on the basis of favoritism or family or political connections. Weber's description was presented as an ideal type, meaning that actual organizations would be found to be more or less bureaucratic. Bureaucratic features tend to increase with organizational size and age. As organizations grow they may find that the bureaucratic features that once enhanced their efficiency now impede it. At that point they may seek to reduce the level of bureaucracy in the organization. Some examples of organizations with bureaucratic characteristics are credit unions with their specialized personnel for different client needs, hospitals with their numerous departmental divisions, and nonprofit social service providers with their documentation requirements and strict procedures for dealing with a vulnerable clientele.

Exhibit 4.1 shows the hierarchical organizational chart for a nonprofit, the Wikimedia Foundation, Inc., which is "a nonprofit charitable organization dedicated to encouraging the growth, development, and distribution of free, multilingual content, and to providing the full content of these wiki-based projects to the public free of charge."[10] The chart shows the reporting relationships and the divisions of the foundation. The chief financial and operating officer reports to the deputy director, as does the chief technical officer. Two individuals report to the chief financial and operating officer and each of them has one person directly reporting to him or her. Contrast this with the chief technical officer who has a much larger span of control, with fourteen direct reports. There are many possible reasons why there is such a difference in span of control in this organization. It may be that the chief technical officer can give his or her direct reports great discretion over their job tasks, reducing the supervisory control needed. Alternatively, there may be technologies that help to control and integrate the work of the technical division so that it can effectively accommodate more subgroups with only one division head to oversee them. The complexity of the work of direct reports may be such that it is relatively easy for their supervisors to monitor it and funnel it to other divisions. The structure may also have simply evolved without strategic attention to what the most effective structure would be to accomplish the mission of the organization.

Looking at their organization's chart, nonprofit leaders should ask these questions:

- Does the organizational chart accurately depict the formal reporting relationships? If not, should the chart or the reporting relationships be changed? Ultimately, they should be aligned.
- Are the spans of control reasonable? In other words, does anyone have too many or too few people to manage given the needs of those being managed? Supervisors should have the time, skills, and systems needed to perform the human relations and work coordination functions related to each person reporting to them.
- Are the individuals operating at the same hierarchical level of the organization relatively equivalent in terms of their discretion, authority, and responsibility within the nonprofit? If not, they should be depicted above or below their current peers.

EXHIBIT 4.1. ORGANIZATIONAL CHART FOR THE WIKIMEDIA FOUNDATION

Executive Director
- Deputy Director
- Executive Assistant
- General Counsel

Chief Technical Officer
- Senior Product Manager
  - Researcher - UX
  - Lead Front-End Developer - UX
  - Software Developer - UX
  - Product Manager - Multimedia Usability
  - Software Developer - Multimedia Usability
- IT Manager
- Software Developer
- Networking Coordinator
- Code Maintenance Engineer
- System Administrator
- Software Developer and Office IT Support
- Engineering Program Manager
- Software Developer - Fundraising
- Software Developer - Mobile
- Data Analyst

Chief Community Officer
- Head of Community Giving
  - Stewardship Associate
  - Development Associate
- Head of Partnerships and Foundation Relations
- Head of Major Gifts
- Head of Public Outreach
  - Education Programs Manager
  - Outreach Officer
  - Project Manager - Bookshelf
- Head of Reader Relations
- Volunteer Coordinator

Chief Global Development Officer
- Head of Communications
- Communications Officer
- Head of Business Development

Chief Human Resources Officer - OPEN
- Human Resources Manager

Chief Financial and Operating Officer
- Accounting Manager and Financial Analyst
- Accounting Specialist
- Head of Office Administration
- Office IT Manager

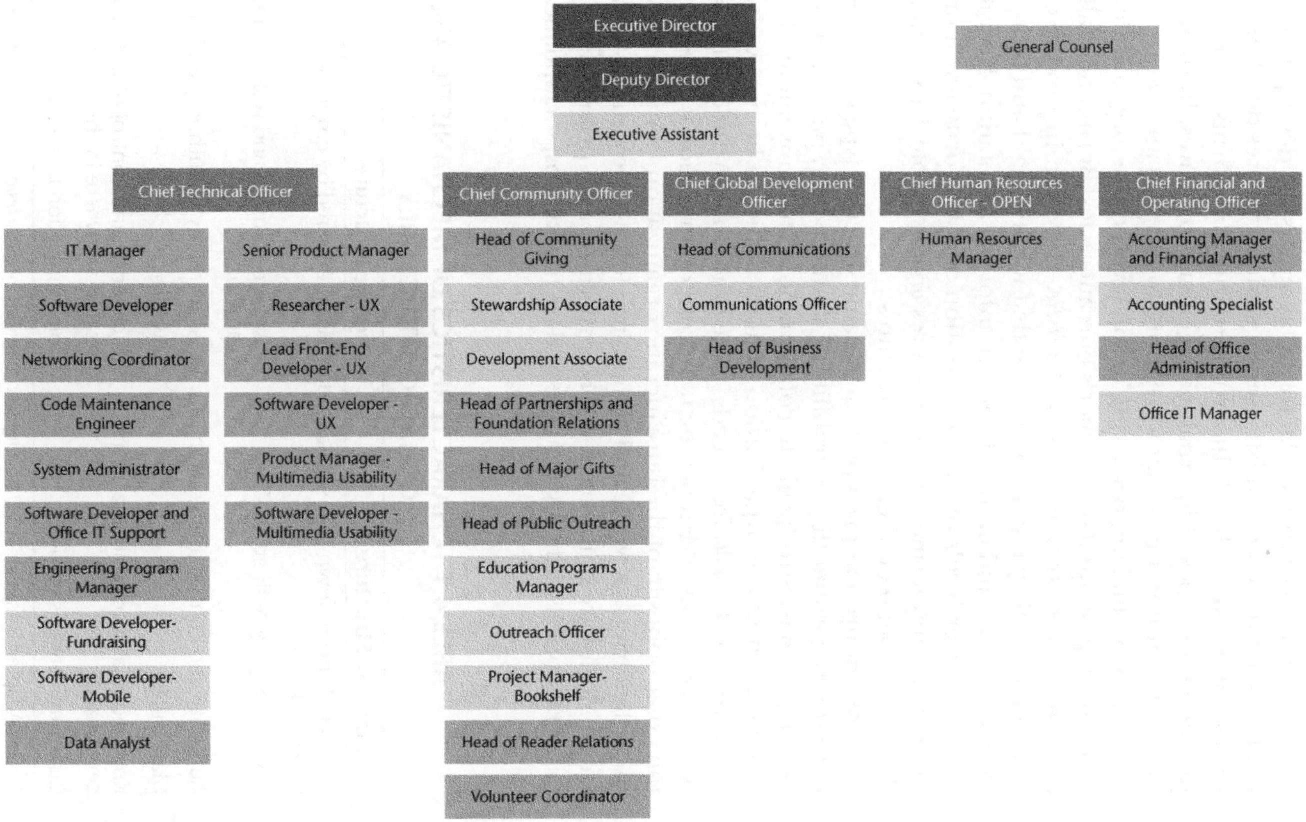

Source: Wikimedia Foundation, *Organizational Chart* (July 2010), http://en.wikipedia.org/wiki/File:Wikimedia_Foundation_organization_chart.png.

A second major influential formulation was the description of the distinctions between mechanistic and organic structures developed by Tom Burns and G. M. Stalker.[11] In a study of industrial firms in England, they identified two types of internal management structures. In stable environments they found firms that were more formalized and centralized, with most decision making occurring at top levels of the organization. These firms were quite similar to Weber's bureaucracies. Burns and Stalker characterized these structures as *mechanistic*. However, in rapidly changing environments they found a structure that was less rigid and more flexible, with fewer rules and more reliance on informal adaptation. Decisions were made at lower levels of the organization and authority was more widely dispersed. They termed these structures *organic*. Table 4.1 summarizes the differences between these two structures.

Many nonprofits exemplify the organic structure type because it appeals to values regarding the desirability of shared power, permeable organizational boundaries to facilitate collaboration, easy movement of members into and out of the organization, and an ability to be innovative and to mobilize quickly to address needs. Joyce Rothschild-Whitt describes an ideal type of a collectivist-democratic nonprofit organization whose features are the polar opposite of the bureaucratic organization.[12] Authority resides in the collectivity as a whole and compliance follows the consensus of the collective. Rules are minimal. Social controls are based primarily on personal or moral appeals. Employment is based on friendships, sociopolitical values,

TABLE 4.1. CHARACTERISTICS OF MECHANISTIC AND ORGANIC STRUCTURES

Mechanistic Structure	Organic Structure
Tasks are broken down into specialized, separate parts.	Tasks are shared by employees.
Tasks are rigidly defined.	Tasks are adjusted and redefined through teamwork.
Authority and control are hierarchical.	Less hierarchy of authority and control.
Many rules.	Few rules.
Knowledge and control of tasks are centralized.	Knowledge and control of tasks can be located anywhere in the organization.
Communication is vertical.	Communication is horizontal.

Source: Adapted from Richard Daft, *Organization Theory and Design*, 9th ed. (Mason, OH: Thomson South-Western, 2007).

personality attributes, and informally assessed knowledge and skills. The concept of career advancement is not meaningful, and there is no hierarchy of positions. There is a minimal division of labor, and jobs and functions are general and flexible. Finally, the primary incentives for participating in the organization are intrinsic (doing something that fits one's values and preferred social benefits), and extrinsic incentives (material benefits such as financial compensation) are secondary.

These features are characteristic of community and grassroots organizations.[13] Such organizations are composed mostly or completely of volunteers or members. Grassroots organizations are often locally oriented, focused on what is happening in participants' neighborhoods. They may be associated with social movements or engaged in advocacy. Some examples are legal collectives, alternative media collectives, food cooperatives, neighborhood beautification or watch groups, self-help groups dealing with diseases, citizen action committees, and recreational clubs. Exhibit 4.2 shows the organizational chart for the Oregon Organic Coalition, a nonprofit trade association with an organic structure that operates with rotating and fluid roles. It was founded to advance the development and growth of the organic industry and community in Oregon. For example, it advocates for using food from local farms in Oregon schools and for federal funding for research on organic crops. The work of the organization is conducted by volunteers, who participate in the leadership council, advisory committees, and task forces. There are no formal members in the legal sense or paid staff. The numerous opportunities participants have to give input and shape the activities of the organization make sense given that it exists to support those participants' interests.

Common Organizational Configurations

Besides these ideal types, we can identify a number of common types of structures. The overall configuration of structural elements indicates how work activities are divided, what the reporting relationships are, and how distinct units or departments are grouped relative to each other. Grouping is used to bring people and units together to facilitate work accomplishment. The configuration establishes the general principles for dividing work, breaking tasks into subtasks, and coordinating activities.[14] It specifies the overall units that are the basis for making decisions and communicating within the organization. The content and direction of information flows within the organization depend in part on the organization's configuration. A number of different bases can be used for nonprofit departmental grouping. It is also likely that changing conditions will lead to new configurations

EXHIBIT 4.2. EXAMPLE OF AN ORGANIC STRUCTURE: OREGON ORGANIC COALITION ORGANIZATIONAL CHART

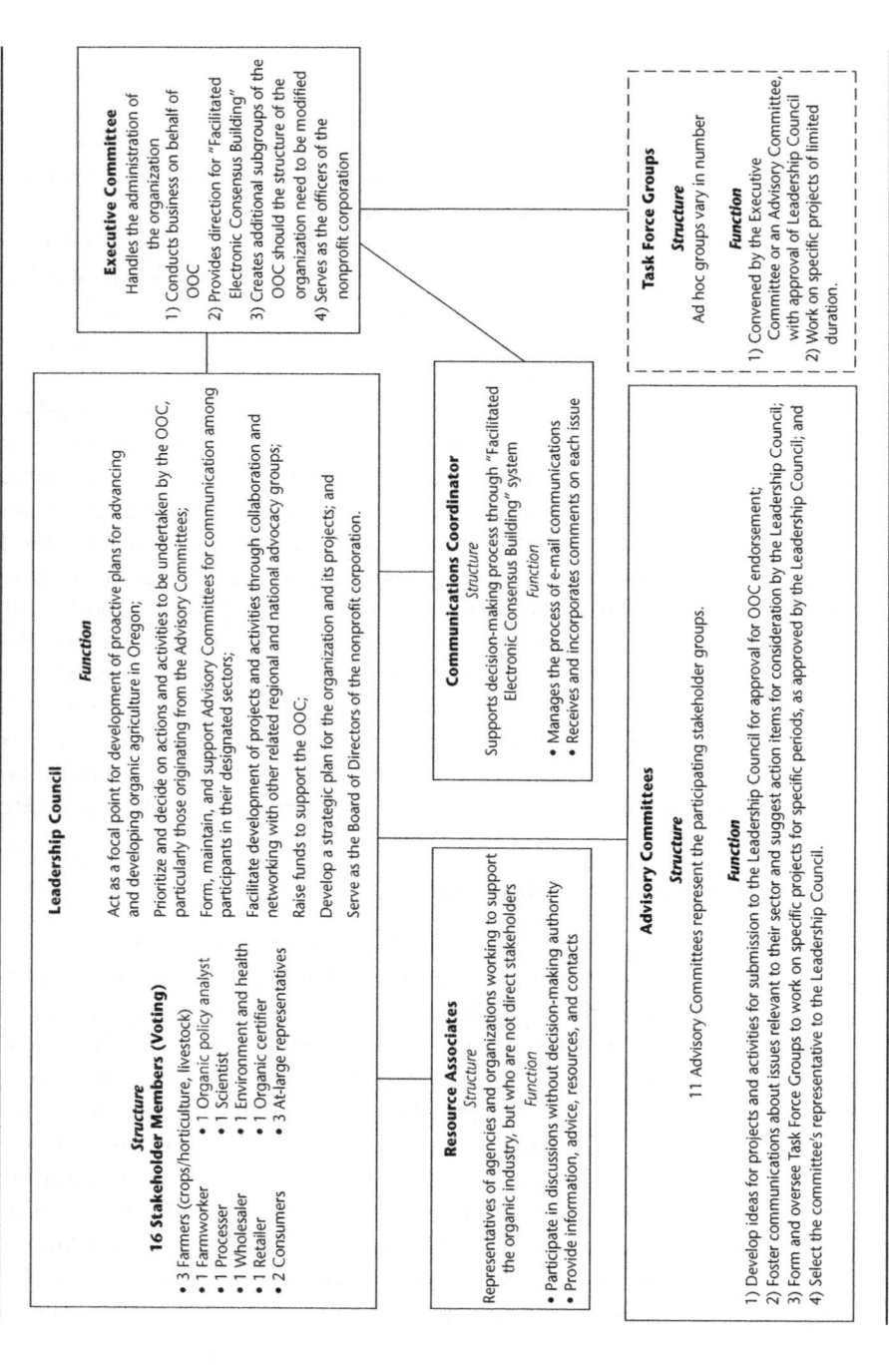

Leadership Council

Structure

16 Stakeholder Members (Voting)

- 3 Farmers (crops/horticulture, livestock)
- 1 Farmworker
- 1 Processer
- 1 Wholesaler
- 1 Retailer
- 2 Consumers
- 1 Organic policy analyst
- 1 Scientist
- 1 Environment and health
- 1 Organic certifier
- 3 At-large representatives

Function

Act as a focal point for development of proactive plans for advancing and developing organic agriculture in Oregon;

Prioritize and decide on actions and activities to be undertaken by the OOC, particularly those originating from the Advisory Committees;

Form, maintain, and support Advisory Committees for communication among participants in their designated sectors;

Facilitate development of projects and activities through collaboration and networking with other related regional and national advocacy groups;

Raise funds to support the OOC;

Develop a strategic plan for the organization and its projects; and

Serve as the Board of Directors of the nonprofit corporation.

Executive Committee

Handles the administration of the organization

1) Conducts business on behalf of OOC
2) Provides direction for "Facilitated Electronic Consensus Building"
3) Creates additional subgroups of the OOC should the structure of the organization need to be modified
4) Serves as the officers of the nonprofit corporation

Resource Associates

Structure

Representatives of agencies and organizations working to support the organic industry, but who are not direct stakeholders

Function

- Participate in discussions without decision-making authority
- Provide information, advice, resources, and contacts

Communications Coordinator

Structure

Supports decision-making process through "Facilitated Electronic Consensus Building" system

Function

- Manages the process of e-mail communications
- Receives and incorporates comments on each issue

Advisory Committees

Structure

11 Advisory Committees represent the participating stakeholder groups.

Function

1) Develop ideas for projects and activities for submission to the Leadership Council for approval for OOC endorsement;
2) Foster communications about issues relevant to their sector and suggest action items for consideration by the Leadership Council;
3) Form and oversee Task Force Groups to work on specific projects for specific periods, as approved by the Leadership Council; and
4) Select the committee's representative to the Leadership Council.

Task Force Groups

Structure

Ad hoc groups vary in number

Function

1) Convened by the Executive Committee or an Advisory Committee, with approval of Leadership Council
2) Work on specific projects of limited duration.

Source: Oregon Organic Coalition, *Procedures Manual* (2006), http://www.oregonorganiccoalition.org/pdf/orgchart.pdf. Reprinted by permission of Oregon Organic Coalition.

within a nonprofit. The common departmental grouping options discussed in the following paragraphs include functional, divisional, matrix, geographical, horizontal, and virtual network structures.

In a *functional structure* activities are grouped together into units or departments by types of work skills and tasks—common functions such as fundraising, marketing, and service provision. This structure can facilitate economies of scale because the organization needs only one unit for each function. Also, grouping all the knowledge and skills for one function together can promote the development of functional expertise. The Wikimedia Foundation is an example of a functional structure, with groupings around technology, community, global development, human resources, and finances. This structure functions best when little horizontal coordination is needed, as horizontal communication or coordination between functional departments will be difficult. Communication between two departments will need to go through a higher organizational level so that decision making can be centralized, with upper-level units deciding on matters that cut across functions in addition to matters that affect the organization as a whole. This communication and coordination pattern can create burdens for the top levels of the organization, resulting in slow response time in changing environments, poor horizontal coordination, and reduced innovation. This structure is therefore best for organizations with relatively few products and working in relatively stable environments.

In a *divisional structure* in contrast, unit grouping is based not on functions but on organizational outputs or products. Each division is organized by the product it produces. Also, the functional departments needed to produce each division's output are contained in that division. This allows for decentralized decision making at the divisional level, freeing the top level of the organization to concentrate on overall decision making and on decisions on issues spanning divisions. For example, top leadership can play the role of organizational banker, deciding the level of resources allocated to divisions. Southend Community Services is an example of a divisional structure, with youth services, child-care, and elderly services divisions. Decentralized decision making and coordination of functions within divisions allows the organization to react quickly to environmental changes, including shifts in customer desires or market conditions. This structure is appropriate for larger organizations with multiple products or services. The major weakness of this structure is that economies of scale within functions are not possible. For example, each division might have a fundraising or marketing department. In addition, coordination across divisions (product lines) may be difficult and would have to be done by higher-level units.

The principle in a *geographical structure* is to organize in terms of the location of the organization's users or customers. With this grouping the organization can address and respond to customer wants and needs that may vary by location (different regions of one country or different countries). For example, large nonprofits such as the Girl Scouts or Boy Scouts, United Way, and Goodwill use semiautonomous local units and a national headquarters. This structure can be extended globally, with nonprofits such as Heifer International having operations in various nations around the globe. A number of options are possible.[15] Multinational organizations have their operations in each country acting as divisions in a decentralized structure. Global organizations, in contrast, centralize knowledge in their headquarters and implement actions through national units, similar to a functional structure. International organizations have hybrid frameworks, with some activities centralized and some decentralized. Finally, transnational organizations are complex structures, with assets and capabilities dispersed, interdependent, and specialized. National units are integrated into a worldwide system.

A number of structures have been designed for situations calling for extraordinary flexibility. A *matrix structure* simultaneously uses aspects of both the functional and divisional structures. This is a complex structure, because it features two types of management and three types of units. Functional managers have responsibility for employees with various skills and expertise, whereas product managers have responsibility for producing outputs. Employees are under the authority of both types of managers. They are assigned by functional managers to various product units, where they are supervised by product managers. For example, a nonprofit providing housing assistance may have

- Functional units organized around expertise in (a) construction, (b) client counseling, (c) financing, or (d) law and policy.
- Product units that may include (a) new house construction, (b) existing housing rehabilitation, (c) financial assistance to home owners, or (d) advocacy.
- Projects that may involve community development in different areas of a city. Some areas may need new housing, others may need rehabilitation, and still others may need action by the city. For each project the best mix of personnel from the functional and product units is chosen for the project team. The team is disbanded after the project is completed.

The matrix structure is appropriate under a variety of conditions, including those where pressure exists to share scarce resources across product lines, environmental pressure exists for two or more critical outputs (such as in-depth technical knowledge and frequent new products), or the environment is both complex and uncertain.[16] Under these circumstances, vertical (functional) and horizontal (team) authority are both given recognition. The advantage of the matrix structure is that it is flexible in terms of both human resources and products. This makes it particularly useful in rapidly changing environments. It is best suited to medium-sized organizations with multiple products. The structure, however, has a number of weaknesses. Employees are responsible to two managers, which violates the principle of the unity of authority. This can cause frustration for employees and managers and requires individuals with good interpersonal skills and a willingness to work in a shifting and ambiguous work setting. Disputes over authority relations are more likely to arise here than in other structures, and time and effort must be expended in resolving them.

Finally, an emerging form termed the *virtual network structure* extends the concept of horizontal coordination and collaboration beyond the boundaries of the traditional organization. This structure is characterized by the outsourcing, or contracting, of some of an organization's functions or activities. With the advent and growth of increasingly extensive and sophisticated electronic communication systems, a network of outside specialists can be located anywhere and coordinated by the core, or central, organization. This allows the core organization to take advantage of the specialized expertise of any number of partner organizations. The organization decides which functions it will outsource and how much control it will maintain or allocate to the partner organizations. This structure gives an organization worldwide access to talent, resources, and capabilities without the need to invest in its own facilities or employees. This reduces overhead and makes the organization highly flexible and responsive to changing environments. For example, the housing nonprofit in the previous example may decide to expand its impact nationally. It has the capacity to use a matrix structure to complete a wide variety of projects locally. Outside of this, however, it may be able to provide only Web-based client education for a national constituency. In order to provide its other services, it could establish partnerships with other nonprofits. In each locale the partners could be linked into a network and coordinated via electronic media. The primary weakness of this structure is the increased difficulty of maintaining control over far-flung partners, including the need to make contracts with these partners and monitor contract compliance. The organization is also dependent on partner performance and potentially vulnerable to partner failure.

Major Influences on Organizational Structure

Many factors have a role in influencing the structure of a nonprofit, including information processing needs and political, cultural, and institutional influences.

Structure and Information Processing

One of the primary activities in an organization is to provide information when and where it is needed in order for the organization to accomplish its tasks. Information needs are contingent on a number of factors, including the technology used to accomplish tasks, the organization's environment, and the organization's strategy. *Technology* here is broadly defined, referring not only to the machines and hardware used to perform work but also to the skills and knowledge of workers. John Galbraith has provided a formulation that holds that information needs are a function of three dimensions of technology: complexity, uncertainty, and interdependence.[17] Information needs increase as the complexity, uncertainty, and interdependency involved in accomplishing tasks increase. Moreover, their influence is multiplicative in that the effect of any one dimension is much greater when another is also present.

- **Complexity** is a function of the number of different items or elements that must be dealt with simultaneously in task accomplishment. It can be measured by the variety of inputs or the degree of customization of outputs. For example, a fundraising event has greater complexity when it involves donors with diverse interests and giving potential. More information needs to be considered and communicated to coordinate an event suited to a wide range of donors.
- **Uncertainty** refers to the variability of the items or elements on which work is performed. This can be measured by the number of exceptions encountered during the production of outputs. A fundraising event scheduled to be held outdoors has uncertainty related to weather conditions. Contingency plans need to be developed in case of bad weather.
- **Interdependency** is the extent to which items or elements on which work is performed or the work processes themselves are interrelated, requiring information sharing. James Thompson relates information use to types of interdependence.[18] The fundraising event, for instance, may have *pooled interdependence* because the program and development staff need to work together as a team to create a report to donors on the organization's achievements. It may have *sequential interdependence* in that

someone must first secure the venue before the food and entertainment can be arranged. Task accomplishment of one person or unit is dependent on the output of another. It may also have *reciprocal interdependence,* with units posing critical contingencies for each other that have to be resolved before action can be taken. For example, tickets cannot be sold until prices are determined, which may depend on estimated costs and revenue goals and an assessment of the market base and opportunities for sponsorships.

In addition, organizational information needs have been linked to organizational environments and strategy.[19] In addition to increasing for technological reasons, information needs increase with increasing environmental uncertainty, complexity, and change. Strategy affects the way an organization is run, which affects organizational structure and decision making. This in turn can affect the degree of information processing needed. As the example of Southend Community Services/Our Piece of the Pie shows, a change of strategy can lead to an increase in the amount of information the organization needs to gather and process.

When information flow in a nonprofit is inadequate, a number of problems can arise. The people who need information may not get it. Or they may get too little information, too much information, or information of the wrong type. In all these cases, job performance will be negatively affected. A nonprofit's structure is key to proper information flow. The design challenge is to create structures that match the demands for information processing. Information needs to flow horizontally as well as vertically through an organization in order to link employees, work units, and organizational levels. As information processing needs increase, an organization can respond by increasing the information handling capacity of its structure. This can be done by increasing the capacity of vertical and horizontal linkages.

Vertical Linkages

Vertical linkages can be used to coordinate activities between the various levels of a nonprofit and are primarily used for control. They ensure that lower levels of the nonprofit are aligned with goals set at higher levels and higher levels are informed of the activities of lower levels. A variety of structural mechanisms can be used to support a nonprofit's vertical linkage requirements. They are ranked here in order of increasing information handling capability:

- Rules, schedules, and plans can be used when problems, issues, or decisions between levels are routine or repetitious. This alleviates the need for direct communication for coordination.

- Hierarchical referral is used when members of a unit (or several units) at one level can't resolve a problem or make a decision. The matter is referred to, or passed to, decision makers at the next higher level in the hierarchy.
- Vertical information systems include periodic reports, written information, and computer-based communications distributed between levels of the hierarchy.

Horizontal Linkages

Horizontal linkages can be used to ensure coordination between units at the same level of a nonprofit, such as divisions or departments within a division (fundraising, marketing, production, and the like). Without horizontal linkages, information sent from one unit to another would have to flow up vertically to a higher unit that oversees both of the lower-level units and then be routed down to the recipient unit. A number of structural alternatives are available to support horizontal information flow. These are ranked here in order of increasing information flow. However, that ranking is inversely related to the cost of the time and human resources needed to establish and maintain each linkage.

- Horizontal information systems can be used to exchange information between units (workgroups, departments, divisions, and so on). Routinized and computerized information systems can provide periodic information about activities and information about problems, opportunities, and needed decisions.
- Direct contact can be established between managers or employees affected by a problem, opportunity, process, or decision. For example, a liaison role may be played by a person in one unit who is given the responsibility of communicating with another unit in order to enhance coordination and cooperation.
- Task forces are useful when linkage is needed between more than two departments. A task force is a temporary group composed of representatives of the units needing to be linked. Each member represents the interests of his or her unit and can carry information about the task force's activities back to that unit. Task forces are typically disbanded after the tasks they were formed to address have been accomplished.
- A full-time integrator differs from a liaison in several respects. This is a position created to link several units. Also, the integrator's position is outside the units being linked. The integrator has the responsibility to coordinate the units. His or her title may be product or program manager when a product's or program's accomplishment requires several units to coordinate.
- A project team is the strongest horizontal linkage, more significant than a task force. Project teams are used when activities among units require

extensive and relatively long-lasting coordination, such as when organizations have a large-scale project or are exploring a major innovation or new product line.

Political, Cultural, and Institutional Influences on Structure

Organizations, including nonprofits, seek to be rational and to design their structures for efficiency and effectiveness. Organizational design, however, is a far from simple process with predictable outcomes. According to Hall and Tolbert, "Organizational design does affect structure, but not in the simple, overly rational manner suggested by the authors of prescriptive solutions for organizations."[20] Organizational structure is also affected by the politics of strategy formation and cultural and institutional factors. Although these topics will be covered in detail in other chapters, it is useful here to mention their relationship to organizational structure.

The strategic choices organizations make are influenced by bounded rationality and the politics of the decision-making process.[21] Organizational choices are made by *dominant coalitions*. Various interest groups within organizations each have preferences for organizational goals. No one interest group is normally powerful enough to impose its preferences on the organization. Consequently it needs to form a coalition with other interest groups who can agree to cooperate (each giving up some part of its preferences in order to form the coalition). The power of a coalition comes from combining the power held by the various parties in the coalition. The power of a dominant coalition is greater than that of other coalitions in the organization. This coalition will form the power center of the organization. Decision makers in the dominant coalition engage in a political process to select those parts of the environment with which the organization will be concerned, strategies to deal with the environment, technologies, and roles and relationships (structure) to control the technologies and implement strategy. In nonprofit organizations such political struggles over strategic choices may be especially pervasive, given the wide variety of stakeholders who might claim to be legitimate members of coalitions.

National culture will also influence organizational structure. Organizations are located in national cultural contexts, and organizational cultures will be a reflection of the larger culture.[22] National culture can be reflected in how organizations structure authority relations; decision-making responsibility; control and communication systems; and employee training, recruitment, evaluation, and promotion. This is important for understanding nonprofits, as they may be structured and operated very differently in different national culture settings. Similarly, the operations of nonprofits with global scope or working in international settings such as development may be structured differently across national cultures.

Organizational culture is the set of key values, beliefs, understandings, and norms shared by organizational participants. It underlies the behavior of the organization as a whole and of the participants. It affects ethical behavior, management commitment to employees, employee commitment to the organization, and the relative importance placed on efficiency or customer service. An organization's culture is unwritten but can be observed in organizational stories, slogans, ceremonies, dress, and office layout. Such cultures are relatively stable and long lasting and are a context within which structures are formed. Culture can affect preferences, such as those for centralization or decentralization, and it interacts with other contextual factors. Nonprofits can have distinct cultures that affect all aspects of their structures and operations. These cultures can be based on mission, a service or client orientation, management preferences, or workplace arrangements. They may also be ideologically based, such as with a focus on feminism, holistic medicine, or environmentalism.

Finally, DiMaggio and Powell note that organizations exist in *fields* composed of other organizations providing the same societal function.[23] Within these fields, social pressures exist for organizations to become homogeneous. This process is termed *institutional isomorphism* and is the result of three possible forces. *Coercive isomorphism* occurs when less powerful organizations conform to the wishes of other, more powerful organizations. For example, funders and regulators can compel nonprofits to adopt particular structures, such as evaluation units. *Mimetic isomorphism* is the result of organizations in uncertain environments copying the structures of organizations perceived to be more successful. For example, a nonprofit may establish a marketing research department if it feels that this has contributed to the success of other similar nonprofits. Finally, *normative isomorphism* is due to the spread and adoption of ideas about appropriate structures that is fostered by professional management schools and consultants. For example, consultants may advise nonprofits to establish accepted models of good governance that specify a particular board structure and way of operation. In each of these cases, nonprofits adopt the structures and processes of other nonprofits in their field.

Structural Deficiency

Nonprofits use valued time, effort, and money designing and redesigning their structures in an effort to enhance their effectiveness and keep abreast of changes inside and outside the organization. The previous discussion reveals that this is far from a simple task and that trade-offs often need to be considered. The consequences of inattention to structural needs or inappropriate structural design can, however, be quite serious. A number of symptoms of structural deficiency have been identified. They manifest themselves when organizational structures are out of alignment with organizational needs.[24] When they occur, nonprofit managers must move quickly to diagnose and correct any underlying structural problems.

- Decision making is delayed or lacking in quality. When this occurs decision makers may be overloaded because the hierarchy funnels too many problems and decisions to them. Delegation to lower levels may be insufficient. Information may not reach the right people because horizontal or vertical information linkages may not be adequate.
- The organization does not respond innovatively to a changing environment. In this situation departments may not be coordinating horizontally. The organizational structure also has to specify departmental responsibilities that include environmental scanning and innovation.
- Employee performance declines and goals are not being met. Employee performance may decline because the structure doesn't provide clear goals, responsibilities, and mechanisms for coordination. The structure should reflect the complexity of the environment and be straightforward enough for employees to work effectively within it.
- Too much conflict is evident. In this case the structure may need to allow conflicting departmental goals to combine into a single set of goals for the entire organization. When departments act at cross-purposes or are under pressure to achieve departmental goals at the expense of organizational goals, the structure is often at fault. Horizontal linkage mechanisms are not adequate.

Concluding Thoughts

Nonprofit organizational structure is both a consequence and a cause. It is a consequence of the nonprofit's external context as well as its work processes and strategy. In turn structure influences many of the internal features of the nonprofit, such as information flow, authority relations, and hierarchy. In addition it has both deterministic elements and flexibility. On the one hand a nonprofit organization cannot survive if its structure is too far out of line with important external or internal contingencies. On the other hand nonprofit organizations usually have a range of design options for accomplishing their tasks.

Given the nature of organizational structure and the diversity of the environments that nonprofits operate in, their missions and strategies, and their internal and external stakeholders, it is not surprising that nonprofit structures take many different forms. For instance, nonprofits may provide public or private goods, get funds from sales or donations, and use employees or volunteers. Each option has several structural implications. Depending on these and other factors, nonprofits may look structurally much like business firms or public agencies, or they may take on hybrid or unique forms. They may also be located in rapidly changing and unpredictable environments, which will have other structural ramifications. All these factors make the structural design tasks for nonprofit organizations continuously challenging.

In the next chapter we consider strategy formation. It is important to remember that this process, as well as the others to follow in subsequent chapters, is intimately interrelated with structure. On one hand the organizational actions required by a strategy that is out of line with existing structure will not be possible. On the other hand a nonprofit may change its structure to facilitate the accomplishment of a new strategic direction. In these ways structure will both influence and be influenced by strategy in a dynamic manner.

Questions for Consideration

1. Nonprofits are sometimes said to have "too much" structure or "too little" structure. Explain what each condition means, how it may come about, and what it might lead to.
2. How might a nonprofit's structural design be influenced by factors outside the organization? How might the design be influenced by factors inside the organization? How might a nonprofit balance these two influences on its structure?

Exercises

Exercise 4.1: Dimensions of Structure

Think of a large nonprofit hospital on the one hand and a small garden club that meets monthly at a member's house for discussions on the other. Describe how these nonprofits are likely to differ in terms of

1. Formalization
2. Complexity
3. Centralization

Why might you expect them to differ on these dimensions?

Exercise 4.2: Structural Design

Organizational structure needs to be aligned with the organization's technology, environment, and strategy. Assume you want to organize one of the following types of nonprofit. After you pick one, answer the questions that follow.

- An agency providing food and clothing to the poor
- A year-round camp for young people
- An art museum and gallery

1. What might your organization's mission statement be?
2. What tasks need to be done to provide its services?
3. Using your answers to the previous questions and information in this chapter, draw an organizational chart illustrating a functional structure for this organization.
4. Draw another organizational chart showing how this organization would look with a divisional structure.
5. What are the pros and cons of these alternative structural configurations?
6. Under what circumstances might it be useful for your organization to have a matrix structure?
7. Under what circumstances might your organization employ a virtual network structure?

Exercise 4.3: Structure and Information

Looking further at the nonprofit you described in Exercise 4.2, discuss its probable information processing needs, and describe the horizontal and vertical information linkages that might meet these needs.

PART TWO
STRATEGIZING, RESOURCING, AND ALIGNING

CHAPTER FIVE

FORMULATION OF STRATEGY

In 1981, the Flinn Foundation in Arizona was focusing its grants on advancing medical education, biomedical research, and a few community health projects.[1] Several years later, sparked by a doubling of bequests, the foundation expanded to support programs in education and the arts. By 2001, it was funding 100 to 150 grants per year for matters as diverse as pregnant teenagers, cross-border issues with Mexico, art exhibitions, scholarships, and endowed chairs. Several factors led the foundation to reevaluate and change this scattered approach, including new board members who questioned it, outside criticism of some of the projects the foundation was supporting, and an economic downturn in Arizona. In response the foundation's leaders began a strategic planning process. They reexamined the foundation's mission and the donors' intent and came to the conclusion that the foundation's money should be spent for the benefit of future generations and long-term systemic changes and not for short-term charitable goals. The board identified three broad areas of focus: health policy, community health, and bioscience research. The board then asked staff and consultants to develop scenarios in each of these areas that would lead to action plans. After a review of these scenarios and a vigorous debate, the board decided to focus on biosciences. A consulting firm was hired to assess the state of biomedical research in Arizona and develop a plan and goals to make Arizona more competitive in biotechnology within ten years. As a result of this strategic planning, Flinn was able to focus its grantmaking on several key strategies—in particular, building the research infrastructure and a thriving bioscience industry. It made fewer but larger grants and now averages about five grants a year. In addition, the foundation acts as a champion for the biosciences and as a coalition builder in this area. Arizona has since seen dramatic increases in jobs, research funding, businesses, and wages in the bioscience sector, and the Flinn Foundation is credited by state leaders with having been instrumental in changing the state's bioscience landscape.

The story of the Flinn Foundation illustrates the key role that strategic planning plays in directing and focusing the activities of nonprofit organizations as they seek to meet their missions and enhance their impact. What is a strategy? How should nonprofits formulate strategies? What factors can make strategic planning more successful? In this chapter we examine the nature of strategy. We present common strategy-related tools and outline a strategic planning process. We also discuss a number of options for thinking about and formulating strategy.

Business Strategy: A Starting Point for Nonprofit Strategy

Strategy is often defined as a plan designed to achieve a particular long-term aim or goal. The word derives from the Greek *strategia*, or "generalship." Sun Tzu's *The Art of War*, written around 500 B.C., is generally acknowledged to be the earliest existing systematic and extensive discussion of military strategy and is still cited as useful reading for managers.[2]

We begin by taking a brief look at the extensive literature on business strategy in order to place nonprofit strategy in perspective. Nonprofit scholars and practitioners have drawn from the frameworks developed for businesses. They have in addition created their own tools for strategic planning, as we will see later in this chapter.

A Brief History of Business Strategy

Strategic planning in American business can be traced to the adoption of a scientific approach to management in the early decades of the 1900s. *Scientific management's* central tenets were rational planning and organizational design based on corporate objectives established by top leaders.[3] Strategy got a big boost in the post-World War II period, when American industry underwent a major expansion, and long-term planning and control became key priorities of large firms wishing to develop new markets.[4] In this business environment, strategy and strategic planning began to take center stage in business thinking. Along with this, prominent academic writers in the 1960s, such as Alfred Chandler and H. Igor Ansoff, insisted that all companies needed an overall corporate strategy.[5]

Alfred Chandler, writing in 1962, is credited with the first use of the term *strategy* in the business context. He provided the classic definition of *strategic management* as "the determination of the basic long-term goals and objectives of an enterprise and the adoption of courses of action and the allocation of resources necessary for carrying out these goals."[6] These and other foundational statements promulgated a view that strategy is about top organizational leaders developing long-range objectives and plans based on the company's desired position in the market.[7] Henry Mintzberg characterizes the thinking in this early period as follows: "When strategic planning arrived on the scene in the mid 1960s, corporate leaders embraced it as 'the one best way' to devise and implement strategies that would enhance the competitiveness of each business unit. . . . Planning systems were expected to produce the best strategies as well as step-by-step instructions for carrying out those strategies so that the doers, the managers of business, could not get them wrong."[8]

The highly rational and analytical models and practices of strategy formation began to be challenged in the mid-1970s.[9] In academia, theorists were developing a variety of less rational or nonrational models of organizations. These models painted a picture of organizational decision making influenced by environmental and social factors. The implications of this for strategy formation were first highlighted in the early 1970s, when research by Henry Mintzberg found that managers were less likely to use analytical planning tools than previously assumed.[10] It was also in the 1970s that the first oil crisis revealed the strategic plans of American businesses to be flawed in that they did not address the possibility of such a crisis in their corporate visions of the future. Around the same time, Japanese companies were experiencing dramatic success despite putting less effort into strategic planning than U.S. companies did. These challenges to formal strategic planning led to a barrage of alternative definitions, models, and practices.

Contemporary Business Strategy

The shifts in thinking that have occurred throughout the history of business strategy have led to a diverse range of theories and models. A 1998 review by Henry Mintzberg, Bruce Ahlstrand, and Joseph Lampel concluded that a variety of general definitions of strategy could be identified in the literature.[11] The dominant view was to see strategy as a *plan*—a guide or course of action into the future or a path to get from here to there. In addition, however, strategy was described in other ways: for example, as a *pattern* of consistent behavior over time, as the *position* of particular products in particular markets, as an organization's *perspective* or fundamental way of doing things, or even as just a *ploy* or specific maneuver intended to outwit an opponent or competitor. These definitions of and approaches to strategy are not conflicting, and they emphasize the different roles that strategy can play in an organization. They also usefully distinguish between strategies and plans. As these definitions suggest, nonprofits may have a strategy with no plan to achieve it or have plans that are not part of any overall strategy. In addition, Mintzberg and his colleagues identify a number of models of strategy formation.[12] The models usually found in textbooks and the practitioner literature explain how to develop a strategic plan by completing a series of prescribed steps and using particular tools. We discuss these steps in detail later in the chapter. These models are based on rational planning in which clear and unique strategies are formulated through a deliberate process of matching internal and external organizational situations. A rigorous set of steps is used. The organization is placed in the context of its industry, and an analysis examines how the organization can improve its strategic positioning in that industry.

An alternative model that is receiving increasing attention is based on organizational learning and holds that strategy formation is an emergent process. In this model, management pays close attention to what does and does not work and incorporates lessons learned into an overall plan of action. Moreover, because the world is too complex for strategies to be developed all at once, they must emerge in small steps as an organization adapts or learns. A vigorous (and at times vitriolic) debate developed in the 1990s between advocates of the more rationally oriented planning models and the emergence model. The result has been an acknowledgment that strategy can result from planning or can emerge without planning and that the increasingly complex world dictates that classical planning approaches need to be adapted to practical circumstances.

Nonprofits and Strategic Planning

Against the backdrop of strategy in business, we next look at strategic planning in the nonprofit context. Formal strategic planning began to appear in the nonprofit sector in the mid- to late 1970s. A number of commentators have noted the differences between nonprofits and for-profits that might influence strategic planning.[13] For nonprofits:

- Service is intangible and hard to measure, and a nonprofit may have multiple service objectives.
- Customer influence may be weak.
- Employees may be strongly committed to a profession or to a cause.
- Resource contributors may intrude into internal management.
- There may be constraints on the use of rewards or punishments.
- A charismatic leader or the mystique of the enterprise may be the means of resolving conflict.

- The existence of multiple stakeholders means that leaders need people skills in addition to or instead of planning skills.
- A nonprofit's ability to change may be limited.

These differences have led some researchers to conclude that nonprofit organizations exist in environments that differ sharply from the environments of for-profit firms and that nonprofits have more values-based goals and missions.[14] This is certainly true for some nonprofits, such as advocacy groups and many environmental and civic organizations, and it limits the usefulness of for-profit rational planning models for these organizations. However, other nonprofit organizations, such as hospitals, day-care organizations, and nursing homes, operate in environments more similar to for-profit environments. For these organizations, adapting business sector strategic planning models can be useful. The benefits of strategic planning for nonprofits include identification of important internal and external influences, the generation of viable options, and understanding of potential effects of strategies on stakeholders.[15] To understand strategic planning in nonprofits, we will first consider a number of general strategic orientations that nonprofits could adopt.

General Strategic Orientations

In this section we look at orientations to organizational strategy. We begin by focusing on strategic positioning.

Strategic Positioning

A nonprofit organization may have a generic overarching strategy, termed its *strategic position*, under which more specific strategies fit. Much work in the corporate and nonprofit strategy field has been devoted to identifying such generic strategies.[16] One of the best-known formulations of strategic positions is Michael Porter's view that there are three generic strategies: cost leadership, differentiation, and focus.[17] In a *cost leadership* strategy, an organization focuses on using efficiency, standardization, and high volume to reduce costs through economies of scale. The organization thrives by selling at a low price to a large customer base. For example, Goodwill Industries is a leader in the secondhand clothing industry with its extensive network of retail stores. A *differentiation* strategy, in contrast, involves positioning the organization to offer unique products for select buyers in a broad market. Specialization can be based on a number of factors, including but not limited to product design, technology, features, dealers, and customer service. These features allow the company to charge a premium price, which buyers (or donors) are willing to pay as long as they perceive added value in the product. Brand loyalty is a critical factor for continued success. Harvard University offers a good example in the nonprofit sector of adopting a differentiation strategy. Finally, an organization with a *focus* strategy relies on a narrow market focus as opposed to the broad market scope of the previous strategies. The organization positions itself to succeed by developing a high level of knowledge and competence in its limited market segment. Competitive advantage can be obtained through innovation and marketing. Among nonprofits, holistic or alternative health clinics may exemplify this strategy.

Raymond Miles and Charles Snow offer another popular framework, in which they differentiate four generic strategy types: defender, prospector, analyzer, and reactor.[18] The most appropriate choice among these strategies depends on an organization's environment, technology, and structure.

Defenders are mature organizations in mature and stable industries. They seek stability and to protect their market position through efficient production, strong control mechanisms, continuity, and reliability. For example, a long-established nonprofit hospital may emphasize doing well what it already does and keeping out new competitors, rather than seeking new entrepreneurial opportunities.

Almost the opposite of defenders, *prospectors* seek to exploit new opportunities in products, services, or markets. A prospector's strength is in innovation and flexibility. This strategy is most appropriate in dynamic and turbulent environments. When Habitat for Humanity began, it was a classic prospector. Its mission of helping low-income individuals build their own homes gave it a unique place in the marketplace.

Analyzers are organizations that seek to minimize risk while maximizing profit through innovation. They typically concentrate on a limited range of products and try to outperform others. This is most appropriate in a changing but not turbulent environment. Some nonprofit schools that delved heavily into distance learning may be seen as analyzers. They figured out how to use their existing strengths profitably to deliver online courses in ways that did not undermine their existing programs delivered in a traditional format.

Finally, *reactors* are organizations that exert little control over their environment. They do not adapt to competition and do not have a systematic strategy, design, or structure for responding to changes in the environment. For example, nonprofits that find their mission is no longer relevant to existing conditions may become reactors. Rather than redefine themselves, they may wait to see if and when conditions might change back in their favor. If conditions do not shift, they risk losing resources and being forced to close their doors. Lack of capacity to

Formulation of Strategy

monitor the environment or initiate changes in the organization may also lead to a reactionary stance. A small grassroots nonprofit that has lost most of its members may find itself in this situation.

MacMillan's Framework

Porter's and Miles's and Snow's frameworks were developed for for-profits. Ian MacMillan has developed a portfolio approach to identifying generic strategic alternatives for nonprofit organizations.[19] MacMillan's framework is based on the assumptions that nonprofit organizations must compete for scarce community resources, that duplication of services should be avoided except when a safety net is needed, and that communities are best served by a high-quality service provider. One implication of these assumptions is that some nonprofit providers or programs should be terminated if they do not provide optimal benefits for the community, opening the way for more effective providers or programs. That is, community benefit should be the primary consideration in choosing whether a nonprofit should collaborate, compete, or end a program.

MacMillan's framework has three dimensions. Each program that a nonprofit offers can be evaluated on these dimensions. *Program attractiveness* is the degree to which the nonprofit sees a program as congruent with a number of positive factors including mission, goals, resources, benefits to clients, and potential to generate revenues or other benefits for the nonprofit. Program attractiveness is classified as high or low. *Competitive position* has to do with how well the nonprofit serves its clients with a program compared to other nonprofits serving those clients with a similar program. Competitive position is classified as strong or weak and may be a function of a nonprofit's resources, skills, locational advantage, or other advantages. Finally, *alternative coverage* is an important dimension because it allows a nonprofit's strategy to take community needs and resources into account by considering whether there are many or only a few alternatives that clients could use to obtain the benefits provided by the nonprofit's program. If few alternatives to a particular service are available and clients and the community need it, a nonprofit might consider providing that service even though it may not be the most attractive option for the nonprofit. Conversely, when there are many alternative providers, community resources may not be put to best use by supporting the nonprofit's provision of that service, especially if the nonprofit is not in a strong competitive position.

MacMillan's framework leads to eight possible types of strategies that a nonprofit could consider in determining an approach to a particular program.[20] Table 5.1 displays these strategy types. The numbered specific actions in the table correspond to the numbered strategies in the following list.

TABLE 5.1. A MODEL FOR IDENTIFYING AN APPROPRIATE STRATEGIC ORIENTATION: BASED ON MACMILLAN'S COMPETITIVE STRATEGIES FOR NONPROFITS

	High Program Attractiveness to Nonprofit's Stakeholders		Low Program Attractiveness to Nonprofit's Stakeholders	
	High Alternative Coverage	Low Alternative Coverage	High Alternative Coverage	Low Alternative Coverage
Nonprofit Has Strong Competitive Position	1. Aggressively compete with other providers.	2. Aggressively grow provision.	5. Collaborate to provide or build up best competitor in order to eventually stop providing.	6. Keep if needed as safety net, strengthen other providers so nonprofit can stop providing if others can be effective providers, find support for provision; or limit scope of provision to make it more attractive for the nonprofit.
Nonprofit Has Weak Competitive Position	3. Stop providing.	4. Decide with other providers who should provide. If chosen to continue, strengthen provision.	7. Stop providing.	8. Consider collaborating to improve offering, encourage other providers, and stop providing when no longer needed.

Source: Adapted from Ian MacMillan, "Competitive Strategies for Not-for-Profit Agencies," in *Advances in Strategic Management,* vol. 1, ed. Robert Lamb (Greenwich, CT: JAI Press, 1983), 69–72.

1. **Aggressive competition.** The nonprofit is among the best at this program and the program is highly attractive to it. Many others are also providing this service, indicating that community resources may be dispersed too widely. Consequently, the nonprofit should compete in order to weed out the weaker providers.

2. **Aggressive growth.** The nonprofit is among the best at this program and the program is attractive to it. The presence of few alternatives is an indication that growth is possible in this area, and the nonprofit should pursue it.

3. **Aggressive divestment.** The nonprofit is in a weak competitive position, and there are many alternative program providers. Even though the program is attractive, there is no good organizational or community reason to keep providing the service.

4. **Build strength or sell out**. Again, the program is attractive, but the nonprofit is in a weak competitive position. In this case, however, few alternative providers are available. It might therefore benefit the community if the nonprofit sought to become a better provider. Alternatively, the nonprofit should step aside and let others, who are better at it, provide the service.
5. **Build up best competitor**. The nonprofit is among the best at this service, but it is not an attractive program for the organization. Given that there are a multitude of other providers for this service, the nonprofit should consider helping the next best organization to take over or share the service.
6. **Soul of the agency**. The nonprofit is among the best at this service. It finds the program unattractive, but there are few alternative providers and the community could suffer if the nonprofit stops providing the service. It is important to understand what makes the program unattractive. If it is a matter of finances, then the nonprofit should seek other ways to finance the program. If it is not a good fit with the mission, then more serious consideration should be given to program termination or the risk of mission drift will increase.
7. **Orderly divestment**. This is not an attractive program, the nonprofit is not good at it, and many alternative providers exist. There are no reasons to keep the program.
8. **Joint venture**. This is not an attractive program, and the nonprofit is not good at it. In this case, however, few alternative providers exist and the community could suffer with the loss of a provider. The nonprofit could consider joining with one of the other providers to benefit the community.

The Strategic Planning Process

In this section we will outline the strategic planning process and present a number of tools that nonprofits have found to be useful. In the general strategic planning model, the strategic plan is the critical link between abstract aspirations and concrete operations, as shown in Figure 5.1.

FIGURE 5.1. GENERAL STRATEGIC PLANNING MODEL

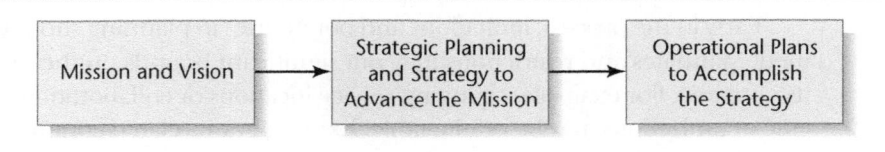

Mission and Vision → Strategic Planning and Strategy to Advance the Mission → Operational Plans to Accomplish the Strategy

Formal strategic planning generally involves a series of steps that include getting ready to plan, assessing the situation facing the nonprofit, linking relevant internal and external factors, identifying strategic issues, and forming strategies designed to address those issues. In this section, we describe how a nonprofit organization takes these steps. We provide examples of what might transpire at each step by walking through a hypothetical strategic planning process for the American Red Cross.

Preparing to Plan

To prepare for strategic planning, nonprofits should answer these questions:[21]

- What is the purpose of the planning effort?
- What will the planning process be?
- What reports will be produced, and when?
- Who will be involved, and what are their roles?
- What are the resources available?

The board and CEO will play a major role in answering these questions. As shown in the example of the Flinn Foundation at the beginning of this chapter, the decision to initiate the planning process is likely to come from these top decision makers. Similarly, in a Red Cross chapter, the board, after a review of performance, may decide that current strategy should be reevaluated. A key question then is whether consultants will be used to guide part or all of this process. Consultants will be useful when specific technical or environmental knowledge is needed. In addition, they may have expertise in the strategic planning process that is lacking in the nonprofit. They may also provide impartial input to the process. Another key question concerns the desired degree of involvement of staff from the operations or service delivery portions of the nonprofit. Although staff will have detailed operational knowledge, they may also feel that they have a stake in the status quo or in an alternative. In general it is important to consider who needs to buy into any strategies developed, including stakeholders from outside the nonprofit. For example, a neighborhood organization would benefit from the input of neighborhood residents. This may dictate who should be involved in the planning process.

Early in the process, limitations and boundaries to planning should be clarified. Mandates and restrictions may put significant bounds on the process or its outcome. For example, changing service locations or collaborating with specific organizations may be off the table. Existing grant-related commitments to deliver specific services may need to be honored. As well, funds and personnel time may be limited or otherwise committed. For example, a Red Cross chapter may need to continue to provide local emergency response services, as this has been the mandate of the American Red Cross since its founding in 1881.[22]

Another key part of the planning process is to review the nonprofit's mission and values. These should be referred to throughout the planning process, and indeed, one of the results of the process may be to refine or revise them. On the one hand a review of the mission and values can help planners to reach agreement on the general direction of the nonprofit and the principles that guide its activities. This in turn can limit possible changes and help planners in giving consistent justifications for new strategies. For example, after reviewing the Flinn Foundation's original mission, the board recognized that the mission had drifted, and it decided to refocus its efforts on creating long-term systemic change, rather than delivering short-term charity. On the other hand a review may show that the mission is appropriate. For example, the Red Cross's mission states that "the American Red Cross, a humanitarian organization led by volunteers and guided by its Congressional Charter and the Fundamental Principles of the International Red Cross Movement, will provide relief to victims of disasters and help people prevent, prepare for and respond to emergencies."[23] This is unlikely to be seen as needing revision.

Situation Analysis: Assessment of External and Internal Environments

The typical next step in strategic planning is a situation analysis, which identifies potentially relevant internal and external factors. At this stage the goal is to provide a complete list of the factors, not to prioritize them. If a factor is not identified at this point, it may not be included in subsequent steps and consequently not be addressed in strategic or operating plans.

A number of tools and techniques can be used for situational analysis. The most common general tool is a *SWOT analysis*, in which internal factors are identified and determined to be strengths (**S**) or weaknesses (**W**) of the nonprofit, and external environmental factors are identified and determined to be opportunities (**O**) or threats (**T**) for the nonprofit. Exhibits 5.1 and 5.2 outline the factors that a chapter of the American Red Cross might see as its strengths, weaknesses, opportunities, and threats. A variety of specific techniques are available to identify the external and internal factors to include in the SWOT analysis.

External Environmental Analysis

The external environment of a nonprofit includes many objective factors as well as the opinions, needs, and attitudes of important external stakeholders, including clients, funders, policymakers, regulators, partners, and community leaders. Many techniques have been developed to help nonprofit organizations describe, explore, and analyze their environments[24] (see the example in Exhibit 5.1).

A common technique for analyzing the external environment is described by the acronym PEST. When using PEST, a nonprofit looks closely at **p**olitical, **e**conomic, **s**ocial, and **t**echnological aspects

EXHIBIT 5.1. EXTERNAL OPPORTUNITIES AND THREATS AT A RED CROSS CHAPTER

An environmental analysis identifies external opportunities and threats to be considered in a SWOT analysis.

Type of Environmental Factor	Opportunity	Threat
Industry factors		A large decline will occur in the oil and gas extraction component of the state's economy.
Economic factors		State and local government will lose about 6,000 workers (3.1%).
Financial factors		Financial distress should increase this year due to problems in real estate.
Government factors	The Red Cross is well supported by government.	Government and public agencies will become less involved in health issues.
Competition factors		Competition exists for first aid, organ donations, safety education, and disaster aid.
Social factors	In times of disaster, the Red Cross gets significant support from the public.	
Demographic factors	Donations to the chapter are higher than the state chapter average.	
Future state trends	It is expected that the state's economy will bottom out this year.	

Source: Adapted from R. Henry Migliore, Robert E. Stevens, David L. Loudon, and Stan Williamson, "Sample Strategic Plans," in *Strategic Planning for Nonprofit Organizations* (New York: Haworth Press, 1995), 161–195.

of the environment that might affect it in a positive or negative way currently and in the future. Within these categories, factors can range from the specific, such as particular regulations or funding streams, to the general, such as demographics or overall economic conditions. For example, for the Red Cross chapter, one of the most important external factors might be the economic resources of the local government that could be mobilized to provide emergency relief. If government resources are lacking, the Red Cross role may need to become more extensive. In addition, the average age of the population and the socioeconomic breakdown of the community may determine the need for Red Cross services. It is not possible to stipulate in advance which specific or general factors will be relevant for any given nonprofit and herein lies the challenge. The technique is only as good as the information available. Also, as the list of factors to examine increases so does the difficulty of the task. Simple environments may be adequately assessed by staff and board members along with knowledgeable outsiders. In more elaborate, complex, or turbulent environments, experts may be needed to provide information to planners. For example, the Flinn Foundation brought in consultants to provide industry data that staff and board members could not have easily obtained on their own.

An *industry analysis* can be used to look at how a nonprofit is operating in one or more industries.[25] The industry analysis is one way in which nonprofits can adopt and adapt a model from the for-profit world. An initial challenge is determining what industry to examine. The Flinn Foundation, for example, could belong to the industry of grantmaking organizations, of community health advocates, of bioscience research supporters, or a number of other industries and subindustries. Likewise, besides providing emergency relief, the Red Cross is also involved in support for military members and their families; community services that help the needy; the collection, processing, and distribution of blood and blood products; and educational programs that promote health and safety.[26] Each of these can be considered a separate industry.

Once an industry of interest is identified, Sharon Oster offers a useful tool that nonprofits can use to identify vulnerabilities and key success factors.[27] Her nonprofit model expands on Porter's for-profit model[28] by including funders and volunteers. It looks at

- Relations among the existing organizations in the industry
- The threat of new entrants
- The threat of new substitutes (competition from alternative services)
- The number and power of user groups
- The power of funding groups
- The power of supplier industries (especially for staff and volunteers)

Several other techniques may prove useful. *Environmental scanning* can be used to examine how imminent or distant the positive or negative impact of an environmental factor is likely to be as well as the magnitude of the impact. For example, a scan might reveal that a reduction in city social service budgets may occur in the next fiscal year. This could significantly affect a nonprofit's city funding for its day-care program. *Scenario analysis* is a technique for developing scenarios describing possible future situations (Exhibit 5.1 illustrates some scenarios). Each scenario is evaluated on the likelihood of occurrence and likely positive or negative impact on the nonprofit. For example, one scenario resulting from reductions in city funding would be for the nonprofit to offset the reduction by imposing fees for its day-care clients. These two techniques can be combined in an *issue impact analysis grid* whose cells range from taking priority actions (for cases of high impact plus high likelihood) to merely tracking (for cases of low impact plus low likelihood). In the example we are considering, if the scenario of reduced funding is seen as likely, the nonprofit might make preparing for this contingency a priority. This preparation might involve appointing a task force to evaluate options. Finally, a *force field analysis* can be used to consider factors in the environment that may promote or inhibit change. In our example, it may not be possible to charge low-income clients fees for services due to their inability to pay. This may make a sliding fee scale the best option.

Internal Factors Analysis

We turn now to the assessment of internal factors, those things inside an organization that may influence strategy. Although all aspects of internal structure and operations may be considered, a nonprofit must be sure to assess its capabilities and resources (see the example in Exhibit 5.2). An analysis of resources can help planners understand current capabilities, potential to meet new needs, and resource gaps. Another key factor is the nonprofit's ability to use its resources to successfully run its programs and meet its mission. The role of resources in helping firms attain competitive advantage has been explicitly considered.[29] Resources can be tangible or intangible. Tangible resources are physical assets and include physical resources (such as buildings, machinery, materials, and productive capacity), financial resources (such as cash balances, debtors, and creditors), and human resources (such as the numbers and types of personnel and their productivity). Intangible resources include knowledge and intellectual resources as well as an organization's reputation and culture. Intellectual resources include patents and copyrights. Knowledge resources include

EXHIBIT 5.2. INTERNAL STRENGTHS AND WEAKNESSES AT A RED CROSS CHAPTER

Continuing the example in Exhibit 5.1, an assessment of internal factors identifies internal strengths and weaknesses to be considered in a SWOT analysis.

Type of Internal Factor	Strength	Weakness
Administrative and human resource factors	Volunteers and staff take great pride in their work. The organization has a culture of service. Staff have extensive training and expertise in providing services.	Youth are not adequately recruited or utilized.
Financial factors	The financial position is excellent and the financial trend is good.	Income funds are generally dependent on the success of the United Way fund drive.
Equipment and facilities factors	The organization has superb, modern facilities. Specialized equipment is available for emergency services.	The organization is absorbing expansion areas of the new facility at a faster rate than planned for.
Line-of-service factors	Disaster services are easily mobilized during times of need.	Compared to other area blood services, the Red Cross carries a high overhead and has a wider area for collection and distribution.

Source: Adapted from R. Henry Migliore, Robert E. Stevens, David L. Loudon, and Stan Williamson, "Sample Strategic Plans," in *Strategic Planning for Nonprofit Organizations* (New York: Haworth Press, 1995), 161–195.

employee knowledge and specialized skills as well as tacit knowledge in the organizational culture.

Although resources are important, it is their configuration that provides organizational competencies. Core competencies provide competitive advantage. They provide access to markets and are perceived by customers to provide benefits. They are difficult to imitate and provide an organization with distinctive capabilities. The Red Cross possesses many of these competencies. It has a strong brand image and reputation for service. It provides extensive training to employees and volunteers and has a strong culture of community service. It has specialized facilities for emergency response (such as buildings, communication equipment, and specialized vans). These factors make the Red Cross the primary emergency response organization in most communities.

Internal analysis can use information from a variety of internal sources, including periodic program or organizational evaluations as well as information gathered specifically for the strategic planning process by consultants or staff. A number of techniques are available for the identification of relevant internal factors.

A major way that internal information is gathered is through evaluations. Evaluation of programs and organizational effectiveness are covered in separate chapters. At this point we stress that periodic evaluations should be linked to strategic planning. These evaluations should assess progress toward achieving performance objectives and point to internal factors enhancing or retarding progress. In addition, organizational assessment tools, codes of practice, and standards are available for use by nonprofits.

Identification of Strategic Issues

Identification of the strategic issues facing the nonprofit is a key step in planning. *Strategic issues* are the small number of very important issues that emerge from evaluation of internal and external factors that currently are affecting or are likely to affect an organization. Once the strategic issues are identified, specific strategies can be formulated to address them. If an important issue is not identified at this stage, strategies may not be formulated to address it.

Strategic issues involve fundamental questions for a nonprofit. For example, a question facing the Flinn Foundation was how to have a longer-term impact on the State of Arizona given the general economic downturn and the foundation's dissatisfaction with its current scattershot approach. Strategic issues might focus on opportunities or challenges. A key point is that there are likely to be consequences at some point if the organization does not deal with them. There may be issues that require no organizational action at present except monitoring, issues that are on the horizon and will require some action at some point, and issues that require an immediate response. For the Flinn Foundation the issues were identified as having moved from the monitoring and horizon stages to requiring immediate action.

Given the diversity of stakeholders and views and values within nonprofits, the process of issue identification will likely require extensive discussion and may entail conflict. For example, in a Red Cross chapter, there may be disagreement on the relative priorities that should be placed on assistance to military families versus youth education. A systematic process will help planners with this stage. John Bryson has identified a variety of procedures that can be used to identify strategic issues.[30] A number of these are quite straightforward and relatively easy to use, especially in smaller nonprofits. In a *direct approach* a discussion of mandates, mission, vision, and SWOT analysis findings leads to the identification of strategic issues, as described in the following section. All potential strategic issues are then evaluated. A simplified *indirect approach* begins with brainstorming to generate a set of options for action that might be entailed in stakeholder expectations, SWOT elements, or other relevant material. These options are then evaluated in more detail. A method that can be employed when there is consensus on organizational goals is a *goals approach*. This technique identifies and evaluates the issues that need to be addressed to reach the goals. Finally, a *vision of success approach* starts with an idea of what success would look like and identifies issues that need to be addressed to reach it.

Using SWOT to Establish Strategic Issues

As noted earlier the SWOT analysis can serve as the basis for establishing strategic issues. Although the use of SWOT in identifying strategic issues appears quite straightforward, Kevin Kearns points to the difficulty of moving from disconnected lists of strengths, weaknesses, opportunities, and threats to a succinct list of prioritized strategic issues, as is required in approaches that rely on SWOT, such as the direct and indirect approaches just outlined. To address this problem, Kearns offers a simple process for extending a SWOT analysis to classify strategic issues.[31] His framework systematically links the internal and external elements of a SWOT analysis. Each internal factor (a strength or weakness) is linked to an external factor (an opportunity or threat), and each external factor is linked to an internal factor.

In this way internal and external elements can be mapped into a four-cell matrix of strategic issue types, as shown in Exhibit 5.3. When opportunities in the external environment are aligned with organizational strengths (cell 1), the generic strategic issue is, *How can the nonprofit leverage its strengths to achieve or enhance its comparative advantage, thereby capitalizing on a perceived opportunity?* When external opportunities are aligned with internal weaknesses (cell 3), the generic issue is, *Should the nonprofit invest its scarce resources in weak programs to become more competitive in relation to a perceived opportunity?* When the environment presents a threat but the nonprofit has strengths connected to that threat (cell 2), the generic issue is, *How can the nonprofit mobilize its strengths to avert a perceived threat or even transform it into an opportunity?* Finally, when threats and weaknesses are aligned and the nonprofit lacks internal capacity or capability to address perceived external threats (cell 4),

EXHIBIT 5.3. USING SWOT ANALYSIS FOR STRATEGIC ISSUE IDENTIFICATION AT A LOCAL RED CROSS CHAPTER

For the Red Cross chapter in our example, a linking of internal strengths and weaknesses and external opportunities and threats could result in the following matrix. This classification could be followed by discussion of critical choices related to each cell.

	Opportunities	Threats
Strengths	1. Organization has a high level of government support.	2. Public agencies will become less involved in health issues.
Weaknesses	3. Youths are not adequately recruited or utilized.	4. Chapter has high overhead costs.

In cell 1 the general issue is how a nonprofit can leverage its strengths to take advantage of an environmental opportunity. For example, the support the Red Cross gets from government (an internal strength) could be used to start or expand services (an opportunity in the environment). A specific strategic issue could be framed this way: Should we use government support to start a new service?

In cell 2 the general issue is how can a nonprofit use its strengths to mitigate an environmental threat? The Red Cross, for example, may have strong programs in health that could in fact benefit from reduced health services from government.

In cell 3 the general issue is whether a nonprofit should invest resources to better address an environmental opportunity. For example, should the Red Cross invest in better recruiting from a growing youth market, an area where its recruiting is currently weak?

Finally, in cell 4 the general issue is how a nonprofit can control or minimize the damage from an environmental threat in an area where the nonprofit is weak. A strategic issue for the Red Cross chapter in this area could be stated this way: Given our high overhead costs, how can we effectively compete with other organizations who can afford to charge less than we do due to their lower overhead costs?

To add to the value of the matrix as a planning tool, each of its cells can be subdivided further. Environmental factors can be subdivided based on their certainty. In this example, it may be uncertain whether government will in fact reduce its involvement in health issues, suggesting that the Red Cross may wish to be cautious about developing new services in affected areas. Strengths and weaknesses can be subdivided based on whether they are actual or potential factors. The chapter may currently have high overhead costs, but it might be that these are likely to come down in the future, turning a current weakness into a potential strength.

then the generic strategy is, *In light of its vulnerable position, how can the nonprofit control or at least minimize the damage that may be inflicted by impending threats?* Exhibit 5.3 returns to the example of the Red Cross chapter to see what strategic issues surface in its SWOT analysis.

In the planning process, board and staff members are likely to identify numerous strategic issues. The final step in this identification process is to rank, or prioritize, these issues to indicate the level of concern they should be given during strategy development. They should be ranked on centrality, urgency, cost implications, public visibility, mission impact, connection to core values, research needed, and feasibility of being effectively addressed. For the Red Cross chapter, the strategic option of using government support to start a new service (cell 1) would rank high on centrality, visibility, and mission impact, whereas the strategic option of dealing with high overhead costs (cell 4) is likely to rank high on urgency, cost implications, and research needed.

From Strategic Issues to Strategies

The next planning step links statements of strategic issues to more concrete choices and actions. Bryson outlines a five-step process for formulating specific strategies once the strategic issues to be addressed have been identified:[32]

1. Identification of alternatives, dreams, or visions for resolving the strategic issues
2. Enumeration of barriers to realizing those alternatives, dreams, or visions
3. Development of proposals for achieving the alternatives, dreams, or visions
4. Identification of actions that need to be taken over the next two to three years to implement each proposal
5. Development of a detailed workplan spanning the next six months to a year to implement the actions

Although the final two steps concern strategy implementation, Bryson makes the point that it is useful to consider them during the planning stage, as strategy development should not be divorced from implementation, and planning should always be done with implementation in mind.

The resulting strategies should meet several important criteria, including technical workability, political acceptability, alignment with important organizational philosophies and core values, and ethical acceptability.

Adopting and Implementing a Strategic Plan

Although the focus of this chapter is on strategy formulation, we should briefly consider the steps to be followed after strategic planning.[33] Once a strategic plan has been formulated by the planning team, it should be adopted officially by the board of directors and endorsed by the staff, especially the CEO. Then the challenge becomes carrying out the strategies. Without proper attention to implementation, intended strategies may never be realized. Successful implementation involves marshalling people and resources in a timely manner. An implementation plan should include the following:[34]

- Implementation roles and responsibilities of oversight bodies, organizational teams or task forces, and individuals
- Expected results and specific objectives and milestones
- Specific action steps and relevant details
- Schedules
- Resource requirements and sources
- Review, monitoring, and midcourse correction procedures
- Accountability procedures

Periodic Review and Reassessment of Strategic Plans

Well-formed strategic plans require the nonprofit to take actions designed to produce specific results over a specified period of time. Strategic plans are usually formulated to span two to five years. Program evaluations will normally address whether the strategies guiding each program have been successful. In addition, the nonprofit should periodically review whether each of its strategies has been successful in creating the intended results. These assessments will provide a basis for maintaining successful strategies and modifying or eliminating unsuccessful ones. They may point to weaknesses in the strategic planning process itself, which may have led to the adoption of poor strategies. Any weaknesses can be taken into consideration during the next strategic planning process. In Chapter Thirteen we will examine more closely how programs are evaluated and assessed and how the evaluation process and strategic planning process are joined.

Challenges to Planning: Emergent Strategy

The purpose of the strategic planning approach we have discussed so far is to develop a systematic, rational, and analytical approach to strategy formation.

This approach is designed to allow nonprofit leaders to appraise the nonprofit and its environment objectively, formulate a strategy that they feel maximizes the chances of success, and implement that strategy through operational plans. As outlined in our earlier overview of the field, however, an alternative view of strategy is that it emerges without planning. In fact, research has shown that organizational success is sometimes *not* due to rational strategic planning.

Although planning is important, an overemphasis on detailed, formal, long-range planning can lead to an underemphasis on continuous learning and flexibility. In his review of the strategy field, Stephen Cummings concludes that it is recognized that in complex and turbulent environments, "A top-down planning and positioning approach tends to make a firm slow, rigid and unresponsive to unforeseen opportunities and threats. It also disengages 'lower level' employees who may have much to add."[35] Mintzberg, Ahlstrand, and Lampel critique planning and positioning approaches by noting that they are double-edged—for every advantage there can be a corresponding drawback.[36] Strategic planning can set the organization's direction, but it can also blind leaders to potential dangers. It may be better to move slowly and focus on the near term so needed adjustments will be easier to make. In addition, although strategic planning can promote consistency and coordinated action, it can also lead to less consideration of alternatives, less creativity, groupthink, or stereotyping. Mintzberg also argues that traditional planning models have three particular difficulties.[37] In the first place, prediction is a problematic process. Mintzberg points out that even though certain repetitive patterns may be predictable, the forecasting of discontinuities, such as technological innovation or a price increase is virtually impossible. For example, a mental health nonprofit may not be able to predict how local government funding for community services might change after an upcoming election. A second potential problem is detachment. This can occur when strategy (thinking) is distanced from operations (doing). Planners may be divorced from the operational details that good strategy relies on. For example, when a nonprofit board engages in strategic planning, it is very important that the board obtains input from operating units. Finally, formalization itself may be a problem. Formal systems may be able to handle more data than informal ones, but sometimes these data are not internalized, comprehended, or synthesized, making learning difficult if not impossible. Formal systems cannot forecast discontinuities, inform detached managers, or create novel strategies. For example, a board strategic planning process that relies on raw data or unanalyzed or unsynthesized reports from a variety of sources in the organization is unlikely to develop an adequate view of operations or alternatives.

Mintzberg has developed the notion of strategy as an *emergent process* and is the foremost advocate of the learning approach to strategy. The roots of this approach can be found in Charles Lindblom's notion of *muddling through*, which portrays policymaking in government as a messy process in which policymakers struggle with situations too complicated for neat, orderly, rational processes.[38] James Quinn's 1980 book, *Strategies for Change: Logical Incrementalism*, is seen as the takeoff point for the learning approach.[39] In charging organizations to focus more on less rational approaches, Mintzberg distinguishes between intended, realized, and emergent strategies (see Figure 5.2).[40]

Intended strategy is planned strategy as conceived and directed by the top management team. *Realized strategy* is the strategy that the organization actually pursues through a pattern of actions. Intended strategies may never be realized, and realized strategies may never have been intended. Unintended realized strategies are termed *emergent strategies*. Emergent strategies are the result of strategic learning through experimentation and discovery. Learning can take place at the individual, team, top executive, and governance levels. It may be driven by conscious desires to seek improvements or by external forces and internal pressures.

This leads Mintzberg to propose a grassroots model of strategy formation.[41] The main tenets of this model are that strategies may grow initially like weeds in a garden rather than like tomatoes in a hothouse; that they can take root in all kinds of places, virtually anywhere people have the capacity to learn and the resources to support that capacity; and that they become organizational when they become collective, that is, when the patterns proliferate to pervade the behavior of the organization at large. An important point is that the process of proliferation may be conscious but need not be and, likewise, strategies may be managed but need not be. Moreover, new strategies, which may emerge continually, tend to pervade the organization during the periods of change that punctuate the periods of more integrated continuity. For leaders, managing this process means not preconceiving strategies but recognizing their emergence and intervening when appropriate.

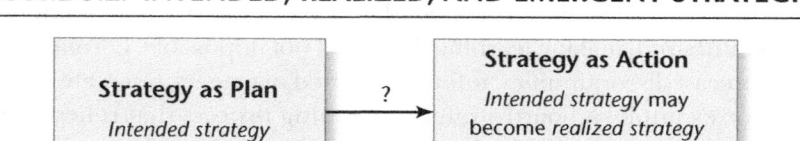

FIGURE 5.2. INTENDED, REALIZED, AND EMERGENT STRATEGIES

Strategy as Plan
Intended strategy

?

Strategy as Action
Intended strategy may become *realized strategy*
When action is unintended it becomes *emergent strategy*

Although learning is an important and necessary process, Mintzberg, Ahlstrand, and Lampel acknowledge that this approach to strategy formation has limitations and weaknesses if carried too far.[42] Actions can spin off in all directions. In a multiservice nonprofit, for example, each department or division could develop services or programs that were unrelated to each other or to any overall organizational plan for growth or development. In addition, in a crisis, the learning approach cannot be relied upon, and a clear strategy may be the key to success. A nonprofit that unexpectedly loses a major source of funding is best off relying on contingency plans prepared expressly for this emergency. Even in stable situations some organizations need strong strategic visions and the coherence that comes from centralized sources rather than decentralized learning. For example, a health services nonprofit contracting with county government needs to provide consistent and reliable services over the term of the contract. For such organizations an overemphasis on learning can undermine a coherent and perfectly viable strategy, and initiatives may be promoted simply because they are new or interesting.[43] The health services nonprofit providing county services should not adopt new or experimental therapies until they have been well tested.

Combining Perspectives

In the previous sections we have considered strategy as planning and strategy as response (emergent). Commenting on the contemporary strategy landscape, Courtney concludes: "With the availability of different approaches to strategy it is difficult for those with responsibility for the management and development of their organizations to make decisions about which approach is best."[44] Similarly, Robert Grant observes that "although the debate between the two schools [planned strategies and emergent strategies] continues, it is increasingly apparent that the central issue is not 'Which school is right?' but, 'How can the two views complement one another to give us a richer understanding of strategy making?' "[45]

Nonprofit organizations need both stability and flexibility, meaning that strategy making should combine elements of control (planned strategy) and of learning (emergent strategy). This combining can take a number of forms. The board and the CEO have important roles in strategy emergence as well as planning strategy. To combine planning and emergence, they could establish broad guidelines, or umbrella strategies, and leave the specifics of strategy to those lower down in the organization.

Nonprofits may pursue a given strategic orientation until they get out of alignment with their environments and a significant strategic reorientation is needed. It is at this point that formally planned and emergent strategies come into contact. For example, mental health services used to be provided largely in institutions until the deinstitutionalization movement dictated that services be provided in community settings. At that point mental health nonprofits that had been providing institutional services needed to learn about and develop new models for service provision.

Much of the time, change is minor and does not need to be addressed strategically. However, managers need to be able to recognize and detect new patterns that may develop into emergent strategies, and deal with them appropriately. This may involve stopping the pattern of developing behavior or watching it to see if it has useful effects on the nonprofit and should therefore be promoted. CEOs often pursue opportunities they perceive that are not in the strategic plan. For example, clients' growing lack of understanding of the increasingly complex housing market may lead a nonprofit housing provider (such as Habitat for Humanity) to start providing educational material to clients on an ad hoc basis. If the amount of effort devoted to this activity increases, the nonprofit should decide if supplying this material detracts from the organizational strategy or if it can usefully benefit the clients. If it detracts it should be dropped, and if it is a benefit then it may be developed into a new strategic focus.

Finally, emergence and learning tend to become relatively more prominent and important as environments become more volatile, complex, and unpredictable. Nonprofits that cannot accurately predict what their environments will be like in the future can only establish general strategic directions and react strategically as events unfold. Nonprofits dealing with illegal immigrants, on the one hand, face such environments and must remain flexible. Nonprofit museums, on the other hand, face far more predictable environments and can develop more specific strategic plans.

Within a nonprofit, strategic approaches may also differ across functions and units. Courtney notes, for example, that fund development efforts, given the high degree of competition for funds, may require traditional strategic planning approaches.[46] The human service delivery component of some nonprofits, in contrast, may operate in a less competitive environment where cooperative and mutually supportive interorganizational relations are beneficial. In this environment, strategies focusing on collaboration, learning, negotiation, and capacity building may be most productive.

Writing on the future of thinking about strategy, Cummings maintains that a new, more open, and flexible mind-set should shape future perspectives on what strategy is or could be.[47] He outlines a new *pragmatic approach* that blends traditional planning with flexible "strategic improvising" approaches and that has these key characteristics:[48]

- Wide participation of staff, trustees, volunteers, and other stakeholders, rather than a top-down approach
- Ongoing support and encouragement of creativity, innovation, experimentation, and learning
- Recognition of the need to negotiate between the various sources of power, inside and outside the organization
- A focus on key strategic issues, or challenges
- Use of a range of scenarios to define potential external situations
- Creation of a strong motivating vision, that is, a strategic intent, which enables an organization and its people to "live deeply in the future while gaining the courage to act boldly in the present"
- Creation of a clear value base for the ethical management of the organization
- Engagement in strategic thinking as a continual process, not just an annual cycle
- Strategic processes that produce commonsense frameworks that will help managers make decisions

Concluding Thoughts

In this chapter we have presented strategy formation as a process that fits, or adapts, the nonprofit organization to its environment. Strategy will help a nonprofit to provide the goods or services the community needs and wants, and as a consequence, to obtain the resources the nonprofit needs to survive. It is the critical link between the general aspirations expressed in vision and mission statements and the more specific goals that direct day-to-day operations. It is important that planning processes not be static and that they not be considered "done" once a strategic plan has been drafted and implemented. Nonprofits need to be adaptable because their environments will inevitably change. They live with a basic tension between their need for both organizational stability and change. We have shown how strategy can provide planned direction and stability on one hand and help the nonprofit learn from unanticipated changes on the other. The challenge is to design processes that foster the type of strategy formation that the nonprofit needs.

In the next chapter we take up the topic of resource acquisition. This is one of the major concerns that strategy will be used to address.

Questions for Consideration

1. At what point(s) in the strategic planning process is it particularly important to get input from top management? From external stakeholders? From service delivery staff?
2. Under what conditions might start-up nonprofits find traditional strategic planning more useful than an emergent strategy approach? When might the opposite be the case?

Exercises

Exercise 5.1: Strategic Orientation

Briefly describe a nonprofit organization with which you are familiar. This could be a club, a church, or a recreational, cultural, or service organization. If need be, you may speculate about a hypothetical nonprofit. Is this nonprofit a defender, a prospector, an analyzer, or a reactor? Explain the reasons for your answer.

Exercise 5.2: Strategic Planning

Continuing to focus on the nonprofit you selected for Exercise 5.1, answer these questions:

1. Using PEST, identify the important aspects of this nonprofit's environment.
2. Identify this nonprofit's strengths, weaknesses, opportunities, and threats.
3. Identify several strategic issues for this nonprofit.
4. Which approach to strategic issue identification did you use in answering the previous question?

Exercise 5.3: Strategy Emergence

How could strategy emerge from the base of this nonprofit (its staff, beneficiaries, or others outside the board and the executive leadership)?

1. What techniques or procedures could the organization's leaders use to encourage emergent strategy?
2. How could these techniques or procedures be integrated with a strategic planning approach?

CHAPTER SIX

RESOURCE ACQUISITION

The Oakes Children's Center was founded in San Francisco in 1963 to provide education and therapeutic treatment for severely emotionally disturbed children.[1] Though it was initially funded by grants from private foundations and fees from parents of the children being treated, it became heavily dependent on state government contracts. In 1992, 97 percent of its revenues came from government, with the remaining portion from ad hoc fundraising and other sources. This was not surprising given that the passage of Public Law 94-142 had guaranteed government funding for education for the children that the center served and had outlawed tuition fees to parents. The result was a steady stream of government funds that brought complacency and little interest in fundraising. The center infrequently mailed solicitation appeals or invited community members to special events. There was no comprehensive strategy for seeking corporate, foundation, and individual donations.

In 1992, the center's leaders saw that shifting political priorities could result in the shrinking of what was still generous government funding. As they began a planning process, the board and staff sensed an urgency to reduce the nonprofit's dependence on government funds but were skeptical that they could make a case to the public for philanthropic support. That year, Robert Tyminski, the executive director, began work on a strategic fund development plan for the center. Tyminski identified numerous challenges that would face the organization as it attempted to change its funding portfolio and increase philanthropic support. The organization had lost its grassroots base of support and full board commitment to fundraising had to be developed. The fundraising message was not clear. The board wondered why individuals and corporations would want to donate to the organization. Working with a marketing consultant, the center's leaders developed a campaign to build visibility, gain strategic partners, and educate the public—all with the hope that donations would follow. They collected and shared their success stories. Over time, more individuals learned how the center's services saved tax dollars and improved the community, and ultimately many of them contributed financial support. Today the center has a more diversified revenue portfolio, continues to seek donations, and works to build an even broader base of philanthropic support. Its Web site now unabashedly links the center and its work to the community. The Mission and Vision section informs site visitors of these aims:

- *We operate Oakes for the benefit of the community and strive to remain flexible and responsive to emerging needs.*
- *We are committed to responsible management of the resources entrusted to us by the community.*[2]

The center persuasively communicates its main message that the children it helps are fellow members of the local community and deserve community members' interest and gifts.

◆ ◆ ◆

Just as there are numerous types of nonprofits, there are numerous types of revenue to support their missions, each with its own challenges. Revenue may come from sales of services and products, licensing agreements, advertising fees, grants, reimbursements, contracts, investment income, membership fees, insurance, sponsorships, and donations. A nonprofit following the model of having all or a large majority of its support coming from one source runs the risk of having to shut down if the funding source goes away.

As the experience of the Oakes Children's Center shows, nonprofits can reduce their financial vulnerability by developing a diversified funding base. The leaders of the center helped ensure its survival by building a fund development program that could supplement shrinking government contracts. The center was then well positioned when it needed to rely on philanthropic support to maintain and grow its services. In order to accomplish this diversification of the funding portfolio, the nonprofit staff and board worked to understand the center's story and constituents, improve its communication strategies, develop strategies for soliciting and stewarding gifts, and convey a persuasive case to motivate individuals and organizations to give to the center. The example of the Oakes Children's Center demonstrates that a fund development plan can be created even in a nonprofit that has existed for many years without significant philanthropic support. The pressure to create and follow such a plan is often dependent on the perceived level and stability of existing revenue sources.

Complacency is a common problem in nonprofits that believe their funding is secure. Taking a hard look at where a nonprofit is currently getting its funding and exploring options for changing this pattern requires time, effort, and a recognition of the concerns associated with potential and existing revenue streams. We encourage nonprofit leaders to examine the vulnerabilities in their revenue portfolio. To that end this chapter reviews revenue sources and presents challenges associated with pursuing and being dependent on them. We then focus on philanthropic support and review types of philanthropic gifts and donors, the fund development process, and fundraising principles.

Revenue Sources and Concerns

Our understanding of the revenue sources of nonprofits in the United States comes primarily from their tax returns. Nonprofits classified as public charities (most of the 501(c)(3) nonprofits) reported over $1.41 trillion in total revenues in 2009, according to the National Center for Charitable Statistics (NCCS).[3] NCCS breaks this total down, finding that it comes mostly from program service revenues, including government fees and contracts (76 percent). An additional 22 percent comes from contributions, gifts, and government grants, and 11 percent comes from other

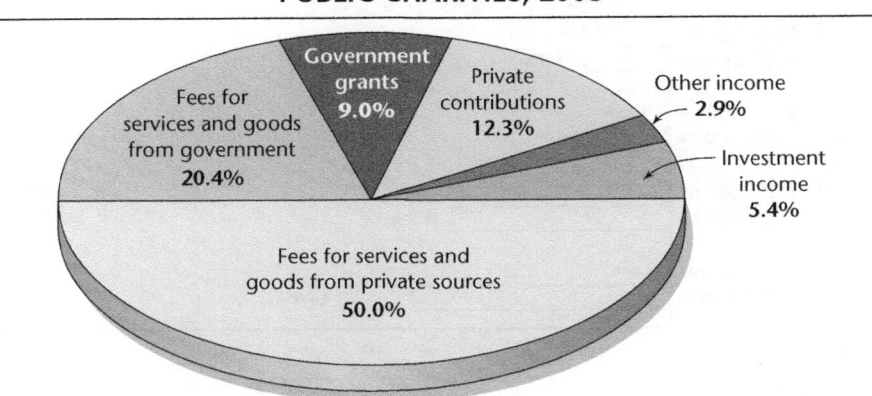

FIGURE 6.1. SOURCES OF REVENUE FOR REPORTING PUBLIC CHARITIES, 2008

- Fees for services and goods from government: 20.4%
- Government grants: 9.0%
- Private contributions: 12.3%
- Other income: 2.9%
- Investment income: 5.4%
- Fees for services and goods from private sources: 50.0%

Source: Kennard T. Wing, Katie L. Roeger, and Thomas H. Pollack, *The Nonprofit Sector in Brief: Public Charities, Giving and Volunteering, 2010* (Washington, DC: Urban Institute, 2010). Copyright © 2008, Urban Institute, National Center for Charitable Statistics.

sources such as dues, rental income, special event income, and goods sold. Another revenue breakdown by NCCS is shown in Figure 6.1; it provides more information by using 2008 tax returns from public charities.

The NCCS breakdowns of revenue for public charities ignore nonprofits with less than $5,000 in annual revenue and religious congregations, due to lack of data on many of these organizations in the IRS tax records. The breakdowns also reflect the presence of nonprofits with very large budgets, which tend to be health care facilities and higher education institutions. Hospitals and primary care facilities account for the lion's share of total revenue, 47.7 percent, and higher education nonprofits make up 11.7 percent of the total revenue. Only about a fourth of public charities reported more than $500,000 in annual expenses, while about 45 percent of the registered public charities filing a tax return in 2008 had expenses under $100,000.[4] Figure 6.2 is a chart from the Urban Institute showing the economic dominance of a relatively small number of public charities. It gives the percentages of public charities by reported expenditures and their proportion in the population of reporting public charities.

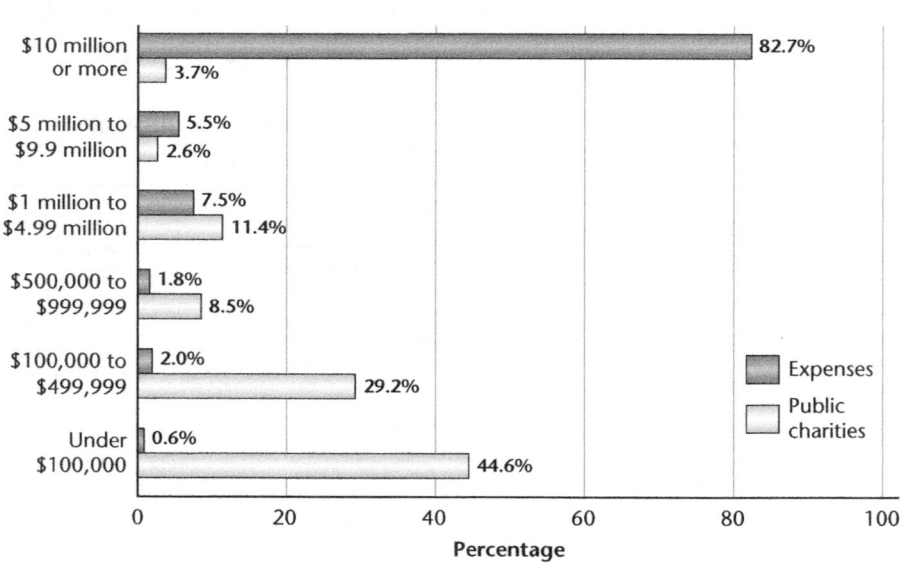

FIGURE 6.2. NUMBER AND EXPENSES OF REPORTING PUBLIC CHARITIES, 2008

Expenses Range	Expenses	Public charities
$10 million or more	82.7%	3.7%
$5 million to $9.9 million	5.5%	2.6%
$1 million to $4.99 million	7.5%	11.4%
$500,000 to $999,999	1.8%	8.5%
$100,000 to $499,999	2.0%	29.2%
Under $100,000	0.6%	44.6%

Source: Kennard T. Wing, Katie L. Roeger, and Thomas H. Pollack, *The Nonprofit Sector in Brief: Public Charities, Giving and Volunteering, 2010* (Washington, DC: Urban Institute, 2010). Copyright © 2008, Urban Institute, National Center for Charitable Statistics.

Of course revenue portfolios vary depending on the type of nonprofit. Churches, for example, tend to rely heavily on donations. Hospitals and universities tend to rely heavily on earned income. Membership-based nonprofits, such as trade and professional associations, rely heavily on earned income from membership fees and sales of goods and services, and many use no philanthropic dollars for their operations. Private foundations set up by families and individuals to make grants or operate programs, such as The William and Flora Hewlett Foundation, Ford Foundation, and The Lilly Endowment, rely on philanthropic gifts from the individuals who established the foundation and income from investment of assets. Grantmaking foundations set up by corporations, such as The Walmart Foundation and the Eli Lilly and Company Foundation, rely on investment income and gifts from their parent corporation. The aggregate numbers for the nonprofit sector fail to indicate the great variation among nonprofits in their revenue sources. Following are closer looks at the most common sources of revenue in the nonprofit sector.

Government Contracts, Grants, and Vouchers

Government is a source of revenue for nonprofits primarily through contracts, grants, and vouchers. Contracts are business transaction agreements. They outline what the government is procuring or purchasing from the nonprofit. A nonprofit may be the prime contractor, and thus do most of the work to secure the agreement, or the subcontractor, hired by the prime contractor to fulfill specific aspects of the contract. Grants are awards of financial assistance to an eligible grantee with no expectation that the funds will be paid back. They involve payments to a recipient nonprofit organization either as part of an allocation formula or for the direct provision of services or products. In the United States, the U.S. Department of Health and Human Services and the U.S. Department of Education are the largest government grantmakers to nonprofits.[5] Government contracts and grants are typically awarded through a competitive process. Government vouchers are coupons issued to individuals who use them to access a service by a qualified provider, which may or may not be a nonprofit. Medicare and Medicaid reimbursements and school tuition and other government vouchers may be important income streams for a nonprofit.

All types of funding have advantages and disadvantages. Government funding typically involves some loss of management control, uncertainty due to unpredictable political processes, heavy reporting requirements, and delays in reimbursements and contract payments.[6] Government contracts demand fiscal and programmatic accountability and transparency.[7] A 2010 study reports that human service nonprofits perceive "serious and widespread problems" with contracts and grants from government agencies. The nonprofits in the study reported that government agencies were often late with reimbursements, with state government checks most likely to be at least ninety days overdue. This left the nonprofits with the challenge of finding other financial resources to pay bills. Many of the nonprofits also complained that their government contracts did not cover the full cost of contracted services. A majority, 57 percent, reported that the government changed the terms of contracts, reduced promised payments, and even cancelled contracts, which forced the nonprofits to figure out whether and how to honor its commitments given the lost government funding.[8]

Still, like the Oakes Children's Center, many nonprofits eagerly seek government contracts and grants as a way to fulfill their missions. In 2009, three out of five of human service nonprofits indicated that the government was their largest source of funding.[9] In countries in which the nonprofit and government sectors are closely intertwined, all funding may come through the government, whereas in other countries no government funding may be available. The Center for Civil Society Studies offers a report indicating how government financial support of the nonprofit sector varies across countries, with data compiled from multiple years (1995 to 2000). For example, on average, over 50 percent of the support of nonprofit organizations in Belgium, Ireland, and Israel is reported to come from government, versus under 30 percent in the United States and under 7 percent in the Philippines, Kenya, and Pakistan.[10]

Not all nonprofits in the United States are eligible to apply for government funding and some do not choose to apply even when they are eligible. In addition to all the reporting demands, in order to receive government funds nonprofits may be required to use professional and even licensed staff, follow government-mandated approaches to service delivery, cover a government-specified geographical area or demographic client base, engage in collaborative activities with other service providers, and otherwise lose some control over how they carry out their missions. Faith-based nonprofits also need to be concerned about not using government funds for overtly religious activities. This may explain why, despite federal initiatives under President Bush's administration to encourage faith-based nonprofits to apply for government funding for social service activities, there was not a huge jump in applications for government funding from these organizations.[11]

Some nonprofits choose not to pursue government funding due to values and principles. Nonprofit leaders may believe that their primary role is to advocate against existing government positions and therefore do not want to have a conflict of interest due to dependency on government funds. For example, the National Association to Protect Children, which fights child abuse and neglect, has a bylaws provision that it will not accept government funds, in order to safeguard its independence and maintain a strong voice in its advocacy efforts.[12] Some nonprofits see even more fundamental concerns with accepting government support, as in the case of the Crazy Horse Memorial, an ongoing project to create a mountain sculpture in South Dakota to honor the Lakota Indian tribal leader and be a beacon for the values of education and humanitarianism. Chief Crazy Horse tried to preserve his tribe from U.S. government interference and persecution. The memorial Web site explains that no government funds have been accepted because the founder believed in individual initiative and private enterprise, and that if members of the public accept the goals of the memorial they will support it financially.[13]

For nonprofits that do seek government funding, here are some recommendations drawn from a report by a San Francisco task force composed of government and nonprofit representatives:[14]

- Encourage government contract sources to coordinate requests for proposals, for example through a shared proposal form for basic information, and to develop systems to facilitate timely payments, for example by reducing government inefficiencies in reimbursement processes. These kinds of activities can reduce the administrative costs of seeking and managing government funds.
- Encourage less duplication of reporting requirements to increase nonprofits' efficiency in demonstrating compliance with contract rules. For example, rather than having to submit evaluation reports and verifications of compliance for the same program to more than one government agency, nonprofits and agencies would benefit from a system in which multiple agencies could access the same paperwork so that the nonprofit does not have to fill out multiple forms with the same information.
- Consider sharing back-office functions with other nonprofits and using management service organizations to assist with government contract management. When more sophisticated accounting expertise is needed to deal with government funding, the nonprofits could share the same accountant. They could also outsource or share human resource management services for contract employees whose employment will end with the completion of grants. Nonprofits may also benefit from sharing the use and cost of facilities and equipment for contract-funded programs.
- Have at least 15 percent of funding provided by a nongovernment source. This broader base of support can add stability if government funds are decreased or withdrawn.
- Keep two months of operating revenue in reserve to help with cash flow management if government funds are delayed. The reserve fund serves as an alternative to borrowing money to honor commitments.

Earned Income

Earning income through sales of merchandise or services has its own set of challenges. It may require a nonprofit to invest in business systems that are not applicable to its mission pursuit and may result in mission drift if priorities begin to be set based on income potential rather than importance to mission.[15] If sales come through government vouchers, a nonprofit may have to agree to government rules and pricing structures to be an approved provider. Entrepreneurial efforts to earn income can suffer many of the same risks encountered by new for-profit businesses. Survival rates for entrepreneurial ventures vary by industry but average about 50 percent after five years.[16]

In nonprofits, profit maximization is rarely the rationale for setting fees for services. Other considerations for pricing are who will be able to take advantage of the service and how the fee will influence perception of the service.[17] A fee for one service may be set higher than the actual cost of the service in order to supplement another service where the cost is too high to be fully covered by the fee charged for that service. Price discrimination can also be used to encourage more sales. Quantity discounts and specially priced bundles of services and products may be offered to increase sales volume and breadth.

Some nonprofits set up sliding-scale or scholarship payment arrangements for services and then use clients or customers and donors who can afford higher fees to subsidize those who require lower fees. However, nonprofits should be sensitive to possibilities for arbitrage, where a good received for a price lower than its actual cost is resold by the receiver rather than used as intended. For example, can free food or event tickets be sold? Can subsidized housing be subleased or sold to others and so no longer serve the mission of being available for lower-income residents? Nonprofits may wish to set up legal and other barriers to the reselling of the goods and services they provide.

Prices can be set to send a signal about the quality of a product or service, with higher amounts often encouraging perceptions that the item is better than that of competitors who charge less. Charging for a product or service can also help to ensure that the client or customer will take advantage of it. When a service or product is free, clients or customers are more likely to fail to show up for appointments or to use a product judiciously.

Many nonprofits are successfully earning income and aligning business activities with their missions. For example, some Habitat for Humanity affiliates offer a ReStore, where customers can buy new or gently used materials at prices below what they would cost from for-profit retailers. Habit for Humanity of Kent County in Michigan describes its ReStore as a win-win venture: sales provide funds for building new homes, donors get tax deductions, materials are kept out of landfills, the store creates opportunities for volunteers to work together, and homeowners and landlords needing low-cost materials get useful products to improve neighborhoods, property values, and community pride.[18] Classic examples of how smaller nonprofits attempt to earn income are bake sales, carnivals, raffles, book sales, and car washes. These activities can be aligned with mission objectives; for example, by running an entrepreneurial activity, teens in a youth development program can learn how to manage projects, take calculated risks, motivate others, track budgets, and celebrate successes.

Some nonprofits' financial and mission models rely on employing or buying from individuals needing income. They may train those who have been recently released from prison, are in recovery from drug addictions, are living in countries with little economic opportunity, or are housed in shelters seeking protection from abusers. The nonprofits then recover the training costs by hiring those they have trained for work that takes advantage of the newly developed skills or by purchasing products the trainees have created that can be sold for a profit to others. According to *Inc.* magazine the earned income model works best when a nonprofit has a valuable product or expertise, the user has some ability to pay, and the nonprofit's mission is job training or skill building.[19] There is a long tradition of using nonprofits to provide job training. Jane Addams, who founded the Hull House Association in 1889, argued that one should work in the community one is trying to serve and that if people are allowed to develop their skills and have an opportunity to earn income through legitimate means then they will not only make a better life for themselves but also contribute to the community as a whole.

Over time, earned income efforts can remain local, low-dollar events, or they can evolve into massive enterprises. The Girl Scouts of the USA now generates more than $700 million in revenue from its cookie sales, an effort that started in 1917 with one troop in Oklahoma. Ten Thousand Villages, a nonprofit program of the Mennonite Central Committee, does not actively seek donations, earning almost all of its operating income through sales of fair trade products at its numerous stores and festivals.[20]

An important consideration when engaging in earned income ventures is to consider the tax implications. If the earned income activity is a regular activity and not substantially related to the exempt purpose of the nonprofit, a UBIT (unrelated business income tax) payment may be required. IRS revenue rulings provide some guidance on whether an earned income activity is likely to be seen as substantially related to the nonprofit's exempt mission. Even when taxes on the income-generating activity are required, the return on the effort may be worthwhile.

For a nonprofit with lists of clients, members, and donors, a key decision is whether to sell its lists to marketers, including other nonprofits. Some nonprofits get more revenue from selling their donor lists than from the actual donations. This is one justification for using premiums to attract donors who give small gifts. Though the cost of the premium (for example, a T-shirt, tote bag, poster, or stationery) may exceed the gift given, the new contact name can be sold. Some nonprofits note on their solicitation materials that they do not share or sell their lists. When a 2004 Charity Navigator survey suggested that sharing of donor lists is pervasive, that organization's executive director commented, "Benevolent individuals who choose to give should not have their generosity punished with unwanted telephone appeals and inundated mailboxes." In defense of the practice, Rebecca Haag, the executive director of the AIDS Action Committee of Massachusetts, said that her organization swaps names with list brokers and other like-minded charities such as the American Red Cross and Planned Parenthood, noting that "this is pretty common practice. It is how you identify new donors."[21]

Before a nonprofit undertakes any earned income strategy, social entrepreneurship scholars Beth Anderson, J. Gregory Dees, and Jed Emerson suggest that it should review a set of feasibility criteria.[22] In summary, they found that an earned income strategy is more likely to be viable when it is aligned with the nonprofit's

- Culture and values
- Core competencies
- Management capacity and time
- Financial stability
- Willingness to take risks
- Access to necessary business skills
- Length of commitment
- Existing or potential markets (customers and clients)
- Competitor relationships
- Capital requirements
- Community perceptions

Membership Fees

Many nonprofits such as unions, trade groups, professional associations, fraternities, and recreational and social clubs are dependent on membership fees for a significant part of their earned income. In 2003, the average 501(c)(3) nonprofit organization in the United States earned less than 1 percent of its revenues from member dues. In contrast, about 60 percent of the revenues of social and recreational clubs (classified as 501(c)(7) nonprofits) came from dues.[23]

In some organizations, revenues called membership fees or dues may actually be donations. For example, individuals who contribute to a pledge drive for public broadcasting may be called members of the radio or television station, but they have no voting rights and the broadcasting they receive for their contribution is a collective good that non-dues-paying individuals can also access. In the United States the value of any acknowledgment "gift" received for a "dues" contribution, such as a book, or any discount, such as half-price admission to a museum, must be deducted from the contribution amount in order to establish the amount the member or donor can claim as a tax deduction.

In a more clear arrangement where donors are differentiated from true members, the nonprofit membership association, rather than selling goods and services individually, sells them as a package to its members for a membership fee. Through affinity agreements the members may also be eligible to receive discounts on products and services offered by other organizations. In addition they may receive discounts on the nonprofit's conferences, merchandise, training programs, and exhibitor charges.

Membership associations may struggle with the issue of who is eligible to become a member. Although an open-door policy may bring more members, each paying a fee, the more exclusive the club, the easier it may be to charge a higher price for membership. The more stringent the qualifications to be a member, the more likely members may be to adhere to the membership requirements and find meaning and identification as members, resulting in greater loyalty and retention.[24] However, as membership fees rise, members may have higher expectations for a return on their investment. Decisions about membership are rarely influenced only by income generation concerns. Exhibit 6.1 provides an excerpt from the Clean Air Partners Membership Strategy for 2008 that illustrates the perceived value of members. As this strategy excerpt shows, there are multiple reasons besides revenue generation for a nonprofit to offer a membership program. Nonprofits that pursue this path should be clear on how much they expect the membership revenue to contribute to the budget and what they are promising members in exchange for their dues.

Partnerships with Business

Nonprofits can earn revenue by partnering with a business. For example, Sesame Workshop, the nonprofit that produces the television show *Sesame Street*, has made money for many years from licensing agreements with for-profit corporations. According to its Web site, licensing partners include but are not limited to Crest, Pampers, Apple & Eve, Random House, Earth's Best, Hasbro, Fisher-Price, Gund, Cardinal Games, Spin Master, and Reader's Digest.[25]

EXHIBIT 6.1. EXCERPT FROM THE CLEAN AIR PARTNERS MEMBERSHIP STRATEGY

As we put together a strategy to drive membership it is important to frame our expectations. With Clean Air Partner's current membership structure, it is unrealistic to rely on membership revenue as a main or even significant source of funding. However, membership can play a very strategic and significant role in helping Clean Air Partners meet its objectives. Clean Air Partners can look at membership as an opportunity to:

- Act as an introduction and relationship-building tool with organizations
- Experience the organization prior to elevating their relationship (such as sponsorships)
- Network and generate leads to other organizations and potential members/sponsors
- Reclaim the hard costs for the materials that go out to each member through membership
- Increase awareness and impact for initiatives such as the Air Quality Forecast, thereby generating larger and more meaningful impacts
- Increase the number of Clean Air Partners advocates
- Give testimony to the significant number of individuals and organizations who support the mission of Clean Air Partners
- Give testimony to the diverse constituency that endorses and supports the work of Clean Air Partners
- Provide training ground for new organization leadership

Source: "Clean Air Partners Membership Strategy for FY 08," prepared for AQAD Meeting, February 1, 2007, http://www.mwcog.org/uploads/committee-documents/oFdfWF820070223083702.pdf. Reprinted with permission of PRR.

Partnerships with for-profit corporations on joint ventures and licensing agreements can come with concerns about weakening the nonprofit's brand because the nonprofit's logo is associated with the corporation's logo.[26] There may also be concerns about what the affiliation is implying about the corporation and its products. For example, the American Medical Association (AMA) came under fire for allowing its name to be used on Sunbeam Corporation's home medical products. Doctors who were members of the AMA were upset that the association appeared to be endorsing the products. In the end the AMA pulled out of the arrangement and agreed to pay Sunbeam millions of dollars to settle the resulting lawsuit.[27]

Some nonprofits have found that their interests in these agreements may be overshadowed by their partner corporation's interests. As nonprofits become more sophisticated in negotiating agreements with corporations, however, the balance of benefits to each party becomes more even.

As in the case of The Nature Conservancy, discussed in Chapter Fourteen, the public perception of how the nonprofit is working with corporations needs to be taken into account in deciding on any business relationship. Having set policies on what types of partnerships are allowable and enforcing mechanisms to ensure that the nonprofit's interests are protected can help the nonprofit avoid criticism that it is the puppet of business corporations.

In addition to understanding the branding and legal implications of partnering with a business to generate revenue, it is important for a nonprofit to understand why a particular business is interested in the partnership and what it can bring to the table. This knowledge may help the nonprofit increase its bargaining effectiveness and strategize about whether and how to evolve the partnership over time. Relationships with businesses may evolve from simple gifts or sponsorships to highly collaborative joint ventures, as described in Chapter Fifteen, on partnerships, alliances, and affiliations. For example, a nonprofit theater may sell advertising in its playbill to a corporation that wants to build awareness of its products among the theater patrons. As the corporation sees more value in connecting its brand to the theater, it may wish to become a major sponsor of a series of performances. Eventually, the corporation may be an investor in a theater production, giving upfront funds needed to stage the play and then sharing in the proceeds from ticket sales.

Partnerships with businesses may open up concerns about a nonprofit's tax exemption and whether unrelated business income tax (UBIT) should be paid. It was a precedent-setting 1980 court case, *Plumstead Theatre Society* v. *Commissioner*, involving a nonprofit theater partnering with private investors to produce a play that opened the door for a myriad of joint ventures between nonprofits and businesses.[28] In the *Plumstead* case the theater's status as a tax-exempt nonprofit was unsuccessfully challenged; although it was working with private investors, the eventual finding was that this partnership arrangement had been entered into at "arm's length" and that the tax-exempt mission had been preserved. In a more recent 2004–2005 revenue ruling, the IRS looked at a limited liability company set up by a tax-exempt university and a for-profit company for the purpose of offering off-campus training. The IRS found that the joint venture's activities were an insubstantial part of the total activities of the exempt participant and thus there were no adverse tax exemption implications.[29]

Nonprofits should choose their business partners carefully, looking for partners whom they can trust, who have a similar level of commitment to sustaining the partnership, who share the same vision, whose values and norms are compatible with the nonprofit's, and who can devote the needed time, resources, expertise, and effort. They also should be careful to avoid relationships with businesses owned by individuals who are disqualified from working with the nonprofit due to prohibitions on private inurement, such as founders, board members, major donors, high-level employees, and any of these individuals' family members.

Nonprofits may choose to partner with a for-profit business in creating a separate legal entity to produce revenue that is then diverted to the nonprofit. Unincorporated nonprofit associations may end up inadvertently creating a separate legal entity if their members divide profits from an income-producing activity. There are a variety of forms of partnership and rules governing them, so legal assistance is recommended for nonprofits considering joint business ventures.

Investment Income

Some nonprofits build investment funds in order to use the returns in future years to subsidize their operations. For example, the Yale University endowment contributed $843 million, 37 percent, of Yale's revenue in 2008.[30] A useful position paper for understanding nonprofit endowment investing strategy and risks is offered by The Vanguard Group.[31]

Spending requirements for foundation assets and endowment assets differ. Foundations are regulated with a requirement that they annually spend 5 percent or more of the average of their asset value for the year, though the IRS allows accounting carryforwards and carrybacks to avoid penalties arising from underspending. Endowments in the United States do not face mandated spending requirements, but there have been proposals to set endowment spending minimums for public charities. For example, U.S. Representative Peter Welch, of Vermont, has proposed that universities be required over a given period of time to spend at least 5 percent of their endowments, in an effort to make college more affordable.[32] Peter Conti-Brown has argued that this proposal and other efforts to force endowment spending were unsuccessful largely because of the effect of the 2007 to 2009 financial meltdown on the value of endowments.[33]

Endowment campaigns are built on the principle that less funding will be needed in the future by building a significant pot of money now; the principal can be invested and preserved and only the earnings spent. Peter Frumkin notes the high price required for the stability of endowment funding, stating that it often requires more than twenty times the amount to be spent on an annual basis.[34] One 2010 poll showed that most nonprofits with endowments have policies requiring them to spend only 4 to 5 percent of the value of the endowment each year. This requires donors to have a high level of trust in the nonprofit's ability to invest the endowment gift well. It also requires careful thinking about the time horizon for the nonprofit's mission. Frumkin asks donors to consider opportunity costs and decide whether their money could be put to better use now in programs to directly achieve the mission rather than being used in a longer-term more incremental strategy that involves placing their gift in an endowment fund.

The question of when to invest and when to spend available funds can become a public relations issue. Some nonprofits have been criticized for building endowments perceived as too large. Boys Town was one of the first nonprofits to face accusations of having an inflated endowment and more interest in building reserve funds than in improving mission effectiveness. The *Omaha Sun*'s 1972 Pulitzer prize–winning investigative report on Boys Town showed that the nonprofit continually solicited donations with the claim that it was in dire straits when actually it was taking in millions of dollars more each year than its annual operating expenses and quietly investing the unneeded funds. It had a net worth larger than Omaha's largest bank and an endowment of $209 million, more than all but a few universities.[35]

Current economic conditions have led some nonprofits to suffer from "underwater endowments," in which the value of the fund is no longer able to support the promised level of withdrawals without reducing the original principal. This is clearly the case for many universities with endowments, with one report finding that 38 percent of university endowment funds were underwater at the end of 2008.[36] Many universities rely on endowments for faculty and student support, with the first evidence for this practice appearing in Athens in A.D. 176, when Roman emperor Marcus Aurelius set up endowed faculty chairs there. Before the recent fiscal crisis, Harvard University was drawing about one-third of its total revenue from its investments.[37] When investment value falls, nonprofits need to determine whether restrictions set by the original donors allow any changes in spending policies and whether changes are necessary and warranted.

The following recommendations are for nonprofits that use investment funds to support their operations:

- Set a policy on what percentage of the endowment should be withdrawn annually to support the organization's mission.

- Determine restrictions on the types of investments that can be made, based on organizational values (for example, some nonprofits serving youth do not invest in companies that sell tobacco products).

- Set investment policies based on how much liquidity is needed and how much risk is tolerable (sample investment policies and guidelines are available).[38]

- Understand and follow the laws regarding investment portfolios and payout requirements (government regulations call for prudent management of investments and specify minimum spending requirements for foundations).
- Set up procedures and accountable parties to oversee the investment manager.
- Schedule regular portfolio reviews.

Donations

Even the pursuit of philanthropic gifts comes with administrative and strategic challenges. There are numerous issues to consider related to honoring donors' intentions in regard to their gifts, and to powerful donors' attempting to control the nonprofit's agenda. Individuals and organizations giving large gifts may expect the recipient nonprofit to give them special treatment and may withdraw support if their interests are not protected. For example, Comcast Corporation pulled $18,000 in funding from Reel Grrls, a nonprofit that teaches girls about media production, after the nonprofit posted a tweet critical of the company. Comcast later apologized and reoffered the money, but the nonprofit refused the gift and went public with the incident.[39]

Struggles with donors may even lead to court cases, as donors attempt to retrieve their gifts, interested parties try to get nonprofits to honor deceased owners' intents, or the nonprofit seeks to make donors honor their pledges. In one case, the Montana Supreme Court dissolved the nonprofit board of the Charles M. Bair Family Museum for breaching its duty to use Alberta M. Bair's family fortune bequest as her will stated it should be used. The board had closed the museum to visitors for periods from 2002 to 2005 in response to low attendance and the declining value of the museum assets. The court said the board had not spent enough money to give a good start to the museum and ordered U.S. Bank, which controlled four of the five board seats, to create a new board to oversee the museum.[40] The new board was more aggressive in its efforts to use available funds to increase the number of visitors. An April 4, 2011, press release announced the opening of a new state-of-the-art museum on the grounds of the Bair family home.[41]

Ethical codes of conduct for professional fundraisers make clear the importance of honoring donors' intentions for their gifts. See Chapter Two for the Donor Bill of Rights compiled by the Association of Fundraising Professionals (AFP). The AFP provides resources to train fundraisers on best practices and offers a certification program to support the professionalization of fundraising.

Revenue Portfolios

Now that we have outlined various sources of revenue, we turn to possible trade-offs among them. Researchers have tried to uncover whether a nonprofit's receipt of government funding or use of earned income strategies reduces individuals' likelihood of making donations or the size of their donations. A core question reviewed by Eleanor Brown and Al Slivinski is whether government grants "crowd out" donations.[42] The argument that seems to have the greatest preponderance of evidence is that as unrestricted grants increase, nonprofits have less interest in seeking donations because they have less need for them, and a reduced effort to fund raise brings fewer gifts.[43] However, government seed grants may spark the creation of new nonprofits and new programs that attract donors' attention and inspire more donations.

Commercial activity also has the potential to crowd out donations and grants. Researchers have found that this effect may vary by subsector. There is some evidence that there is no crowding out from commercialization for educational and medical nonprofits. However, this effect has been found for other types of nonprofits, in particular arts and culture nonprofits.[44]

Nonprofit leaders, like those at the Oakes Children's Center, are wise to review their organization's revenue portfolio to look for vulnerabilities and opportunities. It may reveal that some sources of revenue are crowding out others and whether this is problematic. At the Oakes Children's Center the lack of fundraising was troubling to some of the center's leaders, and they began a concerted effort to generate interest in increasing the nonprofit's capacity in this area.

Nonprofit leaders also should examine whether their nonprofit is sending inconsistent messages about its mission and needs through its different revenue-generating activities. As Howard Tuckman and Cyril Chang discuss, avoidance of mission drift is challenging, given growing commercialization in the nonprofit sector.[45] Nonprofits may find that as they seek earned income, they lose sight of their true purpose and how much revenue is needed to achieve it. If a nonprofit's budget does not clearly reflect a focus on its core purpose, foundation and government funders may not wish to support it. Individual donors may also question why a nonprofit is seeking philanthropic gifts if it appears to be profiting from unrelated business activities. Some individuals may even have trouble distinguishing between for-profit, government, and nonprofit enterprises, given that they all may exist in the same industry. When the revenue-generating activities of organizations in different sectors look very similar, the organizations' sector identities may be unclear to outsiders.

The Philanthropic Impulse

The word *philanthropy* comes from ancient Greek and means "love of mankind." Today we use the word to capture efforts to enhance the well-being of others through financial support or volunteer activity. To quote Robert Payton, philanthropy is "private action for the public good."[46] Philanthropists are those who give their assets to others, whether those assets are their wealth or their talents. *Charity*, not in the legal sense but in the origins of the word, is a subset of philanthropy and focuses on giving to the poor and needy.[47] Eleemosynary activities pertain to acts of charity or almsgiving.

There is a long tradition of philanthropy in the United States and other countries. In the United States many schools, churches, libraries, and colleges were started through private gifts. The earliest recorded instances of fundraising are found in religious texts, and many religions emphasize an obligation to help others through acts of charity. Nonprofits often serve as a vehicle for philanthropic impulses that are nurtured through cultural norms and family traditions as well as religious training and texts.

Not all gifts to nonprofits are given for purely philanthropic reasons. Individual donors' motivations for giving have been studied in depth, confirming that donors give to nonprofits for a variety of reasons.[48] Rarely are gifts purely altruistic. According to social exchange theory, gifts are two-way exchanges that satisfy rational and self-interested motives on the part of both the receiver and giver.[49] Some individuals choose to give out of their own vanity and desire to gain respect and esteem. Others hope to shape outcomes they see as desirable, such as finding a cure for a disease, building a more educated workforce, being able to enjoy artistic performances, and so forth. Giving a gift can help donors influence the success of nonprofits pursuing missions that fit with their interests. They may give in order to "pay forward" gifts or kindnesses they have received. Some donors feel that helping others can help make amends for past misdeeds and atone for sins. Donors may also give as a type of insurance policy, to make sure services are available if they or their loved ones ever need them. They may also give in order to have access to other donors and to enjoy professional or social interactions that come with their giving.

Andrew Carnegie, one of the originators of modern-day foundations, wrote that those with great wealth have a moral obligation to administer their wealth during their lifetime.[50] His sense that philanthropy is a moral duty and a professional endeavor helped to shape giving practices focused on efficient and effective stewardship of one's wealth. Nonprofits were envisioned as accountable for applying donations from wealthy individuals to good effect. According to Carnegie, nonprofits should work to prevent social problems not merely alleviate them.

Types of Philanthropic Gifts

Donations to nonprofits come in a variety of forms. They may be monetary or in kind. An *in-kind* gift is one in which a product or service is donated rather than financial currency. Donations may also come in the form of stocks, bonds, real estate properties, insurance policies, retirement accounts, and other investment vehicles. A gift may be designated for a specific program or for general operating support. It may be a gift to an endowment in which the principal is protected and the nonprofit draws out income generated by the investment of the funds. It may be a percentage of a purchase, in which the donor receives something in exchange for the transaction, but the value of what is obtained is less than the purchase price. A gift may be pledged for the future or immediately given. It may be unsolicited or a response to an appeal, though one of the most common responses to the question of why a donor gave is that someone asked. A gift may be anonymous or come with formal recognition and a title. For example, a gift at a certain level may qualify the donor to be part of a Leader's Circle, to be designated a Platinum giver, or to receive some other status. Gifts may be arranged so that donors receive financial returns from them, as in the case of annuities, in which a nonprofit promises to pay the annuitant a regular income beginning at a future date in exchange for a gift of cash, stock, or property now.

Types of Donors

The Giving USA annual reports track trends in giving patterns in the United States. The proportion of giving by various types of donors has remained relatively stable over the last ten years. In 2010, over $290 billion was donated to nonprofit organizations, according to the Giving USA report. Figure 6.3 shows the breakdown by type of giver.

FIGURE 6.3. BREAKDOWN OF SOURCES OF 2010 CONTRIBUTIONS OF $290.89 BILLION

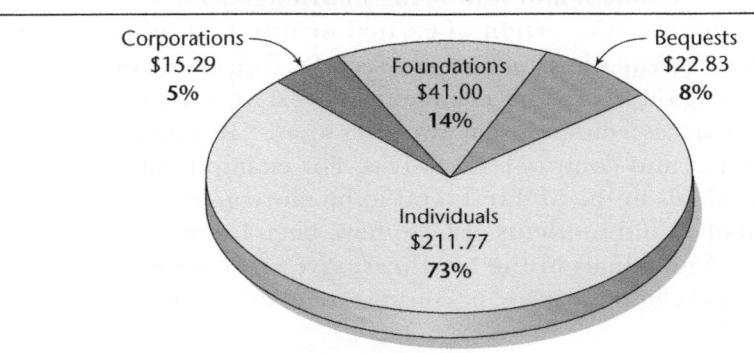

- Corporations $15.29 — 5%
- Foundations $41.00 — 14%
- Bequests $22.83 — 8%
- Individuals $211.77 — 73%

Source: Adapted from Center on Philanthropy at Indiana University, *Giving USA 2011: The Annual Report on Philanthropy for the Year 2010* (Chicago: Giving USA Foundation, 2011).

Individuals

Individuals may give gifts during their lifetimes or in the form of bequests. For those who give while living, Adrian Sargeant and other scholars suggest that nonprofits consider their lifetime value as donors.[51] Rather than seeing each request to an individual as discrete, Sargeant suggests that nonprofits think less about the outcome of a particular appeal to an individual and more about the long-term relationship they are establishing with that individual. Over the course of his or her involvement with a nonprofit, an individual may give cash donations, volunteer, refer others to the organization, sell event tickets, buy merchandise, and otherwise support the nonprofit. The idea of lifetime value comes from the consumer marketing tradition in which someone who purchases a good is understood to have an estimated potential of making a series of such purchases over his or her lifetime. By building donor loyalty and understanding how needs and interests may shift over time, a nonprofit may better manage long-term relationships. Sargeant and others adopt a business orientation and suggest that the greater the expected lifetime value of the relationship with a donor, the greater the expenditure of the nonprofit's time and effort that is warranted to support the relationship.

Much has been written about how to manage relationships with individuals who have given or have the potential to give gifts.[52] Recommendations include customizing appeals to match donors' values and interests, providing tax and legal advice related to gifts, allowing for more and different types of involvement in the nonprofit over time, leveraging positive word of mouth from current supporters, asking for feedback on the nonprofit's performance, and properly stewarding donations to honor each donor's intentions.

Researchers have compiled an impressive amount of work on who gives in the United States, looking at a variety of demographic factors. Havens, O'Herlihy, and Schervish summarize these studies, concluding that higher levels of giving are associated with higher levels of income, wealth, religious participation, volunteerism, age, and educational attainment and with being married, having U.S. citizenship, having a higher proportion of earned wealth than inherited wealth, and having a greater level of financial security. The effects of gender, ethnicity, and religion have more complex patterns; for example, the type of nonprofit makes a difference in who gives more.[53] Researchers have also found regional and country-level effects. For example, in the United States, individuals in the Midwest tend to be more generous than those in the Sunbelt,[54] and residents of Utah have been found to be the most generous.[55] Individuals in the Northeast give more money to secular causes than to religious causes, in contrast to all other regions in the country.[56]

FIGURE 6.4. PYRAMID OF GIVING

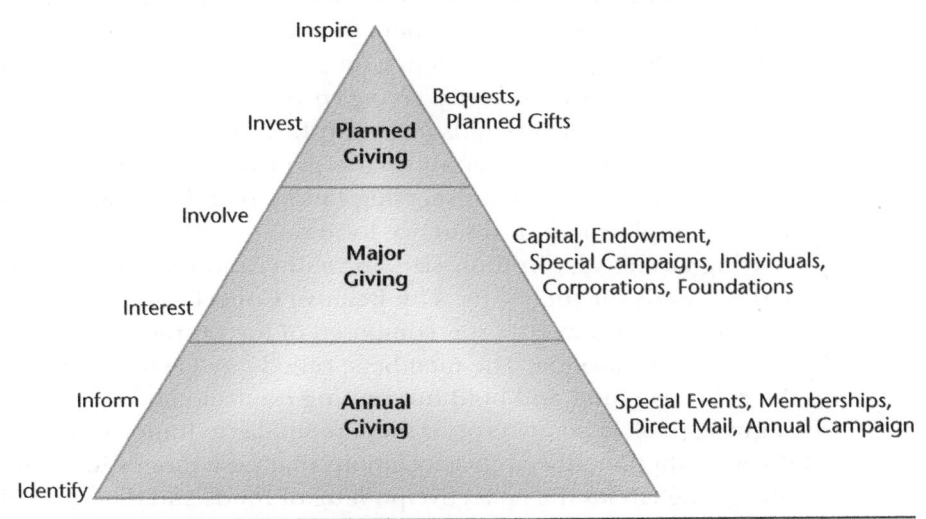

- Inspire / Invest — **Planned Giving** — Bequests, Planned Gifts
- Involve / Interest — **Major Giving** — Capital, Endowment, Special Campaigns, Individuals, Corporations, Foundations
- Inform / Identify — **Annual Giving** — Special Events, Memberships, Direct Mail, Annual Campaign

Source: Barbara L. Ciconte and Jeanne G. Jacob, *Fundraising Basics: A Complete Guide*, 3rd ed. (Boston: Jones & Bartlett, 2009). Copyright © 2009. Reprinted with permission.

The Foundation Center, *Chronicle of Philanthropy*, and Giving USA are several of the organizations that frequently provide reports on giving trends and regional and demographic differences.

Fundraising programs in the United States are typically built on the principle that most of the money in a fundraising campaign comes from a small proportion of the donors. This notion of proportionate giving has resulted in the idea of a gift pyramid and the construction of gift range charts for annual giving, major gifts, planned giving (for example, bequests), and capital campaigns. The largest group of donors is at the base of the pyramid and together they give the fewest number of dollars, while the most money comes from the smallest group of givers at the top of the pyramid. Figure 6.4 shows a gift pyramid developed by Barbara Ciconte and Jeanne Jacob that indicates which types of fundraising appeals are likely to be used at each level.

Appeals to the wealthiest donors, who have the greatest giving capacity, may be best coming from their peers. Bill and Melinda Gates and Warren Buffett are among the most vocal in calling for the wealthy to give more.[57] In 2009, they asked the nation's billionaires to pledge to give at least half their net wealth to charity.[58] Sixty-nine billionaires were listed on the pledge Web site as of August 2011.[59]

Giving Groups

A growing trend among donors is to want both to be more engaged in learning about nonprofits and to pool their gifts to make a greater impact and potentially have more influence on a nonprofit's decision making.[60] One vehicle for doing so is the *giving circle*, in which individuals come together to make collective gifts to nonprofits. The circles may be formed around a particular donor identity such as gender or race, a shared interest such as environmental or youth-serving causes, or a shared affiliation such as place of employment or residence location.

Giving circles vary in their size, formality, and longevity and in how they raise funds for their gifts. The Beehive Collective, for example, was started in 2008, and in 2011 was composed of forty-three young women in Raleigh, North Carolina. The members, called *bees*, each give individually to the collective fund and hold fundraising events to add more dollars to their giving pool. In some respects they are similar to Junior Leagues, Lions Clubs and other membership associations that raise money for causes, but for the giving circles the collective pooling of funds and determination of where to give their money is their core and often sole mission.

One of the largest and most formalized giving circles is Social Ventures Partners, which is itself established as a nonprofit. In 2011, it had twenty-six affiliate organizations with two thousand members across the United States. In the case of Social Ventures Partners and some other giving circles, recipient nonprofits must be prepared to have the donors actively participate and influence their operations. The circles may give advice and volunteer assistance along with funding. They also tend to require extensive information from nonprofits before making giving decisions.

Another source of group-based funding for some nonprofits, particularly for schools, is class or alumni gifts. Donations are solicited and pooled by members of the group and then given to a specific nonprofit. Sometimes the gifts are given to pay for a specific object chosen by the group, such as a bench or artwork. In these forms of giving, peers are instrumental in encouraging gifts to the group fund. They differ from giving circles in that the recipient of the gift is predetermined—it is a nonprofit that has directly helped all members of the giving group.

Foundations

There are three main types of foundations that provide grants to nonprofits: private individual or family foundations, company-sponsored foundations, and community foundations. Briefly, private foundations are set up by one or more individuals. The most typical example is a family foundation, such as the John D. and Catherine T. MacArthur Foundation, established with the personal wealth of family members. A private foundation may be purely a grantmaking organization or may be classified as an operating foundation, which allows it to fund its own programs, not just give out grants to others. A company-sponsored foundation gives out grants using funds generated by a business firm or corporation and not from individuals. For example, the GM Foundation uses funds from General Motors Corporation.

A community foundation creates a fund using contributions from many individuals. Special interest funds are earmarked by a community foundation for designated purposes whereas donor-advised funds are used to allow the donors to influence on an ongoing basis what grants will be given. Donor-advised and designated funds serve as an alternative to private foundations, offering individuals the opportunity to use the infrastructure of the community foundation to manage their gift giving rather than setting up their own independent organization. The Cleveland Foundation was the first community foundation to be established in the United States;[61] in 2009, it reported over $2 billion in assets. Since the establishment of the Cleveland Foundation, community foundations have appeared in every state.

Foundations typically provide support based on assessment of grant proposals. Though foundations vary in what they request in submitted proposals, a good generic proposal outline is offered by the Foundation Center:[62]

- **Executive summary**: no more than one page. Summarizes the entire proposal.
- **Statement of need**: no more than two pages. Explains why the proposed project is necessary.
- **Project description**: no more than three pages. Outlines how the program will be implemented and evaluated.
- **Budget**: no more than one page. Lays out the finances of the project with explanatory notes.
- **Organization information**: no more than one page. Describes the nonprofit's history, structure, primary activities, audiences, and services.
- **Conclusion**: no more than two paragraphs. Summarizes the proposal's main points.

To increase their chances of being funded, nonprofits should show that their request fits the funding interests of the foundation and that they have followed submission instructions. Foundations vary widely on how they manage their grantmaking; however, proposals for foundations tend to be much less detailed than applications for government grants or contracts. Foundations also tend to have fewer instructions and are not as strict about rejecting proposals that don't follow every instruction. Both government and foundation funders may provide information on their funding criteria and eligibility requirements, though government agencies are more likely to do so. Many small foundations may not even advertise that they give out grants and may say that they will review proposals only from nonprofits that have been invited to submit them.

Federated Funders

Federated funders, such the United Way and the Combined Federal Campaign, solicit donations through workplaces and then distribute the funds to the donors' designated nonprofit recipients or, in the case of undesignated contributions, to nonprofits fitting established priorities. Nonprofits agree to participate in the campaign, following rules concerning fundraising during the workplace campaign period. To receive undesignated funds, nonprofits may need to apply for support from the federated funder and later provide evaluations of how the funding was used.

Businesses

For-profit businesses may provide funding to nonprofits through their advertising, marketing, public relations, or philanthropic budgets. They may offer a matching program in which an employee's gift to a nonprofit will be matched by the company. They may also provide sponsorships of events and tie financial gifts to employee volunteer activities. In general, businesses tend to support noncontroversial causes that have wide public appeal or that serve a target market similar to their own. Local causes may be appealing as a way to improve the welfare of employees and their families and provide a high quality of life. In addition to providing financial support, corporations may provide services, goods, and facilities free of charge.

Fund Development

In this section we describe both the process and the principles of fund development.

The Fund Development Process

The fund development process has multiple steps, and each can be critical in attracting and retaining donors. The steps are briefly summarized in the following sections.

Identify Your Nonprofit's Case for Support
Why does the nonprofit exist? What fundamental needs does it address? How are people better off because of what it offers? How do donors and grantmakers benefit from giving to the nonprofit? How does the nonprofit's mission align with potential supporters' values and norms?

In the case of the Oakes Children's Center, its leaders developed the case that the well-being of the community depended on helping the children in the community deal with mental illness and, as the mission expanded, developmental disabilities. With the help of the center the children it serves can become productive members of the community and reduce their need for services when they are adults.

Define What Mission the Fundraising Goal Would Accomplish
How many individuals can be served by the nonprofit? What outcomes can be achieved? What costs need to be covered to accomplish the mission objectives? Do the board and staff agree on what needs to happen now and in the future to fulfill specific objectives related to the mission?

At the Oakes Children's Center the board and staff needed to be convinced that philanthropic support was necessary to move the mission forward and ensure the organization's financial stability, despite the fact that the majority of the center's funding was at that time coming from the State of California. Through the planning process, they laid out what could be accomplished with funds raised.

Assess the Environment for Gift Giving and Determine Markets
Do others outside the nonprofit agree that its mission is valid and its objectives are reasonable? Is there capacity to give at the level required? Who are the most likely supporters? Are they aware of the needs the nonprofit is addressing and the role that the nonprofit can play if adequately funded?

The Oakes Children's Center's grassroots base of support had been neglected. Its board recognized that they needed to make a concerted effort to reinvigorate community interest in the center. In the past, fundraising efforts had been infrequent but still had resulted in gifts, which suggested that, if asked, community members would give.

Assess the Nonprofit's Capacity for Fundraising
Are the staff and board prepared to state the case for support? Are volunteers ready and able to ask for donations? Can gifts be properly stewarded? What budget is available for the fund development process?

The Oakes Children's Center board and staff found that they needed to prepare materials to tell their center's story. Although they had reporting data used for their state grants, it was not in a format that would appeal to individual gift prospects. They also needed to develop mechanisms and procedures to request gifts, acknowledge donations, and use funds according to donors' intentions. All of this required an investment in infrastructure to support the fund development process.

Research and Select Fundraising Vehicles, Prospects, and Approaches

Who will be approached for a gift and how? What is the ability to give and the interest in giving among individuals, corporations, associations, government agencies, local businesses, places of worship, service organizations, foundations, and other groups? How should potential funders be reached? Are they likely to be willing to be approached? Are there any linkages that can be used to connect to them, for example, a board member who works for them? What should the request to them be?

The board and staff of the Oakes Children's Center knew the center would continue to seek government grants. They also knew that the center was restricted from charging the clients' parents for services. The leaders believed that philanthropic gifts would help to diversify their revenue portfolio. With the help of a consultant they were able to identify markets and design materials for their solicitation efforts. The best prospects for the center were those who had an interest in giving, who had the ability to give, and who were accessible through a personal contact.

Prepare the Plan and the Organization

Who will do what? What information, resources, and training do board members, staff, and volunteers need to be effective? How will the fund development plan be integrated into other aspects of the nonprofit's strategic plan? How will the plan be evaluated and modified?

All nonprofits seeking donations, including the Oakes Children's Center, can benefit from having a comprehensive fund development plan that includes strategies, task assignments, and evaluation methods. It is the responsibility of the whole organization to be a worthy steward of gifts. Fundraising staff and volunteers need a validated case for support and research on prospects indicating the gift to be requested and how that gift contributes to the fundraising objectives and goals for the nonprofit.

Solicit Gifts, Thank Donors, Steward Gifts, and Prepare to Renew Gifts If Appropriate

Was the request made? Was it successful? Why or why not? When will it be appropriate to ask for another gift? How can the donor become more involved with the nonprofit? Is more research needed? Does the case for support need to be strengthened before additional solicitations are made?

Eventually someone needs to ask the donor for money. The more personal the approach and the greater the connection of the individual to the nonprofit, the greater is the likelihood of success. With each gift a nonprofit has the opportunity to forge a deeper bond with the giver and further explain how the donor's support is making a positive difference.

Fund Development Principles

There are a few basic principles that can guide fund development. One of the most repeated is that "people give to people to help people."[63] It is humans that make giving decisions, no matter whether they are making decisions about the disposition of their personal or another's wealth or are acting in the interest of a foundation, corporation, or other organization. Fundraising is built on relationships. A gift solicitation is more likely to be successful when there is a basis of trust. Success is also more likely when the person asked for the gift believes that people will genuinely be helped by the gift. Seeing pictures and hearing personal stories from those the nonprofit has reached can be more persuasive than dry statistics in convincing a prospective donor that his or her gift will make a meaningful difference. It can also be helpful to have a volunteer who is a peer of the prospect join a staff member in requests for large gifts. The peer relationship may be a basis for trust. Using a respected celebrity to endorse the nonprofit may also help in building trust.

Another principle is that significant gifts come in all sizes. By offering a wide range of giving opportunities, individuals with different means can give what to them is a generous gift. They may also judge what an appropriate gift is based on what others have given. This is the underpinning of gift pyramids, through which rather than seeking a certain number of donations of the same size, the nonprofit seeks many small and a few large gifts to reach its fundraising goal. For capital campaigns a common rule is to expect 90 percent of the funds to come from 10 percent of the donors. Modest givers should be as welcome as major donors. These modest givers may give more in the future as they become more closely connected to the nonprofit.

It is those closest to the nonprofit who are expected to set the pace for a fundraising campaign. If they are able but unwilling to give leadership gifts, it suggests to others that the nonprofit may not be as worthwhile as it seems.

A third principle is to understand the role of the fundraiser as someone who offers a means for donors to fulfill their aspirations. The means may be through contributions to an annual campaign, endowment campaign, capital or special project campaign, or estate or planned giving. Annual giving programs tend to bring in many first-time donors who identify with the cause, know a little about the nonprofit, and give gifts that do not stretch their giving capacity. They are often reached through less personal vehicles, such as direct-mail letters, telethons, and Web site appeals. Over time, as these donors learn more about the organization and the organization learns more about them, they may be approached with personal visits, more personalized letters, and other approaches. Professional fundraisers cultivate relationships with donors, understanding how their needs can match those of the nonprofit. As the donors' interests change, a good fundraiser will adapt to better support those interests.

Concluding Thoughts

This chapter has reviewed resource acquisition for nonprofits. Choices abound for possible revenue sources and strategies for pursuing them. Each nonprofit has unique contingencies that may affect how its funding has evolved since its establishment. Nonprofit leaders have the responsibility to understand the positives and negatives of their resource acquisition options. They also need to be accountable to their funding sources.

The need to steward a nonprofit's resources brings us to the next chapter on financial management. Building from the understanding of resource acquisition, we turn to how to manage financial resources appropriately.

Questions for Consideration

1. What influences your own giving to nonprofits? What motivates you to give or to stop giving? What does your experience say about how nonprofits should engage with potential and current donors?
2. Should nonprofits and their funders be concerned about growing commercialization in the nonprofit sector? Why or why not?

Exercises

Exercise 6.1: Analysis of Revenue Portfolio

Look at the revenue portfolio of a nonprofit. Is it diversified? What vulnerabilities, if any, do you see related to dependencies on particular funding sources?

Exercise 6.2: Evaluation of Fundraising Solicitation Letter

Analyze a letter from a nonprofit asking for financial support. What case for support does the letter make? How strong is the case? What values is the letter appealing to in asking for a gift? Do you find the letter to be compelling? Why or why not?

Exercise 6.3: Understanding Donor Motivations and Acknowledgment of Gifts

Interview someone you know who gives donations to one or more nonprofits. Ask this person to explain why he or she gives. What motivations for giving did he or she share with you? Focus on one gift the person has recently made. Track the person's engagement with the nonprofit back from the time of the interview to the time he or she decided to make the gift. What types of communications did the person receive from the nonprofit over this timeline? Did the person get thanked for his or her gift? If so, when and how? Do you think the acknowledgment of the gift was sufficient? Why or why not?

CHAPTER SEVEN

FINANCIAL STEWARDSHIP AND MANAGEMENT

With Charles K. Coe, Professor, School of Public and International Affairs, North Carolina State University

The mission of hopeFound is to prevent and end homelessness in the greater Boston area by focusing on helping individuals overcome addiction and find employment, housing, and hope. Its experience helps to show how a nonprofit can turn around its financial management before its mission is put at risk.[1] The board and newly hired executive director of hopeFound identified weaknesses and implemented new strategies and practices with the help of a consulting firm, Nonprofit Finance Fund. Over five years, starting in 2005, hopeFound weathered a recession while revamping its financial approach from perpetual crisis mode to planning. A 2005 financial analysis revealed that it had dangerously low levels of cash and liquid net assets but growing needs to cover amounts owed and purchase property and equipment. It had a short-term debt of $300,000 and continually used all of its line of credit. Its funding portfolio consisted primarily of government cost reimbursements, which did not fully cover program or administrative expenses. It also lacked a director for fundraising. The consulting firm helped hopeFound think holistically about how mission, capacity, and capital affect each other and recommended that the nonprofit develop a strategy for managing liquidity and credit, investigate creating a financial reserve, and consider opportunities for acquisitions.

As a result, hopeFound did a SWOT analysis, examined the cost of doing business, and explored options. Actions derived from goals led the organization to secure pro bono services, develop a comprehensive fundraising campaign, aggressively seek housing vouchers, renegotiate contracts from cost reimbursement to a fee-for-service structure, subcontract the management of its residential units, and reallocate savings to invest in human resources and pay off the line of credit. By 2008, hopeFound had more than three months of cash on hand for operations.

Its 2010 balance sheet was triple and its operating budget more than double what they had been in 2005, and it was able to purchase needed property and equipment. Most important, it was helping more people to get homes and jobs and to overcome addictions. Nonprofit Finance Fund asserts that the transformation from financial distress to financial empowerment was due to three factors: data, discipline, and dialogue. Specifically, hopeFound created and used a dashboard of financial indicators. It began regular board finance committee meetings that identified potential problems and solutions. It also openly discussed how progress would be tracked and gave management and the board equal voices in decision making.

The Harnett County Partnership for Children (HCPC) is a 501(c)(3) nonprofit that provides education and developmental services to children and their families in Harnett County, North Carolina. HCPC contracted with Community Education and Programs, Inc (CEAP), another 501(c)(3) nonprofit, to provide educational services. In 2009, a whistle-blower called the State Auditor's Hotline to allege that CEAP was misusing state funds. CEAP's executive director refused to provide the nonprofit's financial records to the Office of the State Auditor, which then served a subpoena for the records. Examining two contracts totaling $375,000, the state auditor found numerous instances of fraud: HCPC had reimbursed CEAP using state funds, but CEAP had never paid for day-care supplies, employee health insurance, or retiree contributions. Moreover CEAP had fraudulently obtained reimbursements for payroll taxes, payroll expenses, employee bonuses, and supplies. Finally, CEAP had not purchased a fidelity bond sufficient to cover the embezzlement losses. CEAP's bond covered only $10,000, but the nonprofit received nearly $375,000 in contracts. The state auditor made recommendations to HCPC for improving its inadequate financial and contracting practices and referred the audit findings to the Federal Bureau of Investigation and the Internal Revenue Service.[2]

◆ ◆ ◆

This chapter is about nonprofit financial stewardship and management. As our introductory scenarios suggest, proper financial management can help a nonprofit be more successful with its mission, avoid allegations of improprieties, and reduce the risk of unethical and illegal behavior. Through financial analyses and regular monitoring of financial indicators, hopeFound was able to find the resources to expand its programming and develop greater financial security. The Harnett County Partnership for Children was forced to devote resources to changing its financial management systems in response to external scrutiny of its practices. In an extreme case the United Way of America lost financial resources as well as credibility in the eyes of many donors when it was discovered that the organization's financial systems were inadequate and had failed to prevent improprieties by its then CEO, who was eventually sentenced to prison for financial mismanagement and criminal activity. In a more recent case the nonprofit Mosdut Shuva Israel received a $48,000 judgment against it simply for failing to obtain workers' compensation insurance. Other nonprofits, such as Oral Roberts University and the Harlem School for the Arts, have incurred significant debt and faced accusations of financial mismanagement that have threatened their operations.

Nonprofit organizations have a moral obligation to steward resources well, as discussed in Chapter Two. Part of the fallout from the fraud at Enron and other scandals in the for-profit sector was the enactment of the Sarbanes-Oxley Act. Though only two of its provisions apply specifically to nonprofits, the Act has provided guidance to many nonprofits wishing to establish sound financial policies and practices.[3] Financial management systems are critical for demonstrating adherence to the law and accountability to law enforcement agencies, donors, clients, the public, and any members. Toward that end, in this chapter we discuss seven elements of an effective financial management system: financial policies, accounting, budgeting, banking relations, borrowing, risk management, and auditing and financial analysis. By following the basic principles outlined in this chapter, a nonprofit can help to ensure that it remains trustworthy and accountable.

Element One: Financial Policies

A nonprofit board should adopt policies for regulating conflict of interest, protecting whistle-blowers, setting the budget reserve, and managing investments. The need for these and other policies may emerge in strategic planning efforts, as described in Chapter Five; in a board review of the board's ability to carry out its financial oversight responsibilities, as described in Chapter Nine; in efforts to quantify the costs and benefits of program initiatives, as described in Chapter Thirteen; or through other means. In the rest of this section, we review policy areas that every nonprofit should consider.

Conflict of Interest Policy

Nonprofits need to set conflict of interest policies not only to be consistent with the law but also to make their practices justifiable to key stakeholders and to establish enforceable procedures for handling conflicts of interest. As discussed further in Chapter Fourteen, public relations issues may arise over financial policies and practices, so an understanding of public perceptions of policies and expectations for their enforcement is important. Federal law, and also state law in some states, addresses compensation and excess benefit transactions for nonprofit board members and executive staff.[4] Nonprofits in the United States are prohibited from giving private inurement and excessive personal benefit to board members and staff: for example, through contracts overly favorable to a family member of the board chair or excessive compensation of the CEO. Even when the law allows a particular financial arrangement, the public may perceive it to be improper. The Internal Revenue Service (IRS) asks nonprofits to report in their Form 990 whether their conflict of interest policy has been enforced.

Consider a nonprofit that wishes to sell property (a situation we will discuss further in Chapter Fourteen in the context of media coverage of the Nature Conservancy). A board member who wants to buy this property has a conflict of interest. As a private individual she may want it at a cheap price to save herself some money; but as a board member she should want to sell it at the highest price possible to maximize the benefit to the nonprofit. Such financial transactions between nonprofits and board members are surprisingly extensive. A 2006 study revealed that 21 percent of nonprofits bought or rented goods, services, or property from a board member.[5] In some U.S. states, financial transactions between a nonprofit and its board and staff members are illegal. In other states they are legal when the board and staff members of the nonprofit act in the best interest of the nonprofit and contract with someone affiliated with the nonprofit only when that is the best deal possible for the nonprofit. Some nonprofits set policies forbidding sales and purchases that may personally benefit board and staff members, or they establish procedures for handling any conflicts of interest arising from purchase and sales activities.

Nonprofits should supply training for board and staff members (paid and volunteer), with specific examples of the ways in which the nonprofit's conflict of interest policies might be violated and what to do in situations where the policy is unclear. The training should include discussion of the potential consequences for the violator and the nonprofit if policies are not followed. Board and staff members should sign statements affirming their understanding and willingness to comply with the policies. They also should be clear on procedures that will be followed once a conflict of interest is disclosed. For example, the board may vote on whether a conflict of interest exists and whether the person with the conflict of interest is excluded from relevant discussions and votes. When board and staff members understand why the conflict of interest policies are important and what steps will be taken to enforce them, it is more likely that they will follow them.

Employees and board members may have a financial interest in a company doing business with the nonprofit without concern as long as they have placed that financial interest in a blind trust. With a blind trust they do not know their holdings and do not have any discretion over these assets. Politicians, including the president of the United States, use blind trusts when they have control over government funds going to the private sector. Blind trusts are also useful for leaders of nonprofits that do economic development and other types of work from which leaders' investments may benefit.

Gratuities, kickbacks, and loans are ripe for conflict of interest concerns. A gratuity is a gift, monetary payment, favor, free meal, honorarium, and so forth, that is legal but may be perceived as improper. A recommended policy is that nonprofits either set a relatively low limit for acceptable gratuities (for example, up to $25), or ban them altogether. A kickback, which is a payment from a vendor in return for getting the nonprofit's business, is illegal. Nonprofits should also not provide kickbacks in exchange for political favors. A New York state legislator recently resigned from office after he admitted that he took kickbacks from a charity he founded.[6] In response to the scandal the New York Public Interest Research Group called for the State Attorney General's Office to initiate a review to see if other legislators have illegal kickback arrangements with nonprofits in the state. A loan from a nonprofit to a board or staff member can also be considered inappropriate. The Sarbanes-Oxley Act explicitly forbids private loans to insiders in for-profit corporations but does not extend this rule to nonprofits. However, some states recommend or require that nonprofits not provide loans to board members and executives. Examples of nonprofits that ignored this advice can easily be found. For example, Mount Sinai Hospital and School of Medicine gave its president a $2.25 million, interest-free loan as part of its recruitment package and was criticized in the *Chronicle of Philanthropy* for the lost value from the loan. The hospital could have earned significant profit by investing that amount rather than loaning it without charging interest.[7]

Whistle-Blower Protection Policy

A nonprofit must report in its IRS Form 990 whether it has adopted a whistle-blower policy.[8] The Sarbanes-Oxley Act makes it a federal crime for a nonprofit to retaliate against an employee who reports suspected fraudulent activities. This is one of the few provisions of the Sarbanes-Oxley (SOX) Act that must be adhered to by nonprofits as well as for-profit corporations. Nonprofits should give employees and board members options for sharing concerns and should have mechanisms to ensure that the concerns are reviewed and not ignored. Cynthia Benzing and her colleagues review a variety of studies, including their own research, showing that whistle-blower protections are not in place in all nonprofits despite SOX.[9]

As demonstrated in our opening scenario involving CEAP, whistle-blowers are a critical mechanism for uncovering improper financial practices.

Budget Reserve Policy

A nonprofit should set a policy to budget funds in reserve at a certain level. This is fiscally prudent because it protects the nonprofit in the event that revenues are lower or expenses are higher than expected. There are many reasons why a nonprofit might misestimate its revenues and expenses. For example, expectations may not be met due to an economic downturn, unanticipated expense due to an act of nature (such as a tornado or a hurricane), equipment breakdown, reduced funding (such as the early termination of a large grant), or a significant rise in costs (such as a spike in employee health care premiums). As hopeFound discovered, having a reserve fund that is controlled by board vote allows a nonprofit to avoid taking out expensive loans or running a large line of credit.

The bigger a nonprofit's reserve, the greater its ability to weather a downturn; however, funders typically take a dim view of what they perceive as an overly large reserve. They quite understandably want a healthy amount of their funding spent on direct services. For example, as a condition of funding, some United Ways require nonprofits receiving their funding from undesignated gifts to limit their reserve to 25 percent of the annual budget. Having a policy set by the board about the amount of the reserve fund helps in addressing the great variation in opinion that may exist about what it should be. It also helps to focus the board on seeing that the reserve is maintained at the designated level until needed and then replaced when feasible with funds appropriate for this purpose.

Investment Policy

The investment policy designates an investment officer, usually the chief financial officer (CFO) for a large nonprofit or a hired firm for a small nonprofit, to manage the investment program. The board must decide whether to pursue a passive or active investment strategy and spell out the values that will guide investment choices. A *passive* investment strategy, taken by most nonprofits, simply tries to obtain the average rate of return on investments. In contrast, an *active* investment strategy tries to earn a higher rate than the average. Active investing entails more risk. Only a nonprofit that has a sizable amount to invest (for example, an endowment) and that can afford the services of a professional investment adviser should undertake active investing. If the investment officer follows the designated investment strategy and exercises due diligence, he or she is relieved of culpability, legal or managerial, for a decline in value of the investments.[10] In addition to designating the investment risk orientation, the investment policy also specifies the types of investments the nonprofit can use. For example, a nonprofit that advocates for animal rights may make a policy not to invest in companies that use animals for testing products. Environmental conservation nonprofits may choose not to invest in corporations that violate their standards for environmental protection.

Document Retention Policy

Nonprofits should have policies for document retention and destruction that are consistent with local, state, and federal laws. Even if the retention period for documents has passed, the Sarbanes-Oxley Act requires that document purging must stop if an official investigation or bankruptcy proceeding is under way or there is a suggestion that one may be started.

Element Two: Accounting

Every successful organization depends on its accounting system to provide data for financial decision making and reporting. Nonprofit staff and board members should have a basic understanding of the accounts (for example, asset, liability, functional expense, and reserve accounts) used to record information about the operations of the nonprofit and how those accounts relate to the financial position and activities of the nonprofit, the accounting cycle, generally accepted accounting principles, and internal controls.

Accounts

To understand their financial position, organizations need to keep track of what they own (*assets*) and what they owe to others (*liabilities*). A *summary snapshot* of the financial position of the organization is provided by this accounting equation:

$$\text{Assets} - \text{Liabilities} = \text{Net Assets}.$$

Some organizations may need only a few accounts to keep track of their assets and liabilities. For example, a small nonprofit may have assets that include cash on hand and some office equipment. Its liabilities might include an account payable to the local utility and a small loan from a bank. A large nonprofit may own a building (asset) that was financed with a mortgage (liability) and furniture and fixtures (assets) and may have invested some of its funds in stocks or bonds (assets). Some nonprofits may have all their net assets in an unrestricted net asset account, whereas others may have unrestricted net assets and also endowment funds and other types of restricted asset accounts.[11]

In addition to knowing their current financial position, organizations also need to account for their activities. This requires that they be able to identify their revenues (for example, gifts, grants received, program revenues, interest earned, and so on) and their expenses (for example, utility costs, interest payments, salaries, insurance, fees, and so on). The basic accounting equation for summarizing the activities of an organization is

$$\text{Revenues} - \text{Expenses} = \text{Net Income or Net Loss}.$$

Although all organizations need to have detailed accounting records of their assets, liabilities, revenues, and expenses, nonprofit organizations have some additional requirements for tracking different types of expenses (for example, program and fundraising) and for different types of funds (for example, restricted, unrestricted, and temporarily restricted). We address these issues later in this chapter.

The Accounting Cycle

The *accounting cycle* refers to a process that allows for the accurate recording and summarizing of transactions by an organization. Whether accounting records (*the books*) are kept manually or with an automated system, the same basic process applies. Although the official accounting cycle contains several more detailed steps, the gist of the process consists of three key activities:

- **Documenting**. Whenever a transaction takes place, a source document (for example, a bill, invoice, receipt, deposit slip, purchase order, or check) should be generated or received.
- **Recording**. Upon the receipt of a source document, an entry is made to record the data in the appropriate accounts and the source document is filed, consistent with the organization's document-retention policy.
- **Reporting**. Adjusting entries are made and financial statements (described later in this chapter) are prepared.

Numerous accounting software packages are available, including some that help nonprofits conform to generally accepted accounting principles related to fundraising record-keeping rules (see the next section), rules on cost allocations to fundraising versus program activities, rules prohibiting allocations of compensation or fees for fundraising based on amounts raised, and IRS Form 990 reporting requirements.[12] Some commonly used software packages are QuickBooks for Nonprofits, QuickBooks Pro, BlackBaud, Financial Edge, Sage MIP Fund Accounting, Kinters FundWare, and Peachtree.

Generally Accepted Accounting Principles (GAAP)

Uniform accounting standards help to ensure that the financial statements generated by different organizations are consistent and comparable. In 2009, the Financial Accounting Standards Board (FASB) issued the Accounting Standards Codification (ASC, or Codification), which is the source of nongovernmental generally accepted accounting principles (GAAP). The Codification combines thousands of GAAP pronouncements into about ninety topics, organized in a hierarchy of topics, subtopics, sections, and subsections.[13] Many basic accounting concepts and practices are the same in nonprofit and for-profit organizations, but there are some important differences when accounting for contributions and expenses.

One of the most important GAAP standards for nonprofits is Accounting for Contributions (FASB ASC section 958-605-25). Before this standard was established, nonprofits did not have to record the donor's intent for the gift. Now, to assist in keeping track of gifts that must be used in certain ways, nonprofits must put a gift into one of three categories, depending on a donor's intent:

- **Permanently restricted assets** are assets such as endowments, land, and artwork that the donor permanently restricts. In an endowment, the nonprofit must keep intact the corpus of the gift in perpetuity and can spend only the investment income.
- **Temporarily restricted assets** are funds temporarily donor-restricted for a particular use: for example, a contribution received from a capital campaign may be restricted for a new building. The building fund may need to grow over several years before the funds are expended.
- **Unrestricted assets** are funds free of donor-imposed restrictions, such as contributions from individuals and unrestricted grants that are not tied to a particular use.

This categorization scheme helps nonprofits honor donors' wishes. Donors may sue nonprofits to have their gifts returned if they believe their intent for the gift was not honored. Nonprofits obviously have the most discretion with unrestricted assets. If all assets are narrowly restricted, a nonprofit may have difficulty meeting basic operating needs that do not qualify for use of the funds. Therefore nonprofits should be careful to have enough unrestricted assets to be able to carry forth the activities promised as a condition of the restricted assets.

One complication related to accounting for donations is whether a donation should be seen as a *pass-through contribution.* If a nonprofit collects the donation to turn over to another organization to use, the donation is treated as a liability until it is paid to the other organization. For example, a church may collect contributions for disaster relief efforts. The contributions are treated as liabilities if the church does not intend to directly provide the relief services but rather intends to send the contributions to another organization that will use the funds for the relief services.

The issue of restricted and pass-through contributions is especially relevant when we look at the recent review of 9/11 charities published by the Associated Press.[14] Many of these charities delivered what they promised, but others promised to pass on donations to victims or to other nonprofits and failed to do so. One nonprofit, the American Quilt Memorial, promised to construct a quilt with commemorative squares, but out of the $713,000 given to the organization in donations, the founder spent $270,000 on himself and relatives. Urban Life Ministries had its tax exemption revoked by the IRS when it raised $4 million to help victims and first responders but could account for only $670,000 of expenditures. In a classic case of private inurement, and showing why some states prohibit a nonprofit from having contracts with a firm owned by its executive director, a founder of the Flag of Honor Fund raised money to construct a large flag with the names of 9/11 victims. According to the Associated Press review, the flag is produced by a for-profit owned by the founder of the nonprofit and is sold at retail stores, with only a tiny fraction of the money from the sales going to 9/11 charities and most of the profit going to the founder.

GAAP requires nonprofits to report expenses in three categories: (1) *program expenses* related to service delivery; (2) *management and general expenses* that support programs, such as the salary and wages of the CEO and CFO; and (3) *fundraising expenses,* such as postage and paper for a direct-mail solicitation. Some expenses are easily identifiable. For instance, if a staff person works on only one program that can be easily categorized as direct service to clients, administration, or fundraising, then that person's salary can be allocated to that category. Other expenses may be less apparent. For instance, the executive director and staff, although chiefly working on management and general activities, may also work on fundraising and program activities. When that is the case they should keep a time log, recording their time spent in each of the three categories. Time should be recorded at least monthly. Similarly, a portion of building costs (for example, rent and utilities) is allocated to the three expense types, typically based on the number of square feet used for program, management, and fundraising activities.

GAAP's three categories for reporting expenses are important because donors and grantors generally want as much of their funds as possible to be spent on programs, and not on management, fundraising, and general services. For this reason, some funders, such as the United Way, limit the percentage of total expenses that may be spent on management and general activities. Some watchdog groups report how nonprofits allocate their expenses, offering rating schemes based on what these groups suggest are reasonable percentages. These watchdogs include but are not limited to the Better Business Bureau's Wise Giving Alliance, Charity Navigator, and the American Institute of Philanthropy. Some scholars find that the ratios these groups use to rate nonprofits may be misleading to donors and unfairly critical of some types of nonprofits.[15] The watchdogs do not take into account different types of missions, expenses, revenues, and stages of development, which makes it problematic to use their ratios to compare substantially different nonprofits. For example, a very young nonprofit may need to spend more on fundraising than more established nonprofits in order to raise the capital needed to go to scale to gain efficiencies in its operations. Simple comparisons of ratios are likely to make this nonprofit look bad compared to nonprofits that are not actively fundraising because they have large endowments or substantial earned income streams.

Accounting Internal Controls

A sound internal control system improves operational effectiveness, enhances the reliability of financial reporting, ensures compliance with applicable laws and regulations, and reduces the opportunity for fraud. If CEAP and HCPC had had better internal controls, perhaps they could have avoided accusations of financial mismanagement. By establishing a disciplined approach through internal controls, hopeFound moved from crisis mode to a more strategic approach to its mission.

The difference between an error (for example, sloppy accounting) and fraud is that *fraud* is intentional, but an *error* is unintentional. Following are some examples of fraud:

- Theft of receipts, inventory, or donated goods
- Use of organizational assets for personal benefit
- Receipt of kickbacks (for example, cash, gifts, promises of subsequent employment) from a vendor in exchange for preferential treatment

- Overpayments for labor, services, or goods and payments for labor, services, or goods not received
- Overcharging the organization for reimbursements (for example, for travel expenses)
- Collecting donations for one program but using the funds for other purposes

As demonstrated by these examples, nonprofits can suffer from misappropriation of assets, corruption where influence is inappropriately used in a financial transaction, and deliberate falsification of financial statements.[16] More examples of fraud can be found by looking at the uniform occupational fraud classification system developed by the Association of Certified Fraud Examiners and discussed by Janet Greenlee and her colleagues.[17] Greenlee and her colleagues also note multiple abuses of trust by nonprofits or by organizations masquerading as nonprofits. For example, the FBI found that more than two thousand of the Internet sites asking for donations for Hurricane Katrina victims were fraudulent.[18]

As noted in Chapter Two, persons may be unlikely to commit fraud owing to their personal ethical standards, organizational codes of conduct, and societal norms. However, they may feel pressured to commit fraud or rationalize it when they are facing personal financial pressures, feel unfairly paid, are aware that others are doing it, or think no one will notice or care. In their study of investigated frauds committed by nonprofit employees, Greenlee and her research team found that the larger frauds were more likely to be committed by those who were higher in salary, age, tenure with the nonprofit, and educational level attained. Managers were the perpetrators in 25 percent of the cases, and executives in 8.6 percent of the cases. Although many nonprofit employees and volunteers are honest and ethical, it is clear that nonprofit leaders should not assume that everyone working for a nonprofit is immune from temptation. Nonprofits have an obligation as good stewards to reduce if not eliminate opportunities for fraud and to recognize when pressures and rationalizations may lead to motivations for fraudulent activity.

Conditions that can increase opportunities for fraud include having weak internal accounting controls, not obtaining an independent audit, having poorly trained personnel, installing a new accounting or IT system, changing management organization and responsibilities, and being overdependent on one person in areas with opportunities for fraud. Stuart Douglas and Kim Mills argue that it may be easier to commit fraud in a nonprofit than in a for-profit, due to the atmosphere of trust, difficulty in verifying revenue streams, weaker internal controls, lack of business and financial expertise, and reliance on volunteers.[19] For example, it may be easier for volunteers or employees to keep a donation of money or physical items intended for a nonprofit than it is for a cashier at a convenience store to pocket a customer's payment for a purchase of alcohol or help himself to a bottle on the store shelf. There are likely more internal controls at the store, including inventory records, cameras, and cash register records.

There are numerous practices that can help in the prevention and detection of fraud.[20] The most fundamental accounting control is to separate accounting duties among two or more persons to help reduce opportunities for fraud and errors. For example, the person keeping the books should not be the person signing the checks. The check signer should not receive bank notifications and reconcile bank statements. Even with separation, two or more employees can collude to steal. Separating duties is more challenging in a small nonprofit with only one or two employees. Board members may perform one or more of the financial functions to make separation of duties possible. Also, for large transactions, a nonprofit may require two signatures.

Besides separation of duties, these practices may reduce the likelihood of fraud:

- Require background and credit checks on all workers who handle cash or keep records of inventories of supplies, equipment, or donated goods.
- Create a positive ethical environment from the top down.
- Select board members who have no financial interests in the nonprofit's affairs.
- Direct an audit committee to look for fraud.
- Create a whistle-blower protection system.
- Educate workers on the consequences of fraud.
- Develop and test internal financial controls with the help of an expert.
- Watch tax payments carefully; failures to pay these typically go undetected and so they present an easy opportunity for theft.
- Conduct annual audits using an external firm.
- To mitigate losses from fraud, purchase fidelity insurance to cover embezzlement losses.

Nonprofits that are willing to tolerate theft are open to criticism and potentially further financial improprieties. Do not set up confidential repayment arrangements for a perpetrator; instead, contact law enforcement authorities. For example, the executive officers of ACORN discovered that the brother of the nonprofit's founder had embezzled $1 million in 1999 and 2000, but they kept him on the payroll until 2008 after he and his family agreed to repay the embezzled amount in exchange for confidentiality. The executive officers did not inform the board about the situation. This secret arrangement was exposed by *The New York Times*, damaging the reputation of the nonprofit.[21]

Contrast ACORN's response with that of Points of Life officials when they discovered abnormalities in the business practices of a contractor hired to run the nonprofit's eBay store for donated travel packages and other items. As soon as concerns were raised by customers who had not received travel vouchers and certificates they had purchased, the eBay store was shut down. The nonprofit contacted the people who had bought the packages and attempted to make good on their commitments to them. It also contacted the donors and some agreed to help the nonprofit pay back the customers. Points of Light also contacted the U.S. Attorney's Office in Washington, D.C., the jurisdiction of the nonprofit, to report the improprieties.[22]

Element Three: Budgeting

Budgeting is a critical activity for nonprofits. It is impossible to make short- and long-term strategic decisions and guide month-to-month operations without a budget explaining how much money the nonprofit expects to receive and has to spend. A budget can show what funding is available to start a new program or hire a new employee. Checking the annual budget against year-to-date revenues and expenses may show where adjustments in activities and in expectations need to be made in order to finish the year without a deficit. Comparisons of past budgets may reveal trends that show opportunities for growth or best options for managing expenses. For example, a nonprofit may see that fee receipts for certain programs increased over time and expenses decreased, perhaps indicating an opportunity or need for more investment in the program. A budget can show that when a particular contractor was used, the actual expenses exceeded the contractor's budgeted expenses, perhaps indicating that the contractor's estimates should not be trusted. It can show that the nonprofit expects to be highly dependent on a donation or grant from a particular source, thus revealing vulnerabilities and the importance of particular stakeholders in achieving budget goals. Donors, lenders, and grantmaking organizations may evaluate a nonprofit's budget as part of proposals for funding. By creating and monitoring budgets, nonprofits can help to ensure that they will not accrue unwanted debt and that they are stewarding gifts according to donors' intentions. Discrepancies between budgets and actual receipts and expenses may reveal fraudulent activity. The budget is a crucial tool for boards as they fulfill their financial oversight duties. Therefore, developing and then monitoring the organizational budget and specific program budgets is a critical mechanism for nonprofits to ensure that they are effective and ethical.

Producing a Realistic Budget

To be an effective tool, budgets need to be realistic, consistent with strategic objectives, flexible, and measurable.[23] No one person in a nonprofit has all the answers and expertise to achieve these criteria. Therefore the budget should be a team effort of the executive staff, program staff, and board of directors. When a finance committee of the board and a board treasurer have been appointed, they are likely to be involved in helping to develop the budget before it is submitted for approval to the full board. The budget should reflect the programs and activities that are expected or desired for the coming year, so the staff should make program recommendations and get the board's endorsement of programs to be continued and major new initiatives before the budget is prepared. The staff may pull together historical data on expenses and revenues and help the board make assumptions about what the new year will bring in terms of demands for services and economic conditions. If the nonprofit has conducted a SWOT analysis and an action plan as part of its strategic planning effort (see Chapter Five), this information can be used to inform the budget. As the year progresses, the budget should be monitored to see if any flexibility is warranted. This requires accurate accounting to show how closely actual receipts and expenditures are matching the budget.

Estimating and Reviewing Revenues and Expenses

As explained in the previous chapter, a nonprofit can receive revenues from multiple sources. Some revenues are easy to estimate; others are more problematic. For example, it may be difficult to estimate the return from a special direct-mail appeal for donations if this approach has not been tried before. It may also be problematic to know which grant proposals for operating support will be funded over the course of a year. A nonprofit may expect donors to renew their commitments in the coming year, but without formal pledges that funding is uncertain. Business plans for new and continuing earned income ventures should include financial projections that can be used for budgeting purposes.

Typically, as part of the budgeting process for a medium-sized to large nonprofit, the executive director distributes to the program managers a budget calendar, budget request forms, and budget instructions. The budget calendar sets the timetable for preparing and adopting the budget. The program managers should justify their budget requests by explaining how they are consistent with the nonprofit's strategic plan, mission, vision, and priorities as set by the board. For example, university departments may justify budget requests by linking them to the university's strategic priorities. The program managers should submit estimates for the salaries, fringe benefits, supplies, and capital items that they need. The budget instructions tell the program managers how to calculate the cost of salary increases, if any; supplies; and capital items (for example, computers). The cost of fringe benefits (such as Social Security, health care, and pensions), utilities (such as phones, electricity, and gas), and capital equipment may then be added to the expected expenses. For a smaller nonprofit, input for the budget may be more informal, and the individuals who coordinate the programs may be volunteers who are not expected to prepare a detailed program budget, though they should be asked to adhere to the budget they are given.

A budget is simply a plan for the fiscal year. Very rarely are the final financial statements for the year an exact match to the original budget. During the year, revenues and expenses are typically somewhat more or less than budgeted. The executive director or a designated staff member should carefully compare budgeted to actual revenues and expenses, issuing a monthly revenue and expense status report to the board and any program managers. If funds are not available to fund a position or purchase in a particular account, surplus funds may be available in another account. In that case the board can approve a transfer from the surplus account to the deficit account. Moreover, a nonprofit may receive revenues during the year that were not budgeted. In that case the budget can be amended to plan for the increased revenues and expenses. Sixty percent of faith-based organizations make such budget revisions during the fiscal year.[24] The economic downturn from 2008 to 2011 reduced many nonprofits' revenue streams. Fifty-two percent of nonprofits experienced a decline in contributions; 31 percent received fewer grant funds.[25] Such shortfalls may require significant changes to budgets and reconsideration of strategic goals for the year.

Exhibit 7.1 shows a monthly budget status report for a nonprofit for the month of September. This is the type of financial status document that should be reviewed at board meetings. It provides the annual budget figures and year-to-date (YTD) calculations of financial status. For the nonprofit represented in this report, expenses are currently exceeding income (producing a net deficit of $325,540), but the nonprofit's leaders may expect to receive more donations in a future month in response to a

EXHIBIT 7.1. MONTHLY BUDGET REPORT, SEPTEMBER 30

	Annual Budget	YTD Actual	% of Budget	% Spent Prior Year
INCOME				
Charitable foundations	$36,598	$27,449	75%	71%
Contributions	$33,000	$19,800	60%	68%
Government—local	$328,288	$246,216	75%	75%
Government—federal	$531,293	$398,470	75%	75%
Government—state	$931,791	$605,664	65%	70%
Medicaid	$103,182	$51,591	50%	59%
United Way	$224,509	$168,382	75%	75%
TOTAL INCOME	$2,188,661	$1,517,571	69%	70%
UNRESTRICTED NET ASSETS		$52,801		
EXPENSE				
100—Personnel salaries	$1,446,014	$1,209,344	84%	75%
101—Personnel benefits	$278,778	$226,995	81%	75%
102—Professional services	$88,605	$79,745	90%	90%
200—Supplies	$57,009	$48,458	85%	81%
300—Travel and communication	$21,399	$16,049	75%	69%
301—Communication	$38,806	$29,105	75%	75%
302—Staff development: training expense	$39,040	$31,232	80%	75%
303—Facilities: utilities/maintenance	$28,215	$22,572	80%	69%
400—Facilities: rent	$164,063	$123,047	75%	75%
450—Insurance & bonding	$47,999	$35,999	75%	75%
475—Dues & subscriptions	$13,850	$9,695	70%	70%
480—Lease: vehicle/office equipment	$17,034	$10,220	60%	68%
500—Capital outlay	$650	$650	100%	100%
TOTAL EXPENSE	$2,241,462	$1,843,111	82%	77%
NET DEFICIT		−$325,540		

Source: Charles K. Coe, *Nonprofit Financial Management: A Practical Guide* (Hoboken, NJ: Wiley, 2011), 120. Copyright © 2011. Reprinted with permission of John Wiley and Sons, Inc.

planned special event and may also expect new grants to come in before the end of the fiscal year. They had expected to end the year with $52,801 in unrestricted net assets. However, if there is no expectation that income will come in to cover the current net deficit and new expenses, then they should revisit their planned activities in order to cut future expenses or generate more income. The last column of the report shows that the percentage of the budget spent this year is relatively similar to the percentage spent in the prior year for many of the lines. Many of the line items are also at around 75 percent of what was budgeted, which is consistent with the timing of a September report. However, there are some potential areas of concern where the percentage of budget spent at this time of year is higher than in the past (see, for example, personnel salaries and benefits [lines 100 and 101] and facilities: utilities/maintenance [line 303]); these budget lines should be reviewed as potential problem areas.

Element Four: Banking Relations

A nonprofit's use of banking services reflects how prudent the organization is in stewarding its resources. Periodically seeking banking services encourages banks to "sharpen their pencils" to reduce prices and offer more services to a nonprofit willing to change banks. The nonprofit should select a bank by weighing the costs of banking services and the quality of services offered. Core services to review include bill payment, account reconciliation, payroll, electronic funds transfer, check imaging, credit and debit card payments, and security overpayments. Secondary services that may be relevant to a nonprofit include loans, investment assistance, safekeeping of assets, retirement plan management, and insurance. Even a small nonprofit should compare what different banks can provide and the banks' fee structures to determine which should be used.

Element Five: Borrowing

Nonprofits borrow to meet both long- and short-term needs. For example, they borrow long term to purchase a building or buy expensive equipment. They borrow short term to meet cash-flow shortfalls that may result from grants awarded but not received, an unexpected lawsuit judgment, a decline in membership contributions, an economic downturn, an unexpected spike in costs, an act of nature, or a loss of a major funding source. They may also borrow as a matter of course, as hopeFound did before it began to approach its financial management in a disciplined and strategic fashion. For nonprofits with razor-thin reserves, short-term borrowing is commonplace. Other nonprofits, enjoying a healthy cash reserve, borrow only in the event of a rare, precipitous financial downturn. Some nonprofits choose to borrow from a board or staff member. This is not recommended as it creates conflicts of interest and may not be the best business deal for the nonprofit.

Borrowing involves selecting the debt instrument and acquiring the debt. Three features characterize a debt instrument: the funding period, the repayment conditions, and the security against default. A nonprofit's borrowing options include line of credit, loan, bond, and lease.

- **Line of credit (a line)**. This option permits borrowing up to a preset amount over a one-year period. Interest accrues on the borrowed amount until it is repaid. An *uncommitted line* is not put in writing and the lender can terminate it at any time. A *committed line* is a formal, written agreement with established terms and conditions. A *standby letter* guarantees that the lender will lend funds should the nonprofit not be able to pay a major expense.
- **Loan**. This option has fixed repayment terms. A *revolving credit agreement*, also known as a *revolver loan*, permits the nonprofit to continually borrow and repay debt up to an agreed-upon amount. A *term loan* matures in a set number of years, typically one to ten years. A *mortgage* is a loan to purchase a building or land, which then serves as the loan's collateral. The nonprofit pays principal and interest based on a fixed or variable interest rate.
- **Bond**. Some nonprofits—such as private schools, colleges, nonprofit associations, and religious organizations—can issue tax-exempt or taxable municipal bonds, known as *municipals*, for investors to purchase. A state or local government can also issue tax-exempt bonds on behalf of health care organizations, museums, colleges and private schools, and hospitals. Some bonds issued by nonprofits are not tax exempt. For instance, a nursing home or church might issue a taxable bond.
- **Lease**. A nonprofit may lease rather than purchase an asset. Leasing makes sense when an asset, such as a computer, is likely to become technologically obsolete.

Element Six: Financial Risk Management

Every nonprofit faces financial risks and can manage these risks to ensure that it can continue to carry out its mission, protect its assets, and provide a safe environment for workers, volunteers, and others involved in its operations. As discussed in Chapter Fourteen, under the topic of crisis management, nonprofits need to be prepared for unlikely scenarios that can threaten their survival. Financial risks may involve (1) damage to property due to carelessness, fire, natural causes, or faulty mechanisms; (2) lost property due to dishonest acts; (3) loss of income or increased costs due to the malfunction of a revenue-producing facility; (4) liability losses due to accidents; and (5) productivity losses due to health problems, addictions, or other performance barriers. A nonprofit may find value in forming a committee of persons willing to identify risks and find ways to eliminate or reduce their incidence and severity. Exhibit 7.2 offers a sampling of risk reduction methods.

Risks can be transferred to other parties. A *hold harmless* clause in a contract transfers legal liability, holding the other party liable for a loss. The other party must have a certificate of insurance, certifying it has adequate

EXHIBIT 7.2. RISK REDUCTION METHODS

Type of Risk	Risk Reduction Method
Damage to property	Schedule equipment downtime to perform preventive maintenance.
	Make a safety inspection of general operations (monthly), fire extinguishers (monthly), dangerous equipment (daily), and other facilities (yearly).
	Maintain smoke alarms.
	Maintain duplicates of records and computer files off-site.
	Update virus protection software and maintain firewalls.
	Secure and update employee passwords.
	Limit employee access to hardware and software programs.
Loss of property	Keep a duplicate record of checks.
	Prenumber and countersign checks.
	Take an annual inventory of fixed assets.
	Deposit cash daily.
	Install anticrime deadbolt locks, burglar alarms, barred windows, and safes and vaults.
Liability to others	Adopt a policy that defines harassment and ensures no retaliation, confidentiality, and a thorough, impartial investigation.
	Notify employees that they have no right to privacy regarding their e-mail, voice mail, desks, and lockers.
	Conduct safety training.
	Furnish ergonomically designed chairs and desks to avoid health problems.
	Ensure that drivers have a valid license and safe driving record.
	Secure donor records.
	Keep detailed minutes of board meetings and have them approved by the board.

EXHIBIT 7.3. INSURANCE POLICIES

Type of Policy	Coverage
Property damage	
Building and contents	Covers damage to buildings and their contents.
Business interruption	Reimburses for the loss of income if a fire or an act of nature renders a facility inoperable.
Computer	Offers broader coverage than the building and contents policy, including a loss due to a power surge, virus, or equipment and software failure.
Earthquake and flood	Geographically high-risk areas (for example, San Francisco and New Orleans) should insure for their specific risks, typically not covered by the building and contents policy.
Boiler and machinery	Covers accidents to boilers, refrigeration and air-conditioning equipment, electrical power generating machines, and research apparatus.
Liability	
Commercial general liability (CGL)[26]	Protects employees, board members, and volunteers from third-party claims alleging property damage, bodily injury, personal injury, and advertising injury. Covers injuries such as libel, slander, and contract liability.
Improper sexual conduct	The CGL policy may exclude improper sexual conduct coverage. If so, purchase a separate sexual conduct liability policy and include a provision that the policy will cover someone falsely accused of sexual abuse.
Business auto	Covers liability (bodily injury and property damage) and first-party auto physical damage (collision and comprehensive).
Directors' and officers' (D&O) liability	Covers claims against the organization, board members, employees, and volunteers for mismanagement, including libel, slander, third-party harassment and discrimination, and copyright infringement.
Workers' compensation	The federal government requires coverage of full-time and some part-time employees.
Professional liability	Protects against tort liability arising from negligent professional services.
Excess liability	Provides excess coverage, usually in $1 million blocks, to the CGL, business auto, and professional liability policies.
Umbrella liability	Provides excess liability coverage.
Special events	Covers special events such as parades, auctions, and meals that are not protected by the CGL policy.
Cyber liability (also called Internet liability)	Property and commercial liability policies usually do not cover the loss of data suffered when a computer system is breached. This policy pays for staff to reenter data, repair and replace hardware, and resurrect a crashed file server.
Crime	The standard policy covers (1) fidelity loss (loss due to employee dishonesty); (2) loss on the premises of money, securities, electronic records, and so forth; (3) loss off the premises due to theft, damage, or mysterious disappearance; (4) forgery loss; (5) securities loss; (6) computer systems fraud; and (7) counterfeit loss.
Fidelity bond	Insures against theft and embezzlement. Most nonprofits purchase a *blanket position* bond that covers positions (for example, board members, executive director, and CFO), not the individuals.

insurance to cover the liability assumed by the hold harmless clause. A waiver of subrogation, used in a lease agreement, subrogates the lessee's right to recovery when a nonprofit has been negligent.

Risk may be accepted and addressed through self-insurance or by an insurance policy deductible. There are numerous types of insurance policies available to nonprofits, as shown by the list in Exhibit 7.3.

Element Seven: Auditing and Financial Analysis

Auditing and financial analysis help to ensure that a nonprofit stays on track, both in stewarding its resources effectively and in following the law and ethical principles. They aid transparency and accountability, both increasingly demanded by government and the public.

Auditing

The financial audit produces the most comprehensive report for evaluating fiscal condition. Recommendations vary on which nonprofits should invest in an audit. The Better Business Bureau Wise Giving Alliance, a consumer interest group, recommends that a nonprofit with an annual gross income exceeding $250,000 should have an audit.[27] The Panel on the Nonprofit Sector suggests $1 million as the cutoff. Some states require audits for nonprofits with over a certain amount of donations. Audits are required for nonprofits receiving $500,000 or more in a single year in direct or pass-through federal funds. These minimums reflect the fact that audits can be expensive and that for smaller nonprofits with few transactions the audits are unlikely to reveal anything that a good financial system and end-of-year financial analysis cannot uncover.[28]

In 2005, 67 percent of nonprofits had an external audit conducted by an independent auditor, and 91 percent of these audited nonprofits had annual expenses over $500,000.[29] Small nonprofits are less apt to have an audit, because of the cost.[30] The nonprofit's key responsibility in an audit is to close the books and prepare the financial statements for the auditor. The most important feature of the auditor's report is the opinion letter. The auditor will render one of four opinions: (1) an unqualified ("clean") opinion that the financial statements conform to GAAP; (2) a qualified opinion that the financial statements generally conform to GAAP, but with noted exceptions; (3) a disclaimer opinion that refrains from expressing an opinion because of material (serious) departures from GAAP; and (4) an adverse opinion stating that the financial statements do not conform to GAAP.

A nonprofit that cannot afford an audit has four less expensive but also less thorough options. In a *member review* a board member with an accounting, auditing, or finance background reviews accounting procedures and records in selected areas of concern. In a *compilation* the auditor compiles financial information into a set of financial statements but does not verify balances or review internal controls. More extensive than a compilation is an *auditor review*, in which the auditor renders no opinion on the financial statements but issues a letter stating whether the nonprofit has complied with GAAP. Finally, in an *agreed-upon procedure* the auditor evaluates one or more of the nonprofit's accounting procedures (for example, for payroll, bank statement reconciliation, or handling cash receipts).

Financial Analysis

Whether or not a nonprofit purchases auditing services, it should always conduct an internal review of its financial statements. These financial analyses can be helpful in determining whether new systems and strategies need to be developed and whether changes to the budget need to be made before the end of the fiscal year. The statements may be presented at board meetings to show the financial condition of the nonprofit and provide the board with an opportunity to compare actual expenses with budgeted expenses, look for improprieties such as improper use of a restricted gift account, and watch for potential problems such as an inadequate amount in the reserve fund. The board should look for any unexplained differences from the normal patterns. There are four key financial statements that offer important information for making midcourse corrections and determining future financial and program strategies and systems.

Statement of Financial Position

The *statement of financial position* enables stakeholders (for example, management, board members, donors, and creditors) to assess the nonprofit's current financial condition. A typical activity in board meetings is for the treasurer to report on the nonprofit's current financial position. Depending on the report, the board may vote to modify the budget, set new fundraising and program goals, change pricing strategies, or make other changes to affect the nonprofit's financial status. If a nonprofit is in a weak financial position, it may need to seek current-use funding more aggressively. However, if its position is very weak and if it is considering whether to shut down, then donors and creditors may be reluctant to support it.

Statement of Activities

The *statement of activities* summarizes the financial transactions that have increased and decreased net assets, enabling the readers to evaluate fiscal performance, assess the ability to continue services, and evaluate managerial stewardship. This statement also offers the opportunity to look for fraudulent activity: for example, deposits of ticket sales that are too small given perceptions of number of attendees, or an unprecedented increase in travel costs that is inconsistent with travel authorizations.

Statement of Cash Flows

The *statement of cash flows* allows readers to assess the nonprofit's ability to generate future cash flows, its ability to meet financial obligations, and the reasons for the differences between cash receipts and payments. This statement may indicate that the nonprofit will need to seek a loan or ask for a deferral on payment in order to cover its bills and make payroll. Conversely, it may show that there is a healthy cash reserve and that perhaps the nonprofit can increase its services, make capital purchases, or add to its investment portfolio to reduce its available cash.

Statement of Functional Analysis

GAAP requires that voluntary health and welfare organizations prepare a *statement of functional analysis* that classifies expenses by function (for example, program, supporting, and fundraising) and by object or natural classification (for example, salaries, supplies, and travel) in a matrix format. Other types of nonprofits may also find that a statement of functional analysis is useful. This information helps in judging how staff members are allocating their time, supplies, space, and other resources of the nonprofit. It can reveal whether a nonprofit is basically acting as a fundraising operation, with few to no programming operations. If donations are simply funneled back into the nonprofit in order to cover the costs of doing more fundraising, then its tax status may be in jeopardy. The statement of functional analysis can also be used to capture and total the expenses for lobbying activity, to help ensure that the nonprofit does not exceed lobbying limitations set by the government.

Preparing functional analyses for major programs of a nonprofit can be useful in determining whether or not to continue them in their present form, adjust them, or drop them. Though a decision to cut a program is unlikely to be made solely on its financial condition, this may be one factor. Other factors are reviewed in Chapter Thirteen. A functional analysis is helpful in seeing what the fixed and variable costs are in running a program. Pricing and other marketing decisions can be informed by knowledge of these costs.

Financial Indicators and Ratios

With the data in the financial statements, a nonprofit can compute ratios and other financial indicators to evaluate its fiscal well-being. We review a variety of ratios below and some benchmarks for the ratios. In the nonprofit sector these ratios have been used largely as a punitive measure rather than for planning purposes. External agencies calculate the ratios and give nonprofits comparative "scores" that may be more or less useful in evaluating a specific nonprofit. Typically, these scoring activities have revolved around informing donors not to give to nonprofits that spend too little of their budget on programs. This is problematic for nonprofits that don't get good scores but feel that their budget allocations are reasonable.

To judge the value of the ratios and any resulting externally derived scores, board and staff need to apply more sophisticated and comprehensive views of the nonprofit's financial condition. As hopeFound discovered as part of its review of its financial management systems, the board and executive staff need to work together to determine the useful financial indicators for the nonprofit's dashboard. An executive director who inappropriately screens and interprets financial data for the board runs the risk of having board members who cannot make good decisions. And an executive director who overwhelms the board with fine details on the nonprofit's finances runs the risk of disengaging the board and having the board either micromanage the nonprofit or automatically defer to designated experts.

The *program efficiency ratio* (program expenses divided by total expenses) captures the percentage of funds spent directly on program services. For nonprofits the Better Business Bureau recommends that at least 65 percent of expenses be spent on programs. As discussed earlier in this chapter, this benchmark is controversial. It may unfairly disadvantage nonprofits that at particular stages of their life cycle need to raise funds and administrative costs to grow programs. However, if a nonprofit over many years has a low percentage spent on programs, this can be a sign for concern.

The *fundraising efficiency ratio* (fundraising expenses divided by contributions other than grants) measures the percentage of donations going to the nonprofit. It helps us see whether the level of expenses incurred in getting donations is reasonable. The Better Business Bureau recommends a ratio of no more than 35 percent). This ratio is used to consider whether the nonprofit is raising money simply to raise more money—in other words, whether the fundraising program is an end in itself. It is problematic to compare nonprofits using this ratio or to come up with a benchmark that is reasonable for all nonprofits. The smaller a nonprofit's established donor base and the more it relies on a narrow, hard-to-reach population, the higher its fundraising efficiency ratio is likely to be. It takes more money to fundraise for some nonprofits than for others.

The *unrestricted net assets ratio* (unrestricted net assets divided by total expenses) measures a nonprofit's cushion against an unanticipated decrease in revenues or increase in expenses. Some United Ways recommend having three months, or 25 percent, of the annual requirement in unrestricted net assets. Of course, grantmaking foundations are likely to have high reserves and spend only a portion of their principle in a given year. For other types of nonprofits, having a reserve that is too high can be seen as an opportunity for questioning why more funding is not going into programs.

Cash is the lifeblood for any organization. The *number of days of cash on hand* is the number of days the nonprofit could operate if no additional funds were available to cover daily expenses. It is calculated by dividing cash and cash equivalents by total expenses minus depreciation divided by 365.

The *current ratio* (current assets divided by current liabilities) measures the ability to pay current obligations. It is an indicator of liquidity. A ratio of 1.0 means that there are just enough assets to pay current liabilities. A healthy ratio for most organizations is between 2.0 and 4.0.[31]

The *acid-test ratio* (current assets minus inventories divided by current liabilities) is akin to the current ratio and is also called the *quick ratio*. It measures the ability to meet short-term obligations with the most liquid (most easily convertible to cash) assets, such as marketable securities and accounts receivable. Inventories are not included as an asset because they are relatively illiquid. As with the current ratio, experts recommend a quick ratio of 2.0 to 4.0.[32] When there are liquidity problems, a nonprofit may have trouble borrowing or convincing donors and others to invest in the nonprofit, given that the organization may be in danger of closing.

The *days in accounts receivable ratio* (accounts receivable multiplied by 365 and divided by operating revenue) measures the average number of days that accounts are receivable. Receivables should be vigorously collected, particularly when there is a cash shortage and a loan is being considered.

Executive staff and board members should routinely review these ratios and evaluate whether they indicate that any changes are necessary. If the calculated ratios are inconsistent with accepted guidelines, they should consider whether this constitutes a potential crisis that should be managed. Funders and other stakeholders may use the guidelines to make donation and other decisions, thus affecting the nonprofit's ability to carry out its mission. Even if deviance from the guidelines is justifiable, a nonprofit should be prepared for potential backlash and the need to explain itself. If accurate financial information is not readily available to calculate the ratios, that is another area of concern. The board may determine that financial management systems are inadequate and need to be changed or replaced.

Financial Literacy

Financial literacy is an important key to fulfillment of fiduciary duties. All nonprofit chief executive officers need a sound grounding in financial management and the members of the governing board of a nonprofit should understand financial fundamentals. Though all board members do not need to be financial and accounting experts, at least one member of the board should be able to help other members to understand financial ratios and other analysis tools, and should know what financial documents to ask the executive director to provide. Board manuals and learning sessions at meetings can be used to help board members develop their financial literacy. As in our opening scenarios, consultants and auditors can help the nonprofit in reviewing its financial status and practices and can recommend changes based on their analysis. The board should be responsible for making sure that it has access to any recommendations and that board members understand the concerns and suggestions. Nonprofit boards often appoint a treasurer and a finance committee to help make sure the board has and understands the financial documents it needs to make informed decisions.

Concluding Thoughts

Good financial management starts with competent staff and an informed board. Even a nonprofit with no paid personnel should take financial management seriously. If it has financial accounts, it should use QuickBooks or another simple accounting package to record and report transactions. Internal controls over cash receipts and expenses, such as separation of accounting duties, should be in place. A nonprofit board should adopt basic accounting policies and follow a budget. Not all nonprofits have to borrow funds and many have very little risk exposure. Still, all nonprofits should make the time to review their areas of vulnerability, make decisions on how to handle their identified risks, and have a plan to access funds in an emergency. As good stewards of funds, all nonprofits should be prepared to be transparent and accountable in their financial management systems.

In the next chapter we review marketing in nonprofits. It is through the marketing function that nonprofits reach those using their services. Budgeting and financial analyses show the level of resources available for marketing expenditures. Revenues are influenced by the success of marketing efforts. Thus the information in the present chapter can be of assistance to management and boards as they develop rationales for investments in marketing.

Questions for Consideration

1. How can a board's financial literacy be evaluated and improved, if necessary, so that it can make sound financial judgments? In other words, how can one know whether a board has an adequate or an inadequate understanding of the nonprofit's financial management system and current financial condition?
2. How can one train a board to be effective in its financial decision making?

Exercises

Exercise 7.1: Ratio Evaluation

Go to the GuideStar Web site (www2.guidestar.org) and select a nonprofit in your community. Compute the program efficiency ratio, fundraising efficiency ratio, unrestricted net assets ratio, and the quick ratio for the nonprofit. Discuss any potential concerns that are raised by the computed ratios. Would you recommend that the nonprofit's board should discuss any of these ratios? Why or why not?

Exercise 7.2: Policy Evaluation

Interview an executive director about his or her nonprofit's financial policies. Ask to see any policies regarding conflict of interest, whistle-blower protection, budget reserve, and investments. Do you believe these policies can be enforced, and if enforced, are they sufficient to avoid public concern?

Exercise 7.3: Budget Evaluation

Examine a nonprofit's budget and year-to-date totals. Identify any concerns that may indicate that the nonprofit will end the year with a deficit. Do you expect that the nonprofit will have net assets at the end of the fiscal year? If so, why or why not might this be problematic?

Exercise 7.4: Audit Evaluation

Review a nonprofit's audit. Were any concerns identified related to the nonprofit's financial health or the adequacy of its financial management system?

CHAPTER EIGHT

MARKETING

In 2004, the American Heart Association created Go Red For Women—a social initiative designed to empower women to take charge of their heart health. The Go Red For Women's Web site describes the organization's inception, goals, and results, noting that "in the past, heart disease and heart attack have been predominantly associated with men.[1] Historically, men have been the subjects of the research done to understand heart disease and stroke, which has been the basis for treatment guidelines and programs." Yet cardiovascular disease is also the number one killer of women, claiming the lives of nearly 500,000 American women each year. "Go Red For Women encourages awareness of the issue of women and heart disease, and also action to save more lives." It helps women understand their risk for heart disease and gives them the tools they need to lead a heart healthy life. Go Red For Women was launched with a national communication campaign that included media relations, events, promotions, and corporate relations strategies. Actress Daryl Hannah and singer Toni Braxton were recruited as celebrity spokespersons, and billboards and radio public service announcements were used to spread health messages across the United States. As a result, a study showed that 50 percent of consumers named Go Red For Women as the number one cause movement for them in 2007. In addition, $300 million has been raised by Go Red For Women, and twenty-six countries around the world have adopted the campaign and conducted awareness activities. Since the program's inception, over 900,000 women have joined the fight. Research has shown that "a woman who 'Goes Red' follows an exercise routine, has a healthier diet, visits her doctor for important tests, and influences others by talking about heart health."[2] In addition, a number of useful tools have been provided. For example, the Go Red Heart CheckUp, *an interactive online assessment of women's hearth health, has engaged over two million women to learn their risk of heart disease. In addition, Go Red BetterU is a free, twelve-week, online nutrition and fitness program that can improve heart health. It includes an online journal and a downloadable coaching tool. Finally, through a national sponsor, Merck & Co., over 200,000 health care provider offices have received Go Red For Women educational tools to use with patients.*

◆ ◆ ◆

How does a nonprofit organization interact with those it provides services or products to? How does it learn what its clients or customers want and decide on the best way to make these things available to them? If, like Go Red For Women, the nonprofit is seeking to change people's behavior for the better, how does it go about doing that? These are fundamental questions whose answers will determine how a nonprofit relates to its environment to secure vital resources and accomplish its mission. Marketing starts with the nonprofit's mission and strategies and relates the organization to customers, clients, and others that it seeks to provide benefits to or influence. As the case study that begins this chapter shows, Go Red For Women was based on the goals of the American Heart Association. Go Red For Women's marketing efforts relied on knowledge and ideas that were known to be effective. The marketing program made use of extensive promotion and publicity to spread the message, and the results were very successful. In this chapter we will examine the nature and functions of nonprofit marketing. We will consider how marketing helps a nonprofit learn about needs and desires in its environment and then design and deliver products and services to satisfy them.

General Philosophies of Marketing and Nonprofit Organizations

Organizations have always engaged in marketing. Our earliest historical records contain accounts of trade and commerce, including evidence about the availability, price, and distribution of goods and services. The notion of marketing as a distinct business process, however, was only developed in the twentieth century and the most recent ideas about the nature of marketing were developed in the 1950s. Over the course of the twentieth century, the marketing concept has evolved and as it has done so it has become more applicable and acceptable to nonprofit organizations. The formal expansion of marketing ideas to nonprofits began in the late 1960s.

Three orientations toward marketing can be identified, and although they developed at different periods of time, they are all still evident today. The first philosophy of marketing appeared in the early part of the twentieth century and has come to be known as the *product or service orientation*.[3] Appearing in an era of rapidly expanding worldwide customer demand, this orientation focused on the more efficient manufacture and distribution of the goods and services that organizations assumed customers wanted. As demand slumped during the depression, however, and competition increased, sales became an increasingly important function. Consequently, in the 1930s, marketing adopted a *sales orientation* and focused on persuading customers to buy a particular organization's products or services instead of those of its competitors.

In the 1950s, an important shift in orientation took place. Companies increasingly found themselves competing in global markets for consumers with both the information and the means to exercise considerable choice. To thrive in this era of consumer power, organizations had to focus far more on customer needs and desires. In what has come to be known as the *marketing orientation*, or *customer orientation*, the focus shifts to the needs of the customer (sometimes also called the target audience or market). The customer, or target market, has now been given the central role in the marketing process. This is clearly evident in the current definition of *marketing* offered by the American Marketing Association: "Marketing is an organizational function and a set of processes for creating, communicating, and delivering value to customers and for managing customer relationships in ways that benefit the organization and its stakeholders."[4]

The notion of joint value creation for both the consumer and the organization makes the marketing orientation quite compatible with the missions and activities of nonprofit organizations, and ideas about how to employ marketing in nonprofit organizations soon developed. The "birth" of studying how to apply marketing concepts and tools to nonprofit organizations can be traced to a series of articles by Philip Kotler and his colleagues, written between 1969 and 1973.[5] These authors maintained that marketing is a pervasive societal activity, because all organizations are concerned with how their "products" are perceived in the eyes of particular "consumers" and seek to find "tools" for furthering their acceptance.[6] Kotler defined *marketing* as "the social process by which individuals and groups obtain what they need and want through creating and exchanging products and services of value with others."[7] Since the 1970s, nonprofit marketing has developed rapidly and is now both widely taught and practiced.

Distinctive Aspects of Marketing in Nonprofits

Nonprofit marketing, like marketing in for-profits, relies on the marketing mix to accomplish its goals. The *marketing mix* is composed of the four P's: *p*roduct, *p*romotion, *p*rice, and *p*lace (where the product is offered to consumers). These elements can be manipulated by marketing to bring about desired marketing results. In order to completely understand nonprofit marketing, however, we need to consider how the special nature of nonprofit organizations makes nonprofit marketing distinctive.[8]

Nonprofits are likely to have *multiple objectives*. The goal of business firms is long-run profitability. Most nonprofits serve multiple constituencies and therefore have multiple objectives. Moreover, the most important of these objectives may be nonfinancial. As a result, deciding on goals must often involve compromise and consensus building. This makes marketing difficult because time must be spent involving and getting the approval of board members, staff, and volunteers. The results of marketing, in addition, may be difficult to measure for nonfinancial goals. Consequently, it may be hard to convince boards or other decision makers in small nonprofits that it is worthwhile to allocate scarce funds to marketing instead of to activities more directly related to service delivery.

Along with this, nonprofits are likely to have *multiple constituencies*. For-profits are concerned primarily with one constituency—their customer, who is both consumer and revenue source. In many nonprofits there are two separate constituencies: those who subsidize the organization (such as donors) and those who will use or benefit from the nonprofit's services. The effective result is that there are two target markets, which are likely to have very different characteristics, and both markets must be taken into account in marketing plans and programs.

In addition the missions of nonprofits may often entail a long-term view of the welfare of target audiences, which may be somewhat at odds with the desires of current beneficiaries. This may result in tensions between *mission* and *customer satisfaction*. For example, Meals on Wheels may provide nutritious food as opposed to the less healthy offerings their clients may prefer. In this way short-term client satisfaction is sacrificed. The division between resource provider and consumer noted earlier makes this long-term view more feasible when consumers, or target audiences, will not provide resources for long-term objectives.

Most nonprofits provide *services* as opposed to tangible products. Services have a number of distinctive features that will influence the nature and details of marketing. In addition some nonprofits produce neither products nor services but seek instead to change some form of *social behavior* for the better, such as Go Red For Women did.

Finally, nonprofit organizations are under *public scrutiny* because they receive public subsidies (at the least a tax exemption) and may raise money from donors. Administrative costs and the marketing costs of fundraising are frequently the subject of media and watchdog attention. Given the adverse consequences that may follow, nonprofits need to be mindful of potentially negative public opinion as they design and implement marketing programs.

Developing a Marketing Orientation

In both the product and sales orientations described earlier, marketing begins with the organization and what it wants to offer the customer. In the sales orientation this could go so far as to try to change customers' preferences to be more in line with the company's offerings. What is important to note about the marketing orientation is it considers marketing both a philosophy and a function.[9] As a philosophy of management, marketing places the target audience (whomever the nonprofit seeks to influence through its marketing activity) at the heart of a nonprofit's activities.[10] In this way, the nonprofit seeks to accomplish its mission. In a narrower sense, marketing is the set of functions a nonprofit uses to gather research and to design, price, promote, and distribute products or services. Although the discussion is often about these marketing functions, the larger, philosophical significance of marketing for keeping a focus on the nonprofit's mission should not be overlooked.

Andreasen and Kotler describe how marketing will differ depending on a nonprofit's orientation.[11] A nonprofit with a product or sales orientation will believe, based on the nonprofit's own needs and evaluation, that its products or services are inherently desirable. Numerous consequences follow from this belief. A "best" marketing strategy, also based on the nonprofit's own needs and evaluation, is typically chosen and then employed. Any lack of success is attributed to target audience ignorance or lack of motivation. Marketing research is given a minor role, as the organization believes in its offerings. Marketing's job is seen primarily as promotion. A marketing orientation, in contrast, holds that the only way a nonprofit can achieve its own goals is by satisfying the needs of its target market.[12] To do this the nonprofit will need to completely understand that target market (its needs, attitudes, and consuming behavior) and adapt its own outputs accordingly. This will necessitate planning the marketing program as a whole and coordinating all its elements with this in mind. In addition marketing must be closely integrated with the other activities of the nonprofit organization, including strategic planning, production, and evaluation. Heavy reliance will be placed on marketing research to identify potential target markets. These will be analyzed to identify portions of the market (segments) with particular characteristics of relevance to the nonprofit's mission, strategy, and actual or potential products or services. For example, a nonprofit seeking to provide recreational opportunities for children will need to be aware of differences in recreation-related attitudes, desires, and abilities among girls as compared to boys, younger as compared to older children, children from different socioeconomic backgrounds, and possibly even children with different health conditions. To satisfy the desires of these different target market segments, marketing will use all elements of the marketing mix. For each segment, appropriate products, promotion, prices, and distribution will be developed.

The Marketing Planning Process

The development and maintenance of a marketing orientation requires continuous attention to marketing. Nonprofits need to continuously monitor, assess, and react to their customers, clients, and others whom they want to influence. Peter Brinkerhoff has outlined a marketing cycle that embodies the customer orientation:[13]

- Define or redefine the market.
- Answer the question, What does the market want?
- Shape or reshape the products or services.
- Set prices for, promote, and distribute the offerings.
- Evaluate the results of the marketing program.
- Start over.

Go Red For Women is a good example of successfully following these steps. The target market was defined as women, and that market's need for better information and attention to heart care was clearly established. Go Red For Women developed both tools and messages to meet this market's needs and made them available free of charge to women in several convenient ways, including through the program's Web site and information provided to physicians. Finally, the results of the marketing program have been evaluated.

In order to be effective, the marketing cycle needs to be embedded in and supported by a planning framework. The strategic marketing plan will (1) evaluate the nonprofit's environment and current marketing program, (2) set future marketing goals, and (3) develop strategies and tactics for reaching these goals.[14] As Figure 8.1 shows, marketing planning should be consistent with and build upon the nonprofit's mission, vision, and overall strategic plan.

FIGURE 8.1. THE MARKETING PLANNING PROCESS

```
Nonprofit's Strategic Plan:
Vision, mission, internal
and external analysis
        ↓
   Marketing Audit
        ↓
 Marketing Objectives
      and Goals
        ↓
  Marketing Strategies
        ↓
Tactical Considerations:
    Segmentation
   Target audiences
     Positioning
        ↓
 Implementation and
     Assessment
```

A good place for marketing planning to start is with the findings and conclusions of the internal and external analyses prepared for the overall strategic plan. The next stage of marketing planning should be the development of the general approach that will guide the nonprofit's overall marketing program. This will involve setting the basic marketing mission, objectives, and goals. This will be followed by generating key marketing strategies and tactics. These will be based on considerations of the nonprofit's current and future target audiences, its market position, and the use of the marketing mix to reach marketing goals. Setting marketing goals, strategies, and tactics can be complex for nonprofits because their marketing may be aimed (sometimes simultaneously) at current or future customers or clients, donors or other funders, or volunteers. The final portions of the plan will involve implementation details and evaluation.

Marketing Information and Research

Marketing planning, decision making, and control need to be based on accurate information. Target populations must be identified and segmented;

initial service, price, and promotion levels must be set and pretested; and ongoing marketing campaigns must be monitored and assessed. The need for information may, in fact, be greater for nonprofits than for for-profits. When nonprofits use donors' money to provide services to clients, they face two sets of constituencies whose desires and needs are important. They need to market themselves to both funders and service recipients. In addition, when nonprofits provide services to frail or vulnerable populations who may have few alternatives, it is especially important to assess those populations' wishes. This is legitimate information to consider in addition to the ideas that donors or those working in the nonprofit may have about what should be provided for these populations. Nonprofits may need to educate themselves and their donors about the conditions their vulnerable clients face. They may in fact provide their clients with a voice in their organization. For instance, the National Alliance on Mental Illness (NAMI) has a consumer council made up of people who have or have had a mental illness. In addition the boards of local chapters of NAMI may include consumers or their representatives. For example, the board of NAMI in Indianapolis includes a community advocate.

A nonprofit needs a system that routinely collects, analyzes, stores, and disseminates relevant marketing information. Such a *marketing information*, or knowledge, system will provide information to key decision makers and, ideally, will have several subsystems.[15] An *internal reports subsystem* collects information from data sources within the nonprofit, such as program usage levels, demographics of users, contributors, and complaints. A *marketing intelligence subsystem* collects information from routinely available public sources. This will provide insights into possible future developments in target markets. Such a system could include information provided by those inside the organization, by a special person designated with this task, or by outside parties. A *marketing research subsystem*, in contrast, collects and analyzes data about a specific marketing problem or situation faced by the nonprofit. Finally, an *analytical marketing subsystem* organizes general data, performs needed analysis, and provides reports. Usually these are separate from (but support) the marketing research data and analyses used to answer specific marketing questions.

Marketing research is problem oriented and can be defined as the design, collection, analysis, and reporting of reliable marketing information that is relevant to a particular problem faced by an organization in order to reduce uncertainty to tolerable levels at a reasonable cost.[16] To accomplish this, the marketing research process goes through a series of steps.

Problem Identification and Research Objectives

This first step is the most important. Because marketing research is designed to gather information to answer specific marketing questions, it is critical that the right question be asked. This may seem simple, but it might turn out to be quite complex. It is a matter of identifying the most important factors in a marketing situation and the related questions that must be answered. For example, a nonprofit may be concerned about low usage levels for its services and feel this indicates that services need to be redesigned to attract more users. It may then decide that its marketing research objectives are to discover service features that additional users might want. This is premature, however, as there may be a number of reasons for the usage levels that don't have to do with the features of the service itself. It may be, for example, that the demographics of users have changed in particular locations and that what is needed is a new distribution strategy for existing services. It is important not to unduly limit problem definition and the establishment of research objectives. Alternatives should be carefully considered, and some preliminary information or exploratory research may be useful or necessary.

Research Plan Formulation

When research objectives have been set, a research plan can be established to answer specific research questions. In the example just given, the objective could be to identify the cause, or causes, of declining usage. The research might then be designed to assess the influence of particular factors such as service features, new competition, changing demographics, or other factors. The plan will establish the type of information needed to address the research questions, where those data can be obtained, and the most appropriate data acquisition and analysis strategies. It will lay out the steps to be taken to acquire and analyze the needed data.

Data Collection and Analysis

Because marketing research is conducted on human behavior, it uses the methods and statistics of the social sciences—in particular economics, psychology, and sociology. Once the research plan has been specified, standard social science data acquisition and analysis techniques can be used. Standard texts on these techniques as well as their application to marketing are readily available. Researchers can gather their own data (*primary data*) or use data gathered by others (*secondary data*). For example, in designing its messages and tools, Go Red For Women used both data from the medical profession on women's health and data that it had gathered on how women were using its tools and information. Data can be composed of numbers (*quantitative data*) or words and descriptions (*qualitative data*). Researchers may ask people questions in surveys, conduct controlled experiments, or observe behavior in its natural settings. Researchers may be interested in consumer characteristics, attitudes, knowledge, or actions. For example, a nonprofit day-care center considering opening a location in a new part of town will need to know how many families with children are in this service area; which child-care providers in this area are being used; families' satisfaction with these providers; and what programs, services, or other features the nonprofit center will need to provide in order to get parents to send their children to it. Once the data have been gathered, analysis will reveal the patterns in the data. Analysis can range from simple displays and summaries of the data to complex statistically based findings that predict future behavior. For more sophisticated statistical analysis, quantitative data will be needed. To perform these more complex types of data analysis and interpretation, nonprofits that lack qualified staff may employ technically trained consultants.

Interpretation and Reporting of Findings

The results, or findings, of the data analysis are used to answer the research questions. What do the patterns in the data reveal about the behavior that is the cause of concern? For example, is low usage related more strongly to service features or to service location? What are clients' motives for using the service, and what are others' motives for not using the service? The interpretations of the findings are compiled and reported so that they can be the basis of strategies to successfully address the marketing problem.

As the steps described in this section suggest, marketing research can be an extensive, time-consuming, and (by implication) possibly expensive process. It is therefore crucial to understand its importance. Research is at the heart of the marketing orientation that nonprofits need to adopt. A marketing plan is only as good as the research and data it is based on. Given that marketing ties strategy to results, a marketing plan based on flawed or no research can produce poor, no, or negative results and consequences for the nonprofit.

The Marketing Audit

A number of tools have been developed for use in the marketing planning process. A *marketing audit* will answer the question, Where are we now? Marketing audits are detailed reviews of internal and external factors likely to impinge upon the organization in ways relevant to marketing. Consideration should be given not only to the current state of these factors but also to their future change and development. In some cases an audit will focus on particular or marketing-relevant portions of information previously gathered, but in other cases it may require the gathering of new information.

External analysis can be used to gather information on the general environment, including important political, economic, environmental, sociocultural, and technological factors, as the PEST analysis described in Chapter Five does. A nonprofit may have gathered this type of information as part of its strategic planning (Chapter Five). The information should, however, now be examined for its particular relevance for marketing. In addition an analysis of competitors, collaborators, and stakeholders should be carried out. Information on current and potential competitors is especially important. The competitive environment will include other organizations providing similar or substitute products or services. These organizations can be other nonprofits, for-profits, or public agencies. It is also important to consider behavior-level competition.[17] When seeking a certain behavior from the target population, for example, attendance at a classical music concert, a nonprofit will also be competing against other behaviors that are possible for that population. These will include listening to other types of music in other venues, patronizing other classical orchestras, and doing a number of things other than listening to music. Finally, a stakeholder analysis is necessary to examine the characteristics and desires of clients, supporters, and other relevant publics.

An internal analysis will assess the nonprofit's own marketing activity and its marketing strengths and weaknesses. This will provide information about the current ability of the nonprofit to implement marketing objectives. Five areas should be assessed:[18]

- **Trends**. What are the significant trends in the nonprofit's programs, services, participation, and support? Is program participation growing, stable, or shrinking? If it is changing, is this due to external conditions, such as an increase or decrease in the number of potential clients in a service area? Is foundation support changing either for the nonprofit or for the types of services provided?
- **Share of market**. How much of the market does the nonprofit have in relation to competitive organizations? Who are the nonprofit's competitors? How many customers, clients, or other beneficiaries do the competitors have compared to the nonprofit?
- **Stability**. Has the nonprofit demonstrated "staying power"? How old is the nonprofit? Has the nonprofit grown, shrunk, or stayed about the same over the last five (or ten or twenty) years? Has the nonprofit had to abandon programs or services?
- **Efficiency**. Has the nonprofit been cost effective in its use of facilities, personnel, and other resources? What are the benefits provided by the

current configuration of services compared to the costs? Could comparable benefits be provided by alternative, lower-cost services? For example, how many premature births could be prevented by educational services versus more expensive counseling services?

- **Flexibility.** Has the nonprofit been able to adapt to market and environmental changes? If there have been changes in the nonprofit's clients or beneficiaries or in its operating environment, how has the nonprofit responded? For example, has the number of children in a nonprofit's after-school program increased as the number of children in a school district increased? If the school district has been supporting the nonprofit program and has cut funding, has the nonprofit been able to find other support?

In addition, the nonprofit should examine its current marketing activities and the resources it has to carry out these and future marketing efforts. This information should be used to assess the degree to which marketing contributes to the nonprofit's mission and to its competitive advantage or disadvantage. Evaluations of Go Red For Women have found it to be a highly successful program. These positive results will help the American Heart Association design future programs and marketing efforts.

The marketing audit will generate a large amount of information. A number of analytical tools are available to compile this information in ways useful for setting marketing objectives and strategies. In the following discussion we consider two techniques—the product life cycle and portfolio analysis.

Product Life Cycle

The *product life cycle* is based on the idea that products and services pass through predictable usage stages. After a product or service is first introduced, its usage will be low and then will grow slowly as the product or service gains visibility and acceptance. After acceptance, it will have a period of sustained growth. If this continues, the market will eventually become saturated and usage will level off. Eventually a new product or service will emerge as a replacement or substitute, and usage will decline. This pattern is shown in Figure 8.2.

Each stage of the life cycle has implications for the marketing mix. Marketing research is used at the *development* stage. At the *introduction* stage, raising awareness is of key importance and promotion is used to inform potential users about the product or service and its features. During the latter stages of *growth* and during *maturity*, competitors are starting to emerge and marketing is oriented toward differentiating the offering from others emerging in the market. Positioning strategies are also useful at this point.

FIGURE 8.2. PRODUCT OR SERVICE LIFE CYCLE

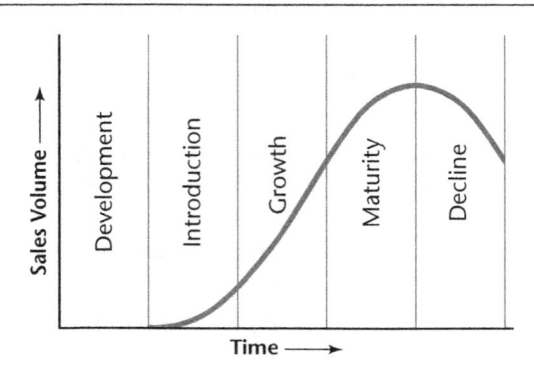

Source: Write a Writing, *Product Life Cycle (PLC): Stages, Development & Process,* http://www.writeawriting.com/business/product-life-cycle-plc-stages-development-process. Reprinted with permission.

During the *decline* stage, there may be a more limited role for marketing. For example, marketing may focus on how distribution channels can be maintained until the product is phased out.

Portfolio Analysis

A *portfolio analysis* considers the main products, services, or programs of a nonprofit and evaluates them against criteria judged to be important for the organization. A number of frameworks for portfolio analysis are available. They differ in terms of the nature and number of the evaluation criteria. The MacMillan framework,[19] a useful portfolio analysis framework for nonprofits, was described in detail in Chapter Five (also see Table 5.1 in that chapter). To summarize, this portfolio technique considers three dimensions: program attractiveness, competitive position, and alternative coverage. Each dimension can have a high or a low value, resulting in an eight-cell matrix. Products, services, or programs are placed on the matrix in accordance with the way they stack up on the three dimensions. The location of a program on the matrix will suggest whether it should be continued or dropped and how marketing might be used. For example, marketing for a program that is highly attractive and with low alternative coverage might focus on distribution, possibly by adding service outlets. This was the situation Go Red For Women encountered, and its response was to make information and tools widely available on the Internet and through physicians' offices. If the same attractive program had faced high alternative coverage, marketing might have focused on promotion or product differentiation.

Marketing Objectives and Strategy

Once a nonprofit has analyzed its current situation, it can address the questions of where it wants to go and how it could get there. It is in a position to set marketing objectives and goals and then strategies and tactics to achieve them. These marketing objectives should be aligned with the organization's overall strategic objectives and contribute to their accomplishment. They should also be consistent with the objectives of key units of the organization, such as the service-providing and communication units. Marketing objectives can include generating income as well as changing the awareness, attitudes, or behaviors of target audiences. The American Heart Association's goals were to change women's behavior, and the marketing goal of Go Red For Women was to provide education designed to lead to that end. Once objectives have been established, marketing strategies will express, in general terms, what the nonprofit's broad approach to meeting its marketing objectives will be. Tactics will specify how strategies will be carried out through the marketing mix.

Identifying Offerings and Markets

A useful approach to setting overall objectives is to consider the services, products, or messages the nonprofit can offer as well as the markets in which they might be offered. The offering and market opportunity matrix shown in Exhibit 8.1 provides an illustration. In this matrix each cell represents a different marketing objective.

In any approach it is important to analyze the *competitive environment* the nonprofit will face. Michael Porter has outlined three strategic options for competition.[20] These are discussed in detail in Chapter Five. In summary, a *differentiation strategy* entails offering something that few or no others offer, and a *cost strategy* entails seeking to be the lowest-cost provider in the market. Both of these strategies are oriented toward large markets. A *focus strategy* leads the nonprofit to select a limited market segment and provide a unique offering.

Adrian Sargeant draws out the implications of cost and differentiation strategies.[21] A nonprofit will need a sustainable cost advantage over its competitors to succeed with a cost strategy. For this strategy it is important that services or products are standardized, so that consumers can select on the basis of price. In addition, consumers should be readily able to switch to lower-priced offerings. A differentiation strategy is possible when services or products can be modified to appeal to consumers. This differentiation can be identified or applied to any product aspect, including design, the imagery associated with it and how it is promoted, or where and how it is available.

EXHIBIT 8.1. OFFERING AND MARKET OPPORTUNITY MATRIX

	Existing Offering	New Offering
Existing Market	1. *Market penetration.* The nonprofit seeks greater impact in its current market. It could do this through reductions in price, further promotion, or increased distribution. For example, the Red Cross may decide to have bloodmobiles start visiting sites in different parts of a city.	3. *Product or service development.* The nonprofit seeks to enhance its offerings in its current markets. This could be due to the lack of growth of its current offerings or due to customer demand. For example, Go Red For Women was a new program of the American Heart Association in the health care market.
New Market	2. *Market development.* The nonprofit seeks to extend its offerings to new markets. It could explore new uses for its offerings or market to new segments. In the case of the American Red Cross, it could start offering instructions in lifesaving to senior citizens or junior high school students.	4. *Diversification.* The nonprofit seeks to offer new products to new markets. New offerings could be related or unrelated to current offerings. Related diversification may be due to the desire to expand. Unrelated diversification may be due to necessity if a service area ceases to exist (as when a cure is found for a disease or condition). For example, in a related diversification a nonprofit providing job training in classroom settings may start a landscaping service that employs its own clients.

Source: Adapted from Adrian Sargeant, *Marketing Management for Nonprofit Organizations* (New York: Oxford University Press, 2009), and based on H. Igor Ansoff, *Corporate Strategy* (New York: Penguin Books, 1968).

Segmenting Markets

Marketing efforts are directed toward target audiences. These audiences are chosen to allow a nonprofit to use its limited resources so as to most effectively accomplish its mission and goals. The identification of these audiences is accomplished through *market segmentation.* Segmentation involves identifying groups of potential consumers based on some meaningful criteria. These segments can then be evaluated for their marketing attractiveness. There are of course many ways to identify groups of people, and marketers have come up with a very large number of criteria that may be used for segmentation, including objective and psychological factors. These criteria can be categorized as follows:

- **Demographic criteria** include people's age, generation, gender, sexual orientation, race and ethnicity, family life cycle, income, occupation, and social class. Data are often relatively readily available on these characteristics.

A nonprofit's mission and strategies will lead it to serve market segments with particular demographic characteristics. For example, the Boy Scouts provides services to boys in particular age ranges. Market segments may also be defined by income, a factor important to nonprofits dealing with inner-city poverty for example. In a similar fashion, virtually any demographic could be the basis of a nonprofit market segment.

- **Geographical criteria** identify the locations of potential consumers. This information is especially useful when used in conjunction with other factors such as demographics or psychographics. For example, nationwide nonprofits, such as Goodwill Industries and the United Way, have local divisions or chapters in defined geographical areas, including major cities. In addition, local nonprofits, such as religious or educational organizations, are likely to draw their clients or members from particular neighborhoods.
- **Product or service criteria** include benefits that are being sought, loyalty to the brand, and user status. For example, a symphony orchestra may evaluate to what degree different patrons may prefer different styles of classical music, and tailor its offerings accordingly.
- **Psychographic criteria** are factors such as lifestyle, values, attitudes, opinions, and personalities. For example, an environmental nonprofit may seek to recruit middle-class, politically left-leaning members.

Market segments are then analyzed to select those segments that appear most appropriate to pursue with a marketing effort. *Targeting* uses a variety of basic criteria to evaluate segments.[22] Most important, the segment should fit with the mission of the nonprofit and, given its present and future capabilities, the nonprofit should then be able to develop a marketing mix that will appeal to the segment. In addition the characteristics of the segment should be measurable and distinct enough to differentiate it from other segments, and its members should be accessible to the nonprofit. Also, the segment should be large enough to justify a marketing effort, and the behavior of people in the segment stable enough for planning purposes.

A number of broad strategic targeting choices are available:[23]

- **Undifferentiated (mass) marketing**. Go after the whole market with one offer and marketing mix, and try to reach as many members of the target audience as possible. For example, the Humane Society of the United States provides animal protection services to anyone, and its public service announcements about its work against abuse of animals are designed to appeal to the general public.

- **Differentiated marketing.** Go after all or several market segments with an offer and market mix for each. For example, a local chapter of the American Red Cross may offer a variety of programs that appeal to different market segments. These programs might include blood collection, support for the Armed Forces, transportation to medical appointments, first aid training, and youth education.[24]
- **Concentrated marketing.** Go after one market segment with a unique offer and marketing mix. Go Red For Women has identified its market segment as women and provides information and tools to promote heart health.
- **Mass customization.** Customize the offering to individuals. This is a recent development characterized by organization and customer interaction that results in customized fabrication or assembly.[25] Communication with individual customers is made more feasible by consumers' access to the Internet. For-profit examples include Dell's "build to order" model for marketing computers and tourism companies' offers of package holiday alternatives. Although mass customization could be used by nonprofits, a recent report notes that most mass customization applications are still in business-to-business industries.[26]

Positioning

Positioning involves creating and maintaining an image of an organization's offering, relative to its competitors' offerings, in the minds of target audiences.[27] Consumers can evaluate and compare products and services on many dimensions. Nonprofit marketers need to understand which dimensions their target audiences use to evaluate the nonprofit's offering and to compare it to others. Alternative or competitive offerings can then be placed on a continuum of these dimensions. Two or three dimensions can be displayed on perceptual maps and used to assess the relative positions of the nonprofit's offering and the alternative or competitive offerings.

Positioning can be used strategically to help a nonprofit build on its present strengths, search for a market niche, or reposition the competition (through messages characterizing the competition).[28] The following process can be used to develop and choose among positional alternatives for each market segment of interest:[29]

- Determine the factors that are important to each market segment.
- Survey the market to uncover the current positions of each competitive offering (including the nonprofit's own).
- Create a perceptual map for each segment of interest, and analyze the nonprofit's present or planned positioning compared to that of competitors.
- Analyze the alternative attractive positions available and the marketing resources required to achieve them.

- Decide what position is most strategically beneficial.
- Create an integrated marketing program to achieve the position.

Positioning can become quite complex. The position a nonprofit has in the minds of its constituencies can be due to perceptual as well as objective factors. It is necessary to determine which factors are important in order to design marketing programs appropriately. In addition, nonprofits often deal with multiple constituencies, such as different types of clients or patrons and various funder types. It is likely that different constituencies will use different dimensions to rate a given provider or will rate alternative providers differently on any given dimension. When different constituencies are important, positioning must be considered for each. Finally, it is unlikely that a nonprofit can excel on every dimension of importance to its segments. Therefore the position that a nonprofit decides to strive for will, most likely, involve trade-offs on various dimensions. The nonprofit will need to decide which dimensions it is best off excelling on relative to its competitors.

Branding

The American Marketing Association defines a *brand* as "a name, term, design, symbol, or any other feature that identifies one seller's good or service as distinct from those of other sellers."[30] A nonprofit's brand is a way for the public to identify and recognize the nonprofit. Brands may take the form of a name, trademark, logo, or slogan. There are numerous examples of nonprofits whose names we probably all know and encounter regularly, including the United Way, American Red Cross, Humane Society of the United States, and Salvation Army. Ideally brands will be memorable, meaningful, likable, transferable, adaptable (meaning that their use can be extended and customized), and legally protectable.[31] It is important to stress, however, that brands are only symbols. What is important is that they are designed to influence perceptions and convey complex psychological and emotional messages about the nonprofit to target publics. These perceptions and messages can hold a variety of meanings about the nonprofit, including its attributes, benefits, values, culture, personality, and the nature of its users.[32] A nonprofit's brand, therefore, both reflects the nonprofit's mission and unique social contribution and makes a promise of performance to target audiences and other stakeholders.[33]

Developing a brand involves defining what is distinctive about the nonprofit and what it does and why the nonprofit deserves consideration by the various audiences it seeks to influence. This information guides the construction of the images the nonprofit wishes to convey in relation to its attributes and the decisions to be made about how these images are to be conveyed.

Successful branding can lead to these benefits:[34]

- **Differentiation**. Users will know what they will get from the nonprofit.
- **Enhanced performance**. Users will come to trust the nonprofit and that should lead to more use of its products and services.
- **Reputation insurance**. Users will have confidence in the nonprofit, enabling it to better weather any short-term problem or crisis.
- **Enhanced loyalty**. Users will develop emotional ties with the nonprofit.
- **Partnerships**. Other organizations will be more likely to want to associate with the nonprofit.

Branding can, however, involve a number of challenges. Branding may require complex planning and implementation. Going far beyond appropriate names and logos, its success also depends on the consistency of all other communication the nonprofit has with its publics as well as the degree to which the nonprofit's actions reinforce or undercut the images and messages conveyed in that communication. A good deal of effort and substantial resources might be needed to establish and maintain the communication flow needed to build and reinforce the brand. In addition, behavior in all elements and at all levels of the nonprofit must reinforce the brand, and this may be difficult in large or geographically dispersed nonprofits.

Branding for members of the Millennial generation (roughly classified as individuals born between 1979 and 1994) is a good example of these challenges. In a recent report on twenty-two- to thirty-year-olds, Patricia Martin noted: "Young people of each generation have unique characteristics. . . . Millennials are genuinely different from the Boomer generation in its youth. Much of this can be attributed to the rapid rise of technology from generation to generation."[35] A major differentiating characteristic for Millennials is their increased use of social media for communication and interaction. Martin's report offered three insights on how marketers can interact with this generation:

- The brand is no longer at the center of the universe—the user is. Millennials will need to be given vehicles to provide input on the marketing mix. A brand manager for Ford observes: "We want their unbiased, unfiltered opinion . . . good, bad, or indifferent. It can't be in-your-face branding or they'll be turned off."
- Have something meaningful to say. Millennials' deep-seated desire for authentic experiences needs to be met by content that is emotionally intense and rings true. Brands increase their emotional appeal by staying committed to intensely dramatic story lines and characters.
- Help them belong to the brand. Millennials crave knowledge that can be shared. It empowers and makes them influential. Brands that understand and appreciate the need to learn and exchange information can

make a strong connection. Helping Millennials to connect with the organization and each other can be done by such things as soliciting and responding to consumer comments, engaging bloggers, interviewing Millennials, and inviting reviews and commentaries.

Managing Offerings

After target markets have been chosen based on the considerations and analyses outlined above, marketing can move to the next stage of formulating tactics, which uses the four elements of the marketing mix—the four P's. As discussed earlier these four variables, or tools, that marketing has at its disposal are product, promotion, price, and place (distribution channels).

Product

The organization's product is usually the first consideration, as its parameters will shape or determine the other elements of the mix. The use of the term *product* in the marketing mix comes from for-profit marketing, which is, indeed, often devoted to the sale of products. For nonprofits, the meaning of the product category in the marketing mix must be expanded to include services and programs. As we noted previously, even though some nonprofits provide tangible products, most nonprofits provide services instead. In addition, some nonprofits carry out marketing programs aimed at changing behaviors. Termed *social marketing*, these programs don't offer anything tangible to target audiences and rely on communication to fulfill their function.

Products

Products are tangible items delivered to recipients in target markets. Marketing products involves a number of strategic considerations. Products are designed to provide core benefits to recipients, satisfying the needs and desires of recipients that led them to patronize the nonprofit in the first place. A nonprofit can also provide additional value to recipients by augmenting, or enhancing, a product. Augmentation can further differentiate a nonprofit from competitors by meeting more target market needs or wants.

A nonprofit's mix of products can be described and strategically manipulated in terms of (1) length, width, and depth; (2) mission relevance; and (3) ability to attract customers, or patrons.[36] Length refers to the number of product types or lines. Width refers to the number of basic offerings in each product line. Depth refers to the number of variations each offering has. These factors can be varied to meet target market desires. Goodwill is an interesting example. Goodwill takes in used goods and resells them in its retail outlets. Goods can be almost any type of nonperishable material, including all varieties of clothes, furniture, household goods, sporting goods, electronics, books, and so forth. Goodwill's products, therefore, are high on length, width, and depth. Products designed to play a major role in attracting patrons are called *product leaders* or *flagship products*. A nonprofit might add a highly prestigious product to its product line in order to establish a product leader.

Services

Services have a number of distinguishing features with implications for marketing:[37]

- **Intangibility**. Services do not exist until they are consumed, and each instance of a service goes out of existence as soon as it is consumed. Service producer claims cannot be assessed beforehand, making it difficult to differentiate offerings. For example, a counseling session starts and ends at particular times, and neither its quality nor its results can be assessed until the service is delivered.
- **Perishability**. Services cannot be produced in advance and stored during slow times. Excess capacity is lost, and it is difficult to ensure optimal utilization. It is not possible to have counseling sessions sitting on the shelf during periods of slow demand. During these periods, counselors will be idle.
- **Simultaneity**. Services are produced and consumed at the same time. This means that the producer and consumer need to interact and be in the same place at the same time. Counseling sessions, for example, require the presence of both parties.
- **Heterogeneity**. Service quality will vary among organizations, providers, and occasions. This makes it difficult to guarantee performance standards and quality. For example, different counselors providing the same type of therapy are likely to conduct their sessions in somewhat different manners, depending on such things as their personalities and training. Even the sessions with the same counselor will vary depending on the counselor's mood, the client's feelings, and the stage of the therapy.

Given these features, marketing services requires different approaches than marketing products does. A key issue is the assurance of quality. The target audiences will perceive and judge the quality of services by comparing their expectations of service quality with the actual service delivered. This makes it critically important to understand what a target market's perceptions of service quality are and what they are based on. This may require obtaining information from target audience members, which they themselves might find difficult to provide.[38] For example, those new to counseling may not have a good idea of what forms positive outcomes can take. Once such information is obtained, however, a nonprofit can then develop objective measures of service quality and monitor its performance against these measures. Target audiences can also be provided with indirect signs of service quality, such as high-quality facilities; knowledgeable, courteous, and helpful employees; and certificates or giveaways. For instance, the Red Cross has obtained a well-deserved reputation as this country's premier private sector responder to disasters. This reputation has been built up over the years by well-publicized performances in responding to both human-caused and natural disasters. To maintain the quality of its response the Red Cross has developed extensive recruitment, training, and logistical procedures that allow it to respond quickly and effectively.

Social Marketing

Social marketing refers to an attempt to change some form of social behavior for the benefit of target audiences or society at large. This may sometimes entail large shifts in target market behavior, such as increasing healthy behavior as the American Heart Association has sought to do. Nonprofits carry out social marketing through communication with target audiences. They can also provide incentives and use other means to facilitate or encourage behavioral change. Social marketing emerged as a distinct concept in the early 1970s. As the story of Go Red For Women at the beginning of this chapter shows, social marketing can deal with important social issues and can have significant positive results. A wide variety of social issues have been addressed by social marketing, and well-known campaigns have been carried out to, for example, counter drug and alcohol abuse, persuade students to stay in school, and urge expectant mothers to obtain prenatal care.

Social marketing seeks to have target markets do one of four things: (1) accept a new beneficial behavior (by composting food waste, for instance), (2) reject a potentially undesirable behavior (by not starting smoking, for instance), (3) modify a current behavior (by getting more exercise, for instance), or (4) abandon an old undesirable behavior (by stopping texting while driving, for instance).[39] Social marketing has a number of unique features and challenges. On the one hand target audiences may be indifferent to the issues behind the target behaviors, or they may not see any direct personal benefits from the behavioral change. On the other hand the behavior may involve controversial topics, or the target audience may actually be opposed to the behavioral change. A number of dimensions will determine how difficult it may be to achieve change. Change will be more difficult when people are highly involved in the behavior, when the behavior is continual (rather than occurring once or a few times), and when the behavior is exhibited by groups (rather than individuals).[40]

Given its complexity and difficulty, social marketing requires careful planning. Appropriate marketing objectives and target markets must be identified. The offering (messages or incentives, or both) must be based

FIGURE 8.3. ONLINE INTEGRATION MODEL TO PROMOTE BEHAVIORAL CHANGE

1	Awareness of Behavior →	Audience-Targeting →	Online Advertising and Web Sites
2	Contemplate Behavior Change →	Audience Engagement →	Interactive Features—Individual to Site
3	Share Behavior Intentions →	Audience-Sharing →	Interactive Features—Individual to Individual
4	Sustain Behavior →	Audience Ownership →	Interactive Features—Community Interactivity

Source: Leah King, "Using the Internet to Facilitate and Support Health Behaviors," *Social Marketing Quarterly* 10, no. 2 (2004): 72–78. Copyright © 2004 Routledge. Reprinted with permission.

on solid research about the determinants of current and desired behaviors and how appropriate behavioral change may be made. Likewise the other elements of the marketing mix, especially promotion, must be designed and implemented to be consistent with the behavioral models.

Currently, social marketing campaigns rely heavily on the Internet. Leah King reviews a major social marketing campaign to promote behavioral change that was developed by Schwartz and Hardison and that employs an online integrated model (Figure 8.3).[41] In this model, online resources—such as Web sites, e-mails, blogs, and electronic interactions—are used to bring about behavioral change. Web sites can be used to provide information about particular behaviors, such as the dangers of smoking. Target audiences can be engaged and given tools to help them contemplate behavioral change. For example, online tools can be provided to assess smoking behavior and health status. In addition, other audience members can share their experiences and intentions to change their behavior—for instance by cutting down on or quitting smoking—via blogs or other individual communications. Finally, this behavioral change can be sustained by facilitating self-help or support groups.

Commenting on the use of this model, King concludes:

- Offline behavioral change activities should translate to the online environment, making it a definitive *place* for audiences to go to understand, share, and sustain a behavioral change. A comprehensive Web site can be a frequent destination point where the evolving mix of information, activities, and community can support a change in a particular health behavior.

- To effectively reach an audience on the Internet, with the intent to support or change behavior, an organization must understand the audience members' online habits, such as where they go on the Internet and why, what information they want and how they seek it, and how they will communicate what they learn to others.
- Interactive advertising and marketing promotions on complementary Web sites can send visitors to a site, as well as deliver audience members who have already moved past awareness and may be ready for the Web site to help them make or sustain a health behavior change.
- Nonpaid partnerships with complementary sites are valuable in building message awareness and sending traffic to a site.

King describes a major social marketing campaign that used this model. The National Youth Anti-Drug Media Campaign was created by Congress in 1998.[42] The campaign's target audiences include teens, their parents, and other influencers (the press, entertainers, and educators). Six different Web sites were designed to provide information to these different target audiences. Messages in numerous media (radio, TV, and print) were used to present drug prevention messages and to invite target audiences to visit these Web sites for more information. The Web sites also provide a place for audiences to exchange information, advice, and support. Over a five-year period, the Web sites garnered a total of more than 50 million visitor sessions and 150 million page views. For example, Freevibe.com was developed for teens fourteen to sixteen years old. It had 1 million visitors per month in 2004.

Promotion

Promotion is communication to the market about the availability and benefits of the service or product the nonprofit offers. In general, promotion is held to have a number of objectives. Promotion is used to inform target audiences. This could involve telling new users about an offering or informing current users about new features of an ongoing offering. In addition, promotion is used to persuade current and potential users to engage in some form of behavior. This could be positive, as in buying or using a service or product, or negative, as in refraining from some detrimental behavior. Promotion can also be used to remind users that a service or product is available or has certain features. This is useful when a service has been available for some time or a product is at the mature stage of its life cycle. Finally, promotion can be used to differentiate a specific offering from others the nonprofit or its competitors has. Particular features making a product or service better or more appropriate than alternatives would be stressed.

It is important to recognize that promotion is a form of communication with current and potential users. This goes beyond thinking solely about the wording of an advertisement. The communication process entails a sender or source (the nonprofit) intending to convey a particular thought, encoding that thought in a message of words or symbols, transmitting that message via some communication channel or medium (for example, television or a brochure) to a receiver (target user), who subsequently decodes the words or symbols into thoughts. In addition, receivers always provide feedback to senders (another message), and the whole process can be affected by noise, or distortions, at all stages of the process.

To be effective, promotion must take all aspects of the communication process into account. An understanding of the receiver will suggest the decoding process that he or she will use and the potential for interpretations of the message that will differ from those intended. For example, adolescents are likely to interpret a message from what they perceive as an authority figure quite differently from the way older people would. These considerations influence the design of important message characteristics such as theme and style.[43] Given the overall marketing objective and the more specific promotional objective, the overall theme, or broad idea or subject matter, of the message needs to be determined. Following this, a consistent style or tone needs to be established by using appropriate symbols. For a message about providing homes for abused dogs, for example, to what extent should the dogs be shown in their abused state as opposed to after they are happily established in their new homes?

Marketers also need to decide on the tools they will use to deliver promotion. Taken together, these tools are referred to as the *promotional mix*. A major option in the promotional mix is *paid advertising*. Advertising can produce dramatic messages. These can, however, be expensive to produce. In addition, paid advertising is impersonal because the message cannot be customized or made specific to small segments of the target market. The nature of the medium used and the need for efficient distribution will determine the size and diversity of the audience. Television advertising, for example, will go to anyone watching television at the particular time the advertisement appears.

It might also be possible for a nonprofit to get its services or programs featured in a *public service announcement* (PSA). PSAs are messages deemed to be in the public interest, and a nonprofit may be able to get some parts of the message development, production, and distribution donated free of charge by other concerned parties.

Another option is *sales promotion*. Sales promotions provide short-term incentives designed to stimulate demand, such as gifts, discounts, premiums, and contests. Although short-term demand may increase, sales promotions have several potential drawbacks. They may be linked in users' minds to the many sales promotions that for-profits carry out, thereby making the nonprofit appear less special. In addition, users may become accustomed to the promotion feature and react negatively when it is over (for example, when prices go back to normal).

More directed methods for promotion may also be used. The most common of these is *direct mail.* Using its own files on users or large consumer and other databases, a nonprofit can customize its mailings to particular recipients. These can be made to appear almost as one-to-one messages and be quite cost effective.

The most recent development is the growth of *electronic formats* for promotion. They take advantage of the dramatic and rapid rise of computer technology, the Internet, and social media. These vastly enhance the ability of nonprofits to communicate with target audiences and of audience members to communicate with each other. Data from the World Bank show that in 2009, 78 percent of the U.S. population were Internet users.[44] This was up from 44 percent in 2000. Nonprofits have responded to the increased Internet use. A 2004 study by GuideStar of over six thousand nonprofits found that about 97 percent used the Internet to provide information, such as mission statements, financial reports, and instructions, and about 55 percent used it to gather support, such as memberships, donations, and volunteers.[45] The chief electronic channels for marketing are Web sites and social media.

Web sites have become virtually mandatory for nonprofits today. Web sites are used to provide information and engage audiences. A 2004 study by the Network for Good of over two thousand individuals found that 49 percent said that they had visited nonprofit Web sites and searched for information about specific causes or volunteer opportunities.[46] Of these, more than 75 percent said they engaged in some further activity while visiting the Web site. In terms of what makes a Web site good, respondents reported that the top five characteristics were significant content about the nonprofit's cause, information about how donations were spent, ease of use, information about how to get involved, and information about how to become a member. In addition, a Web site should[47]

- Be easy to navigate.
- Be able to tailor itself to different users.
- Provide the potential for two-way communication.
- Provide related links.
- Have a look and feel that is consistent with the organization's brand identity.

Social media are personal communication channels that link friends, family members, and associates. These channels include blogs, e-mails, podcasts, YouTube, MySpace, Twitter, and Facebook. Social media have tremendous potential for mobilizing people. For instance, communication over social media played an important role in the overthrow of the government of Egypt in early 2011.[48] The power of connection can also be used by marketers. A recent study found that whereas one influential person's word of mouth tends to influence the buying behavior of two other people, the influence jumps to eight others when communication is online.[49]

The example of the National Youth Anti-Drug Media Campaign presented earlier is a good example of how Web sites and social media can be interwoven to support and reinforce promotional campaigns. The previous discussion about marketing to Millennials clearly illustrates how this socially connected age group is leading organizations to incorporate and integrate social media into the promotion of products and services. In order to facilitate the use of social media by their consumers, it is now commonplace for nonprofits to be on Facebook, YouTube, Twitter, and other social media.

Price

Pricing for nonprofits involves a number of complexities that for-profits do not normally encounter. The missions of nonprofits involve nonfinancial goals. In addition, there may be multiple ways of pursuing a mission and these may entail incompatible ramifications for pricing. Also, target audiences may be unable to pay for the full (or any) value of the services they receive.

There are a number of general considerations when thinking about whether or not to charge prices.[50] Charging prices will of course bring in income. It may also promote more customer awareness of the nonprofit, help the nonprofit to measure output, discourage overuse of a product or service, promote feelings of ownership among users, and preserve users' dignity. However, prices should not be charged if doing so will threaten the mission or if beneficiaries will have significant difficulties paying.

More specifically, a pricing strategy can be established to accomplish a number of different objectives. Prices may be set to bring in as much revenue as possible, thereby maximizing profitability. For this, it will be necessary for the nonprofit to understand the demand its users have. Another objective may be to recover the cost of production, either the full cost or some part of the cost if the remainder is covered by internal or external subsidies. The nonprofit may also seek to maximize market share and attract as many users as possible. This objective could entail being the lowest-priced provider in the market. Considerations of social equity may also influence pricing strategy. This may entail charging less to those who are less well off and more to those who are wealthier. Finally, pricing may be used as a negative incentive, for example to encourage people not to engage in some behavior—similar to what the government tries to do by setting high taxes on cigarettes.

Generally speaking, there are three approaches to setting prices. The *cost of producing* the service, good, or program may be used as a basis for establishing price. Pricing to just cover that cost (break-even pricing) is one example of this approach. Pricing to provide a set percentage over cost (a markup) is another. This approach to setting prices is most feasible when costs can be accurately determined. For example, a nonprofit providing information on the available homes in a neighborhood to prospective home buyers could use this strategy because its costs for the material it provides (standard housing information) will be clear. This is not always the case, however, and when it is difficult to allocate costs to specific services or programs, cost-based pricing will be difficult or inaccurate.

There can be a number of difficulties in determining costs.[51] Organizations have both fixed and variable costs. Variable costs can usually be attributed to each product. For example, the cost of each piece of the housing material described above can be known. Fixed costs, however, do not change with the volume of sales. These costs include such things as rent, monthly salaries, and other overhead items. Fixed costs are divided by total sales to provide the average fixed cost for each item, so this average cost will vary with sales volume. In addition, when an organization produces more than one product or service, it must decide how to allocate overhead to each of the products or services. For example, the housing nonprofit may also provide financial management training and home repair programs. The allocation of overhead to the various programs may be somewhat arbitrary.

Setting prices based on *user demand* is a second approach. It is divorced from costs and may bring in either more or less than cost-based pricing. It does, however, put the nonprofit more in touch with its users. For example, a food bank may price its goods so that low-income people can afford them. To use this technique well, a nonprofit will need to understand the elasticity of demand among its users. This refers to the amount that demand will decrease as price increases. If a nonprofit seeks to benefit as many users as possible, then decreases in demand due to higher prices will be an important consideration.

The third approach is to set prices in relation to the *competition*. For example, this type of pricing can be found among nonprofits in the highly competitive day-care or nursing home industries. This option is relatively easy to implement, as competitors' prices should be readily available. Competitors' prices may be a way to gauge what prices a market might bear and so to establish a "ceiling" for a nonprofit's price. Competitors' prices are also targets for undercutting, providing a way for a nonprofit to try to increase its market share. It is important to ensure, however, that beating a competitor's price does not lead to sacrificing quality or to mission drift.

Place

This portion of the marketing mix addresses the question of how the product, service, or program is made available, or distributed, to target audiences. Distribution channels have been defined as "conduits for bringing together the marketer and target customer or market at the same place and time for the purpose of facilitating a transaction."[52] A number of functions need to be accomplished in distribution channels, including transporting, storing, sorting, buying, selling, and financing. Two basic aspects of distribution channels are (1) the design of the physical and logistical details of the channel and (2) the performance of the channel in meeting the needs and desires of the target market.

A major decision in channel design is whether distribution should be direct or indirect. In *direct distribution* the nonprofit will control all aspects of getting the service, product, or program to the user. This will afford the nonprofit the most control of the design and performance of the channel. This design can, however, require significant resources and a high degree of expertise. It may be more economical and effective for a nonprofit to use *indirect distribution* and a number of specialized intermediaries to fulfill some of the distribution functions.

Another important decision in distribution channel design is how many locations will be used and what will be available at each location. This decision is related to both the characteristics of users and the expenses of establishing multiple locations. Three options are usually considered. *Convenience* goods or services are those that users will not make much of an effort to acquire. These must be made widely available at many locations. A nonprofit example might be antismoking literature. Most people would not go out of their way to acquire this material. Consequently, it must be made widely available to them at places they are likely to frequent for other purposes. Conversely, users will make some effort to acquire *shopping* goods or services, and these can be located at fewer and farther apart locations. An example would be Goodwill retail outlets. Finally, *specialty* goods and services are considered by shoppers to be so special that they will make significant efforts to acquire them. For these items, the nonprofit can choose a location pattern that is most economical for the organization. For example, the Humane Society of the United States provides specialized animal protection services and normally has only one facility in a city.

A second broad concern is the way in which the distribution channel affects the target market's experience as it acquires the service or product. In the for-profit world this might be called the *buying experience*. Distribution channels can enhance the experience users have in several ways.[53] Factors such as the number, location, and characteristics of outlets can make things easier for users by saving them time and expense. Having everything needed available at all locations will also help. Of course, this is likely to require additional expenses for the nonprofit. Another factor is the *atmosphere* of the place of delivery. The design of a health facility, for instance, might try to create feelings of professionalism as well as caring in the minds of patients.

Concluding Thoughts

In this chapter we have examined one of the most important ways that nonprofits relate to their environments. Marketing is usually responsible for generating the resources nonprofits need to survive while at the same time providing the services, products, or programs the nonprofit uses to fulfill its mission. To successfully initiate and maintain these important transactions, marketers match the target audience's needs and desires with the organization's mission and capabilities in creative ways to produce value for both. Research, planning, strategy, and tactics need to align to produce these results.

In the next chapter we begin the next section of the book. In that section we cover the topics of leading, managing, and delivering. Chapter Nine begins the section by considering the top levels of the nonprofit and discussing boards and governance.

Questions for Consideration

1. Based on the marketing principles described in this chapter, can local community-based nonprofits with limited marketing budgets effectively compete with national, better-resourced nonprofit and for-profit organizations for the same clients? How?
2. Identify a nonprofit with a highly visible and successful brand. What perceptions are associated with this brand?
3. Identify and discuss both a successful social marketing effort and an effort that has not been successful. What might be the reasons for success on the one hand and lack of success on the other in these cases?

Exercises

Exercise 8.1: Marketing Opportunities

What steps might Go Red For Women take if its objectives fell in each of the four cells of Exhibit 8.1? Consider each cell separately.

Exercise 8.2: Services

Identify a nonprofit service that appears to be at the introductory stage of its life cycle. Compare it to nonprofit services that are at later stages of the life cycle. From a marketing standpoint, what would you recommend for each of these services?

Exercise 8.3: Marketing Penetration Versus Diversification

Identify a nonprofit pursuing a market penetration strategy and another nonprofit pursuing a diversification strategy. Compare the two nonprofits: How do their marketing efforts differ?

Exercise 8.4: Segments

How might the market for child care be meaningfully segmented? Suggest a position in this market for a nonprofit provider, using three criteria. How might this position and the criteria differ from those adopted by a for-profit provider?

PART THREE
LEADING, MANAGING, AND DELIVERING

CHAPTER NINE

BOARDS AND GOVERNANCE

The National Association for the Advancement of Colored People (NAACP) is the oldest and largest civil rights association in the United States, and it has gone through some challenging times. Since its establishment in 1909, this nonprofit has had a succession of executive directors and board members, some of whom have been more effective in leading the organization than others. Myrlie Evers-Williams is one of the board members standing out from the pack. A divided board, tensions between the board and the executive director, scandals resulting in legal action against the organization, and lack of strategic attention to membership interests had left the organization weakened. As chair of the NAACP board, Evers-Williams led the board in a successful effort to save the organization from a perilous situation in which its reputation and finances were at a dangerous low point. She regained financial support from donors by admitting the organization's problems and arguing that the organization was worth saving due to its historic civil rights contributions. She revised management structures to increase efficiency and accountability and inspired board members to change their policies and practices from a somewhat self-interested and subgroup orientation. Under her direction, they worked together for the good of the organization. In sharp contrast to her predecessor, she relied on reasoned arguments rather than threats of retribution to influence board members. In commenting on her role in saving the organization, she stated: "I've always built a team. I did not do it; we did it together. How sad that so many people perceived that there was only one person that could save the organization. I did not possess all the required talents, so like any good manager you surround yourself with the best talent possible."[1]

◆ ◆ ◆

In the United States the governing board is legally designated as holding the fiduciary responsibility for a nonprofit organization. Board members are expected to ensure that the nonprofit operates according to the rules under which it was established and is accountable for expending resources appropriately. For a 501(c)(3), public-serving organization, this means the nonprofit is responsive and accountable to community interests and does not exist to serve the organizational founders. For nonprofits classified by the Internal Revenue Service as member-serving (mutual benefit nonprofits), the board is responsible for honoring members' interests and giving them the rights assigned to them in the bylaws. For grantmaking foundations, the board primarily acts to see that the organization pursues the wishes of the funding source(s) within legal guidelines. For all types of nonprofits, the board is expected to oversee the executive director, set and protect the mission of the nonprofit, ensure that laws are followed, and decide what overall strategies will be effective in achieving the nonprofit's mission and realizing its vision. As illustrated by the NAACP, the governing board of a nonprofit is not always successful in these tasks but can be reinvigorated with a common vision and can once again become a key driver for success in an organization.

Governing boards for nonprofits are an important channel for civic participation[2] and for establishing the legitimacy that allows nonprofits to receive financial support and operate without heavy government regulation. Stakeholders may judge a nonprofit by the individuals who serve on its board.[3]

Ideally, the governing board and executive director forge an effective partnership, working in sync to lead the nonprofit organization. On the one hand boards can be dysfunctional and contribute little to a nonprofit's success in achieving its mission and gaining financial stability. A board may be limited or undermined by an executive director who is uncomfortable or unskilled at supporting the board's governance role. On the other hand boards may be critical to a nonprofit's effectiveness and survival, particularly when the organization is experiencing a change of executive director, challenges to its mission, and financial and reputational stresses, as the NAACP found when Evers-Williams was elected by that organization's board as the board's leader.

This chapter explores nonprofit leadership by the governing board. We examine board responsibilities and effectiveness and review options for board configuration and composition. We also examine tools to aid board functioning. Owing to the board's role as a decision-making group that needs to consider potentially conflicting interests and approaches, we have also included a discussion of conflict management. Finally, we take a broad look at the concept of governance, going beyond the idea that governance is solely the board's role and responsibility.

Responsibilities of Nonprofit Governing Boards

In many countries, including the United States, government establishes a nonprofit governing board's responsibilities, but those looking to nonprofits for beneficial products, services, and programs typically have hopes, if not expectations, that a board will go beyond what is legally required.[4] The following list of board responsibilities is adapted from a practical guide published by BoardSource, one of the leading resource centers for boards:[5]

1. **Set the organization's mission and purpose.** The board is responsible for creating and reviewing mission statements and articulating the goals and means for pursuing the mission.
2. **Select the chief executive.** The executive director reports to the board, and it is the board's responsibility to hire and, when justified, fire the director.
3. **Provide proper financial oversight.** Boards are legally responsible for seeing that proper financial controls are in place. They should help to develop the annual budget and regularly review financial statements to see that resources are being handled appropriately.
4. **Ensure adequate resources.** Boards have the responsibility of seeing that the nonprofit has the resources needed to pursue the mission. Goals set by the board should emerge from an understanding of the resources required to meet them.
5. **Ensure legal and ethical integrity and maintain accountability.** The board should make sure that the nonprofit honors the law and meets ethical standards.
6. **Ensure effective organizational planning.** The board should be involved in strategic planning and in monitoring the achievement of strategic goals.
7. **Recruit and orient new board members and assess board performance.** The board is responsible for its own functioning and development and should evaluate its own performance.
8. **Enhance the organization's public standing.** The board members serve as representatives of the nonprofit. The board should act to attract support for the organization.
9. **Determine, monitor, and strengthen the organization's programs.** The board should determine what programs should be offered and review them to ensure that they are effective and consistent with the mission.
10. **Support the chief executive and assess his or her performance.** The board is responsible for ensuring that the executive director has the resources and professional support to be effective, and the board should evaluate the director's performance.

Legally Required Board Duties

According to U.S. law for incorporated nonprofit organizations and charitable trusts, there are three standards to which members of the board are accountable. In meeting these standards, the board fulfills its fiduciary duties. The legal standards for nonprofit boards are duty of care, loyalty, and obedience.

Duty of Care

Board members are required to participate in making well-informed decisions on behalf of the nonprofit. This involves holding adequate meetings, prudently reviewing material facts necessary to make reasoned decisions, consulting experts if needed, and ensuring that a quorum is in attendance to make official decisions. So long as board members are operating in good faith and demonstrating that they are trying to make prudent decisions, they are likely to be seen as exhibiting duty of care. In the case of *Queen of Angels Hospital* v. *Younger*, the board was seen to have violated its fiduciary duty of care by entering into an inappropriate settlement. The board approved financial payments to Catholic sisters who had not worked for the hospital, in response to an unjustified claim that the sisters were owed compensation for past services. The board never asked for evidence of hours worked and the sisters' work could be reasonably seen as donated, therefore the court ruled that the board did not exercise good business judgment.[6]

Naomi Ono suggests that nonprofit boards should carefully document their decision-making processes to show that they exercised due care. They should create and retain background materials, meeting notes, minutes, and statements explaining their decisions for any actions that may be scrutinized. In addition to showing that material facts were reviewed, the board should show that the decision was made with active board participation. Meetings should be held with prior notice and the bylaws should be followed in regard to quorums and voting procedures. Boards should also monitor any committees that have been delegated important roles related to board decision making to ensure that the board is acting responsibly when it uses committee information or recommendations.[7]

Duty of Loyalty

Board members need to set aside their personal and business interests and make decisions in the best interest of the nonprofit. Once a board has made a decision, each board member is expected to stand behind it or resign from the board. However, board members may still wish to record their dissent from a decision for the record. This may protect them from personal liability if this decision is later found to be in violation of board duties or connected to illegal activities. Board members are also expected to respect confidentiality in relation to the nonprofit's legitimate activities.

Examples of violations of duty of loyalty are numerous. For example, a director who convinces a board to buy unneeded insurance from her firm and pay her a commission is getting improper personal benefit. A director who sits on the boards of two nonprofits that compete with one another for grants and gifts is likely to be unable to show duty of loyalty to both organizations. Even a board member who invests in a for-profit corporation that competes with the nonprofit may have a conflict of interest. Board members who capitalize on an opportunity available to the nonprofit are also likely to be in violation. For example, a board member who buys artwork or other property that was first presented for sale to the nonprofit is in violation unless the nonprofit has already rejected the opportunity. In the seminal case of *Stern* v. *Lucy Webb Hayes National Training School for Deaconesses & Missionaries*, the board was found to violate duty of loyalty by mismanaging hospital funds. The board members had voted to invest the funds in banks where some of them had personal interests, despite the opportunity to obtain better returns elsewhere. The disinterested board members were not made aware of the conflicting interests held by the members who could benefit from the transactions, and they had not sought to uncover any relevant conflicts of interest.[8]

A simple method that boards can use to prevent violations of the duty of loyalty standard is to have a conflict of interest policy and have each board member sign a statement that he or she understands and will comply with the policy. The policy and statement should be reviewed annually. During the policy review and annual statement signing, as well as when relevant situations arise, board members should disclose conflicts. When a conflict arises, the board may choose to have the member abstain from voting and not be present during board discussion of the issue. The board may also take extra care and appoint a special independent committee to investigate options not involving benefits to board members.[9] Boards should also have policies for dismissing and replacing individuals whose conflicts make it impossible for them to be effective board members.

Duty of Obedience
Board members are responsible for ensuring that the nonprofit remains true to its purpose as stated in its charter or articles of incorporation when it was established. Donated funds should be used to fulfill the nonprofit's mission. Board members should make decisions that keep the nonprofit within the bounds of its stated mission. This means that boards should get legal advice if they wish to substantively change the mission. To illustrate the importance of caution, consider a New York court ruling that a hospital board was violating its duty of obedience by voting to close the hospital's teaching, research, and acute care facility and sell the real estate to another hospital.[10]

Boards also should be careful about which donations they accept. If the use of the donation is highly restricted or open to multiple interpretations, they may be better off either refusing the gift or requiring a modification of the gift contract in order to avoid future legal battles over the donor's intent. Interpreting a donor's intentions can become especially tricky when the donor is deceased, as demonstrated by the case of The Barnes Foundation. The foundation endured numerous lawsuits related to duty of obedience when it decided that it was essential to move a deceased donor's art collection from its original location. The terms of the trust setting up the foundation specified that the artworks be left in place, that the institution stay in its present home, and that no new facilities be constructed. The board of trustees claimed that for the foundation to survive, the collection needed to be taken out of its suburban location and relocated for greater public access and increased fundraising opportunities.[11]

Protection from Liability

Board members who do not fulfill their fiduciary duties may face legal action. Penalties can be imposed on individual board members who receive excess financial benefits from a nonprofit. Board members are legally required to avoid *private inurement*, which is related to the *non-distribution constraint* for nonprofits. Board members should not distribute any profits of the organization to themselves, nor should they enter into contracts with the nonprofit that are not in the best interest of the nonprofit. In some states, board members are forbidden from *self-dealing*, that is, contracting with the nonprofit they serve. Board members can be compensated and reimbursed by the nonprofit for expenses incurred for board service, but the compensation and reimbursement must be considered reasonable.

Some nonprofits have insurance policies to at least partially protect their board members from having to suffer personally if the organization is sued or has other financial difficulties. The policy may cover penalties to the nonprofit or the board members when the board is found to have violated its duties and the individual board members are not accused of criminal activity. It may also pay for legal representation for board members when their performance or private benefits come under scrutiny.

Some nonprofit boards in the United States have adopted provisions of the 2002 Sarbanes-Oxley Act, although the U.S. government requires nonprofit compliance with only two of these provisions. The Act was developed in response to scandals in the for-profit arena and places new requirements on corporate boards. Following Sarbanes-Oxley, some states added their own regulations to constrain nonprofit boards. The Act requires nonprofits to protect whistle-blowers and sets rules regarding destruction of documents. Other provisions of the Act that have led to voluntary or state-level changes to some nonprofit board practices include mandated use of audit committees and prohibitions on loans to board members and executive directors.[12]

Executive Director Roles Versus Board Roles and Responsibilities

One of the most common challenges in nonprofits is differentiating between the roles of the board and of the executive director. A simple rubric is that the board focuses on the big picture and overall strategies for the organization and the executive director focuses on the day-to-day implementation of the strategies and general work routines. More concretely, this means that the board sets major policies, such as the mission, code of ethics, service philosophy, and fundamental mandates, for the nonprofit along with broad strategies and goals. This may be easier said than done, given that most boards meet fewer than four times a year, most boards have limited information, and some members may have been on the board for only a short time. Nonprofit staff are usually deemed responsible for minor procedures, standard operating plans, and work rules that guide day-to-day operations. Under this division of labor, there is a blurring of responsibilities in some areas: for example, in setting marketing and financial policies.

Not all scholars agree on how best to set up board and executive director relations to support a high level of board and organizational effectiveness. John Carver, one of the most vocal critics of traditional approaches to nonprofit boards, is not alone in stating that most boards perform work that is best left to the executive director.[13] In his policy governance model, Carver outlines a framework for differentiating between board and executive director tasks. He designed this model as a means of preventing boards from veering away from strategic, big-picture decisions on the one hand or simply rubber-stamping the staff's recommendations on the other. Overall, Carver's model states that the board should[14]

- Set *ends policies* that describe what the organization is supposed to accomplish.
- Give the executive director discretion in the methods for achieving ends, although the board should set *means statements* indicating boundaries the director cannot cross.
- Explicitly delineate the responsibilities of the board and of the executive director.
- State the procedures the board will follow.
- Determine to whom, ultimately, the board is accountable.

In contrast to Carver's position, other scholars suggest that blurring the boundaries between board tasks and executive director tasks is appropriate.

Richard Chait, William Ryan, and Barbara Taylor argue that the executive director and board should work together on what is most important to the nonprofit. Acting as a team, they should be concerned with fiduciary responsibilities and ensure that laws are followed and resources are properly stewarded. In addition, the board should work with the executive director and other top staff on strategic planning, setting long-term directions, and establishing goals. The board should also work with the executive director to engage in generative, or "out of the box," thinking.[15] Researchers see this blurring of board and executive director roles most often in younger, volunteer-based, grassroots organizations. These organizations tend to have boards that are more involved in the daily operations of the nonprofit.

Few nonprofits ever achieve the ideal set out by Carver, and typically boards are strongly guided by the executive director. Research has found that the power balance between the board and the executive director varies across nonprofits and even within the same nonprofit over time. Developmental stage, age, size, and distance from the original donors and founders can affect what roles and responsibilities are assumed by the board.[16] Francie Ostrower and Melissa Stone found that boards tend to have more power than the executive director when the nonprofit is not heavily reliant on government resources and when a nonprofit is in crisis, small, nonbureaucratic, or young. Executive directors tend to have more power when they have professional credentials and seniority and their board members do not have high socioeconomic status. Boards composed mostly of women tend to have less power than boards composed mostly of men do.[17]

In actuality there is a great deal of variation in how boards operate, and strong predictors of division of responsibilities do not exist. The full NAACP case, only sketched in the opening chapter scenario, offers a historical review of how the power dynamics of the board chair, board, and executive director shifted over time.[18] It illustrates the power struggles that one nonprofit experienced between its board and executive director and the negative outcomes of lacking a clear policy about board and staff responsibilities and expectations. Unfortunately for the NAACP, when one individual pursued a great deal of control over the organization, the imbalance of power led to improprieties that put the NAACP in jeopardy. We see the old adage that power corrupts in operation in this case, as well as the way a crisis can emerge when a board does not effectively resist a powerful executive director or board chair and fails to act as a whole to exercise duty of care, loyalty, and obedience.

One model that can be useful for assessing board and executive director dynamics has been offered by Miriam Wood and then revisited by Julia Classen.[19] Wood suggests that board behavior is cyclical. Following the founding period, boards tend to go through operating phases of super-managing, focusing on corporate responsibility, and ratifying, as elaborated in Table 9.1. There is no set time frame for each of the phases of this cycle, and boards

TABLE 9.1. PHASES OF BOARD AND EXECUTIVE DIRECTOR DYNAMICS

Phase	Board Concerns	Board Recruitment
Founding: collective subphase	The board of directors is personally and professionally invested in creating the new nonprofit. Directors tend to serve as both board members and volunteers and to work side by side with the nonprofit's executive director, if one exists. The board is concerned with whether and how the nonprofit will survive. The potential problem is that board and staff roles are intertwined, making it difficult to have proper checks and balances.	Board members are the founders or friends of the founders. They are drawn to the nonprofit by their passion for the mission or are chosen by the founders from the founders' existing network.
Founding: sustaining subphase	The board sees the nonprofit as relatively stable. A concern is what types of board member skills, expertise, and contacts are needed to sustain the organization. Directors' responsibility in this phase is to establish a board to support the nonprofit and executive. Potential problems are that new board members may not have as strong a passion for the nonprofit mission as the founders do and may not understand their governance role.	The initial board members step off, making way for new members chosen for the skills, resources, and contacts they can bring to the nonprofit.
Super-managing	Board members brought on for their expertise and skills begin to question the executive leader and attempt to influence the nonprofit in their governance role. The board begins to feel more independence from the executive. It spends time managing in addition to governing. The potential problem is that the board may attempt to micromanage, challenging the executive director's authority over operations.	New members begin to see their primary role to be stewardship and oversight, but some board members are still acting as volunteers under the supervision of the executive director or other staff.
Focusing on corporate responsibility	The board is focused on its governance responsibility and expects accountability and transparency from the executive leader. The executive director manages systems to provide the board with needed information for decision making, but the board may use additional information sources. There is a clear separation of board and executive director responsibilities. The potential problem is the board's dependency on the executive director for information and transparency.	The board acts to recruit and guide new members, who are chosen to govern and support, not to manage the nonprofit.
Ratifying	The board performs its duties in a cursory manner. Its focus is on running efficient meetings. The board is functional but largely disengaged. The potential problem is that the board does not fully address its governance responsibilities, assuming that all is well. It becomes a "rubber-stamping" board.	Increasingly busy and prestigious board members are chosen, who have limited time to devote to board affairs.

Source: The information in this table is adapted from Miriam M. Wood, "Is Governing Behavior Cyclical?" *Nonprofit Management & Leadership* 3, no. 2 (1992). Copyright © 1992. Adapted with permission of John Wiley and Sons, Inc.

may return to an earlier phase in response to the types of challenges they are facing. Though not all nonprofits experience these phases as described in the table, the phases illustrate some common ways that boards and executive directors may relate and how the relationship may evolve over time.

Effectiveness of the Governing Board

As part of their responsibilities, boards should assess their own performance and consider ways to improve the contributions they make to the governance of the nonprofit. A simple activity is to rate the board's success with its responsibilities and to identify and address barriers to more successful performance. More comprehensive tools for identifying a board's strengths and weaknesses include but are not limited to BoardSource's online self-assessments, which can be used by board members to see how well they are fulfilling their responsibilities and achieving board diversity and inclusion. In addition to a generic tool for nonprofits, BoardSource offers specialized, online board self-assessment tools, so that membership associations, community foundations, schools, and credit unions can more specifically address the unique features of their mission and context.[20] Assessment tools that have been adopted by researchers looking at nonprofit and board effectiveness include one offered by the National Center for Nonprofit Boards[21] and two published in academic research journals.[22] All these tools share the basic assumption that nonprofit boards should fulfill core responsibilities and their fiduciary duties.

There is no one measure of effectiveness to apply across all nonprofit boards. Executive directors and board chairs are likely to prioritize different criteria in assessing the performance of individual board members and the board as a whole.[23] The priorities and achievements of a board may vary depending on funding sources, program challenges, and other factors. For example, the board of a nonprofit that relies heavily on donations from individuals may designate fundraising as a major priority and consider itself to be effective if it brings in large financial gifts. Nonprofit executive directors who are actively engaged in advocacy may judge their board on how well it provides access to and legitimacy with important policymakers. Boards that are governing long-established, well-functioning nonprofits will likely place little emphasis on mission development and establishing policies and parameters for operations, but boards governing newly formed struggling nonprofits that are still determining their purpose and methods may judge their effectiveness on their internal policy creation and enforcement. A board of a new nonprofit may judge itself on how successful it is in building the nonprofit's visibility and reputation.

There are a limited number of research studies examining the influences on particular dimensions of board effectiveness and the ways in which boards influence organizational effectiveness.[24] Robert Herman and David Renz are among the researchers who have systematically attempted to link board and nonprofit effectiveness. Following are some of the findings from a review of studies:

- Having major donors on a board was connected to organizational efficiency.[25]
- The kind of activities board members emphasized was linked to dependency on donations and government support.[26]
- Boards whose members received training on how to be a good board member were more effective than boards that did not train members.[27]
- Nonprofits with boards involved in formal planning had higher performance.[28]
- Nonprofit financial strength and growth was related to board formalization and common vision.[29]
- General board effectiveness was unrelated to board size and number of committees and related to involvement in strategic planning.[30]
- Greater board size was linked to a greater number of donations[31] and to a lower percentage of funds spent on projects.[32]
- Organizational effectiveness was positively related to the activity level of the board in strategic planning, board development, resource development, financial management, and conflict resolution.[33]

Scholars debate the importance of nonprofit boards to overall organizational effectiveness.[34] Boards vary greatly in the degree to which they simply follow the instructions and recommendations of their executive director versus developing and making their own decisions. They also vary in what responsibilities they handle beyond basic fiduciary duties. This makes it difficult to do large-scale studies. There are too many variations among board structures, strategic orientations, and responsibilities to come to strong conclusions about the influence of boards on organizational effectiveness. What is clear is what distinguishes actively engaged boards with the potential to positively contribute to organizational effectiveness from more passive and inactive boards whose efforts make little difference to the nonprofit's success.

Chait, Holland, and Taylor suggest that boards are likely to be high performing and to make positive contributions to nonprofit organizational effectiveness when they demonstrate six competencies:[35]

1. **Contextual competency.** Boards demonstrate contextual competency by considering the organization's culture, norms, values, principles,

and history when making decisions. For example, Evers-Williams helped the NAACP board to invoke the NAACP's civil rights mission and values in order to regain the support of funders who had withdrawn their funding due to the organization's mismanagement.

2. **Educational competency.** Boards that take time to educate themselves about the organization and its environment and that analyze their own functioning are more likely to have the information needed to recognize poor performance and address emerging concerns about effectiveness. Evers-Williams demonstrated educational competency by directly confronting the subgroups on the NAACP board and showing them that the organization could survive only if board members worked as a whole rather than competed for power.

3. **Interpersonal competency.** Boards need to operate as a group of individuals, taking advantage of individual board members' skills and knowledge, building cohesiveness, and grooming future board leaders. As discussed in more detail later in this chapter, Evers-Williams used her interpersonal skills to develop board consensus and increase the motivation and participation of the more passive members of the NAACP board.

4. **Analytical competency.** Boards are likely to make better decisions when they seek multiple perspectives and feedback to help them recognize complexities in situations and issues the organization is facing. As the NAACP board worked to save the nonprofit, it sought feedback from various internal and external stakeholders to understand their interests and what the nonprofit could do differently to better address their needs.

5. **Political competency.** Boards need to understand and be sensitive to the interests of the organization's key constituents. This helps them develop and maintain healthy relationships. For example, in recruiting a new executive director for the NAACP, the board had to negotiate what authority the director would have in relation to the board. The interests of the new director had to be weighed against needs for accountability and transparency.

6. **Strategic competency.** Given that a main responsibility of boards is setting strategies, boards need to concentrate their time on key strategic priorities and not be waylaid by less important concerns. One of the challenges for the NAACP board was transitioning from a short-term crisis orientation focused on developing strategies to save the organization into a more optimal situation where the board could develop longer-term strategies focused on mission achievement.

Nonprofit boards vary in the tools they use to build their competencies and the amount of attention they give to improving their effectiveness and accountability. Thomas Holland explains what boards can do to help ensure that they are acting appropriately:[36]

- **Set explicit statements of expectations and responsibilities**. These statements should be written for individual board members as well as the board as a whole. For example, the board can write board job descriptions that specify obligations and values to be honored.
- **Emphasize adherence to conflict of interest policies**. For example, the board can insist that board members who have personal or business interests in a decision be transparent about those interests and refrain from voting when they can directly benefit from the board's decision.
- **Foster effectiveness and accountability by staying focused on priorities**. By setting goals for the board and periodically revisiting its progress on these goals, a board may be able to keep itself focused.
- **Make it a practice to have two-way communication with constituencies**. The board should report what it is doing and solicit feedback. For example, the board can invite visitors to board meetings and have open comment periods, and can also seek informal feedback on the nonprofit's reputation.
- **Conduct assessments of themselves and formal evaluations by outsiders**. Assessments can improve accountability and give guidance for needed improvements. For example, boards can use an annual retreat to review performance standards and the outcomes of their efforts, and then board members can brainstorm and experiment with alternative approaches to their work.

Each board must develop its own approach to its governance role.[37] There is no single best way to organize and operate, though some states set basic parameters on choices of design, policies, and practices. For example, some states have laws that set the minimum number of board members and forbid self-dealing (contracting with a board member's firm by the nonprofit). To go beyond what is legally required for nonprofit boards, we suggest a *structural contingency theory* approach.[38] In other words, the board should fit itself to the contingencies of the nonprofit's situation. In the next section we review some of the options for boards and examine the way in which contingencies influence the best choice.

Determining Board Configuration by Contingency

A useful list of board types is provided by Patricia Bradshaw. She argues that the environment of a nonprofit suggests what type of board it should have, and she reviews five basic board configurations.[39]

Policy Governance Configuration

The *policy governance* configuration is found in boards that follow Carver's model and other frameworks in which there is a clear delineation between board and staff roles and the board is focused on big-picture strategy and policy setting. In this model the structure is formalized and there is a strict hierarchical arrangement between the board and staff. Board committees tend to be permanent with clear mandates. The board tends to be focused mostly on defending the nonprofit's position in its niche. Many large, established nonprofits focused on service delivery have this type of board. It is typical of nonprofit hospitals and universities.

Constituency/Representative Governance Configuration

The *constituency/representative governance* configuration is similar to the policy governance configuration in that it is formalized, with clarity of roles and responsibilities, and uses permanent committees with clear mandates. However, it tends to be more decentralized in its decision making, giving more power to committees and staff. It also has a more diverse membership, as board members are elected or appointed to designated seats by constituency groups. Board members may feel that they are representing particular interest groups. The NAACP has this type of board, with seats assigned to specific geographical regions. A focus of this type of board is making sure constituent voices are heard.

Entrepreneurial/Corporate Governance Configuration

A board with an *entrepreneurial/corporate governance* configuration is less formalized and bureaucratic than the previously described boards. It tends to use short-term task forces and project groups more than permanent committees. There is less clarity and more overlap in the roles of board and staff. The focus is on efficient work processes and getting things done. Planning processes tend to informally emerge rather than being formally structured. Board members contribute an entrepreneurial perspective, reflecting an interest in innovation to improve the performance of the nonprofit. Many new nonprofits have boards fitting this configuration, until they establish more formal and structured ways of operating.

Emergent Cellular Governance Configuration

The *emergent cellular governance* configuration is the most informal of the types. This board has organic, emergent ways of operating. There is little formalization and bureaucracy. The board regularly seeks input and involvement from nonboard members. This configuration is most likely to be present in nonprofits with alternative or nonmainstream ideologies, such as feminist, social justice, and anti-oppression organizations. The board may clearly articulate the value of shared leadership and avoid giving too much power to any one individual.

Hybrid Configuration
Some boards do not fit cleanly into any of these configurations. They may have characteristics of each type. These *hybrid* boards may be the result of adaptations to environmental pressures and preferences of nonprofit leaders.

◆ ◆ ◆

Bradshaw argues that when external environments are uncertain and unstable, the entrepreneurial/corporate or the emergent cellular configuration is the best choice. These boards have fewer fixed structures, allowing them to more quickly mobilize to deal with environmental changes. Their more diverse memberships may help them recognize and deal with changing issues. The constituency/representative or emergent cellular configuration may be best when a nonprofit's external environment is complex, containing multiple stakeholders with potentially competing interests rather than a simple environment with a homogeneous set of stakeholders who share the same expectations. These structures encourage a diversity of voices on the board. The policy governance board, the most traditional one in the United States, may be best suited to a stable, noncomplex environment with well-known, predictable challenges and consistent stakeholder expectations.[40]

Another useful framework of board types is suited to member-serving nonprofit organizations, such as professional and trade associations like the National Association of Manufacturers and the Association of Fundraising Professionals. These nonprofit organizations are established to serve members, and thus there are pressures on the boards of these types of organizations to reflect member interests. Georg von Schnurbein identifies the following four general types of association boards.[41]

Satellite Governance
A *satellite governance* structure can emerge in membership associations that have affiliates who are individuals. The affiliates may control the national organization through their designated seats on the national board. The board acts somewhat like a parliament, with individuals on the board voting primarily to support the interests of their home base rather than the interests of the national association. The national association is weak compared to the regional affiliates.

Delegate Governance
Delegate governance is similar to satellite governance in that the board is based in a federalist structure, with strong influence by affiliates of the national association. However, in the delegate type of governance the members that the national organization exists to serve are organizations whereas in the satellite type the members are individuals. The national board is composed

of individuals appointed by the member organizations as organizational representatives. The representatives tend to be chosen for their skills in political negotiation and ability to protect their home organization's interests.

Executive Governance

An association board that features *executive governance* has little power and defers to paid staff of the association. The staff carry out much of the work of the organization with the assistance of advisory groups. Board members act more like clients of the organization than like individuals with governance authority.

Inner-Circle Governance

Associations may have a small number of members who dominate the board through the power they have in their industry domain. Regional affiliates of the association have minimal influence compared to these powerful elite members. In this *inner-circle governance* model a core subgroup of the board is in control.

◆ ◆ ◆

The framework offered by von Schnurbein helps us see that it is not enough to consider the power of the board in relation to the executive director. In nonprofits serving members, the power of the nonprofit's members is also relevant and should be considered a key strategic contingency in deciding on board structure. In federalist structures, where board seats are reserved for specified affiliates, the affiliates are likely to have greater influence over the national organization than the executive director does. In more centralized structures in membership associations, the executive director or a few powerful members have an opening to take more control. The more important the nonprofit is to members, the more they are likely to want representation and power on the board.

Determining Board Composition

Board members bring knowledge, skills, perspectives, and connections to their boards. Which of these assets are most valued will vary from board to board. Not all board members can be expected to individually offer everything that a nonprofit requires. A high-capacity board will be able to turn to individual board members to fulfill specific needs. For example, though all board members should be able to read their nonprofit's financial statements, not all may be good at understanding complicated loan arrangements. Therefore the board of a nonprofit that borrows and lends funds may benefit from including an accountant on the board to assist in making sure that loan operations are appropriate. A grid showing current and desired assets of board members can be a useful tool for evaluating the composition of a board and considering the types of individuals that should be recruited to fill open board seats. Exhibit 9.1 offers a board composition analysis grid used by the United Way of King County, Washington.

EXHIBIT 9.1. BOARD COMPOSITION ANALYSIS GRID

Sphere of Influence	Other									
	Access to community leaders, groups									
	Access to neighborhood leaders, groups									
	Access to people with expertise									
	Access to people with money									
Area of Expertise	Real estate/property management									
	Public relations									
	Financial management									
	Fundraising									
	Human resources									
	Legal									
	Evaluation									
	Program									
Geographic Area Represented	South King County									
	North King County									
	King County									
	Greater Seattle									
	East King County									
Sector	Medical									
	Small business									
	Local media									
	Faith-based									
	Corporate									
	Political									
	Education									
	Law enforcement									
	Neighborhood									
	Union									
Race or Ethnicity	Other									
	Native American									
	Hispanic/Latino									
	Caucasian									
	African/African-American									
	Asian/Pacific Islander									
Gender and Age	Self-identifies as gay, lesbian, bi, or transgender									
	Self-identifies as disabled									
	65 and over									
	55–64									
	45–54									
	35–44									
	25–34									
	18–24									
	Male									
	Female									
	Years on Board									
	Board Member									

United Way of King County

Note: This grid helps the Nominating Development Committee in their selection of new board members, [allowing the committee] to match community expertise, skills, experience, professions, etc., with the agency needs as defined by the board and committees.

Source: United Way of King County, Washington. Reprinted by permission of the United Way of King County.

Research suggests that demographic heterogeneity on a board can facilitate sensitivity to stakeholders and innovativeness.[42] Having board members with access to diverse information and contacts can position a nonprofit to take advantage of opportunities. Through their connections with different communities, board members can monitor perceptions and expectations of the nonprofit and learn about external changes affecting the organization's ability to carry out its mission. Boards that draw members from a homogeneous, tightly connected pool of individuals may be limiting the perspectives and information that can be brought to board discussions as well as opportunities to communicate with constituent groups. Therefore a common recommendation for boards is to recruit candidates who have connections to important constituent groups and can bring new, relevant perspectives to board meetings.

Some boards, recognizing the value of having certain viewpoints and experiences at the table, have designated seats for certain types of board members. For example, an individual may be appointed to a board as the designated representative of a particular geographical region, client group, age group or social class, or agency partner. Some boards seek to proportionally reflect the demographics of the population the nonprofit serves, sometimes due to pressure from external stakeholders. For example, Habitat for Humanity International encourages minority and local community representation on the boards of its affiliates.[43] The funding decisions of some grantmaking foundations, such as the Z. Smith Reynolds Foundation, are influenced by how well the composition of the board of a grant-seeking nonprofit reflects the population the nonprofit serves.

Boards may be dominated by particular types of identity groups.[44] For example, the boards of the YWCA and the Junior League, both with missions related to women, have been found to be dominated by females. Social service agencies and hospitals with a religious affiliation tend to have boards dominated by members of that religion. Alumni organizations for private schools, not surprisingly, are dominated by individuals with academic degrees from those schools. Studies have shown that, overall, nonprofit boards tend to be dominated by males, especially for the larger and more prestigious nonprofits,[45] and by individuals with managerial and professional experience and management education.[46] Some evidence suggests that although there is no apparent gender bias in nonprofit organizations' recruitment of board members with graduate management degrees, a bias for males is seen when comparing male and female board members without graduate education.[47] By understanding the types of identity groups on their boards, nonprofit leaders can better identify coalitions among board members that form because of shared backgrounds and interests. The minorities on a board may require extra support and encouragement if they are to bring any unique perspectives and talents to board activities.

Board composition should reflect consideration of the reputation and values of board members. Having board members who are well respected suggests that the nonprofit is legitimate and trustworthy, which may be especially helpful at times when stakeholders may be in doubt about what the nonprofit is actually doing. By selecting board members that embody certain values, the nonprofit is sending a signal about the kind of organization it is. For example, Rikki Abzug and Joseph Galaskiewicz argue that having board members with high levels of education along with management and professional backgrounds signifies to external constituents that the nonprofit is committed to being efficient.[48]

Who is asked to serve on boards and who does the asking depends on the type of board. Some boards are self-perpetuating. The current board members elect individuals to fill empty seats, often after a nomination committee offers its recommendations. Member-serving nonprofits often have boards elected by the organization's members. Sometimes subgroups of members elect representatives to serve in designated seats on the board. Boards may also have ex officio members appointed by an external authority. For example, bylaws may specify that a sponsor of the nonprofit or a government agency has the right to appoint a board member. A certain number of board seats may also be reserved for clients. For example, federally qualified health centers that are neighborhood clinics for underserved populations require 51 percent of the board to be clients of the clinic. Recruiting board members from the client base may require special efforts to find interested individuals willing to learn how to be an effective board member. The Bron Afon Community Housing charitable organization in the United Kingdom devotes space on its Web page to board recruitment and training materials, demonstrating the type of information that may help persuade clients to serve on a board.[49]

The average size of boards differs across the nonprofit sector. Nonprofits with larger budgets and staffs tend to have larger boards, as do nonprofits that have particularly complex operations. There is no clear empirical link between board size and the effectiveness of the board and nonprofit. Factors to consider in deciding on the size of the board include legal minimum size requirements and the nature of the work of the board. Smaller boards may have an easier time scheduling meetings and getting a quorum. They also may find it easier to serve as a cohesive unit and have fewer costs associated with the management of board affairs. Larger boards have a greater challenge in ensuring that all board members are actively engaged and informed, especially if the board relies heavily on committees to do much of its work. However, larger boards provide greater breadth and depth of experience and contacts.

Using Board Tools

A variety of tools are available to help boards be more effective. The bylaws are required at the incorporation stage and, if changed, should be sent to the appropriate state government authority. Other tools may be created and evolve over time to serve board needs and challenges.

Bylaws

The *bylaws* of a board are the rules under which it operates. For example, bylaws provisions are likely to cover board size, qualifications for candidates for board seats, officer positions, and voting processes. By following these rules a board can avoid having to reinvent procedures and can act consistently, thus minimizing impressions of unfairness or confusion in procedures, such as how conflicts among board members are handled. Most states offer model bylaws for nonprofits that can be adopted in full or modified by a board. Some of these state model bylaws are derived from the Revised Model Nonprofit Corporation Act developed by the American Bar Association.[50] States adopting the Act in whole or in part for model bylaws include Indiana, Mississippi, Montana, North Carolina, South Carolina, Tennessee, Washington, and Wyoming. If a nonprofit does not develop and follow its own bylaws, the state government will consider the nonprofit responsible for acting in accordance with the model the state has adopted.

Officers

Boards are traditionally led by a board chair or president who runs the meetings and may be given the authority to sign contracts and checks for the nonprofit. Other popular officer positions are vice chair or chair-elect, treasurer, and secretary. The vice chair typically leads board meetings when the chair is absent. The treasurer coordinates the board's review of financial statements and may have the authority to sign organizational checks. The secretary is often responsible for seeing that minutes of meetings are taken and then approved by the board at a subsequent meeting. Some boards appoint a parliamentarian or ask the secretary to monitor the board to ensure that it follows its bylaws and meeting rules, such as *Robert's Rules of Order*.

Committees

Many boards use committees to perform tasks between board meetings that are better suited to a small group than the whole board. Board committees may or may not include staff and nonboard members. William Brown and Joel Iverson found that nonprofits emphasizing innovation and experimentation, rather than defending their current niche, were more likely than other boards to make greater use of committees and to have nonboard members serving on board committees.[51]

Standing committees are permanent groups established in the bylaws as part of the board structure. Popular standing committees are an audit and finance committee to oversee the auditing of financial statements and review monthly financial reports, a nominating committee to recommend new board members, a fund development committee to bring in donations, a program committee to monitor services, a human resource committee to attend to staffing issues including reviews of the executive director, and an executive committee made up of officers of the board to make decisions between board meetings. Ad hoc committees or task forces may be used to deal with short-term or special needs.

Orientation, Training, Self-Assessments, and Organizational Reports

As mentioned earlier in this chapter, it is important that board members are well educated about the nonprofit and its environment. Boards that offer orientations to new board members can give them a good start on learning what they need to know to be effective board members. Useful documents for board members include the organization's constitution and bylaws, mission statement, plans, annual reports, goals, budget, financial reports, program descriptions, organizational chart, and policies. Additional useful materials for board members are relevant laws, a contact list for board members and committees, committee descriptions, the board member job description, board officer job descriptions, meeting agendas and procedural rules, event schedules, meeting minutes, organizational evaluations, and needs assessments. Board self-assessments can help members to understand their weak areas and identify needs for board development.

Advisory Groups

A nonprofit may have advisory groups in addition to its governing board. There are many names for these groups, including advisory board or council. Some may be attached to specific projects, such as a special event or a pilot program supported by a grant, or to a need, such as fundraising. These groups may take some of the pressure and workload off the governing board. They can also serve as a grooming ground for prospective governing board members or as a place for governing board members to serve after their term on the governing board has ended. This type of group may attract individuals who are willing to help the nonprofit in a limited capacity without fiduciary responsibility.

Managing Board Conflict

A board is a group of unique individuals so inevitably there will be opportunities for disagreements and miscommunications among board members. Conflict is natural in any group, and it is a sign of a passive and disengaged board if disagreements among board members or between the board and the executive director never surface. By managing conflict well, a board can help to ensure effective leadership.

Conflict occurs in stages. In the first stage, *latent conflict*, conditions are ripe for conflict but people lack awareness of the conflict. Some of the conditions that encourage conflict are resource scarcity, discomfort with power differences, lack of consensus on goals and strategies, competing values, and underdeveloped norms for interaction. Boards can find it helpful to make sure there are no latent conflicts related to board decisions. Latent conflict may be exposed by assigning someone to act as devil's advocate and to raise possible opposing viewpoints, and by a board chair who assures board members that it is appropriate to raise concerns and questions.

In the *perceived conflict stage*, individuals are aware that conflict exists. During this stage it is helpful to analyze the sources of the conflict. Is it due to personal differences, informational deficiencies, incompatible roles, or environmental stress? Is the focus of the conflict on an issue or on the people involved in the issue? To remove emotional intensity from a conflict, it is useful to try to turn the focus away from the people involved and reframe the conflict as a disagreement on an issue rather than a personal dispute. Once a conflict becomes personal it may be difficult to resolve it without hurt, frustration, and anger. Ideally, a conflict will be used constructively to share information, negotiate differences, and creatively improve situations for all parties.

When individuals feel tense or anxious as a result of misunderstandings or disagreements, there is *felt conflict*, which can turn into *manifest conflict* if the individuals act to pursue their positions or interests. This may involve acting aggressively or withdrawing from the situation. In some cases, in order to avoid perceived conflict or when conflict remains latent, members of a board will engage in groupthink, showing agreement with an initial decision in an effort to avoid honest discussion of an issue. Exhibit 9.2 presents symptoms of groupthink. In some cases an individual will knowingly escalate a conflict in order to increase the likelihood that it will be addressed. This escalation may take a variety of forms, including getting third parties involved, for example by leaking information to the media. When a conflict is not resolved effectively, frustration and dissatisfaction can result.

Kenneth W. Thomas offers a review of five conflict-handling modes and recommendations for their use (see Exhibit 9.3). How best to handle conflict will vary across situations. The choice of a conflict-handling style depends on the personalities involved, norms for interacting, perceived interests at stake, time demands, and perceptions about the outcomes of past conflicts.

EXHIBIT 9.2. SYMPTOMS OF GROUPTHINK AMONG BOARD MEMBERS

Invulnerability	Members feel safe and protected from ineffective action.
Overrationalization	Members ignore warnings and rationalize their board's behavior.
Moral superiority	Members believe the board is inherently moral and ethical.
Stereotyping	Members view those holding opposing viewpoints as incompetent or unworthy of consideration.
Pressure dynamics	Members encourage conformity and do not allow exploration of alternatives.
Self-censorship	Members fail to express questions or concerns.
Perception of unanimity	Members perceive that everyone on the board has the same view.
Use of mind guards	Members keep from others information that could undermine consensus and cause concerns and questions to be raised.

Source: Adapted from Irving Janis, "Groupthink," *Psychology Today*, June 1971.

An effective board will establish a culture in which members feel free to express opinions about issues and do not let conflicts turn personal. Encouragement of differences of opinion can help the board members to avoid groupthink and reach better decisions. The board members will also understand that once a board decision is made, the full board should support it, even those members who voted against the decision. Individual board member divisiveness and lack of commitment to board decisions can create confusion among staff asked to follow through on the board's directives.

One of Myrlie Evers-Williams strengths as the NAACP board chair was her ability to bring the board together for effective decision making. Rather than use threats or shut individual board members out from decision making, she used logical, rational arguments to persuade them to agree with her positions. Under crisis conditions, when a common but ineffective response is to be defensive, she openly shared information and asked for input from stakeholders. By role-modeling discussion behaviors, she helped to change the board's culture so that members became more open to diverse viewpoints and challenges to the status quo. Her experience demonstrates the possibility of turning around even very entrenched boards and making them more effective in managing conflict and ultimately in governing their nonprofit.

EXHIBIT 9.3. FIVE CONFLICT-HANDLING MODES AND WHEN TO USE THEM

Mode	When to Use This Mode
Competing or forcing	When quick, decisive action is vital
	When unpopular actions need implementing
	When you know you are right about issues vital to the nonprofit's welfare
	When facing people who take advantage of noncompetitive behavior
Collaborating	To find an integrative solution when all concerns are important
	When you wish to learn
	To merge insights from people with different perspectives
	To gain commitment through a consensual process
	To work through feelings negatively affecting a relationship
Compromising	When a goal is not worth the time and effort to collaborate or compete
	When opponents with equal power have mutually exclusive goals
	To achieve temporary settlements
	To arrive at a solution under time pressure
	As a backup when collaboration or competition is unsuccessful
Avoiding	When an issue is trivial or more important issues are pressing
	When you perceive no chance of satisfying your concerns
	When potential disruption outweighs the possible benefits of resolution
	When people need to cool down and regain perspective
	When information gathering is needed
	When others can resolve the situation more effectively
	When an issue is tangential or symptomatic of other larger issues
Accommodating	When you find you are wrong
	When issues are more important to others than to you
	To build social credits for later use
	To minimize loss
	When harmony and stability are especially important
	To allow others to develop by learning from mistakes

Source: Adapted from Kenneth W. Thomas, "Toward Multi-Dimensional Values in Teaching: The Example of Conflict Behaviors," *Academy of Management Review* 2, no. 3 (1977): 487.

A Broader Conception of Governance

This chapter should not leave the impression that boards are the only entity responsible for governing nonprofit organizations. As David Renz explains, the domain of "governance" has moved beyond the domain of "the board."[52] Renz argues that when communities confront complex problems, they address them through a network of organizations. No one nonprofit provides all the leadership to address the problem. A single nonprofit may provide the services to address the problem, but the overall approach is designed, organized, resourced, and coordinated (in Renz's word, "governed") through the overarching network of relationships among the relevant entities. The structure of these relationships and the leadership existing within this structure may constantly evolve. The boards of nonprofits that are part of these overall networks need to understand their role in the context of this system of leadership. Within this shared power dynamic, effective boards understand the need to cross organizational boundaries and share accountability for community impact.

Judy Freiwirth suggests that in this broader governance framework, nonprofit boards may contribute through four functions: planning, advocacy, evaluation, and fiduciary care.[53] As planners they may assist in strategic direction setting and coordination and may provide input on trends and priorities. As advocates they may help with needs assessments and contribute to decisions about policies and advocacy activities. For the evaluation function, they may participate in evaluation design and implementation, offering resources, feedback, and expertise. Their fiduciary care activities may include defining resource needs, developing resource streams, and stewardship of resources. For an example of this shared governance in action, consider Freiwirth's example of Homes for Families, a statewide organization in Massachusetts that serves the homeless. Each year, its board and staff hold a visioning session with a range of constituents and partner organizations that helps to shape its own and others' initiatives. As part of the network serving the homeless, Homes for Families delivers a leadership development program whose graduates share responsibility for devising and implementing advocacy strategies.

Concluding Thoughts

Not all of us are called to serve on the board of a nonprofit organization. Those who do serve need to understand the legal and moral responsibilities entailed in board governance. This chapter has outlined basic responsibilities and the duties of care, loyalty, and obedience for board members. It has presented competencies and tools that can be drawn upon to create an effective board. This chapter has also outlined choices for board composition and structure and reviewed basic approaches to conflict. Boards have the opportunity to take active roles in guiding and supporting their organizations. Those that do can provide a critical factor by ensuring that their nonprofits stay accountable to key stakeholders.

The next chapter helps us learn more about the executive director role in nonprofits. Ideally, the board and executive director work as a team to forward the best interests of the nonprofit and the communities it serves. Understanding the executive leadership role can help boards prepare for executive transitions and for their responsibilities in reviewing the performance of the executive and providing support for the operations of the nonprofit.

Questions for Consideration

1. Are there common characteristics desirable for all nonprofit board members? If so, what are they? Beyond any common characteristics, what types of diversity should be sought for a board?
2. In a shared governance system, boards need to understand their nonprofit's role as part of a larger system of relationships. How can boards prepare themselves to be effective in contributing to governance in a network of organizations addressing the same social problem?

Exercises

Exercise 9.1: Comparing Boards

Compare the boards of two nonprofits. What are the similarities and differences in their size, composition, officers, and use of committees? What factors do you think may explain these similarities and differences?

Exercise 9.2: Bylaws

Read the bylaws of a nonprofit board. How are the bylaws helpful in increasing board efficiency and reducing the possibility of conflict? Are there any recommendations you would make for amending the bylaws?

Exercise 9.3: Managing Board Conflict

Attend a board meeting for a nonprofit organization. Did the chair of the board encourage board members to express their views and differences of opinion? Were any conflicts manifested during the meeting? If so, what was the conflict and was it handled effectively?

CHAPTER TEN

EXECUTIVE DIRECTORS AND LEADERSHIP

*S*antropol Roulant is a nonprofit in Montreal, Canada, providing critical services to those in need and a space for diverse people to be deeply and meaningfully involved in their community. It has always been run by young people living in the community. The core service is a Meals on Wheels delivery program. The nonprofit also offers a rooftop garden (in partnership with other agencies) and workshops on cooking and bicycles. Information on its Web site reflects its thoughtful approach to its leadership structure and the roles and responsibilities of its executive director and board based on legal needs and democratic principles.[1] After its first nine years of existence it converted to a membership-based organization, with members electing the board. The executive director is encouraged to run for a board seat. Unlike the many nonprofits that have a narrow conception of who is a member and requirements that members pay dues, Roulant treats as a member anyone who within the past year has received meals, made a donation, volunteered, or been an employee.

Santropol Roulant was founded in 1995 by Chris Godsall and Keith Fitzpatrick, when both were under the age of twenty-eight. They led the organization until 1997. To staff the organization, they took advantage of government funding for six-month contracts for youth needing employment. This set the organization on its path of dealing with regular staff transitions, including those in the job of executive director. Since its founding the nonprofit has gone through a succession of directors, some leading during rocky times and even on the verge of bankruptcy. Despite financial challenges and the high turnover of executive directors and staff, the Roulant has continued to survive, winning awards for its involvement of youth and level of community service.

A video posted on YouTube outlines the organization's planned approach to one of its executive leadership transitions. In the video the focus is on the change from a *highly charismatic leader to Jane Rabinowitz, who was seen to offer a more managerial orientation.*[2] *Rabinowitz worked for five years for Santropol Roulant before assuming executive leadership of more than five hundred volunteers and ten full-time and two part-time employees. She describes the nonprofit as a functional family where volunteers, staff, and clients are equally valued. Job duties are flexible, and everyone pitches in when work is to be done. Staff and volunteers feel empowered to try new ideas and are meaningfully involved in decision making.*

After taking over, Rabinowitz set out to establish human resource policies and procedures with the advice of the board. She interviewed staff individually to understand the lack of consistency and transparency in how human resources were handled and then brought the staff together to discuss shared concerns. She treated this challenge and other "growing pains" as opportunities for the young staff to learn. Another of her priorities was to involve the nonprofit in larger networks. As one mechanism for this, employees were encouraged to sit on boards of local organizations where they could exchange ideas helpful to the Roulant and the community. The nonprofit has developed a document outlining its core principles of engagement, which it shares with its fellow network members. The nonprofit's leaders believe these principles, presented later in this chapter, are the key to its success.

Rabinowitz sees her role as enabling others who come to the organization with a desire to do good work. She states, "It is important for us at the Roulant to help the young people who are involved in the organization to understand what it is to make intentional choice—to choose to do something because it resonates with who you are as a person. To enable them to choose to do something good and to obtain joy through this work. This is a big part of what Santropol Roulant is about."

◆ ◆ ◆

What makes the perfect leader? When we look at Santropol Roulant under Rabinowitz's leadership, we see a leader who has her own ideas but is working to draw out and implement the ideas of others. Should we blame her if the organization fails to thrive? Is she truly a leader if we cannot say that she personally set the direction for the organization and then found individuals willing to follow that direction? In a nonprofit organization, particularly one established to serve members, traditional notions of a leader as someone who individually crafts a vision and motivates others to pursue it may not be the best model.

This chapter examines leadership, focusing on the role of the executive director rather than the board. We review individual and group characteristics, power dynamics, and environmental factors that can affect the choice and effectiveness of leadership efforts. In addition, we examine shared leadership and substitutes for formal leadership in nonprofits. The chapter closes with thoughts about executive director development and succession.

The Nonprofit Executive Director

According to the legal framework in many countries, including the United States, the executive director is subordinate to the board, even when the director is the founder of the organization. In some nonprofits the executive director has a seat on the board and votes in board decisions. This may be in a seat designated for the director or, as in the case of Santropol Roulant, a seat that the director has won in an election. Typically in the United States, individuals fulfilling the executive director role who also have voting rights on the board are called presidents; otherwise they tend to be called executive directors or chief executive officers (CEOs).

Nonprofits usually have one person in charge of the overall management of the organization. This chief staff person, whom we are calling the executive director or CEO throughout this book, may be paid or unpaid.

However, as discussed in Chapter Four, on the structure of nonprofits, some nonprofits have two top leaders with management responsibilities. For example, in arts organizations there may be an artistic director and an administrative director.[3] The artistic director manages the artistic programming, and the administrative director manages such other functions as marketing and accounting, and neither director has authority over the other. At the Metropolitan Opera, a general manager and a music director fill the top executive roles. We can also find examples of dual-executive structures in religious, educational, health, and other types of nonprofit organizations. Dual leadership structures tend to occur in nonprofits where special expertise, often obtained through education from a specialized institution such as a seminary, medical school, or music conservatory, qualifies an individual to have an executive-level role in managing the pursuit of the core mission but does not give that person the administrative know-how to manage a complex organization. The administrative side of the nonprofit is therefore split from the mission side, with both executive-level directors reporting as equals to the board.[4]

Some nonprofits based on feminist or democratic principles of empowerment and equal participation and voice exist without hierarchical structures that place one individual in charge with power over other organizational members.[5] Usually in these types of organizations, there is a decision-making team that manages the operations of the organization, with no one in clear authority over the others. An executive decision-making team is also typical of all-volunteer, grassroots organizations that have a single executive director but tend to frequently rotate volunteers in and out of that top leadership role.

The authority of the executive director may change over time as a nonprofit gets more complex or the experience and expertise of the director grows. For example, the Burning Man organization, which coordinates a free expression festival, adopted an informal shared leadership structure in its early days but found that over time a clearer hierarchy of authority was needed.[6]

The festival grew from an experimental art experience project on a beach in California, coordinated by a group of volunteers, to a bustling temporary city of over forty-eight thousand people living for a week in an experimental community in the Black Rock desert. As the complexity of the weeklong event grew, so too did the need for formal leadership embedded in the position of a single executive director, now in charge of an incorporated for-profit organization.

Responsibilities of the Nonprofit Executive Director

Scholars tend to place the burden of ensuring a nonprofit's growth and survival on the executive director rather than on the board, arguing that the person in the director's role generally has the greatest familiarity with the complexity of the organization's internal operations, environment, and growth opportunities.[7] As Herman and Heimovics put it, the executive director has *executive centrality*. It is up to the director to enable the governing board to carry out its duties. Compared to the board, the executive director has easier access to information on how well the organization is functioning, has greater expertise related to the organization's mission, and often serves as the public face for the nonprofit; and thus he or she carries the burden of responsibility for the organization's successes and shortcomings.[8]

Nonprofit operating manuals and textbooks tend to talk about the executive director's role as administering the day-to-day affairs of the organization while the board makes the bigger-picture decisions affecting the nonprofit.[9] In actuality, as discussed in the previous chapter, these roles are often blended. Some "rubber-stamping" boards, in fact, make no decisions independent of their executive director's advice and desires. Michael Worth presents the ten basic responsibilities of a nonprofit executive director as compiled by BoardSource:[10]

1. Commit to the mission.
2. Lead the staff and manage the organization.
3. Exercise responsible financial stewardship.
4. Lead and manage fundraising.
5. Follow the highest ethical standards, ensure accountability, and comply with the law.
6. Engage the board in planning, and lead implementation.
7. Develop future leadership.
8. Build external relationships, and serve as an advocate.
9. Ensure the quality and effectiveness of programs.
10. Support the board.

A search of job advertisements and job descriptions for nonprofit executive directors shows that they often reflect these responsibilities but also reveal a wide range of emphases or priorities in what is desired. Exhibit 10.1 gives Santropol Roulant's description of what it wants in an executive director.

EXHIBIT 10.1. JOB DESCRIPTION FOR THE SANTROPOL ROULANT EXECUTIVE DIRECTOR

Santropol Roulant is a young organization with a history of innovation and creative development, whose mission is to bring people together across generations and cultures through food initiatives and to build a healthy and dynamic community. The executive director is responsible for leading Santropol Roulant through the next stages of its organizational development while ensuring program excellence, relevance and creating new opportunities for involvement in the community. She will do so with vision and imagination to both develop the internal capacity of the organization, and the scope and depth of the organization's voice in local and national issues. Ultimately, her role is to imagine new and dynamic ways of providing essential social services that have a larger vision for social change, act as a catalyst for community development and are empowering to individuals and communities.

The executive director manages all aspects of, and has general authority and responsibility for, Santropol Roulant's activities and operations in accordance with the vision, mission, policies and goals established by the board of directors. The executive director works with the board of directors on strategic planning and policy development and implements those directives within board guidelines and she provides leadership and direction to [the] organization's staff and volunteers. The executive director is accountable to the board of directors.

Source: Santropol Roulant, *The Government of Santropol Roulant—Roles and Responsibilities* (2009), http://santropolroulant.org/2009/E-membership.htm. Reprinted by permission of Santropol Roulant.

As the Roulant job description reflects, an executive director's responsibilities include management as well as leadership tasks. It is a management task to ensure that work is performed in an effective and efficient manner. It is a leadership task to decide *what* the work should be and to motivate others to pursue the vision that drives the work. A useful summary of the distinctions between managers and leaders is provided by John Kotter. He explains that leaders focus on change by setting direction and vision, aligning people to that vision, and motivating people to achieve the vision. In contrast, managers plan and budget to produce results. They organize, staff, and structure jobs and reporting relationships to implement plans; and they control, problem solve, and correct deviations from the plan.[11] In other words it is a leadership task to develop a shared plan and a management task to coordinate its implementation. For example, Jane Rabinowitz of the Roulant was acting as a leader when she set as a priority the development of human resource management policies in order to ensure fairness and transparency. She acted as a manager when she coordinated the process for developing and implementing the policies.

Leadership Responsibilities

A generic list of leadership responsibilities applicable to nonprofit executive directors can be drawn from James Kouzes and Barry Posner's framework.[12] These authors argue that successful leaders need to engage in the following five key leadership activities.

Challenge the Process
Leaders should experiment and take risks to encourage innovation and find better alternatives to the status quo. For example, the Robert Wood Johnson Foundation (RWJF) is challenging its process by soliciting feedback from grantees and comparisons with other foundations to get ideas for improving its operations. RWJF executive director Risa Lavizzo-Mourey used the foundation's "B" grades to motivate information gathering and changes to operations, even though the benefit of the changes may not be apparent for years.[13]

Inspire a Shared Vision
Leaders should have an end picture in their mind and share it to enlist others to realize their vision. As a founder of the Southern Christian Leadership Conference and a great orator, Martin Luther King Jr. was a master at inspiring others. His "I Have a Dream" speech continues to be a compelling vision statement.[14]

Enable Others to Act
It is not all about them. Leaders should collaborate, build teams, and support coalitions. Darell Hammond, the founder and director of KaBOOM!, designed his nonprofit to encourage and support community-based organizations interested in working together to create playgrounds. He understands that by building connections and social capital among the individuals he touches, they may work together to address local problems long after his involvement ends.

Model the Way
Leaders should behave in ways consistent with their beliefs and values. Mahatma Gandhi lived his values. As the leader of the Indian National Congress he did not ask any of its members to do anything he would not do himself. His day-to-day activities reflected the values he espoused: nonviolence, truth, and modesty.

Encourage the Heart
Leaders should celebrate accomplishments and believe in and care for their workers and their organization's mission. The HR Council for the

Nonprofit Sector offers the following advice for recognition: don't delay praise, do it because you are truly appreciative, give details of the achievement, do it in person or use a handwritten note, don't mix in criticism, and don't wait for perfect performance.[15]

Understanding Leadership

Scholarship on leadership offers many ideas with applicability to the nonprofit sector. We review the most promising by organizing them around five basic principles of leadership:

- Effective leaders are not all the same.
- Effective leaders change their style to fit the situation.
- Effective leaders are self-aware and operate out of a strong value system.
- Effective leaders integrate and balance roles and perspectives.
- Effective leaders use power and influence wisely.

Effective Leaders Are Not All the Same

Early scholars introduced *trait theories* of leadership, arguing that some people have innate characteristics, constant across time and situation, that make them great leaders. After decades of research, no common set of stable personality traits had emerged that distinguished effective leaders from followers, and these *great person* theories were discredited.[16] Academic scholars and practitioners continue to come up with lists of common leadership characteristics and behaviors, but there is now an assumption that individuals can be taught to be great leaders, whether or not they are born with specific traits.

Nonprofit leaders come in all physical forms and personality styles. However, some people still have leadership prototypes or mental images of leadership that affect their perceptions of who is or is not an effective leader. Research has shown that individuals are more likely to be seen as effective leaders when they exhibit physical traits that are consistent with stereotypes about leaders, including, for example, stereotypes related to race, gender, and height.[17] Stereotypes can be culturally and historically specific. For example, in the early years of the United States, tall, white, extroverted males were assumed to be more leaderlike than other males, and their greater access to leadership opportunities served to reinforce these perceptions.

The nonprofit sector has helped to weaken leadership stereotypes. In the United States, women and minorities rose to positions of influence in nonprofits even when they faced career barriers in other sectors.[18] Jane Addams, founder of the nonprofit Hull House and the first American woman to be given a Nobel Peace Prize (awarded in 1931), Clara Barton, founder of the American Red Cross (established in 1881), and Martin Luther King Jr., cofounder in 1957 of the Southern Christian Leadership Conference, are just a few of the historical figures who led nonprofits and shaped the nonprofit sector as we experience it today. Even when they could not vote or were excluded from membership in influential societies, women, African Americans, Catholics, Jews, and other disenfranchised or otherwise marginalized individuals created and led nonprofits and thus participated in American civic life. Many of the nonprofit institutions they established as alternative power structures still exist today. But the traditional leadership prototypes may still partially explain why, in some nonprofit subsectors, white males have historically held more top leadership positions.[19]

Though people no longer believe there is only one personality and physical profile for successful leaders, scholars are finding that certain personality characteristics tend to be common among them. Successful leaders tend to be ambitious, high energy, tenacious, trustworthy, reliable, open, intelligent, and self-confident. They have a desire to lead and are able to integrate large amounts of information. They know their industry and relevant technical matters, trust in their own abilities, take initiative, are creative, and have the ability to adapt to the needs of followers and the requirements of situations.[20] They tend to be more cooperative, verbal, and well educated than their followers.[21] They are admired for being honest, forward looking, inspiring, and competent.[22] In a survey of what makes a good leader in the nonprofit and for-profit sectors, characteristics distinguishing strong nonprofit leadership were effective relationship management, empathy and inclusiveness, transparency and confidence, and patience and flexibility.[23]

Effective Leaders Change Their Style to Fit the Situation

Effectiveness of a given leadership style depends on situational factors. Therefore, leaders need to have different styles in their repertoire. Leaders first need to choose how task and relationship oriented they should be. They also need to choose whether to take a more transactional or transformational approach to their leadership.

Task- and Relationship-Oriented Leadership
One of the most basic leadership frameworks suggests that leaders should vary their approach depending on the situation and have in their portfolios the following three styles of behavior:

- **Task-oriented leadership**. Leaders define and organize work relationships, determine roles and responsibilities, and establish communication channels and procedures. For example, Jane Rabinowitz, executive director of Santropol Roulant, exhibited a task-oriented leadership style when developing human resource management policies by setting up an interview schedule and asking everyone to contribute individually and in a group to the review of existing practices and analysis of possible policies to develop.

- **Relationship-oriented leadership**. Leaders nurture friendly and warm working relationships, encourage trust and respect, and satisfy social and emotional needs. Rabinowitz demonstrated relationship-oriented leadership in ensuring that young volunteers felt welcomed and valued for their contributions.
- **Laissez faire leadership**. Leaders are nondirective, are neither task nor relationship oriented, and may be empowering by staying out of the way. Rabinowitz took a laissez faire approach in the Roulant's efforts to have its staff serve on other agency boards. Staff had independence in deciding what boards to join and what information to exchange during board meetings.

Studies show that a task-oriented style tends to be most effective in highly unfavorable situations for the leader and also in highly favorable ones, such as being trusted and respected by subordinates and having formal authority. A relationship-oriented style is more effective when the situation is more moderate. In situations where tasks are ambiguous, task-oriented leadership tends to work best.[24]

For a nonprofit executive director, this means that if he or she is not well trusted or respected by the staff or board, it may be best to demonstrate competency and gain credibility by focusing on assigning tasks and scheduling activities so that formal goals can be achieved, rather than spending a lot of time trying to get to know individuals on a personal basis in order to try to satisfy their social and emotional needs. In this kind of situation, staff and board members are likely to be cynical about immediate attempts to focus on improving relationships rather than technical work outcomes. As staff confidence grows in a leader's ability to produce task-oriented results, more of the leader's time and effort should be spent on nurturing work relationships.

For leaders who are well liked and respected, adopting a task-oriented approach is likely to be effective. Workers already feel they are in a supportive environment, so a task-oriented approach can improve efficiency while not undermining a positive work culture. This does not mean that relationship-oriented behaviors should be avoided. They can be combined with more task-oriented ones, as Rabinowitz did in leading the Roulant. For activities where staff and volunteers are fully competent to carry out the tasks, as in routine meal delivery, Rabinowitz's best use of time is to engage in friendly interactions that demonstrate that she values others' contributions to the organization.

The Hersey and Blanchard *situational leadership* theory elaborates when to use task- and relationship-oriented leadership styles. It has the premise that leadership behaviors should be chosen based on the job maturity or readiness of followers to carry out tasks.[25] There are four main leadership behaviors in this model: delegating, supporting, coaching, and directing. If followers have low competence and low commitment to perform, coaching is suggested. Leaders using coaching combine task-oriented and relationship-oriented behavior, giving direction to the worker and also being encouraging as the worker learns how to perform. When a worker has high competence and high commitment, delegating is appropriate. The leader can take a hands-off approach and the worker is likely to be successful at the task. For workers with moderate to high competence and variable commitment, leaders should use a supporting style to encourage the behavior without directing it. When workers have low competence but high commitment, the workers can benefit from and are likely to welcome the directing style, in which the leader tells them how to do a task.

Transactional Versus Transformational Leadership Styles

Another useful leadership style framework contrasts *transactional* and *transformational* leadership styles.[26] Transactional leadership is well suited to organizations that do not need major changes. Transactional leader behaviors involve working within existing systems to ensure that the mission is appropriately pursued. An individual acting as a transactional leader promotes organizational stability and incremental improvements. In contrast, transformational leadership behaviors involve inspiring followers to work to achieve a new vision and implement major change in an organization. A transformational leadership style is called for when a nonprofit is first founded or faces a major crisis or environmental changes that undermine the value of its current mission and approach.

Santropol Roulant has moved back and forth between transactional and transformational leaders. For example, when it faced its first fiscal crisis and was left without a formal leader, it brought back one of the initial founders who had proven his ability to radically transform the organization by taking it from concept to reality. He left the executive director position when the need for a transformational leader ended and someone more comfortable with a transactional style could be appointed. Leaders who can easily switch styles offer the most versatility for a nonprofit.

Effective Leaders Are Self-Aware and Operate Out of a Strong Value System

Knowing and accepting oneself is necessary for personal well-being, growth, self-confidence, and general success in life. It is also a critical first step in knowing and accepting others.[27] Individuals are unlikely to be good at creating and maintaining inclusive and diverse organizations without being aware of how they perceive themselves as similar and as different from others.[28] Scholars argue that only by understanding themselves can individuals hope to be successful as leaders. According to Frances Hesselbein and Alan Shrader, "Leadership is a matter of how to be, not how to do."[29] Robert Quinn provides us with the thought that "each leader is different. Each one has her own unique approach. It is not what they do. It is who they are that matters."[30]

Nonprofit executive directors need to understand their own values, how those values align with the missions of their organizations, and that others may be acting based on different sets of values. For all of us, our values are the "deep-seated, pervasive standards that influence every aspect of our lives: our moral judgments, our responses to others, [and] our commitments to personal and organizational goals."[31] It is by consciously surfacing our values that we connect deeply to a nonprofit's mission and become passionate in our work. Clarifying our values helps us make decisions and stay on course.

Without a mission that attracts workers and other supporters, a nonprofit, no matter its leader's skills, is likely to fail. Executive directors need to understand, believe in, and clearly communicate their organization's mission. By linking it to shared values, they can inspire others to work to achieve that mission. For example, individuals who value safety may be inspired to support nonprofits that reduce criminal behavior. Some individuals value education and health, and leaders may call on that value in inspiring them to help schools and hospitals. By emphasizing values that others share, leaders gain widespread support.

Executive directors have a responsibility to leave their nonprofit if they no longer believe in its mission or values. Their effectiveness is undermined when they stay without agreeing with what the nonprofit stands for and hopes to accomplish. This was the case for Candy Lightner, the founding president of MADD (Mothers Against Drunk Driving). She left the organization when it changed its goals to emphasize problems with drinking alcohol that were unrelated to drunk driving. She explained, "It has become far more neo-prohibitionist than I ever wanted or envisioned. I didn't start MADD to deal with alcohol. I started MADD to deal with the issue of drunk driving."[32]

Exemplary leaders embody the values that they promote. When their vision for what they hope to accomplish in life aligns with an organizational vision, they can act with integrity on their own behalf as well as on behalf of the organization, nurturing relationships that help them and the organization at the same time. Santropol Roulant's nine core principles of engagement (Exhibit 10.2) show the values one nonprofit is attempting to embed as the fundamental basis for all its actions. Its leaders believe that the nonprofit's successes are due to its following these principles.

EXHIBIT 10.2. SANTROPOL ROULANT'S NINE CORE PRINCIPLES OF ENGAGEMENT

1. People as gifts—Each person who comes in contact with Santropol Roulant is seen as a whole person with many dimensions that, when given space to flourish, feed the organization's vibrancy, capacity to innovate, and overall effectiveness.
2. Relational productivity—Creating the space and skills for healthy interpersonal and group communication are essential and highly productive aspects of organizational life.
3. Comfort with change—We embrace change and uncertainty as opportunities to learn and evolve. For a youth-run organization such as Santropol Roulant, staff and volunteer turnover are necessary and positive elements of our organizational rhythm.
4. Cultivating individual learning and organizational creativity—We value personal growth, curiosity, and play as essential to Santropol Roulant's dynamism and productivity.
5. Collaborative leadership—We strive to be deeply participatory, sharing decision-making and leadership in a way that contributes to everyone's learning and growth while we deliver on our mission.
6. The importance of space—We pay attention to the state and arrangement of the physical space as it affects the way people relate to the organization and to each other.
7. Gravitational structuring—We invite people to involve themselves in the tasks, projects, conversations, and decisions that they are drawn to based on their own interests and curiosities.
8. Coherence—We aim to live our deepest values in all our relationships: with clients, staff, board members, volunteers, funders, partners, neighbors, etc.
9. Community building—We strive to become a living expression of the change we want to see in the world, rather than simply an instrument for that change.

Source: Santropol Roulant, "Santropol Roulant's Core Principles of Engagement" (n.d.), http://hrcouncil.ca/hr-toolkit/documents/SR_Core_Principles.pdf. Reprinted by permission of Santropol Roulant.

It has long been known that building and maintaining trust is a critical leadership skill. People are more likely to collaborate and follow the directions of others when they view those others as trustworthy.[33] When leaders' values guide them and are transparent to others, their actions become predictable and their decisions understandable. This leads to the development and maintenance of trust. Jurkiewicz and Massey explain that leaders should not be preoccupied with trying to please others. Instead, they can earn respect by making tough decisions based upon principled criteria, taking responsibility for those decisions, and proceeding on their chosen path with conviction.[34] The ability to demonstrate consistent adherence to values and ethical standards may be even more important for a leader of a nonprofit organization than for one in the for-profit business sector. Thomas Jeavons argues that in order to be entrusted with scarce resources, nonprofit executive directors need to appear trustworthy, ethical, and willing to uphold higher values in their organization's operations.[35]

In addition to being aware of their personal values and how those fit with their nonprofit's values, leaders should be aware of their weaknesses and strengths. Rather than focusing energy on trying to improve their weak areas, leaders can compensate for them.[36] For example, if leaders know they are not great at setting standards, they can join with someone who is good at spearheading that activity. If they are aware that they tend to sound overly authoritarian, they can delegate decisions to teams and take a laissez faire approach to give the teams the space and freedom to reach consensus without a leader's involvement. Knowing their strengths, they can devote time and effort to developing situations that work well with their strongest leadership styles. For example, when leaders know they are good at motivating others through passionate speeches, they can seek out opportunities for public speaking.

Being self-aware is also a critical component of cultural competency, which is the ability to understand, communicate with, and interact effectively with people of different cultures and backgrounds. Cultural identities may be related to race, ethnicity, nationality, gender, age, sexual orientation, physical abilities, class, job status, language, religion, and immigrant status. To have an inclusive workplace, nonprofit leaders need to be aware of their assumptions, beliefs, and biases and the ways in which these traits may affect who feels welcome and respected in their organization and who does not.[37] By being self-aware of their intuitive approach to diversity, they can better counter any of their tendencies that might undermine inclusion. CompassPoint Nonprofit Services presents lessons from its Cultural Competence Learning Initiative, including one that emphasizes the importance of leader self-awareness. It tells the story of an executive director who was able to move multiculturalism forward only after recognizing that she was not asserting needed leadership because she was white and thought she should allow people of color to lead the effort. Once she recognized that she needed to champion diversity and inclusion just as she championed other initiatives, the nonprofit was able to make more progress.[38]

Effective Leaders Integrate and Balance Roles and Perspectives

Lee Bolman and Terrence Deal tell us that effective leaders use multiple frames or ways of looking at and interpreting a situation.[39] These frames present different lenses for understanding and responding to their organization's challenges. Depending on the frame, different leadership behaviors may be chosen, so it is important to integrate all the frames before strategizing about how to respond to a situation. The frames are

- **Structural**: attention to goals, expectations, procedures, and policies
- **Symbolic**: attention to shared beliefs, values, and norms
- **Human resources**: attention to hopes, relationships, and preferences
- **Political**: attention to power, conflict, and shared interests in relationships

These frames have been applied to nonprofits by Roger Herman and Richard Heimovics.[40] In their research, Herman and Heimovics found that effective nonprofit executive directors are more likely than their less effective counterparts to use a political frame. The political frame gives them a perspective on how conflicts, power relationships, and external factors influence decisions and policies. In using this frame they apply conflict resolution skills and work with coalitions and interest groups. The researchers found that in general, nonprofit executive directors tend to strongly emphasize the structural frame. When using the structural frame, they set clear goals, expectations, procedures, and policies. Frames found to be used less frequently by nonprofit executive directors are the human resources and symbolic frames. When using the human resources frame, they are responsive to hopes, relationships, and preferences and act to empower others. Their use of the symbolic frame involves creating shared beliefs, values, and norms, in other words, fostering a shared organizational culture.

The most effective nonprofit leaders are those that can look at a situation from multiple frames and act in ways that address the needs highlighted by each view. For example, an effective executive director may show staff and board members how being responsive to powerful external interest groups is consistent with organizational values (symbolic frame) and can result in rewards for staff members (human resources frame), and that established procedures are being followed (structural frame) that improve the bargaining position of the nonprofit (political frame).

Sometimes applying multiple frames leads executive directors to act in seemingly incompatible roles. They exhibit *behavioral complexity*, a term that captures how leaders respond to competing expectations of numerous constituencies by assuming numerous roles.[41] Behavioral complexity theory and related empirical findings suggest that leaders need to balance roles rather than see them as either-or options,[42] just as they need to look at situations from multiple perspectives.

Effective Leaders Use Power and Influence Wisely

Given the importance of political skills to a nonprofit executive director, it is useful to review sources of power that the director and others may possess as well as influence strategies that they may adopt. Effectiveness in influencing others can be predicted by organizational and personal sources of power as well as strategies used.[43]

Many people have negative reactions to the idea of strategizing about building and using power. Some worry that too much power held by an individual may lead to abuses of power and may not be in the best interest of the collective group. Their concerns are valid. Research has shown that the more power an organizational leader has, the less likely he or she is to listen to others and consider their advice.[44] Powerful people tend to have an excessive belief in their own judgment. Astute executive directors understand that politics and use of power are inevitable and that by understanding power dynamics, and being open to others' ideas, they can better forward the interests of their organization.[45] As Rosabeth Moss Kanter and other scholars have explained, leaders can use their power to intercede favorably for someone in trouble, attract resources, get access to other decision makers, set agendas, acquire useful information, and build a high-performing workforce.[46]

Personal and Positional Sources of Power

Personal as well as organizational characteristics affect how much power one person has over another. In analyzing the power dynamics in a situation it is useful to use the list developed by John French and Bertram Raven to look at the types of personal and positional power leaders have: legitimate, reward, coercive, referent, expert, effort-related, centrality-related, criticality-related, flexibility-related, visibility-related, and relevance-related.[47]

Legitimate power comes from having authority from followers to exert influence over them. Individuals who are seen as legitimate leaders tend to be perceived as able to make good on their commitments to followers. Legitimate power often comes from the position one holds. Thus executive directors have a ready source of legitimate power over their staff by virtue of their job title. However, executive directors can lose legitimacy despite their title if they act outside the values and norms of their followers or appear to be ineffectual in getting tasks done. They also may lose power as soon as they lose their title. Their staff may be doing what they ask because of their position, not them, so when they change roles they may find that their influence over certain people is lost. Thus a founder who moves from an executive director role to a board member or other volunteer role may find that he or she now has less influence over the daily operations of the nonprofit.

Reward power arises from the ability to control rewards and positive outcomes for others. It is closely related to *coercive power*, the ability to influence others through fear of punishment. In response to reward power, people comply in order to receive positive benefits, whereas coercive power leads to compliance to avoid negative consequences. Rewards and punishments that may be under a nonprofit executive director's control include but are not limited to money, information, work assignments, work shifts, acceptance, and praise and criticism. In Chapter Twelve we will discuss in detail the use of rewards and punishments (that is, positive and negative incentives) as a motivating tool.

Executive directors with *referent power* have influence over others because they are personally liked by them. Charismatic individuals have high referent power. People enjoy being around them, admire them, and want to please them. Agreeable people also tend to have referent power. They make friends easily, and their friends are willing to support them out of friendship and personal liking. There is evidence that an attractive appearance is linked to referent power. Attractive people have been found to be more successful, which may be due to assumptions by followers that they have socially desirable personality characteristics and are virtuous and effective.[48] Those with high referent power are more likely to serve as role models than are those with low referent power. By increasing their referent power, executive directors may find that others are more likely to emulate their attitudes and behaviors.

Executive directors with *expert power* have technical knowledge and expertise that others rely upon. Having unique and useful knowledge is a source of power. Individuals are likely to follow the direction or instructions of someone who, they believe, understands an issue or problem better than they do. However, there is a downside to an executive director's development of highly specialized knowledge. The investment required for a high level of expertise may not be worth the benefits if having a general understanding is sufficient given one's other sources of power. Also, when the director is the only person with a particular expertise, then the nonprofit has no one who can monitor for improprieties or serve as a backup to handle situations when the director cannot be involved due to being on vacation or sick leave, having a conflict of interest, or having to resolve other priorities. Having an executive director with strong expert power can also add to the difficulties faced by a nonprofit when that director leaves unexpectedly and there is no succession plan in place. The knowledge the director has may be lost. Succession planning should involve developing individuals who share or can replace the current executive director's expertise.

Individuals can obtain *effort-related power* through active, dependable performance. The more that they can show useful effort, the more they are likely to be relied on by others and given discretion to act without supervision. They may be sought out for new opportunities or deferred to because of their past performance and willingness to work hard. There is also a sense of indebtedness or obligation that can build over time out of gratitude for past effort. This can explain reluctance to fire an executive director with long years of experience in a nonprofit even when current performance is poor. The extraordinary effort that the director exerted in the past carries power into the present.

There are five forms of power that individuals can acquire through their position in an organization or network. One is *centrality-related power*, which comes from controlling how others interact and gain information. As described earlier in this chapter, executive directors typically have centrality-related power with their boards, what we called *executive centrality*. They tend to have more information than the board does on the nonprofit's operations and performance outcomes. They can present this information in a way that makes them look effective and encourages others to go along with their recommendations. They may also control the flow of important information to staff, clients, and other stakeholders.

Criticality-related power comes from performance of tasks critical to others' performance. The more one's performance affects others' performance, the more power one has. If others can work around a person without much trouble or concern, that person lacks criticality-related power. This explains why volunteers sometimes feel powerless in a nonprofit when employees' work does not depend on the volunteers' performance. Volunteer tasks are peripheral to the employees' tasks. If an executive director has criticality-related power, others understand that the director's success is critical to the nonprofit's success. There are many ways an executive director can increase criticality-related power, for example, by being responsible for acquiring and allocating resources for others to perform their jobs, composing work teams, and approving and contributing to others' assignments.

Discretion over what one does provides *flexibility-related power*. It is important for a nonprofit to have checks and balances so that this source of power is not abused. Directors who have too much flexibility can create situations that are unethical and ineffective. For example, William Aramony of the United Way of America had discretion to use funds to pay for expenses unrelated to the nonprofit's mission and to implement practices that ended up being inconsistent with the organization's values and the law. As a *Time* magazine article stated, "In a way, William Aramony was a victim of his own success—and excess."[49] The United Way board had provided Aramony with much independence. Perhaps the board felt comfortable with this given that he had been president of the nonprofit for twenty-one years and was credited with dramatically increasing its receipts.

Visibility-related power comes from being in a position where one can be known and seen by influential others. Executive directors who become popular with the media have power because of this. Others are reluctant to challenge them given how well they are known. They become highly identified with their nonprofit. If they do fall in stature, it can have serious repercussions for their nonprofit, as the United Way found with President Aramony when his indiscretions were uncovered and he was convicted of embezzlement. Donations to United Ways across the country dropped. However, the visibility-related power of an executive director can also be a benefit to a nonprofit. The visibility can lead to doors being opened for the director that bring more resources to the organization. Positive attention and awareness can help with mission achievement.

Executive directors can also have *relevance-related power*. The ability to control the tasks and outcomes of high priority to others gives power. The more relevant a nonprofit's mission is to community leaders and funders, for example, the more power its executive director is likely to have with them. At Santropol Roulant the executive director is highly relevant to the volunteers who use the nonprofit as a way to connect to the community, and to the clients who rely on meal deliveries as a source of physical and social sustenance.

Strategies for Influencing Others

We now turn to a review of three general strategies for influencing others: retribution, reciprocity, and reason.[50] These strategies are not foolproof, and their ethical appropriateness will vary across situations. It may be possible for each strategy to be thwarted by the person who is the object of the influence attempt.[51] Still, it is useful for executive directors to be able to use these strategies wisely and recognize when others are using them.

Retribution involves forcing others to do what the influencer wants. This can take the form of intimidation or coercion. For example, an executive director may threaten to fire an employee if the employee's performance does not improve. An advantage of the retribution approach is that it can result in quick action. A disadvantage is that it may raise concerns about violation of rights and may engender resentment, harming the relationship of the influencer and the person being influenced. Others observing the influence attempt may see it as exploitative, too aggressive, or uncooperative. The desired behavior may be unsustainable without an escalation of threats. A retribution strategy typically requires a continual threat to maintain behaviors, unless the individual being influenced gets over any resentment and finds intrinsic value in the performance of the desired behaviors. It may be possible to weaken a retribution strategy by pointing out mutual dependencies and making counterthreats.

An influence strategy with less risk is *reciprocity*, in which the individual encourages others to want to do what the individual desires. Reciprocity can involve obligating others or bargaining with others. For example, an executive director may offer to increase the budget of a department if the department head takes on additional tasks. For this strategy to work, the actors involved typically need to be seen as trustworthy and to hold resources seen as valuable by the other party. It is helpful if there are established norms for exchanges and adequate time for negotiating. This strategy may encourage an instrumental, "what's in it for me?" view and the assumption that interactions with the influencer are negotiable. In response to reciprocity influence attempts, the person being influenced may find it helpful to his or her interests to point out any manipulative and high-pressure bargaining tactics and suggest alternative exchange processes.

Reason is the third general influence strategy. Through reason a leader can appeal to personal values and present facts that stress merits and needs. For example, the executive director can show an employee that showing up late for work is a hardship for clients and goes against the employee's belief that one should always show respect for others. The desired behavior may be sustainable without further intervention when a reasoning strategy is used and is based on shared goals and values. With a reason strategy the person being influenced may accept the inherent merit of performing the desired behavior and internalize the desire to see it performed. This strategy may require more time than retribution or reciprocity, due to the need to build trust, discuss the common goals and values related to the situation, and resolve any disagreements or misunderstandings. As trust builds, this strategy may become more effective and efficient to use. A reasoning influence strategy may be undermined by highlighting those beliefs, values, and goals that are not shared; affirming a right to refuse a request; and ending the discussion before any agreement is reached.

Strong Leaders and Shared Leadership

Some of the same characteristics that make for a strong leader may in fact weaken a nonprofit. In this section we discuss ways in which a dominant leader may jeopardize an organization, and we suggest that nonprofits encourage sharing of leadership responsibilities.

Charismatic Leadership

Leaders with charisma have personal magnetism, a quality that inspires uncritical devotion from followers. Under charismatic leadership, followers are swayed by the force of their leader's personality, seeing the leader as having exceptional, sometimes even superhuman qualities. Followers' enthusiasm for a charismatic leader can bring them to rally around the leader's vision and work under the leader's direction. At the same time, followers' fervent devotion and enthusiasm may result in their overlooking any negative qualities of the leader and may create resistance to anyone opposing or replacing the leader.

Although charismatic leaders can be quite effective in the short term, some scholars argue that a charismatic leader can pose a risk to the organization in the long term. Followers want the approval of charismatic leaders, and are motivated to please the leader rather than to act based on shared vision or values. The long-term sustainability of a nonprofit can be harmed when individuals affiliate with the organization because they are drawn to its charismatic leader rather than feeling a commitment to the organization's mission. Some authors go so far as to suggest that too much dependence on the personal talents of any leader may be harmful. As John Gardner explains, some "leaders are, perhaps, very talented to solve problems personally, but if they fail when it comes to institutionalizing this process, their departure severely weakens the organizations they leave behind."[52]

Leaders do not have to be charismatic to inspire followers. Numerous examples exist of effective leaders who lacked charisma. This point is reinforced in Shirley Sagawa and Deborah Jospin's book on charismatic nonprofit organizations.[53] They find that a nonprofit can develop a high degree of social capital even when its leaders are not individuals that attract followers through the force of their own personalities. Leaders can build strong connections among their nonprofit's core constituents and create bridges to other groups or individuals outside this core group. The strength of these connections can motivate the individuals involved to pursue activities that support an organizational vision. The individuals are not drawn to each other due to their desire to follow a single charismatic leader's direction but rather because of coherence with the organizational mission.

Founder Executive Directors

Some of the most charismatic leaders of nonprofits also happen to be the founders. They possess the talents, knowledge, and skills needed to bring their dreams to life. Many nonprofits owe their establishment and continued existence to the deep personal commitment their founders brought to them, as well as to the founders' personal magnetism that attracts followers. However, having a strong founder may leave a nonprofit open to *founder's syndrome*, in which the founder has too much control over the organization, leaving it vulnerable. A founder's weaknesses may haunt an organization even after the founder's departure.

Because of the strong personal investment that founders who are executive directors have in their organizations, they may have trouble sharing power with others in the nonprofit. In one of the few available studies of founders versus nonfounders, Stephen Block and Steven Rosenberg discovered that founders tended to have more control over the board than nonfounders did.[54] Founder-led nonprofits had boards that met less frequently than boards in nonprofits run by nonfounders did, and the founder executive director was more likely to set the board agenda and have more influence in swaying board votes. Founders also tended to have a stronger belief than nonfounders that they should play an instrumental role in recruiting board members. When a board does not have adequate power over a founding executive director, the founder may see the board as accountable to him or her rather than the other way around.

A founder may have leadership traits that are more appropriate for the founding of a nonprofit than for its long-term management. Looking at nonprofits working in developing countries, L. David Brown and Archana Kalegaonkar discuss how gifted visionaries and entrepreneurial founders can be amateurs at organizing and managing organizations.[55] Susan Chambre and Naomi Fatt also noted managerial and technical failings among charismatic leaders in their study of newly established nonprofits addressing AIDS.[56] Although founders may have a talent for rallying others around a vision, in doing so they may focus more attention on gaining external support than establishing effective internal procedures.

What happens in the formative years of a nonprofit is critical to its long-term survival. A founder can imprint his or her agenda and vision on an organization, and initial policies and practices can endure for many years. Allowing a dominant founder to have too much control in a nonprofit may result in embedded managerial challenges, legacies of whatever weaknesses the founder had. If the founder was highly skilled and competent, other staff may have relied too heavily on him or her, making it difficult to fill the skills gap when the founder leaves. A founder who does not build capacity in others as a backup to his or her own abilities may leave the nonprofit with staff who have difficulty adjusting to the greater levels of power and responsibility they have after the founder's departure.

By proactively preparing for the departure of a founder, or in fact any executive director, a nonprofit may be able to avoid some of the vulnerabilities that can arise from these transitions, especially if efforts are made to avoid overdependence on the director in the first place. In some cases the departure of a founder who has been serving as the executive director gives the organization an opportunity to become stronger. Miriam Wood found that when organizations lose a founder, they tend to hire executive directors who focus on internal management, which is a common area of weakness in a founder-led nonprofit.[57]

Shared Leadership

Relying heavily on a charismatic leader or founder is clearly not a sustainable model. Even having a highly respected executive director can have a downside for a nonprofit. The deference given the director may make it difficult to encourage wide representation in decision making and build broad leadership capacity. Some scholars argue that leadership needs to be embedded in a community, not in a single individual with an agenda.[58] Sonia Ospina, Bethany Godsoe, and Ellen Schall explain that leadership creation is a collective process; it should not be left in the hands of one individual.[59] The message for nonprofit executive directors from this line of thought is that leadership should be shared.[60] Co-leadership and empowerment of others is critical for nonprofit executive directors to be effective in the short and long term.

This is the approach taken by Santropol Roulant. Nobody serving as its executive director expects to be in this job for long. Executive directors at the Roulant know they have to prepare the next generation of leaders. Therefore they push decision making down through the organization. The Roulant defines itself as a youth-led organization, and plans on executive directors aging out of the position. New executive directors know there are others in the organization whom they can rely on to have useful skills, knowledge, and contacts. They see it as their responsibility to ensure that power is shared with others in the organization with leadership interests.

As Santropol Roulant has learned, leadership can be found and should be fostered throughout an organization. Chairs of committees and program heads can take on leadership tasks. Advisory groups and task forces can provide leadership through their contributions of advice and other resources. Interim directors, drawn from leaders previously retired from the nonprofit, may serve in temporary leadership roles. By reducing the importance of any one person to the organization, a nonprofit can develop a strong, broad-based foundation of current and future leaders.

Leadership Transitions and Leader Development

A change of executive director can be a trying time for a nonprofit. Staff and board members who have come to rely on a strong executive director may find that the organization does not have the internal capacity to fill the departing leader's shoes. The departure may also come with a loss of supporters, those who were involved in the organization because they were drawn to the director rather than to the organizational mission. When an executive director is asked to resign by a board, a different array of challenges may emerge. The requested resignation may signal dissatisfaction with the situation but not necessarily a plan for moving forward. The board may attempt to take over management functions if the executive position is left vacant. An interim or new executive director may need to assess the situation quickly and determine whether he or she agrees with the views of the board, staff, and other stakeholders about what is needed and feasible. A poor choice of a new executive director or a long period without one may compound problems and make it difficult for the nonprofit to survive the transition and regain momentum.

Managing nonprofit executive transitions has become an industry. Numerous consulting firms and transition guides are available to assist nonprofits in addressing leadership succession proactively or responding quickly to an emergency need for a new executive director. Still, few nonprofits have an executive succession plan. A recent survey of a random sample of U.S. nonprofits showed that even though respondents recognized the importance of succession planning, few were in organizations that were ready for a transition. No internal pipeline for talent had been developed, no emergency succession plan was available, the board and the director had not discussed the possibility of succession, and no procedures had been established to handle an executive leadership change.[61]

As when hiring for any position, it is helpful to have procedures for identifying potential candidates, encouraging interest, screening prospects, preparing a realistic job preview, interviewing, orienting the person chosen for the position, and supporting the new hire. It may also be necessary to select an interim director to fill the void while a permanent choice is being identified and recruited. Boards should consider whether the previous executive director can and should be on hand to help with the selection and orientation process and reduce any tensions from the transition.

It is the responsibility of the board to hire the executive director, leaving the director to hire all other staff members. A key transition task is for the board to assess the organization, determine what type of director is needed at this stage of the nonprofit's development, and define the existing and projected organizational and environmental challenges. The board should also plan to be on hand to offer support to the director as he or she adjusts to new responsibilities. Asking the director for thirty- and ninety-day workplans for the first months on the job may facilitate the director's prioritization of tasks and ensure that the board's and the director's expectations for early job performance are consistent.

According to research by Michael Allison, boards face three typical threats to successful transitions: (1) they underestimate the risks and costs of bad hires; (2) they are unprepared for the hiring task; and (3) they fail to take advantage of the opportunities in executive director transitions.[62] Hiring a new executive leader can be a time for reflection and renewal. Boards can benefit their nonprofits by using the loss of a director as an impetus for a careful assessment of the organization and the priority roles and responsibilities for the new leader.

Candidates for the executive director position may be internal or external. There is some evidence, though largely anecdotal, that nonprofit executive directors are unlikely to move to the director's slot in another nonprofit.[63] Perhaps more typically, executive director roles are filled by nonprofit employees who move up the ranks inside a nonprofit or move from one nonprofit to another to gain more leadership responsibility. Although many employees in the nonprofit sector stay in that sector for their entire working careers, sector shifting is not unusual.[64] Some scholars expect that the sector may see an influx of formerly retired individuals to replace Baby Boomers who retire. These new leaders may have leadership experience in government or for-profit businesses. In addition, there has been tremendous growth in higher education programs to prepare individuals for work in the nonprofit sector.[65] Graduates of these programs may add to the labor pool for nonprofit executives.

The 2006 *Daring to Lead* report created intense interest in a projected leadership deficit for the nonprofit sector. The study revealed that many nonprofit executives planned to leave their jobs within five years.[66] That same year The Bridgespan Group estimated that a large number of senior managers would be needed in the sector over the next decade.[67] Adding to concerns about future shortages of qualified leaders are 2007 and 2008 study reports that suggest younger workers are reluctant to become nonprofit CEOs. Some of the reasons given for this reluctance are the same as those given for why current leaders plan to leave their jobs: lack of adequate compensation, difficulty in maintaining a healthy work-life balance, and fundraising demands. In addition, some young nonprofit professionals reported that they were frustrated by lack of mentoring from senior executives.[68]

Although the projected leadership deficit has produced a range of recommendations for nurturing future leaders, there are doubts about how serious this so-called crisis actually is. In 2009, Janet Johnson suggested that the labor market and nonprofit organizations will adjust in response to supply and demand. She expects higher executive pay, increased labor market participation by older workers, skill acquisition among younger workers, skill sharing among volunteers and board members, venture philanthropy, and even a reshaping of the composition of the sector to mitigate Baby Boomer retirements.[69] Not all current executive directors will retire at once. As younger individuals rise to executive positions, they will have the opportunity to slowly reshape expectations about the nature of the work of a nonprofit executive director. Increasing professionalization of the sector through college programs, accreditation systems, and regulatory environments may also shift the general nature of the work and the rewards and challenges of it.

Internal leadership development programs may encourage and prepare current staff to take over executive director positions, as demonstrated by the experience of Santropol Roulant. To encourage movement up the ranks, staff can be given opportunities to impress board members with their leadership abilities and encouraged to enroll in courses to improve their leadership abilities and credentials. Promising staff members can be supported in efforts to develop their networks. Identifying and nurturing staff with the potential to take on the executive director role can help to ensure that an internal leadership succession goes smoothly.

Many university programs explicitly train students for jobs as nonprofit leaders. Current executive directors have been surveyed to find out what they believe are the most important training topics and the results used to design educational programs.[70] The choice of topics has remained relatively stable over time, with slight variations based on the characteristics of the organization to be led and each respondent's background. In one study the following topics were ranked as highly important to nonprofit executive directors: leadership, ethics and values, long-term planning, financial management, conducting effective meetings, creativity, public relations, interpersonal skills, short-term planning, managing change, conflict management, program evaluation, collaboration and networking, fundraising, quality management, public speaking, needs assessment, managing a diverse workforce, personal growth and stress management, volunteer management, marketing, staff compensation and evaluation, board recruitment and development, and grantwriting.[71] We can easily add to this list, for example by including cultural sensitivity and entrepreneurial skills, both of which are topics receiving a fair amount of attention from writers interested in leadership and capacity building.[72] The NASPAA and NACC standards for nonprofit management programs, discussed in Chapter One and outlined in the Appendix, also provide a sense of what is needed to prepare future leaders.

It is the rare executive director who has a full range of highly developed leadership skills. Effective directors will look for ways to develop needed skills and to empower others who have skills that they are lacking. They can also find ways to mitigate their weaknesses through *substitutes for leadership*. These substitutes are organizational factors that reduce the need for active leadership. For example, a strong organizational culture may carry shared values and norms that shape behaviors and beliefs. Formal policies, rules, and standardized procedures can reduce the need for task-oriented leadership. Professional training and certifications can guide behaviors, making it less necessary for leaders to inspire commitment to high work quality. Nonprofit workers with high self-confidence and competence may feel less need for an emotional connection with and support from a leader than workers do who are unsure of expectations and their own abilities. Highly cohesive teams may find that they can guide and support each other without the help of someone with hierarchical authority over them.

Concluding Thoughts

Executive directors are symbols for their organizations. They need to have a repertoire of styles, perspectives, roles, and behaviors from which to draw depending on the situation. It is their responsibility to share leadership with others to ensure the long-term sustainability of the organization. Effective leadership requires skills in influencing others, either directly or indirectly, and using power wisely. Whether it is fair or not, our human tendency is to hold nonprofit executive directors accountable for everything about their nonprofits' performance, whether praiseworthy or blameworthy. By developing leadership skills in both themselves and potential successors, encouraging shared leadership, and using leadership substitutes, nonprofit executive directors can strengthen their organizations and build sustainability.

In the next chapter we discuss human resource management. All nonprofit leaders, no matter the size of their organization, can benefit from strategically involving individuals to carry out the mission. Human resource management systems and strategies can help with this endeavor.

Questions for Consideration

1. This chapter argues that there are dangers in having a very powerful and dominant executive director. Do you agree with this argument? Why or why not?
2. What are your leadership strengths and weaknesses? In what types of situations do you think you excel as a leader?

Exercises

Exercise 10.1: Leadership Lessons

Interview a nonprofit executive director and ask what lessons he or she has learned about leading a nonprofit. Report back on how this person's leadership lessons fit with the ideas in the chapter.

Exercise 10.2: Leadership Style

Select and watch a video on YouTube featuring an executive director of a nonprofit. What type of leader do you think this person is—transformational, transactional, or both? Were any task-oriented or relationship-oriented leadership behaviors illustrated in the video?

Exercise 10.3: Management and Leadership Tasks

Find a job listing for a nonprofit executive director. What management tasks are described in the ad? What leadership tasks are described? How attractive is this job to you? Which features are most attractive, and which are least attractive?

CHAPTER ELEVEN

STRATEGIC HUMAN RESOURCE MANAGEMENT

*L*iz O'Neill, executive director of Big Brothers Big Sisters: Edmonton & Area (BBBSE), understands the importance of human resources to her organization.[1] In 2010, the nonprofit was able to serve 3,500 children with 2,700 volunteers.[2] To provide effective one-on-one mentoring to children in need and their families, BBBSE puts the right people in the right places to do the right things. Under O'Neill's tenure the organization has thrived. In one year alone, it doubled the number of children served without doubling or overtaxing the BBBSE staff. The continual, demand-driven growth has been managed by careful attention to human resources, participating in a shared services arrangement with other agencies, and building an organizational culture that values paid and volunteer employees and has a strong client and service delivery focus.

O'Neill credits a reinvented human resource management system with being a key factor in the organization's success. BBBSE participated in a pilot program that provided assistance and best-practice advice on all areas of human resource management to executive directors of six nonprofits in the Edmonton area. The directors reviewed their organizations looking for opportunities to increase efficiency without sacrificing quality. During the pilot, O'Neill was able to find ways to partner with other agencies to better meet client needs, and to design a staffing structure that would increase the engagement of employees and the technical and social support given them. She got the encouragement and insight she needed to step back and look at the big picture, rather than focusing only on immediate staff issues. As a result, she streamlined the service delivery process, resulting in financial savings. Some of the savings were used to create new positions for a manager of human resources and a manager of mission effectiveness. Eventually, staff who no longer fit the new delivery approach were let go in a process that gave them support as they looked for other employment. This was a difficult but needed process, as O'Neill describes in a video about the BBBSE.[3]

The more intentional focus on human resources and its integration with other functions has been worth the effort. Volunteer and paid staff retention is high, though the nonprofit struggles to retain individuals with child-care challenges. Workers have a common understanding of what needs to be done and a shared vision of what they want to achieve. They have opportunities to give feedback, voice concerns, participate in the development of new programs, and engage in the annual budgeting and planning process. Local advisory committees and representatives from area agencies contribute their ideas to help BBBSE. Everyone involved with the nonprofit is invited to training sessions to ensure that board members, staff, and volunteers all share a common language. O'Neill continues to work to build capacity in her workforce, in agencies sharing services with BBBSE, and in other Big Brothers Big Sisters chapters.

◆ ◆ ◆

The two previous chapters examined nonprofit boards and executive directors. This chapter focuses on the workers who carry out the operations of the organization, primarily the paid and volunteer staff. Boards and executive directors depend on the capacity of these workers to effectively pursue their nonprofits' missions. Therefore human resource management considerations should be integrated into strategic planning processes, evaluation practices, and decision making on budgets and action plans. O'Neill discovered with BBBSE that taking a proactive and comprehensive approach to human resources, rather than simply reacting to day-to-day staff issues, increased her nonprofit's ability to grow without requiring additional financial resources. Other nonprofits may benefit similarly from looking for ways to improve human resource capacity while taking into account financial constraints, labor supply, and service demands.

In this chapter we define human resource (HR) capacity and strategic HR management. Then we look at how to estimate HR capacity needed for the future. Next, we explain the cycle of involvement for workers, a four-stage model that incorporates basic HR functions and activities, beginning with initial involvement and moving through development, maintenance, and separation. The next chapter will add more information and examples on the topic of influencing worker motivation and performance in the nonprofit sector.

Human Resource Capacity and Human Resource Management

Human resource capacity refers to the abilities, experience, and talent of the people who conduct the work of the organization internally—the board, executive director, paid staff, and volunteers, and for some nonprofits, the members. HR capacity may also incorporate *contingent workers*, those individuals who work for the nonprofit on a nonpermanent basis. Contingent workers include consultants, independent contractors, freelancers, temporary contract workers hired through an external labor firm, student interns, loaned executives, workers paid with government stipends (for example, AmeriCorps VISTA, RSVP, and Peace Corps members), court-assigned community service workers, and welfare recipients required to do community service.

Human resource management refers to the policies and practices in place to mobilize and maximize this capacity. HR management influences the workplace culture and working conditions as well as the skills, knowledge, and abilities that individuals bring to their jobs and that can be developed through training and other means. Strategic HR management provides managers with tools and techniques to motivate their workers and to reduce risks for the workers, the organization, and those served. For example, it can enforce reward systems that are fair and ensure that worker safety and any rights to dispute resolution are protected.

If the nonprofit's current HR capacity does not match its current or projected HR needs, then new individuals need to be started on the cycle of involvement or current workers' abilities need to be developed and better leveraged so service demands can be met with the existing workforce. Key questions are: Which tasks should be contracted out and which performed in-house? and, What types of workers should be recruited for the tasks—for example, should they be paid or volunteer? In cases where resources are severely constrained—due to the loss of a large grant, for example—a nonprofit may have to scale back its HR capacity. Key questions then are: How, if at all, can capacity be maintained at less cost? or, What type of HR capacity should be let go if a shortage in at least one skill, knowledge, or ability area is unavoidable? BBBSE offers us an example of how a review of HR capacity and HR management gave its executive director the idea that she could serve more clients with the same number of volunteers within the existing budget, but only if the volunteers were better supported through a new HR director position and redesign of the service delivery system.

Assessing Current HR Capacity

To assess HR capacity, nonprofit leaders need a clear understanding of what current workers are able and willing to do. A simple way to evaluate a nonprofit's current HR capacity is to list the main tasks that need to be done in the organization and match each task to the abilities required to perform it. The next step is to conduct an *abilities inventory*. This inventory captures the abilities that workers are or could be demonstrating. The abilities may be recognizable from a review of job descriptions for filled positions as well as from individual worker characteristics such as education obtained, certificates and licenses earned, work experience (volunteer and paid), hobbies, and demonstrated abilities such as foreign language skills.

Even when workers have the ability, they may not be willing to perform particular tasks. Performance assessments, worker surveys, individualized development plans, and personal interviews can help to determine whether a person is ready and motivated to take on different responsibilities. Additional training or mentoring may be required to increase confidence and competency with particular work tasks. Motivational tools may be helpful in increasing the desire to perform assigned tasks well.

An HR matrix can capture gaps between current and desired HR capabilities. Tasks that need to be completed to achieve the nonprofit's mission are identified on the vertical axis, and available workers are listed on the horizontal axis. Information can be entered for each individual to indicate the abilities they currently have that relate to the task needs, as well as their available time for the desired task activity. The matrix can also show the abilities each individual could be asked to develop based on readiness and time available, and how those potential abilities match tasks that need to be assigned. At BBBSE, O'Neill's assessment of current HR capacity revealed that no one had adequate time or skills to strategically coordinate and support the volunteers and thus that the hiring of a manager of human resources was justified.

Forecasting Demand for Services

A variety of internal and external factors may influence future demands for services and thus the HR capacity and HR management that will be needed. Typically, only large, well-resourced nonprofits have the time and dollars to conduct sophisticated forecasting of demands for services. However, even the smallest nonprofits can track when their services are being used and determine whether demand is exceeding what can be made available given current HR capacity. By collecting data on services delivered and waiting lists, patterns may be identified that explain peak and low demand times through the year as well as longer-term trends.

All nonprofits can look for environmental changes that may lead to significant increases or decreases in service demand. Simple scans of mass media and industry-specific reports can reveal external conditions likely to affect service demands, such as the forthcoming closure of an agency that will result in its clients searching for new service providers. Questionnaires can be used to see if current clients plan to return for more services. The Internet can be used to find reports on immigration and other trends affecting the geographical community served. What follows is a sampling of factors that can affect service demand. We encourage nonprofits to look for additional factors that are important in their specific context.

Economic Conditions

Economic conditions are a key driver of demand for many nonprofit services and the size of the available labor pool. For example, as unemployment rises, demands on nonprofits that provide food, shelter, and job hunting services rise. When unemployment is low, nonprofits may need to pay more to compete with other employers for the most qualified workers and may find it more difficult to attract volunteers from a reduced supply. Some federal government data point to great resilience in the nonprofit sector in the United States, despite recessions. One study states that total nonprofit sector employment grew by 8.8 percent from 2009 to 2010, a period with staggering job losses in the private business sector. There was greater need for services offered through nonprofits and funding available to increase HR capacity. Laid-off workers added to the pool of potential paid employees and volunteers available to nonprofits. Only one category of nonprofits, those with fewer than ten employees, showed a drop in employment. For nonprofit health care organizations with over a thousand employees, employment was up 16.7 percent,[4] due at least partially to the influx of government economic recovery funds.[5]

Population and Demographic Shifts

In areas facing population and demographic shifts, nonprofits may discover that their current HR capacity either exceeds or is insufficient for the projected demand for their services. If they have excess capacity, they may respond by either reducing the workforce or expanding their service area or mission. In the Washington, D.C., area, for example, nonprofits serving low-income immigrants shifted their HR capacity to reach those in need in surrounding counties, moving their focus away from the area near their home offices, where the greatest need once existed but where now there are few low-income immigrants.[6] Demographic shifts can also change the abilities workers need to have. For example, in a community with an influx of immigrants with limited English language skills, local nonprofits may seek bilingual staff who can serve this group.

Realization of Mission

Some nonprofits are fortunate to see the need for their services decline because they or others have been successful in resolving the problem they were founded to address. For example, once polio prevention measures were in place, the March of Dimes needed to figure out what to do with its excess HR capacity. Other nonprofits find that mission success leads to greater not lesser demand. Nonprofits that offer well-received artistic performances may find that future shows are sold out. Nonprofits that improve understanding and reduce the stigma of an addiction, such as gambling, or a disease, such as mental illness, may find, as they desired, that more individuals seek treatment services.

Natural Environment

Some nonprofits' service demands change with conditions in the natural environment. For example, extreme temperatures, storms, and natural disasters can leave individuals in need of services for shelter. Emergency rooms and health clinics experience demands for different types of health services based on time of day and season.

Other Actors in the Service Network

A nonprofit's service demands are likely to shift when other organizations start, expand, or end the same or similar services. Marketing and awareness campaigns by organizations that complement or compete with a nonprofit may change demand for the nonprofit's services. A public information campaign by government to encourage exercise and better nutrition, for example, may have ripple effects on demands for recreational facilities, community gardens, health clinics, and other nonprofit services tied to health-related behaviors.

External Funding and Government Reimbursement Policies

As discussed in Chapters Six and Fourteen, the government may determine which organizations are approved providers of services. Government agencies may also dictate what quantity of service a nonprofit must make available if it receives government funding. The geographical and demographic scope of a nonprofit's service provision may also be set by a funding source. The availability of government grants and reimbursements to a potential client may influence whether or not services are affordable and therefore pursued, as well as the type of professional qualifications providers must have for the client to take advantage of the government funding.

Technological and Cultural Shifts

New technologies and public attitudes can affect demand. Some nonprofits' approaches can become outmoded while others come into fashion. For example, younger generations tend to prefer to get a nonprofit's information from its Web site rather than in personal meetings. Forms can be completed online and data sets automatically updated, reducing the demand for staff time. Additional examples are that innovative medical interventions are reducing the need for major surgery and universities are finding a greater interest among students in distance learning over traditional courses, changing HR capacity needs.

Forecasting HR Capacity Needs

Once a nonprofit has a sense of its current HR capacity and likely changes in demands for services, it can better predict its future HR capacity needs. Key questions to be answered are

- What skills and knowledge will be needed to meet our strategic goals?
- What kinds of workers and how many of them are needed to fulfill the various needs?

- What new jobs will be needed, and what existing jobs will no longer be needed?
- Can our current workforce fill the needed jobs?
- How successful are we likely to be in retaining current workers?
- What do we need to do to develop workers for these jobs?
- Do we have enough managers and trainers to develop and support the workers?
- Are our current HR resources and practices adequate for future needs?

HR capacity-building decisions should be informed by an understanding of what each type of worker is likely to be able to provide and what resources will be needed to manage different types of workers. For example, BBBSE relies heavily on volunteers. A nationwide study by Big Brothers Big Sisters showed that what mattered to the children was that they had a caring adult in their lives, not the activities they did with the person matched to them.[7] If these adults were paid to be caring, they likely would not have as much impact. The children know that the adults matched to them are volunteers; this reinforces the idea that they care.

Most volunteers work within the nonprofit sector, and some nonprofits rely completely on volunteer labor.[8] Volunteers and paid staff can differ in how they enhance the capacity of a nonprofit. A variety of studies have examined how values and norms affect decisions about the use of volunteers versus paid employees. For example, Donileen Loseke found considerable ambivalence about using paid workers in a domestic violence shelter.[9] Paid employees can be seen as incongruent in self-help and self-empowerment programs that foster peer-to-peer support networks. Use of paid workers in nonprofits may also be seen as undermining the idea that nonprofit work reflects an altruistic calling and supporting the idea that work in a nonprofit should be treated as an instrumentally rewarding career. Economic formulas are inadequate for calculating the costs and benefits of using volunteers versus paid staff. Many nonprofits use volunteers despite the lack of obvious economic benefit,[10] but there is evidence that the demand for volunteers is influenced by calculations of volunteer productivity, outputs, and economic cost.[11] This suggests that, as Woods Bowman concludes, volunteers are not simply replacements for paid workers.[12]

The Cycle of Involvement

Effective human resource management has multiple activities. These activities can be categorized by their place in the cycle of involvement. As shown in Exhibit 11.1, the activities in the cycle fit into four stages: initial involvement, development, maintenance, and separation.

EXHIBIT 11.1. CYCLE OF INVOLVEMENT FOR PAID AND VOLUNTEER EMPLOYEES

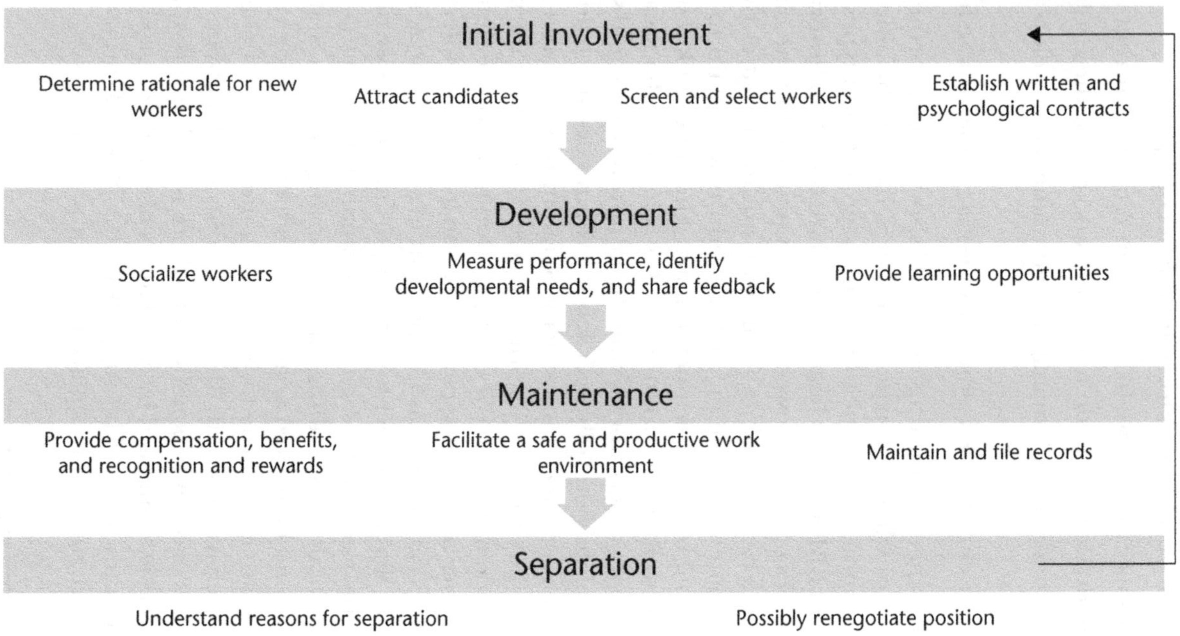

Initial Involvement
- Determine rationale for new workers
- Attract candidates
- Screen and select workers
- Establish written and psychological contracts

Development
- Socialize workers
- Measure performance, identify developmental needs, and share feedback
- Provide learning opportunities

Maintenance
- Provide compensation, benefits, and recognition and rewards
- Facilitate a safe and productive work environment
- Maintain and file records

Separation
- Understand reasons for separation
- Possibly renegotiate position

Stage 1: Initial Involvement

The initial involvement stage includes four activities: determining the rationale for new workers, attracting candidates, screening and selecting new workers, and establishing written and psychological contracts.

Determine Rationale for New Workers

At the initial involvement stage the rationale for involving new workers should be determined and clearly articulated. This requires a thorough understanding of the mission, goals, strategies, and structure of the nonprofit—topics we discussed in previous chapters. When explaining why more workers are needed, nonprofit leaders should be able to clearly link the HR needs to the organization's mission and plan. At BBBSE, for example, Liz O'Neill justified hiring a manager of human resources because past experience demonstrated that without permanent staff to provide continuity, insufficient attention was likely to be given to HR issues. She also recognized that there was unmet demand that could be handled if someone were available to better leverage the volunteers' time. Fortunately, due to costs saved with the redesign of the service delivery process, BBBSE was able to add the position without increasing the budget.

The argument for filling the new position with a volunteer, paid staff member, student intern, or contracted temporary worker should be integrated into the rationale for the position. Even when funding might be available to hire paid staff, there may be good reasons for choosing another type of worker. Jeffrey Brudney offers numerous reasons for choosing a volunteer over a paid staff member, including cost effectiveness, improved ability to obtain external grants, enhanced community access, better connections with clients, and fundraising benefits.[13] If the rationale for using a volunteer instead of a paid staff member is that the volunteer will be better able than a paid professional to establish a peer-to-peer relationship with a client, then relevant characteristics of the clients should determine the type of volunteer sought. For example, survivors of domestic abuse may work best as volunteers with battered women seeking shelter. If it is argued that volunteers are better fundraisers than paid staff for major gifts, then those who are more comfortable in this fundraising role and who have personally made a financial gift to the nonprofit should be sought.

Nonprofits may be able to significantly increase their HR capacity by outsourcing tasks to consulting firms or using other types of temporary contingent work relationships. Consultants, temporary labor firms, loaned executives, student interns, stipended workers such as AmeriCorps VISTA or Peace Corps personnel, and other types of workers who can handle short-term or specialized assignments for the nonprofit can increase the nonprofit's capacity without adding permanent paid employees or volunteers. A benefit is that the nonprofit does not need to offer insurance and retirement benefits to these types of workers. It also does not need to worry about these workers expecting advancement opportunities in the nonprofit, although the workers may be informally evaluated for their potential for permanent positions. Use of temporary or contingent work relationships is popular in the United States[14] and is likely to grow in the nonprofit sector.[15] Scholars in other countries have also noted the contributions of this type of labor to the nonprofit sector.[16] Research indicates that HR professionals who provide pro bono work to nonprofits, such as Eldon Emerson, who advised Liz O'Neill of BBBSE as part of the pilot program described in the opening case, are an especially valuable resource and their ranks are growing.[17]

Attract Candidates

The initial involvement stage may also involve attracting potential new workers to the nonprofit. Though it is usually easier and more cost effective to retain and retrain workers than to recruit new ones, it is not always possible. Individuals can be promoted, demoted, or moved laterally to new positions within an organization in response to capacity needs. However, at times an inadequate HR capacity may make it impossible to draw only from the current workforce. In addition, contracts, union rules, government regulations, and employment policies may prevent changing a current employee's responsibilities.

To recruit new workers, a first step is to consider the characteristics needed for the position and the types of individuals who are likely to have those characteristics. Rather than taking a scattergun approach where the nonprofit broadly promotes the opportunity and invites anyone interested to apply, it may be more cost effective and less frustrating for everyone involved if the nonprofit adopts a more targeted appeal so that applicants better fit its needs. If the job requires certain skills, credentials, and time availability, that can be made clear. Written *job descriptions* should be used to determine which qualifications and commitments are required and which are preferred. Essential elements of job descriptions for both volunteers and paid employees are the following:

- Job title
- Supervisor's title and contact information
- General description of position, including responsibilities and duties
- Overview of task assignments and their connection to the nonprofit's mission

- Qualifications required and qualifications desired
- Assessments and training needed (for example, criminal background check, confidentiality agreement, health assessment, and required orientation and training participation)
- Time commitment
- Benefits (tangible and intangible)

There are numerous mechanisms for finding individuals suited to nonprofit work positions.[18] Searches outside the organization may involve print advertisements, radio and television promotions, Web site postings, social media communications, placement agencies, executive recruiters, professional search firms, career centers on university and college campuses, internship program listings, executive loan programs of corporations, government placement programs, announcements in newsletters of professional and trade associations, and volunteer centers. Nonprofits can also seek referrals from staff, boards, other agencies, and clients. Word-of-mouth advertising is often effective because current workers can recruit individuals from their professional and personal circles and share stories of what it is like to work at the nonprofit.[19] Another recruitment mechanism may be labor unions. Though union members are not common in most of the nonprofit sector, when they are needed the appropriate trade union may be critical in finding these qualified workers.[20]

When identifying appropriate methods for soliciting potential workers, nonprofits can benefit from thinking broadly. Demographic and generational shifts in labor pools and greater competition for workers as Baby Boomers retire suggest that nonprofits will need to be increasingly attentive to the need to create a welcoming and supportive environment for workers with diverse backgrounds and interests. One of the risks of relying primarily on word-of-mouth advertising is that the pool of candidates identified is likely to be less diverse than it would be if multiple methods of advertising were used to attract potential workers. There are few studies comparing discrimination across sectors, but what is available suggests that there may be less discrimination affecting wages and other work aspects in the nonprofit sector than in other sectors.[21] Still, when nonprofit staff draw job candidates from their personal networks rather than through more broad-based advertisements, they are likely to attract individuals who are more rather than less similar to them. This can initiate a negative spiral—the more a nonprofit lacks diversity, the more difficult it may be to attract diverse candidates. Those who do consider working for the nonprofit may see it as an organization for people of a certain age, ethnicity, gender, or other easily observable characteristic. In recruitment strategies, nonprofits should also consider how disabilities may be accommodated so that lack of such accommodation does not prevent the nonprofit from having the best candidates for positions.

No matter whether a nonprofit is seeking a paid employee or a volunteer, it is important to find people with a good fit to the characteristics of the job and the organization's culture, norms, and values.[22] Workers with a good fit are most likely to demonstrate high performance, satisfaction, and commitment. Simply believing in the nonprofit's mission is not enough to ensure a good fit. Nonprofits should offer realistic previews of the job, work atmosphere, and organizational culture. Individuals who have more accurate information are better at selecting a work setting that will keep them motivated and committed. For example, someone who wants to work to help children in a youth-serving agency may not apply for an advertised position if he understands that the responsibilities will involve little contact with children. Someone who is concerned about career advancement may recognize that a job is not a good fit if she understands that it offers few opportunities to demonstrate leadership abilities.

It is perhaps obvious that nonprofits should seek individuals who are qualified to perform a job at the desired level or who can be trained to meet the standards for the position. However, some nonprofit leaders may engage in nepotism or feel that they need to hire unqualified individuals recommended by their donors. To understand the qualifications for the position, the nonprofit may perform a job analysis to determine what is required for effective performance. The desired KSAs (knowledge, skills, and abilities) can be written into a job description and noted in position announcements to help in the attraction and screening of candidates and, ultimately, to be used in performance appraisals.[23]

One of the special challenges for nonprofits is to carefully manage the volunteer recruitment process. Having more individuals on the volunteer list than can actually be employed is problematic. The volunteers may feel disappointed not to be called to action or may feel that they are not given meaningful work because there are too many volunteers. Having backup support can be useful but can result in workers called in and then left with no worthwhile tasks to perform. Volunteers can be frustrated when they expect to perform tasks at the core of the mission but are assigned administrative or other types of tasks that are peripheral even though necessary for accomplishment of the mission. Although their idealism may have driven them to work for the nonprofit, it is unlikely to sustain them if they see their tasks as not meaningful because they are not exposed to direct mission outcomes. Though it may be tempting to amass a long list of individuals who wish to volunteer, recruiters should be careful to be honest about what work opportunities truly exist.

Crowdsourcing, outsourcing a task to a large group in an open call for assistance, typically over the Web, is a relatively new approach to increasing capacity, but nonprofits have been experimenting with it.[24] Netsquared.org used crowdsourcing to find a new logo through an online design contest. A New York public radio show used listeners as researchers and citizen reporters. HopeLab asked the kids it was trying to reach to come up with ideas for increasing physical activity. Some may say that crowdsourcing is just an alternative method for finding and using volunteers, but typically it is for a short-term, one-task engagement. With crowdsourcing, there is little investment in the activities of the cycle of involvement, in contrast to what we encourage for more committed volunteer or paid workers who want to contribute to the mission on a longer-term basis and be more integrated into the nonprofit.

Screen and Select Workers

Screening and selection processes for workers vary in their formality and value. Though interviews are a popular means for screening a pool of candidates, research shows they are not that useful in predicting job performance. They can convey information for judging whether there is likely to be a good fit and clearing up misconceptions about the job and organization. Checking references can also be misleading, given that some reference providers limit the information they provide due to fear of lawsuits or other reasons. Still, references can be useful in verifying facts and providing examples of observed and recorded behaviors, such as unexcused absences, public speaking experiences, and success in meeting deadlines. Licenses to practice and educational degrees should be checked to ensure that a job candidate does have needed credentials. In some cases, criminal background checks are legally required, for example, when the prospective worker will have close contact with youth.

Nonprofits should have systems in place to ensure legal compliance in the selection process. Paid employment in the nonprofit sector is subject to the same set of rules as employment in for-profits. For example, in the United States, Title VII specifically prohibits employment discrimination based on race, skin color, religion, sex, and national origin. Other Acts address other forms of illegal discrimination, such as discrimination owing to age or pregnancy. Immigration laws establish hiring limitations for noncitizens. Though the use of volunteers is not as regulated as the use of paid workers, there are still legal guidelines that should be followed for volunteer screening and selection to avoid claims of negligent hiring if the volunteer should happen to do harm. For some work assignments, background checks need to be run on volunteers as well as paid employees. In addition to addressing hiring practices and eligibility, laws affect what contract provisions can be offered, such as wages, hours, leave benefits, safety, and insurance coverage. For additional information, nonprofits can consult the Web sites of such government agencies as the Department of Labor and the Internal Revenue Service's tax-exempt division, and also state and local government Web sites.

Establish Written and Psychological Contracts

Before a mutual decision to enter into a working relationship is made, it is important that the initial responsibilities of the position and related performance expectations are clearly understood by both parties. Although the tasks and objectives associated with the position should be aligned with the nonprofit's mission, a variety of different work arrangements can be designed, depending on the needs of the organization and the prospective worker. For example, workers may split time across organizations. For some situations, the nonprofit may need to negotiate how the same job can be shared by more than one worker. At the initial involvement stage, work times and sharing policies should be coordinated and agreed to by the worker and the nonprofit.

Once choices are made about which persons to bring into the organization as new workers, any required permissions must be obtained as part of the contracting process. Nonprofits should be clear on who is legally required to be treated as a paid employee and who is a contract worker and then file the appropriate paperwork. In the United States, the Internal Revenue Service provides resources for classifying workers and determining the appropriate information to file (www.irs.gov). Sometimes, special permissions are required. Nonprofits seeking to hire temporary foreign professionals on H-1B visas are subject to wage rules and must demonstrate inadequate domestic labor supplies in formal requests for H-1B hires.[25] For youth workers, permissions should be obtained from a parent or legal guardian. Internship and loaned executive arrangements may require special paperwork.

With paid employees, deciding on compensation can be tricky. Wage surveys can be used to find averages for different types of nonprofit positions in different parts of the country and for nonprofits with different types of missions and budget sizes. Going outside these norms may result in criticism. Many nonprofits can be found that were attacked by the press and the public for overcompensating workers. For example, for months in 2008 the board of the United Way of Central Carolinas defended its $1.2 million pay package to its executive director but eventually unanimously asked the longtime director to resign or be fired in response to community pressure.[26] This nonprofit is not alone in originally seeing no wrong in a pay package and then backing down in the face of public outcry or a government investigation. In 2011, the board of the Young Adult Institute, a nonprofit serving people with developmental disabilities, took action to remediate the nearly $1 million pay packages it gave to its former executive director and other high-level executives.[27] Additional examples can easily be found.

Although a written contract may provide information about the tasks and performance expectations of a position as well as information about any compensation or benefits the worker will receive, it is unlikely that any written contract will be extensive enough to incorporate all of the expectations that the nonprofit has for the worker or that the worker has for the organization. Research has shown that whenever an individual agrees to work for an organization, in addition to any explicit legal contract, an implicit *psychological contract* comes into play that captures that individual's perceptions of the obligations he has to the organization and the obligations the organization has to him.[28] These psychological contracts exist for all types of workers.[29] When a formal written contract does not exist, the psychological contract may gain importance in capturing perceptions of mutual obligations. If a worker perceives a breach in the psychological contract—for example, not being given training that was expected or being passed over for a promotion—possible consequences include reductions in satisfaction, productivity, and desire to continue with the nonprofit.

A manager can make an effort to avoid psychological contract breaches by encouraging prospective and new workers to reveal their understanding of reciprocal obligations. If any of the perceived obligations cannot be honored, the manager can explain this and potentially mitigate any negative consequences. For example, a manager can explain to a prospective volunteer who might be expecting to use volunteer work as an entry to paid work that even if she does a great job it is unlikely that she can be hired into a paid employment position.

Instead of using internal workers, nonprofits may outsource tasks to business firms or other nonprofits, minimizing the demands of later stages of the cycle of involvement but making the contracting stage particularly critical in dictating the work arrangement. When outsourcing tasks, nonprofits need to be attuned to any laws prohibiting them from contracting with individuals or firms associated with their board members or paid staff. The use of a competitive bidding process can help in avoiding accusations of giving some individuals or firms an unfair advantage in obtaining a contract.

Stage 2: Development

The development stage involves helping workers to define themselves as part of a nonprofit and to hone the skills, knowledge, and abilities to perform effectively. Basic development activities, which can be repeated throughout an individual's time with a nonprofit, include socializing, measuring performance, identifying developmental needs, sharing feedback, and providing learning opportunities.

Socialize Workers

Early in the socialization process, as one task in a performance management system, workers need to be given a clear understanding of their job responsibilities and performance expectations.[30] Creating an explicit performance plan with workers helps to align their activities with the organizational mission and provides the foundation for future performance evaluations. The socialization process should also reinforce values in the organizational culture. For example, many organizations make valuing diversity part of their mission and recognize the importance of creating and sustaining a culture that is supportive for all members of a diverse workforce. Thus socialization activities should be inclusive and should encourage workers to embrace their own individuality as well as the individuality of others. A nonprofit's cultural values may be explicitly shared with new workers through orientation materials, welcoming speeches, and other communications that make clear the ethical foundation and operating principles for the organization.

Over time, individuals are socialized to their new roles. Workers engaging with a nonprofit for the first time as well as workers who are transferred or promoted to a new position have the status of outsiders until they are accepted by those in their work unit. In the development stage they gain what they need to be productive workers, and learn the values and norms of their work unit. John Wanous, Arnon Reichers, and S. D. Malik offer a four-stage integrative approach to socialization (see Figure 11.1).[31] The time it takes to go through the stages will vary by individual, job, and organization. It is important for managers to recognize that workers need time to understand and accept organizational realities, be clear on their role, see how they fit into the larger organization, and feel successfully integrated. Orientations, introductions to fellow workers, mentoring programs, tours, team-based assignments, and briefings can speed up the socialization process. Each of these activities gives workers opportunities to engage with coworkers, ask questions about the nonprofit, and observe other workers.

Eventually, a worker may come to identify himself with the nonprofit. His self-image may be tied to his role and involvement in the organization. This is sometimes the case with founders. They may find it hard to leave their nonprofit or see it change from what they created. They may feel a loss of themselves as the nonprofit transforms and may leave them behind. Other highly socialized workers may also feel their personal identity threatened by the loss of a founder. Understanding this socialization dynamic can help in managing transitions from a founder to a new leader. There may be a grieving process, and workers may need time to alter their self-image to fit with the reality of the changed nonprofit. New rituals and interpersonal relations will take time to develop and become the new norm.

FIGURE 11.1. SOCIALIZATION OF WORKERS

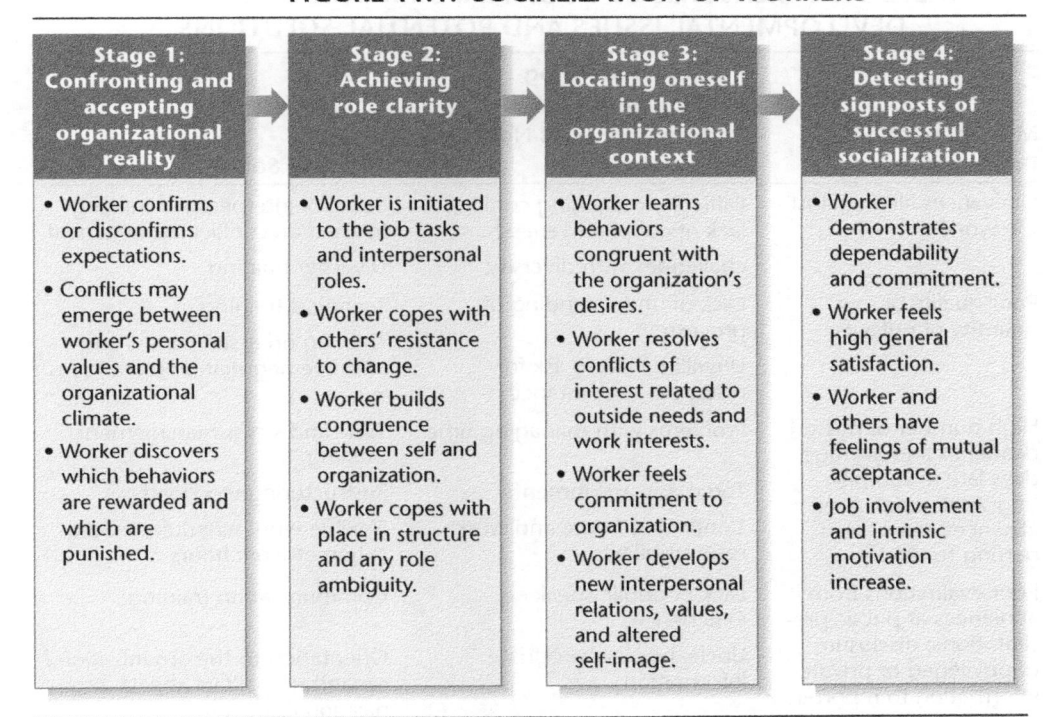

Stage 1: Confronting and accepting organizational reality	Stage 2: Achieving role clarity	Stage 3: Locating oneself in the organizational context	Stage 4: Detecting signposts of successful socialization
• Worker confirms or disconfirms expectations. • Conflicts may emerge between worker's personal values and the organizational climate. • Worker discovers which behaviors are rewarded and which are punished.	• Worker is initiated to the job tasks and interpersonal roles. • Worker copes with others' resistance to change. • Worker builds congruence between self and organization. • Worker copes with place in structure and any role ambiguity.	• Worker learns behaviors congruent with the organization's desires. • Worker resolves conflicts of interest related to outside needs and work interests. • Worker feels commitment to organization. • Worker develops new interpersonal relations, values, and altered self-image.	• Worker demonstrates dependability and commitment. • Worker feels high general satisfaction. • Worker and others have feelings of mutual acceptance. • Job involvement and intrinsic motivation increase.

Source: Adapted from John P. Wanous, Arnon E. Reichers, and S. D. Malik, "Organization Socialization and Group Development Toward an Integrative Perspective," *Academy of Management Review* 9 (1984): 674.

Measure Performance, Identify Developmental Needs, and Share Feedback

It is the rare worker whose performance is excellent starting with the first day on the job. Even those performing simple tasks are likely to need to figure out where to get needed supplies, when rest breaks are appropriate, and what their coworkers are like. Identification of any developmental needs may come from the workers themselves, supervisors, peers, mentors, or others aware of performance weaknesses, such as clients.

A variety of tools can help with measuring performance, identifying developmental needs, and sharing feedback. Some of the most common tools are performance appraisals, self-evaluations, benchmarking, balanced scorecards, outcome measurement, peer reviews,[32] and career counseling. Quality improvement systems in nonprofits can also provide workers with performance data and set them on a path of continuous improvement.[33] Using specific behavioral measures that are tied to a worker's performance objectives, rather than making general observations, can pinpoint what, if anything, the worker needs to change going forward. Table 11.1 gives some examples of performance measures that can be used, some developmental

TABLE 11.1. MEASURES OF POOR PERFORMANCE UNDERLYING DEVELOPMENTAL ISSUES AND POTENTIAL SOLUTIONS

Measures of Poor Performance	Possible Underlying Developmental Issues If Performance Does Not Meet Expectations	Potential Solutions
Grievances filed against the worker	Difficulty managing conflict; lack of cooperativeness;	Social or interpersonal training focused on conflict management
	challenges with diversity	Diversity training
Poor quality or low quantity of outputs	Lack of understanding of processes	Technical training
	Unwillingness to ask for resources or assistance	Training on assertiveness and effective negotiation techniques
High number of missed deadlines and average days late in submitting work; unexcused absences; lateness in getting to work	Problems with managing time	Time and stress management training
	Too many assignments	Restructuring workload
	Conflicting home and work responsibilities	Flexible work schedule; modification of work hours
Poor evaluations from audiences at public presentations; disclosure of privileged or private information to reporters or others	Lack of public speaking experience	Communication training
	Unclear or inappropriate information	Orientation to the organization, organizational fact sheets, organizational spokesperson
	Lack of organization-wide communication plan and crisis management procedures	Guidance on privacy laws and organizational procedures

Source: Adapted from John P. Wanous, Arnon E. Reichers, and S. D. Malik, "Organization Socialization and Group Development: Toward an Integrative Perspective," *Academy of Management Review* 9 (1984).

issues that may be responsible for poor performance, and some potential solutions to help the worker improve.

Poor performance may not be the fault of the worker. Influences on performance will be discussed in more detail in the next chapter. In brief: unclear division of labor, conflicting objectives, lack of resources, and other organizational factors may result in poor performance. It is important to identify the root cause of poor performance before determining a solution. Holding a performance review meeting provides an opportunity for discussion with the worker to identify the most appropriate developmental activities to improve future performance, based on the root cause of the problem.

Of course the level of investment in performance objective setting, performance review, and feedback has to be justified by the likely benefits. For some short-term work engagements, these processes are unlikely to be worth much time or effort. Still, there may be some opportunity to provide useful feedback to the worker and to consider how the next engagement of this nature can be more productive for the nonprofit and whoever is involved. For example, a nonprofit leader who is disappointed or pleased with the quality of a student work project should inform the students and the supervising faculty member of that conclusion. Perhaps changes could be made for future assignments to bring more benefits to all involved.

Research suggests that performance evaluation is one of the most uniformly disliked organizational processes,[34] and it is often viewed as having little benefit for the organization, the manager, or the employee.[35] Performance evaluation often is assumed to be a negative process, focused on finding fault and assigning blame. A good performance evaluation system, however, might be better described as providing a process for celebrating past successes and identifying opportunities for future growth. This reframing of the performance evaluation process does not mean that performance problems are ignored—both negative and positive variances between actual and desired performance need to be addressed. The focus, however, is not on punishing poor past performance but on facilitating excellent future performance.

To help set the right tone in a feedback meeting, it is best for the manager to start out with positive behaviors and performance outcomes. After celebrating these successes, asking the worker to identify areas that she would like to improve on and inquiring about what the manager could do to help her be more successful are also helpful for maintaining a positive, collaborative tone. Managers should keep in mind that the main goal of the feedback discussion is to come up with an action plan that will benefit the organization and the worker. That action plan may include making some organizational changes (for example, revising the service delivery process to streamline the work required) and some modifications to managerial behaviors (for example, providing more explicit directions when giving assignments) as well as providing some developmental opportunities for the worker. In keeping with the positive tone set at the beginning of the performance evaluation meeting, the developmental opportunities identified should reflect the interests of the worker as well as the needs of the organization.

Provide Learning Opportunities
Most individuals are motivated by the desire to improve themselves. This is discussed in more detail in the next chapter. What is relevant here is that HR management should incorporate learning opportunities for workers. These opportunities can take a variety of forms. Coaching, counseling, mentoring, and training can all be used as interventions to improve performance and keep motivation high. *Coaching* tends to focus on developing abilities

whereas counseling focuses on changing attitudes. Coaches share advice and information and help in setting standards and goals. In *counseling*, workers recognize problems and come up with solutions. Both coaching and counseling can be effective when workers are ready to change, are nondefensive, and feel supported rather than offended by the intervention. *Mentoring* involves matching a senior worker with a junior one. The senior worker can serve as a role model and can facilitate the junior worker's development by offering advice, making useful introductions, and providing opportunities for the junior worker to participate on important projects. *Training* tends to focus on addressing needs for task-related knowledge and skills.

Coaching may be especially helpful for executive directors when they come into their position without much preparation and do not have an adequate peer support network. CompassPoint found that within six months of a coaching program for nonprofit executives, these leaders displayed improvements in their communication with staff, stronger leadership abilities, and greater self-confidence. The coaching was also positively correlated with retention.[36] Positive results were also reported by Robert Fischer and David Beimers in their review of a pilot coaching program for nonprofit executives.[37]

For many workers, job changes may satisfy developmental interests. *Job rotation* involves rotating workers among jobs at the same organizational level. This allows them to use different skills and gives them exposure to multiple aspects of the nonprofit. For example, interns at a hospital may change departments in order to get a better sense of their work preferences and a broader picture of how the departments interact. *Job enlargement* involves adding tasks to a job to make it more complex and meaningful. For example, workers may be asked not only to stuff envelopes for a fundraising solicitation but also to keep track of donations received and to send thank-you letters, helping them to see the results of their envelope-stuffing efforts. *Job enrichment* involves giving workers more responsibility and decision-making authority. Workers may be asked to plan and prioritize their tasks, allocate resources to and implement the tasks, evaluate the outcomes, and decide whether to continue with the tasks. For example, as part of a job enrichment program, a worker involved in processing fundraising mail solicitations may be asked to decide the frequency of the mailings and to provide input on the content of the solicitation letters.

Stage 3: Maintenance

The maintenance stage of involvement includes the many routine human resource activities that facilitate the ongoing work relationship. Examples of these activities are providing compensation and benefits, recognizing and rewarding workers, facilitating a productive and safe work environment, and keeping records and submitting paperwork.

Provide Compensation, Benefits, and Recognition and Rewards

Workers need to be compensated according to contractual agreements. Compensation schemes vary widely in the nonprofit sector, but concerns that the sector does not offer living wages are generally unfounded for nonprofits with paid full-time employees. For some jobs, nonprofits may even pay better than employers in the government and for-profit sectors do. Laura Leete offers a variety of explanations for why pay in the nonprofit sector may be lower or higher than pay in other sectors for the same jobs.[38] One explanation for lower pay is that nonprofit workers are willing to accept it because they derive well-being or can pursue their ideological goals from their participation in the nonprofit. They may also accept lower pay because they do not think that the nonprofit enterprise is using them to make a profit. Another explanation is that differences in pay are due to differences in the size and resources of the employer and are not related to whether or not it is a nonprofit. An explanation for why nonprofit salaries and wages are sometimes higher than those for the same jobs in another sector is that the nonprofit has the benefit of lower taxes, fewer regulatory costs, and lack of profit-maximizing pressures, all of which can lead to having more resources to devote to compensating workers.

Many organizations provide nonprofit salary information that can be considered in setting appropriate pay. Examples of salary information providers searchable on the Internet are salary.com, GuideStar Nonprofit Services (for information on top executive salaries), Professionals for Nonprofits, Charity Navigator, and payscale.com. The *Philanthropy Journal* offers links to a variety of 2010 nonprofit salary reports.[39] A review of the reports demonstrates that average salaries depend not only on job title but also on mission, location, budget size, and the methodology of the salary study.

Formal and informal acknowledgments of performance and intrinsic and extrinsic rewards are part of maintaining involvement. Whether serving in a paid or volunteer capacity, workers are likely to appreciate being treated in a manner that shows their contributions are valued and promises made to them are being honored. For paid employees there is clear evidence that how they are treated affects organizational performance and worker well-being. Anna Haley-Lock and Jean Kruzich list studies demonstrating that nonprofits offering more generous and flexible benefits have higher worker retention, job performance, and worker satisfaction, whereas employee dissatisfaction, burnout, and turnover are more common in nonprofits with low pay, irregular work hours, and limited insurance and retirement pensions.[40] Studies do not find consistent differences in benefits between the nonprofit and other sectors but do provide evidence of wide variation in what benefits are offered for similar positions.[41] In the next chapter we discuss ways to show workers that they are appreciated.

Recognition opportunities are countless, from a simple verbal expression of thanks to performance bonuses, volunteer of the year celebrations, and other awards and rewards that require an investment in recording performance information and producing fair evaluations.

Facilitating a Safe and Productive Work Environment

The maintenance stage also involves facilitating a safe and productive work environment. For example, in the United States, work conditions should conform to the standards and rules outlined in the Occupational Safety and Health Administration (OSHA) Act. Accommodations may need to be made for workers with disabilities, as outlined in the Americans with Disabilities Act (ADA). All workers should be protected from harassment by coworkers as well as by other individuals who interact with the organization, including clients and board members. Workers should be given the resources needed to perform their jobs. A work culture should be established that promotes ethical standards and the values of the organization. One challenge that volunteers and contingent workers who are being paid by other organizations may face is that they may be wrongly perceived as being cost free and thus may not be given what they need to perform well. They should be given office space, access to other workers, training opportunities, supplies, performance feedback, and other needed resources.

Maintain and File Records

Nonprofits should keep appropriate records for each worker. This should be done not just to meet legal requirements but also to track information useful for understanding HR capacity and providing performance feedback. Certain employment information such as health checks and Social Security numbers should be kept private and protected to avoid identity theft and violations of privacy.

Robert Mathis and John Jackson offer a list of ratios that may be helpful in identifying HR potential problem areas.[42] For example, it is useful to know how long it typically takes to fill certain types of job vacancies and recruitment costs per applicant hired. This may help nonprofits in judging the value of different types of job advertising options and may also provide information on the likely necessity of adjusting others' work assignments to cover important tasks until a position is filled. It may also be useful to keep track of the percentage of employment offers accepted out of the offers extended. If the percentage is low, perhaps the compensation and benefits offered are not competitive. Keeping track of compensation costs over total revenue, particularly compensation for those who are not directly delivering services, can be helpful in judging whether the nonprofit is vulnerable to public criticism of the proportion of the budget devoted to salaries. Another useful ratio to examine is the number of resignations per year over the number of employees per year. If voluntary turnover is high, perhaps the selection process is not encouraging good fits or perhaps other problems exist, such as poor working conditions, frustration with coworkers, or other issues that may be correctable. Of course it may be, as we found in Chapter Ten with Santropol Roulant, that high turnover is expected owing to the types of workers attracted to the nonprofit, such as the Roulant's youth workers.

Stage 4: Separation

At this stage of the cycle of involvement the individual leaves the nonprofit or is directed to another position. A termination of a work relationship may be voluntary or involuntary, planned or unplanned. The goal of the nonprofit should be to have amicable separations, where workers feel fairly treated and have good feelings toward the organization. Workers should leave with an accurate understanding of the nonprofit and acceptance of the need for the separation.

Understand Reasons for Separation

Some human resource management systems will have a mechanism, such as an exit interview, to debrief the worker and gain information on the reasons for the separation. The exit interview is an opportunity to reduce any negative feelings from the departure of the worker. Positive feelings can be enhanced by thanking the worker for his contribution and discussing ways he can continue to be involved with the nonprofit. The nonprofit may have the ability to offer outplacement services such as career counseling, résumé assistance, job hunting workshops, job listings, and referrals. Discussing these resources during the exit interview may improve the departing worker's attitude about the organization.

When a worker is leaving because of dissatisfaction, information obtained in the exit interview may be especially helpful for identifying areas for organizational improvement. Disgruntled or frustrated workers may be more willing to honestly express their opinions once they know they are leaving the organization. For example, a worker who has been feeling overwhelmed may not have communicated this to his supervisor but in an exit interview may indicate that his tasks were too complicated or that he was poorly trained. Once this information is known, it may be possible to remedy that problem for future workers, or it may even open an opportunity to delay or prevent the separation of the current worker.

Possibly Renegotiate Position

Losing a valued volunteer or paid staff member can negatively affect the nonprofit's ability to achieve its mission. It may be worthwhile to find a way to retain an individual who wishes to voluntarily separate from the organization. Perhaps an alternative arrangement might be acceptable to the worker.

For example, a full-time staff member might be willing to continue on a part-time basis or as a volunteer. An individual who feels that her work is not challenging enough may be moved to a new position or given additional responsibilities, consistent with overall HR capacity needs.

Concluding Thoughts

As noted in the opening case on BBBSE, the success of any organization depends on having the right people, in the right place, doing the right things. Good HR management is about aligning workers to the mission. At the initial involvement stage, the mission is the driving force behind the rationale for adding new workers, finding workers with a good fit, and setting job expectations. In the development stage, socialization reinforces workers' commitment to the mission. Measuring performance, identifying developmental needs, and providing feedback help to ensure that workers' activities are consistent with the mission. In the maintenance stage, providing compensation and benefits creates a sense of reciprocal obligation on the part of the worker. Recognizing and rewarding workers for their efforts to achieve the organizational mission further heightens workers' commitment. Separation is inevitable, but can be managed in a way that ensures wise use of HR resources and gives input for improving HR capacity for mission achievement.

In the next chapter we continue to examine performance issues. We add more information on theories of motivation and offer practical guidance on how to create and maintain a motivated, high-performing workforce. Combined with a strategic HR management system, efforts to motivate workers are likely to be fruitful in enhancing HR capacity.

Questions for Consideration

1. Does a nonprofit have an ethical responsibility not to violate its volunteers' psychological contracts? Why or why not? How can a nonprofit try to avoid breaches of the psychological contract?
2. Under what circumstances should nonprofits offer compensation that is competitive with what for-profit employers are offering for the same position? When, if ever, is it all right to pay less?
3. Think about the economic and social environment today. What implications do current conditions have for the ability of a nonprofit to attract new volunteers and paid staff?

Exercises

Exercise 11.1: Cycle of Involvement

Consider the last job you held. Apply your experience to the cycle of involvement. What occurred at each of the four main stages? What was done well at each stage? What could have been improved at each stage?

Exercise 11.2: Recruitment Ads

Find and compare two job ads for similar nonprofit positions. Using the ideas in this chapter, consider whether one ad is more likely than the other to attract applicants with a good fit to the nonprofit. Explain why one ad is better, or why both ads will have similar results.

Exercise 11.3: Paid Versus Volunteer Workers

Analyze the composition of a nonprofit's workforce. Concentrate on the paid and volunteer workers. How do these two types of workers differ in their work assignments and in the activities and resources that support them in each stage of the cycle of involvement?

CHAPTER TWELVE

MOTIVATION AND PERFORMANCE

The High Line is a park in Manhattan built on the infrastructure for a long-unused elevated rail line. The High Line railway opened in 1934, and the last train ran on the tracks in 1980. Using the High Line for a new purpose was the brainchild of Robert Hammond and Joshua David, who met at a community meeting and shared a desire to save the rail line.[1] In 1999, they formed Friends of the High Line to prevent the demolition of the historical structure and to turn it into something that the neighborhoods it ran through could enjoy. The founders of the Friends group were committed to changing residents' minds from seeing the neglected railway as an ugly problem to viewing it as a unique asset for the city. Groundbreaking on the park was celebrated in 2006, after seven years of building a coalition of supporters, collecting design ideas, conducting economic analyses to show benefits greater than the cost of construction, convincing CSX Transportation, Inc., to donate the elevated structure to the city, and gaining the approval of city, state, and federal authorities. The first section of the High Line Park was opened in 2009 and the second in 2011. For twelve years these founders, along with the friends and staff they recruited, maintained their motivation and momentum to preserve the High Line and make it into a destination site. In the words of actor Edward Norton, the park demonstrates that "things that ought to be, can be." The success of the Friends of the High Line serves as inspiration for other groups interested in urban, historical, and environmental preservation.

The High Line has been described as representative of the next generation of public parks, urban spaces where communities work together to define how to use them to benefit their neighborhoods. Motivations of supporters of the High Line vary. The designer Diane Von Furstenberg calls it a "ribbon" through the city that is "beautiful and romantic." For some the appeal is less aesthetic and more about keeping a reminder *of the city's industrial past. Others see it as a place to educate schoolchildren and where people with diverse backgrounds can come together for recreation. Still others are motivated by the tax revenues and increased property values that the High Line generates.*

The founders were able to successfully bring together numerous parties with varying motivations to act to preserve the structure and build this urban oasis. Starting as a small group of like-minded volunteers, the Friends of the High Line is now a nonprofit with over fifty-five staff members, twenty-eight board members, and fourteen ex officio and emeritus board members. It provides 70 percent of the annual operating budget for the public park. The Friends maintain the High Line Park under an agreement with the City of New York and cultivate a vibrant community around the High Line through tours, lectures, performances, public art projects, and other activities.

◆ ◆ ◆

This chapter is about motivation and performance in nonprofit settings. As our opening story suggests, for nonprofit organizations the desire to motivate others typically extends beyond the formal employment setting. In addition to paid employees, nonprofit leaders may need to motivate volunteers, collaboration partners, government officials, legislators, donors, service recipients, and other stakeholders. To make High Line Park a reality, Robert Hammond and Joshua David motivated artists, architects, business owners, civic leaders, grantmaking foundations, neighborhood residents, schoolteachers, and others to join together to brainstorm uses for the High Line, contribute financial support to make the vision happen, lobby government, personally use the redeveloped space, and entice others to enjoy its benefits. However, motivation was not sufficient in itself. The leaders needed to provide resources and training to ensure that individuals who were willing to help with the park were able to do so effectively.

In this chapter we review how motivation combined with ability affects behavior. The previous chapter examined human resource management systems for nonprofits and discussed recommended management practices for both paid employees and volunteers. This chapter concentrates on understanding human dynamics in order to encourage peak performance. It also offers information useful in diagnosing reasons for poor performance and creating conditions that can improve work attitudes, behaviors, and outcomes.

Influences on Performance

Three simple formulas are useful for those who wish to influence performance.[2] A model based on the formulas is shown in Exhibit 12.1. The model illustrates that performance is dependent on ability and motivation to perform. Ability depends

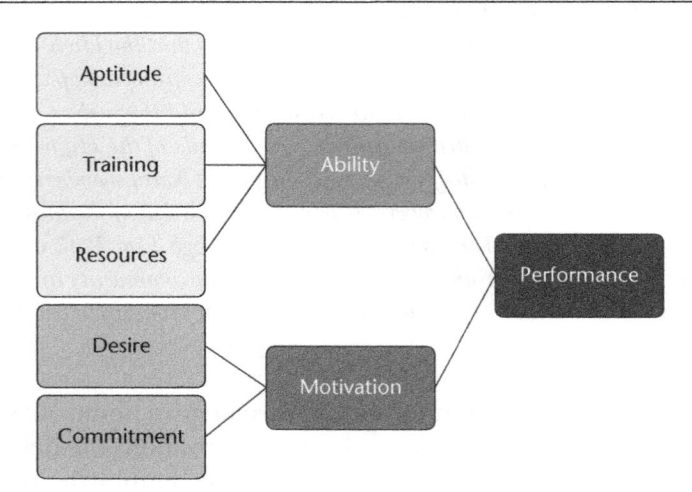

EXHIBIT 12.1. INFLUENCES ON PERFORMANCE

[Diagram: Aptitude, Training, Resources → Ability; Desire, Commitment → Motivation; Ability and Motivation → Performance]

Three Formulas
Performance is a function of ability and motivation.
Ability is a function of aptitude, training, and resources (capacity and opportunity to perform).
Motivation is a function of desire and commitment (willingness to perform).

---

on having the capacity and opportunity to perform through one's aptitude, training, and resources. Motivation is a function of one's desire and commitment. So, for example, the founders of Friends of the High Line had to figure out who had the ability to turn over the rail line to the city and then motivate them to do so. They also had to persuade government officials to perform the actions necessary to turn the rail line into a park. The founders recognized that they did not have the aptitude or the resources to design the park and therefore turned to others who were more qualified to do so. In order to motivate the designers, the founders inspired them with ideas drawn from a design competition and established a contract with due dates and payment schedules. This helped to encourage the designers' desire and commitment.

When an individual's performance is inadequate, managers can diagnose the cause (or causes) of the problem. One of the first questions to ask is whether the poor performance is due to a lack of ability or lack of motivation to perform a task. If it is due to a lack of ability, that may in turn be due to lack of aptitude, training, or resources. If it is a motivational problem, the person may not have the desire or commitment to perform.

- **Aptitude to perform.** Individuals may not have the skills, knowledge, or personality traits to excel. If a task requires a high level of collaboration and communication, they may not have the capacity to build trust or share tasks with others. They may also not have adequate physical strength or intellectual understanding. An example from the High Line project is that Hammond and David knew they did not have the aptitude to figure out the best use for the old railway, and therefore they commissioned studies and held a design competition.

- **Training to perform.** An individual may have the innate aptitude to perform but may not know how to perform. A person may be trained to perform a task a certain way, but the training may be incorrect or insufficient or may become out of date over time, leading to performance problems. In the case of the High Line, in order to help schoolteachers to use the park effectively in their courses, the Friends offer curriculum guides and training sessions for educators.
- **Resources to perform.** The opportunity to perform is dependent on what the environment offers or doesn't offer that is needed to perform. Lack of resources can lead to poor performance. Individuals may be unable to perform a task well because they don't have needed materials, supplies, technology, instructions, access, or other resources. The Friends of the High Line had videos, reports, and drawings for advocates to use for fundraising and lobbying purposes. Without these materials the advocates' efforts would likely have been less successful.
- **Desire to perform.** Individuals may not want to perform. They may believe the benefits of not performing outweigh the benefits of performing. They may not see the value of the positive outcomes of performing and therefore may be unwilling to perform. For example, initial resisters to the use of the High Line as a park thought that the structure was an eyesore and could not be saved. Once convinced that saving it was possible, however, some offered their financial and volunteer support.
- **Commitment to perform.** Individuals may have the desire to perform but lack the drive to persevere. They lack commitment to perform. For example, volunteers and donors can experience fatigue, believing that their efforts are making only a little dent in a complex social problem. Their motivation to continue to invest in the cause can weaken over time as they get distracted with other demands for their attention. The founders of the Friends of the High Line were able to maintain commitment through rallies, progress reports, and celebration of milestones.

Leaders and managers can use a variety of methods and tools to address aptitude, training, resources, desire, and commitment. Table 12.1 offers some general suggestions for each.

TABLE 12.1. GENERAL RECOMMENDATIONS FOR INFLUENCING HIGH PERFORMANCE

Predictor of Performance	Recommendations
Aptitude	Recruit those who already have the needed knowledge, skills, and abilities.
	Reassign or train individuals lacking aptitude.
	Form teams to have complementary aptitudes available.
Training	Design and deliver training so that individuals understand how and when to perform certain behaviors.
	Provide manuals and relevant reference material.
	Encourage individuals to identify their weaknesses in knowledge, skills, and abilities so that the nonprofit can address them to avoid performance problems.
Resources	Modify technology to compensate for aptitude or training needs.
	Ensure that information needed to perform well is provided.
	Provide adequate space, time, coworkers, and physical supplies.
Desire	Help the individual understand the benefits of their performance for themselves and others.
	Create a work context where individuals see the outcomes of their performance.
	Highlight the underlying values of the organization or program so that individuals can better understand the meaningfulness of their work.
Commitment	Chop large, long-term tasks into smaller, short-term ones so that individuals can see progress.
	Rotate jobs to avoid boredom and fatigue.
	Reduce distractions.
	Ensure that jobs are challenging but not frustrating or discouraging.
	Celebrate small wins along the way to the big accomplishments.

Theories of Motivation

Theoretical treatments of motivation typically focus on *content theories* of motivation, which give primary emphasis to variables inside the individual that affect motivation, and on *process theories* of motivation, which look at the environment as well as the individual to explain motivation. Classic motivation theories are Abraham Maslow's needs hierarchy, Clayton Alderfer's ERG theory, Frederick Herzberg's two-factor theory, David McClelland's learned needs theory, and also public service motivation theory, expectancy theory, operant conditioning theory and behavior modification, social learning theory, goal-setting theory, and equity theory.

Though these classic theories of motivation typically are applied to for-profit settings, there is evidence that they fit nonprofit workplaces.[3] For example, René Bekkers examined motivations for volunteering and found that incentives, value orientations, and role modeling all explain the motivation to volunteer.[4] Catherine Schepers and her coauthors found that the basic premises of the classic theories are consistent across the nonprofit and for-profit sectors but the actual motivating factors may differ; nonprofit employees tend to have stronger preferences than those in for-profit settings for social rewards, work that helps others, growth opportunities, and intrinsic rewards.[5] Volunteers tend to have strong needs for personal growth, external recognition, and social affiliation.[6] In the next sections we draw out basic lessons from each classic theory of motivation and use them as jumping-off points for elaborating what research tells us about motivation and performance in the nonprofit sector. The basic lessons are the following:

- People are motivated to satisfy their needs and may not have the same needs as others.
- If some needs cannot be satisfied, people focus on satisfying other needs.
- People are motivated by both intrinsic and extrinsic incentives.
- The work environment affects the needs people seek to satisfy.
- Nonprofits attract people with altruistic impulses.
- People act on what they expect to bring the most good and least bad results.
- People's behavior is influenced by positive and negative reinforcements.
- People modify attitudes and behaviors to match those of role models.
- Goals can be motivating—when set appropriately.
- People want rewards to be fair.

People Are Motivated to Satisfy Their Needs and May Not Have the Same Needs as Others

Maslow's *hierarchy of needs* provides insights on the needs that individuals may attempt to satisfy through their paid and volunteer work.[7] Maslow arranges these needs in pyramid form, according to priority, arguing that individuals attempt to satisfy the lower-level survival needs before the upper-level needs. Individuals strive to move up the pyramid due to a fundamental need to grow and develop. According to Maslow, unsatisfied needs cause conflict, stress, and frustration, which can negatively affect performance. Researchers have been unable to substantiate Maslow's claim that fulfilled needs cease to motivate behavior and that workers' behaviors are dominated by a desire to fulfill the lowest order need that has not yet been fulfilled. Though no empirical evidence has been found to support the idea of a hierarchy of need satisfaction behavior, the idea that individuals get involved in nonprofit organizations to satisfy needs is clearly established. It is also clear that managers in nonprofit organizations should not assume that all individuals have the same needs. Maslow identified physiological, safety and security, social, esteem, and self-actualization needs, as represented in Figure 12.1.

Being involved with a nonprofit, such as the Friends of the High Line, enables individuals to pursue the basic needs identified by Maslow. These needs are reflected in the mission statements of a large number of nonprofits. Many nonprofits are established to help individuals with their physiological, safety, and security needs. Thus one sees shelters and soup kitchens in cities throughout the United States. Many nonprofit recreational clubs primarily serve people's social needs, and clubs for youth are often established with esteem as well as social needs in mind. For example, Boys and Girls Clubs and other youth-serving membership organizations, such as the Girl Scouts, work to build confidence and create social networks for positive peer support. Many staff, volunteers, and donors contribute to nonprofits in ways that fulfill their personal self-actualization needs. Through involvement with nonprofits, they find meaning and develop their knowledge and skills.

FIGURE 12.1. MASLOW'S HIERARCHY OF NEEDS

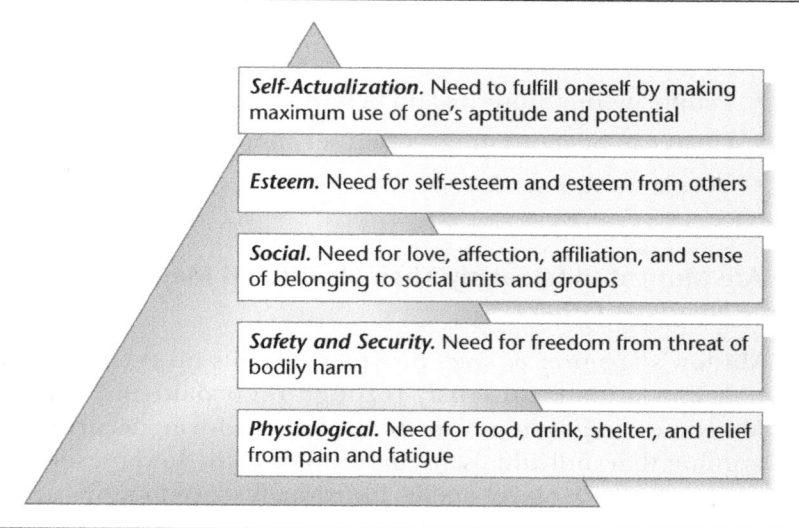

Self-Actualization. Need to fulfill oneself by making maximum use of one's aptitude and potential

Esteem. Need for self-esteem and esteem from others

Social. Need for love, affection, affiliation, and sense of belonging to social units and groups

Safety and Security. Need for freedom from threat of bodily harm

Physiological. Need for food, drink, shelter, and relief from pain and fatigue

Source: Adapted from Abraham H. Maslow, *Maslow on Management* (New York: Wiley, 1998).

The same behaviors may satisfy different needs as well.[8] For example, a volunteer act, such as serving meals or tutoring a child, may fulfill any of the following needs captured in E. Gill Clary and his colleagues' Volunteer Functions Inventory (VFI):

- **Social**: satisfied by spending time with friends and gaining approval from those we admire
- **Career**: satisfied by gaining job-related benefits or advancement
- **Understanding**: satisfied by learning, practicing skills, and honing abilities
- **Values**: satisfied by expressing altruistic or humanitarian concern
- **Protective**: satisfied by reducing guilt over feeling more fortunate or by escaping personal problems
- **Enhancement**: satisfied by a sense of personal growth or esteem

It is not always easy to know what needs specific employees, volunteers, donors, and others are fulfilling through their involvement with nonprofits. Rather than designing all available tasks, and the conditions under which they are performed, to satisfy multiple needs, it may be better to allow for some self-selection of tasks and flexibility in how they are performed. If a worker seems to lack motivation, managers and leaders wishing to motivate him may find it helpful to try to determine his most important needs and help him choose tasks or adjust task conditions to better satisfy those needs. Individuals with high social needs, for example, may choose tasks that are performed as part of a group. Individuals with high esteem needs may ask for tasks where they are likely to get a lot of positive feedback.

If Some Needs Cannot Be Satisfied, People Focus on Satisfying Other Needs

Alderfer's *ERG theory* is consistent with the basic idea that humans act to satisfy their needs.[9] Alderfer argues that the needs in Maslow's hierarchy should be combined into three basic sets of needs: *existence needs* satisfied by food, air, water, compensation, and safe working conditions; *relatedness needs* satisfied by meaningful social and interpersonal relationships; and *growth needs* satisfied by an individual making creative or productive contributions.

Alderfer gets credit for the idea, backed up by research, that multiple needs may be affecting an individual's behavior at the same time. People typically have multiple motivations for acting in a certain way. When an individual is frustrated in satisfying one set of needs, she will likely focus on satisfying another set of needs. For example, if satisfaction of her need for growth is blocked because there is no opportunity to get a more challenging position, her manager might encourage her to focus on relatedness needs by providing opportunities to socialize and affiliate with others in work teams, task forces, or employer-organized volunteer groups or sports teams.

Richard Waters and Denise Bortree offer some useful conclusions about motivating work environments in nonprofits. Finding that trust and inclusion are highly critical in maintaining the commitment of teen volunteers, they recommend that paid staff show respect and appreciation by including volunteers in the workgroup, welcoming them to meetings, supporting their efforts to perform, involving them in decision-making opportunities, and understanding their needs and concerns.[10] These recommendations are consistent with standard advice for volunteer management programs. If paid staff do not see volunteers as making valuable contributions and think that the volunteers are a resource drain, integrating volunteers with staff can negatively affect staff members' sense of satisfaction and commitment. Asking paid staff to invest their time, effort, and resources in poorly performing volunteers can lead to low morale and staff turnover. Conversely, asking staff to invest in high-performing volunteers can lead to greater staff retention and well-being.[11] A key lesson for integrating staff and volunteers is that neither the employees nor the volunteers want to feel that their time is being wasted.

People Are Motivated by Both Intrinsic and Extrinsic Incentives

Herzberg's *two-factor theory* proposes that there are some factors that lead to job dissatisfaction when they are insufficient but do not lead to high levels of satisfaction no matter how abundant they are.[12] *Hygiene factors* are extrinsic incentives, such as supportive supervisors and safe working conditions and externally given rewards such as salaries and benefits. In contrast, *motivators* are intrinsic incentives, operating inside an individual. These intrinsic incentives include enjoyment of the work, sense of importance of the work, interest in the tasks, feeling of personal growth, and fulfillment of higher-order needs such as esteem and self-actualization. Though researchers have not confirmed the idea that intrinsic and extrinsic incentives work differently to affect satisfaction and motivation, they have found that both types can affect attitudes and behavior of paid employees and volunteers. In particular, it is clear that altruistic (other-serving) as well as instrumental (self-serving) motivations help to explain interest in volunteering[13] and in having paid employment in the nonprofit sector.[14]

As mentioned in Chapter Ten on executive directors and leadership, national studies suggest that nonprofits will be facing significant challenges in retaining their current executive directors and recruiting younger generations to leadership roles. The 2006 *Daring to Lead* study report found that directors were planning to leave their jobs due to inadequate compensation, burnout, lack of contributions to retirement accounts, and overwhelming fundraising responsibilities.[15] The 2008 *Ready to Lead?* study report looked at the nonprofit leadership pipeline and found that next generation leaders are frustrated by a lack of mentorship and unclear internal career paths.[16] Some find the prospect of becoming a nonprofit executive director unappealing due to fundraising responsibilities, long hours, and low pay and retirement benefits. These studies reinforce the idea that there are disincentives (hygiene factors) for work in the nonprofit sector that managers can attempt to ameliorate or avoid to better recruit and retain nonprofit workers.

Putting Herzberg's ideas into action, nonprofits should seek to make work more interesting, meaningful, and personally fulfilling in order to boost motivation and satisfaction. They should also provide extrinsic rewards such as praise from supervisors and pleasant working conditions. Some nonprofit leaders have a tendency to rely on intrinsic motivators rather than extrinsic ones. They feel that the opportunity to contribute to achieving the mission of the nonprofit should be a sufficient motivator. Therefore they may choose to pay low salaries, not invest in staff development, and assume that employees and volunteers will perform at a high level without needing much positive feedback or encouragement. Unfortunately, this may lead to those pursuing careers in the nonprofit sector feeling underpaid and overwhelmed with work demands.

There is much discussion in the nonprofit sector about the greater presence of intrinsic motivation in this sector than in the others. Studies have found that nonprofit paid employees tend to have weaker monetary orientations than their counterparts in the for-profit sector do.[17] For example, in a study of nonprofit careers and sector switching, nonprofit paid employees were found to place more importance on having work that helps others and less importance on high salary than for-profit paid employees did.[18] This high level of intrinsic motivation is often used to explain why nonprofit workers are willing to accept low wages. When extrinsic rewards are increased, intrinsic motivation is theorized to drop.[19] John Deckop and Carol Cirka found this in their examination of the introduction of a merit pay system in a nonprofit. The employees who had the highest level of intrinsic motivation were the ones who experienced the greatest decline in this type of motivation when faced with a merit pay system.[20] However, other studies, such as a study of AmeriCorps members, have not found that intrinsic motivation drops in the presence of extrinsic rewards.[21]

Some of the simplest and least expensive rewards can have a great influence on satisfaction and motivation. For example, one study of volunteers for Meals on Wheels found that a hot, fresh cookie given to volunteers each day they volunteered generally was more valued by them than occasional drawings for fuel cards, snacks on holidays, appreciation events, acknowledgments in newsletters, meetings with celebrities, and other tangible rewards. Some of the volunteers studied were actually less likely to continue volunteering if they perceived that they were being paid or somehow compensated, however little, for their time and effort. Overall, this study showed, like many others, that volunteers and paid staff tend not to want the same rewards to the same degree. Making a positive difference, being able to help others, and receiving small, tangible rewards like a cookie were generally very useful in keeping most volunteers motivated.[22]

The Work Environment Affects the Needs People Seek to Satisfy

McClelland's *learned needs theory* says that performance is based on needs for achievement, power, and affiliation. It also offers the insight that needs are learned through cultural influences, and therefore the work environment can reinforce the pursuit of certain needs.[23] For example, being rewarded by a supervisor for being dominant and taking charge strengthens a person's need for power and his subsequent efforts to get power. Extending this idea of learned needs, if a for-profit company encourages and rewards volunteering, its employees are more likely to be motivated to volunteer. Working alongside their boss on a community service project can satisfy for-profit employees' needs for affiliation and achievement, and having the opportunity to serve in a volunteer leadership role can satisfy needs for power.[24] Even his occupation can influence a person's desire to volunteer. Natalie Webb and Rikki Abzug found that occupational groups vary in the likelihood that they will do volunteer work, and concluded that norms and values within occupations help shape desires to volunteer.[25]

This premise that needs are learned can be linked to the massive literature on how leaders can affect organizational culture.[26] The culture of an organization reflects the shared beliefs, attitudes, values, and norms that guide behavior and attitudes within that organization. Artifacts of the culture include the organization's mission statement, slogans, codes of conduct, visible awards and recognitions, and facilities; the ways members dress; and their manner of interacting. Something as simple as how the phone is answered and what is displayed on office walls can suggest the values and norms that are shared in an organization. Nonprofit leaders need to understand their organization's culture and the behaviors that are reinforced by it. For example, workers are likely more willing to be creative and to experiment when innovation is a cultural value than they are when the culture is more bureaucratic and rule following is valued. A leader can strengthen a culture by setting up reward systems consistent with shared beliefs, values, and norms. For example, by praising paid staff for working collaboratively with volunteers and ensuring that rewards are given to teams of volunteers and staff, some of the typical power differences between staff and volunteers may be weakened and the idea that all workers are equally valued may be reinforced. The organizational culture can reinforce or reduce staff and volunteer tensions, depending on how well volunteer management systems are understood and appreciated by employees.[27]

Nonprofits Attract People with Altruistic Impulses

Public service motivation (PSM) theory was originally developed to be applied to government employees, though it subsequently has been applied to the nonprofit and for-profit sectors. James Perry and Lois Wise suggested that public employees have four main dimensions of motivation: attraction to public service, commitment to the public interest, compassion, and self-sacrifice.[28] Work in the nonprofit sector can serve as an outlet for these altruistic impulses. Research on public service motivation has found that individuals vary in their willingness to put others' interests above their own and put themselves at risk in order to help others. Individuals with higher levels of public service motivation are more likely to work in the nonprofit or government sectors than the for-profit sector.

Researchers find high rates of burnout in the nonprofit sector, as individuals put their work-life balance at risk in order to help others. They may feel guilt about going on vacation or accepting salary or other rewards when those they are trying to help are still suffering. As John Brauer and Jed Emerson put it in their article on burnout of nonprofit staff: "Plenty of people come to the 'do-good' professions with the belief that they, along with others, should do no less than change the world. They can't seem to do enough to help their agencies pursue their missions. But this beautiful passion can lead straight to burnout when the issues of poverty don't end, the environment continues its decline, and a realization dawns that no one person or agency can solve such complicated and overwhelming issues."[29] To avoid burnout, nonprofit managers can insist that staff take vacations and work reasonable hours. They can also help workers focus on small wins where they can see that they are making a positive difference, so that they are not discouraged.

People Act on What They Expect to Bring the Most Good and Least Bad Results

Expectancy theory has been relatively well supported by empirical research since its introduction by Victor Vroom. It says that individuals calculate the probability and value of their achievement of good and bad outcomes as a result of their actions. Then they behave in a way likely to result in the most good and the least bad results.[30] The theory assumes that individuals are rational and follow utilitarian principles. More recent formulations of the theory look at two types of expectancies: the likelihood that effort will lead to a certain performance level and the likelihood that the performance level will result in receiving a certain level of reward. The theory guides managers to learn what expectations workers have regarding the link between effort and performance and between performance and rewards. It also suggests that managers should learn what workers see as the most preferred rewards. They can then help a worker see that performing at a certain level is possible and that this performance will result in rewards the worker values.

Any time a nonprofit takes on a challenging mission in which individuals doubt whether success is possible, expectancy theory is useful. It helps managers understand that sometimes perceptions of what is possible need to be changed to encourage peak performance on tasks. For example, to rally initial detractors around the idea of making the High Line into a positive asset, the leaders of the effort had to first convince them that an ugly eyesore could be made beautiful. Without belief that the nonprofit can actually succeed, behavior is likely to be lackluster, even counterproductive. Many nonprofits have ambitious missions and are dealing with complex, difficult social problems. Leaders need to be able to show progress in achieving these missions to keep workers motivated. Noting milestones is critical for keeping volunteers and staff engaged when the final destination appears far away.

Expectancy theory also helps managers to understand the phenomenon of burnout, common among volunteers and staff dealing with the toughest social problems. After years of seeing little progress in addressing social ills or helping individuals who cannot seem to make progress or who frequently regress, workers can feel burnt out. They stop expecting to be able to be of help or no longer see that the rewards are worth the effort. Nonprofit workers may experience burnout when they are faced with pressures to quantify their successes even though achievements are hard to document. Sometimes single stories about someone who was helped can remind workers that their work is meaningful and feasible despite being under-resourced. This relates to the often repeated story of the person who justifies throwing stranded starfish back into the ocean by saying that even though all the starfish can't be saved, his actions make a difference to the few starfish that are saved.

People's Behavior Is Influenced by Positive and Negative Reinforcements

Operant conditioning and behavior modification approaches draw from the work of behavioral psychologists such as B. F. Skinner. They explain how managers can reinforce desired behaviors and extinguish less desired ones.

For example, if a volunteer is routinely ignored by her supervisor every time she asks for a new assignment, the volunteer is unlikely to keep asking for new work. The lack of attention by the supervisor is a negative reinforcement. The behavior of asking for more volunteer work will eventually be extinguished. However, if the volunteer is enthusiastically greeted and thanked when she turns in an assignment and asks for more work, she is likely to want to finish her work and get more tasks to complete. The supervisor is providing a positive reinforcement.

Operant conditioning and behavior modification research offers important implications for managing workers. An important finding is that positive reinforcement is more efficient in influencing behavior than punishment. Also reinforcement after each occurrence of a behavior produces more rapid acquisition of the desired behavior, but the behavior is also more likely to stop when the reinforcement ends. Intermittent reinforcement is likely to take longer to establish the desired behavior, but once the reinforcement stops the behavior is likely to continue longer.[31]

Reinforcements may be as simple as being thanked, praised, scolded, embarrassed, rewarded with a token of appreciation, or presented as a positive role model. An important caution is that it is easy to reward one behavior while hoping for another.[32] For example, a nonprofit may say it wants good customer service but may actually reward employees for speed in moving to the next customer. In order to be effective in encouraging desired behaviors, any performance management system needs to be sensitive to what it is incentivizing.[33]

People Modify Attitudes and Behaviors to Match Those of Role Models

Social learning theory helps managers to understand how individuals motivate themselves by choosing a role model and copying that person's behavior and attitudes.[34] An implication of this theory for nonprofit managers is that workers can benefit from having individuals to observe and admire. Managers can expose workers to potential positive role models, but it is the workers' choice whether they emulate these models. Learning by observing is common. In addition to formal training, people learn by watching fellow team members and others in their work and social environments. Conferences, shared interest meeting groups, reading circles, and job shadowing are just a few of the avenues for observing others and finding role models.

Mentoring programs may be very effective in increasing performance in nonprofit organizations. Mentors can help with technical training and knowledge sharing, thus improving the abilities of those mentored. Mentors can also affect motivation by serving as role models. One study of employees of a nonprofit elder-care program found that those with mentors had significantly stronger motives to help others and reported higher boosts in self-esteem, more understanding of social problems, and greater reflection of their values in their work. They had stronger beliefs in the organization's mission, a greater desire to be supportive of peers, and less stress in their caregiving tasks.[35] This nonprofit's positive results from a formal mentoring program suggest that an investment in coordinating mentoring may be worthwhile. By sharing their lessons learned and perspective gained from experience, mentors can ease the challenges facing less seasoned workers and model positive attitudes and behaviors.

All those involved in a nonprofit should be aware that whenever they are being observed, their behaviors and attitudes may be a model for others. Even clients can be role models. Many employees and volunteers report that they learn much from interacting with service recipients. In our chapter on executive directors we explore how they are role models and the importance of their behavior in setting the tone for the organization. In Chapter Two we discuss why it is important for unethical behavior of employees to be stopped when discovered; otherwise these behaviors may be modeled by others. Part of the value of leaders getting out of their offices and "walking around" is that they can reflect positive attitudes and behaviors and observe others. If they see negative role models, they can try to change the behaviors of these individuals or remove them from the workplace.

Goals Can Be Motivating—When Set Appropriately

Goal-setting theory outlines how goals can influence behavior.[36] We reviewed in Chapter Two how clear and meaningful goals enable stakeholders to judge organizational effectiveness by whether or not these goals have been met. In this chapter our focus is on individual and team-level goals. To encourage high performance, goals should be specific and challenging yet reachable. When goals are not achieved, commitment to goal-related tasks and similar tasks may falter. For example, fundraisers who do not reach a fundraising goal may enter the next campaign with less motivation than fundraisers for successful campaigns have.

When a nonprofit fails to reach certain goals, leaders should actively manage future expectations. They can do this by helping workers see that current conditions allow new goals to be reached. If necessary, they can diagnose with the worker why a goal was not met. If it was due to lack of ability, they can see that the worker has adequate resources and training to meet the goal. If it was due to lack of motivation, they can see what might change the worker's desire and commitment to achieve the goal.

People vary in how they respond to goals but, in general, as the perceived value of a goal increases so does the commitment to the goal. Feedback about progress in achieving a goal is usually necessary for the goal to positively influence performance. A difficulty in applying this theory is that goals may be hard to specify or counterproductive, particularly when dealing with high-level strategy or in situations with multiple, complex, and competing goals.[37]

Using a goal-setting framework, Mary Tschirhart and colleagues looked at the importance of initial goals set by AmeriCorps members working in nonprofit organizations and then at their perceived accomplishment of these goals.[38] The researchers found evidence for five general goals and linked them to desire to volunteer one year later. Those AmeriCorps workers who had not achieved their goals had less intention to volunteer in the future. The researchers also found that when these workers did not believe their work had helped them to feel good about themselves or feel needed, they were less likely to report high levels of achievement of other important goals. It seems that the level of satisfaction with achievement of self-esteem goals can affect the pursuit and achievement of other goals. A practical implication from this research is that managers can benefit from understanding workers' goals and helping to ensure that they are reachable, either by providing adequate training and resources for goal achievement or by persuading workers to change their goals when they are unrealistic.

People Want Rewards to Be Fair

Equity theory brings the insight that workers compare their efforts and rewards to others in similar work situations.[39] Most individuals have a need to be treated fairly and are likely to change their behavior if they perceive an inequity. If others seem to be getting greater rewards for the same work, or the same rewards for lesser work, workers are likely to respond in one of several ways. They may put less time or effort into their work. They may decide to try to achieve greater outputs to call attention to their superior performance. They may change which people they are comparing themselves with or reevaluate their calculation of inputs, outputs, and outcomes. Other options they may pursue are to quit or to decide that the inequity is tolerable.

In the nonprofit sector, workers may not be able to make exact comparisons, and they may see inputs and outcomes as multifaceted, making it difficult to calculate and compare ratios to see whether equity is being preserved. For example, a paid staff member working as a fundraiser may compare herself to a volunteer who is raising funds for the same campaign. The staff member may have different kinds of relationships to nurture with prospective donors and more or fewer resources to support fundraising activities than the volunteer does. The rewards these workers receive for their efforts also vary greatly. In particular the staff member has pay as an extrinsic reward. The value of the theory is in helping managers to see the possible negative consequences of perceptions of inequity. It also suggests that managers should be aware of the comparisons that workers are making and their sensitivity to perceived inequity.

Laura Leete finds that equity concerns are stronger in the nonprofit sector than in the for-profit arena.[40] A sense of what is fair affects many dimensions of nonprofit work, particularly pay systems. In Deckop and Cirka's examination of a merit pay system in a nonprofit, they found that equity and expectancy concerns were prevalent. Some individuals felt that performance appraisals were not accurate and that the pay was not distributed to reward those with the highest performance, though that was the stated purpose of the merit pay program.[41] These types of beliefs can have negative effects on performance.

Not being consistent in types of rewards used for workers in different jobs also can be problematic. Anna Haley-Lock explains that nonprofit managers risk under-rewarding the individuals who are assumed to be intrinsically motivated and whose work is directly related to the nonprofit's mission while over-rewarding those who are not in mission-focused functions, do not appear to be "called" to work in the nonprofit, and are assumed to be doing the job for the money.[42] The inequity that results can cause motivational and performance problems.

Concluding Thoughts

In general, worker satisfaction is high in the nonprofit sector.[43] Numerous studies have shown that nonprofit employees in general are satisfied and more loyal than their for-profit counterparts, even in the presence of lower wages, excessive workloads, and stress from inadequate resources. They tend to stay with their organizations because they feel attached to the mission and are satisfied with their experience.[44] Most individuals have stable preferences for employment in one sector over another. These preferences are linked to personal values as well as to educational and work backgrounds.[45] Even though the nonprofit sector may have to compete with the for-profit sector for talented leaders, there will always be individuals who have a passion for nonprofit projects and who are eager to work toward achieving a mission that fits their value system.

The fundamental dynamic that performance is predicted by ability and motivation should not be ignored. This chapter has outlined a variety of ideas for influencing ability and motivation based on classic theories and empirical research. These concepts, combined with ideas from the preceding chapter on human resource systems, form a foundation of basic knowledge on how to encourage high levels of performance among paid staff and volunteers. In the next chapter on program evaluation, we reveal more insights on performance by looking not at individual workers' effectiveness but at the effectiveness of programs as a whole.

Questions for Consideration

1. Should compensation for equivalent jobs be lower in the nonprofit sector than in government or the for-profit sector? When is this appropriate? Why or why not?
2. How would you determine whether the poor performance of someone you are supervising is due to a problem of ability or of motivation?

Exercises

Exercise 12.1: Satisfying Needs

Consider a job you know well. Prepare an inventory of the personal needs that might be satisfied through performing this job. How could the work environment be changed to allow more of these needs to be satisfied through the job?

Exercise 12.2: Positive and Negative Reinforcements

Observe your own behavior for three days. During this time period, how often did you use positive and negative reinforcements with others? Did their reactions differ depending on what type of reinforcement you used? When were you most likely to use negative reinforcements, and when were you most likely to use positive reinforcements?

Exercise 12.3: Responding to Inequity

Think about a time when you experienced inequity in a work situation. How did you respond to the inequity? Could you or the organization have addressed the inequity in other ways? If so, how?

PART FOUR
EVALUATING, CONNECTING, AND ADAPTING

CHAPTER THIRTEEN

PROGRAM EVALUATION

The Nurse-Family Partnership (NFP) program was founded by physician David Olds, professor of pediatrics, psychiatry, and preventive medicine at the University of Colorado Denver.[1] While working in an inner-city day-care center in the early 1970s, Olds was struck by the endemic risks and difficulties in the lives of low-income children. He realized the children needed help much earlier and, basing his effort on the work of both academics and practitioners, designed a unique home visitation program that would rely on registered nurses and begin during pregnancy. The program's goals included improving pregnancy outcomes by improving women's prenatal health, improving child health and development by reducing dysfunctional caregiving, and improving each mother's life course by helping her develop a vision for her future, which would involve planning any future pregnancies, staying in school, and finding employment.

Over the next thirty years, he tested the program in randomized, controlled trials. The first trial was with poor, white, and rural families in Elmira, New York, in 1977. The program was found to produce positive impacts. In order to test the generality of the model, a second test was conducted in Memphis, Tennessee, among inner-city African American families. Similar positive results were found. A third trial was conducted in Denver, Colorado, in order to test the model on Hispanic families and also to test the efficacy of using paraprofessionals instead of nurses (this had been suggested as a cost-saving measure). The test showed that the program was effective for Hispanics but that using paraprofessionals produced inferior results. The analysis of the results of these trials resulted in thirteen academic papers that, taken together, demonstrated positive results. This convinced funders and policymakers to support expansion of the program, and in 1996, the program was established in sites in

Ohio, Wyoming, California, Florida, Missouri, and Oklahoma. The Nurse-Family Partnership National Service Office, a national nonprofit, was established in 2003 to facilitate quality replication of the Nurse-Family Partnership program across the United States and to provide implementing agencies with ongoing support in nursing education and practice, program quality assurance, marketing, government relations, and more. The program has continued to grow tremendously. By 2005, it was operating in twenty states and serving twenty thousand families. As of August 2010, the program had expanded to thirty-two states. In addition, since 2006, inquiries have been received from a number of other countries about instituting the model.

◆ ◆ ◆

As our opening case example shows, the Nurse-Family Partnership program was carefully designed. It was based on theories of behavior and extensively evaluated before being widely disseminated. Evaluation results were used to determine the final program configuration. The result is a program that is widely respected for delivering consistently positive results. Nonprofits are facing increasing demands that they demonstrate their impact. Foundations and philanthropists are seeking to be more strategic as they seek *social impact*, government agencies are requiring information on program results, and board members want information on organizational activities.[2] How can nonprofit organizations determine how well they are doing in their pursuit of their mission? How can they determine if their programs are benefitting their clients? How can they provide information to funders and other stakeholders who want evidence of impact before making funding or other decisions of importance to the organization? In this chapter we will examine how nonprofits evaluate the effectiveness of their programs in order to answer these questions. We focus here on the evaluation of specific programs and not the evaluation of the effectiveness of the nonprofit as a whole, which is considered in detail in Chapter Two. For nonprofits with single programs, nonprofit and program effectiveness are closely related. In larger nonprofits with multiple programs, however, the assessment of organizational effectiveness is more complex and goes beyond the results of any one program evaluation.

Program Evaluation and Accountability Management

The evaluation of programs has a long history. In her review of evaluation, Susan Paddock points out that in the United States, formal evaluations of organizations and programs began with student assessment in the late 1800s.[3] Following World War II, evaluation began to be applied to public program administration. The social programs of the Great Society in the 1960s, which led to significant increases in public expenditures, were accompanied by an increase in attention to evaluation.[4] Legislators sought independent, thorough analysis of the performance of such programs as the War on Poverty, Model Cities, and the like. For many programs, Congress mandated that funding be set aside for program evaluation. Evaluations of programs had been performed before this, but they had usually been carried out in-house by agency staff. A key feature of the new evaluation model was the insistence on outside evaluators.

Legislation requiring regular review of federal programs was enacted in the early 1970s, when the federal government devolved the provision of many federal programs to the states.[5] Formal evaluation was a requirement of the funding. In addition, the Office of Management and Budget established its Evaluation and Program Implementation Division. As a result of these developments, program evaluation has boomed, both among practitioners and academics. Today a number of professional journals, such as *Evaluation Quarterly*, focus on this area, and a professional association, the American Evaluation Association, is available to students and professionals in this field.

The evaluation of government programs started with a relatively simple rational model. The research assessed the degree to which the initial goals of the program had been accomplished by the end of the program. Over time, however, the methodology was augmented in important ways to take into account the realities and complications of public programs. For example, programs often had multiple goals, and programs could change over time due to unforeseen circumstances. In addition, evaluations began to be used to improve program performance while programs were still under way.

Program evaluation has been widely adopted in the nonprofit sector as well. Since the 1980s, nonprofits have faced cutbacks in government funding, economic slowdowns and recessions, the rise of a conservative political ideology favoring market-based solutions to social problems, and an increase in the competition for funding as the number of appeals has increased. In this environment, funders and other external stakeholders have increasingly demanded that nonprofits provide evidence that they are making a difference and producing impact. As a result, accountability has become a major concern for nonprofits. Program evaluation is a central aspect of accountability and has therefore become increasingly important for nonprofits.

In its most general sense, *accountability* refers to an obligation or willingness to accept responsibility or to account for one's actions.[6] Following from this, organizational accountability is usually defined as an organization being answerable to someone or something outside itself and accepting responsibility for activities and disclosing them.[7] Organizations can also be accountable to internal standards. The standards may be expressed through codes of conduct and the mission statement.[8] Accountability involves four core components:[9]

- **Transparency**: collecting and making information available for scrutiny
- **Answerability or justification**: providing clear reasons for actions and decisions so that they may be questioned

- **Compliance**: adhering to rules or standards through the monitoring and evaluation of procedures and outcomes
- **Enforcement**: applying sanctions for shortfalls in transparency, justification, or compliance

In practice, accountability involves three fundamental questions. To whom is the organization accountable? For what is the organization accountable? By what means can the organization be accountable? Alnoor Ebrahim reviews nonprofit accountability and notes that nonprofits are expected to be accountable to multiple actors, including upward to funders and patrons, downward to clients, and internally to themselves and their mission.[10] In addition, nonprofits are accountable for finances, governance, performance, and mission. Finally, nonprofit accountability mechanisms include disclosure statements and reports, evaluation and performance assessment, self-regulation, participation, and adaptive learning.

Program evaluation plays an important role in accountability. Kevin Kearns notes that "accountability, in essence, is the obligation of public and nonprofit organizations to serve a higher authority—the public trust—which is the ultimate source of their mandate, their authority, and their legitimacy."[11] This public trust is served by the outputs and outcomes of nonprofit organizations, and accountability requires the evaluation of these results. For the NFP, evaluation was essential not only for developing the program but also for convincingly demonstrating to funders and policymakers what the value of the program was and that the program was worthy of support.

The 1990s saw several major initiatives to promote evaluation in the nonprofit sector. The Government Performance and Results Act of 1993 emphasized accountability in nonprofits receiving federal support.[12] In addition, in 1996, the United Way of America (UWA) launched its outcome measurement initiative to evaluate program outcomes in United Way–funded agencies.[13] The model developed for the UWA has become the most widely used approach to outcome measurement in the nonprofit sector, with a reported 450 local United Ways encouraging about 19,000 United Way–funded agencies to measure outcomes in 2008.[14] The basis of the UWA model is the clear specification of program inputs, activities, outputs, and outcomes, as shown in Figure 13.1. Some important strengths of the UWA model that have been widely incorporated into current program evaluation practice include an emphasis on outcomes, program improvement as a primary motivator, and the use of logic models as an important tool.[15] These will be discussed in detail in the following sections.

FIGURE 13.1. BASIC ELEMENTS OF PROGRAMS: THE NFP EXAMPLE

Programs consist of
Inputs → Program Activities → Outputs → Outcomes → Impacts

Examples of NFP program elements are
Inputs: nurses, mothers, children, other caregivers
Program activities: home visitation, prenatal health care, counseling and education
Outputs: appropriate child care, job search
Outcomes: planning pregnancies, employment
Impacts: healthy and functioning families

Understanding Basic Program Theory

Before we discuss the details of program evaluation, we need to define the basic elements of programs (see Figure 13.1). *Inputs* include those to be served by the program as well as the resources needed for program activities, such as labor and capital. *Program activities* are the steps an organization takes to bring about the intended program results. This could include instruction, counseling, or medical procedures. *Outputs* are the most direct consequences of program activities. In a vocational education program, for instance, program activities could include holding a number of classes. Outputs in this case would be the number of hours of instruction the students received over the course of instruction. Outputs, it is hoped, will produce outcomes. *Outcomes* are the short-term and intermediate changes that occur in program participants as a result of the program activities. Outcomes can involve changes in knowledge, skills, attitudes, intentions, or behavior. In our example, student outcomes would be an increase in vocationally relevant knowledge and skills. Outcomes are not the ultimate goals of programs, however. *Impacts* are the broader changes that program outcomes are designed to bring about within program participants or their surroundings, including the community, society, or environment. Graduates of the vocational education program should be able to obtain better jobs, which will benefit not only their well-being but also their communities.

The Program Evaluation Process

The program evaluation process should proceed through a series of logically related steps, including preparing for evaluation, securing agreement and commitment by leaders and stakeholders, choosing an appropriate evaluation design, collecting and analyzing data, and reporting the results of the evaluation. This basic model can be used by both large and small nonprofits.

Preparing for Program Evaluation

Nonprofits must have both the will and the ability to evaluate their programs. They must build capacity, define purposes, set goals, and get all necessary buy-in.

Building Evaluation Capacity

To build evaluation capacity, an organization needs to "continuously create and sustain overall organizational processes that make quality evaluation and its use routine."[16] This requires allocating adequate human capital and material and financial resources to evaluation. Boris Volkov and Jean King describe three elements of evaluation capacity:[17]

- **Resources devoted to evaluation**: personnel, facilities, funds, equipment, software, and time, along with staff and volunteer skills, knowledge, experience, and motivation
- **Structures conducive to evaluation**: an evaluation capacity-building plan, inclusion of evaluation in organizational policies and procedures, a system for reporting and monitoring evaluations, and effective communication and feedback systems
- **Organizational context supportive of evaluation**: internal support for evaluation integrated with the demands of external stakeholders for evaluation

Determining Program Evaluation Purpose

If evaluation findings are to be used to achieve greater accountability and enhanced performance, the evaluations themselves need to be carefully planned and a number of important questions should be addressed. Paddock points out that program evaluation can[18]

- Inform planning decisions.
- Determine whether more detailed, full-blown evaluations are needed.
- Track program progress.
- Determine whether a program has accomplished its goals (*outcome evaluation*).
- Determine whether a program has been implemented as planned (*process evaluation*).
- Measure the effectiveness or efficiency of units or practices.
- Determine whether there are unintended consequences.
- Assess the degree of stakeholder satisfaction.
- Compare programs or approaches to determine which might be best in a new setting.

Evaluations of the NFP program were used for all of these purposes. The first evaluation was used to test the initial program design. Subsequent evaluations tested the effectiveness of the program for other service recipients and geographical areas. In addition, two different service delivery modes were tested to determine which was more effective and efficient. Finally, the results of the evaluations were the basis for planning program expansion and the establishment of a national nonprofit organization.

Given these diverse purposes, it is clear that evaluations can be performed for a variety of stakeholders. For any evaluation, however, stakeholders may have diverse agendas and favor different performance criteria and indicators. In these situations, program evaluation is likely to involve disputes and political games. A consideration of NFP stakeholders and interests clearly illustrates this point. These stakeholders obviously included the mothers and families who were getting services as well as the nurses who were providing the services. These stakeholders would want services that were effective and easy to deliver. The agencies implementing the program would be interested in how well their programs were being run and the outcomes obtained. Other child welfare providers might be interested in the degree to which some portion of the services could be adopted by their agencies. Local government officials and social service providers would be interested in how the services could make good use of public resources. Finally, academics would be interested in identifying exactly what program activities produce which results and what that might mean for theories of child welfare. To mitigate the possibility of conflict, it is important that agreement among stakeholders is reached before an evaluation begins. No matter which type of evaluation is being considered, it is important to identify major stakeholders and involve them in the process.

Getting Full Stakeholder Buy-In
Those responsible for the future of the programs must be included in the evaluation process and must believe that the process will lead to positive results. It is important therefore that the first step in evaluation planning be the commitment of organizational leaders. This commitment should entail both the provision of support for the evaluation as well as an agreement to give serious consideration to the evaluation results. It is also important that stakeholders for whom the program is important be included in the planning and possibly the design process for the evaluation. These stakeholders are likely to include representatives of various staff functions and possibly clients or others outside the organization. The program staff have detailed knowledge of program operations and are in the best position to both pinpoint key aspects of the way programs are actually run and help interpret findings. Clients can identify program successes and problems as well as other, possibly unintended, program effects.

Establishing Clear Goals

It is crucial at this time to clearly establish the specific goals and eventual use of the evaluation. This may well involve negotiation among key stakeholders. However, it is important at this stage that negotiation be followed by agreement, as that (1) signals to stakeholders that this is a serious effort and worthy of the time and effort required, and (2) secures the cooperation of those expected to act on the findings. Finally, adequate resources and time frames need to be established. The best evaluation goals and designs can be undermined by inadequate resources or time. This will then lead to frustration on the part of those involved in the process and potentially cynical attitudes about the commitment of organizational leaders to program improvement. For the NFP program, evaluation goals changed over time. The early evaluations were concerned with testing the program that David Olds had designed. He had based the program details on his and other practitioners' experiences as well as on the academic literature. It was important to establish that the expectations drawn from these sources were borne out in practice. A test of alternative service providers (nurses versus paraprofessionals) was also conducted, and evaluations were used to test the degree to which the program could be used for a range of communities and ethnic groups.

Determining the Evaluation Approach

Once the purpose and goals of the evaluation have been established, a number of options are available for the shape the evaluation will take. Space precludes a detailed discussion of program evaluations for each of the purposes we listed previously. We will instead focus on process and outcome evaluations, because they are the two most general types and are most likely to be used by nonprofit organizations.

Two general evaluation approaches have been distinguished. The approach taken will have consequences for the types of questions the evaluation can answer, who will do the evaluation, and the types of data gathered. John Thomas describes an *objective scientist approach*.[19] This approach is based on the natural science model of research, and it has particular implications for program evaluation. A key feature of this approach is the quest for objectivity. Procedures to ensure this include distance between the evaluator and the program, in order to minimize the influence of potentially biased program staff. Consequently, outside evaluators are used. In addition, quantitative data are gathered. These data are seen as objective in that they do not require the subjective interpretation that qualitative data do. The goal of the evaluation is to assess whether program goals were accomplished. The internal workings of the program are not considered, and the evaluation is performed at the end of the program. Thus this evaluation has a *summative* purpose, and the model it follows is described as an *outcome evaluation* process.

The objective scientist approach was developed in the early days of program evaluation in public agencies. It was based on the idea that program goals were clear and could be objectively measured and that data on goal accomplishment was sufficient for decision makers. This may have been the case for legislators debating program renewal, but it was not sufficient for those concerned with program improvement. They needed more information about program details. To provide this information, an alternative approach, termed *utilization-focused evaluation*, was developed.[20] In this approach the goal is a more comprehensive evaluation that includes the insights of program staff and the details of program operations. Although the objective views of outsiders have value, program staff have intimate knowledge of how a program actually operates and can identify problems in cause-and-effect relationships in program logic, clarify intermediate program steps, provide details on subjective program goals, and assist in interpreting results. To support these evaluations, fine-grained qualitative data are used in addition to objective data. The evaluation is designed to produce the knowledge that will allow staff to modify a program to enhance its outcome and impact. The knowledge may be used before the program ends. Thus this evaluation has a *formative* purpose, and the model it follows is described as a *process evaluation* process.

The NFP initial program model was founded on a core principle that registered nurses, by virtue of their education, were best qualified to conduct home visits. As the program gained acceptance, however, funders sought to reduce program costs by using paraprofessionals, who were expected to have a high school education but no bachelor's degree or any college preparation, instead of registered nurses. To test this, a study was done in Denver in which the outcomes for paraprofessional-visited mothers were compared with those for nurse-visited mothers. The evaluation of this study showed that nurse-visited mothers had the same positive outcomes as found in previous evaluations whereas paraprofessional-visited mothers had far fewer positive outcomes. Moreover, a process evaluation was also conducted. This showed that the quality of interactions between mothers and nurses was higher than between mothers and paraprofessionals (for example, nurses provided more information and were more trusted). This was held to be responsible for the difference in outcomes between the two ways of delivering the program. These results were used to justify the continued use of nurses.

Understanding Theories of Change and Logic Models

Programs are essentially tests of ideas about making something happen. Once support is gathered for particular goals, a program to bring about the necessary conditions or changes to accomplish those goals can be established. For example, if there is enough support for reducing smoking, an antismoking program can be established. Social programs, in turn, are based on *theories of change* about how modification of behavior or social impact can be produced. These theories of change specify relationships between causes and effects and serve as the foundation for determining program activities and outcomes. For example, the theory of change that underlies an antismoking program consisting of distributing educational material is different from the theory of change that underlies an approach consisting of raising tobacco prices. The first program relies on the theory that people can be educated to do what is healthy, whereas the second relies on the theory that people are rational calculators and will pay only so much for any commodity. Although both theories have been shown to work in some contexts, it may not be clear which would work better in the case of smoking. Social behavior is complex, and the best way to bring about changes in behavior may often be unclear or contested.

How does this relate to program evaluation? Outcome evaluation can tell the nonprofit whether its program outcomes are as desired. If they are, the organization has evidence that the cause-and-effect relationships assumed by the program's theory of change are supported and useful. For example, the positive evaluations of the NFP programs strongly supported a conclusion that the underlying theories of prenatal health and caregiving and parental support were valid and useful in bringing about the desired results. When desired program outcomes are not obtained, however, outcome evaluation alone will not help a nonprofit to distinguish between two possible causes for the failure. One cause might be that the program's theory of change is not appropriate, meaning that the cause-and-effect relationships are not as expected, and consequently, program activities do not bring about the changes in behavior desired. We could call this a *theory failure*. In the case of an antismoking program relying on education, if the expected reduction in smoking does not come about, it may be that education is of limited use for this type of addiction. Alternatively, the theory of change may be appropriate, but the program may not have been correctly run. For example, perhaps the educational material in the antismoking program was not distributed to the right people or in the right manner. A problem often encountered is that budgets levels are not adequate or are compromised in the course of running the program. We could call this a *program administration failure*. In this case, supplementing the outcome evaluation with a process evaluation, in order to closely evaluate the way the program is run, will help to determine whether the lack of impact is due to theory or program administration failure.

Our discussion points to the need to base programs on well-articulated theories of change. On the one hand these theories may be extensive, complex, and based on academic research, like those used by the NFP. On the other hand they may be more modest in scope and also based on experience and practice. A good example of the latter can be seen in Project Superwomen, a program designed to help female abuse survivors find employment.[21] Theories of change can be developed through a series of steps, beginning with *identifying assumptions and outcomes*. Project Superwomen involved the assumptions that (1) nontraditional jobs for women (electrician, for instance) have better wages and so should be the target of training, and (2) women who have been through abuse need coping skills in addition to job training. Desired outcomes included (1) long-term employment, (2) coping skills, (3) marketable skills in nontraditional jobs, and (4) workplace behavior skills. This step is followed by *backward mapping* and connecting outcomes. Backward mapping involves looking at the desired outcomes and specifying the antecedents (program steps) needed to produce them. For Project Superwomen, backward mapping found the following descending series of antecedents:

- The final outcome, women's long-term employment, is brought about by the intermediate outcomes of women attaining coping skills and job and workplace skills.
- Coping skills are taught through peer-to-peer counseling and counseling and practical support for crises. Skills are taught in internships, which are preceded by training about workplace expectations and classes in job skills. In addition, employers are educated about how to use interns.
- Getting access to this teaching requires that women enroll in the program, which requires that women are ready to commit and attend as well as able to access child care if needed.
- Before any of this can happen, women need to hear and learn about the program, which requires that a variety of sources (such as social service agencies) provide information to them.

Finally, the mapping is displayed in a *logic model*. The logic model should make clear the assumptions, interventions, and other conditions associated with producing the outcomes. In addition to the basic program elements, the logic model can be used to specify antecedent and mediating variables. These variables are important in establishing the parameters within which the program operates and that may have an impact on program performance and results. For example, the program is likely to have different results for women of different educational levels (an antecedent variable). In addition, the commitment of employers to providing quality internships is likely to be important in the attainment of outcomes (a mediating variable). Logic models make the theory of change and the basis for producing impacts clear and provide a sound basis for program evaluation. Exhibit 13.1 displays the theory of change and logic model for Project Superwomen.

EXHIBIT 13.1. THEORY OF CHANGE AND LOGIC MODEL FOR PROJECT SUPERWOMEN

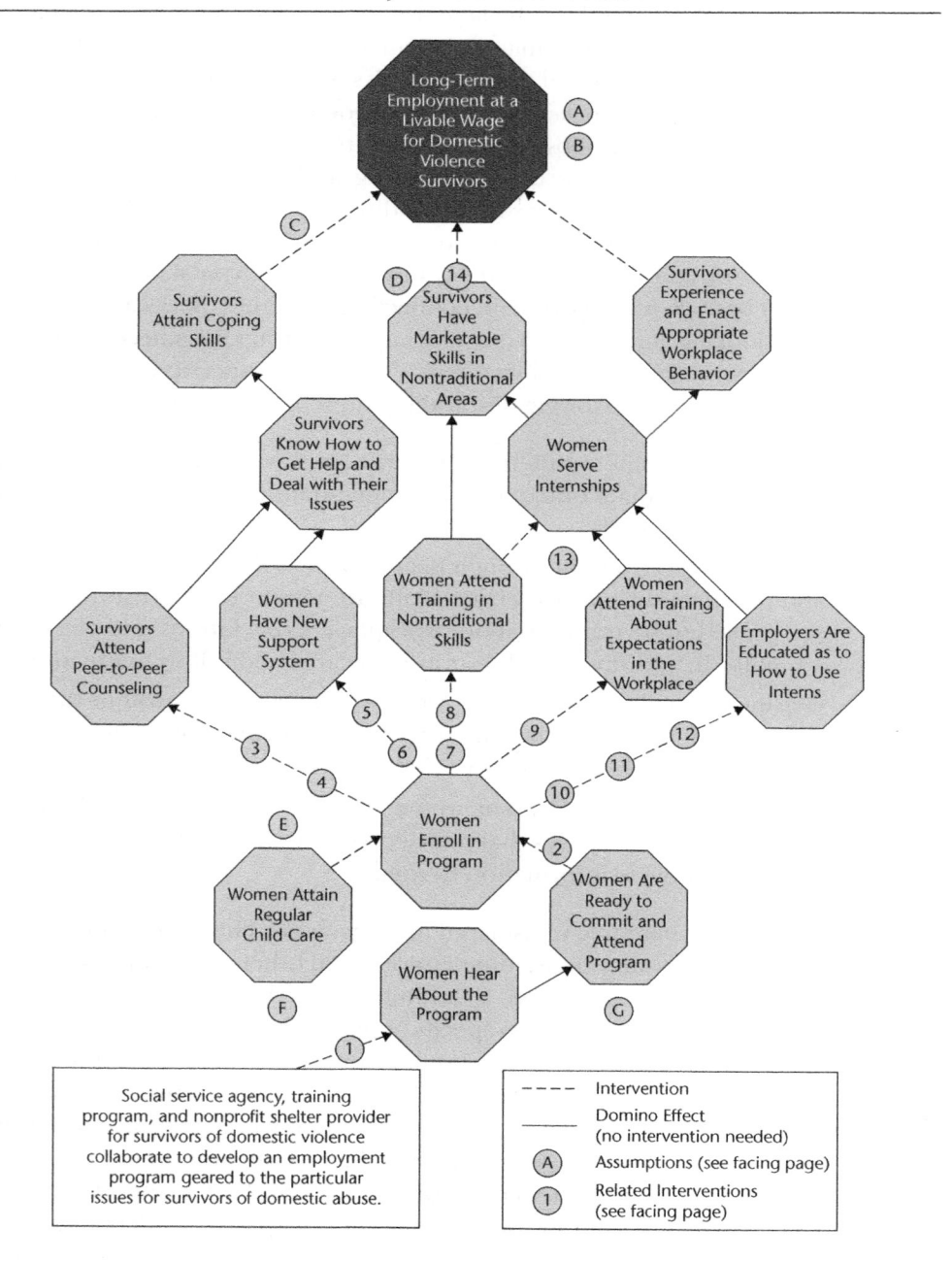

Long-Term Employment at a Livable Wage for Domestic Violence Survivors (A, B)

- Survivors Attain Coping Skills (C)
- Survivors Have Marketable Skills in Nontraditional Areas (D) (14)
- Survivors Experience and Enact Appropriate Workplace Behavior
- Survivors Know How to Get Help and Deal with Their Issues
- Women Serve Internships
- Survivors Attend Peer-to-Peer Counseling
- Women Have New Support System
- Women Attend Training in Nontraditional Skills
- Women Attend Training About Expectations in the Workplace
- Employers Are Educated as to How to Use Interns
- (3) (4) (5) (6) (7) (8) (9) (10) (11) (12) (13)
- Women Enroll in Program
- (E) Women Attain Regular Child Care
- (2) Women Are Ready to Commit and Attend Program
- (F) Women Hear About the Program (1)
- (G)

Social service agency, training program, and nonprofit shelter provider for survivors of domestic violence collaborate to develop an employment program geared to the particular issues for survivors of domestic abuse.

Legend:
- ---- Intervention
- —— Domino Effect (no intervention needed)
- (A) Assumptions (see facing page)
- (1) Related Interventions (see facing page)

Assumptions

A. There are jobs available in nontraditional fields for women.

B. Jobs in nontraditional areas of work for women, such as electrical, plumbing, carpentry, and building management, are more likely to pay livable wages and are more likely to be unionized and provide job security. Some of these jobs also provide a ladder for upward mobility, from apprenticeship to master, giving entry-level employees a career future.

C. Women who have been in abusive relationships need more than just skills; they need to be emotionally ready for work as well.

D. Women can learn nontraditional skills and compete in the marketplace.

E. The program cannot help all women, and so entry into the program must include screening so that women who have sufficient literacy and math skills to take the training and have lives stable enough to attend classes are admitted. The program does not have the resources to handle providing basic skills or major social services.

F. Women who have left abusive situations are often single mothers and therefore cannot work unless they have child care.

G. Women must be out of the abusive situation. The program assumes that women still in abusive situations will not be able to attend regularly, may pose a danger to others, and will not be emotionally ready to commit.

Interventions

1. Implement outreach campaign.
2. Screen participants.
3. Set up counseling sessions.
4. Lead group sessions.
5. Provide help for short-term crises, such as housing evictions or court appearances.
6. Provide one-on-one counseling.
7. Develop curricula in electrical, plumbing, carpentry, and building maintenance.
8. Conduct classes.
9. Develop curricula and experiential learning situations.
10. Conduct classes.
11. Identify potential employers.
12. Create employer database.
13. Match women to internships.
14. Help women secure permanent jobs.

Sample Indicators

Outcome
Long-term employment at a livable wage for domestic violence survivors.

Indicator
Employment rate.

Target population
Program graduates.

Baseline
47% of program attendees are unemployed. 53% are earning minimum wage.

Threshold
90% of the graduates remain in job at least six months and earn at least $12 per hour.

Source: Andrea Anderson, *The Community Builder's Approach to Theory of Change: A Practical Guide to Theory Development* (Washington, D.C.: Aspen Institute Roundtable on Community Change, 2005), Resource Toolbox, p. 33. Reprinted with permission of The Aspen Institute.

Specifying Program Goals

Specifying measurable goals is a crucial activity in program evaluation—it links the logic model and the evaluation process. We can distinguish between impact goals, outcome goals, and activity goals. *Outcome* and *impact goals* serve as the basis for outcome evaluation; *activity goals* serve as the basis for internal program activities and process evaluation. The latter might include numbers of hours of instruction, counseling, or internships. In the NFP program, we have an example of clearly specified outcome and activity goals. Program activity would begin during pregnancy. Nurses would visit mothers to build trust and provide education on prenatal care, diet, and the dangers of drug use.[22] In all, nurses try to make fourteen visits during pregnancy and twenty-eight visits during infancy. Nurses provide information, encourage family members to help, assist mothers in envisioning a future consistent with their values and goals, and help mothers to evaluate contraception, child-care options, and career choices. The activity goals were established and refined though extensive research in which alternative activities were evaluated and rejected, such as the use of paraprofessionals instead of nurses. Activity goals will often be the easiest to articulate, achieve, and measure—hence the pressure to restrict program evaluation to process evaluation.

For program and evaluation purposes, an additional type of goal has been designated by Carol Weiss.[23] *Bridging goals* are defined as falling between activity and outcome goals. Bridging goals are seen as relying on activity and leading to outcome. For example, in the NFP program's effort to get mothers to stay in school, the bridging goal between conversations with mothers (the activity) and mothers staying in school (the outcome) might be an increased awareness by mothers of the lifelong negative consequences of dropping out. Bridging goals are the links between program activities and outcomes and hence are at the heart of the theory of change the program is seeking to embody. Therefore they represent the conceptual basis on which the program is built. To demonstrate that the program's theory of change is appropriate, it is necessary to show that the bridging goals have been accomplished and have led to the outcome. For the NFP the theory of change is based on the notion that appropriately provided support and education can lead to positive behavioral change. Changes in mothers' attitudes and motivations could be assumed to be crucial links and can serve as bridging goals.

Collecting Data

Proper data collection in the three NFP trials was essential to the success of the overall evaluation of the NFP. Given the goal of establishing the NFP as a major public health initiative, it was important to gather support from funders, community leaders, practitioners, and academics. These stakeholders would assess the value of the program using evidence found in program evaluations, and this evidence was only as strong as the data it was based on. Program improvement and development also depended on convincing data on program operation and impact.

Program evaluation data collection and analysis is based on the various research methodologies that have been developed in the social sciences, including psychology, sociology, and economics, to name a few. This is an extensive topic, and many good texts, some geared specifically toward evaluation, are available. Here, we can provide only some basic guidelines. Jane Wei-Skillern and colleagues have provided a useful way of relating data acquisition to evaluation, as shown in Figure 13.2. They note that as one moves from inputs to impacts, one tends to go further out in time, away from the center of the organization, down in degree of control, down in measurability, up in abstraction, and down in the degree to which one can confidently attribute causation. A lot of data are normally collected in zone 1 for program administration. Data for process evaluation are also readily available. Data availability in zone 2 is more questionable. The question becomes, how far "outside" the organization should data routinely be collected on the results of the organization's activities (that is, what is the *normal data horizon*)? The question of how far outside the organization to go for data is also relevant for an assessment of impacts (zone 3).

FIGURE 13.2. ZONES OF THE VALUE CHAIN, PERFORMANCE MANAGEMENT, AND EVALUATION

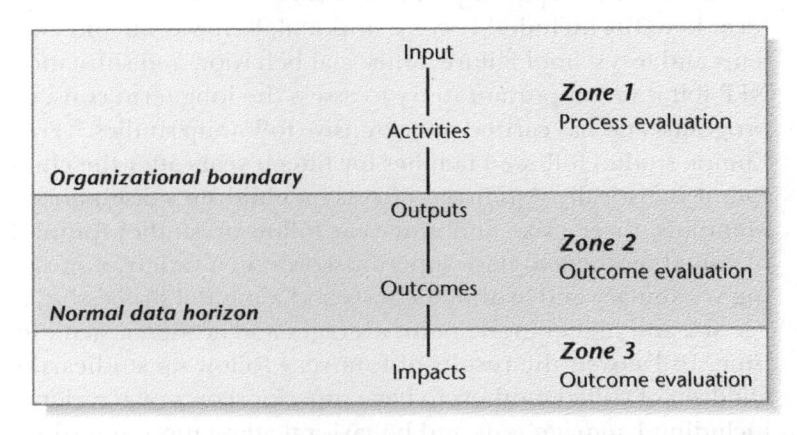

	Input	
	|	Zone 1
	Activities	Process evaluation
Organizational boundary	|	
	Outputs	
	|	Zone 2
	Outcomes	Outcome evaluation
Normal data horizon	|	
	Impacts	Zone 3
		Outcome evaluation

Source: Adapted from Jane Wei-Skillern, James Austin, Herman Leonard, and Howard Stevenson, *Entrepreneurship in the Social Sector* (Thousand Oaks, CA: Sage, 2007), 332.

Data in this zone would be expensive to come by and attributions of causality would become more difficult. Nonprofits may find it difficult to gather and use zone 3 data.

The NFP started carrying out evaluations immediately after the initiation of its program in each of the three study sites. We would place these studies in zone 2. These evaluations quickly found positive results. In Elmira, New York, women in the program trial were enrolled prior to their thirtieth week of pregnancy.[24] They were subsequently given four different levels of service. These will be described when we discuss experimental designs in the section below. For the women who received nurse visits, the visits began during pregnancy (ideally within the first trimester) and were conducted weekly, biweekly, or monthly over a two-year period. To gather data to assess program outcomes, women were interviewed at enrollment and at six, ten, twelve, twenty-two, and twenty-four months after the birth of their child. At six, twelve, and twenty-four months, children were weighed, measured, and given developmental tests. Medical and child abuse and neglect records were also checked over the two years. Data from this study showed that mothers who received nurse visits smoked less during pregnancy and had fewer preterm deliveries than mothers who received no services. In addition, they neglected or abused their children less and provided more appropriate child care, and their children were seen less frequently in emergency rooms or by physicians to be treated for accidents and poisoning.

The NFP model, however, hypothesized longer-term benefits from the program.[25] These effects would be found in zone 3. For mothers, the hypothesized benefits included reduced substance abuse, less welfare dependence, and more widely spaced pregnancies. For their children, projected long-term benefits included fewer emotional, behavioral, and cognitive problems and less school failure, antisocial behavior, and substance abuse. The NFP felt it was important to try to assess the long-term consequences of its programs and has carried out extensive follow-up studies.[26] For example, in Elmira, studies followed families for fifteen years after the child's birth and found statistically significant effects on children's disciplinary records. In Memphis, three-, six-, and nine-year follow-up studies found the children of visited mothers to have superior scores on a variety of measures, including vocabulary and arithmetic tests and a mental processing composite at age six, and higher grade point averages and academic achievement at age nine. In Denver, the results of four-year follow-up studies also found the children of visited mothers to have superior scores on a variety of measures, including language tests and behavioral adaptation in testing. Because of the care that was given to the initial testing of the programs, subsequent testing could be carried out (clients could be located, and so forth). The program was also able to secure funding for further evaluations.

Understanding Different Types of Data

The data used in evaluations may come from a variety of sources. Program administration requires the keeping of *records* on program inputs, activities, and outputs. Statistics based on this information are also routinely computed. These are, however, usually quantitative measures useful for running the program, and they do not convey any subjective or interpretive information. These data may be useful in process evaluations but are seldom detailed enough to be the primary source of information. Data on outcomes may be periodically or sporadically gathered as part of other organizational activities, such as strategic planning or marketing.

Information may be obtained directly from *service recipients*. In some cases, client records may be available from other sources. More typically, client perceptions about the services they received and their satisfaction with these services are assessed through surveys. Surveys can be administered in personal interviews, through the mail, by phone, or over the Internet. The advantage of surveys is that they can be tailored to the data needs of the evaluation. For example, additional relevant client information can also be obtained through these surveys, such as demographics, related activities, or other services or organizations used. Downsides of surveys include potentially low response rates for mail or phone surveys, given the deluge of advertising and solicitations that people receive; varying rates of responses to Internet surveys owing to limited computer use among some populations; and questions about the accuracy of self-reported information. People may be hesitant to divulge information on sensitive or controversial topics, such as drug or alcohol use, for example. They may also be concerned about confidentiality or worried about the use to which their information may be put. In addition, the design of even a moderately extensive survey requires careful attention to technical factors such as question wording and survey layout. These technical details are covered in texts or guides on conducting survey research.

Finally, several *qualitative* data collection techniques are available, primarily observation and in-depth interviewing. These techniques are usually carried out by trained experts. Observers need to be aware of the various ways in which the information they are looking for can be displayed. For example, in observing a group interaction, they need to know how group cohesion might be manifested. In-depth interviewers need to be sensitive to times when probes should be used to solicit more detailed information or allow respondents to branch out to other, related, aspects of the topic. These techniques are worth the effort, however, because they can provide very detailed information on the way programs were run or clients were affected.

Collecting Outcome Evaluation Data

Outcome evaluation requires data on the degree to which program outcome goals were realized. These goals have to do with changes brought about in recipients due to program activities. Consequently, data on recipient changes attributable to program activity must be obtained. A variety of data collection designs are available. They all compare program outcomes with what would have happened without the program. Adele Harrell and her colleagues provide a good overview of these designs.[27] They vary in terms of the degree to which causation can be inferred. They also vary in terms of the difficulty of data collection and analysis. Organizations with limited resources or expertise may not be able to carry out the more sophisticated designs. They could, however, consider some of the less elaborate ones.

To show that program activity caused behavioral change, it is necessary to show that the behavioral change varied in tandem with the program activity (*covariation*), that the program occurred before the behavior changed (proper *time order*), and that the behavioral change was not caused by any other factors (*nonspuriousness*). The first two conditions can usually be dealt with in a fairly straightforward manner through program design. The final requirement, however, may be extremely difficult to address.

Experimental designs have been developed to explicitly address all three requirements. Individuals or groups are assigned to one of two groups at random. This is to ensure that the two groups are similar at the start of the experiment. Each group is given a pretest, measuring the behavior of interest. One group is then subject to the experimental treatment (the NFP program in our example). The other group, the *control group*, does not receive the treatment. Both groups are tested again in a *posttest*, and any differences between the two groups can be attributed to the impact of the treatment. Although such experiments are the gold standard for assessing causation, their use in real-world settings is limited. The major problem is the ability to make random assignments to control and treatment groups and the appropriateness of this. Some programs, such as youth curfews, cannot be selectively given to a subset of the target population. In addition, ethical questions may be raised against withholding benefits to the control group.

The NFP used an experimental design in testing its program. The Elmira study is typical.[28] Four hundred pregnant women were recruited through the health department antepartum clinic, the offices of private obstetricians, Planned Parenthood, the public schools, and a variety of other health and human services agencies. These women had at least one of the following maternal characteristics that predispose infants to health and developmental problems: (1) young age (less than nineteen years old),

(2) single-parent status, or (3) low socioeconomic status. The families were assigned at random to one of four treatment conditions:

- **Treatment 1**. These families served as a control group. During pregnancy no program services were provided. Infants were screened for sensory and developmental problems at one and two years of age. If needed, referrals to specialists were made.
- **Treatment 2**. Families were provided free transportation for regular prenatal and well-child care at local health care providers. Screening for infants was provided at one and two years.
- **Treatment 3**. Families were provided nurse home visits during pregnancy in addition to transportation and screening services. Nurses visited families about every two weeks and made an average of nine visits during the pregnancy.
- **Treatment 4**. Families received the same services as those in treatment 3. In addition, the nurse continued to visit until the child was two years old. Initial visits were every week. The frequency declined to once every six weeks over the course of the two years.

This experimental design made sophisticated statistical analysis of the impacts of the different treatments possible and was responsible for the acceptance of the findings, which were published in numerous academic journals.

Although objections to experimental designs can sometimes be addressed with creative design or follow-up services to a control group, outcome evaluations are often carried out using *quasi-experimental* designs. These designs relax the requirements of experimental designs. The most common variation is the relaxation of random assignment to treatment or control groups. Usually, evaluators use existing groups that are as similar as possible for comparison purposes. For example, two classes in the same school could be used. Multivariate statistical techniques are then used to control for the remaining differences between the groups.

There are, in addition, a number of *nonexperimental* designs, departing further from the experimental ideal. They do not have comparison groups or individuals not exposed to the program. Although they are relatively easy and inexpensive, they have numerous methodological shortcomings. A major limitation is that they cannot estimate the full impact of the program as no data are available for people receiving no services. These designs include

- Before and after comparisons of program participants
- Time series designs based on repeated measures of outcomes before and after the program for groups that include program participants

- Panel studies based on repeated measures of outcomes in the same group of participants
- Postprogram comparisons among groups of participants

Given their resources and expertise, small, community-based nonprofits may find that these simpler, nonexperimental designs are most appropriate for them. These designs can be used as long as some measure of the participant characteristics of interest can be obtained. For example, to what degree did people smoke before and after a smoking cessation program? Simple questions can be used to assess this. Other measures based on observations may also be used. For example, did participants increase their strength and endurance after a physical fitness program?

Collecting Process Evaluation Data

Harrell and colleagues also describe designs for the collection of data for process evaluations. These data are collected to show to what degree programs are being implemented as specified, to identify any unintended consequences and unanticipated outcomes, and to understand the program from the perspectives of staff, participants, and the community. Designs include case studies, focus groups, and ethnography.

Case studies entail in-depth studies of programs to determine how the program is operating, what barriers to program implementation have been encountered, what strategies are the most successful, and what resources and skills are necessary for program operations. Case studies can also be used to evaluate competing program models in order to identify the best alternative. The information gathered will help program designers choose or develop key program elements most in line with the program's theory of change and logic model. Case studies produce qualitative data, gathered from semistructured interviews, focus groups, or researcher observations. Semistructured interviews ask specific questions but allow respondents to answer in as much detail as they want to provide. In addition, probes can be used to solicit additional material. In this way, respondents can reveal complex and unanticipated descriptions and explanations of program realities.

Focus groups are useful for examining both attitudes and behavior. A number of stakeholders are brought together for a focused discussion. These group discussions are guided by a facilitator. Another researcher is present to take detailed notes. The conversations are also recorded. Several general questions are used to direct the conversation among group members. The goal of the discussion can vary. It may be to arrive at consensus on an issue or to surface as many divergent viewpoints as possible. Given the goal, the composition of the group should be carefully chosen to provide relevant viewpoints and characteristics. Afterward the conversations are summarized by the researcher, using both the detailed notes and the recording. If numerous focus groups are held, an overall summary is also produced.

Ethnography uses observation and unstructured interviews to study program processes, the community context of the program, causal processes as participants view them, and models of decision making. The goal is to understand the subjective experience of the staff, participants, and others and then use this information to understand whether and how program goals are being achieved. Researchers observe program operations, make detailed field notes, and analyze their observations and notes to identify themes and trends. This flexible, unstructured approach is useful for identifying unintended consequences and unanticipated outcomes. Unexpected observations may lead to entirely new theories of change.

Analyzing Data and Presenting Results

Data need to be analyzed before they are meaningful. Evaluations begin with particular purposes, and analysis must be adequate to address the questions an evaluation set out to answer. Data analysis is a highly specialized field, and if the analysis is to go beyond simple descriptions and breakouts, specially trained staff or outside expertise is likely to be needed. Outcome evaluations rely on comparisons of groups or individuals. Statistical analysis will be needed to determine the results of the experimental and related designs discussed above. These analytical techniques are used extensively in psychological research and are well developed. Process evaluation relies in whole or part on the analysis and interpretation of qualitative data. Reasons for success or failure are sought. Statistical analysis plays a lesser part in these analyses, which rely heavily on description, summarization, and interpretation. Researcher experience with these methods is an important factor for obtaining useful results. The fields of sociology and anthropology have developed and employ these methods.

When results have been obtained, they need to be distributed to the evaluation stakeholders, including organizational leaders, board members, program staff, and funders or other outsiders involved in or concerned about the evaluation. The information needs of these various groups are likely to differ, and results should be configured and reported accordingly. For some groups, such as funders or government agencies, outcome data are most relevant and sufficient for their decision making. For others, such as program managers, process data are most relevant. They seek to make judgments about and improvements in program activities and need highly detailed information. Higher-level organizational leaders, such as board members, may want some of each type of data. Summary outcome data are important for them, but their decisions also concern program activities.

For any stakeholder group, it is important to provide neither too little nor too much information. Too little information will leave questions unanswered and frustrate decision making. Too much or overly complex information will confuse and possibly mislead those getting it. Finally, besides being shaped to stakeholder needs, results also need to be provided in a timely manner. Decisions may need to be made in particular time frames, which then need to be accommodated by evaluators.

Challenges to Evaluation in Practice

Nonprofits face a number of challenges when it comes to program evaluation. Many community-based nonprofits lack the will, expertise, and resources for the kind of large-scale, substantially funded evaluations conducted by experts that occur in the government context.[29] In the nonprofit context, evaluations demanded by stakeholders can be seen as intrusive diversions from the real work of the organization.[30] Comments gathered by Joanne Carman and Kimberly Fredericks from a study of human service nonprofits attest to these difficulties:[31]

> "The amount of time and money we spend on program evaluation is not worth it."
>
> "We simply don't have the knowledge or expertise to do quality program evaluation."
>
> "Much of what we do for program evaluation is symbolic."
>
> "Spending time and resources on evaluation takes away from what we do best—provide services."
>
> "Program evaluation requirements are just hoops that our funders make us jump through."

In spite of the challenges, most nonprofits are concerned about evaluating their programs. Carman and Fredericks found that 90 percent of the nonprofits in their study reported that they evaluated their programs. The extensiveness of evaluations, however, varied considerably. About a third reported that they did very little or only some evaluation. At the other extreme, only 18 percent reported that they went out of their way to evaluate all of their programs. Evaluation results were used for strategic management as well as for external reporting or program promotion. The most frequent strategic management uses of evaluation information included helping to make changes in existing programs (93 percent of the nonprofits) and establishing program goals or targets (75 percent). In addition, between 60 percent and 70 percent used the information for each of the following: strategic planning, developing new programs, making decisions about staffing, and making decisions about fiscal allocations. Use of evaluation information for reporting purposes included reporting to the board (82 percent) and reporting to funders (67 percent), outreach and public relations (59 percent), and seeking new funding (53 percent).

As these findings show, program evaluation provides practical benefits to nonprofits.[32] Evaluation can help to provide feedback and direction to staff, focus boards on program issues, identify service units or participant groups that need attention, compare alternative service delivery strategies, identify partners for collaborations, allocate resources, recruit volunteers and attract customers, set targets for future performance, track program effectiveness over time, increase funding, and enhance a public image. In order to realize these benefits, however, leaders in nonprofits and funding agencies must foster an appreciation of the benefits of evaluation as well as provide the support and resources necessary.

Small and midsized nonprofits should not forgo program evaluation. Although their evaluations need to follow appropriate procedures, their programs and services are likely to be simpler and smaller in scope than those of larger nonprofits. This makes following the steps in this chapter easier. Fewer staff will be needed, and it might be possible to use volunteers.[33] Data will be easier to gather, and analysis can be less elaborate. In addition, assistance for program evaluation is available from a variety of sources. These resources explain program evaluation logic and design in everyday terms, provide practical guidance for carrying out the steps needed, and contain links to further resources. Nonprofits can use these to educate their staff members and guide the evaluations. Some examples of useful online resources for program evaluation include the following:

> Foundation Center, *Tools and Resources for Assessing Social Impact*, (http:trasi.foundationcenter.org)
>
> Delaware Association of Nonprofit Organizations, *Info Central: Program Evaluation*, (http://www.delawarenonprofit.org/infocentral/programeval.php)
>
> The Free Management Library, *Basic Guide to Outcomes-Based Evaluation for Nonprofit Organizations with Very Limited Resources*, (http://managementhelp.org/evaluation/outcomes-evaluation-guide.htm)
>
> University of Wisconsin-Extension, *Program Development and Evaluation*, (http://www.uwex.edu/ces/pdande/evaluation/index.html)

Evaluations can become embroiled in political tensions. A nonprofit's stakeholders, including the board, staff, volunteers, consumers, funders, community leaders, and regulators, may have different, and possibly competing, views on the desirability, goals, and techniques of program evaluation. Nonprofit leaders must balance these multiple viewpoints when making decisions about program evaluation. In order to make program evaluation the basis of organizational improvement and a cornerstone of organizational learning, leaders must motivate and mobilize internal stakeholders. Salvatore Alaimo characterizes this as an *internal push* for evaluation.[34] Leaders should communicate that evaluation is an effective tool for helping the organization accomplish its mission and should provide resources for evaluation capacity building. In addition, demands from external stakeholders must also be addressed. Moreover, these *external pulls* must be integrated with the internal push for evaluation. The need to satisfy external stakeholders and acquire resources may need to be balanced with the desire to retain autonomy.

An in-depth evaluation of a workforce development project for the James Irwin Foundation provides the basis for some useful recommendations for addressing some of the key internal challenges to successfully organizing evaluations in nonprofits:[35]

- Involve leaders of the organization: their sustained endorsement is especially critical for buy-in by others in the organization and for follow-through as the evaluation proceeds.
- Establish a high level of trust between funders and the nonprofit: nonprofits need to feel free to expose weaknesses in their performance without fear that their funders will use this against them when considering future funding.
- Clarify roles, responsibilities, and expectations: this involves having clarity about such things as what the steps in the process will be, who will do them, and when they will be done.
- Allocate sufficient time for technical assistance that might be needed: if specialized knowledge is needed for evaluation design or data acquisition and analysis but it is not obtained, serious errors in interpretation may occur and lead to inappropriate action.
- Involve a broad range of staff: incorporate staff from throughout the organization in creating a culture supportive of evaluation.
- Ensure that staff can devote sufficient time: make evaluation tasks part of the regular work of the staff, instead of adding them on top of existing workloads.

Funders have played a key role in the spread of nonprofit outcome evaluation. However, as noted earlier, tensions can arise between funders and nonprofits. To address these issues, nonprofits can work with funders to establish a more collaborative evaluation environment.[36]

- To be most constructive, funders should be encouraged to view their role as helping agencies to develop evaluations that will provide the most useful information for programs.
- Funders serve their own best interests by helping agencies to develop evaluation capacity. This includes support for hands-on, experiential training and ongoing technical assistance.
- Local funders can collaborate with each other to support agency evaluation efforts. This could include pooling funds as well as establishing common terminology, methodologies, or reporting requirements.
- When funders make outcome data a reporting requirement, they should drop other requirements that do not relate to this focus. When process information is required, it should clearly relate to outcomes and not general agency operations.

Concluding Thoughts

Nonprofit organizations are given a number of benefits. They receive exemptions from taxes, individuals and corporations give them financial contributions, and individuals also give of their time and volunteer efforts. These benefits are provided so that nonprofits, through their services and activities, can contribute to the welfare of individuals and society. This chapter has covered the questions at the heart of the nonprofit missions and operations: What have we been able to do? and, What have the results been? These questions are of crucial importance to those running nonprofit programs and to other nonprofit stakeholders. Program evaluation is both a logical approach and a set of techniques that allows nonprofits to answer these questions. It is the basis for documenting a nonprofit's value, justifying public confidence and support, and improving programs.

The next chapter considers major stakeholders in nonprofit environments. It discusses government and public relations. Government and key portions of the public can significantly affect nonprofit organizations, and their understanding of the outcomes of nonprofit programs is likely to play an important role in their decision making about nonprofits.

Questions for Consideration

1. Are accountability and program evaluation likely to differ for nonprofits, for-profits, and government agencies? Why or why not?
2. Can all nonprofit programs and services be evaluated? Think of some types of nonprofit programs or services that might be very difficult or

impossible to evaluate. What accounts for the difficulties? How might evaluation design be used to address these difficulties?

Exercises

Exercise 13.1: Accountability

Select a nonprofit organization you are familiar with, and then answer the following questions about it:

1. To which stakeholders might this organization be accountable?
2. How could this nonprofit comply with the four core components of accountability?
3. How could this nonprofit use program evaluation for accountability?

Exercise 13.2: Evaluation Design

Select a nonprofit program you are familiar with, and then respond to the following:

1. In one sentence, describe the program's goal.
2. What is the program's theory of change?
3. Draw a logic model of the program.
4. Design an outcome evaluation for the program.
5. Design a process evaluation for the program.

Exercise 13.3: Evaluation Challenges

Considering the nonprofit you selected in the first exercise, answer the following questions:

- What might its key internal challenges be when doing a program evaluation?
- What external challenges might it encounter?
- How could it successfully address these challenges?

CHAPTER FOURTEEN

PUBLIC AND GOVERNMENT RELATIONS

The Nature Conservancy is one of the world's leading conservation organizations. Founded in 1951, it has done much to protect land and water through a nonconfrontational, collaborative approach. Unlike the World Wildlife Fund and other conservation nonprofits that, at least initially, treated for-profit businesses as adversaries, The Nature Conservancy has tried to forge partnerships with businesses, founded on scientifically based approaches to sustainability. Over the years its working relationships with businesses have led to accusations that it is not staying true to its mission: "Protecting nature, for people today and future generations." One of its greatest challenges was salvaging its image after a series of critiques in The Washington Post. *Following are some of the headlines and related statements from that series, showing the numerous ways in which the practices and policies of the nonprofit were attacked.*

> ***Nonprofit Land Bank Amasses Billions***
> *The Conservancy is the world's richest environmental group, amassing $3 billion in assets by pledging to save precious places. But recently it has aligned closely with corporations. In addition to land conservation, it pursued drilling, logging and development. Its approach has led to strange bedfellows.*
>
> ***$420,000 a Year and No-Strings Fund***
> *Officials at The Nature Conservancy say their finances are an open book, a stance charity experts describe as essential to promoting public trust. Still, simple answers can prove difficult to get.*
>
> ***Image Is a Sensitive Issue***
> *A look inside The Nature Conservancy reveals a whirring marketing machine that has poured millions into building and protecting the organization's image, laboring to transform the charity into a household name.*

The Washington Post *attempted to show that The Nature Conservancy was "transforming from a grassroots group to a corporate juggernaut."*[1] *The newspaper claimed that corporations, board members, and major donors were inappropriately benefiting from the policies and practices of the large nonprofit. As a result of the comments in the paper's series, The Nature Conservancy was investigated by a U.S. Senate committee, the Environmental Protection Agency (EPA), and the Internal Revenue Service. The negative exposure contributed to concerns of the U.S. Congress about nonprofits and debate on whether to further regulate the nonprofit sector.*[2] *The Nature Conservancy made a press release available that explained its position on* The Washington Post *series. Here is an extract from that release:*[3]

> *We want to set the record straight—both about the risks we've taken, our mistakes and how we propose to correct them; but also about our record of achievement, grossly neglected and misrepresented by* The Washington Post *"Big Green" series. We must and will continue to take risks in our work to protect lands and waters today, before they and their wealth of life are lost to us and to our children. The Washington Post "Big Green" series about The Nature Conservancy was based on a two-year investigation conducted by reporters from* The Washington Post. *The Nature Conservancy cooperated fully with* The Washington Post, *providing literally thousands of pages of requested documents and scheduling interviews with dozens of staff, partners and other experts, including four separate interviews with our president, Steve McCormick. Instead of a balanced report, however,* The Washington Post *"Big Green" series lacked a fair contextual description of our accomplishments and simplified complex issues, explored in depth in the following pages. Although* The Washington Post *"Big Green" series was fraught with mischaracterizations and omissions of fact, we at The Nature Conservancy recognize some mistakes we have made in pursuit of innovation and conservation change. Many of these we had begun correcting and learning from before* The Washington Post *investigation began. We take full responsibility for our actions, as we always have. Through intensive self-examination across The Nature Conservancy, as we have done throughout our history, we know we will emerge a stronger organization, one better able to accomplish our conservation goals. . . . By reviewing our mission, strategy and values, and summarizing the steps we are taking to correct our missteps, we hope to convert the criticism leveled at us into a real dialogue about the future of how we do conservation [Reprinted with permission from The Nature Conservancy].*

❖❖❖

The strategic response of The Nature Conservancy to the media attacks and government investigation reveals the benefit to nonprofits of having strong public relations and government relations programs. As The Nature Conservancy discovered, actions may be interpreted by others as inappropriate even when a nonprofit's board and staff believe that they are ethical. Once a nonprofit's reputation is under scrutiny, government may step in to further regulate its behaviors or impose penalties. The public may withdraw its support or demand greater accountability. In The Nature Conservancy's case, negative attention by *The Washington Post* newspaper resulted in a government probe. As a large well-resourced nonprofit, The Nature Conservancy was able to devote considerable resources to responding to allegations and advocating to protect its interests.

No nonprofit, whatever its size, is immune to public relations challenges, and any nonprofit may wish to engage in advocacy. As we saw in Chapter Two, not all stakeholders will evaluate the ethics and effectiveness of a nonprofit in the same way using the same criteria. No matter the size and perceived vulnerability to criticism of a nonprofit, we recommend proactively developing public and government relations skills and strategies and having a crisis management plan in place. In this chapter we will focus on how nonprofits can strategically communicate to establish and maintain a positive image and reputation, manage a crisis, advocate for their cause and organizational interests, and lobby for desired legislation.

Image and Reputation

Image and reputation are important intangible resources for nonprofit organizations.[4] A negative image or tarnished reputation can harm relationships with both internal and external stakeholders. Image and reputation reflect the knowledge and opinion that stakeholders hold about the organization.[5] *Reputation* reflects perceptions of the organization's actions over its lifetime[6] and may consist of three aspects: familiarity with the organization, beliefs about what to expect from the organization in the future, and impressions about the organization's favorability.[7] A positive reputation, therefore, requires consistently positive action over an extended period of time. *Image* relates to external stakeholders' current knowledge, feelings, and beliefs about an organization.[8] Image involves the mental pictures or associations that are formed when stakeholders see or hear the organization's name or see its logo, symbol, or trademark.[9] Image is therefore more malleable and can change quickly. Chapter Eight, on marketing, elaborates on this discussion by focusing on how to create and maintain a positive brand.

Image and reputation are critical to nonprofit organizations, given that they are granted discretion to operate by the government and may be rewarded with donations and tax benefits. Although IRS rules and regulations (such as the *non-distribution constraint*) provide legal guidelines for nonprofits, the general public and other stakeholders typically have standards and expectations for nonprofit behavior that exceed those required by law. Nonprofits' legitimacy is based on being perceived as trustworthy stewards of the public's resources (donations, tax exemptions, and so forth) and reliable providers of social benefits. A positive image and reputation helps nonprofits to attract and retain employees, volunteers, and donors and maintain good relations with other stakeholders such as clients, media, and legislators.

Understanding how changes to their image can affect them, some nonprofits strategically promote a positive and coherent image through their fundraising, marketing, and public relations communications. For example, a hospital may present itself as highly concerned about patient care. If the hospital ranks high in a patient satisfaction or surgery outcomes survey, it may share this information with the public to reinforce that positive image.

Nonprofit leaders protect their organization's reputation by ensuring that they understand the expectations and values of the public and government, and by recognizing and responding to potential crises when their organization's purposes, actions, and outcomes are not aligned with those expectations and values. For example, The Nature Conservancy carefully and quickly responded to government inquiries, demonstrating that it was transparent and eager to adjust its practices to be consistent with the U.S. Senate's desires and expectations. It issued press releases and other communications to reassure stakeholders that it would seek continual improvement and was committed to its founding values.

A variety of tools and techniques are available for reputation management such as reputation scorecards, key performance indicators, competitive benchmarks, media content analysis, journalism surveys, opinion polls, branding guidelines, and measurement of Web page usage.[10] These tools and techniques provide information on how the nonprofit is representing itself and how others are viewing the organization. Even small organizations can keep track of the extent and tone of their media coverage, Web site hits, client satisfaction, staff and volunteer turnover, and goal achievement. They can use this information to assess whether they are likely to be meeting expectations and whether their image and reputation are in jeopardy.

Strategic Communication

Communication to enhance image and build reputation should be part of a nonprofit's strategic plan. A nonprofit should be able to clearly present what it stands for and hopes to accomplish. Its values should be apparent in its actions and words. The Nature Conservancy demonstrated its appreciation of the importance of values in reiterating what it stands for throughout its press release responding to the negative *Washington Post* coverage. For example, the opening paragraph states, "We must and will continue to take risks in our work to protect lands and waters today, before they and their wealth of life are lost to us and to our children."

Communication plans should be established to further organizational goals and reinforce a consistent brand. For each strategic goal, the communication plan should outline the change that is sought for a particular target audience.[11] Communication objectives may be to create awareness, engage the audience, move the audience to act, maintain relationships, or all of these. Good communication objectives specify the following types of objectives:

- **Target audience**: for example, U.S. senators
- **Nature of the desired change in the target audience**: for example, greater approval of The Nature Conservancy
- **Specific knowledge, attitude, or behavior to be achieved**: for example, understanding of the appropriateness of The Nature Conservancy's policies related to the selling of land
- **Amount of change desired**: for example, enough change in senators' perceptions to avoid government regulation or penalties
- **Target date**: for example, by the end of the U.S. Senate probe

A communication plan should be built around these objectives. Further steps include conducting research, developing messages, producing materials, assessing resources, and writing workplans.[12] We next discuss public relations as a communication process.

Public Relations

The Public Relations Society of America (PRSA), the nation's largest community of public relations and communication professionals, notes that both the definition and the practice of public relations have evolved from the field's formal inception in the early twentieth century. Early definitions of public relations focused on press agentry and publicity. More contemporary definitions incorporate notions of engagement and relationship building. In 1982, PRSA adopted a definition that is now widely used and accepted: "public relations help an organization and its publics adapt mutually to each other."[13] The term *publics* refers to all the audiences that are relevant to an organization. Kotler defines a *public* as "a distinct group of people and/or organizations that has an actual or potential interest and/or impact on an organization."[14]

It is important to emphasize that public relations is more than the flow of information between an organization and its publics. It is a communication process that engages and informs key audiences, builds important relationships, and brings vital information back into an organization for analysis and action. Nonprofits need to listen to their publics, scan their policy environments, and bring this information back for discussion about whether any action is necessary in response to what was learned. Public relations therefore involves the following management functions:[15]

- Anticipating, analyzing, and interpreting public opinion, attitudes, and issues that might impact, for good or ill, the operations and plans of the organization.
- Counseling management at all levels in the organization with regard to policy decisions, and courses of action and communication, taking into account their public ramifications and the organization's social or citizenship responsibilities.
- Researching, conducting, and evaluating, on a continuing basis, programs of action and communication to achieve the informed public understanding necessary to the success of an organization's aims. These may include reviewing marketing; financial; fundraising; employee, community, or government relations; and other programs.
- Planning and implementing the organization's efforts to influence or change public policy. Setting objectives, planning, budgeting, recruiting and training staff, developing facilities—in short, managing the resources needed to perform all of the above.

Staff and volunteers in nonprofit organizations perform these functions in order to gain acceptance for the organization's mission, create and maintain a climate favorable for action, and inform and motivate key stakeholders.[16] Some nonprofits invest in a public relations professional or department to guide these functions. Whether or not it has public relations experts on staff, every nonprofit engages to some extent in public relations, whether formally or informally. All board members, staff, and volunteers of a nonprofit serve as its representatives and can offer useful information about how the organization is perceived. Even clients and donors may affect a nonprofit's image and reputation. All bear some responsibility for what the public believes about the nonprofit.

The Public Relations Process

A nonprofit's process of guiding its public relations begins with an assessment and proceeds through setting goals, objectives, and strategies; learning about target audiences; developing, delivering, and determining the effectiveness of its messages; and throughout, ensuring that its messages and approaches are ethical.

Assess Internal and External Factors Affecting Public Relations

A public relations plan starts with an assessment of the nonprofit's *public relations context*. This assessment considers general internal and external factors and their relevance for public relations. Building from questions developed by Smith, Bucklin & Associates, here are some things to ask as part of this assessment:[17]

- What are the strengths and weaknesses of the nonprofit organization?
- How do perceptions square with realities? Are perceptions of strengths and weaknesses accurate and consistent across audiences?
- How do important constituencies feel about the nonprofit? Does the nonprofit organization elicit respect, excitement, frustration, anxiety, disappointment, or some other emotion?
- How do important constituencies share information about the nonprofit?
- How does the nonprofit compare to similar organizations? Are the comparisons favorable?
- How would the nonprofit operate in an ideal world? How would it be perceived? How would it work with its most important publics, such as supporters, donors, volunteers, members, the news media, lawmakers, and community leaders?

Set Goals, Objectives, and Strategies

Specific public relations goals, objectives, and strategies should be developed in conjunction with a nonprofit organization's strategic plan. The public relations goals should support other goals and the overarching vision for the organization. For example, increased awareness (a public relations goal) may have to come before an endowment fund can be built (a fundraising goal). Success in increasing the geographical reach of a program (a program goal) may depend on motivating individuals who have tried the service to refer others to it (a public relations goal). Measurable public relations objectives come out of these goals; for example, one objective may be to have fifty referrals to a program in the first year of its operation.

The best strategies to accomplish objectives will depend on what resources are available for public relations. Resources include staff, facilities, and funds for researching audiences; producing material (such as press releases, public announcements, mailings, and media kits); and contacting and responding to media and other stakeholders. The organization should assess the degree to which these tasks could and should be done by employees, volunteers, or consultants. Community leaders may be willing to speak on behalf of the organization. Also, other organizations, including businesses or nonprofits, may be willing to provide facilities and audiences for speeches, produce informational material, or give donations for public relations activities.

Identify and Research Target Audiences

Once objectives have been established and resources inventoried, *target audiences* should be identified. Eileen Wirth explains that "the essence of all public relations is targeting strategic messages to audience segments that the organization needs to advance its goals."[18] For nonprofit organizations, target audiences usually include current and potential service recipients, volunteers, funders, and in some cases government bodies. In most cases leaders and program directors will be able to identify target audiences. Volunteers, clients, and consultants also may provide useful information about relevant audiences. For each target audience the nonprofit should have a communication goal, specifying what it hopes to accomplish with the public relations effort.

Once audiences have been identified, *image research* can be used to assess specifically what the audience members know and feel about the organization, what images of the organization they hold, and where they get their information. For audiences that are well known, this information may be easy to obtain. Information can be collected on a regular basis from user satisfaction surveys; searches for media coverage; phone logs of inquiries; and recruitment and exit interviews with staff, board members, and volunteers. For audiences that do not usually have interactions with the nonprofit, formal research methods, if affordable, can be used. Focus group sessions and surveys can be used to uncover potential public relations issues. Outside consultants may be used to provide the expertise needed to collect reliable and valid information. Nonprofits that cannot afford extensive image research can at least assign someone, such as a volunteer or student intern, to ask staff, volunteers, board members, and those using the nonprofit's services if their opinions of the organization are positive or negative and why.

Develop Messages

Once research is completed and audiences understood, it is time for *message development*. For each target audience, messages should be based on the public relations goals and audience research. On the one hand, if research shows that awareness is low, educational messages can be developed that help individuals learn about the nonprofit. On the other hand, if research shows that opinions of the organization are poor, then the message may be crafted to change opinions rather than build awareness. If the goal is to inspire action, such as the signing of a petition, then the message may be designed to encourage the desired behavior, rather than build awareness or change opinions.

Janet Weiss and Mary Tschirhart summarize the extensive literature on how people process communications, and note some key influences on the success of a message:[19]

- **Source credibility**. The more trusted the source, the more likely the message will be heeded and accepted.
- **Message clarity**. The message must be understandable, which typically means that a simpler message is likely to have more impact.
- **Fit with prior knowledge**. Messages are more likely to be accepted when they are consistent with what is already known or believed.
- **Exposure**. It may be necessary to repeat messages before they are noticed. The message needs to compete with other demands for attention. It can be helpful to vary the way the message is delivered, while retaining its meaning.

Consider a campaign by Edelman, a PR firm, and the American Heart Association (AHA) targeting women. The award-winning campaign focused on generating awareness that heart disease is the number one killer of women and encouraged women to visit GoRedForWomen.org to join and take heart checkups. The campaign raised the percentage of women aware that heart disease is a top killer of women and also resulted in an increase in donations to AHA and in heart checkups. The campaign designers credited the use of spokesperson Marie Osmond, whose mother and grandmother died of heart disease, along with stories shared through online forums from "women like me," for helping to make a convincing message. The message that heart disease is a killer was noncontroversial, but research had found that women did not see the disease as a personal threat and also that they tended to act on information delivered by their peers. The campaign aimed to inspire action by telling multiple motivating stories that personalized the disease statistics.

Not all nonprofits have the luxury of working with firms to create their campaigns. However, low-budget efforts can also demonstrate positive results. For example, Google AdWords can build awareness and drive visitors to nonprofit Web sites, and can be free for nonprofit organizations. A staff member at the Northern Clay Center, a nonprofit dedicated to advancing the ceramic arts, has explained in YouTube videos how his use of AdWords, based on a whim, resulted in more individuals becoming aware of his nonprofit's offerings. By using AdWords to put the nonprofit's message through keywords, images, and photos on the Google search page, new audiences were reached.

Choose Communication Outlets and Deliver Messages

A wide variety of print media outlets are available to reach targeted audiences and accomplish the goals set out for each. Each type of media has distinct features, advantages, and limitations.[20] Print media, such as newspapers, magazines, newsletters, and bulletins, may offer a better opportunity for an organization to tell its story in depth than a television news interview or talk show. General newspapers may provide the greatest audience coverage, but more highly targeted publications offer the opportunity to refine messages and provide details of interest to special audiences. Nonprofits can research which reporters cover relevant issues and offer themselves as resources. Executive directors or experts affiliated with the nonprofit can position themselves to be a source of useful quotes for reporters. Nonprofits can also submit letters to the editor or opinion pieces. Over time, relationships can be built with reporters and editors that can help a nonprofit to get repeated and positive coverage.

A variety of broadcast options are available. These include public radio and television, cable public access channels, all-news radio and television stations, and public affairs programs. A nonprofit can develop a story and pitch it to an appropriate reporter or assignment editor. For television, usually the more visuals made available the better. In addition, the organization can make representatives available for interviews. A public service announcement (PSA) can be developed to be broadcast on local radio and television stations. Clear Channel Communications, a large media conglomerate, has a Web site where nonprofits can post a PSA to be used by radio stations.[21]

A nonprofit can use wire and video services to broadcast press releases. These may reach large audiences as the services disseminate information to a variety of media outlets. This information is often picked up by journalists and disseminated in their media. Services may, however, charge a per-release or membership fee. Major wire services include Associated Press, MediaLink, Reuters, and PR Newswire.

The Internet is growing rapidly as a communication vehicle, especially among younger audiences. Web site blogs and text messages on mobile phones have attracted donations and votes. For example, you can tell your friends to text "HAITI" to 90999 to donate $10 to Red Cross relief efforts in that country. A video game, *Darfur Is Dying*, was created by college students to put players into the role of Sudanese refugees—the game has been played millions of times, raised thousands of dollars, and attracted mainstream news coverage.[22] Urban Ministries of Durham has a video game where players put themselves in the shoes of the homeless or unemployed. Games and videos can help the public better understand the nature of the need the nonprofit is addressing. For example, affluent individuals may better understand how challenging it is to find and retain a job when one has no money for transportation or no place to shower and safely store work clothes. Some nonprofits have virtual world avatars that can help spread their messages. Second Life offers space for nonprofits to set up display and meeting spaces that can be used to help educate visiting avatars. For example, Second Chance Trees has a place where avatars can learn about the value of different types of trees, plant a virtual one, and get a real one planted for them for free.

At the minimum, a nonprofit should develop a Web site and refresh it regularly with news releases, information about upcoming events, and other items of interest to constituencies. It should take advantage of free social media such as Twitter and Facebook to help spread its news. Nonprofits may also be able to get their stories out via Web sites hosted by YouTube for nonprofits, and by *The NonProfit Times*, *The Chronicle of Philanthropy*, and *Philanthropy Journal*.[23]

Evaluate Effectiveness and Ethics of the Communication

Once messages are delivered, it is important to try to assess their impact. Did they reach the intended audience? Did they accomplish what was intended, for example, build awareness or inspire action? If not, they may need to be changed, repeated, or even delivered through different outlets. Did they have unintended consequences? For example, antismoking messages from health organizations were at times found to have boomerang effects, as some messages actually encouraged rather than discouraged smoking. A boomerang effect in social psychology is a message recipient's reaction of defiance to or rejection of the message because he feels his freedoms are being restricted. This reaction may be conscious or unconscious.[24]

In addition to considering whether the messages were effective, nonprofits should ask, Were the messages ethical? For example, were the outcomes of the organization honestly portrayed? Were privacy concerns honored? Did the nonprofit avoid exploiting clients for their public relations value? Did all individuals portrayed in photos give their permission to have their image shared by the nonprofit?

Ethics in Public Relations

If public relations activities are perceived as advertising or narrow self-serving behavior, they may encounter skepticism from audiences. People are becoming increasingly wary of efforts to justify, take undue credit for, or escape blame for actions and outcomes. It is therefore very important that public relations is carried out ethically. In Exhibit 14.1 we offer a summary of the main issues in the ethics framework created by the Public Relations Society of America. It is relevant to nonprofit organizations of all sizes that have individuals acting in public relations roles, whether or not these individuals are trained public relations professionals.

EXHIBIT 14.1. SUMMARY OF SELECTED PROVISIONS IN THE PUBLIC RELATIONS SOCIETY OF AMERICA CODE OF ETHICS

Building Principles on Core Values

The Code of Ethics, created and maintained by the PRSA Board of Ethics and Professional Standards (BEPS), sets out principles and guidelines built on core values. Fundamental values are advocacy, honesty, expertise, independence, loyalty, and fairness.

Translating values into principles of ethical practice, the Code advises professionals to

- Protect and advance the free flow of accurate and truthful information.
- Foster informed decision making through open communication.
- Safeguard confidential information.
- Promote healthy and fair competition among professionals.
- Avoid real, perceived, or potential conflicts of interest.
- Work to strengthen the public's trust in the profession.

Code guidelines, like tactics supporting strategies, zero in on putting value and principles into play for working professionals facing everyday tasks and challenges. Guidelines for public relations professionals include the following:

- Be honest and accurate in all communications.
- Avoid deceptive practices.
- Reveal sponsors for represented causes and interests.
- Act in the best interest of clients or employers.
- Follow ethical hiring practices to respect free and open competition.
- Avoid conflicts between personal and professional interests.
- Decline representation of clients requiring actions contrary to the Code.
- Accurately define what public relations activities can accomplish.
- Report all ethical violations to the appropriate authority.

Source: Adapted from Public Relations Society of America, "Member Code of Ethics," http://www.prsa.org/AboutPRSA/Ethics/CodeEnglish.

Many nonprofits do not have public relations professionals on their staff. They often do, however, have individuals such as staff, board members, volunteers, vendors, and consultants who feel passionately about the nonprofit's cause and wish to tell others about the positive work of the organization. An ethical practice is to disclose one's relationship to an organization when publically praising it. For example, news editorials, blogs, posted comments, and speeches should be clear on the relationship of the writer or speaker to the organization.

In addition to using inappropriate endorsements by those who have a financial stake in a nonprofit's product or service, there are a variety of irresponsible actions that may be taken by a nonprofit in its effort to positively showcase itself and advocate for its cause. These include falsely claiming celebrity endorsements, overstating the number of supporters, inflating numbers or types of clients served, claiming success for services without backup documentation, claiming the need for services is greater than can be justified, naming partners and collaborators that are such in name only or that have not agreed to be recognized in this way, misrepresenting competitors and competing perspectives, and not disclosing conflicts of interest.[25] To help prevent these practices, a nonprofit may enforce comprehensive policies for public communications on its behalf or on behalf of those individuals and organizations with which it is affiliated. For example, a review process can be used for public communications to ensure that more than one individual approves the content, audience, and delivery method. Policies to protect whistle-blowers may help to ensure that questionable communications are brought to light when first observed.

Risk and Crisis Management

Shortly after the terrorist attack on 9/11, the American Red Cross, a nonprofit used to dealing with the crises faced by others, found itself embroiled in a crisis of its own.[26] The Red Cross set up a "Liberty Fund" for 9/11 victims and quickly raised $547 million in donations. Widespread criticism was then leveled at the Red Cross when it was learned that the Red Cross planned to use some of the funds for non-9/11 purposes, contrary to donor expectations. However, it had long been Red Cross practice to raise funds for subsequent disasters, and it did not intend for donors to think that all funds donated would be for 9/11 victims. Another issue was that the Red Cross collected more blood than it could use. Because it was perishable, the excess blood had to be destroyed. In addition, the Red Cross president and CEO abruptly resigned. Throughout the crisis, critics charged that the information the Red Cross released was unclear and not timely. The Red Cross subsequently took steps to deal with the issues raised by its critics. For a more nuanced understanding of this situation, see Paula DiPerna's case study.[27]

The Red Cross's experience, like that of The Nature Conservancy, shows that even the most well-intentioned and experienced nonprofit organizations can encounter a potential crisis. The Nonprofit Risk Management Center defines an *organizational crisis* as a sudden situation that threatens an organization's ability to survive. It is an emergency, disaster, or catastrophe that may involve death or injury, lost access to the use of facilities or equipment, disruption or significantly diminished operations, unprecedented information demands, intense media scrutiny, or damage to an agency's reputation.[28]

Problems and issues can quickly come to the public's attention. The press is notoriously successful at telling the public what to think about, though less successful in telling them what to think. Press coverage of nonprofits varies, but researchers have found that it is generally favorable, unless reporters are framing a situation as a scandal.[29] The public is often ill informed and therefore may not be able to grasp the complexities of a situation. Some argue that this was the situation with The Nature Conservancy and that the news articles presented an oversimplified picture. Rather than argue against the complaints and try to fully explain the complexities, The Nature Conservancy's message across a range of communication mechanisms was that it promised to do a better job. Although some might argue that The Nature Conservancy was "guilty" in its dealings with corporations and therefore could take no other position, others might contend that the leaders understood that it was in their best interest to accept the concerns and move forward rather than position The Nature Conservancy as argumentative and unwilling to accept criticism.

Risk Assessment and Management

Though crises usually come as a surprise, nonprofit organizations should try to identify their risks. This is part of overall risk assessment and management. *Risk management* is a process that helps an organization deal with uncertainty. The process includes an assessment of internal and external factors bearing on possible risks (such as staff expertise, risk history, and financial and political environments), the identification of relevant risk types and specific risks, and the evaluation of risks in terms of likely frequency and severity. Once potential risks have been identified, the nonprofit can develop a plan for responding to each of them. Nonprofits can also develop systems to monitor and improve their risk identification and management process.[30]

As part of risk management, a nonprofit should create an inventory of risks. These include but are not limited to avoidable risks such as financial difficulties, actual or alleged client maltreatment, service or product failure, accidents, transportation-related mishaps, guilt by association, employment disputes, and criminal conduct. The nonprofit should also consider unavoidable risks, including such things as natural disasters, civil unrest, and unexpected loss or death of key personnel. In addition, it should look at risks that come with being involved with organizations and individuals external to the nonprofit, such as collaboration partners, donors, and even detractors who may try to infiltrate and sabotage the organization.

As noted in Chapter Seven in the discussion of financial risks, there are four main options for responding to identified risks:

- **Avoidance**. Eliminate the risk: for example, stop a controversial or unsafe behavior.
- **Transfer**. Contract the risk to others: for example, buy insurance or contract out the risky activity.
- **Reduction**. Take preventative measures: for example, require criminal background checks for all staff and volunteers.
- **Retention**. Assume the risk: for example, prepare a plan for a possible backlash from a risky activity.

Crisis Management

One of the most serious types of risks is an attack on an organization's reputation. The news media can play a major role in this. Larry Lauer notes that a crisis becomes more dangerous for the reputation of an organization if the situation changes from news organizations reporting a balanced story to news organizations using an alleged scandal to compete with each other for readers and viewers.[31] Also, the longer that news stories are reported, the more potential there is for reputational damage.

An important goal for crisis management is to help the organization's leadership to deal effectively with the crisis and thereby contain the reporting to as short a time period as possible. This will involve analyzing the risk that a problem will grow to be a crisis, having procedures in place to mobilize if a crisis should occur, and providing appropriate communications to relevant audiences. An often repeated recommendation is to be as concerned about perceptions as reality. It is particularly important for an organization to avoid looking defensive and instead to display that it is dealing as quickly and effectively as possible with the crisis. If the nonprofit is at fault, the best approach is likely to be to apologize and promise to do better. Though it may be tempting to conceal information, scapegoat, or accuse the accuser, this is rarely successful in reassuring the nonprofit's stakeholders and avoiding escalation of the situation.

Crises may fall into several types, including

- **Rapidly or slowly developing**. A natural disaster can take an organization by surprise, whereas a financial crisis may be years in the making.

- **Externally or internally focused.** Crises may be caused by forces outside organizations, such as economic or social turmoil. Factors inside nonprofits, such as embezzlement by an employee or a product defect causing injuries, may also cause crises.
- **Preventable or unavoidable.** Steps can be taken to mitigate the likelihood of some crises, such as those stemming from workplace safety. Other crises, such as natural disasters, can occur despite any steps that might be taken.
- **Isolated or linked.** A crisis may affect a single nonprofit in isolation, as when a client starts a lawsuit, or involve several organizations, as when payments to social service providers by a government agency are delayed. When more than one organization is likely to respond to the same potential crisis, it is useful to coordinate responses. Coordination may help in avoiding audience confusion and reinforcing the shared message.

Given the diversity of potential crises, every nonprofit can benefit from having a crisis management plan that inventories risks and looks at what may or may not be available to address a crisis.[32] Committees can be used to create the plan and implement it if a potential crisis emerges. As part of the crisis management plan, nonprofits may include a risk financing strategy, which lays out sources of funds to use if necessary. Even though commercial insurance is a common source of financing, it may not be an option and alternatives may need to be considered. Every nonprofit should try to have a financial cushion to pay for unexpected expenses. As part of crisis management planning, contingencies should be developed to guide organizational action. For example, what can the organization do to continue operations during inclement weather or after the loss of certain facilities?

Having general communication policies and practices can help when facing a potential crisis.[33] Managers should be aware of the need for and be proficient at effective communication. General written communication policies and procedures should include guidelines for privacy and for liability, addressing the kinds of information that will and will not be disclosed. Rules should be established for the ways in which the organization responds to media and public requests for information and comments. Spokespersons for various aspects of organizational activity should be designated. Numerous guides are available for preparing for and managing during a crisis.[34] Scrambling to respond while the crisis unfolds is likely to be ineffective and may even worsen the problem. A series of steps are commonly recommended:

- **Assign overall responsibility for managing the crisis.** The crisis manager will operate in consultation with the crisis management committee if the organization has one.

- **Establish the facts**. The facts should be immediately investigated. Responsibility for this should be assigned to those closest to the events that transpired. The facts should be established before any substantive statements are made.

- **Decide what information to share and prepare a fact sheet**. A fact sheet should be prepared; the information should adhere to what the investigation of the facts reveals and decisions about disclosure.

- **Prioritize audiences**. Targets for communication should be identified and prioritized. Internal audiences should be notified first and informed of the facts and the response. Those directly affected by what happened should also be quickly notified. Communication with the news media may follow. Ideally, those most directly affected will not hear the news first from the media and be unprepared for media inquiries.

- **Select one or more spokespersons**. If necessary, several spokespersons can be used, each representing one aspect of a complex situation. For example, one person may speak to the impacts of the crisis on the finances of the organization, another about implications for clients, a third about any effects on the community, and so on. It is important, though, that the messages are coordinated and consistent.

- **Prepare public statements and spokespersons**. Prepare lists of questions that might be raised and also suggested responses. Presentations should be rehearsed. Not talking may be appropriate when there are good reasons for it, including lack of information, inappropriate questions, or news stories that are not legitimately related to the crisis.

- **Determine methods of public release of information**. These could include statements to the media, interviews, dissemination of fact sheets, or press conferences. Procedures should be developed for handling requests for follow-up information. The objective for all public statements should be to contain the story within a reasonable time frame.

- **Respond appropriately**. If possible the crisis should be turned to the organization's advantage. Lauer notes that the public will judge an organization in large part on how well it handled the crisis.[35] Will the organization be perceived as one caught off guard and ineffective or as one with strong values that knows what it is doing? A positive image will be portrayed if the organization has strong values, clear policies, known procedures, a readiness to act quickly, and confident and prepared leadership.

- **Evaluate and plan improvements**. Evaluation of the management of the situation should be conducted to reveal lessons for the future. The crisis should be monitored to be sure that it is not escalating and to reduce the possibility that it could emerge again. Given their recent experience, the crisis management team and organizational leaders should consider possible improvements to the general crisis management plan and to the organization.

Effective and appropriate communication is the key to crisis management. But as the Colorado Nonprofit Association suggests, at times no action is needed.[36] There is no need to respond when the situation of concern is not directly connected to the nonprofit. Another organization may be more suited to responding to the situation, especially if the nonprofit does not have unique information to share. For example, if a nonprofit is asked to comment on the supposed wrongdoing of another nonprofit, it may be better off staying silent than talking without knowing all the facts and perceptions related to the situation.

Government Relations

We now turn to a discussion of government relations. This can involve *advocacy*, a broad term signifying the act of pleading or arguing in favor of a cause, idea, or policy, and *lobbying*, a type of advocacy in which actions are taken to affect specific legislation by influencing decisions of legislators and officials in the government. As with public relations, planning and strategic communication are at the core of government relations. In Chapter Six, we reviewed government as a potential source of revenue. Here we focus on efforts to influence government opinion, actions, and policies by nonprofits working alone or as part of a coalition or movement.

Importance of Nonprofit Lobbying

It is nonprofits that have pushed for many significant changes in the United States and other countries. Consider Amnesty International, whose mission is to demand human rights for all. By mobilizing its members the organization has been able to convince governments to commute death sentences, free political prisoners, and bring torturers to justice. Mothers Against Drunk Driving (MADD) has lobbied for laws to discourage underage drinking. In North Carolina the NC Center for Nonprofits used lobbying to help defeat a proposal that would have allowed state agencies to retain 2 percent of nonprofits' state government grants to pay for oversight activities. The Nature Conservancy has been pushing for legislative action on climate change. These organizations are just a few of the many nonprofits that have active advocacy agendas.

Many individuals and organizations have called for more nonprofits to get engaged in the political process. Some argue that rather than limit themselves to a Band-Aid approach to social problems, nonprofits should take the opportunity through lobbying to attempt to change the conditions that lead to those problems. They also point out that lobbying can result in greater funding coming to nonprofits and other organizations engaged in researching and addressing the problems. J. Craig Jenkins suggests that nonprofits have an important role to play in facilitating civic participation and helping broaden representation in the public policy arena.[37]

Bob Smucker also emphasizes the importance of lobbying, quoting the religious leader Paul H. Sherry who said: "The primary role of voluntary associations in American life is not service delivery but to continuously shape and reshape the vision of a just social order . . . to argue for that vision with other contenders in the public arena, and to press for its adoption and implementation. For voluntary associations to do less than that is to abdicate their civic responsibility."[38]

Although it is easy to give reasons why nonprofits should lobby and to list nonprofits that lobby, the nonprofits that do so are in the minority. Of those that do lobby, most are classified as 501(c)(4) or (c)(6) organizations. Most 501(c)(3) nonprofits are ambivalent about or fearful of lobbying.[39] Rather than risk breaking the rules about their permitted activities, many nonprofits choose to avoid lobbying activity. They may also avoid lobbying because they think it puts them at a higher risk of being audited or subjected to other types of investigations, a fear that the U.S. government says is unfounded.

Clarifying the opportunities and risks involved may help in encouraging staff and board members to advocate on behalf of their organization's cause and interests. To this end, it is important to distinguish between political activities and legislative activities.

Political Activities

In the United States, all 501(c)(3) nonprofits (including unregistered religious organizations) are prohibited from political activities.[40] They are banned from directly or indirectly participating in or intervening in any political campaign on behalf of or in opposition to a candidate for elective office. This includes a prohibition against providing campaign contributions, fundraising for a candidate, or issuing verbal or written statements for or against a candidate. These nonprofits can encourage individuals to register or vote in elections but cannot show any bias that would favor one candidate over another. They can also distribute a candidate's voting records if this is done throughout the year and not just prior to an election. If a 501(c)(3) organization violates these prohibitions, that is, engages in electioneering, it could lose its tax-exempt status or be penalized, with taxes imposed on the nonprofit and its managers.

The government's position against political activities by 501(c)(3) nonprofits has been in effect for over half a century. In every recent presidential election, the IRS has investigated nonprofits for allegedly violating its rules. For example, the NAACP received a note from the IRS saying that agency was commencing an investigation to see if the 501(c)(3) component of the organization had intervened in a political campaign. The IRS wrote: "We have received information that during your 2004 convention in Philadelphia, your organization distributed statements in opposition of George W. Bush for the office of presidency. Specifically in a speech made by Chairman Julian Bond, Mr. Bond condemned the administration policies of George W. Bush on education, the economy and the war in Iraq." The note included a warning that extra taxes could be imposed on the NAACP and a personal tax could be imposed on any manager who agreed to the forbidden activities.[41] After a two-year investigation, the IRS found that the NAACP did not violate the ban on partisan electioneering in 2004.

Not all nonprofits face such a strict prohibition against political activities. U.S. nonprofits with greater latitude include civic and social welfare groups, which are classified as 501(c)(4) nonprofits; labor unions, which are 501(c)(5) nonprofits; and chambers of commerce and trade associations, which are typically 501(c)(6) nonprofits. Adding to the possible confusion about which activities are legal is the U.S. Supreme Court's January 21, 2010, decision in *Citizens United v. Federal Election Commission*. This landmark decision stated: "Government may not suppress political speech on the basis of the speaker's corporate identity. No sufficient governmental interest justifies limits on the political speech of nonprofit or for-profit corporations." However, this decision did not apply to 501(c)(3) nonprofits, which remain banned from political speech that could influence elections.

The 2010 decision was the result of an appeal of a lower court decision in 2008 that prevented Citizens United, a 501(c)(4) conservative nonprofit, from airing a film critical of Hillary Clinton within thirty days of the 2008 Democratic primaries. The Supreme Court overturned the 2008 decision against the airing of the film but upheld provisions related to disclosures of sponsors of advertisements for the film. Citizens United had a long-standing interest in films aired during political campaign periods. In 2004 and 2005, it filed unsuccessful complaints with the Federal Election Commission, arguing that ads for Michael Moore's *Fahrenheit 9/11*, a film that was critical of the Bush administration, constituted political advertising during the 2004 presidential campaign. Given the remaining ambiguity in the relevant court decisions, nonprofits that are interested in using political films before elections should seek expert legal advice.

Legislative Activities: Lobbying

All nonprofits registered in the United States can take action to support or oppose specific legislation at the national, state, and local levels. Limitations on lobbying are greatest for 501(c)(3) organizations. However, even there the limits are generous, allowing much higher expenditures on lobbying activity than are typically reported by this category of nonprofit.[42] Legislators have attempted to make the relevant laws less ambiguous in order to encourage these types of nonprofits to lobby. To this end, the 1976 Lobby Law clarified and expanded the amount of allowable lobbying expenditures for 501(c)(3) organizations. Later, the Lobbying Disclosure Act of 1995 required organizations that engage in lobbying to register and report their activities. In 1990, the IRS put forth a variety of regulations that help to distinguish what is allowable and what is not for different types of nonprofits.

An explanation for the differences in treatment across nonprofit types is that the 501(c)(3) organizations have the benefit that donations to them are tax deductible for the donor.[43] This is a form of government subsidy, intended to encourage support of nonprofit missions. The government is forgoing the tax revenue that it could have derived from these donor funds. Therefore the government wants to ensure that this untaxed revenue will in fact be used to support nonprofits' activities that directly relate to their missions and not to pay for political activities or lobbying. Other nonprofits do not have the benefit of receiving donations that are tax deductible for the donors, and therefore the government is less likely to be seen as helping to support their political activities or lobbying efforts.

To understand lobbying limits, we first need to distinguish between grassroots and direct lobbying. In *grassroots lobbying* a nonprofit attempts to influence the opinions of the general public, ultimately in order to influence legislation. To be seen as engaging in grassroots lobbying, a nonprofit must spend funds to encourage the general public or a segment of the public to contact legislators in reference to specific legislation. The nonprofit must also convey a point of view on the merits of the legislation. In *direct lobbying* a nonprofit expends funds to communicate directly with legislators or government officials who may participate in formulation of legislation.

Under the law it is not considered lobbying for a nonprofit organization to engage in activities that involve

- Appearing before or communicating with any legislative body about a possible decision on matters that might affect the organization's existence, powers, or duties or the exemptions or deductibility of contributions to it. For example, the funds that The Nature Conservancy spent on defending its land-selling practices during the Senate probe were not counted as lobbying.

- Giving members information on legislation, as long as the nonprofit is not encouraging its members to lobby their legislators or asking these members to urge nonmembers to attempt to influence legislation.
- Responding to written requests from legislative bodies for technical advice on developing or pending legislation.
- Examining and discussing broad social, economic, and similar problems.

The federal government offers two regulatory regimes for 501(c)(3) public charity nonprofits that wish to engage in lobbying. These nonprofits can operate under the *insubstantial* rule or elect to lobby using IRC Form 5768, "Election/Revocation of Election by an Eligible 501(c)(3) to Make Expenditures to Influence Legislation." The option to elect to lobby is highly recommended due to inherent problems with the insubstantial rule. Also, it is very easy for a nonprofit to elect. All it must do once its board votes to elect, is submit the form, and track and report its lobbying expenditures.

Under the insubstantial rule, lobbying may be permitted as long as it is an insubstantial part of the nonprofit's total activity, but expenditure restrictions and what counts as an insubstantial part are unclear. For example, volunteer hours may be included in the determination of whether or not the lobbying activities are substantial, not just the amount of direct expenditures on lobbying. If questioned by the IRS, the nonprofit must show that it had an insubstantial amount of lobbying, but there is ambiguity in how to show this. Evaluation of compliance to the rule is subjective and therefore record-keeping requirements increase. Details on all activities that could be seen as affecting legislation must be tracked, not just direct expenditures.

It was the uncertainty and vagueness in the insubstantial rule that led to the more specific restrictions laid out in the 1976 Lobby Law. Once a nonprofit formally elects to lobby, the limits and penalties for violations are clear. For example, a 501(c)(3) public charity nonprofit will not lose its tax-exempt status unless its "normal" total lobbying expenditures for each tax year exceed more than 150 percent of the limit or its grassroots lobbying expenditures for the tax year are more than 150 percent of the grassroots limit.

As of February 2011, the expenditure limits for a nonprofit that elects to lobby are calculated as a percentage of the nonprofit's total expenditures to accomplish its exempt purposes. This total does not include costs associated with a separate fundraising unit and capital expenditures. Under these limits, the per-tax-year lobbying expenditure that is nontaxable is the lesser of $1 million or

1. 20 percent of the total exempt purpose expenditures if they are no more than $500,000

2. $100,000 plus 15 percent of the excess of the exempt purpose expenditures over $500,000 but not over $1,000,000

3. $175,000 plus 10 percent of the excess of the exempt purpose expenditures over $1,000,000 but not over $1,500,000

4. $225,000 plus 5 percent of the excess of the exempt purpose expenditures over $1,500,000 [44]

Of the total amount available for nontaxable lobbying, only 25 percent can be used for grassroots lobbying.

This means that a nonprofit expending $100,000 for its exempt purposes could spend $20,000 on lobbying and only $5,000 of that could be used for grassroots lobbying. A nonprofit expending $1 million for its exempt purposes could spend $175,000 on lobbying ($100,000 plus 15 percent of $500,000), of which only $43,750 could be used for grassroots lobbying. A nonprofit expending $4 million for its exempt purposes could spend $400,000 ($225,000 plus 5 percent of $2,500,000), with $100,000 of that amount available for grassroots lobbying. The IRS Web site offers instructions for calculating limits and identifying lobbying expenditures.

It is important to emphasize that if a nonprofit elects to lobby, it is the expenditures that are counted to see if limits are honored, not the extent of the activity itself. Moreover, these expenditures cannot be paid for out of private, earmarked grants. In other words, the 501(c)(3) cannot get a grant specifically for lobbying from a private foundation or corporation. However, it can use general support grants from private foundations and grants earmarked for lobbying from community foundations. In general, it cannot use federal funds to lobby, but special definitions and rules apply.

These very generous rules suggest that 501(c)(3) nonprofits should not be fearful that they will exceed lobbying limitations. The government has repeatedly demonstrated that nonprofits are welcome to participate in shaping legislation. By adding their voices to the political process, nonprofits can ensure that legislators consider multiple perspectives and understand the interests of individuals who are unable or reluctant to speak for themselves. Nonprofits can use the power of collective action to gain attention and credibility for their causes. They can work with their constituents to determine what makes a good society and, through lobbying, act to achieve this vision.

Planning and Implementing Government Relations

There are numerous books, articles, and guides to help nonprofits develop effective lobbying campaigns. Information on this topic can easily become outdated. The growth in social media and networking, for example, has dramatically changed lobbying practices. Power shifts among political parties and special interest groups can change the lobbying environment. Still, there are some general ideas that appear to have lasting value. We outline these in the following discussion, focusing first on steps in the general government relations process. We then provide ideas for engaging individuals in a lobbying campaign and discuss designing and delivering effective messages.

The general steps outlined at the beginning of this chapter for public relations can be adapted for government relations. Once a nonprofit learns of a legislative or government policy issue of importance to the organization and its clients, it can take these steps:

1. **Assess internal and external factors.** What are the strengths and weaknesses of the various positions on the issue and who are the actors likely to take a particular side? What emotions does the issue raise? How is information shared on the issue? What organizations are likely to want to work with the organization on the issue and with whom would it like to work? What is the legislative process and timeline for the issue? What are the financial and political implications of working on this issue?

2. **Set goals and objectives.** What does the nonprofit want to accomplish relative to the issue? Is the goal to raise awareness, educate a particular audience, or inspire action? How should success be measured? How do the goals related to the issue fit with the nonprofit's strategic goals? Should the nonprofit allocate resources and management systems to lobbying and other forms of advocacy? What should the budget and sources of funds be for the effort?

3. **Identify and research target audiences.** What groups or individuals need to be reached? What is their current understanding of and position on the issue? What values and interests do they have that are aligned with or contrary to the nonprofit's position on the issue? Which individuals and organizations are they likely to see as credible sources of information on the issue? What should the mix be between grassroots and direct lobbying?

4. **Develop messages.** What is the message for each target audience? Is it as noncontroversial as possible? Can be it be repeated with slight variations?

5. **Choose communication outlets and deliver messages.** What are the best mechanisms for reaching the targets: social networking, postal mail, phone calls, personal meetings, radio shows, television ads, op-eds, letters to the editor, concerts, public forums and speeches, online maps, text messaging, e-mail, brochures, protests, marches, petitions, blogs, wikis, virtual worlds, billboards, yard signs, videos, or yet another approach? Who has access to each target audience and should deliver the message?[45]

6. **Evaluate effectiveness and ethics.** Is the campaign working? Is it legal and ethical? What should be continued and what changed? Has the overall mission of the organization been advanced or hindered by the advocacy activity? Have there been any unintended consequences?

On the one hand, political mobilization can be *decentralized*, occurring through informal grassroots organizations and multisector coalitions that mobilize volunteers, as was the case in the origins of the civil rights movement and the women's movement.[46] On the other, it may be *centralized*, occurring through established nonprofits with their own registered lobbyists. There is ongoing debate about the advantages of conducting advocacy through decentralized versus centralized organizations.[47]

Decentralized advocacy organizations may best embody democratic values and maximize civic involvement. They offer more points of access for involvement through the loosely connected cells of the advocacy structure than does a campaign run in a highly centralized fashion, where access and control come through a single or lead organization. Decentralized campaigns are better at empowering grassroots leaders and are more difficult for powerful actors to repress. However, the more decentralized the advocacy campaign, the more likely it is to suffer from inefficient decision making, coordination problems, resource constraints, message confusion, and conflicts in viewpoints. For example, when a campaign goes viral, as in the case of tell-a-friend campaigns or unauthorized viral ads, the message may be controversial and the nonprofit may need to deny developing or approving it. For example, viral messages encouraging condom use among teens to prevent HIV/AIDS may create problems for the nonprofit originating a campaign to increase awareness of the disease. Negative messages about a politician in relation to a particular policy may be made and electronically disseminated independently of the nonprofit that started the campaign to discuss that policy.

More *centralized advocacy structures* tend to come with a sharper focus on organizational survival, which can divert resources from the advocacy activities. However, because there are fewer stakeholders who need to debate the issues and agree on acceptable responses to them, centralization can lead to faster preparation, more consistent messages, more professional communications, and greater ease in negotiating compromise positions. In addition, when resources can be held by a single organization, it may be easier to find and allocate them in response to an opportunity or threat. However, as discussed in Chapter Nine, many nonprofits operate in a shared governance system. To effectively address complex social problems they need to cross organizational boundaries and work collaboratively, making highly centralized advocacy structures unattractive or even infeasible. By operating as part of an advocacy coalition, a nonprofit may be more effective in encouraging systemic changes.

The differences between decentralized and centralized efforts are reflected in the origins of the pro-life and pro-choice movements. John McCarthy describes the pro-life movement as relatively decentralized, rooted in networks of local churches. In contrast, the pro-choice movement historically did not have a preexisting infrastructure, such as networks of churches, that could serve as the organizing force for its advocacy activities. It took a more centralized approach, relying more on professionals than volunteers.[48] Today, both sides attract grassroots volunteers as well as professional paid lobbyists.

Engaging Advocates

A nonprofit's advocates are those who will speak and write to promote the organization's position and well-being. Barry Hessenius offers a useful review of what it takes to engage advocates in a lobbying campaign.[49] He notes that people need to clearly understand what they are being asked to do, have the necessary tools, feel they have the needed skills or will be trained, and have a realistic goal. They are more likely to participate if they feel they will be acting in concert instead of alone. Although it is important that they feel they are part of a coordinated effort, they also should feel that their individual contribution is essential. The campaign should be organized on the principle that everybody counts. It also helps if the activity is fun and successful. Showing measurable results throughout the campaign can create a sense of excitement and achievement. More folks are likely to want to join the effort if they think it will be pleasurable and worthwhile. Hessenius also recommends that the campaign tap into a sense of outrage. People who have a personal stake in the outcome of the campaign are more likely to want to participate.

But how do you find the constituents who will agree with your issue and feel a personal stake in it? Katya Andresen suggests a telescoping approach to identifying people likely to support a cause. She advises nonprofits to start at the broadest level with people likely to be interested and then narrow the focus down to those most interested and able to participate. For national issues she suggests looking first at recruiting at the national level, then at the state, city, and neighborhood levels. Starting broadly and zeroing in can help in ultimately identifying those with strong stakes.[50]

Saul Alinsky championed a different approach that focuses in on local communities and then links these communities together if appropriate. The idea is to empower local leaders who can work within their communities to identify common interests. As they gain strength they can negotiate agreements with public and private sector institutions.[51] Rather than recruiting individuals to follow a previously established cause, the causes emerge from the local communities. Using the networks of existing participants to grow the effort can be effective no matter what general organizing approach is taken.

Typical of many nonprofits with missions focused on social change, Common Cause expects to retain only a small majority of members from year to year. A classic problem is that over time advocates lose sympathy for the cause and drop out, or limit their contributions to a donation. It may also be challenging to convert sympathizers into active participants, so some "members" may join but never play active roles in a campaign. To fill the holes left by departing and passive members, Common Cause recruits broadly and keeps membership dues and time commitments low. As Common Cause's experience demonstrates, to sustain a long-term campaign it is important to continually build membership.

To build and sustain active participation, it is helpful to frame a campaign's focus as a broad moral issue that appeals to generally accepted standards and legal equity, and also to highlight material benefits for participants. For example, in the welfare rights movement, most welfare mothers initially got involved to gain material benefits but then became committed to the ideology of the movement and the solidarity of the group. Other movements have also been successful in stressing both desirable societal outcomes and personal benefits for advocates.[52]

Once the passion for a cause is tapped, advocates need to be prepared and organized for the effort. Nonprofits need to be able to guide advocates so that they can reach the right legislators and legislative aides with the right message at the right time. Bob Smucker argues that to be effective lobbyists, individuals need only three things: a few basic facts, belief in the cause, and common sense.[53] Nonprofits can prepare advocates by educating them on the substance of the legislation at issue, why it is important, what the costs will be if it is enacted, and what the likely outcomes will be if it is passed or does not pass. The Center for Lobbying in the Public Interest is one of the leading organizations that provide training and other resources to help staff and volunteers associated with 501(c)(3) nonprofits to be effective with their advocacy efforts. There are also numerous consultants and grassroots organizers who know how to attract, prepare, and manage staff and volunteers for advocacy campaigns.

Designing and Delivering the Advocacy Message

Few advocates can effectively handle more than one issue. When a nonprofit keeps advocates focused on one issue, the communications of those advocates are likely to be more effective in persuading others to take their position. Popular advice for advocates includes the following:[54]

- Be brief, in both written and verbal communications.
- Be clear, which may mean simplifying complex subjects without losing accuracy.

- Be informative; share facts and stories that are compelling and that illustrate your point.
- Make the case that action is needed now.
- Be persuasive, polite, and relentless but not argumentative or demanding.
- Be grateful; thank people for their time and, if the effort is effective, later for their vote.
- Make personal contact, the more personalized the communication, the better.
- Plan on small wins and long-term strategies rather than quick, decisive victories.

Concluding Thoughts

This chapter has examined public and government relations. For both, strategic communication plans are a key to success. Nonprofit leaders can listen to constituents and design strategies and messages that will reach desired audiences, but it is not only these leaders who will influence the success of a campaign. All individuals associated with a nonprofit have the opportunity to shape the image, reputation, and perceived advocacy positions of the nonprofit. Coordination and control of messages can be pursued, but there can be value in more decentralized approaches to communication. Contingency plans should be developed to address any concerns that may arise that could result in full-blown crises.

In our next chapter we explore partnerships, alliances, and affiliations. Not only can these be instrumental for advocacy efforts but they may also be of benefit to general public relations efforts. In this increasingly networked world, funders and other resource holders consistently call for collaborative initiatives. Finding the right organizations to work with on the right projects is often critical to mission achievement.

Questions for Consideration

1. Some say there is a special burden on nonprofits to do good and be good. Therefore when a nonprofit's image or reputation is tarnished, it tends to reflect badly on the whole nonprofit sector. Still, nonprofits are typically assumed to be operating with good intentions. Why, if at all, is it important for a nonprofit to invest resources in public relations when its mission clearly states that it exists to serve the public? Couldn't these resources be better devoted to program delivery?

2. Nonprofits and government agencies often complement one another in addressing complex social problems. Many nonprofits do not formally engage in lobbying yet they have visions for a better world. Should government increase its encouragement of them to engage in the political process? If so, how? Do you agree with the existing limits on lobbying activity for various types of nonprofits?

Exercises

Exercise 14.1: Link Between Reputation and Image

Identify a nonprofit organization that is widely recognized as having a good reputation. Upon what is this reputation based? How does the organization's image reinforce the organization's reputation?

Exercise 14.2: Crisis Management Review

Identify a nonprofit organization that has recently undergone a crisis. Evaluate the organization's response based on the principles described in this chapter. Alternatively, read "Shark Fundraising at the Foundation," by David Paas, published in *Nonprofit Management & Leadership* 5, no. 4 (1995): 433–438. Develop a crisis management response to the situation faced by the foundation featured in the article.

Exercise 14.3: Advocacy Opportunity

Identify one piece of pending legislation at the local, state, or national level that deals with an issue important to some nonprofits. What types of nonprofits might wish to lobby for or against this legislation, and why? For a national-level perspective on legislative issues affecting nonprofits, see the INDEPENDENT SECTOR's *Word on Washington* Web page at http://www.independentsector.org/hot_on_the_hill.

CHAPTER FIFTEEN

PARTNERSHIPS, ALLIANCES, AND AFFILIATIONS

The Cancer Vaccine Collaborative (the Collaborative) is a joint program of the Cancer Research Institute (CRI) and the Ludwig Institute for Cancer Research (LICR).[1] *CRI's mission is to support and coordinate laboratory and clinical efforts that will lead to the immunological treatment, control, and prevention of cancer. CRI is headquartered in New York City, with volunteer offices in California, Connecticut, Massachusetts, New Mexico, Texas, and Virginia. LICR is a nonprofit research organization committed to improving the control of cancer through integrated laboratory and clinical research and novel therapeutic strategies based on the emerging understanding of cancer. The core of the LICR is concentrated at ten research locations: two each in Australia, Sweden, and the United States, and one each in Belgium, Brazil, Switzerland, and the United Kingdom. The Collaborative was founded to address the multiple challenges of cancer vaccine development. Research over the last twenty years has established that an optimal cancer vaccine must include several components (or* immune agents*) each with a distinct function. Moreover, due to product development agendas, supply scarcity, and proprietary concerns, corporations may limit academic researchers' access to vaccine components. Academics therefore have great difficulty in gaining access to promising vaccine components and securing permission to combine them in an investigative cancer vaccine. Finally, identifying optimal combinations of multiple vaccine components is a complex and time-consuming clinical task. The Collaborative is a coordinated global network of clinical trial sites with special expertise in immunology that conduct parallel, early stage clinical trials to identify the optimal composition of* *successful therapeutic cancer vaccines. The Collaborative is the world's only international network of cancer vaccine clinical trial sites and immune monitoring laboratories. It was established by CRI and LICR to address their shared goal of accelerating the development of therapeutic cancer vaccines. "The formation of the Collaborative was motivated by our realization that our two organizations share common objectives," says CRI executive director Jill O'Donnell-Tormey. "These goals—understanding the immunological response to cancer, harnessing that knowledge for patient benefit, and accelerating the translation of basic research into new cancer therapies—could best be achieved by combining our resources and requiring that our scientists collaborate rather than compete." The Collaborative includes eminent clinical investigators from leading research and medical clinical trial sites and first-class immune monitoring laboratories. These are supported by an extensive and comprehensive independent trials management infrastructure that provides regulatory, safety, and compliance expertise and oversight, trial management, shared data collection software, intellectual property management, and funding. By designing complementary trials to be run in parallel at multiple sites, and by standardizing the types of immunological measurements taken, the Collaborative helps to extract the immunological knowledge necessary to eventually optimize a therapeutic vaccine at a significantly accelerated pace compared to efforts carried out solely by competing industry interests The results have been groundbreaking, and the Collaborative has produced some of the most comprehensive knowledge available today about cancer. The Collaborative has established collaborations with more than fifteen companies to obtain vaccine components. The clinical trials network has been expanded from six sites in New York to nineteen sites on four continents. Since 2001, more than forty clinical trials have been completed or are ongoing, and nearly seven hundred patients have been treated. In addition, more than 120 scientific papers have been published in peer-reviewed journals.*

◆ ◆ ◆

The Cancer Vaccine Collaborative described in our opening case links two major cancer research centers into a global network to carry out cancer vaccine trials. Although this collaboration is larger in scope and operations than a more typical collaboration between local nonprofits, it is nevertheless a striking example of how nonprofits with shared goals can take advantage of the expertise and capabilities they each possess to produce far-reaching results. All nonprofits face decisions about with whom they should work. Nonprofit organizations cannot accomplish their missions and goals alone. Like all organizations they need others to provide them with vital inputs and services. Other organizations may also use a nonprofit's output. In addition, in many cases nonprofits will work with other organizations in arrangements designed to benefit both by taking advantage of their relative strengths. The Cancer Vaccine Collaborative is an example of such a joint effort. In this chapter we will discuss a wide variety of such cooperative arrangements. We address a number of questions: Why do nonprofits seek partners? What factors determine the scope and intensity of a collaborative relationship? What role does governance play in collaboration? What factors increase the chances for successful collaboration? What challenges need to be addressed to successfully establish and manage the relationship?

Why Collaborate?

Why would a nonprofit seek a cooperative relationship with another organization? A wide variety of benefits stemming from collaboration have been cited.[2] For example a nonprofit may gain access to new facilities, such as when a youth-serving nonprofit partners with a church in order to get the use of the church gymnasium. Also, a nonprofit may become more efficient, such as when a nonprofit shares office space or administrative personnel with another in order to cut costs. Two small nonprofits providing similar services might combine to expand the service into different neighborhoods. Another benefit may be increased visibility and political clout. Collaborating nonprofits may each know different local politicians or community leaders. However, beyond the particular benefits that might result from specific collaborations, we need to also look at the internal and external factors that influence the decision to collaborate.

Darlyne Bailey and Kelly Koney, building on research on collaboration in for-profits and government, have laid out six perspectives on nonprofit collaborative activity: they center on social responsibility, operational efficiency, resource interdependence, environmental validity, domain influence, and strategic enhancement.[3] These perspectives inform most listings of the bases and types of collaboration that are found in the literature. David Campbell, Barbara Jacobus, and John Yankey discuss the implication of these perspectives for nonprofit mergers.[4] These perspectives are, however, relevant for all cooperative relationships.

Social Responsibility

The *social responsibility* perspective emphasizes the nonprofit's goal and responsibility to solve social problems. Risk and responsibility are shared by the community actors who have a stake in the issue or problem.

Key Factors to Consider for Social Responsibility

- What are the specific social problems in the community?
- What services or activities does the community need to solve these problems?
- How can the nonprofit best contribute to solving this problem?

As social responsibility is the key basis for nonprofit activity, we will consider its implications for nonprofit cooperation further. Nonprofit missions normally transcend organizational boundaries, and shared interests in social issues can lead to cooperation if collective action will produce more social benefits. This should lead nonprofits to behave more like a community of organizations than like business firms in a for-profit industry.[5] In a for-profit industry, organizational and cooperative action (for example, a joint venture) is designed to benefit industry businesses. Nonprofits, however, should be concerned about the benefits their independent and cooperative actions provide to their publics over and above just the benefits for their own organizations. For example, this driver would lead nonprofits to consider how many alternative providers are available relative to community needs, and the degree to which their organization is a community asset or liability. Ian MacMillan's framework, which we introduced in Chapter Five, on strategy, is useful for this type of decision making.[6] Decisions on partnership formation can be made based on the three dimensions of the framework. *Competitive position* considers how well the nonprofit is doing relative to the other providers of like services in a given area. *Program attractiveness* is the degree to which the program meets a variety of internal and external factors, such as the organization's mission and the skills of its personnel and also whether the program is well supported, has a growing client base, and is sustainable. *Alternate coverage* takes into account the number of other providers with similar programs in the same region.

Being in a strong competitive position indicates that a nonprofit is well accepted and, presumably, doing a better job than its competitors at providing the program or service. It is therefore effectively using community resources. Community benefit should be considered even when the program is not very attractive to the nonprofit. In this situation a for-profit would most likely abandon the service. A nonprofit would likewise seek to exit this unattractive service but would want to see its program delivery skills (which are responsible for its strong competitive position) maintained in the community. It could do this by transferring skills or program coverage to the best of the other agencies providing this service. If these other organizations require assistance, the nonprofit would collaborate with them to build their capacity. For example, an environmental nonprofit that has decided to move out of a garden refuse collection program that is not generating any revenue might consider making its specialized collection bins available to another nonprofit, such as one providing recycling services.

Conversely, from the community's standpoint, nonprofits in a weak competitive position are not the most effective users of resources. In general, options for these weaker nonprofits are to either seek partners or abandon the service or program. Partnership is especially important when alternative coverage is low, meaning that the community would benefit from the nonprofit's presence. MacMillan notes that these situations may result in new programs to meet needs that have only recently developed but are rapidly growing. A nonprofit may not have the skills to be a strong competitor, but given the attractive program, it could seek resources or a partner to build that program. In the early days of the AIDS/HIV epidemic, many nonprofits sought to provide services. Given the complex nature of the disease and treatment, many of these early entrants ended up collaborating with others.

Operational Efficiency

The operational efficiency perspective makes the point that collaboration can be undertaken to produce economies of scale and that such collaboration is often driven by funders or other stakeholders seeking to increase service volume. Funders' interest in collaboration may be driven by a concern about the duplication of services and the duplication of appeals for resources that result from numerous competing providers. Government agencies, foundations, and federated funders such as the United Way all feel this pressure.

Key Factors to Consider for Operational Efficiency

- Where are operations least efficient?
- To what degree are these inefficiencies also a concern of stakeholders?
- Are these inefficiencies best addressed alone or through collaboration?

Resource Interdependence

The resource interdependence perspective focuses on the idea that organizations need resources from each other to meet objectives and survive. For example, grant-makers and service providers may need each other to meet mission objectives. Also, nonprofits may cooperate in service delivery. For example, a nonprofit addressing the needs of the homeless may refer its clients to other providers for help with particular problems related to their homelessness, such as addiction or unemployment. These providers may refer clients in return. In this way agencies become interdependent as they benefit themselves and their partners.

Key Factors to Consider for Resource Interdependence

- What are the critical resources the nonprofit needs?
- From which organizations might these resources be acquired?
- What is the nature of the interdependence that would result from these resource exchanges?

Environmental Validity

The environmental validity perspective holds that legitimacy is a key resource and that nonprofits will pursue strategies to acquire and bolster it, including collaboration with others. Nonprofits are rewarded for living up to social expectations that they provide community benefits. However, they often provide services that are hard to evaluate, and the benefit of these services may not be clear to the community. A loss of legitimacy in the eyes of key stakeholders will likely be detrimental for future funding.

Key Factors to Consider for Environmental Validity

- What is the basis of legitimacy in the eyes of prominent community stakeholders?
- Can legitimacy be acquired by the organization's efforts alone?
- What are other sources in the community from which the nonprofit could acquire legitimacy?
- What community pressures might affect cooperating with these sources?

Domain Influence

The domain influence perspective focuses on power as a reason for collaboration. An organization can secure resources by enhancing its power or influence in its domain, or sphere of activity. Collaboration can be used to increase and control resources, set standards for service, and influence funder priorities. This is a political model, in which organizations seek to align with others who share common interests to enhance their power over other organizations.

Key Factors to Consider for Domain Influence

- What are the ways in which the nonprofit lacks power to accomplish its goal?
- Could the presence of other organizations be used to enhance the nonprofit's power?

Strategic Enhancement

The strategic enhancement perspective emphasizes the use of collaboration as a means of increasing competitive advantage. Nonprofits must respond to externalities, such as funder or marketplace demands, and these may prove problematic for individual nonprofits. In this case a joint venture could be used to produce benefits that two organizations could share but that neither alone could produce. Joint fundraising is one example of this approach. In addition, government or third-party funders may seek more comprehensive services. Several nonprofits, each providing a narrow range of services, could collaborate to provide the continuum of services desired by funders.

Key Factors to Consider for Strategic Enhancement

- After assessing the level and type of competitive advantage likely to be needed in the future, can the nonprofit attain that competitive advantage by itself?
- What other organizations might be available for a collaboration designed to enhance competitive advantage?

◆ ◆ ◆

A number of these perspectives are usually at work in every collaboration decision. Jessica Sowa conducted a study of twenty interagency collaborations among early childhood education providers.[7] These nonprofits reported that their collaborations were established to: improve core organizational services; use the resources of the collaboration to strategically address existing service gaps; and address organization-level needs that included enhancing organizational survival, achieving legitimacy, and improving the strategic position of each nonprofit within its field of endeavor. The Cancer Vaccine Collaborative, for example, provides a number of these benefits to its cooperating partners. It helps each partner advance the social goal of developing cancer treatment. The complementary resources provided by each partner allow the Collaborative to provide a much more efficient way to conduct clinical trials, thereby addressing an important need in the field. And the status of the well-respected nonprofits forming the Collaborative give it, and the researchers associated with it, legitimacy. This facilitates the work of the Collaborative and is instrumental in the establishment of cooperative relations with corporate partners.

Defining Types of Collaborative Relationship

Up to this point we have been using the terms *cooperation* and *collaboration* loosely to refer to any joint efforts of two or more organizations. Joint relationships vary greatly, however, and a variety of terms have been used to classify them, including: *cooperation, coordination, collaboration, alliance, joint venture, partnership,* and *merger*. We have found that these terms are not consistently defined (except for *merger*, which has a legal definition). In addition, the bases of these classifications vary in terms of the nature of the relationship, the autonomy of the partners, and the outcome (such as the significance of the resources exchanged). However, what the types we have described do have in common is that in all of them, the activities of two organizations are more or less closely intertwined.

In this section, we will examine the work of James Austin and David La Piana, who provide useful frameworks for describing and analyzing the range of relationships that organizations can engage in. In both frameworks, relationships vary from less to more extensive. Each framework, however, provides readers with a different useful set of factors for understanding the range of relationships possible. For the remainder of the chapter, except when noted, we will refer to all of these relationships as *collaborations*. This will help to avoid terminological confusion. Moreover, the factors we discuss in the remainder of this chapter in relation to collaboration development, success, and challenges are relevant to all types of relationships. It is typically the extensiveness of the relationship that determines the portions of the factors that may be more or less significant and the amount of effort organizations may invest in particular factors. Finally, owing to their special characteristics, in this section we will also examine mergers and cross-sector collaborations in detail.

The Collaboration Continuum

A framework that is useful for understanding the range of collaborative relationships is James Austin's *collaboration continuum*. Although formulated to describe relationships between nonprofits and for-profits,[8] the continuum is useful in describing the relationship between any two types of organizations. Austin finds that collaboration intensity varies along seven dimensions. These dimensions are listed in the first column of Table 15.1. Each dimension varies in degree as the collaboration type varies, as shown in columns 2, 3, and 4.

TABLE 15.1. THE COLLABORATION CONTINUUM

Relationship Dimension	Simple Collaboration	Transactional Collaboration	Integrative Collaboration
Level of engagement	Low	⟶	High
Importance to mission	Peripheral	⟶	Central
Magnitude of resources	Small	⟶	Big
Scope of activities	Narrow	⟶	Broad
Interaction level	Infrequent	⟶	Intensive
Managerial complexity	Simple	⟶	Complex
Strategic value	Minor	⟶	Major

Source: Adapted from James Austin, "Strategic Collaboration Between Nonprofits and Business," *Nonprofit and Voluntary Sector Quarterly* 29 (2000): 69. Copyright © 2000, Association for Research on Nonprofit Organizations and Voluntary Action. Reprinted by permission.

Austin uses seven dimensions to characterize three types of collaborations. He notes, however, that these types are only three of the possible points on this continuum. Depending on their location on the continuum, collaborations will vary in terms of the collaboration mind-set, the strategic alignment of the partners, the value that the collaboration has for each partner, and the management of the relationship. We should note, in addition, that there may be cases where all seven dimensions will not vary in tandem. For example, a nonprofit's mission may be significantly affected by a collaboration involving a relatively low level of interaction or management complexity. This might occur, for instance, when a key staff member participates in a coalition that provides valuable information or knowledge.

Simple collaborations are at one end of the spectrum. These collaborations involve only little contact between partners. Writing in terms of collaborations between nonprofits and for-profits, Austin labels these as *philanthropic collaborations*. They usually involve only a donation from the for-profit to the nonprofit. If we generalize to a nonprofit collaborating with other nonprofits or public agencies, we would label these relationships as simple collaborations. They are characterized by minimal collaboration in defining activities, minimal fit beyond a shared interest in a particular issue, generic resource transfer, and a low level of contact between designated organizational personnel. An example is EmployAlliance, a collaborative project that won the U.S. Secretary of Labor's Fifth Anniversary New Freedom Initiative Award. It is a collaboration among six nonprofits that find employment leads for their disabled clients. As Dave Stevens, a career counselor at the Chicago Lighthouse, describes his part in this effort, "I now work with people who are blind, so when I get a job requiring sight, instead of letting it go fallow, I pass it along to other local agencies for people with disabilities via EmployAlliance, which in Chicago is under the Chamber of Commerce."[9] These collaborations may also be short-lived, such as when two or more nonprofits participate on a team or task force to address a specific problem or short-term issue. For example, representatives of relevant nonprofits may be called together to come up with a plan to assist in a new citywide plan to deal with homelessness. Or nonprofits may meet to discuss how to address proposed changes in government funding or policy. These short-term collaborations can be contrasted with the longer-lasting relationships that characterize the more extensive collaborations discussed next.

Transactional collaborations have a higher level of involvement between partners. These collaborations involve a more extensive partnering mind-set with increased understanding and trust; an overlap in mission and vision; a more equal exchange of resources (possibly involving core competencies); and extended relationships throughout the organization. Jane Arsenault provides an example of the development of such a collaboration. Three chamber music groups with declining audiences discovered through audience research that there was considerable overlap in their audiences. Their initial collaborative effort was to convert their mailing lists to the same software and develop a single mailing list, which they then all used. This simple collaboration expanded to allowing audiences of one group to get discounted tickets to the performances of the other groups. Further collaborative development included coordinating their concert calendars by negotiating concert dates. A final step was for the groups to develop a common calendar of events and mail it to the entire combined audience. Future efforts may include joint fundraising and board development.[10]

Finally, *integrative collaborations* entail extensive, multidimensional partner involvement. These collaborations are characterized by a joint or merged mind-set. They have, in addition, a broad range of activities of strategic significance, high mission alignment and shared values, and joint benefit creation. Projects are identified and developed at all levels of the organizations. Deep personal relationships develop across the organizations, and the culture of each organization influences the culture of the other. The Cancer Vaccine Collaborative is a good example of an integrative collaboration and clearly illustrates the benefits that can result from this level of interaction. The Collaborative has an identity beyond that of its participants. It addresses the core missions of the partners and integrates their core capacities and facilities, including trial sites and laboratories. It has developed a shared system that supports all aspects of the scientific work.

The Partnership Matrix

Another well-known framework for understanding the types of collaborations nonprofits engage in has been developed by David La Piana (see Figure 15.1).[11] His partnership matrix distinguishes between partnerships based on programs (such as health care, counseling, or recreation services) and those based on administration (functions such as accounting, facilities management, or human resources). Partnerships may also be based on a combination of program and administration activities.

The horizontal axis describes the degree of partner integration. At one end of this spectrum are loose partnerships where each organization retains a great deal of autonomy. In this framework, *collaborations* are only one type of partnership. They are not permanent relationships and decision-making power remains with the individual organizations. Sharing information and referring clients are examples of this type of relationship and are seen quite frequently among nonprofits of all types. For example, nonprofits providing counseling services will routinely refer clients to other agencies for other needs their clients have (such as housing or nutrition).

Strategic alliances are more extensive partnerships and entail a degree of restructuring of the partner organizations. They are based on an agreement that commits them to future joint activities and a degree of shared decision-making power. This agreement is usually a formal one.

FIGURE 15.1. THE PARTNERSHIP MATRIX

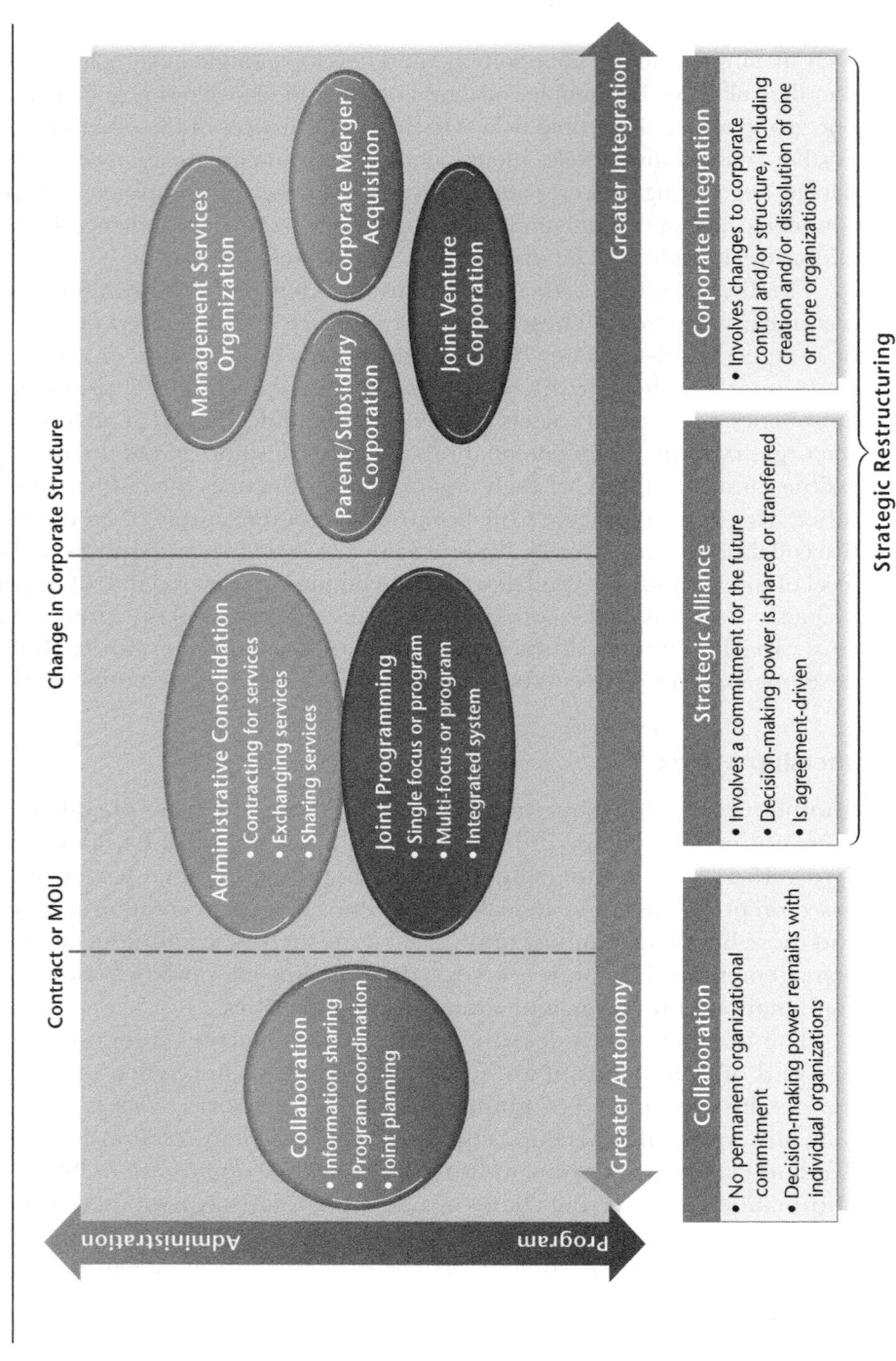

Contract or MOU | **Change in Corporate Structure**

Greater Autonomy ← → Greater Integration

Administration / Program

- **Collaboration**
  - Information sharing
  - Program coordination
  - Joint planning

- **Administrative Consolidation**
  - Contracting for services
  - Exchanging services
  - Sharing services

- **Joint Programming**
  - Single focus or program
  - Multi-focus or program
  - Integrated system

- **Management Services Organization**

- **Parent/Subsidiary Corporation**

- **Corporate Merger/Acquisition**

- **Joint Venture Corporation**

Collaboration
- No permanent organizational commitment
- Decision-making power remains with individual organizations

Strategic Alliance
- Involves a commitment for the future
- Decision-making power is shared or transferred
- Is agreement-driven

Corporate Integration
- Involves changes to corporate control and/or structure, including creation and/or dissolution of one or more organizations

Strategic Restructuring

Source: La Piana Consulting, *The Partnership Matrix* (2011), http://www.lapiana.org/downloads/ThePartnershipMatrix_LaPianaConsulting_2011.pdf. Copyright © 2011, La Piana Consulting. Reprinted with permission. www.lapiana.org.

Alliances can involve the sharing, exchanging, or contracting of administrative functions to increase administrative efficiency or the joint launching and managing of programs to further mission:

- **Joint programming** describes two organizations sharing in the operation of a program or the provision of a service. An example can be found in Spokane, Washington, where a neighborhood action program and a business development association have teamed up to recruit, educate, and provide loans to low-income adults interested in starting a business. This is an example of a single-purpose, joint collaboration.
- **Administration consolidation** describes two organizations sharing administrative functions. An example can be found in Wooster, Ohio, where a substance abuse program and a shelter for abused women undertook a joint capital campaign and now jointly own the building that houses their offices.

Corporate integrations are partnerships that involve changes in corporate control or structure, possibly involving the creation or dissolution of one or more organizations:

- **Management services organizations** are established to integrate administrative functions. For example, a management service organization was created by two multipurpose human service organizations in Springfield, Massachusetts. This new organization provided all the back-office functions for the agencies and also provided some administrative support for four smaller organizations.
- **Joint venture corporations** are created to further specific administrative or program goals. Governance is shared by the partners. A case in point is a joint venture formed by three major visual arts organizations in Louisville, Kentucky. They established a new limited liability company to jointly operate a gift store and gallery. In addition, the Cancer Vaccine Collaborative is a good example of a new organization that was formed from a joint venture that involved both merging programs and establishing new administrative functions.
- **Parent-subsidiary relationships** involve the integration of administrative or program functions, with one partner overseeing the activities of the other. For example, a multipurpose human service organization in Cincinnati, Ohio, formed a parent-subsidiary relationship with a mental health agency (the subsidiary). All administrative functions, policies and procedures, and some programs have been consolidated. The mental health agency's board is appointed by and its executive director reports to the human service organization.

Mergers

Mergers are the most significant collaborations, and so we consider them in more detail. *Mergers* involve the integration of all administrative and program functions of two or more organizations through the dissolution of one or more of the organizations or the creation of a new merged organization. One example of a merger involves two organizations providing educational, mental health, and other services to children with physical and mental disabilities in the San Francisco Bay Area. They dissolved their organizations and merged all of their functions in a new agency. David La Piana has written extensively about nonprofit mergers. He notes that "the success of an increasing number of mergers is inspiring other nonprofit leaders to take a closer look at this strategy. Though these leaders may have previously considered a merger but abandoned the idea as too risky, they now feel more comfortable going where others have gone before."[12] We will consider some of the main points made by La Piana.

Under the term *merger,* La Piana includes a variety of nonprofit restructuring options. *Outright mergers* can be accomplished either by dissolving one organization and leaving its assets to another or dissolving both organizations by merging them into a new third organization. Another option is an *asset transfer.* In this transaction the organizations remain separate, but the valuable assets of one (which may include money, real property, a name, or other intangibles) are "purchased" by the other. The purchase may be for cash or (more commonly) for some other consideration, such as a commitment to continue the organization's mission. Alternatively, nonprofits may form *interlocking boards.* This option allows the organizations to maintain their separate legal identity. The nonprofits can, nevertheless, merge their operations by reconfiguring their boards so that the same individuals are on each board. A joint executive director may also be appointed.

The Arizona's Children Association (AzCA) provides a good example of a nonprofit that has pursued mergers and acquisitions (M&A) strategically and realized substantial value from doing so. Its efforts are discussed in a report on mergers published by The Bridgespan Group.

> Fifteen years ago, AzCA was a $4.5 million organization, focused primarily on offering residential services in Tucson. As they looked to the future, AzCA's leaders realized that they would need to modify their mission to have the kind of impact they wanted. As Fred Chaffee, AzCA's president and CEO, put it, "We were primarily a residential treatment organization, and we didn't have any services in primary prevention and early childhood work. From a mission perspective of protecting kids and preserving families, we needed to be serving kids earlier to give families the tools and reach kids before they arrived at residential services."

But AzCA didn't have the staff expertise, donor relationships, or "brand" to build a new effort to serve families. So 10 years ago, AzCA acquired an organization that did, marking the beginning of a rapid, strategic expansion through M&A. Six acquisitions later, AzCA has grown into a $40-million state-wide nonprofit with a broad continuum of care for children and their families. This growth did not just come from the "purchase" of other organizations. Each acquisition allowed AzCA to add new services and skills, and to spread them to every office and program across the organization. Then, once the organization achieved "critical mass" in a given area, it engaged in competitive bidding to further organic growth. (Critical mass, according to Chaffee, "means more than just numbers of people; it's reputation, community and brand awareness.") But all of this rested on the success of AzCA in using M&A to gain footholds in new services, geographies and beneficiary populations. Arizona's Children Association's approach has proved prescient, as the trend in recent years has been to move more children from residential to out-patient or in-home care. As a result, AzCA's diversification has positioned the organization well to weather the corresponding changes in funding priorities.[13]

Given what is at stake, serious self-assessment is needed before making a decision to seek a merger. Organizations should have clarity on why a merger might be sought. Normally, the reasons involve improving finances, gaining access to a larger skill set, or enhancing mission pursuit. In addition, the expected outcomes of the merger should be clear. Additional factors that enhance the prospects of merger success include the nonprofit's being able to keep a focus on its mission, having a unity of strategic purpose, having leadership that speaks with one voice, having solid board-management relationships, having a history of successful risk taking, having a growth orientation, and being familiar with other successful mergers. Whether or not the organization is in crisis needs to be considered. A crisis will create strain in the organization, use resources and staff time, and put the organization in a weak bargaining position with potential partners. Nevertheless the merger may be a significant opportunity and may in fact help to resolve the crisis. Finally, the state of the executive leadership needs to be considered. For example, mergers may occur more easily when one organization has lost its executive leader. When both leadership teams are intact, then the organizations must determine who will lead the merged organization. Difficult decisions about the leaders in the separate organizations may need to be made.

Potential partner assessment is also of vital importance and has some special features. Potential merger partners usually know each other. For a merger to advance through the early negotiation stage, they must also trust each other. It is important that knowledge and trust be based on valid, firsthand information rather than secondary information or rumor. It is also better if the organizations have a history of working together successfully. This experience can provide the most useful information for building trust; assessing the skills, assets, and potential contributions of the partner; and designing future programs.

Negotiation is necessarily complex in mergers. The organizations should form a joint merger negotiation committee. The committee needs to consider all of the issues each partner deems important. It needs to decide on the particular form the merger will take. It also needs to communicate regularly with the boards and management teams of the organizations. When all issues and details have been considered and a decision made, the committee will draft a proposed merger agreement. The board of each organization will then vote on the agreement. If the vote of each board is affirmative, the merger can be implemented.

The Bridgespan report on the Arizona's Children Association addresses this:

> As Arizona's Children Association has gained experience with M&A, its leaders have integrated the topic into their discussions about strategy. Five or six times a year, the management team convenes to discuss when and where the organization should grow, and if there are any potential M&A candidates to evaluate as a means to achieving their goals. Arizona's Children Association's leaders also have developed a robust internal capability with staff members seasoned in vetting and integrating acquisitions, and solid benchmarks on the cost/benefits of merging, which they can use to raise funding for merger-related expenses. Arizona's Children Association probes any merger possibility with a set of 10 key questions that its leaders use as a high-level filter to assess how well a candidate organization fits with AzCA's strategic goals in terms of service, geography and brand. These questions also assess organizational fit and financial impact. Once a candidate has passed this test, AzCA deploys a "swat team" of 10 internal staff representing finance, clinical staff and programming, IT and HR that meets with their counterparts when a merger or acquisition is being seriously considered. This group has developed a template used to identify both the costs for undertaking a merger and the cost efficiencies from supporting it. Arizona's Children Association's leaders have used these figures as an aid in raising the funds to support several of its most recent deals.

> Finally, AzCA also deploys this team during postmerger integration, understanding that the majority of the work—and the greatest challenge to ensuring a successful merger—stems from joining two cultures. Arizona's Children Association's leaders see the organization's strength as an M&A partner as essential to its ongoing M&A efforts. [President and CEO Fred] Chaffee says, "The biggest fears as a CEO or board member when you get acquired are, 'I'm going to lose my sense of identity and I'm going to lose my mission.' We have people on the AzCA board

who represent every acquisition, and we have two of the five former CEOs still on staff. When we go in to have an initial discussion, we say: 'Here are the names of former CEOs who either worked for us or in the community of agencies we acquired.' They don't sugarcoat it, but they give positive feedback and help to allay those fears."[14]

Cross-Sector Collaborations

Nonprofits work in partnership with for-profits and government agencies in *cross-sector collaborations*. These collaborations are necessary for solving the most difficult public challenges, such as dealing with environmental concerns, providing health care, or revitalizing communities. John Crosby, Barbara Bryson, and Melissa Stone define cross-sector collaborations as the "linking or sharing of information, resources, activities, and capabilities by organizations in two or more sectors to achieve jointly an outcome that could not be achieved by organizations in one sector separately."[15] They point out that a basic reason for cross-sector collaboration is the shared-power approach to many issues in American society, where many groups and organizations are involved in dealing with public challenges. Although most of the points made in this chapter pertain equally well to nonprofit collaborations with any organizations, cross-sector collaborations involving nonprofit organizations involve some special features.

Nonprofit and Government Collaborations

To examine nonprofit and government collaborations, we need to consider the motives that government agencies have to collaborate with organizations in other sectors. H. Brinton Milward and Keith Provan discuss four types of networks that government agencies establish, and we will review these types here.[16] Nonprofit organizations can be partners in any of these networks. *Service implementation networks* are used to deliver services that a government agency funds but does not directly deliver, such as many health and welfare services. Services are jointly produced by two or more other organizations, and integration is important to ensure that services are reliably produced and that vulnerable clients do not fall through the cracks. Government funding to private sector providers is normally arranged by contract. These contracts can be major sources of funding for nonprofits, and we discuss nonprofit contracting with government in Chapter Six on resource acquisition.

Information diffusion networks are established between government agencies to share information across organization and department boundaries. They are used to help agencies anticipate and prepare for problems that involve high uncertainty, such as disaster response. Although the bulk of collaboration in these networks is likely to be among government agencies, nonprofits may also be valuable sources of information that government agencies find helpful. Milward and Provan give the example of cooperation between the National Institutes of Health and medical foundations to manage the flow of knowledge from government-funded research so that everyone in a program that involves this research is informed of problems, protocols, and findings.

Problem-solving networks are designed to solve immediate and pressing problems, such as disasters. As such, these networks can grow out of information diffusion networks. Public managers confront demands for quick action, and this shapes the nature of the network that is established. Collaborations may be temporary, and after the problem or issue is dealt with the network may disband or become dormant. As disaster or emergency response often involves nonprofit organizations, they can be important members of these networks. A major example is the American Red Cross, whose resources are important components of the emergency response plans of local communities. Although the exact Red Cross activities will vary for each particular emergency, the Red Cross will nevertheless be a partner in community preparedness planning.

Finally, *community capacity-building networks* are established to help communities build the social capital they need to deal with both current and future needs, such as economic development or prevention of alcohol or drug abuse. Networks and partnerships build social capital in that they promote trust and norms of reciprocity between organizations.[17] This makes coordinated or joint action between organizations easier. Given their important roles in communities, nonprofit organizations will be important partners in these networks. For example, Milward and Provan report on a federal grant that created an agency whose goal was to weave together all the substance abuse prevention resources in an urban county. The number of agencies was large and included municipal agencies such as police and schools as well as specific nonprofit, for-profit, and government drug and alcohol prevention agencies. Goals included bringing isolated agencies to the table and bridging the various worlds of substance abuse prevention to bring about a more coordinated community response.

Nonprofit and For-Profit Collaborations

Joseph Galaskiewicz and Michelle Colman discuss four types of nonprofit and for-profit collaborations.[18] Both nonprofits and business firms have economic and noneconomic incentives to engage in collaboration. Nonprofits can get a variety of resources from firms, and firms can enter into collaborations with the goal of increasing sales. In addition, the collaboration will be designed to enhance social welfare. Although this aligns with the rationale for nonprofit existence, it can benefit firms as well, who also experience pressures to be concerned with more than the financial bottom line. Firms engage in *philanthropic collaborations* in order to help nonprofits deliver mission-related services. This assistance usually takes the form of donations of money or company products, but more extensive collaborations are also found. These can take the form of firm employees volunteering for the nonprofit, the firm sharing expertise with the nonprofit, or the firm participating in the nonprofit's program. KaBOOM! a well-known nonprofit builder of children's playgrounds, has a variety of corporate partnerships that illustrate the range of collaborations possible.[19] KaBOOM! combines the efforts of corporate and community (nonprofit) partners to build the playgrounds. Corporate partners provide contributions and employee volunteers. KaBOOM! has used contributions from a wide variety of corporate partners to build over two thousand playgrounds across the country with this model.

In *strategic collaborations*, firms seek to realize benefits for themselves while also advancing social welfare through the activities of nonprofits. These types of collaborations have also been labeled *social investing* or *strategic philanthropy*. Collaboration activities can include a firm's sponsorship of nonprofit events and donations of firm products or equipment. Having the firm's name prominently displayed is expected to give the firm credibility and legitimacy in the eyes of community stakeholders. In addition, donations may give prospective customers exposure to the firm's products. For example, major computer manufacturers have made donations of equipment to schools. One effect of these donations was that students became familiar with these products.

KaBOOM! engages in strategic collaborations with a number of corporations. As recently described on the About KaBOOM! Web page, "This year, Dr Pepper Snapple Group (DPS) introduced Let's Play, a community partnership designed to get kids active nationwide. The first Let's Play initiative is a three-year commitment to KaBOOM! Together, through Let's Play, DPS and KaBOOM! will build or fix up 2,000 playgrounds by the end of 2013, benefiting an estimated five million children across North America. With the launch of Let's Play, DPS will continue to promote fit and active lifestyles, a key component of ACTION Nation, DPS' corporate philanthropy program."

Commercial collaborations are focused primarily on increasing revenues for the firm and the nonprofit. These collaborations have fewer direct connections to service delivery and instead involve cause-related marketing and the licensing of nonprofit names and logos. In cause-related marketing the firm typically aligns itself with a cause and a nonprofit by providing a portion of sales revenue to the organization. The firm hopes to gain sales by advertising its association. In a licensing arrangement the nonprofit sells a firm the right to use the nonprofit's name or logo in the firm's promotional activities. The nonprofit gains the licensing fee as well as increased exposure through the firm's promotion. A question that may come up in these collaborations is the degree to which the nonprofit endorses the superiority of the firm's products or services.

KaBOOM! is involved with several corporations in cause-related marketing arrangements. For example, through a licensing agreement, Ben & Jerry's created KaBerry KaBOOM! ice cream, for which KaBOOM! received a per-purchase contribution.

Finally, *political collaborations* are aimed at advancing the political aims of partners. Corporate motives may include improving business conditions, avoiding negative publicity or investor or customer dissatisfaction, and demonstrating that the firm is addressing social and environmental concerns. Firms can combine lobbying and contributions to similarly interested nonprofits in order to garner advantageous political support. In addition, corporations may use alignments with nonprofits to provide access to the policy process. As Galaskiewicz and Colman note, "many companies view philanthropic contributions as a tactic to become credible and ensure that the firm and its interests are taken into account when policies are formulated or decisions are made." Collaborations can go beyond donations, as in the case of FedEx and the Environmental Defense Fund (EDF) collaboration on the development of hybrid diesel-electric delivery trucks.[20] FedEx had the purchasing power to attract manufacturers and provided test facilities. The EDF provided the metrics for environmental performance. Through the collaboration, FedEx established itself as an industry leader in clean truck technology and enhanced its brand value. The EDF advanced its mission and helped to reduce air emissions and transform the market for clean truck technology.

◆ ◆ ◆

Although there are clearly benefits to the partners in cross-sector collaborations, they also face a number of issues. Austin points out that as partnerships become more integrative, they involve more and more significant elements of each organization and increasing levels of interaction. As a result, the organizations will face increasing challenges.[21] A primary challenge is that the partners have different ends. Nonprofits are created to provide social benefits, for-profits must respond to their owners, and public agencies are tied to the political process. At some point in the collaboration, these divergent ends may lead to conflicts. For example, the relative emphasis placed on creating social versus economic return in a collaboration may well differ for the nonprofit and the business partner. Austin also notes that for collaborations to work, each partner must perceive that it gains enough value to continue the relationship, and this may prove difficult. In any nonprofit and for-profit collaboration, the corporate partner may conclude that the marketing benefits of the collaboration do not justify the effort expended. In addition, partners may have unequal power, misconceptions about one another, and different decision-making styles.[22] These differences can lead to feelings of inequality and mistrust. Although these issues can plague any collaboration, when combined with differences in ends and values, they become especially problematic. Nevertheless, careful attention to the factors important for collaboration formation and management can lead to successful cross-sector collaborations. In the sections that follow, we discuss how nonprofits can successfully address the challenges of forming and maintaining collaborations.

Developing a Process for Collaboration

Collaboration is the result of a process that develops over time. Numerous authors have investigated this development and identified a general pattern in the nature of the process and how it unfolds. A number of models have been developed that describe the process as a series of stages or steps. These models vary in the specific number of stages, how these stages are labeled, and the boundaries between stages.[23] However, all the models describe a sequential process that moves from initial planning and a decision to seek a collaboration to generating and evaluating specific potential partners and then to forming and implementing a formal collaborative relationship and finally to evaluating the operation of the collaboration. We will consider several key points in this process.

Initial Planning

Each stage of collaboration development is important, and the outcomes of a given stage depend upon successfully meeting the challenges of the previous stage. Given this, it is hard to overemphasize the importance of the initial stages of the process. Arsenault discusses aspects of preliminary planning, partner identification, and initial negotiation.[24] The planning process should result in clear collaboration goals for the nonprofit, based on its needs. Preliminary planning and the assessment of organizational readiness should include the following activities:

- Make sure internal constituencies understand the organization's situation in its environment.
- Identify the goals that leaders would like to accomplish as a result of collaboration.
- Determine the degree of support for these goals among board members, leaders and managers, key staff, funders, key donors, important political supporters, and existing collaboration partners.
- Educate the board and management about the collaboration options for reaching goals.

- Carefully think through the potential impact on the organization if the initiative succeeds.
- Determine the funds available to pay for any professional services that might be needed.
- Identify clear parameters and roles and responsibilities for internal and external communication in the search for a partner and in early negotiations.
- Determine the members of the negotiating team.
- Define what the nonprofit organization brings to the table.
- Establish clear roles for partner identification and the early negotiation process.
- Determine initial screening criteria.

The Arizona's Children Association described earlier is a good example of an organization taking initial planning very seriously. This is to be expected given the scope of the mergers it has engaged in. These procedures, however, are also crucial for other types of collaborations.

Identifying Potential Partners

It is also important to assess what the organization will bring to the table. What can partners stand to gain by collaborating? Organizational strengths should be assessed in relation to

- Cash assets
- Leadership expertise: such as business skills, fundraising ability, and political clout
- Administrative capacity: such as management information, accounting, and human resources
- Physical plant: real estate and location
- Donor access: personal connections, history, and recognition
- Volunteers: volunteer base and its management
- Unique competencies: such as intellectual property, staff skills, and program models
- Public presence and community image

Several methods are available for identifying potential partners. The organization may develop its own information and then select and approach a specific candidate for collaboration. Collaborations can grow out of the personal relationships of executive directors and board chairs.

Board members and managers are likely to have personal knowledge of potential collaborators as well as contacts with others who might have this type of information. Their personal knowledge and networks are important in that they are likely to contain specific and relevant information. If such personal knowledge is not available, information about potential partners can be obtained from relevant secondary sources such as IRS reports (especially Form 990 information), industry data on high-performing organizations, or the annual reports of particular organizations.

Forming the Collaboration

Once specific potential partners are identified, they can be approached by organizational representatives to assess their interest in collaboration. A second method is for the organization to issue a formal request for proposal (RFP). In this latter case the negotiating team identifies a list of possible collaborators. Material is prepared describing the organization, what it is trying to do, and what its criteria are for collaboration. This material is provided to the potential collaborators, and interested organizations are requested to respond with a letter of interest.

Once potential collaborators are identified, representatives of the organizations meet to assess the degree of mutual interest and compatibility. This can be done through a side-by-side analysis that addresses aspects of each organization deemed relevant to the collaboration.[25] This could include a comparison of missions, visions, values, cultures, governance, programs, human resources, and other assets.[26] It is important to assess the degree of congruence between the collaboration goals of the prospective partners as well as their backgrounds, current situations, and future potentials. This examination will be more extensive for collaborations that are expected to be more extensive and long lasting. For example, two substance abuse programs that seem to have similar goals may find at this stage that they are not congruent, perhaps because one is faith based and the other is not.

If the two organizations agree to collaborate, negotiations will be needed to establish the general terms of the basis for collaboration and to formalize the relationship. The extensiveness of the negotiations and the degree of formalization will depend on the type of collaboration. For simple collaborations a *memo of understanding*, laying out the general points for future cooperation, may suffice. For more extensive collaborations, such as joint ventures, detailed plans for future joint action will need to be negotiated and legal documents may be required. For example, the Cancer Vaccine Collaborative involves extensive, long-lasting, and multifaceted interactions between numerous aspects of each partner. When specific interactions need to be specified in advance, such as coordinated lab trials in the case of the Collaborative, detailed schedules or even contracts can be drawn up.

Evaluating the Collaboration

When the functional details have been formalized, collaboration can be implemented, and joint action can begin. Once again, the type of collaboration will determine the type and degree of interaction of personnel and processes. The results of these interactions should be the collaboration benefits expected. At some point, there should be an assessment of the benefits each partner receives through collaboration. This will lead to a decision to continue the collaboration as is, to expand or contract particular aspects of it, to renegotiate its basic terms, or to terminate the collaboration.

As noted previously, the Arizona's Children Association deploys a team to evaluate postmerger integration, focusing particularly on the integration of the cultures of the two organizations. Amelia Kohm and David La Piana provide other examples of the ways in which collaboration evaluations have been used by partners. In one case a human service nonprofit in Spokane, Washington, formed a microenterprise program with a business development association. The program resulted in increased services for low-income clients, including access to capital and business education. The staff at both organizations were quite happy with the program and saw only relatively minor adjustments needing to be made to the program in the future. In contrast, the collaboration between a substance abuse treatment center and a shelter for abused women in Wooster, Ohio, was more challenging. The organizations agreed to develop a joint facility but were hampered by leadership transitions. These were eventually resolved, and the facility opened with shared staff and costs. The clientele of both organizations seemed to like the facility and location. Most of the people interviewed felt that the relationship between the organizations would continue and grow, perhaps with the organizations merging in the future.[27]

It is important for nonprofit boards and managers to understand that the depiction of collaboration development as a simple linear series of stages is somewhat of an oversimplification. The process can be iterative, and the collaboration may not reach the final stage.[28] Unexpected complications may arise during the course of implementation that necessitate a return to negotiation or the selection of a different potential partner. In addition, dysfunctional interpersonal dynamics during negotiation or implementation may make further progress difficult or impossible.

The Role of Governance

Suzanne Feeney discusses the strategic roles that nonprofit boards play in collaborations and mergers.[29] These roles are an extension of the governance and stewardship roles that boards play in their individual organizations. The degree to which the board has responsibilities and tasks in a collaboration will vary with the scope of the collaboration. Informal collaboration will require little, if any, board involvement, whereas joint ventures or mergers will require extensive involvement. The responsibilities can be understood in relation to five board functions. The functions and examples of board activity during collaboration are the following:

- **Executive director and board interactions**. The board's role may include assessment of planning, reviewing and approving contracts or commitments, and hand-in-hand planning or leading.
- **Stakeholder outreach and boundary spanning**. The board's role may include partner assessment, gathering and interpreting information, communicating with stakeholders, and building community support. This may be an extensive process, as stakeholders include funders, clients, regulators, and others, and each stakeholder is likely to have a different orientation toward any collaboration.
- **Fiduciary and financial responsibility**. The board's role may include assessing risk potential and resource commitments, playing a governance role when required by a formal agreement, dissolving and transferring assets, and ensuring legal compliance.
- **Policy development and monitoring**. The board's role may include ensuring program and mission alignment and also mission consistency and congruence.
- **Ensuring organizational health**. The board's role may include monitoring staff morale and program or service delivery, monitoring organizational impact, supporting the CEO and staff, and monitoring culture change.

Factors Promoting Collaboration Success

Paul Mattessich, Marta Murray-Close, and Barbara Monsey have reviewed the research on collaboration and have compiled for the Amherst H. Wilder Foundation a comprehensive inventory of twenty factors influencing successful collaboration.[30] The breadth of the factors included in the inventory attests to the difficulty of establishing and maintaining successful collaboration. The Wilder Foundation provides a workbook for using the inventory to assess current or potential collaborations. The workbook recommends that relevant personnel rate the degree to which they feel the collaborative group or situation possesses each of the twenty factors. The assessment is not designed to provide a single numerical score but rather to identify factors that may be missing or problematic in a collaboration. The twenty factors are organized into six categories. We present the six categories of the Wilder framework here, along with paraphrased questions that illustrate each of the twenty factors.

1. Factors related to the environment:
   - Do the potential partners have a history of collaboration or cooperation in the community that provides them with an understanding of the roles and expectations required in collaboration?
   - Is the collaborative group seen as a legitimate leader in the community and is it perceived as reliable and competent (at least in relation to the group's goals)?
   - Do political leaders, opinion makers, persons who control resources, and members of the public support (or at least not oppose) the mission of the group?
2. Factors related to membership characteristics:
   - Do members of the group share an understanding and respect for each other and their respective organizations, including how each organization operates, its cultural norms and values, its limitations, and its expectations?
   - To the extent that they are needed, does the group include representatives from each segment of the community that will be affected by its activities?
   - Do the partners believe that they will benefit from their involvement in the collaboration and that the advantages of membership will offset costs, such as loss of autonomy and turf?
   - Do members have the ability to compromise? Members will need to compromise because the many decisions made within the collaborative effort cannot possibly fit the preferences of every member perfectly.
3. Factors related to process and structure:
   - Do members of the group feel "ownership" of both the way the group works and the results or products of its work?
   - Does every level of each partner organization have at least some representation and ongoing involvement in the collaboration?
   - Is the group open to varied ways of organizing itself and accomplishing its work?
   - Do the partners clearly understand their roles, rights, and responsibilities, and understand how to carry out those responsibilities?
   - Does the group have the ability to sustain itself in the midst of major changes, even if it needs to change some major goals, members, or the like, in order to deal with changing conditions?
   - Can the structure, resources, and activities of the group change over time to meet the needs of the group without overwhelming its capacity, at each point throughout the collaboration?

4. Factors related to communication:
   - Do group members interact often, update one another, discuss issues openly, and convey all necessary information to one another and to people outside the group?
   - Do members establish personal connections—producing a better, more informal, and cohesive group working on a common project?
5. Factors related to purpose:
   - Are the goals and objectives of the group clear to all partners, and can they realistically be attained?
   - Do partners have the same vision, with a clearly agreed-upon mission, set of objectives, and strategy?
   - Do the mission and the set of goals, or the approach, of the group differ, at least in part, from those of the member organizations (that is, does it have a unique purpose)?
6. Factors related to resources:
   - Does the group have an adequate financial base, along with the staff and materials needed to support its operations?
   - Does the individual who provides leadership have organizational and interpersonal skills, and does he or she carry out the role with fairness?

Challenges to Collaboration Success

In general, any problems in relation to the success factors outlined in this chapter could limit the success of the collaboration. In addition, a number of factors have been considered particularly important.[31] The more extensive the collaboration is, the more potentially problematic these factors will become.

- **Incompatible mission, vision, and values.** Mission, vision, and values are the basic building blocks upon which specific nonprofit activities are built. If these fundamental ideological and value orientations are not congruent, significant disagreements are likely regarding any joint activities.
- **Culture.** Organizational culture is of major importance because it affects the behavior of organizational participants, has both visible and unobservable elements, and is difficult and slow to change. Nonprofits, given their focus on missions to serve people, are likely to have distinctive cultures. It is important to assess the culture of each partnering organization and to attend to cultural incompatibilities.

- **Ego**. Collaboration may involve the modification or giving up of some responsibility or activity. Both leaders and members may resist if they feel that their organization or group is somehow "lessened" in this process. This can pertain to a perceived loss of prestige or power as well as to a perceived diminishing of the values or worldviews that organization members are invested in. For example, executive directors and boards are particularly influential in mergers, and McLaughlin has paraphrased some typical expressions of ego by board members, such as, "This organization has been around for 112 years, and it's going to be around for the next 112," and, "I refuse to be known as the last president of this organization."[32]
- **Turf**. Each organization has established itself in a particular domain or sphere of operation that it may tend to defend. For example, a nonprofit may resist giving another nonprofit access to its clients or treating its partner as an equal.
- **Cost**. Costs can be incurred in both time and resources. As we have noted, collaboration development can be very time consuming. It may take a significant time to complete a partnership agreement, and much staff time can be used during search and negotiation stages. Complex or extensive collaborations may also involve expenditures for information gathering, analysis, and due diligence. Resources will also be needed if the collaboration involves new or altered programs or services. Finally, opportunity costs inherent in the collaboration should also be considered.

Several reports on unsuccessful collaborations point to the corrosive impact of these factors. A report on the merger between three well-established Jewish groups, for example, alleged that the first years of the merger had been marked by "unclear expectations, unshared visions, mixed motivations, and multi-layered power games."[33] It also alleged that problems resulted from an inadequate understanding, by consultants, of the cultures of the organizations. Another report on a failed merger between a university medical center and health maintenance system in Pennsylvania pointed to three interrelated issues, including dysfunctional leadership, distrust among board members, and different organizational cultures.[34]

Concluding Thoughts

Collaboration is a fact of organizational life. The diverse missions of nonprofit organizations may lead to collaborations with partners in any sector, and thus the collaborations can take a wide variety of forms. However, a number of important characteristics of collaborations can be identified. In this chapter we examined the reasons why nonprofits might collaborate, the forms that collaborations can take, the process by which collaborations are established, and factors leading to collaboration success. Understanding these factors will enhance the likelihood that a collaboration will meet the nonprofit's expectations.

In the next chapter we explore change and innovation. Change often comes about through and as a result of collaboration. Therefore planning for greater mission impact or responding to changes may entail establishing, nurturing, and managing a collaboration.

Questions for Consideration

1. Six reasons why nonprofits might collaborate were identified (social responsibility, operational efficiency, and so on). Might it be possible for a particular collaboration to advance one of these objectives while detracting from another? In the case of this kind of conflict, what factors might lead a nonprofit to favor one objective over another?
2. If the answers to the questions posed in the "Factors Promoting Collaboration Success" section are yes, how will this mitigate the factors discussed in the "Challenges to Collaboration Success" section?

Exercises

Exercise 15.1: Types of Collaboration

Identify a nonprofit collaboration that exemplifies one of the six perspectives on nonprofit collaboration presented in the chapter.

Exercise 15.2: Austin's Collaboration Continuum

Select a nonprofit that you are familiar with or define a hypothetical nonprofit. Using Austin's collaboration continuum, discuss how this nonprofit might form a transactional or an integrative collaboration with another nonprofit.

Exercise 15.3: Cross-Sector Collaboration

Looking again at the nonprofit you selected for the previous exercise, discuss how it might form a transactional or integrative collaboration with a for-profit organization. How might it form such a collaboration with a public agency?

CHAPTER SIXTEEN

ORGANIZATIONAL CHANGE AND INNOVATION

*T*each For America was started in 1989 with a novel approach to remedying the achievement gap between rich and poor students in the United States.[1] Its founder, Wendy Kopp, proposed having graduates of top universities spend two years teaching disadvantaged students. Teach For America would provide recruits with intense training over the summer and then place them in schools in low-income communities. Low-income students would benefit by having bright, energetic teachers, and the recruits would become lifelong advocates for education. The idea caught on rapidly. By June 1990, the organization had trained five hundred new university graduates, or corps members. The following year, helped by positive news stories, the organization attracted three thousand applicants for seven hundred positions. The budget jumped to $5 million and prominent corporations and foundations endorsed Teach For America. Success led Teach For America to start two other organizations under its umbrella. TEACH! was started to help school districts improve their new teacher recruitment and support, and the Learning Project was begun to develop innovative summer school programs in inner cities. As it grew, however, Teach For America failed to build adequate organizational capacity and remained overly reliant on too few large foundations and individual donations. Expenses outstripped income, and by 1995, the organization was in debt, enrollments were dropping, and it had been criticized in an academic journal, further eroding financial support and morale.

Teach For America, though, was able to rebound from this low point through a concerted effort to stabilize finances, refocus on its mission, and bolster its structure and culture. It trimmed its budget by 25 percent to more closely match income and *expenditures and charged its regional offices to broaden the funding base. As a result, the organization went from 275 funders in 1993 to more than 1,400 in 1998. The organization refocused on accomplishing its original mission. This led it to spin off TEACH! and the Learning Project. Teach For America dedicated itself to clear organization- and constituency-building goals and instituted quantifiable performance goals. Organizational structure was enhanced by moving from a relatively flat organization and fairly informal interactions to a more hierarchical structure with a senior management team composed of vice presidents for major internal units and more formal interactions. The culture had become diffused as the organization grew, with different units developing different understandings and outlooks. A consistent culture was revived by having everyone participate in the generation of eight core values. The staff buy-in that resulted set a new, positive, tone in the organization.*

The changes made by Teach For America greatly strengthened the organization. By 1997, it was covering its operating expenses and had retired its long-term debt. Staff felt more committed, and morale and relations between staff and managers had improved. Performance goals were set and reviewed and programs had been strengthened. In 2000, now on a firm financial footing, it launched an expansion plan, and by 2003, 3,400 corps members reached more than 250,000 students. Teach For America is not sitting on its laurels and is aware of the need for future change. Everyone in the organization is charged to continuously ask two questions: Are the members and alumni of the corps truly expanding educational opportunities? Is the organization building the internal capacity to realize its goals today and in the future?

◆ ◆ ◆

The story of Teach For America shows us an example of the kinds of changes a nonprofit can go through. Although young organizations such as Teach For America are particularly vulnerable to pressures for major change, older organizations are not immune. In this chapter we will examine how nonprofits change and innovate. To change means to make different. What is the impetus for change, or making something different, in a nonprofit? What kinds of changes do we find in nonprofits, and how do these changes come about? We will also discuss innovation, an important type of change for nonprofits. To innovate is to begin something new. Nonprofits are frequently faced with new ways to accomplish their missions and serve their constituencies. How do they innovate and adopt new ways to address challenges and opportunities?

Change is an ubiquitous feature of the natural and social world. The Greek philosopher Heraclitus wrote over 2,500 years ago that "nothing endures but change."[2] Although it may be ubiquitous, change is not easy for individuals, organizations, communities, or society. For organizations, change can take many forms, including growth, decline, or alteration in structures or processes. In addition, each form of change has different characteristics. An organization's founding is quite different from its dissolution. Moreover, there are risks involved, as not all changes are beneficial and organizations may run into difficulties before they achieve success. In addition, change, even if beneficial, will always involve costs in such things as time, personnel effort, and possibly resources. Finally, change upsets the status quo, which can be threatening. Consequently, organizations and the people in them may resist change, even if in the long run it is likely to be beneficial.

As these observations indicate, change will be challenging for organizations. This is all the more so in light of the fact that the pace of environmental change and the pressure on organizations to adapt are increasing. In a recent report, McKinsey & Company expressed the situation currently facing organizations: "Today, the overriding problem for every organization is how to change, deeply and continually, and at an accelerating pace. We live in a world where change is 'shaken, not stirred.' Yet in most organizations, practices and structures reflexively favor the status quo over change and renewal." The report goes on to say: "In most organizations, innovation is still mostly an afterthought. It's a project, an initiative, or a function, but it's not an activity that involves everyone, every day."[3]

The need to change certainly affects nonprofit organizations. This is so, in part, due to a number of trends that have been felt in the nonprofit sector for some time. As the pace of population growth, resource scarcity, and global interdependence increase, social problems are becoming increasingly intense and complex. Nonprofits worldwide are under pressure to contribute to the solutions to these problems, but also to do more with less. Financial pressures on nonprofits have increased. Costs have been rising faster than inflation while government funding has decreased, and private donations and grants have not made up the difference.[4]

These trends are reflected in a recent report in *The Chronicle of Philanthropy* on emerging forces in the nonprofit sector.[5] The forces include governments in crisis, strains on the safety net, and falling donations and volunteerism as a result of the recession and the meager recovery of the last few years. In addition, nonprofit employees have been hit by layoffs, salary freezes, and benefit cuts and are ripe for burnout. On the donor side, donors are increasingly specifying how their contributions should be used and are looking for new ways to determine that their contributions have made a difference. Moreover, few nonprofits have discovered how to use the new social media to raise money. In spite of these challenges, however, Lester Salamon notes that there are also opportunities for nonprofits.[6] These include demographic shifts, such as the growth of the elderly population, that increase the demand for nonprofit services, and the increased visibility and credibility of nonprofits that has resulted from nonprofit involvement in major social and civic events, such as disaster relief efforts. What is clear is that, in this rapidly changing world, nonprofit organizations will need to search for new ways to both address the challenges the nonprofit sector faces and take advantage of its opportunities.

Understanding Change in Nonprofits

In this section we will examine the nature of change in nonprofits. We will first consider the general processes and specific forces that lead to change in nonprofits. We will then discuss the parts of a nonprofit that can change, how large or significant changes can be, and the resistance to change that a nonprofit may encounter.

Process-Driven Change

In the most general sense, we can define organizational change as the adoption of a new or different idea or behavior by an organization.[7] The literature on organizational change is huge. In a search using the key words *change* and *development*, Andrew Van de Ven and Marshall Poole identified over one million articles, from a variety of disciplines, and at least twenty specific theories.[8] This literature shows that change can be associated with general organizational processes as well as a number of specific driving forces. General organizational processes that entail change include life cycles, goal setting, conflict, and evolution.[9] Each of these can be seen at work in nonprofit change.

Organizational Life Cycles

Organizational life cycles have been associated with change. The idea that organizations have life cycles is borrowed from biology and posits a sequence of stages occurring during the existence of an organization. These stages vary predictably as they are based on an underlying process of growth and development (analogous to birth, growth, and death in a biological organism). A popular organizational life cycle model has been developed by Larry Greiner. In this model, organizations go through five stages as they grow. Challenges develop at each stage, and these must be overcome if the organization is to grow further and advance to the next stage. The life cycle stages in this model are outlined in the following list:[10]

- **Creativity, or start-up.** This stage requires strong leadership and vision to marshal the resources, energy, and commitment needed to launch the organization. The organization is likely to be fairly informal, with people helping out and pitching in as needed to get the work done. As the organization grows, however, this flexibility and informality that helped launch the organization becomes less productive, and more professional management and formal structures are needed.
- **Direction.** Further growth will be facilitated by the introduction of more formalized structures and systems. These rules and procedures are used by top leaders to direct action. As growth proceeds, however, the system of control becomes unwieldy and lower-level units and managers push for more autonomy. Delegation is the solution for this, but top managers may be unwilling to give up the control they have.
- **Delegation.** The discretion needed by lower levels of the organization will result in the formation of semiautonomous subunits (divisions or departments) that are given targets or goals and the discretion to accomplish them in the ways they see as best. Top management is responsible for overall strategy and direction. Delegation, however, can lead to parochial attitudes in subunits, duplication of efforts, communication problems, and inconsistent strategic action.
- **Coordination.** The problem of delegation can be met by centralizing operations. A head office provides coordination of human resources, marketing, production, and other functions across the different divisions and operating units. Over time this will lead to the proliferation of rules and red tape, which will inhibit operations, perhaps to the point where the coordinating systems and programs become dysfunctional. The activity of following rules can become more important than producing results. In this case the organization has become too large to be centrally controlled through formal and bureaucratized systems.
- **Collaboration.** In order to overcome the crisis of red tape, the organization needs to find ways to enhance innovation. This will involve simplifying structures and procedures and installing coordination through flexible, collaborative means, such as task forces, cross-functional teams, or matrix structures.

Teach For America is a good example of an organization moving through the first two stages. The early days of the organization were characterized by a great deal of creativity, energy, and enthusiasm. During this period, operations were quite informal. This informality, however, proved dysfunctional as the organization grew, and as a consequence, a more hierarchical and formal system of control was put in place to manage a larger and more diverse organization. A life cycle approach that is particularly relevant for nonprofit organizations has been developed by Paul Light. Termed the *development spiral,* it will be discussed later in this chapter.

Organizational Evolution

Organizational evolution also uses ideas about change from biology. In the biological world, change at the species level takes place through the natural selection processes of variation, selection, and retention. Analogously, organizational change can take place through the replacement of one form, or type, of organization by another. In the organizational world, change results as types of organizations compete for scarce resources. New types of organizations are constantly being developed, and those that are better at acquiring resources will replace types of organizations that are less able to do so. For example, in the child welfare field, changes in funder priorities have resulted in the decline of orphanages and the rise of community-based options for custodial care (such as foster care).

Organizational Goal Setting

Organizational goal setting may lead to purposive strategic change in individual organizations. Goals are continuously changed to respond to external and internal changes. For example, nonprofits evaluate their missions periodically, create and review strategies yearly, and assess goal accomplishment even more frequently. In setting the agendas for these changes, leadership at a number of levels is involved. Board members and top leaders have responsibilities for changing mission and strategy, whereas changes in operational goals and plans are made by lower-level leaders. In all cases, any changes made will be the result of the dynamics of decision-making processes at these levels. These decision-making processes could unfold relatively harmoniously or be characterized by conflict. Teach For America was able to reverse its downward spiral by setting goals to bolster finances, establish new structure, and revitalize its culture.

Organizational Conflict

Organizational conflict may lead to organizational change driven by opposition and disputes. Organizations are composed of interest groups, each seeking to have its viewpoint expressed in organizational action. For example, even though top leaders may propose major changes the board may not approve them. Board members may disagree with the direction of the organization proposed by top leaders and these disagreements may be negotiated. In these situations the changes that result may be compromises. In addition, new leaders often come to a nonprofit with specific plans and these may, likewise, be considered and approved by the board. Subunits of the nonprofit may attempt to influence decisions. For example, a nonprofit's service staff may want the nonprofit to expand its programs and serve more clients. The finance department, however, may have concerns about how to finance the growth and may want to maintain the status quo, put off growth, or grow very slowly. These conflicts may need to be resolved by decision makers higher up in the organization. External conflicts can also drive change. Nonprofits may need to negotiate with funders or meet a competitor's actions.

Specific Drivers of Nonprofit Change

In addition to the organizational processes just considered, organizational change can be the result of more specific environmental pressure and internal forces.[11] Patrick Dawson outlines a variety of internal and external drivers, or *triggers*, that can be expected to influence all organizations, including nonprofits.[12]

External Drivers

External drivers include general factors as widespread as the globalization of markets, which will present new opportunities as well as challenges. Drivers on a somewhat smaller scale include government laws and regulations, fluctuations in the business cycle or the economy, major political and social events or changes, and advances in technology. All types of organizations can be influenced by these drivers. For example, some nonprofits have global operations, and all nonprofits in the United States are subject to IRS rules. Moreover, the downturn in the U.S. economy in the last few years has reduced contributions for many nonprofits, and a change of presidential administrations can result in increases or reductions in federal programs that support nonprofits. Nonprofits can expect yet other drivers and inhibitors of change.[13] A nonprofit's *mission* can be an important driver of change. Nonprofits expect to affect individuals and communities. If the desired social change is accomplished, nonprofits may need to redefine their missions or strategies to stay relevant. However, given the large social issues that nonprofits usually seek to address, it is more likely that they or their external stakeholders may judge progress in mission accomplishment to be insufficient. This will lead to pressure to reevaluate strategies or programs or redefine the mission.

Changes in *external constituencies* may also result in nonprofit change. Nonprofits are closely tied to external constituencies, and any changes in these groups may generate pressures for change. For example, the increase in the number of elderly people in the United States may result in more needs for services. Or a worsening economy may result in higher community poverty, unemployment, and health care needs. Likewise, changes in government policy could result in more or fewer social needs, as well as changes in government funds available for nonprofits. Even major natural disasters may require a prolonged response by nonprofits. For example, New Orleans is still dealing with problems caused by Hurricane Katrina, which struck in 2005. In addition, *donor preferences* may change. Donors may change their funding priorities as new issues or problems arise and capture the public's attention. A nonprofit significantly reliant on donations will be affected by these shifts and may need to change in response. In addition, nonprofits may rely on national or international donors, whose priorities may be quite different from the priorities of the local community. Nonprofits have a number of options to address funding shortfalls resulting from the loss of funders. They may seek income from other sources, such as fees or charges. In addition, they may cut costs, drop or alter services, or establish partnerships with other service providers.

Finally, a nonprofit's *visibility and accountability* can lead to pressure for change. As a nonprofit gains visibility and prominence, expectations for transparency and accountability may increase. These expectations can come from a variety of external actors, including the general public or citizen groups, government agencies or regulators, professional associations, and other nonprofits. The nonprofit may find itself the target of conflicting expectations and demands. Irrespective of the choices that might be made, these pressures will result in the need for organizational change. For example, a nonprofit providing chemical dependency services for the homeless may be obligated to open a facility in a certain neighborhood by a city contract or grant. Clients, however, may want and advocate for other services, and residents may seek to block the establishment of a facility in their neighborhood.

Internal Triggers

Internal triggers exert pressure for change from inside the organization. In the organizational change literature, four general internal triggers to change are typically identified: the organization's technology, primary task, personnel, and administrative structures.[14] For example, significant changes can be expected if an educational nonprofit moves to all online instruction, a day-care center becomes a preschool, a legal services nonprofit replaces lawyers with paralegals, or a nonprofit cooperative becomes bureaucratic.

Besides these general drivers, nonprofits can be expected to face additional internal forces for change. These include values, performance, and leadership.[15] Nonprofit missions and the strategies to accomplish them are *values* driven. Significant differences and conflicts can arise within the organization about the most desirable means and ends. For example, should a community services nonprofit work toward short- or long-term solutions to neighborhood problems? Helping residents repair their houses would be the former whereas enhancing the economic development of the community would be the latter.

In addition, should it help all community residents or only low-income ones? The outcomes of these debates will likely entail changes in goals and operations. A second factor is that as nonprofits grow and gain experience and capabilities, they may experience internal pressures for *improving performance* as well as demands to demonstrate results. Each of these has implications for change. Improving performance may involve refining or expanding programs to serve more clients, serve them better, or establish services in a new location. It may also, as in the case of Teach For America, result in eliminating some services in order to refocus and improve others. Demands to demonstrate results can be met by instituting or improving outcome evaluation. Finally, nonprofits will face *leadership transitions.* As a nonprofit grows, founders must normally step aside to be replaced by a new leadership team. This may entail a change in vision, goals, or strategies as well as the establishment of new procedures. Any subsequent major changes in leaders may likewise entail similar changes.

Elements That Can Be Changed

As we have seen, there are a multitude of reasons *why* a nonprofit would want or need to change. It is also important to examine *what* a nonprofit might want to change. The literature on strategic organizational change has focused on four general types of change, corresponding to the major elements of an organization: change in strategy and structure, change in technology, change in products and services, and change in people and culture. Richard Daft discusses the unique properties of these types of changes.[16]

Strategy and Structure Change

Strategy and structure change involves the elements that provide administration, supervision, and management. This includes changes in structural arrangements and strategic plans as well as in features such as policies, coordination techniques, control systems, and accounting and budgeting. Such changes can affect major aspects of the organization and are therefore normally made from the top down. The top leaders of an organization have the authority needed to make this type of change, and this type of change is most easily adopted by an organization with a mechanistic, or more bureaucratic, formalized, and centralized structure. Such an organizational structure is best for facilitating changes in structures, rules, and procedures throughout the organization. For example, the establishment of a more formal, hierarchical structure at Teach For America was initiated by Wendy Kopp. In addition, we can see this type of change in major nonprofit reorganizations, such as mergers.

Mergers are strategy driven and under the control of top management and are discussed in detail in Chapter Fifteen.

Technology Change
Technology change involves the instituting of different techniques for producing products or services. This may entail new knowledge, skills, or other competencies. This type of change normally occurs from the bottom up. Those in the research or production levels of the organization are most likely to have the expertise to evaluate and propose technology changes. If approved, these changes are then instituted in the organization. Ways to promote and encourage technology change include flexible (or organic) structures that allow participants freedom to be creative and develop or introduce new ideas, creative departments, venture or collaborative teams, and corporate entrepreneurship. For example, a change to the Montessori method of education in a nonprofit preschool will be led by and be under the direction of the teaching staff.

Product and Service Change
Product and service change involves the outputs of the organization. For nonprofits these outputs will often be the services provided to constituencies. Changes can be made to provide for new or additional needs of clients, respond to competitors, or take advantage of new opportunities for mission accomplishment. Successful product or service change occurs on the horizontal level. It entails (1) linking the different, specialized units or groups that develop, produce, and market new products or services, and (2) linking these units or groups with relevant sectors in the external environment. In this way the nonprofit can become aware of the need or opportunity to respond to its environment and can acquire the ability to turn ideas into new products and services. For example, Goodwill Industries of Central Indiana recently started a charter school. This nonprofit sought to combat a root cause of unemployment, lack of education, by establishing this new school for the children of its clients and for other students. Starting this school required extensive horizontal activity and coordination. Teams had to study client needs, develop business plans, recruit instructors, market services, recruit students, and integrate the school into the Goodwill organization at the level of other major Goodwill operations and services.[17]

People and Culture Change
People and culture change involves change in regard to the behavior, values, attitudes, or beliefs of organizational participants. For nonprofits, these participants could include volunteers as well as employees. Changing people and culture

is typically more difficult than changing other aspects of the organization. Numerous difficult-to-change factors are involved, including individual psychology and personality as well as the norms and values embedded in organizational practices. Teach For America went through an elaborate process to arrive at core values that were shared by organizational participants. An initial list was generated by top management. This was distributed to and amended by other levels of the organization until agreement was eventually reached. As change requires the actions of people, any change involving one of the other three types of change almost always requires some change in people and culture. A major approach to bringing about change in the human and social aspects of organizations is organizational development, which will be considered later.

Degree of Change

An important aspect of organizational change is that it can vary dramatically in scope and significance. For a nonprofit, we can see this by contrasting a minor change in how services will be delivered with a change in mission. The former is an example of what Warner Burke calls *evolutionary* change, whereas the latter can be considered *revolutionary* change—a complete overhaul that could affect all of the categories just described, from strategy and structure to people and culture.[18]

David Wilson provides a helpful framework that identifies four degrees of change.[19] The first degree, *status quo*, refers to no change in current practice, operations, or strategy. *Expanded reproduction* involves producing more of the same goods or services. This level of change affects mainly operations. An example would be the opening of additional Goodwill retail outlets in different areas of a city. Changes in organizations tend to be resisted, and it can be expected that more significant changes may encounter the most resistance. Consequently, most changes in organizations tend to be expanded reproduction, relatively small incremental steps or adjustments to address a problem or take advantage of an opportunity. *Evolutionary transition* is a more significant degree of change. It occurs within existing parameters of the organization (such as structure and technology) and affects mainly the direction, strategy, and goals of the organization. An example would be a youth counseling agency that has focused on mental health issues adding drug counseling services for its clients. Finally, *revolutionary transformation* involves shifting or redefining existing parameters and making major changes in strategy, structure, or technology. Nonprofit transformation is discussed in detail in a later section.

Change efforts can have a time imperative. At times, change needs to be dramatic and significant, altering major aspects of organizational functioning. Stephen Jay Gould has proposed a *punctuated equilibrium* model of organizational change.[20] In this model, organizations exist in steady states for a period of time. During this period only small or minor changes are made. This period, however, can be interrupted (punctuated) by the need for a sudden dramatic change, which is then followed by another period of equilibrium. Significant changes in the environment can bring about dramatic nonprofit changes. As noted earlier in this book, the March of Dimes offers a classic example. It was founded in 1938 with a mission to eliminate polio. When medical science perfected a vaccine against polio in the 1950s and 1960s, the March of Dimes needed to transform itself. Today, the mission of the March of Dimes is to help mothers have full-term pregnancies and to research the problems that threaten the health of babies.[21]

Resistance to Change

As the discussion so far reveals, nonprofits face a variety of pressures to change. Change, however, alters and disrupts established patterns of activity in organizations. It creates uncertainty and threatens some organizational participants. Resistance can arise on every organizational level, including individual, subgroup, organizational, and environmental levels. As the degree of change increases, it can be expected that resistance will likewise increase. At the *individual* level, Dawson identifies a number of general factors that can inhibit change. A change in jobs may require changes in skills. A change may pose a threat to employment or result in a reduction in economic security or job displacement. Or a change may result in a disruption of social relations due to new work arrangements or a lowering of status due to redefined authority relationships.[22]

Tony Eccles identifies a number of more specific reasons why employees may resist change. Employees may fail to understand the problem given as the reason for change. They may have a preference for an alternative solution to the problem or feel that the proposed solution will not work. The proposed solution may have unacceptable personal costs or insufficient rewards. They may find the required new values and practices personally unacceptable or repugnant. Finally, management motives themselves may be questioned.[23]

Change may be resisted by other levels, including subunits, the organization, and even the organization's environment. These levels bring in a set of additional factors.[24] Within workgroups, norms, cohesion, or groupthink may lead to resistance. A host of factors at the organizational level may inhibit change, including power relations and conflict, differences in functional orientations between subunits, a rigid or mechanistic structure, lack of resources or sunk costs, and finally, the organizational culture itself. Resistance can also be found in the organization's environment. The organization may have contractual agreements with others that prohibit change. In addition, public or community beliefs and opinions may limit the amount of change that an organization feels it can engage in.

A nonprofit's special characteristics may also pose particular challenges for change. Jacquelyn Wolf identifies a number of factors that may inhibit nonprofit change:[25]

- **Nonprofits' nature.** Nonprofits are characterized by a culture of integrity, an altruistic mission, and the creation of social benefits. Evaluations may be based on personal experience with the organization. Policies, programs, clients, staff, and volunteers may be as important to participants as goals and results, or even more important. For example, a program to mentor inner-city youth may be based on long-term personal relationships. These relationships are likely to be idiosyncratic and based on the personalities of mentors and mentees. The dedication and commitment of mentors may be the key to both program success and the satisfaction of both parties, and any changes that might inhibit mentor dedication are likely to be resisted.
- **Breadth of purpose.** Nonprofits tend to have very general mission statements that don't provide clear criteria for program decisions. Nonprofits need to take stakeholder expectations into account, and these can vary significantly. For example, the stakeholders of a reentry program for released prisoners include the professional staff, the released prisoners, the public and private funders, and neighborhood residents. Professional staff may want to provide accepted levels of service, the former prisoners might want a program with fewer obligations or restrictions, funders may want more demonstrated outcomes, and the neighborhood may not want the facility at all. Changes favoring one of these stakeholder groups may well be resisted by the others.
- **Demanding environment.** For nonprofits, demands for services have gone up while donations have not kept pace. In addition, operating grants are down while contracts and project funding are up. The sector is more professionalized than in the past, and funders expect administrative efficiency and entrepreneurship. Wolf observes that nonprofits must show hard-hitting business capacity as well as compassionate concern and advocacy for the needy. Changes to facilitate the former may conflict with the latter. For example, in a food bank that has provided free food, there may be resistance to the idea of charging for food, on the grounds that this might hurt those most in need.
- **Volunteer and staff mix.** Volunteers have motivations and needs different from those of paid staff. Nonprofits must address how to meet these needs with their mission, values, and policies for volunteer recruitment and management. They must also integrate the volunteers into the work of the staff.

In some cases, staff may be more professional and have a larger overview and information base. A nonprofit that uses a large volunteer base will need to assess the impact that changes in structure, programs, or technology will have on its volunteers. For example, if a nonprofit were thinking of computerizing more of its operations, it might need to consider how this change could affect the extent to which it could use volunteers.

- **Increasingly mixed structure.** Nonprofits are seeking more earned income. This can produce conflicting cultures in the organization. A traditional culture characterized by an altruistic or charity orientation and devotion to services and advocacy for the less advantaged will likely conflict with an entrepreneurial, market-oriented culture that might arise in a program of the nonprofit that receives commercial income, competes with for-profits, and has a better-off clientele. Implementing programs or administrative changes that satisfy both cultures is difficult.[26] For example, in a nonprofit dedicated to helping the homeless, one department might provide free mental health and addiction services to those just entering the program and another department might employ the most able clients in an income-producing venture (such as lawn care). The commercial side of the organization may resent the reallocation of its revenue to fund an expansion of the mental health program.

These difficulties do not lessen the need for nonprofits to change, and nonprofit managers need to understand how changes take place in organizations and must have frameworks and tools to successfully implement needed changes.

Managing the Change Process

Given the importance of change, its complexity, and the resistance that may be encountered, good management of the change process is essential for success. In general, the organizational change process typically proceeds through a number of stages. Burke identifies four primary phases: prelaunch, launch, postlaunch, and sustaining the change.[27]

The *prelaunch* phase establishes important initial conditions, including basic management orientations toward change. Managers should be aware of their personal disposition, motives, and values in regard to the factors needed for successful change. These include ambition, the need to achieve, tolerance for ambiguity, ability to effectively handle challenging circumstances, appreciation of shared decision making, and strong values that can be communicated to others. In addition, managers should have a thorough knowledge of the organization's environment. Not only are many changes brought on by environmental shifts but most will also entail some action in regard to the environment. For example, the organization will likely need to establish changed or new relationships with funders, clients, or other stakeholders. Although the awareness of the need for change may come from a variety of sources, top management should be convinced of the need and establish the organizational commitment to proceed. This should be accompanied by a vision that provides a clear direction for the change process to follow.

The decision to change starts the *launch* phase. At this point, management should take responsibility for communicating the need for change to the organization. Top management normally does this, but other leaders who will be directly involved in the change can be brought in to promote buy-in. In addition, it may be useful to hold an initial event to capture attention, provide focus, and establish that the change effort is now under way. This could take the form of workshops, meetings, or the establishment of task forces. Finally, action should be taken to head off and overcome resistance. Wolf discusses techniques for dealing with the following causes of resistance.[28]

- **Loss of control.** People in nonprofits are concerned about what will happen with both their careers and the organization's mission. Widespread involvement of organizational participants can be used to address these concerns: for example, by establishing task forces to deal with aspects of the change.

- **Excessive uncertainty.** There may be more uncertainty than necessary if information is not shared widely enough. Excessive rumors are a clear symptom of this. Uncertainty can be addressed by providing more information and establishing better communication: for example, by offering briefings and question-and-answer occasions.

- **Real threats.** With any change, some people will be adversely affected. The best policy is to let them know as soon as possible and not pretend otherwise.

- **Valuing past contributions.** Although the change will be presented as an improvement, the past should not be painted as all bad. People in the organization will have worked hard on past programs and are likely to be emotionally involved. Managers should praise what was good in the past.

- **Concern about future competence.** People may fear that they will not have the skills needed after the change. Managers should assure people that they will be supported if new skills are needed or that there will be training and a break-in period.

- **Past resentments.** Change brings up an opportunity to air grievances, even if they are not directly related to the current situation. Managers need to acknowledge individuals' feelings but should stress that everyone now needs to be part of the solution to the current situation.

Burke makes the point that the *postlaunch* phase can be difficult and uncertain. Actions must be taken to ensure that the change proceeds. Once unleashed, change may seem to take on a life of its own. Top leaders may feel they lack control, and participant reactions may range from enthusiastic support to skepticism. Change, especially in large organizations, is often too complex to be accomplished by one action alone. As a result, multiple levers of change may need to be employed in tandem. These levers can include new mission or strategic statements, the institution of training and development, new compensation systems, or the establishment of teams or task forces. Change leaders face some particular challenges during this phase. They can expect to come under fire from those unhappy with the change, even if it was successful. The behavior of a change leader will be scrutinized for consistency with earlier statements about the change. Inconsistency will damage trust in the change leader. It is essential that the change leader perseveres, especially as the initial enthusiasm for the change wanes. The change leader needs to remind participants of what they are doing and why. The vision should be repeated in as many ways as possible.

Burke's final phase involves *sustaining* the organizational change effort. One goal in this phase is the establishment of a momentum that will lead to further change. The tendency of a changed organization to settle into a new equilibrium (where change does not happen) needs to be countered. Appropriate changes will enhance organizational operations and should be maintained as long as useful. However, environments are constantly changing, and changes made at one point in time will not eliminate the need for future changes. Organizations must be ready to make further changes as needed. Change leaders must constantly monitor the environment for forces that will require adaptation. Another way to counter equilibrium is to prevent homogeneity in the change leadership. New change leaders from outside the organization or other functional units will infuse the change process with new blood and counter tendencies toward groupthink. Finally, new change initiatives, in line with the original change objectives, may be deliberately launched by the change leader to keep the organization moving forward. The point is that although particular change initiatives may end, the change process itself does not.

Models of Planned Change

A large number of frameworks, recipes, and models have been proposed to help managers understand and guide the change process. They may focus on change at the individual level or at the larger organizational level. In general, individual change models rely on the analysis of factors promoting or inhibiting the integration of individuals and groups into organizational systems or processes. In contrast, organizational change models rely on the use of structure or strategy to enhance the alignment, or fit, between the organization and its environment. We present some of the major frameworks in the remainder of this section.

Lewin's Force Field Model

Kurt Lewin developed an early model of change in organizations.[29] The model relies on a process of *unfreezing, change,* and *refreezing.* The model is centered on the balance among the forces driving and restraining, or inhibiting, organizational change. If these forces are roughly in balance, a quasi-stationary *equilibrium* will exist in the organization, during which little or no organizational change will take place. This is a temporary state, however, as the balance is not perfect and cannot be maintained, due to changing external or internal circumstances. To bring about positive change, managers need to identify the driving and restraining forces and unfreeze the equilibrium. This is done through selectively removing restraining forces and increasing appropriate driving forces. This will change behavior in the desired direction. Refreezing is an essential final step and can be accomplished through the judicious application of restraining forces to keep change from going too far, thereby reestablishing the equilibrium. The establishment of the desired behavior is not seen as a lasting solution, in any sense. Future changes will be required, which will require a repeat of the process. Lewin's model remains the central feature of many planned change models, the essence of which is recognition of driving and restraining forces and the taking of appropriate action to manage the balance in the desired direction.[30]

The force field diagram in Figure 16.1 illustrates the situation of a nonprofit seeking to enhance the economic attainment of its clients through, for example, neighborhood economic development. The nonprofit currently lacks revenue to expand its programs. By enhancing commercial revenue through its development activities or raising donations, it could shift this undesirable equilibrium in a positive direction.

Organizational Development

Organizational development (OD) is a major approach to implementing organizational change. OD originated in the late 1950s and has become a standard field of academic study and research as well as an applied practice. As David Jamieson and Christopher Worley note, most definitions of *organizational development* describe it as (1) a planned process intending to

FIGURE 16.1. LEWIN'S FORCE FIELD MODEL APPLIED TO AN ECONOMIC DEVELOPMENT NONPROFIT

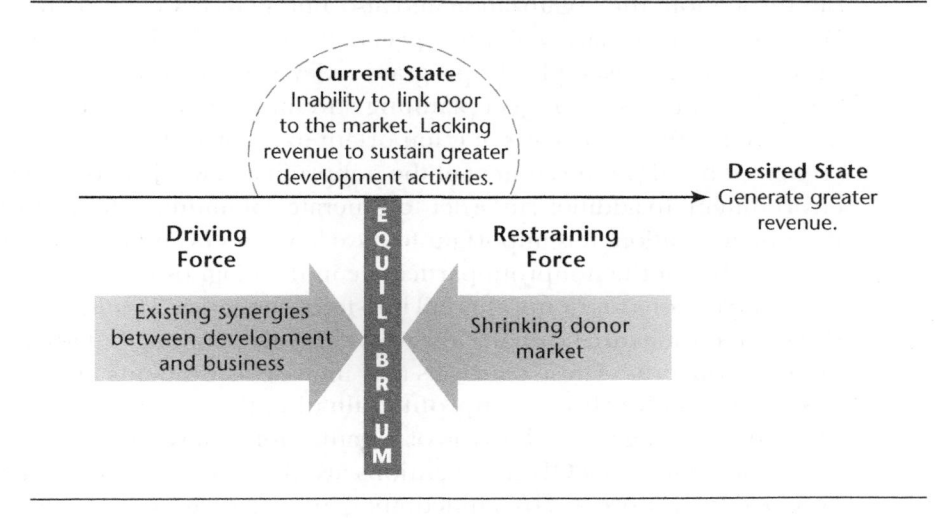

Current State: Inability to link poor to the market. Lacking revenue to sustain greater development activities.

Desired State: Generate greater revenue.

Driving Force: Existing synergies between development and business

Restraining Force: Shrinking donor market

EQUILIBRIUM

bring about change, (2) through the use of various interventions, (3) using behavioral science knowledge, (4) having an organization or systemwide focus, and (5) typically involving a third-party change agent.[31]

The basic OD model involves three stages: diagnosis, intervention, and monitoring. Diagnostic devices are used to determine the need for intervention and primarily include individual and group interviews and surveys.[32] Surveys can assess job satisfaction, organizational climate, job assessment, and leadership. Interventions are crucial for effective OD and typically involve relationship-building techniques. These could include individual counseling and sensitivity training. T-group training involves individuals focusing on their actions, how these actions are perceived by others, and how these others react. The goal is to identify unintended consequences of behavior. Team building helps members of a workteam diagnose task, process, and interpersonal problems within the team and develop solutions. Intergroup training can be used to help groups or teams learn to work better together. In addition, OD may be used for job redesign, management by objectives, enhancing communication channels, and establishing other problem-solving processes. After interventions, changes are evaluated and monitored to assess the success of the OD effort and determine if additional OD is needed.

Tandon discusses the use of OD for nonprofit organizations.[33] Typically, recognition of the *need* for change is felt initially by field project staff, headquarters staff, leaders, or a major donor. Project evaluations can also turn up the need for change. Both the recognition of the need for change and the commitment for OD should occur not just among top leaders but throughout the organization and also among its key external partners. Diagnosis typically starts with the aspect of the nonprofit that prompted the need for OD. For example, if a program review surfaced the need, the diagnosis should focus on project planning and implementation. Irrespective of where the diagnosis starts, it is important to consider the elements to be enhanced by OD in the context of the nonprofit as a whole and its external environment. In addition, in order to generate commitment to the OD and its implementation, it is important to have key leaders and the widespread membership of the nonprofit participate in the diagnosis.

Interventions for nonprofits fall into four categories. *Identity and strategy* OD interventions are normally linked to strategic planning but will involve broader concerns. These concerns may include assessments of planning, design, and staff roles. A nonprofit evaluating the results of its strategic planning may engage in this type of organizational development.

Human dimension OD interventions are the most common. They are designed to improve internal functioning in such areas as communication, participation, decision making, conflict resolution, motivation, morale, and so forth. They also include role clarification and team building. These interventions are particularly important for nonprofits given their people-centered nature and need to operate harmoniously. Nonprofits involved in mergers will find this type of OD useful as human resources will need to be combined or reconfigured in some way.

Technostructural OD interventions are concerned with congruence between a nonprofit's technology (the core functions of the organization) and structure. These interventions will address the introduction of new technology and its integration into the nonprofit. In addition, these interventions may consider the formalization of roles and procedures; program planning, monitoring, and evaluation; and job and work design. Goodwill Industries could have used this type of OD during the establishment of its charter school, because teaching was not the central focus of its existing operations.

Finally, *external relations* OD interventions focus on strengthening the nonprofit's external relationships. Partnerships and relationships will be assessed with an eye toward enhancing joint initiatives and organizational networks. These interventions focus on the enhancement of interorganizational relationships in terms of the allocations of time and resources needed to establish and maintain them. Besides other civil society organizations, nonprofits also need to deal with government, the media, and for-profits, and these relationships will also be considered with an eye toward how they could be strengthened for mission accomplishment. We must remember, however, that network partners must cooperate with any changes proposed. This could put limits on what an external relations intervention can accomplish. Important decisions about the roles of network partners may be made within the network, not by individual organizations.[34] For example, in a coalition to address homelessness, providers may be assigned services or areas of the city to work in.

Building Adaptive Capacity

Carl Sussman provides an organizational level approach that nonprofits can use to build their capacity for change.[35] *Adaptive capacity* is the ability of a nonprofit to take the initiative in making adjustments that will result in improved performance, relevance, and impact. Adaptive capacity involves not only the ability to respond to change but also the ability to generate and initiate change. Nonprofits thus will not be mere reactors but can themselves seek to influence their environments in their favor. This more proactive approach will often require forging new external relationships.

Four qualities are essential for building adaptive capacity. These qualities will create a nonprofit that is both flexible and linked to the most important parts of its environment. To maintain vital connections to its environment, a nonprofit needs an external focus and network connections. An *external focus* allows a nonprofit to focus continually on environmental dynamism and complexity. *Dynamism* refers to the degree to which the environment is changing, and *complexity* refers to the number of environmental elements simultaneously needing attention. An external focus is developed through external contacts that provide rich information about the environment. Such contacts are developed by an active board, strategic partnerships, and other personal, professional, or organizational affiliations.

The environment, however, is more than just a source of information. In today's complex and interconnected environments, action is increasingly taking place not in individual organizations but in formal or informal networks of organizations. *Network connections*, therefore, are becoming more important for mission accomplishment. For example, Sussman describes the National Children's Facilities Network. It was formed by four community development organizations to advocate for funding for childcare centers in low-income communities. Despite not having any staff, the network currently has twenty-four members and has secured $2.5 million in federal appropriations.

Being connected to the environment is only part of what is needed for adaptive capacity. Nonprofits must have internal properties that let them take advantage of these connections. They must be inquisitive and innovative. To be *inquisitive* is to be knowledge seeking. Inquisitive nonprofits seek out data and information. They use this to learn, and then they apply and share what they have learned. Nonprofits attain and enhance inquisitiveness through outcome measurement, knowledge management, and organizational learning. Outcome measurement is covered in Chapter Thirteen. For knowledge management it is important to distinguish between raw data and information that conveys meaning, and knowledge (which allows action).[36] Sussman defines learning as the process of collecting data and transforming it into knowledge. Data and information become organizational knowledge when they are used to improve organizational actions. For example, a nonprofit may become aware that local government seeks to revitalize particular neighborhoods in the city. The nonprofit could use this information to design new programs or enhance existing ones. To do this, it will need to ascertain such factors as which government agencies will be involved, how new revenues will be distributed, and how client needs could be better addressed.

Finally, nonprofits need to be *innovative*. Innovation is covered in detail later in this chapter, but we can point out here that it is important for adaptive capacity for several reasons. It entails the creation of new or improved programs and services. This goes hand in hand with challenging conventional or accepted wisdom. Sussman calls innovation the generative component of adaptive learning in that it gives nonprofits the ability to initiate change and not just react. Adaptive nonprofits promote innovation to ensure that they continually change in order to remain relevant and effective.

The Development Spiral

Paul Light provides an integrated life cycle model for sustaining nonprofit performance.[37] In his model, nonprofit development proceeds through five stages (Light refers to these stages as *landings*). In each stage the nonprofit's goal expands. To reach these expanded goals, the nonprofit must address questions and challenges regarding its environment, structure, leadership, and systems. These questions are outlined in Table 16.1.

The questions Light poses represent the major considerations and challenges a nonprofit will encounter at each stage. Unless the nonprofit takes successful actions to address these questions, the nonprofit cannot move to the next stage. In this sense the model is similar to Greiner's, which we considered at the beginning of the chapter. The factors and issues Greiner considers in his model can be seen reflected in the questions about structure in Light's model. For example, Light's first structural question ("Who does what?") is addressed in Greiner's discussion about the *creativity* stage. Likewise, the question, "How much can we do?" corresponds to Greiner's

TABLE 16.1. THE DEVELOPMENT SPIRAL

Stage	Goal	Questions We Need to Ask Ourselves at Each Stage			
		Environment	Structure	Leadership	Systems
Organic nonprofit	Presence	How will we make a difference?	Who does what?	Why do we exist?	How will we know success?
Enterprising nonprofit	Impact	Where will we expand?	How much can we do?	How do we remain authentic?	How do we cope with breadth?
Intentional nonprofit	Focus	How do we fit?	Can we increase our impact by concentration?	How do we remain faithful?	How have we done thus far?
Robust nonprofit	Endurance	What are our futures?	How do we stay agile?	What are our values?	How do we insure against vulnerabilities?
Reflective nonprofit	Legacy	How can we lead?	How do we get younger?	How do we change the future?	How do we manage freedom?

Source: Adapted from Paul Light, "The Spiral of Sustainable Excellence," in *Sustaining Nonprofit Performance* (Washington, DC: Brookings Institution, 2004), 142.

direction stage; "Can we increase our impact by concentration?" corresponds to *delegation*; "How do we stay agile?" corresponds to *coordination*; and "How do we get younger?" corresponds to *collaboration*. Light's model, however, goes on to assess the implications for nonprofit growth and development of other dimensions, including the nonprofit's environment, leadership, and systems, in this way providing a more integrated model.

The most important questions are asked at Light's *organic* stage. The answers to these questions will establish direction and early momentum toward impact. The answers to "How will we make a difference?" and, "Why do we exist?" establish the nonprofit's mission. "Who does what?" sets the initial scope of operations and the division of labor. "How will we know success?" establishes the basis of evaluation and subsequent changes. Although not all the answers will be clear yet, many nonprofits do not address these questions adequately. As a result, they may fail to become visible enough to attract support or build the infrastructures needed for further development. Of course some nonprofits have founders with very clear answers to these initial questions. These nonprofits will move quickly to the next stage. Teach For America started with a very clear vision of success and a simple operating model. Both of these resonated with funders, and the nonprofit was able to expand rapidly.

If nonprofits develop to Light's *enterprising* stage, they face a different set of challenges. Growth and expansion, especially if driven by funder priorities, can result in loss of focus, mission drift, confusion, underinvestment in core administrative functions, and employee burnout. To overcome these difficulties, nonprofits must regain a focus on *intentional* action. This will require revisiting both priorities and capacities and likely result in divesting programs and releasing staff that do not align clearly with the major agendas chosen. This in turn may create resistance internally and among external constituencies. If the nonprofit can successfully address these challenges, it can move to the *robust* stage. Light defines robustness as the ability to withstand and exploit uncertainty. This is accomplished by hedging against vulnerabilities and shaping the environment to one's benefit. This entails having a focus on the longer term, identifying various alternative futures, and being willing to prepare for multiple futures simultaneously by adapting organizational structures and processes. Nonprofits must be able to assess risks realistically. However, they must also act opportunistically and take leaps of faith when outcomes warrant it. Teach For America illustrates the problems caused by rapid growth accompanied by underdeveloped administrative capacity and mission drift. These almost led to the failure of the organization. Intentional action to address the problems, however, resulted in a turnaround and left the organization poised to move into the robustness stage.

The independent actions taken at the robust stage can lead a nonprofit to become isolated, less accountable, imperialistic, or self-righteous. To overcome this, nonprofits need to reach the *reflective* stage. At this stage larger questions again come into play. For example, the nonprofit may think about how it can contribute to the future of its service area. It may revisit the initial reasons for its founding to reconcile these reasons with the enhanced capabilities it currently has. It will seek to stay relevant by streamlining, spinning off, or assisting newer organizations; entering into alliances and partnerships; and otherwise engaging with the environment. Reflective nonprofits stay reflective by constantly revisiting the mission as well as the techniques that helped them move up the spiral. In this stage a stable and sustainable Teach For America might turn to thinking about the field of education more broadly. It might, for example, seek to influence education policy and establish new partnerships to give itself a national policy voice.

Nonprofit Transformation

Transformations are extreme, or revolutionary, changes in organizations. Transformations affect the core form or essential competencies of organizations. These competencies are what define an organization—the primary reasons for its existence—and what make it distinct. For example, the American Red Cross provides a well-known set of disaster relief and human services in a particular way. If it were to undergo a transformation, these services would change significantly. This is far different from incremental or evolutionary changes such as organizational development or building adaptive capacity.

Transformations have been studied in for-profits. Ralph Kilmann and Teresa Covin offer a number of conclusions about corporate transformations. These findings should also pertain to nonprofit organizations. Transformations are often "no other choice" adaptations to the environment, driven by concern for survival. In addition, the most important part of the process may be formulating a new vision fundamentally different from the present state. Both executives and other personnel must be convinced that the old ways are not working anymore and that a new organization can be created to replace the current inadequate one. Major efforts must be focused on behavioral changes, which are likely to involve some pain for everyone, including senior management. Change must focus on the entire organization, although different subunits will absorb the changes differently. Transformations should be led by line managers, preferably senior managers, to ensure resources and commitment. Finally, an increase in both vertical and horizontal information flow and communication is needed for success.[38]

Felice Perlmutter and Burton Gummer discuss the transformation process in nonprofit organizations. Transformations pose a particular challenge for nonprofit organizations as they must continue to serve their fundamental purpose and the mission they presented to the IRS. In the extreme case, a fundamental change in mission may necessitate the dissolution of a nonprofit and the formation of a new one. Perlmutter and Gummer point out that transformation is the result of dramatically changing circumstances in the environment. They outline a variety of factors that are particularly relevant for bringing about transformations in nonprofits.[39]

- **Change in legitimacy**: when an informal group, such as a self-help group, obtains formal recognition by incorporating as a formal nonprofit.
- **Change in sector**: when organizations change the part of society or the social economy under which they operate. Although the conversion of a nonprofit to a for-profit is most common, for-profits or public sector organizations may also convert to nonprofit status.
- **Change in professionalism**: when the professional credentials of a nonprofit's staff change. This could entail going from nonprofessional or paraprofessional to professionally credentialed staff or shifting from one type of professional to another.
- **Change in technology**: when the means by which activities are accomplished change. Given the pace of technological change, this change is becoming increasingly common. It may involve the introduction of new treatment models or changes in hardware or software for either service provision or administration.
- **Change in mission**: when nonprofits, through necessity or choice, change the basic ends they are pursuing. For example, the mission of the March of Dimes shifted to a concern with birth defects when its original mission, working to eradicate polio, was accomplished.
- **Change in structure**: when a nonprofit significantly redesigns its subunits or major processes for accomplishing work. For example, as a nonprofit grows and takes on additional activities it could divide those activities into specialized divisions.
- **Change in funding**: when a nonprofit's resource base changes. This is perhaps the most common type of change, given the volatility in income sources. Old sources of revenues may dry up, as when a nonprofit loses the support of a major funder. Or new revenue sources may emerge, as when government agencies or foundations decide to put more resources into a service area.
- **Change in charismatic leadership**: when the individual who has led the nonprofit primarily through the force of his or her personality or vision leaves the organization. This person may be the organization's founder. Another

charismatic leader, with perhaps a different vision, may then take over, or the organization may need to find a leader who is more focused on establishing rules and procedures.

- **Change in societal values**: when a change occurs in the views and beliefs of major parts of the society. Nonprofits in related areas will need to respond to such a change. For example, the movement to deinstitutionalize the mentally ill resulted in significantly enhanced opportunities for community-based, nonprofit mental health organizations.

As we can see from this discussion, transformations involve major changes in nonprofits. Perlmutter and Gummer go on to discuss a number of strategies that leaders can use to deal with nonprofit transformations: political, organizational, professional, and individual.

Political strategies employ organizational politics and the use of power to accomplish goals. These strategies may be particularly important for nonprofits due to the presence of competing values, goals, and interests in their environment. Moreover, these competing views are also likely to be mirrored by stakeholders within the organization. To deal with these political environments, nonprofit leaders need to be watchdogs for their constituents' needs and advocates for their organizations. In addition, they need to network with key interest groups and community leaders.

Organizational strategies will need to be used when the consequences of change require altered modes of operating or interacting within the nonprofit. For example, a shift to a more decentralized structure may require more flexible and creative interactions between individuals or subunits. These will need to be learned and accepted by participants. In the extreme case of mergers, staff and cultural adjustment will need to be addressed in addition to the structural and process changes.

Professional strategies involve responding to the environment by changing the conceptual, ideological, and technical underpinnings of the work of professional staff. For example, the services to mentally ill clients in a deinstitutionalized context include assistance with a variety of additional issues, such as housing and employment. Professional staff will need to be willing and able to provide such assistance in addition to psychiatric treatment.

Finally, *individual strategies* address the characteristics and actions of successful change managers. These managers will need to understand the importance of initiative, innovation, and risk taking. They need to display these characteristics as they analyze alternatives and then plan and implement change.

Innovation

An *innovation* is the adoption of an idea or behavior that is new to an organization, its industry or market, or the general environment.[40] It is a departure from existing practices or technology and often represents a significant departure from the state of the art at the time it appears.[41] Innovations can involve products, services, processes, or structures and can range from minor variations to radical departures.[42] Minor variations might involve changes to existing products or services, including cost reductions, repositioning, and new applications. For example, a nonprofit that helps neighborhood residents with minor home repairs could ask residents to start donating part of a weekend day to helping its staff expand services. More innovation is involved in product improvements or revisions and additions to product or service lines. In this case the nonprofit could decide to start helping small retailers improve their facilities.

New products or services entail the most innovation. These can be new to the company, new to the market, or new to the world. Process innovations can involve any processes in administration, support, production, or service delivery. Innovation can include modest improvements or significant revisions of existing processes as well as the development of minor or major new processes. For example, Nonprofit Shopping Mall is a new online service that turns consumer dollars into charitable donations.[43] The organization partners with major online retailers such as Target, Amazon, Home Depot, Bloomingdale's, Expedia, Petco, and iTunes. These companies donate a percentage of each purchase to the shopper's nonprofit of choice. A shopper begins by visiting Nonprofit Shopping Mall, choosing a charity, and then clicking through to a retailer.

What is important from an organizational standpoint is whether or not an innovation is ultimately adopted. Without this, it is merely a good idea. Innovation adoption is a complex matter, involving the characteristics of the innovation itself in interaction with organization characteristics and the environmental context.

Characteristics of Innovation Affecting Adoption

Gerald Zaltman, Robert Duncan, and Jonny Holbek summarize the characteristics of innovations that will influence their adoption. The list is very long, but the factors are important considerations for those in a nonprofit who are involved in developing adoptable innovations. The length of the list also attests to the complex nature of innovation. In a very real sense, there are no shortcuts, and the factors that follow will be relevant for success.[44]

- **Cost.** There may be both initial and continuing financial costs. It will take an initial outlay of resources to start a new nonprofit service as well as continuing costs as the service is produced. In addition, nonfinancial social costs may involve power, status, or social position in the organization. The status of those in a nonprofit responsible for a new service may be influenced by the success or failure of that service. The reputation of the CEO may suffer if a new nonprofit program proves unsuccessful.

- **Return on investment.** The "payoff," the benefits gained as a result of expenditures on the innovation, is especially important when scarce resources are involved. In addition, the benefits of new nonprofit services (such as neighborhood cohesion) may be hard to measure, thereby leading to an underestimate of return.
- **Risk and uncertainty.** A successful innovation may provide opportunities for other, related, innovations. If unsuccessful, an innovation may result in damage. Marshall Becker, in a study of public health officials, identified political risks to innovation, including opportunities for political opponents and risk to reputation and position.[45]
- **Communicability.** It is important to be able to communicate the results and benefits of an innovation—especially in processes where a number of activities or processes are at work. In those cases it is important to show which part of the result is due to the innovation. For example, is higher student achievement the result of a student mentoring program (the innovation) or some other factor?
- **Compatibility.** How similar is an innovation to an existing product or service that it may eventually supplement, complement, or replace? The degree to which an innovation requires changes or adjustments on the part of other elements of the organization will influence the speed of adoption. An innovation involving only a simplification of delivery techniques will be more readily adopted than one that also requires new funding, accounting, or facilities.
- **Complexity.** The more complex an innovation is in terms of the operations required, the slower its acceptance is likely to be. In an educational nonprofit, for example, adding new computers to allow for self-paced learning of existing lessons is less complex than changing the curriculum.
- **Perceived relative advantage.** The new feature that an innovation provides over its alternatives is a central feature. The visibility of the relative advantage and the ability to demonstrate that advantage are important. This will be the major focus of program and outcome evaluations, which are used for internal decision making and external funding.
- **Status quo ante.** The reversibility of the innovation, or the degree to which the previous state (the status quo ante) could be reestablished matters. When

alternative innovations are being considered, the more reversible ones will be adopted sooner. Can the innovation be adopted without abandoning current practice? Can the innovation be broken down into components that can be adopted gradually with the benefit of feedback?

- **Commitment**. Successful innovation use requires commitment and also the endorsement of higher authority as well as the attitudinal and behavioral acceptance of users. If partial commitment can be made, this will help in obtaining later commitment.
- **Interpersonal relations**. An innovation will affect relations within and between organizations. Innovations may be more or less disruptive or integrative. Depending on the success or failure of an innovation, the position of an individual supporting the innovation will be strengthened or weakened.
- **Publicness**. Public goods are produced and available to everyone (as fluoridation of the public water supply is, for example) and must be accepted even by those opposing them. Nonprofits need to be prepared for opponents to mount stiff resistance.
- **Gateway features**. An important question is the number of gatekeepers who need to approve an innovation. Having to get many approvals may delay or possibly stop the adoption of the innovation. An accepted innovation's gateway capacity is its ability to make the adoption of future innovations easier. Therefore nonprofits that desire large-scale social change might ask, What kinds of initial innovations are most likely to bring this about? It is possible that even small social changes can set the stage for large-scale innovation.

Environmental Sources of Innovation

General environmental features have been linked to higher levels of innovation in organizations. External actors may offer incentives for innovation by directly providing resources (such as foundation funding) or instituting favorable policies (such as tax incentives).[46] External actors may not just encourage innovation, they may require it. For example, changing federal regulations may require changes in industry performance standards for hospitals.[47] Finally, involvement in networks has also been positively linked to innovation.[48]

In Chapter Three we reviewed a number of sources of entrepreneurial opportunities for nonprofits. Entrepreneurial nonprofits will seek innovations (their own or those of others) to address these opportunities. We summarize these sources of innovative opportunity here: general environmental and industry sources;[49] technological, public policy, public opinion and taste, and social and demographic changes;[50] economic or social market failures;[51] and market barriers, weakened populations, lack of voice, and negative externalities.[52]

Management of Innovation

Michael Morris, Donald Kuratko, and Jeffrey Covin point out that innovation poses dilemmas for organizational leaders.[53] For example, innovation is about the unknown whereas management is about control. Innovation is about breaking the rules, but rule breakers may not last long in organizations. In addition, failure is likely if an organization does not innovate, but the more an organization innovates, the more it fails. Innovation is risky, but not innovating can be even more risky. An organization that innovates may make its own products or services obsolete. Morris, Kuratko, and Covin go on to provide guidelines for fostering an innovative organization: Have unreasonable expectations, which will facilitate the search for breakthrough ideas. Create elastic business definitions, and define the organization not by what it does but by its core competencies and strategic assets. Consider the organization a cause and not a business. Draw strength from worthwhile visions and causes that go beyond profits or growth. Allow new voices to be heard. Those who are young, are newcomers, or are on the periphery may have ideas you have not heard before. Create an open market for ideas and capital. Allow entrepreneurial ideas to compete, and establish small funds for prototypes or market trials. Finally, foster low-risk experimentation. Don't try only for high-risk innovations. Strike a middle ground between being a cautious follower and a high-risk taker.[54]

Writing for social entrepreneurs (particularly nonprofit organizations), Gregory Dees provides a number of more specific guidelines for facilitating organizational innovation.[55] Cultural norms that support innovation include a restless drive for continuing improvement, receptivity to new ideas at all levels and sources, rigorous screening and testing of new ideas, respect for honest mistakes and calculated risk taking, and responsibility and authority for innovation at lower levels of the organization. Individual and organizational capabilities are also needed. These include skills in information gathering and processing; working across functional lines and organizational boundaries; thinking creatively, critically, and constructively; thinking into the future; and managing risk, uncertainty, and timing. Mechanisms to support and reinforce innovative behavior include a clear and compelling shared vision, systems for reliably measuring organizational performance, strong signals supporting innovation from senior management, rewards in the form of recognition and resources, funding to support innovation, incorporation of innovation into individual performance evaluation, accountability for innovation all the way up to the board level, and willingness to create new units when new ventures are based on potentially threatening innovations that cannot be accommodated by the existing organization.

The value of these supporting mechanisms is borne out in a study by Paul Light of eighteen innovative nonprofit organizations in Minnesota. These organizations provided services in the arts, community development, housing, social services, education, and the environment. They were committed to being innovative by design and had histories of innovativeness. Light's major findings included the following:[56]

- Innovative organizations *stayed thin*, with a minimal number of managerial layers in their middle and upper levels. This made hierarchy less of a barrier to innovation. For example, Theatre de la Jeune Lune established two self-managed teams, one dealing with artistic decisions, the other with administrative decisions. These two teams reported to and interacted with each other to make decisions for the organization.
- They *created room to experiment*: for example, by setting up task forces charged with innovation. The Phoenix Group, whose mission was to get the homeless off the streets and into a productive life, is an example. The organization structured itself as an incubator of innovation. It started a mix of housing, employment, and counseling programs. Besides renovating housing, the organization started a grocery store, a café, an auto repair shop, and an upholstery business. In the process, it employed two to three hundred people, most of whom were recovering from addiction.
- They were particularly good at *pushing authority downward*, allowing frontline employees the authority to come up with new service delivery approaches. For example, the Dowling School (a magnet school) included teachers, students, and staff in decision making. Students from first to sixth grade had a formal voice in making school policy. They were organized into teams that made software recommendations and participated in a system for generating suggestions about changes to the way the school operated.
- They *lowered barriers to internal collaboration*, assuming that creativity was spread throughout the organization and that the ability to share ideas and exchange information was an important way to harness this creativity for organizational innovation. Some organizations created common spaces where people could interact—sometimes at the facility and at other times off-site. Luther Theological Seminary evaluated what its

students needed as today's Christian leaders. It came to the conclusion that its calendars, department lines, and governance structures needed to change. It created interdisciplinary course construction teams to design a new curriculum, grouped its academic departments into three new divisions, modified the calendar and course sequence to give students more options, changed the faculty appointment and promotion policy to emphasize a common mission, and created a new academic leadership team at the top.

- A large number of the organizations *shifted to a more democratized structure.* A majority of the organizations went through leadership transitions during the course of the study, and all but one shifted to a more participative style. Organizational democracy has numerous benefits, creating a shared sense of commitment, pushing authority downward, and creating more channels for good ideas to flow to the top. For example, under new leadership in 1991, the Walker Art Center moved to a more democratic approach. In the process, Walker staff and volunteers were consulted about the future of the organization. Achieving one of the center's new goals ("manage staff creatively and progressively") meant emphasizing a participative management style to improve internal communication and staff recognition.

- The innovative organizations *primed themselves for innovativeness* by making funds available to support innovative initiatives. Most created an innovation investment fund. There are two questions when creating an innovation investment fund. The first is how much money to put at risk (because innovations are risky ventures). The size of the organization's budget is the primary factor here. The second is how to choose among competing ideas. The nonprofits in the study made deliberate choices, often following an investment banking model or establishing an internal foundation.

- The availability of resources for innovation *supported an internal marketplace of ideas.* Ideas competed against each other and were evaluated on their merits, as opposed to organizational politics or happenstance. The organizations in the study used hard questions to evaluate the merits of innovations. They assessed the priority of the needs the innovation addressed, what the long-term payoff for the organization would be, how reasonable the budget was, whether other sources were contributing to the project, and the anticipated timing of the project.

- These innovative organizations also *prepared for stress.* Facing the challenges of external and internal drivers for change puts people, subunits, and the organization as a whole under pressure. To be successful, organizations need to be able to channel the challenges and stress in productive ways. For example, WomenVenture was formed through a merger, for financial reasons, of two radically different organizations. The organizations were initially unwilling to give up their old identities; however, the lack of a common identity and the associated organizational stresses and strains almost led to the failure of the new organization. A new president addressed a severe financial crisis, and issues such as the new organization's name, location, budgets, staffing, policies, and procedures were eventually managed. The result was that WomenVenture was able to emerge as a strong organization able to start new, innovative programs.

Concluding Thoughts

The pace of change in the areas where nonprofits are active is increasing. Changes pose challenges and offer opportunities to nonprofits. Nonprofits have no choice but to respond to these changes. If they do not change, nonprofits will lose touch with their environments and stakeholders and will decrease the chances that they will accomplish their missions. The result will be rapid or eventual organizational decline. A changing world may surprise an unaware nonprofit, forcing it to respond in a rapid, unsystematic fashion. This response may address the immediate situation yet fail to make the most of the underlying changes in the nonprofit's world. A better response is to develop the nonprofit's capacity to understand change, analyze situations calling for change, and take the steps necessary to lead change with positive consequences.

This chapter concludes our consideration of specific nonprofit management techniques and tools. In the next and final chapter we turn to larger questions and ask readers to think about what the future might hold for nonprofits and to reflect upon what this might mean in light of what they have learned in the last sixteen chapters.

Questions for Consideration

1. Funders are important stakeholders for nonprofits. What aspects of change in nonprofits can they affect? How can they make change easier for nonprofits?
2. Where do you see a lot of innovation occurring now in the nonprofit sector? Why is this change happening? Are there positive benefits?

Exercises

Exercise 16.1: Force Field Model

This chapter considers both internal and external forces for change. Discuss one or more examples of nonprofits where internal and external forces are driving forces. Discuss examples where internal and external forces are restraining forces. Finally, discuss examples where internal and external forces oppose each other.

Exercise 16.2: Transformation

If your school or academic department were to undergo a transformation, what would likely change? Of the factors listed by Felice Perlmutter and Burton Gummer (changes in legitimacy and so forth), which, if any, could bring such a transformation about?

Exercise 16.3: Innovation

Suggest an innovation for Teach For America, another nonprofit you are familiar with, or a hypothetical nonprofit. What characteristics of this innovation would facilitate adoption? Might any characteristics hinder adoption? How might the nonprofit's leaders make adoption more likely?

CHAPTER SEVENTEEN

THE FUTURE OF NONPROFIT LEADERSHIP AND MANAGEMENT

This book ends where it started, with a focus on the mission. It is the mission that determines whether an organization will be recognized by the government as a nonprofit or a for-profit, and thus what discretion and mandates it will have. It is the mission that should guide the board and executive director in setting and pursuing strategies and evaluating the outcomes of the organization's efforts. And it is the mission that inspires the strongest form of commitment among volunteers, donors, and others who choose to add their contributions to forward that mission's achievement.

When leaders and managers lose sight of the mission, and the values behind it, they lose an ethical guidepost and run the risk of accusations that they are using the nonprofit as simply a commercial enterprise or instrument for government contracts, or even worse, putting their personal interests above those of the nonprofit and the public to whom it is accountable. Peter Frumkin might frame this as having an instrumental rationale, which if taken to the extreme might result in a nonprofit acting as a vendor focused solely on responding to government funding opportunities or as a competitive market actor neglecting underserved communities in favor of activities that can better contribute to the nonprofit's or an individual's earned income revenue stream.[1]

When well defined, a mission gives the nonprofit's leaders and managers a sense of the *current reality*, the *social problem*, and the *organization's approach* to the problem. It also inspires a sense of what is possible, leading to a *vision of a better world.* Peter Senge claims that effective leaders manage the creative tension between the current reality and the vision.[2] When individuals are content with current reality, they can become complacent. When they see the vision as too far from reality, they may become cynical or experience burnout and disengage. The right amount of tension can create energy that can be directed toward pursuing the vision. The nonprofit leader's job is to help others dream of what is possible and show them a path, or at least the obvious first step, to achieving it. The nonprofit manager's job, then, is to coordinate resources and action so that this path is pursued as effectively and efficiently as possible.

The Challenge of Understanding Current Reality

But what if current reality is constantly shifting or unknown? This book helps leaders to address the problem of discovering the current situation a nonprofit is facing, internally and externally. For example, we reviewed how to do a SWOT analysis, complete a needs assessment, and prepare a program portfolio. We noted that stakeholders may have distinct views of a situation based on their values, interests, and limited information, and we discussed how to gather multiple perspectives on a situation and manage conflicting viewpoints. These activities aid leaders, managers, and other stakeholders in getting a shared sense of the current reality. The challenge is how to deal with realities that are frequently shifting.

The pace of change is accelerating. The world is experiencing exponential advances in communication, computing, and other technologies that affect the nature of today's social problems and possible approaches to them. Institutions are increasingly interdependent. Some nonprofits are involved in multi-actor, systemic approaches that were impossible decades ago. The ability to access and analyze information has dramatically increased. This means that the reality leaders see today may not be the reality of next month. Even if leaders can get a firm grasp of current reality, it is hard for anyone to imagine what the future will hold a decade from now, or some may say, even a few years from now. Once it was common to have ten-year strategic plans; now organizations tend to have one-year plans or at most three-year plans. As William Shakespeare wrote, "we know what we are, but know not what we may be."

Imagining the Future

In this chapter we encourage readers to think about what kind of leaders and managers nonprofits of the future will need. To aid this effort, we note what some thought leaders and futurists are imagining and discuss some trends that are likely to affect nonprofits. Some of the predicted changes apply to all sectors and others are specific to nonprofits. Although managers and leaders can try to prepare themselves and their organizations for what the trend lines say is to come, as an observation often attributed to physicist Niels Bohr warns us all, "prediction is very difficult, especially about the future."

General trends noted in 2010 by the U.S. National Intelligence Council and the European Union's Institute for Security Studies include a more globalized interdependent economy, a wealth and power shift from West to East, a reduction in the world influence of the United States, climate change, and greater threats to global security and stability from scarcities, infectious diseases, and terrorism.[3] In addition, international migration is affecting the demographics of particular regions, changing social needs and increasing the diversity of interests, norms, and values. Nonprofits operating in the world arena may find suspicion of global governance efforts and more global-level players emerging from countries such as India, Russia, Brazil, and China.

Community-based nonprofits operating in the United States may find that migration flows and generational shifts are changing the composition of the populations who seek their services and their talent pools for staff and volunteers. For example, needs for services for older Americans are likely to grow as Baby Boomers age. As more Generation Y's enter the workforce, nonprofits will need to aggressively attract and retain them by offering meaningful tasks and empowerment and by an embracing of diverse backgrounds and interests.

In the United States, intergenerational wealth transfers, the increasing economic power of other countries, and new communication tools are affecting fundraising strategies and outcomes. As wealth is passed on to younger generations, philanthropic priorities change, leaving some nonprofits floundering. Fund development prospects increasingly include individuals from other countries who traditionally have not contributed significantly to U.S.-based nonprofits. Peer-to-peer fundraising using social media is increasing in its variations and total dollars raised.[4] More donors have an investment orientation to their philanthropy and expect two-way communication.

When we asked some thought leaders in the nonprofit sector to contribute to this chapter by giving us a sense of what they thought the future would hold for nonprofits, we heard a lot about accountability. Putnam Barber, author of *Nonprofits in Washington* and editor of *Nonprofit FAQ*, wrote:

> Accountability is only going to get more and more important. Nonprofits of every size and type are going to be asked—by governments, by ratings groups, by actual and potential grantors and donors, and, most importantly,

by those they seek to serve—to demonstrate publicly the strengths and value of what they do. With thought, determination, and—let's face it—a little luck, this emphasis can be a plus for everyone. It's going to be up to nonprofits, though, to change the rules of the game. Let's call it proactive accountability. Here's what's needed: First, board commitment to efforts like "Charting Impact" that structure the definition and description of the work (www.chartingimpact.org). Second, complete and accurate transparency about finances, including doing what is required and expected by government agencies with responsibility for oversight and regulation. Third, rejection of game playing in fundraising appeals and other communications—no more bragging about meaningless "stars" or presenting results that distort reality in pursuit of support or acclaim. Fourth, active engagement in efforts to break the pattern of wasteful and misleading forms of "accountability" that have been tolerated and ignored—while growing ever more burdensome—for way too long. In other words, commit to being known and respected for doing good work and candid and clear about what it takes to do it.

To follow Barber's advice, managers and leaders are going to have to publically and programmatically recognize their nonprofit's dependency on other actors to achieve mission outcomes. It is unlikely that nonprofits addressing entrenched, complex social problems can effectively do this work alone. They also need to understand the growing sophistication and interconnectedness of those who work to evaluate nonprofits' efforts. Information on a nonprofit's inputs and outputs may be accessible from multiple sources, not all controlled by the nonprofit. Honest, authentic communication will, as always, be critical to maintaining stakeholders' trust.

John Graham, the CEO of ASAE: The Center for Association Leadership, reminded us of the effect of changes in the workforce on nonprofits. He commented:

As the workforce continues to evolve, nonprofits' ability to maintain relevancy in a changing demographic landscape will be more important than ever. We now have a multigenerational workforce that includes Gen X workers, Millennials, and Baby Boomers who are postponing retirement. With multiple generations in the workforce, we face the challenge of reconciling a range of professional development needs, work-life balance expectations, and value propositions. The workforce is also becoming more ethnically diverse, so managing and encouraging a diverse and inclusive workplace—with pathways to management and other leadership positions—is essential for the future success of associations.

There are numerous writings on how the multiple generations living and working today differ from one another, giving nonprofits guidance on how their leadership and management approaches need to change as each new generation enters the workforce.[5] But a cautionary note is in order: more than ever nonprofits are in a world where quick and easy categorizations of the generations may lead them down faulty paths. The members of Generation Y are more diverse than members of previous generations; diversity is one of this generation's defining characteristics. This means that leaders and managers should be careful about making assumptions about Generation Y members' specific work styles, interests, and values. They also will be working side by side with older workers who may have become comfortable with certain workplace practices and policies. Leaders and managers who can treat each worker as an individual with unique motivations and abilities will have a leg up in building their HR capacity and an advantage over those who want to compartmentalize their workforce, limiting their workers' potential contributions.

Lastly, we share some thoughts from Jonathan Reckford, chief executive officer of Habitat for Humanity International. He told us:

> One of the challenges that nonprofit groups must sometimes address is the assumption that we are somehow less than professional—that we are driven by passion for a cause rather than a bottom line. This is not an either/or. Nonprofits often arise out of grassroots movements where people are motivated by a sense of calling and mission. However, we are also accountable to donors, to the community (in the case of Habitat for Humanity, a global community) and to those whom we serve. We are using other people's money to help those in need. We need to have higher standards than businesses because more is at stake. The same skills that make leaders successful in the private sector are needed in the nonprofit world. You can't run a nonprofit like a business, but all nonprofits require leaders with great competence, drive, humility and character.

Mr. Reckford returns us to the idea that this is a book about leading and managing nonprofits. Although we encourage the use of for-profit business tools and orientations, they must be tempered with an understanding of the limits of their applicability to the nonprofit setting. Social entrepreneurship efforts are blooming in many countries, and their leaders may choose to operate them as nonprofits, for-profits, hybrids (for example, B Corporations), or government entities. We also know that nonprofits in some industries have long competed and collaborated with business and government organizations. In these arenas it may be difficult for the public to understand what distinguishes a nonprofit provider from a provider in another sector. There is a responsibility to honor the trust and discretion afforded nonprofit organizations by virtue of their legal status. To preserve the integrity of the nonprofit sector, its leaders and managers must uphold high standards.

Leadership Development

Educators are well aware of the growth in career opportunities in the nonprofit sector and of the professional development needs of individuals wishing to take advantage of these opportunities. In higher education there is an increasing number of undergraduate and graduate programs in nonprofit management.[6] As mentioned in our opening chapter, the Nonprofit Academic Centers Council (NACC) and the National Association of Schools of Public Affairs and Administration (NASPAA) offer guidelines on the subject areas these programs should cover. A perusal of the NACC list (see the Appendix) suggests the breadth and depth of knowledge and skills areas that nonprofit managers and leaders are encouraged to develop. In addition to formal degree programs, there are workshops, seminars, and other learning opportunities to build leadership and management capacity.

As the future unfolds, new development needs will be revealed. Recall, for example, that just twenty years ago, a person getting an MBA degree was not exposed to the value of social media in building business relationships. There will always be new ways for nonprofits to touch lives and make positive differences. An orientation to continual learning will help nonprofit leaders and managers to ensure that worthwhile opportunities are not missed and that their organizations remain open to the most effective ways to forward their missions.

APPENDIX

MAPPING OF CHAPTER CONTENT TO NACC GUIDELINES FOR STUDY IN NONPROFIT LEADERSHIP, THE NONPROFIT SECTOR, AND PHILANTHROPY

NACC Curricular Topics for Undergraduate Study*	NACC Curricular Topics for Graduate Study*	Corresponding Book Chapter(s) and Notes
Comparative Perspectives on Civil Society, Voluntary Action, and Philanthropy	Comparative Perspectives on the Nonprofit Sector, Voluntary Action, and Philanthropy	Our focus is primarily on the United States, but we provide international comparisons. We discuss international trends in Chapter 17.
Foundations of Civil Society, Voluntary Action, and Philanthropy	Scope and Significance of the Nonprofit Sector, Voluntary Action, and Philanthropy; History and Theories of the Nonprofit Sector, Voluntary Action, and Philanthropy	Each of the chapters covers material that fits under these topics; however, most coverage is in Chapters 1 and 3. Dynamics between the nonprofit sector and other sectors are covered primarily in Chapters 6, 14, and 15.
Ethics and Values	Ethics and Values	Most coverage of this topic is in Chapter 2, but discussion of ethics is woven throughout the book.
Public Policy, Law, Advocacy, and Social Change	Public Policy, Advocacy, and Social Change; Nonprofit Law	The legal framework is covered in Chapter 3. Advocacy and lobbying is covered in Chapter 14. Legal and tax implications of charitable giving and commercial activity are covered in Chapter 6.
Nonprofit Governance and Leadership	Nonprofit Governance and Leadership Leadership, Organization, and Management	Nonprofit boards and governance are covered in Chapter 9, and executive directors and leadership theory in Chapter 10. Innovation and change are covered in Chapter 16.
Community Service and Civic Engagement		We cover the involvement of students in nonprofits in Chapter 11, on human resource management.

Leading and Managing Organizations		Subtopics under this topic are covered in Chapters 2, 3, 4, 5, 10, 12, 13, and 15.
Nonprofit Finance and Fundraising	Nonprofit Finance Fundraising and Development	Subtopics under this topic are covered in Chapter 6.
Financial Management	Financial Management and Accountability	Financial management is covered in Chapter 7. Issues of accountability are woven throughout the book.
Managing Staff and Volunteers	Nonprofit Human Resource Management	We cover human resource management and human resource capacity in Chapter 11, and motivation and performance theories are in Chapter 12.
Nonprofit Marketing	Nonprofit Marketing	Most of the material on marketing is in Chapter 8.
Professional and Career Development		Some subtopics under this topic are covered in Chapter 2 with the discussion of professional norms.
Assessment, Evaluation, and Decision-Making Methods	Assessment, Evaluation, and Decision-Making Methods	Chapter 13 covers program evaluation. Organizational evaluation is addressed in Chapter 2, and worker performance review is in Chapters 11 and 12.
	Nonprofit Economics	Social entrepreneurship is covered in Chapter 3; pricing schemes are covered in Chapter 8.
	Information Technology and Management	Public relations and communication are covered in Chapter 14.

*Note: This table lists the curricular topics identified in the guidelines; each topic has a number of subtopics. This book covers many of these subtopics but not the entire set.

NOTES

Chapter One

1. The statistical information in this chapter is from the National Center on Charitable Statistics, *Quick Facts About Nonprofits* (2009), accessed November 25, 2011, http://nccs.urban.org/statistics/quickfacts.cfm; *501(c)(3) Public Charities* (n.d.), accessed November 25, 2011, http://nccsdataweb.urban.org/PubApps/nonprofit-overview-segment.php?t=pc; and *501(c)(3) Private Foundations* (n.d.), accessed November 25, 2011, http://nccsdataweb.urban.org/PubApps/nonprofit-overview-segment.php?t=pf.
2. National Center on Charitable Statistics, *Quick Facts About Nonprofits*.
3. David H. Smith, "Some Challenges in Nonprofit and Voluntary Action Research," *Nonprofit and Voluntary Sector Quarterly* 24 (1995): 99–101.
4. Lester M. Salamon, *America's Nonprofit Sector: A Primer*, 2nd ed. (New York: Foundation Center, 1999).
5. Peter Frumkin, *On Being Nonprofit: A Conceptual and Policy Primer* (Cambridge, MA: Harvard University Press, 2002).
6. Lester M. Salamon, ed., *The State of Nonprofit America* (Washington, DC: Brookings Institution Press, 2002).
7. More information on B corporations is available at the B Lab Web site, http://www.bcorporation.net; B Lab is the nonprofit that certifies B corporations.
8. Bradford Gray and Mark Schlesinger, "Health," in *The State of Nonprofit America*, ed. Lester M. Salamon (Washington, DC: Brookings Institution Press, 2002), 65–106.

Chapter Two

1. Case details are from Dan Immergluck's report "What Happened to CANDO and What's Needed Now?" unpublished manuscript (prepared for the Local Initiatives Support Corporation, Chicago, 2003).
2. Alan Fischer, "Elderly Couple Pays Dearly for Baptist Fund's Trouble," *Arizona Star*, September 26, 1999; and Terry Sterling's series of articles in the *Phoenix New Times*: "In the Name of the Father and the Son and the Wholly Owned Subsidiary," May 22, 1997; "The Moneychangers," April 16, 1998; "A Shaky Foundation," April 23, 1998; "Poring a Foundation," December 10, 1998; and "Savings Bondage," September 10, 1998. Also see "Baptist Foundation of Arizona," *Wikipedia* (n.d.), accessed June 30, 2011, http://en.wikipedia.org/wiki/Baptist_Foundation_of_Arizona.
3. Kim S. Cameron was one of the first to lay out multidimensional frameworks for assessing effectiveness; see especially, "Critical Questions in Assessing Organizational Effectiveness," *Organizational Dynamics* 9 (1980): 66–80, and "Effectiveness as Paradox: Consensus and Conflict in Conceptions of Organizational Effectiveness," *Management Science* 32 (1985): 539–553. Robert Herman and David Renz explored effectiveness in nonprofits using a multidimensional framework in "Multiple Constituencies and the Social Construction of Nonprofit Organization Effectiveness," *Nonprofit and Voluntary Sector Quarterly* 26 (1997): 185–206.
4. Jim Collins explores the difference between the for-profit and nonprofit sectors in the ways they view money as an indicator of effectiveness in his book *Good to Great in the Social Sectors* (New York: HarperCollins, 2004).
5. For a rich discussion of this dynamic see Steven Kerr, "On the Folly of Rewarding A, While Hoping for B," *Academy of Management Executive* 9, no. 1 (1995): 7–14 (original article published 1975).
6. Jonathan Weill, "Andersen Agrees to Pay $217 Million to Settle Suits over Audits of Baptist," *The Wall Street Journal*, May 6, 2002.
7. John M. Bryson and Barbara C. Crosby offer instructions on how to identify stakeholders involved in policy domains in *Leadership for the Common Good: Tackling Public Problems in a Shared-Power World* (San Francisco: Jossey-Bass/Wiley, 1992). Their technique can be helpful in considering the multiple stakeholders affecting or affected by a particular nonprofit.
8. The triangle was inspired by Harvard professor Mark Moore's strategic triangle. It suggests the need for a balanced approach to effectiveness. Another example of the need for balance is the *competing values* approach introduced by Robert E. Quinn and John Rohrbaugh. For one of their earliest treatments of the topic see "A Spatial Model of Effectiveness Criteria: Toward a Competing Values Approach to Organizational Analysis," *Management Science* 29, no. 3 (1983): 363–377.
9. Peter Panepento, "Ethical Standards Erode at Nonprofit Groups, Study Finds," *Chronicle of Philanthropy*, March 27, 2008. See the survey results at http://www.ethicsworld.org/ethicsandemployees/nbes.php#2007nnes.
10. David Shulman, "More Lies Than Meet the Eyes: Organizational Realities in Nonprofit Organizations," *International Journal of Not-for-Profit Law* 10, no. 2 (2008): 5–14.
11. For more information about the examples discussed here see Robert H. Doktor, "Asian and American CEOs: A Comparative Study," *Organizational Dynamics* 18, no. 3 (1990): 46–56; Rosalie L. Tung, "Handshakes Across the Sea: Cross-Cultural

Negotiating for Business Success," *Organizational Dynamics* 19, no. 3 (1991): 30–40; and Debra L. Nelson and James Campbell Quick, *Organizational Behavior: The Essentials* (New York: West, 1996).

12. The review of personality factors is drawn from Nelson and Quick, *Organizational Behavior*.
13. Amar Bhidé and Howard H. Stevens, "Why Be Honest If Honesty Doesn't Pay?," *Harvard Business Review*, September–October 1990, 121–129.
14. The review of contextual factors for unethical behavior is drawn from Nelson and Quick, *Organizational Behavior*.
15. The Ethics Resource Center, http://www.ethics.org, offers trend data on organizational ethics programs and ethical behavior and attitudes of employees. It also has resources for ethical training and evaluating workplace ethics.
16. This list of training goals builds on the idea that ethical conduct is based on moral awareness. For more information see James R. Rest, ed., *Moral Development: Advances in Research and Theory* (New York: Praeger, 1994), 26–39.
17. Kenneth Blanchard and Norman Vincent Peale, *The Power of Ethical Management* (New York: Fawcett Crest, 1988).
18. See World Wildlife Fund, *WWF Code of Ethics: How We Behave Towards Our Mission, Our World, and Ourselves* (n.d.), accessed December 3, 2011, http://wwf.panda.org/who_we_are/organization/ethics.
19. Thomas H. Jeavons, "Ethical Nonprofit Management," in *The Jossey-Bass Handbook of Nonprofit Leadership & Management*, 2nd ed., Robert D. Herman & Associates (San Francisco: Jossey-Bass/Wiley, 2005), 204–229.
20. "Detroit Zoo Director to Lose a Month's Pay," *Chronicle of Philanthropy*, July 3, 2007, accessed July 10, 2011, http://philanthropy.com/blogs/philanthropytoday/detroit-zoo-director-to-lose-a-months-pay/13521.
21. Panel on the Nonprofit Sector, *Strengthening Transparency, Governance, Accountability of Charitable Organizations: A Final Report to Congress and the Nonprofit Sector* (Washington, DC: INDEPENDENT SECTOR, June 2005); and *Principles for Good Governance and Ethical Practice: A Guide for Charities and Foundations* (Washington, DC: INDEPENDENT SECTOR, October 2007).
22. Maryland Association of Nonprofit Organizations, *The Standards for Excellence: An Ethics and Accountability Code for the Nonprofit Sector* (2009), accessed January 12, 2012, http://www.marylandnonprofits.org/dnn/Strengthen/StandardsforExcellence/ExploretheCode.aspx.
23. Mary Tschirhart, "Self-Regulation at the State Level by Nonprofits: The Membership Association Form as a Self-Regulatory Vehicle," in *Nonprofit Clubs: Voluntary Regulation of Nonprofit and Nongovernmental Organizations*, ed. M. K. Gugerty and A. Prakesh (New York: Oxford University Press, 2010), 85–99. Other chapters in this book also speak to accountability mechanisms for nonprofits.
24. Panepento, "Ethical Standards Erode at Nonprofit Groups, Study Finds."
25. Lester M. Salamon, S. Wojciech Sokolowski, and Associates, *Global Civil Society: Dimensions of the Nonprofit Sector*, vol. 2 (Bloomfield, CT: Kumarian Press, 2004).
26. René Bekkers, "Trust, Accreditation, and Philanthropy in the Netherlands," *Nonprofit and Voluntary Sector Quarterly* 32 (2003): 596–615.
27. Doktor, "Asian and American CEOs"; Tung, "Handshakes Across the Sea"; and Nelson and Quick, *Organizational Behavior*.

Chapter Three

1. Leslie R. Crutchfield and Heather McLeod Grant, *Forces for Good: The Six Practices of High-Impact Nonprofits* (San Francisco: Jossey-Bass/Wiley, 2007).
2. Wendy Kopp, *One Day, All Children . . . : The Unlikely Triumph of Teach For America and What I Learned Along the Way* (New York: PublicAffairs, 2003); Wendy Kopp, *A Chance to Make History: What Works and What Doesn't in Providing an Excellent Education for All* (New York: PublicAffairs, 2011).
3. *Wendy Kopp: Advice for Social Entrepreneurs,* video posted by Stanford University's Entrepreneurship Corner (n.d.), accessed November 26, 2011, http://www.youtube.com/watch?v=TUAS1iY1f7s.
4. Kennard T. Wing, Thomas H. Pollak, and Amy Blackwood, *The Nonprofit Almanac 2008* (Washington, DC: Urban Institute Press, 2008).
5. For information on the size and scope of the nonprofit sector in a range of countries see Lester M. Salamon, S. Wojciech Sokolowski, and Associates, *Global Civil Society: Dimensions of the Nonprofit Sector,* vol. 2 (Bloomfield, CT: Kumarian Press, 2004).
6. Bill McKelvey and Howard Aldrich, "Populations, Natural Selection, and Applied Organizational Science," *Administrative Science Quarterly* 28 (1983): 101–128.
7. Stephen R. Block, *Why Nonprofits Fail* (San Francisco: Jossey-Bass/Wiley, 2004).
8. Howard Aldrich, *Organizations Evolving* (Thousand Oaks, CA: Sage, 1999).
9. Dan H. McCormick, *Nonprofit Mergers: The Power of Successful Partnerships* (Gaithersburg, MD: Aspen, 2001).
10. Anthony J. Filipovitch, "Organizational Transformation of a Community-Based Clinic," *Nonprofit Management & Leadership* 17, no. 1 (2006): 103–115.
11. Jacques Delacroix and Glenn Carroll, "Organizational Foundings: An Ecological Study of the Newspaper Industries of Argentina and Ireland," *Administrative Science Quarterly* 28 (1983): 274–291.
12. W. Richard Scott and Gerald Davis, *Organizations and Organizing: Rational, Natural, and Open System Perspectives* (Upper Saddle River, NJ: Pearson Prentice Hall, 2007).
13. Howard Aldrich and Martin Ruef, *Organizations Evolving,* 2nd ed. (Thousand Oaks, CA: Sage, 2006).
14. Richard H. Hall, *Organizations: Structures, Processes, and Outcomes,* 8th ed. (Upper Saddle River, NJ: Pearson Prentice Hall, 2002), 186.
15. Dennis Young, "Entrepreneurship and the Behavior of Nonprofit Organizations: Elements of a Theory," in *The Economics of Nonprofit Institutions: Studies in Structure and Policy,* ed. S. Rose-Ackerman (New York: Oxford University Press, 1986), 162.
16. Paul Light, "Reshaping Social Entrepreneurship," *Stanford Social Innovation Review* 4 (Fall 2006): 47–51.
17. J. Gregory Dees and Peter Economy, "Social Entrepreneurship," in *Enterprising Nonprofits: A Toolkit for Social Entrepreneurs,* ed. J. Gregory Dees, Jed Emerson, and Peter Economy (New York: Wiley, 2001), 12–13.
18. James Austin, Howard Stevenson, and Jane Wei-Skillern, "Social and Commercial Entrepreneurship: Same, Different, or Both?" *Entrepreneurship Theory & Practice* 30, no. 1 (2006): 1–22.
19. William A. Sahlman, "Some Thoughts on Business Plans," in *The Entrepreneurial Venture,* ed. William A. Sahlman, Howard H. Stevenson, Michael J. Roberts, and Amar Bhidé (Boston: Harvard Business Press, 1999), 138–176.

20. Kathi Jaworski, "Massachusetts Takes Another Step Toward Social Impact Bond Funding for Social Programs," *Nonprofit Quarterly*, June 29, 2011, accessed December 5, 2011, http://www.nonprofitquarterly.org/index.php?option=com_content&view=article&id=13581:massachusetts-takes-another-step-toward-social-impact-bond-funding-for-social-programs&catid=155:nonprofit-newswire&Itemid=986; Nonprofit Finance Fund, "What Is a Social Impact Bond (SIB)?" (n.d.), accessed December 5, 2011, http://nonprofitfinancefund.org/social-impact-bond-initiative.
21. Teach For America, Web site, accessed July 14, 2011, http://www.teachforamerica.org/what-we-do/our-approach.
22. William Bygrave, "The Entrepreneurial Process," in *The Portable MBA in Entrepreneurship*, ed. William Bygrave and Andrew Zacharakis (Hoboken, NJ: Wiley, 2004), 1–28; Peter Drucker, *Innovation and Entrepreneurship* (New York: Harper Business, 1985).
23. See Carol Moore's model in her paper "Understanding Entrepreneurial Behavior," in *Academy of Management Best Paper Proceedings*, ed. J. A. Pearce II and R. B. Robinson Jr., 46th Annual Meeting of the Academy of Management (Briarcliff Manor, NY: Academy of Management, 1986).
24. Bygrave, "The Entrepreneurial Process."
25. Robert Hisrich, Michael Peters, and Dean Shepherd, *Entrepreneurship*, 6th ed. (Boston: McGraw-Hill/Irwin, 2005), 62.
26. Arthur Brooks, *Social Entrepreneurship: A Modern Approach to Social Value Creation* (Upper Saddle River, NJ: Pearson Prentice Hall, 2009).
27. Peter Drucker, *Innovation and Entrepreneurship* (New York: Harper Business, 1985), 35.
28. Jerry Kitzi, "Recognizing and Assessing New Opportunities," in *Enterprising Nonprofits: A Toolkit for Social Entrepreneurs*, ed. J. Gregory Dees, Jed Emerson, and Peter Economy (New York: Wiley, 2001), 45–46.
29. Kitzi, "Recognizing and Assessing New Opportunities," 52–59.
30. For a comparison of business and strategic plans see Charles A. "Chip" Brethen, "The Business Plan Versus the Strategic Plan—Part 1" (Bizquest, n.d.), accessed July 24, 2011, http://www.bizquest.com/resource/the_business_plan_versus_the_strategic_plan__part-31.html.
31. Web sites offering nonprofit business plans include The Bridgespan Group, *Sample Nonprofit Business Plans* (March 30, 2009), accessed December 5, 2011, http://www.bridgespan.org/sample-nonprofit-business-plans.aspx; and Bplans, "Nonprofit Youth Services Business Plan" (n.d.), accessed December 5, 2011, http://www.bplans.com/nonprofit_youth_services_business_plan/executive_summary_fc.cfm.
32. See *NPower Basic Business Plan April 2005* (2005), accessed December 4, 2011, http://faculty.maxwell.syr.edu/acbrooks/pages/Courses/Documents/Soc%20Ent/NPowerNY.pdf, for the complete plan.
33. Alexander Tübke, *Success Factors of Corporate Spin-Offs* (Boston: Kluwer, 2005), 4.
34. Joseph W. Cornell, *Spin-Off to Pay-Off: An Analytical Guide to Investing in Corporate Divestitures* (New York: McGraw-Hill, 1998), 40–42.
35. Michael H. Morris, Donald F. Kuratko, and Jeffrey G. Covin, *Corporate Entrepreneurship & Innovation* (Mason, OH: South-Western/Cengage Learning, 2008), 244–245.
36. See the Quaqua Society's news Web page at http://www.quaqua.org/news.htm.
37. David Garvin, "Spin-Offs and the New Firm Formation Process," *California Management Review* 25 (1983): 3–20.

38. "Entrepreneurs: Will They Stay or Will They Go?," *Capital Ideas* 3, no. 3 (2002), accessed December 6, 2011, http://www.chicagobooth.edu/capideas/win02/entrepreneurs.html.
39. Peter Dobkin Hall, *A History of Nonprofit Boards in the United States* (BoardSource E-Book Series, 2003), accessed December 6, 2011, http://www.boardsource.org/dl.asp?document_id=11.
40. Courtney Macavinta, "Scientologists Settle Legal Battle" (CNET News, March 30, 1999), accessed December 6, 2011, http://news.cnet.com/2100-1023-223683.html.
41. Examples are from Liz Galst, "Nonprofit Groups Spin Off Green Ventures," *The New York Times*, October 28, 2009, accessed December 6, 2011, http://www.nytimes.com/2009/10/29/business/smallbusiness/29sbiz.html.
42. The Vera Institute's Spin-Off Tool Kit may be accessed at http://www.vera.org/download?file=1469/Vera_Tool_Kit_Final.pdf.
43. Brad J. Caftel, *Forming a Subsidiary of a Nonprofit, Charitable Tax-Exempt Corporation* (Oakland, CA: The National Economic Development & Law Center, 2002), accessed January 30, 2009, http://www.insightcced.org/uploads/publications/legal/720.pdf.
44. Caftel, *Forming a Subsidiary of a Nonprofit, Charitable Tax-Exempt Corporation*.
45. Sharon M. Oster, "Nonprofits as Franchise Operations," *Nonprofit Management & Leadership* 2, no. 3 (1992): 224.
46. Oster, "Nonprofits as Franchise Operations," 226.
47. Sharon Oster, "Nonprofit Organizations and Their Local Affiliates: A Study in Organizational Forms," *Journal of Economic Behavior & Organization* 30 (1996): 83–95.
48. Brennen Jensen, "Housing Charity Settles Lawsuit with Texas Affiliate," *Chronicle of Philanthropy*, July 24, 2008.
49. "Manitou Girl Scout Council Proves to Be One Tough Cookie," *JS Online: Milwaukee-Wisconsin Journal Sentinel*, May 31, 2011.

Chapter Four

1. Case details are from The Bridgespan Group case study of the organization, in Alex Cortez and Alan Tuck, "Our Piece of the Pie (Formerly Southend Community Services): Making the Biggest Difference in Hartford" (April 1, 2006), accessed December 6, 2011, http://www.bridgespan.org/LearningCenter/ResourceDetail.aspx?id=360.
2. Bob Searle, Alex Neuhoff, and Andrew Belton, "Clients at the Center: Realizing the Potential of Multi-Service Organizations" (The Bridgespan Group, July 7, 2011), accessed January 5, 2012, http://www.bridgespan.org/clients-at-the-center-for-mso.aspx?resource=Articles.
3. Jeffrey Bradach, Nan Stone, and Thomas Tierney, "Four Questions for Charities to Answer as They Seek to Thrive in Hard Times," *Chronicle of Philanthropy*, January 2009, 29.
4. Henry Mintzberg, *The Structure of Organizations* (Upper Saddle River, NJ: Pearson Prentice Hall, 1979).
5. Richard Daft, *Organization Theory and Design*, 9th ed. (Mason, OH: South-Western/Cengage Learning, 2007).
6. Peter Hall and Pamela Tolbert, *Organizations: Structures, Processes, and Outcomes*, 9th ed. (Upper Saddle River, NJ: Pearson Prentice Hall, 2005).

7. W. Richard Scott and Gerald Davis, *Organizations and Organizing: Rational, Natural, and Open System Perspectives* (Upper Saddle River, NJ: Pearson Prentice Hall, 2007).
8. Jerald Hage, "An Axiomatic Theory of Organizations," *Administrative Science Quarterly* 10 (1965): 289–320.
9. Max Weber, *The Theory of Social and Economic Organization*, trans. A. M. Parsons and T. Parsons (New York: Free Press, 1947).
10. Wikimedia Foundation, "Home," accessed December 6, 2011, http://wikimediafoundation.org/wiki/Home.
11. Tom Burns and G. M. Stalker, *The Management of Innovation* (London: Tavistock, 1961).
12. Joyce Rothschild-Whitt, "The Collectivist Organization: An Alternative to Rational-Bureaucratic Models," *American Sociological Review* 44 (August 1979): 509–527.
13. Carl Milofsky, *Community Organizations: Studies in Resource Mobilization and Exchange* (New York: Oxford University Press, 1988); David Horton Smith, *Grassroots Associations* (Thousand Oaks, CA: Sage, 2000).
14. Richard M. Burton and Borge Obel, *Strategic Organizational Diagnosis and Design: The Dynamics of Fit*, 3rd ed. (Boston: Kluwer Academic, 2004).
15. Burton and Obel, *Strategic Organizational Diagnosis and Design*.
16. Daft, *Organization Theory and Design*.
17. John Galbraith, *Designing Complex Organizations* (Reading, MA: Addison-Wesley, 1973); John Galbraith, *Organizational Design* (Reading, MA: Addison-Wesley, 1977).
18. James Thompson, *Organizations in Action* (New York: McGraw-Hill, 1967).
19. Burton and Obel, *Strategic Organizational Diagnosis and Design*.
20. Hall and Tolbert, *Organization*, 19.
21. Herbert Simon, *Administrative Behavior* (New York: Free Press, 1957).
22. Geert Hofstede, "Intercultural Conflict and Synergy in Europe," in *Management in Western Europe: Society, Culture and Organization in Twelve Nations*, ed. David J. Hickson (New York: de Gruyter, 1993), 1–8.
23. Paul Dimaggio and Walter Powell, "The Iron Cage Revisited: Institutional Isomorphism and Collective Rationality in Organizational Fields," *American Sociological Review* 48 (1983): 147–160.
24. Daft, *Organization Theory and Design*.

Chapter Five

1. Case details are from Judith A. Ross, *Becoming Strategic: The Evolution of the Flinn Foundation*, CEP Case Study No. 3 (Cambridge, MA: Center for Effective Philanthropy, March 2009), accessed June 1, 2009, http://www.effectivephilanthropy.org/assets/pdfs/CEP_Flinn.pdf.
2. Sun Tzu, *The Art of War*, trans. Lionel Giles (El Paso, TX: Norte Press, 2007).
3. See, for example, Frederick Taylor, *The Principles of Scientific Management* (New York: HarperCollins, 1911); Henri Fayol, *General and Industrial Management*, trans. Constance Storrs (London: Pitman, 1949); Ralph Davis, *The Principles of Factory Organization and Management* (New York: HarperCollins, 1928); Ralph Davis, *The Fundamentals of Top Management* (New York: HarperCollins, 1951).
4. Roger Courtney, *Strategic Management for Voluntary Nonprofit Organizations* (New York: Routledge, 2002).

5. Alfred Chandler, *Strategy and Structure: Chapters in the History of Industrial Enterprise* (Cambridge, MA: MIT Press, 1962); H. Igor Ansoff, *Corporate Strategy* (Gretna, LA: Pelican, 1965).
6. Chandler, *Strategy and Structure*, 13.
7. Stephen Cummings, "Strategy: Past, Present, and Future," in *The Sage Handbook of New Approaches in Management and Organizations*, ed. Daved Barry and Hans Hansen (Thousand Oaks, CA: Sage, 2008).
8. Henry Mintzberg, "The Fall and Rise of Strategic Planning," *Harvard Business Review*, January–February 1994, 107.
9. Roger Courtney, *Strategic Management for Voluntary Nonprofit Organizations*.
10. Mintzberg's research is summarized in Henry Mintzberg and James Waters, "Of Strategies, Deliberate and Emergent," *Strategic Management Journal* 6, no. 3 (1985): 257–272.
11. Henry Mintzberg, Bruce Ahlstrand, and Joseph Lampel, *Strategy Safari: A Guided Tour Through the Wilds of Strategic Management* (New York: Free Press, 1998).
12. Mintzberg et al., *Strategy Safari*.
13. Courtney, *Strategic Management for Voluntary Nonprofit Organizations*.
14. David Gerard, *Charities in Britain: Conservatism or Change?* (London: Bedford Square Press, 1983); J. Malcolm Walker, "Limits of Strategic Management in Voluntary Organizations," *Journal of Voluntary Action Research* 12, no. 3 (1983): 39–55.
15. Courtney, *Strategic Management for Voluntary Nonprofit Organizations*.
16. Courtney, *Strategic Management for Voluntary Nonprofit Organizations*.
17. Michael Porter, *Competitive Strategy* (New York: Free Press, 1980).
18. Raymond Miles and Charles Snow, *Organizational Strategy, Structure, and Process* (New York: McGraw-Hill, 1978); the types are also summarized in "Four Strategic Types (Raymond Miles and Charles Snow)," *12Manage: The Executive Fast Track* (n.d.), accessed May 20, 2009, http://www.12manage.com/methods_miles_snow_four_strategic_types.html. Also see Courtney, *Strategic Management for Voluntary Nonprofit Organizations*.
19. Ian MacMillan, "Competitive Strategies for Not-for-Profit Agencies," in *Advances in Strategic Management*, vol. 1, ed. Robert Lamb (Greenwich, CT: JAI Press, 1983), 65.
20. The description of MacMillan's strategy types is adapted from Michael J. Worth, *Nonprofit Management: Principle and Practice* (Thousand Oaks, CA: Sage, 2009).
21. John Bryson, "Strategic Planning and the Strategy Change Cycle," in *The Jossey-Bass Handbook of Nonprofit Leadership and Management*, 3rd ed., David O. Renz and Associates (San Francisco: Jossey-Bass/Wiley, 2010). 230–261.
22. American Red Cross, Web site, accessed July 12, 2011, http://www.redcross.org.
23. American Red Cross of Greater Indianapolis, "About Us" (n.d.), accessed July 15, 2011, http://www.redcross-indy.org/AboutUs/default.aspx.
24. The discussion of environmental assessment techniques draws on Courtney, *Strategic Management for Voluntary Nonprofit Organizations*.
25. Sharon M. Oster, "Nonprofits as Franchise Operations," *Nonprofit Management & Leadership* 2, no. 3 (1992): 223–238.
26. American Red Cross, Web site.
27. Oster, "Nonprofits as Franchise Operations."
28. Porter, *Competitive Strategy*.
29. For more on the resource-based view of strategy, see Jay Barney, "Firm Resources and Sustained Competitive Advantage," *Journal of Management* 17, no. 1 (1991):

99–120; Robert M. Grant, "The Resource-Based Theory of Competitive Advantage: Implications for Strategy Formulation," *California Management Review* 33, no. 3 (1991): 114–135; Gary Hamel and C. K. Prahalad, "Strategy as Stretch and Leverage," *Harvard Business Review*, March–April 1993, 75–84; John Kay, *Foundations of Corporate Success* (New York: Oxford University Press, 1993); Margaret Peteraf, "The Cornerstone of Competitive Advantage: A Resource-Based View," *Strategic Management Journal* 14, no. 3 (1993): 179–191.
30. Bryson, "Strategic Planning and the Strategy Change Cycle."
31. Kevin Kearns, "From Comparative Advantage to Damage Control: Clarifying Strategic Issues Using SWOT Analysis," *Nonprofit Management & Leadership* 3, no. 1 (1992), 3–22.
32. Bryson, "Strategic Planning and the Strategy Change Cycle."
33. Work done under the label of *strategic management* is concerned with how strategy is incorporated and integrated into all aspects of organizational action. See, for example, Garth Saloner, Andrea Shepard, and Joel Podolny, *Strategic Management* (Hoboken, NJ: Wiley, 2000).
34. Bryson, "Strategic Planning and the Strategy Change Cycle."
35. Cummings, "Strategy: Past, Present, Future."
36. Mintzberg et al., *Strategy Safari*.
37. Mintzberg, "The Fall and Rise of Strategic Planning."
38. Charles Lindblom, "The Science of Muddling Through," *Public Administration Review* 19, no. 2 (1959): 79–88.
39. James Quinn, *Strategies for Change: Logical Incrementalism* (Homewood, IL: Irwin, 1980).
40. Henry Mintzberg, "Crafting Strategy," in *Understanding Nonprofit Organizations*, ed. J. S. Ott (Boulder, CO: Westview Press, 2001), 158–166.
41. Henry Mintzberg, *Mintzberg on Management: Inside Our Strange World of Organizations* (New York: Free Press, 1989).
42. Mintzberg et al., *Strategy Safari*.
43. Mintzberg et al., *Strategy Safari*.
44. Courtney, *Strategic Management for Voluntary Nonprofit Organizations*, 102–103.
45. Robert Grant, *Contemporary Strategy Analysis*, 5th ed. (Malden, MA: Blackwell, 2005), 25.
46. Courtney, *Strategic Management for Voluntary Nonprofit Organizations*.
47. Cummings, "Strategy: Past, Present, Future."
48. Courtney, *Strategic Management for Voluntary Nonprofit Organizations*.

Chapter Six

1. Case details are from the Oakes Children's Center Web site, http://www.oakeschildrenscenter.org; and Robert Tyminski, "Reducing Funding Risk and Implementing a Fundraising Plan: A Case Study," *Nonprofit Management & Leadership* 8, no. 3 (1998): 275–286.
2. Oakes Children's Center, "Mission & Vision" (n.d.), accessed December 13, 2011, http://www.oakeschildrenscenter.org/mission.htm.
3. National Center for Charitable Statistics, *Quick Facts About Nonprofits* (n.d.), accessed December 13, 2011, http://nccs.urban.org/statistics/quickfacts.cfm.
4. Kennard T. Wing, Katie L. Roeger, and Thomas H. Pollack, *The Nonprofit Sector in Brief: Public Charities, Giving and Volunteering, 2010* (Washington, DC: Urban Institute, 2010).

5. Angela L. Bies, "Public Philanthropy," in *Philanthropy in America: A Comprehensive Historical Encyclopedia*, 3 vols., ed. Dwight F. Burlingame (Santa Barbara, CA: ABC-CLIO, 2004), 402–404. This encyclopedia has short entries on many topics relevant to this chapter.
6. Kirsten A. Gronbjerg, *Understanding Nonprofit Funding: Managing Revenues in Social Services and Community Development Organizations* (San Francisco: Jossey-Bass/Wiley, 1993).
7. Steven R. Smith and Michael Lipsky, *Nonprofits for Hire: The Welfare State in the Age of Contracting* (Cambridge, MA: Harvard University Press 1993).
8. Elizabeth T. Boris, Erwin De Leon, Kaitie L. Roeger, and Milena Nikolova, *Human Service Nonprofits and Government Collaboration: Findings from the 2010 National Survey of Nonprofit Government Contracting and Grants* (n.d.), accessed December 13, 2011, http://www.urban.org/publications/412228.html. Additional materials from this survey are available at http://www.urban.org/nonprofitcontracting.cfm.
9. See Rick Cohen, "Undone by Public Funding? New Study Points to Reasons," *Nonprofit Quarterly*, October 7, 2010, accessed December 13, 2011, http://www.nonprofitquarterly.org/index.php?option=com_content&view=article&id=6316.
10. See Lester M. Salamon, S. Wojciech Sokolowski, and Associates, *Global Civil Society: Dimensions of the Nonprofit Sector*, vol. 2 (Bloomfield, CT: Kumarian Press, 2004), accessed November 5, 2011, http://ccss.jhu.edu/pdfs/CNP/CNP_table401.pdf, for international comparisons from 1995 to 2000.
11. Robert J. Wineburg, *Faith-Based Inefficiency: The Follies of Bush's Initiatives* (Westport, CT: Praeger, 2007).
12. See Protect (a joint website of Protect & the National Association to Protect Children), "Who We Are, " accessed December 14, 2011, http://www.protect.org/about-protect; and the National Association to Protect Children's Facebook profile, in which this organization emphasizes its rejection of government funding: http://www.facebook.com/protectnow/posts/194007363977025. Concerns that government funding suppresses nonprofits' political activity were not supported in a study reported by Mark Chaves, Laura Stephens, and Joseph Galaskiewicz, "Does Government Funding Suppress Nonprofits' Political Activity?" *American Sociological Review* 69 (2004): 292–316.
13. Crazy Horse Memorial, "Frequently Asked Questions" (n.d.), accessed December 14, 2011, http://www.crazyhorsememorial.org/faq. Additional explanations for the decision not to use government funding are discussed by Maxwell Wallace, "Crazy Horse Memorial Information" (n.d.), accessed December 14, 2011, http://www.ehow.com/about_6466627_crazy-horse-memorial-information.html.
14. *Partnering with Nonprofits in Tough Times: Recommendations from the San Francisco Community-Based Organizations Task Force* (April 2009), accessed December 14, 2011, http://stridecenter.org/articles/CBOTaskForceReporFinalSFF.pdf.
15. For a thoughtful review of mission drift, see Howard P. Tuckman and Cyril F. Chang, "Commercial Activity, Technological Change and Nonprofit Mission," in *The Nonprofit Sector: A Research Handbook*, 2nd ed., ed. Walter W. Powell and Richard Steinberg (New Haven, CT: Yale University Press, 2006), 629–644.
16. Amy E. Knaup, "Survival and Longevity in Business Employment Dynamics Data," *Monthly Labor Review* 128, no. 5 (May 2005): 50–56.
17. For a comprehensive treatment of pricing see Dennis R. Young and Richard Steinberg, *Economics for Nonprofit Managers* (New York: Foundation Center, 1995).

18. See Habitat for Humanity of Kent County, "About" (n.d.), accessed December 14, 2011, http://www.habitatkent.org/ReStore.aspx, for a local chapter's description of its ReStore.
19. Issie Lapowsky, "The Social Entrepreneurship Spectrum: Nonprofits with Earned Income," *Inc.*, May 2011, accessed January 12, 2012, http://www.inc.com/magazine/20110501/the-social-entrepreneurship-spectrum-nonprofits-with-earned-income.html.
20. Ten Thousand Villages, *Annual Report* (2010), http://www.tenthousandvillages.com/pdf/Annual_Report_2010.pdf.
21. Bruce Mohl, "Group: Most Charities Sell Donor Lists," *Boston Globe*, December 1, 2004.
22. Beth Battle Anderson, J. Gregory Dees, and Jed Emerson, "Developing Viable Earned Income Strategies," in *Strategic Tools for Social Entrepreneurs: Enhancing the Performance of Your Enterprising Nonprofit*, ed. J. Gregory Dees, Jed Emerson, and Peter Economy (Hoboken, NJ: Wiley, 2002), 191–233.
23. R. Steinberg, "Membership Income" in *Financing Nonprofits: Putting Theory into Practice*, ed. D. R. Young (Lanham, MD: Altamira Press, 2006), 121–156.
24. Mary Tschirhart, "Nonprofit Membership Associations," in *The Nonprofit Sector: A Research Handbook*, 2nd ed., ed. Walter W. Powell and Richard Steinberg (New Haven, CT: Yale University Press, 2006), 523–541. Also see Mary Kay Gugerty and Aseem Prakesh, eds., *Nonprofit Accountability Clubs: Voluntary Regulation of Nonprofit and Nongovernmental Organizations* (New York: Oxford University Press, 2010).
25. Sesame Workshop, *Licensees* (n.d.), accessed December 16, 2011, http://supportus.sesameworkshop.org/site/c.nlI3IkNXJsE/b.2748689.
26. Mary Tschirhart, Robert K. Christensen, and James L. Perry, "The Paradox of Branding and Collaboration," *Public Productivity and Management Review* 29, no. 1 (2005): 69–87.
27. Shirley Sagawa and Eli Segal, *Common Interest, Common Good: Creating Value Through Business and Social Sector Partnerships* (Boston: Harvard Business Press, 2000).
28. *Plumstead Theatre Society v. Commissioner*, 74 Tax Court 1324 (1980), aff'd 675 F. 2d 244 (9th Cir. 1982).
29. P. *Promotion of Fine Arts and the Performing Arts: Analysis of the Goldsboro Art League and Plumstead Theatre Society Cases, and UBIT Considerations*, 1982 EO CPE Text, accessed January 12, 2012, http://www.irs.gov/pub/irs-tege/eotopicp82.pdf.
30. Kimberly A. Stockton and Daniel W. Wallick, "Endowment and Foundation Investing: The Challenge of Defining the Liability" (Vanguard Investment Counseling & Research, 2009), accessed December 14, 2011, https://advisors.vanguard.com/iwe/pdf/FASENF.pdf.
31. Stockton and Wallick, "Endowment and Foundation Investing."
32. Chetan Narain, "Congressman to Propose Mandating Endowment Spending," *Daily Princetonian*, October 10, 2008, accessed January 12, 2011, http://www.dailyprincetonian.com/2008/10/10/21744.
33. Peter Conti-Brown, "Scarcity Amidst Wealth: The Law, Finance, and Culture of Elite University Endowments in Financial Crisis," *Stanford Law Review*, March 6, 2011, 699–749.
34. See Peter Frumkin, *Strategic Giving: The Art and Science of Philanthropy* (Chicago: University of Chicago Press, 2006).
35. An article in *Time* magazine helps to tell the story: "Education: Rebuilding Boys Town," *Time*, August 5, 1974.

36. David Bass, *Management of Underwater Endowments Under UPMIFA: Findings of a Survey of Colleges, Universities, and Institutionally Related Foundations* (Washington, DC: AGB in partnership with Commonfund Institute and NACUBO, 2009).
37. "Universities' Financial Straits: A Moody's Retrospective," *Harvard Magazine,* June 18, 2010.
38. See, for example, Presbyterian Endowment Education & Resource Network, *Investment Policies and Guidelines* (n.d.), accessed December 14, 2011, http://www.presbyterianendowment.org/information/library/investment/investment-policies-and-guidelines.
39. Jennifer Sokolowsky, "Seattle Nonprofit Refuses Comcast Funds After Tweet Controversy," *Puget Sound Business Journal,* May 20, 2011, accessed January 12, 2012, http://www.bizjournals.com/seattle/blog/2011/05/seattle-nonprofit-refuses-comcast.html.
40. Stephanie Strom and Jim Robbins, "Montana Museum Board Breached Duty, Court Says," *The New York Times,* April 30, 2008, accessed December 14, 2011, http://www.nytimes.com/2008/04/30/us/30museum.html.
41. Bair Museum, "New Bair Museum Slated to Opening Memorial Day Weekend," press release (April 4, 2011), accessed December 14, 2011, http://www.bairfamilymuseum.org/press/20110404.aspx.
42. Eleanor Brown and Al Slivinski, "Nonprofit Organizations and the Market," in *The Nonprofit Sector: A Research Handbook,* 2nd ed., ed. Walter W. Powell and Richard Steinberg (New Haven, CT: Yale University Press, 2006), 140–158.
43. This conclusion is supported by the following discussions: Susan Rose-Ackerman, "Do Government Grants to Charity Reduce Private Donations?" in *Nonprofit Firms in a Three-Sector Economy,* ed. Michelle White (Washington, DC: Urban Institute, 1981), 95–114; and James Andreoni and A. Abigail Payne, "Do Government Grants to Private Charities Crowd Out Giving or Fundraising?" *The American Economic Review* 93, no. 3 (2003): 793–812.
44. Tuckman and Chang, "Commercial Activity, Technological Change and Nonprofit Mission."
45. Tuckman and Chang, "Commercial Activity, Technological Change and Nonprofit Mission."
46. Robert Payton, *Philanthropy: Voluntary Action for the Public Good* (New York: MacMillan, 1988).
47. For an overview discussion of the concept of charity see Frumkin, *Strategic Giving.*
48. See, for example, Jerry D. Marx and Vernon Brooks Carter, "Hispanic Charitable Giving: An Opportunity for Nonprofit Development," *Nonprofit Management & Leadership* 19, no. 2 (2008): 173–188.
49. Peter M. Blau, *Exchange and Power in Social Life* (New York: Wiley, 1964).
50. Andrew Carnegie, *The Gospel of Wealth* (1889), accessed December 14, 2011, http://carnegie.org/publications/search-publications/pub/272.
51. See Adrian Sargeant, "Using Donor Lifetime Value to Inform Fundraising Strategy," *Nonprofit Management & Leadership* 12, no. 1 (2001): 25–38; Wesley E. Lindahl and Christopher Winship, "Predictive Models for Annual Fundraising and Major Gift Fundraising," *Nonprofit Management & Leadership* 3, no. 1 (1992): 43–64; and Adrian Sargeant and Elaine Jay, *Fundraising Management: Analysis, Planning and Practice* (New York: Routledge, 2010).
52. For examples, see Karen Maru File, Russ Alan Prince, and Dianne S. P. Cermak, "Creating Trust with Major Donors: The Service Encounter Model," *Nonprofit Management & Leadership* 4, no. 3 (1994): 269–284.

53. John J. Havens, Mary A. O'Herlihy, and Paul G. Schervish, "Charitable Giving," in *The Nonprofit Sector: A Research Handbook*, 2nd ed., ed. Walter W. Powell and Richard Steinberg (New Haven, CT: Yale University Press, 2006), 542–567.
54. See Dwight Burlingame, ed., *Critical Issues in Fundraising* (Hoboken, NJ: Wiley, 1997), and in particular Julian Wolpert's chapter "The Demographics of Giving Patterns," 75–80.
55. John J. Havens and Paul G. Schervish, *Geography and Generosity: Boston and Beyond* (Boston: Boston College, Center on Wealth and Philanthropy, 2005).
56. Analysis of regional variations is based on data from the Center on Philanthropy at Indiana University, *Giving USA 2005* (Chicago: Giving USA Foundation, 2005).
57. For a YouTube video of Melinda Gates talking about her and her husband's giving and their call to government and other donors to do more, see *Melinda Gates: Rich Should Give Half* (n.d.), http://www.youtube.com/watch?v=wFyY91p_JdA&feature=relmfu.
58. Carol J. Loomis, "The $600 Billion Challenge," *Fortune*, June 16, 2010, accessed December 14, 2011, http://features.blogs.fortune.cnn.com/2010/06/16/gates-buffett-600-billion-dollar-philanthropy-challenge.
59. The Giving Pledge, Web site, accessed December 14, 2011, http://givingpledge.org/#enter.
60. Angela M. Eikenberry, "Fundraising in the New Philanthropy Environment: The Benefits and Challenges of Working with Giving Circles," *Nonprofit Management & Leadership* 19, no. 2 (2008): 141–152.
61. For more information on the history of community foundations, see Peter Dobkin Hall, "The Community Foundation in America, 1914–1987," in *Philanthropic Giving*, ed. Richard Magat (New York: Oxford University Press, 1989), 180–199.
62. See Foundation Center, *Proposal Writing Short Course* (2011), accessed December 14, 2011, http://foundationcenter.org/getstarted/tutorials/shortcourse/components.html.
63. Stanley Weinstein, *The Complete Guide to Fundraising Management*, 2nd ed. (New York: Wiley, 2002).

Chapter Seven

1. Case details are from a slide presentation and case study: Nonprofit Finance Fund, *hopeFound: Finding the Way Through Data, Discipline & Dialogue (Case Study)* (SlideShare, 2011), accessed December 14, 2011, http://www.slideshare.net/nonprofitfinancefund/hopefound-case-study. This presentation was prepared by the firm that helped the nonprofit.
2. Beth Wood, *Investigative Report: Harnett County Partnership for Children, Inc., Community Education and Programs, Inc., Lillington, North Carolina, May 2010* (Raleigh, NC: Office of State Auditor, 2010), accessed January 12, 2012, http://www.ncauditor.net/EPSWeb/Reports/Investigative/INV-2010–0357.pdf.
3. BoardSource, *The Sarbanes-Oxley Act and Implications for Nonprofit Organizations* (2006), accessed January 15, 2012, http://www.boardsource.org/clientfiles/sarbanes-oxley.pdf.
4. Board Source, *The Sarbanes-Oxley Act and Implications for Nonprofit Organizations*.
5. Francie Ostrower and Marla Bobowick, *Nonprofit Governance and the Sarbanes-Oxley Act* (Washington, DC: Urban Institute 2006), 8.

6. Rebecca Harshbarger and Brendan Scott, "State Pol Guilty of Charity Scam," *The New York Post*, January 17, 2011, accessed December 14, 2011, http://www.nypost.com/p/news/local/state_pol_guilty_of_charity_scam_8OcezPDKqKqXyrv6sAFroL.
7. Harvey Lipman and Grant Williams, "Charities Bestow No-Interest Loans on Their Well-Paid Executives," *Chronicle of Philanthropy*, February 5, 2004, accessed January 15, 2012, http://philanthropy.com/article/Charities-Bestow-No-Interest/61934.
8. See Internal Revenue Service Form 990, "Return of Organization Exempt from Income Tax," Part VI, line 13.
9. Cynthia Benzing, Evan Leach, and Charles McGee, "Sarbanes-Oxley and the New Form 990: Are Arts and Culture Nonprofits Ready?" *Nonprofit and Voluntary Sector Quarterly* 40, no. 6 (2011): 1132–1147.
10. Resources for understanding investment choices for nonprofits include Robert P. Fry Jr., *Who's Minding the Money? An Investment Guide for Nonprofit Board Members*, 2nd ed. (Washington, DC: BoardSource, 2009).
11. See Charles K. Coe, *Nonprofit Financial Management: A Practical Guide* (San Francisco: Jossey-Bass/Wiley, 2011), for more information on accounting and charts of accounts.
12. See Janet S. Greenlee, "Nonprofit Accountability in the Information Age," in *Approaching Foundations*, New Directions for Philanthropic Fundraising, no. 27, ed. Paul P. Pribbenow (San Francisco: Jossey-Bass/Wiley, 2000).
13. Richard F. Larkin and Marie DiTommasso, *Wiley Not-for-Profit GAAP 2009: Interpretation and Application of Generally Accepted Accounting Principles for Not-for-Profit Organizations* (Hoboken, NJ: Wiley, 2009).
14. Associated Press, "Over Past Decade, Some 9/11 Charities Failed Miserably," SILive, August 25, 2011, accessed January 15, 2012, http://www.silive.com/september-11/index.ssf/2011/08/over_past_decade_some_911_char.html. For a slightly different take on the AP story, see Rick Cohen, "AP Report Finds Many 9/11 Charities Failed Miserably," *Nonprofit Quarterly Newswire*, August 29, 2011, accessed January 15, 2012, http://www.nonprofitquarterly.org/index.php?option=com_content&view=article&id=15386:ap-report-finds-many-911-charities-failedmiserably&catid=155:nonprofit-newswire&Itemid=986.
15. For example, see the executive summaries of two August 2010 studies commissioned by the Direct Marketing Association Nonprofit Federation: Jessica Sowa, "Charity Rating Scales: The Challenge of Developing 'Effective' Measures of Nonprofit Organizational Effectiveness" (August 2010), accessed December 14, 2011, http://www.nonprofitfederation.org/sites/default/files/Executive_Summary_Charity_Rating_Scales.pdf; and George Mitchell, "Reframing the Discussion About Nonprofit Effectiveness" (August 2010), accessed December 14, 2011, http://www.nonprofitfederation.org/sites/default/files/Executive_Summary_Reframing_the_Discussion_about_Nonprofit_Effectiveness.pdf.
16. Joseph T. Wells, *Principles of Fraud Examinations* (Hoboken, NJ: Wiley, 2005).
17. Janet Greenlee, Mary Fischer, Teresa Gordon, and Elizabeth Keating, "Investigation of Fraud in Nonprofit Organizations: Occurrences and Deterrents," *Nonprofit and Voluntary Sector Quarterly* 36 (2007): 676.
18. Diana Aviv's September 28, 2005, testimony to the U.S. Senate Finance Committee, "Hurricane Katrina: Community Rebuilding Needs and Effectiveness of Past Proposals," is cited in Greenlee et al., "Investigation of Fraud in Nonprofit Organizations."
19. Stuart Douglas and Kim Mills, "Nonprofit Fraud: What Are the Key Indicators?" *Canadian FundRaiser*, August 16, 2000, accessed September 1, 2011, http://www.charityvillage.com/cv/research/rlegal16.html.

20. See Michael DeLucia, "Preventing Fraud: From Fiduciary Duty to Practical Strategies," *New Hampshire Bar Journal*, Summer/Autumn 2008, 6–12; also see Edward McMillan, *Preventing Fraud in Nonprofit Organizations* (Hoboken, NJ: Wiley, 2006).
21. DeLucia, "Preventing Fraud."
22. Stephanie Strom, "Funds Misappropriated at 2 Nonprofit Groups," *The New York Times*, July 9, 2008, accessed December 14, 2011, http://www.nytimes.com/2008/07/09/us/09embezzle.html?pagewanted=1.
23. Clifton Gunderson LLP, *Best Practices of Nonprofit Budgeting and Cash Forecasting* (2008), accessed December 14, 2011, http://www.cliftoncpa.com/Content/5HQ5OYA9WU.pdf?...NonprofitBudgeting.
24. John Zietlow, Jo Ann Hankin, and Alan Seidner, *Financial Management for Nonprofit Organizations* (Hoboken, NJ: Wiley, 2007), 255.
25. GuideStar Publications, *The Effect of the Economy on the Nonprofit Sector: A June 2010 Survey* (Washington, DC: GuideStar, 2009).
26. For an in-depth discussion of CGL, refer to Melanie L. Herman, "Risk Management," in *The Jossey-Bass Handbook of Nonprofit Leadership and Management*, 2nd ed., ed. Robert D. Herman & Associates (San Francisco: Jossey-Bass/Wiley, 2005), 560–584.
27. Better Business Bureau Wise Giving Alliance, *Standards for Charity Accountability* (2003), accessed January 12, 2012, http://www.bbb.org/us/Charity-Standards.
28. These figures are reported in Terrie Temkin, "Audits for Smaller Nonprofits," *Philanthropy Journal*, February 7, 2009, accessed December 14, 2011, http://www.philanthropyjournal.org/resources/managementleadership/audits-smaller-nonprofits.
29. Ostrower and Bobowick, *Nonprofit Governance and the Sarbanes-Oxley Act*.
30. Temkin, "Audits for Smaller Nonprofits."
31. Steven H. Berger, *Understanding Nonprofit Financial Statements*, 3rd ed. (Washington, DC: BoardSource, 2008), 46.
32. Berger, *Understanding Nonprofit Financial Statements*.

Chapter Eight

1. Case details are from American Heart Association, "About the Movement," *Go Red for Women* (n.d.), accessed July 5, 2011, http://www.goredforwomen.org/about_the_movement.aspx; information about the communication campaign is from Cone Communications, "AHA Go Red for Women" (n.d.), accessed July 5, 2011, http://www.coneinc.com/aha-go-red-for-women.
2. Information from the Fall 2007 Go Red For Women Database Survey, reported on American Heart Association, *Go Red for Women*.
3. See C. Whan Park and Gerald Zaltman, *Marketing Management* (New York: Dryden Press, 1987); and Alan Andreasen and Philip Kotler, *Strategic Marketing for Nonprofit Organizations* (Upper Saddle River, NJ: Pearson Prentice Hall, 2008), for the historical development of these orientations.
4. American Marketing Association, *Dictionary*, definition of *marketing* (n.d.), accessed March 10, 2010, http://www.marketingpower.com/_layouts/Dictionary.aspx?dLetter=M.
5. Philip Kotler and Sidney Levy, "Broadening the Concept of Marketing," *Journal of Marketing*, January 10–15, 1969; Philip Kotler and Gerald Zaltman, "Social Marketing: An Approach to Planned Social Change," *Journal of Marketing*, July 3–12, 1971; Benson Shapiro, "Marketing for Nonprofit Organizations," *Harvard Business Review*, September–October 1973, 223–232.

6. Paulette Padanyi, "Operationalizing the Marketing Concept: Achieving Orientation in the Nonprofit Context," in *The Routledge Companion to Nonprofit Marketing*, ed. Adrian Sargeant and Walter Wymer (New York: Routledge, 2008), 12.
7. Philip Kotler, *Marketing for Nonprofit Organizations*, 2nd ed. (Upper Saddle River, NJ: Pearson Prentice Hall, 1982), 6.
8. See Eugene Johnson and M. Venkatesan, "Marketing," in *The Nonprofit Management Handbook: Operating Policies and Procedures*, ed. Tracy Connors (Hoboken, NJ: Wiley, 1993), 132–133; Adrian Sargeant, *Marketing Management for Nonprofit Organizations* (New York: Oxford University Press, 2009); and Andreasen and Kotler, *Strategic Marketing for Nonprofit Organizations*.
9. Sargeant, *Marketing Management for Nonprofit Organizations*.
10. The term *target audience* is adopted by Andreasen and Kotler, *Strategic Marketing for Nonprofit Organizations*.
11. Andreasen and Kotler, *Strategic Marketing for Nonprofit Organizations*.
12. Johnson and Venkatesan, "Marketing."
13. Peter Brinkerhoff, "The Marketing Cycle for a Not-for-Profit," *Journal of Voluntary Sector Marketing* 2, no. 2 (1997): 168–175.
14. Sargeant, *Marketing Management for Nonprofit Organizations*.
15. Walter Wymer, Patricia Knowles, and Roger Gomes, *Nonprofit Marketing: Marketing Management for Charitable and Nongovernmental Organizations* (Thousand Oaks, CA: Sage, 2006); Andreasen and Kotler, *Strategic Marketing for Nonprofit Organizations*.
16. Wymer et al., *Nonprofit Marketing*.
17. Andreasen and Kotler, *Strategic Marketing for Nonprofit Organizations*.
18. Johnson and Venkatesan, "Marketing."
19. Ian MacMillan, "Competitive Strategies for Not-for-Profit Agencies," in *Advances in Strategic Management*, vol. 1, ed. Robert Lamb (Greenwich, CT: JAI Press, 1983), 65.
20. Michael Porter, *Competitive Strategy* (New York: Free Press, 1980).
21. Sargeant, *Marketing Management for Nonprofit Organizations*.
22. Brenda Gainer and Mel Moyer, "Marketing for Nonprofit Managers," in *The Jossey-Bass Handbook of Nonprofit Leadership & Management*, 2nd ed., Robert D. Herman & Associates (San Francisco: Jossey-Bass/Wiley, 2005), 277–309.
23. Andreasen and Kotler, *Strategic Marketing for Nonprofit Organizations*.
24. American Red Cross of Greater Indianapolis, "Services" (n.d.), accessed July 15, 2011, http://www.redcross-indy.org/Services/default.aspx.
25. Andreas M. Kaplan and Michael Haenlein, "Toward a Parsimonious Definition of Traditional and Electronic Mass Customization," *Journal of Product Innovation Management* 23, no. 2 (2006): 168–182.
26. Gb3group.com, "Mass Customization" (n.d.), accessed August 1, 2011, http://www.gb3group.com/mass-customization.php.
27. Jack Trout with Steve Rivkin, *The New Positioning: The Latest on the World's #1 Business Strategy* (New York: McGraw-Hill, 1997).
28. Andreasen and Kotler, *Strategic Marketing for Nonprofit Organizations*.
29. Wymer et al., *Nonprofit Marketing*.
30. American Marketing Association, *Dictionary*, definition of *brand* (n.d.), accessed February, 10, 2010, http://www.marketingpower.com/_layouts/Dictionary.aspx?dLetter=B.
31. Brad VanAuken, *The Brand Management Checklist: Proven Tools and Techniques for Creating Winning Brands* (Eastbourne, UK: Gardners Books, 2004).
32. Jennifer L. Aaker, "Dimensions of Brand Personality," *Journal of Marketing Research* 34, no. 3 (1997): 347–356.

33. Sargeant, *Marketing Management for Nonprofit Organizations.*
34. Sargeant, *Marketing Management for Nonprofit Organizations.*
35. Patricia Martin, *Tipping the Culture: How Engaging Millennials Will Change Things* (Chicago: LitLamp Communications, 2010).
36. Andreasen and Kotler, *Strategic Marketing for Nonprofit Organizations.*
37. See Eugene M. Johnson, Eberhard E. Scheuing, and Kathleen A. Gaida, *Profitable Service Marketing* (Homewood, IL: Dow-Jones-Irwin, 1986); Valarie A. Zeithaml, A. Parasuraman, and Leonard L. Berry, "Problems and Strategies in Service Marketing," *Journal of Marketing* 49, no. 2 (1985): 33–46.
38. Assessing perceived service quality can be quite complex if done well. See Sargeant, *Marketing Management for Nonprofit Organizations,* for a discussion of various techniques.
39. Philip Kotler and Nancy Lee, *Social Marketing: Influencing Behaviors for Good* (Thousand Oaks, CA: Sage, 2008).
40. Andreasen and Kotler, *Strategic Marketing for Nonprofit Organizations.*
41. Leah King, "Using the Internet to Facilitate and Support Health Behaviors," *Social Marketing Quarterly* 10, no. 2 (2004): 72–78.
42. Office of National Drug Control Policy, "National Youth Anti-Drug Media Campaign," accessed January 18, 2012, http://www.whitehouse.gov/ondcp/anti-drug-media-campaign.
43. Brenda Gainer and Mel Moyer, "Marketing for Nonprofit Managers," in *The Jossey-Bass Handbook of Nonprofit Leadership & Management,* 2nd ed., Robert D. Herman & Associates (San Francisco: Jossey-Bass/Wiley, 2005), 277–309.
44. World Bank, "World Development Indicators" (last updated July 28, 2011), accessed July 30, 2011, http://www.google.com/publicdata/explore?ds=d5bncppjof8f9_&met_y=it_net_user_p2&idim=country:USA&dl=en&hl=en&q=internet+usage.
45. Wymer et al., *Nonprofit Marketing.*
46. Wymer et al., *Nonprofit Marketing.*
47. Kotler and Lee, *Social Marketing.*
48. L. Gordon Crovitz, "Egypt's Revolution by Social Media: Facebook and Twitter Let the People Keep Ahead of the Regime," *The Wall Street Journal,* February 14, 2011.
49. Kotler and Lee, *Social Marketing.*
50. Wymer et al., *Nonprofit Marketing.*
51. BlacksAcademy.net, "Cost-Based Pricing" (n.d.), accessed August 1, 2011, http://www.blacksacademy.net/content/4001.html.
52. Wymer et al., *Nonprofit Marketing.*
53. Andreasen and Kotler, *Strategic Marketing for Nonprofit Organizations.*

Chapter Nine

1. Case details are from J. E. Austin, Elaine V. Backman, Paul Barese, and Stephanie Woerner, *The NAACP,* Harvard Business School Case 9-398-039, November 7, 1997.
2. Francie Ostrower and Melissa M. Stone, "Governance: Research Trends, Gaps, and Future Prospects," in *The Nonprofit Sector: A Research Handbook,* 2nd ed., ed. Walter W. Powell and Richard Steinberg (New Haven, CT: Yale University Press, 2006), 612–628; Ruth McCambridge, "Underestimating the Power of Nonprofit Governance," *Nonprofit and Voluntary Sector Quarterly* 33, no. 2 (2004): 346–354.

3. Rikki Abzug and Joseph Galaskiewicz, "Nonprofit Boards: Crucibles of Expertise or Symbols of Local Identities?" *Nonprofit and Voluntary Sector Quarterly* 30, no. 1 (2001): 51–73.
4. BoardSource, *The Nonprofit Board Answer Book*, 2nd ed. (San Francisco, Jossey-Bass, 2007).
5. BoardSource, *The Nonprofit Board Answer Book*.
6. N. Ono, "Boards of Directors Under Fire: An Examination of Nonprofit Board Duties in the Health Care Environment," *Annals of Health Law* 7, no. 3 (1998): 107–138.
7. Ono, "Boards of Directors Under Fire."
8. Ono, "Boards of Directors Under Fire."
9. Ono, "Boards of Directors Under Fire."
10. Jeremy Benjamin, "Reinvigorating Nonprofit Directors' Duty of Obedience," *Cardozo Law Review* 30, no. 4 (2009): 1677–1708.
11. Benjamin, "Reinvigorating Nonprofit Directors' Duty of Obedience."
12. Michael J. Worth provides a useful discussion of Sarbanes-Oxley in *Nonprofit Management: Principles and Practices* (Thousand Oaks, CA: Sage, 2009).
13. Others commenting on board effectiveness include Michael Klausner and Jonathan Small "Failing to Govern? The Disconnect Between Theory and Reality in Nonprofit Boards and How To Fix It," *Stanford Social Innovation Review* 43 (Spring 2005): 42–49.
14. John Carver, *Boards That Make a Difference: A New Design for Leadership in Nonprofit and Public Organizations*, 3rd ed. (San Francisco: Jossey-Bass/Wiley, 2006).
15. Richard Chait, William P. Ryan, and Barbara E. Taylor, *Governance as Leadership: Reframing the Work of Nonprofit Boards* (San Francisco: Jossey-Bass/Wiley, 2005).
16. Miriam M. Wood, "Is Governing Behavior Cyclical?" *Nonprofit Management & Leadership* 3, no. 2 (1992): 139–163; David O. Renz, "Leadership, Governance, and the Work of the Board," in *The Jossey-Bass Handbook of Nonprofit Leadership and Management*, 3rd ed., David O. Renz and Associates (San Francisco: Jossey-Bass/Wiley, 2010), 125–156.
17. Ostrower and Stone, "Governance."
18. Austin et al., *The NAACP*.
19. For a fresh treatment of Miriam Wood's model (described in Wood, "Is Governing Behavior Cyclical?"), see Julia Classen, "Here We Go Again: The Cyclical Nature of Board Behavior," *Nonprofit Quarterly*, Spring 2011, 16–21.
20. See BoardSource, *Assessment Tools* (n.d.), http://www.boardsource.org/Assessments/selfassessments.asp, for descriptions of BoardSource materials.
21. Larry Slesinger, *Self-Assessment for Nonprofit Governing Boards* (Washington, DC: National Center for Nonprofit Boards, 1996).
22. Douglas K. Jackson and Thomas P. Holland, "Measuring the Effectiveness of Nonprofit Boards, *Nonprofit and Voluntary Sector Quarterly* 27, no. 2 (1998): 159–182; Mel Gill, Robert J. Flynn, and Elke Reissing, "The Governance Self-Assessment Checklist: An Instrument for Assessing Board Effectiveness," *Nonprofit Management & Leadership* 15, no. 3 (2005): 271–294.
23. In an exploratory study Kevin Kearns found that board chairs and executive directors weighted criteria differently when comparing the effectiveness of board members: "Effective Nonprofit Board Members as Seen by Executives and Board Chairs," *Nonprofit Management & Leadership* 5, no. 4 (1995): 337–358.
24. Ostrower and Stone, "Governance." Also see William A. Brown, "Exploring the Association Between Board and Organizational Performance in Nonprofit Organizations," *Nonprofit Management & Leadership* 15, no. 3 (2005): 317–339.

25. Jeffrey L. Callen, April Klein, and Daniel Tinkelman, "Board Composition, Committees, and Organizational Efficiency: The Case of Nonprofits," *Nonprofit and Voluntary Sector Quarterly* 32, no. 4 (2003): 493–520.
26. Mayer N. Zald, "Urban Differentiation, Characteristics of Boards of Directors, and Organizational Effectiveness," *American Journal of Sociology* 73, no. 3 (1967): 261–272; Jeffrey Pfeffer and Gerald R. Salancik, *The External Control of Organizations: A Resource Dependence Perspective* (Stanford, CA: Stanford University Press, 2003; originally published 1978).
27. Jeffrey L. Brudney and Patricia Dautel Nobbie, "Training Policy Governance in Nonprofit Boards of Directors," *Nonprofit Management & Leadership* 12, no. 4 (2002): 387–408.
28. Julie I. Siciliano, "The Relationship Between Formal Planning and Performance in Nonprofit Organizations," *Nonprofit Management & Leadership* 7, no. 4 (1996), 387–403.
29. Pat Bradshaw, Vic Murray, and Jacob Wolpin, "Do Nonprofit Boards Make a Difference? An Exploration of the Relationship Among Board Structure, Process, and Effectiveness," *Nonprofit and Voluntary Sector Quarterly* 21, no. 3 (1992): 227–249.
30. Bradshaw et al., "Do Nonprofit Boards Make a Difference?"
31. David E. Olson, "Agency Theory in the Not-for-Profit Sector: Its Role at Independent Colleges," *Nonprofit and Voluntary Sector Quarterly* 29, no. 2 (2000): 280–296.
32. Pablo de Andrés-Alonso, Natalia Martin Cruz, and M. Elena Romero-Merino, "The Governance of Nonprofit Organizations: Empirical Evidence from Nongovernmental Development Organizations in Spain," *Nonprofit and Voluntary Sector Quarterly* 35, no. 4 (2006): 588–604.
33. Jack C. Green and Donald W. Griesinger, "Board Performance and Organizational Effectiveness in Nonprofit Social Services Organizations," *Nonprofit Management & Leadership* 6, no. 4 (1996): 381–402; Brown, "Exploring the Association Between Board and Organizational Performance in Nonprofit Organizations."
34. The following articles are among the discussions that have informed the debate on the importance of a board to nonprofit effectiveness: Brown, "Exploring the Association Between Board and Organizational Performance in Nonprofit Organizations"; Robert D. Herman and David O. Renz, "Board Practices of Especially Effective and Less Effective Local Nonprofit Organizations," *American Review of Public Administration* 30, no. 2 (2000): 146–160; Katherine O'Regan and Sharon M. Oster, "Does the Structure and Composition of the Board Matter? The Case of Nonprofit Organizations," *Journal of Law, Economics & Organization* 21, no. 1 (2005): 205–227.
35. Richard P. Chait, Thomas P. Holland, and Barbara E. Taylor, *Improving the Performance of Governing Boards* (Phoenix, AZ: Oryx Press, 1996).
36. Thomas P. Holland, "Board Accountability: Lessons from the Field," *Nonprofit Management & Leadership* 12, no. 4 (2002): 409–428.
37. See, for example, Maureen K. Robinson, *Nonprofit Boards That Work: The End of One-Size-Fits-All Governance* (Hoboken, NJ: Wiley, 2001); and Candace Widmer and Susan Houchin, *The Art of Trusteeship: The Nonprofit Board Member's Guide to Effective Governance* (San Francisco: Jossey-Bass/Wiley, 2000).
38. See Lex Donaldson, *The Contingency Theory of Organizations* (Thousand Oaks, CA: Sage, 2001), for a summary of contingency theory.
39. Patricia Bradshaw, "A Contingency Approach to Nonprofit Governance," *Nonprofit Management & Leadership* 20, no. 1 (2009). 61–81.

40. Brudney and Nobbie, "Training Policy Governance in Nonprofit Boards of Directors," find that Carver's policy governance model is less likely to be successfully implemented in organizations with more than fifteen board members and where the board members also function as staff.
41. Georg von Schnurbein, "Patterns of Governance Structures in Trade Associations and Unions," *Nonprofit Management & Leadership* 20, no. 1 (2009): 97–115.
42. For an overview of board diversity and inclusion issues, see William A. Brown, "Inclusive Governance Practices in Nonprofit Organizations and Implications for Practice," *Nonprofit Management & Leadership* 12, no. 4 (2002): 369–385.
43. See, for example, D. Mark Austin and Cynthia Woolever, "Voluntary Association Boards: A Reflection of Member and Community Characteristics," *Nonprofit and Voluntary Sector Quarterly* 21, no. 2 (1992): 181–193.
44. Abzug and Galaskiewicz, "Nonprofit Boards."
45. Ostrower and Stone, "Governance"; Francie Ostrower, *Nonprofit Governance in the United States: Findings on Performance and Accountability from the First National Representative Study* (Washington, DC: Urban Institute, 2007).
46. Abzug and Galaskiewicz, "Nonprofit Boards."
47. Mary Tschirhart, Kira Kristal Reed, Sarah J. Freeman, and Alison Louie Anker, "Who Serves? Predicting Placement of Management Graduates on Nonprofit, Government, and Business Boards," *Nonprofit and Voluntary Sector Quarterly* 38, no. 6 (2009): 1076–1085.
48. Abzug and Galaskiewicz, "Nonprofit Boards."
49. See Bron Afon Community Housing, *Board Member Recruitment* (n.d.), accessed December 17, 2011, http://www.bronafon.org.uk/Home/Workingwithus/BoardMemberrecruitment/tabid/623/Default.aspx.
50. See the Revised Model Nonprofit Corporation Act (1987) at http://www.muridae.com/nporegulation/documents/model_npo_corp_act.html.
51. William A. Brown and Joel O. Iverson, "Exploring Strategy and Board Structure in Nonprofit Organizations," *Nonprofit and Voluntary Sector Quarterly* 33, no. 3 (2004): 377–400.
52. David O. Renz, "Reframing Governance," *Nonprofit Quarterly*, Winter 2010, 50–53.
53. Judy Freiwirth, "Community-Engagement Governance: Systems-Wide Governance in Action," *Nonprofit Quarterly*, Spring 2011, 40–50.

Chapter Ten

1. Case details are from HR Council for the Nonprofit Sector, "Workplaces That Work, Case Study #2: Santropol Roulant" (n.d.), accessed December 21, 2011, http://hrcouncil.ca/hr-toolkit/santropol-case-study.cfm.
2. *Santropol Roulant—Leadership and Transitions*, video posted by The J. W. McConnell Family Foundation (June 2008), accessed December 21, 2011, http://www.mcconnellfoundation.ca/en/resources/multimedia/video/santropol-roulant-leadership-and-transitions.
3. Wendy Reid and Rekha Karambayya, "Impact of Dual Executive Leadership Dynamics in Creative Organizations," *Human Relations* 62 (2009): 1073–1112.
4. Gary M. Romano, "Dual-Executive Structures in Religious Non-Profit Organizations" (master's thesis, Virginia Polytechnic Institute and State University, June 1995); Reid and Karambayya, "Impact of Dual Executive Leadership Dynamics in Creative Organizations."

5. Patricia Yancey Martin, "Rethinking Feminist Organizations," *Gender & Society* 4, no. 2 (1990): 182–206.
6. Katherine Kang-Ning Chen, *Enabling Creative Chaos: The Organization Behind the Burning Man Event* (Chicago: University of Chicago Press, 2009).
7. Robert D. Herman and Richard D. Heimovics, "Executive Leadership," in *The Jossey-Bass Handbook of Nonprofit Leadership and Management*, 2nd ed., ed. Robert D. Herman & Associates (San Francisco: Jossey-Bass/Wiley, 2005), 153–170; Robert D. Herman and Richard D. Heimovics, *Executive Leadership in Nonprofit Organizations: New Strategies for Shaping Executive-Board Dynamics* (San Francisco: Jossey-Bass/Wiley, 1991).
8. Herman and Heimovics "Executive Leadership."
9. Arnold J. Olenick and Philip R. Olenick, *A Nonprofit Organization Operating Manual: Planning for Survival and Growth* (New York: Foundation Center, 1991); Michael J. Worth, *Nonprofit Management: Principles and Practices* (Thousand Oaks, CA: Sage, 2009).
10. BoardSource, *The Source: Twelve Principles of Governance That Power Exceptional Boards* (Washington, DC: BoardSource, 2005), cited in Worth, *Nonprofit Management: Principles.*
11. John Kotter, "What Leaders Really Do," *Harvard Business Review*, May–June 1990, 103–111.
12. James M. Kouzes and Barry Z. Posner, *The Leadership Challenge*, 4th ed. (San Francisco: Jossey-Bass/Wiley, 2007).
13. Shahryar Minhas and Susan Parker, "The Robert Wood Johnson Foundation" (Center for Effective Philanthropy, n.d.), accessed December 21, 2011, http://www.effectivephilanthropy.org/assets/pdfs/CEP_RobertWoodJohnson_RepeatCase.pdf.
14. To listen to the speech go to Internet Archive, http://www.archive.org/details/MLKDream.
15. See HR Council for the Nonprofit Sector, "Keeping the Right People: Employee Recognition" (n.d.), accessed December 21, 2011, http://hrcouncil.ca/hr-toolkit/keeping-people-employee-recognition.cfm, for this list as well as other resources on employee recognition.
16. Gary A. Yukl, *Leadership in Organizations*, 2nd ed. (Upper Saddle River, NJ: Pearson Prentice Hall, 1989).
17. Angelo J. Kinicki, Peter W. Hom, Melanie R. Trost, and Kim J. Wade, "Effects of Category Prototypes on Performance-Rating Accuracy," *Journal of Applied Psychology* 80, no. 3 (1995): 354–370.
18. See David C. Hammack, *Making the Nonprofit Sector in the United States* (Bloomington: Indiana University Press, 1998).
19. For a review of labor in the United States see Laura Leete, "Work in the Nonprofit Sector," in *The Nonprofit Sector: A Research Handbook*, ed. Walter W. Powell and Richard Steinberg (New Haven, CT: Yale University Press), 159–179. For a discussion of the underrepresentation of women in nonprofits in Norway, see Dag Wollebaek and Per Selle, "The Role of Women in the Transformation of the Organizational Society in Norway," *Nonprofit and Voluntary Sector Quarterly* 33, no. 3, suppl. (2004): 120S–144S.
20. Jerald Greenberg and Robert A. Baron, *Behavior in Organizations*, 5th ed. (Upper Saddle River, NJ: Pearson Prentice Hall, 1995).
21. Debra L. Nelson and James Campbell Quick, *Organizational Behavior: Foundations, Realities, and Challenges*, 4th ed. (Mason, OH: South-Western/Cengage Learning, 2003).
22. Kouzes and Posner, *The Leadership Challenge.*

23. See Ray & Berndtson, *Successful Leaders in the Nonprofit Sector: Ten Qualities for Top Performance* (2005), accessed December 21, 2011, http://www.odgersberndtson.ca/fileadmin/uploads/canada/Documents/PDFs/NonProfitE.pdf.
24. Fred E. Fiedler and Martin M. Chemers, *Leadership and Effective Management* (Glenview, IL: Scott, Foresman, 1974); the path-goal theory advances Fiedler's earlier work. See also Chester Schriesman and Mary Ann Von Glinow, "The Path-Goal Theory of Leadership: A Theoretical and Empirical Analysis," *Academy of Management Journal* 20, no. 3 (1977): 398–405, for research support for employing task-focused leadership in ambiguous task situations.
25. Paul Hersey, Kenneth H. Blanchard, and Dewey E. Johnson, *Management of Organizational Behavior* (Upper Saddle River, NJ: Pearson Prentice Hall, 2008).
26. James MacGregor Burns, *Leadership* (New York: HarperCollins, 1978).
27. Erich Fromm, "Selfishness and Self-Love," *Psychiatry* 2 (1939): 507–523; Carl R. Rogers, *On Becoming a Person* (Boston: Houghton Mifflin, 1961).
28. Barry Cross Jr., "Perspective Then and Now: Making the Invisible Visible," *Diversity Factor* 16, no. 2 (2008): 9–15.
29. Frances Hesselbein and Alan Shrader, *Leader to Leader 2: Enduring Insights on Leadership* (San Francisco: Jossey-Bass/Wiley, 2008), xii.
30. Robert E. Quinn, "Building the Bridge as You Walk on It," *Leader to Leader* 34 (2004): 21–26.
31. Kouzes and Posner, *The Leadership Challenge*, 212.
32. "MADD as Hell and Not Going to Take It Anymore," *Broadcasting*, April 1985, 58.
33. Hyejin Bang, "Leader-Member Exchange in Nonprofit Sports Organizations: The Impact on Job Satisfaction and Intention to Stay from the Perspectives of Volunteer Leaders and Followers," *Nonprofit Management & Leadership* 22, no. 1 (2011): 85–106.
34. Carole L. Jurkiewicz and Tom K. Massey Jr., "The Influence of Ethical Reasoning on Leader Effectiveness," *Nonprofit Management & Leadership* 9, no. 2 (1998): 173–186.
35. Thomas H. Jeavons, "When the Management Is the Message: Relating Values to Management Practice in Nonprofit Organizations," *Nonprofit Management & Leadership* 2, no. 4 (1992): 403–417.
36. Daniel Goleman, "Leadership That Gets Results," *Harvard Business Review*, March–April 2000, 78–90.
37. See Patricia St. Onge et al., *Embracing Cultural Competency: A Roadmap for Nonprofit Capacity Builders* (Nashville, TN: Fieldstone Alliance, 2009).
38. CompassPoint Nonprofit Services, *Multicultural Organizational Development in Nonprofit Organizations: Lessons from the Cultural Competence Learning Initiative* (2010), accessed October 5, 2011, http://www.compasspoint.org/sites/default/files/docs/research/CP%20Cultural%20Competence%20Lessons%20FINAL%20RPT.pdf.
39. Lee G. Bolman and Terrence E. Deal, *Reframing Organizations: Artistry, Choice, and Leadership*, 3rd ed. (San Francisco: Jossey-Bass/Wiley, 2003).
40. Herman and Heimovics, "Executive Leadership."
41. Robert Hooijberg and Robert E. Quinn, "Behavioral Complexity and the Development of Effective Managers," in *Strategic Leadership: A Multiorganizational-Level Perspective*, ed. Robert L. Phillips and James G. Hunt (Westport, CT: Quorum Books/Greenwood, 1992), 161–175.
42. Robert E. Quinn, Sue R. Faerman, Michael P. Thompson, Michael McGrath, and Lynda S. St. Clair, *Becoming a Master Manager: A Competing Values Approach*, 5th ed. (Hoboken, NJ: Wiley, 2011).

43. John R. P. French Jr. and Bertram Raven, "The Bases of Social Power," in *Studies in Social Power*, ed. Dorwin Cartwright (Ann Arbor, MI: Institute for Social Research, 1959), 150–167.
44. Kelly E. See, Elizabeth W. Morrison, Naomi B. Rothman, and Jack B. Soll, "The Detrimental Effects of Power on Confidence, Advice Taking, and Accuracy," *Organizational Behavior and Human Decision Processes* 116, no. 2 (2011): 272–285.
45. David A. Whetten and Kim S. Cameron, *Developing Management Skills*, 5th ed. (Upper Saddle River, NJ: Pearson Prentice Hall, 2002).
46. Rosabeth Moss Kanter, "Power Failures in Management Circuits," *Harvard Business Review*, July–August 1979, 65–75.
47. French and Raven, "The Bases of Social Power."
48. Whetten and Cameron, *Developing Management Skills*.
49. Michael Duffy, "Resignation Charity Begins at Home," *Time*, June 24, 2001, accessed December 21, 2011, http://www.time.com/time/magazine/article/0,9171,159170,00.html.
50. David Kipnis, "Psychology and Behavioral Technology," *American Psychologist* 42 (1987): 30–36.
51. Ideas on neutralization are taken from Whetten and Cameron, *Developing Management Skills*.
52. John W. Gardner, *On Leadership* (New York: Free Press, 1990); Alfred Vernis, Maria Iglesias, Beatriz Sanz, and Angel Saz-Carranza, *Nonprofit Organizations: Challenges and Collaboration* (New York: Palgrave Macmillan, 2006).
53. Shirley Sagawa and Deborah Jospin, *The Charismatic Organization: Eight Ways to Grow a Nonprofit That Builds Buzz, Delights Donors, and Energizes Employees* (San Francisco: Jossey Bass/Wiley, 2009).
54. Stephen R. Block and Steven Rosenberg, "Toward an Understanding of Founder's Syndrome: An Assessment of Power and Privilege Among Founders of Nonprofit Organizations," *Nonprofit Management & Leadership* 12, no. 4 (2002): 353–368.
55. L. David Brown and Archana Kalegaonkar, "Support Organizations and the Evolution of the NGO Sector," *Nonprofit and Voluntary Sector Quarterly* 31, no. 2 (2002): 231–258.
56. Susan M. Chambre and Naomi Fatt, "Beyond the Liability of Newness: Nonprofit Organizations in an Emerging Policy Domain," *Nonprofit and Voluntary Sector Quarterly* 31, no. 4 (2002): 502–524.
57. Miriam M. Wood, "Is Governing Behavior Cyclical?" *Nonprofit Management & Leadership* 3, no. 2 (1992): 139–163.
58. In addition to Vernis et al., *Nonprofit Organizations*, see Mary Tschirhart, *Artful Leadership* (Bloomington: Indiana University Press, 1996); and Wilfred H. Drath and Charles J. Palus, *Making Common Sense: Leadership as Meaning-Making in a Community of Practice* (Greensboro, NC: CCL Press, 1994).
59. Sonia Ospina, Bethany Godsoe, and Ellen Schall, "Co-Producing Knowledge: Practitioners and Scholars Working Together to Understand Leadership," in *Building Leadership Bridges*, ed. Cynthia Cherrey and Larraine R. Matusak (New York: International Leadership Association, 2002), 59–67.
60. Vernis et al., *Nonprofit Organizations*.
61. Karen Froelich, Gregory McKee, and Richard Rathge, "Succession Planning in Nonprofit Organizations," *Nonprofit Management & Leadership* 22, no. 1 (2011): 3–20.

62. Michael Allison, "Into the Fire: Boards and Executive Transitions," *Nonprofit Management & Leadership* 12, no. 4 (2002): 341–351.
63. Allison, "Into the Fire."
64. Mary Tschirhart, Kira Kristal Reed, Sarah J. Freeman, and Alison Louie Anker, "Is the Grass Greener? Sector Shifting and Choice of Sector by MPA and MBA Graduates," *Nonprofit and Voluntary Sector Quarterly* 37, no. 4 (2008): 668–688.
65. Roseanne M. Mirabella, *Nonprofit Management Education: Current Offerings in University-Based Programs* (Seton Hall University, 2009), http://academic.shu.edu/npo.
66. Jeanne Bell, Richard Moyers, and Timothy Wolfred, *Daring to Lead 2006: A National Study of Nonprofit Executive Leadership* (San Francisco: CompassPoint Nonprofit Services, 2006).
67. Thomas J. Tierney, "The Leadership Deficit," *Stanford Social Innovation Review*, Summer 2006, 26–35.
68. See Josh Solomon and Yarrow Sandahl, *Stepping Up or Stepping Out: A Report on the Readiness of Next Generation Nonprofit Leaders* (New York: Young Nonprofit Professionals Network, 2007). Also see Marla Cornelius, Patrick Corvington, and Albert Ruesga, *Ready to Lead? Next Generation Leaders Speak Out* (San Francisco: CompassPoint Nonprofit Services with the Annie E. Casey Foundation, the Meyer Foundation, and Idealist.org, 2008).
69. Janet L. Johnson, "The Nonprofit Leadership Deficit: A Case for More Optimism," *Nonprofit Management & Leadership* 19, no. 3 (2009): 285–304.
70. For examples see Drew A. Dolan, "Training Needs of Administrators in the Nonprofit Sector: What Are They and How Should We Address Them?" *Nonprofit Management & Leadership* 12, no. 3 (2002): 277–292; and Michael O'Neill and Kathleen Fletcher, eds., *Nonprofit Management Education: U.S. and World Perspectives* (New York: Praeger. 1998).
71. Mary Tschirhart, "Nonprofit Management Education: Recommendations Drawn from Three Stakeholder Groups," in *Nonprofit Management Education: U.S. and World Perspectives*, ed. Michael O'Neill and Kathleen Fletcher (New York: Praeger, 1998), 62–80.
72. For example, see Terence Jackson, "A Critical Cross-Cultural Perspective for Developing Nonprofit International Management Capacity," *Nonprofit Management & Leadership* 19, no. 4 (2009): 443–466.

Chapter Eleven

1. Case details are from HR Council for the Nonprofit Sector, "Workplaces That Work, Case Study #3: Big Brothers Big Sisters—Edmonton" (n.d.), accessed December 21, 2011, http://hrcouncil.ca/hr-toolkit/BBBS_Casestudy.cfm.
2. Big Brothers Big Sisters: Edmonton & Area, "History" (2010), accessed December 22, 2011, http://www.bbbsedmonton.org/ABOUT/History/tabid/60/Default.aspx.
3. *Big Brothers Big Sisters: Edmonton & Area*, video posted by HR Council for the Nonprofit Sector (2008), accessed December 22, 2011, http://www.youtube.com/watch?v=9rkPfHK8cP4.
4. Agency for Healthcare Research and Quality, *Medical Expenditure Panel Survey* (July 2011), accessed December 22, 2011, http://www.meps.ahrq.gov/mepsweb/survey_comp/Insurance.jsp.

5. Rick Cohen, "HHS Data: Nonprofit Jobs Picture Mixed, Faster Job Growth Than in For-Profit Sector, Small Nonprofits Hit Hard by Recession," *Nonprofit Quarterly*, October 5, 2011, accessed December 22, 2011, http://www.nonprofitquarterly.org/index.php?option=com_content&view=article&id=16496:hhs-data-nonprofit-jobs-picture-mixed-faster-job-growth-than-in-for-profit-sector-small-nonprofits-hit-hard-by-recession&catid=153:features&Itemid=336.
6. Venture Philanthropy Partners, *Greater Than the Sum of Its Parts, Part 1: A Regional Perspective on Changing Demographics* (January 2009), accessed December 22, 2011, http://www.vppartners.org/sites/default/files/reports/VPP-Greater-than-the-Sum.pdf.
7. Joseph P. Tierney and Jean Baldwin Grossman, with Nancy L. Resch, *Making a Difference: An Impact Study of Big Brothers Big Sisters* (Philadelphia: Public/Private Ventures, 2000), accessed December 22, 2011, http://www.ppv.org/ppv/publications/assets/111_publication.pdf.
8. Laura Leete, "Work in the Nonprofit Sector," in *The Nonprofit Sector: A Research Handbook*, 2nd ed., ed. Walter W. Powell and Richard Steinberg (New Haven, CT: Yale University Press, 2006), 159–179.
9. Donileen Loseke, *The Battered Woman and Shelters: The Social Construction of Wife Abuse* (Albany: State University of New York Press, 1992).
10. Woods Bowman, "The Economic Value of Volunteers to Nonprofit Organizations," *Nonprofit Management & Leadership* 19, no. 4 (2009): 491–506.
11. Femida Handy and Narasimhan Srinivasan, "The Demand for Volunteer Labor: A Study of Hospital Volunteers," *Nonprofit and Voluntary Sector Quarterly* 34, no, 4 (2005): 491–509.
12. Bowman, "The Economic Value of Volunteers to Nonprofit Organizations," 504.
13. Jeffrey L. Brudney, "Designing and Managing Volunteer Programs," in *The Jossey-Bass Handbook of Nonprofit Leadership and Management*, 2nd ed., ed. Robert D. Herman & Associates (San Francisco: Jossey-Bass/Wiley, 2005), 310–344.
14. Susan N. Houseman, "Why Employers Use Flexible Staffing Arrangements: Evidence from an Establishment Survey," *Industrial and Labor Relations Review* 55, no. 1 (2001): 149–170; Mary Tschirhart and Lois R. Wise, "U.S. Nonprofit Organizations' Demand for Temporary Foreign Professionals," *Nonprofit Management & Leadership* 18, no, 2 (2007): 121–140; Arne L. Kalleberg, "Nonstandard Employment Relations: Part-Time, Temporary and Contract Work," *Annual Review of Sociology* 26 (2003): 341–365.
15. Joan E. Pynes, *Human Resources Management for Public and Nonprofit Organizations* (San Francisco: Jossey-Bass/Wiley, 1997).
16. Stephen Almond and Jeremy Kendall, "Taking the Employees' Perspective Seriously: An Initial United Kingdom Cross-Sectoral Comparison," *Nonprofit and Voluntary Sector Quarterly* 29, no, 2 (2000): 205–231.
17. James W. Shepard Jr., *Strengthening Leadership and Human Resource Capacity in the Nonprofit Sector: Pro Bono as a Powerful Solution: National Research Findings* (San Francisco: Taproot Foundation, n.d.), accessed December 22, 2011, http://www.taprootfoundation.org/docs/Taproot-Strengthening-Leadership-HR-Capacity.pdf.
18. For good ideas see Mary R. Watson and Rikki Abzug, "Finding the Ones You Want, Keeping the Ones You Find," in *The Jossey-Bass Handbook of Nonprofit Leadership and Management*, 2nd ed., ed. Robert D. Herman & Associates (San Francisco: Jossey-Bass/Wiley, 2005), 623–659.

19. See Michael A. Zottoli and John P. Wanous, "Recruitment Source Research: Current Status and Future Directions," *Human Resource Management Review* 10 (2000): 353–382, for a review of research on recruitment sources.
20. Pynes, *Human Resources Management for Public and Nonprofit Organizations*.
21. Pynes, *Human Resources Management for Public and Nonprofit Organizations*.
22. For reviews of the literature on fit see Amy L. Kristof-Brown, Ryan D. Zimmerman, and Erin C. Johnson, "Consequences of Individuals' Fit at Work: A Meta-Analysis of Person-Job, Person-Organization, Person-Group, and Person-Supervisor Fit," *Personnel Psychology* 58, no. 2 (2005): 281–342; and Benjamin Schneider, "Fits About Fit," *Applied Psychology* 50, no. 1 (2001): 141–152.
23. The example comes from Lawrence Kleiman, *Human Resource Management*, 2nd ed. (Mason, OH: South-Western/Cengage Learning, 2000).
24. The examples come from Rebecca Leaman, "Crowdsourcing: How Business and Nonprofits Tap into the Wisdom of Crowds" (June 11, 2008), accessed December 22, 2011, http://www.wildapricot.com/blogs/newsblog/2008/06/11/crowdsourcing-how-business-and-nonprofits-tap-into-the-wisdom-of-crowds.
25. Tschirhart and Wise, "U.S. Nonprofit Organizations' Demand for Temporary Foreign Professionals."
26. Eric Frazier and Kerry Hall, "United Way's Challenge: Rebuilding a Region's Trust," *Charlotte Observer*, August 27, 2008, accessed December 22, 2011, http://www.charlotteobserver.com/2008/08/27/153812/united-ways-challenge-rebuilding.html.
27. Barbara Benson, "Pay Scandal Shakes Nonprofit's Board," *Crain's New York Business*, September 12, 2011, accessed December 22, 2011, http://www.crainsnewyork.com/article/20110912/FREE/110919989.
28. Denise M. Rousseau, *Psychological Contracts in Organizations: Understanding Written and Unwritten Agreements* (Thousand Oaks, CA: Sage, 1995). For a discussion of the applicability of psychological contracts to volunteers see Steven M. Farmer and Donald B. Fedor, "Volunteer Participation and Withdrawal: A Psychological Perspective on the Role of Expectations and Organizational Support," *Nonprofit Management & Leadership* 9, no. 4 (1999): 349–368.
29. Matthew A. Liao-Troth, "Attitude Differences Between Paid Workers and Volunteers," *Nonprofit Management & Leadership* 11, no. 4 (2001): 423–442.
30. A detailed discussion of strategy-based performance management systems can be found in Dick Grote, *The Performance Appraisal Question and Answer Book: A Survival Guide for Managers* (New York: AMACOM, 2002). For a summary of Grote's system and guidelines for giving feedback, see Robert E. Quinn, Sue R. Faerman, Michael P. Thompson, Michael McGrath, and Lynda S. St. Clair, *Becoming a Master Manager: A Competing Values Approach*, 5th ed. (Hoboken, NJ: Wiley, 2011), 60–63.
31. John P. Wanous, Arnon E. Reichers, and S. D. Malik, "Organization Socialization and Group Development Toward an Integrative Perspective," *Academy of Management Review* 9 (1984): 674.
32. Martin E. Purcell and Murray Hawtin, "Piloting External Peer Review as a Model for Performance Improvement in Third-Sector Organizations," *Nonprofit Management & Leadership* 20, no. 3 (2010): 357–374.
33. For a discussion of these programs see Ben Cairns, Margaret Harris, Romayne Hutchison, and Mike Tricker, "Improving Performance? The Adoption and Implementation of Quality Systems in U.K. Nonprofits," *Nonprofit Management & Leadership* 16, no. 1 (2005): 135–151.

34. Gina Imperato, "How to Give Good Feedback," *Fast Company*, August 31, 1998, accessed December 22, 2011, http://www.fastcompany.com/magazine/17/feedback.html.
35. Charles S. Jacob, *Management Rewired: Why Feedback Doesn't Work and Other Surprising Lessons from the Latest Brain Science* (New York: Penguin, 2009), cited in Quinn et al., *Becoming a Master Manager*, 60.
36. CompassPoint Nonprofit Services, *Executive Coaching Project: Evaluation of Findings*, study conducted by Harder+Company Community Research (2003), accessed December 22, 2011, http://www.compasspoint.org/sites/default/files/docs/research/2_cpcoachingexecsumm.pdf.
37. Robert L. Fischer and David Beimers, "Put Me In, Coach: A Pilot Evaluation of Executive Coaching in the Nonprofit Sector," *Nonprofit Management & Leadership* 19, no. 4 (2009): 507–522.
38. Leete, "Work in the Nonprofit Sector."
39. Terrie Temkin, "Nonprofit Salaries in 2010," *Philanthropy Journal*, July 26, 2010, accessed December 22, 2011, http://www.philanthropyjournal.org/resources/managementleadership/nonprofit-salaries-2010.
40. Anna Hayley-Lock and Jean Kruzich, "Serving Workers in the Human Services: The Roles of Organizational Ownership, Chain Affiliation, and Professional Leadership in Frontline Job Benefits," *Nonprofit and Voluntary Sector Quarterly* 37, no. 3 (2008): 443–467.
41. Hayley-Lock and Kruzich "Serving Workers in the Human Services."
42. Robert L. Mathis and John H. Jackson, *Human Resource Management: Essential Perspectives*, 2nd ed. (Mason, OH: South-Western/Cengage Learning, 2002).

Chapter Twelve

1. Case details are from the High Line Web site, http://thehighline.org; see especially the "History" and "Friends of the High Line" pages. The site also includes videos.
2. These formulas and the scholars who have used them are presented in David A. Whetten and Kim S. Cameron, *Developing Management Skills*, 5th ed. (Upper Saddle River, NJ: Pearson Prentice Hall, 2002).
3. Assessments of the empirical grounding for the theories and their value to the evolution of management thought are drawn from a variety of textbooks. The most useful for this chapter are John M. Ivancevich and Michael T. Matteson, *Organizational Behavior and Management*, 6th ed. (Boston: McGraw-Hill/Irwin, 2002); Hal G. Rainey, *Understanding and Managing Public Organizations*, 3rd ed. (San Francisco: Jossey-Bass/Wiley, 2003); and Debra L. Nelson and James Campbell Quick, *Organizational Behavior: The Essentials* (New York: West, 1996).
4. René Bekkers, *Giving and Volunteering in the Netherlands: Sociological and Psychological Perspectives* (Utrecht, Netherlands: Interuniversity Center for Social Science Theory and Methodology, 2004).
5. Catherine Schepers, Sara De Gieter, Roland Pepermans, Cindy Du Bois, Ralf Caers, and Marc Jegers, "How Are Employees of the Nonprofit Sector Motivated? A Research Need," *Nonprofit Management & Leadership* 16, no. 2 (2005): 191–208.

6. Joan E. Pynes, *Human Resources Management for Public and Nonprofit Organizations* (San Francisco: Jossey-Bass/Wiley, 1997); Matthew J. Chinman and Abraham Wandersman, "The Benefits and Costs of Volunteering in Community Organizations: Review and Practical Implications," *Nonprofit and Voluntary Sector Quarterly* 28, no. 1 (1999): 46–64.
7. Abraham H. Maslow, *Maslow on Management* (Hoboken, NJ: Wiley, 1998).
8. This is a basic premise of functional theory that has strong empirical backing. See Daniel Katz, "The Functional Approach to the Study of Attitudes," *Public Opinion Quarterly* 24 (1960): 163–204, for a basic statement of the theory. For an application to volunteers, see E. Gil Clary and Mark Snyder, "A Functional Analysis of Altruism and Prosocial Behavior: The Case of Volunteerism," in *Review of Personality and Social Psychology*, vol. 12, ed. M. Clark (Thousand Oaks, CA: Sage, 1991), 119–148.
9. Clayton P. Alderfer, *Existence, Relatedness and Growth: Human Needs in Organizational Settings* (New York: Free Press, 1972).
10. Richard D. Waters and Denise S. Bortree, "Building a Better Workplace for Teen Volunteers Through Inclusive Behaviors," *Nonprofit Management & Leadership* 20, no. 3 (2010): 337–356.
11. Steven G. Rogelberg, Joseph A. Allen, James M. Conway, Adrian Goh, Lamarra Currie, and Betsy McFarland, "Employee Experiences with Volunteers: Assessment, Description, Antecedents, and Outcomes," *Nonprofit Management & Leadership* 20, no. 4 (2010): 423–444.
12. Frederick Herzberg, Bernard Mausner, and Barbara Bloch Snyderman, *The Motivation to Work* (Hoboken, NJ: Wiley, 1959).
13. Debra J. Mesch, Mary Tschirhart, James L. Perry, and Geunjoo Lee, "Altruists or Egoists? Retention in Stipended Service," *Nonprofit Management & Leadership* 9, no. 1 (1998): 3–22.
14. Mary Tschirhart, Kira Kristal Reed, Sarah J. Freeman, and Alison Louie Anker, "Is the Grass Greener? Sector Shifting and Choice of Sector by MPA and MBA Graduates," *Nonprofit and Voluntary Sector Quarterly* 37, no. 4 (2008): 668–688. Also see Paul Light, "The Content of Their Character: The State of the Nonprofit Workforce," *Nonprofit Quarterly* 9, no. 3 (2002): 6–16; Shawn Teresa Flanigan, "Factors Influencing Nonprofit Career Choice in Faith-Based and Secular NGOs in Three Developing Countries," *Nonprofit Management & Leadership* 21, no. 1 (2010): 59–75.
15. Jeanne Bell, Richard Moyers, and Timothy Wolfred, *Daring to Lead 2006: A National Study of Nonprofit Executive Leadership* (San Francisco: CompassPoint Nonprofit Services, 2006).
16. Marla Cornelius, Patrick Corvington, and Albert Ruesga, *Ready to Lead? Next Generation Leaders Speak Out* (San Francisco: CompassPoint Nonprofit Services with the Annie E. Casey Foundation, the Meyer Foundation, and Idealist.org, 2008).
17. See Philip H. Mirvis, "The Quality of Employment in the Nonprofit Sector: An Update on Employee Attitudes in Nonprofits Versus Business and Government," *Nonprofit Management & Leadership* 3, no. 1 (1992): 23–42; Jenny Onyx and Madi Maclean, "Careers in the Third Sector," *Nonprofit Management & Leadership* 6, no. 4 (1996): 331–346.
18. Tschirhart et al., "Is the Grass Greener?"
19. Edward L. Deci, *Intrinsic Motivation* (New York: Plenum, 1975).
20. John R. Deckop and Carol C. Cirka, "The Risk and Reward of a Double-Edged Sword: Effects of a Merit Pay Program on Intrinsic Motivation," *Nonprofit and Voluntary Sector Quarterly* 29, no. 3 (2000): 400–418.

21. Mary Tschirhart, Debra J. Mesch, James L. Perry, Theodore K. Miller, and Geunjoo Lee, "Stipended Volunteers: Their Goals, Experiences, Satisfaction, and Likelihood of Future Service," *Nonprofit and Voluntary Sector Quarterly* 30, no. 3 (2001): 422–443.
22. Laura C. Phillips and Mark H. Phillips, "Volunteer Motivation and Reward Preference: An Empirical Study of Volunteerism in a Large, Not-for Profit Organization," *SAM Advanced Management Journal*, Autumn 2010, 12–39.
23. David C. McClelland, "Business Drive and National Achievement," *Harvard Business Review*, July–August 1962, 99–112.
24. Mary Tschirhart and Lynda St. Clair, "Diversity Issues in Workplace Volunteer Service Programs: Participation and Perceptions," paper presented at the Association for Research on Nonprofit Organizations & Voluntary Action Conference, Atlanta, GA, November 15–17, 2007.
25. Natalie J. Webb and Rikki Abzug, "Do Occupational Group Members Vary in Volunteering Activity?" *Nonprofit and Voluntary Sector Quarterly* 37, no. 4 (2008): 689–708.
26. For more detail on how to guide organizational culture in nonprofits see Paige H. Teegarden, Denice R. Hinden, and Paul Sturm, *The Nonprofit Organizational Culture Guide: Revealing the Hidden Truths That Impact Performance* (San Francisco: Jossey-Bass/Wiley, 2011).
27. Steven G. Rogelberg, Joseph A. Allen, James M. Conway, Adrian Goh, Lamarra Currie, and Betsy McFarland, "Employee Experiences with Volunteers," *Nonprofit Management & Leadership* 20, no. 4 (2010): 423–444.
28. James L. Perry and Lois R. Wise, "The Motivational Bases of Public Service," *Public Administration Review* 50 (1990): 367–373; James L. Perry, "Measuring Public Service Motivation: An Assessment of Construct Reliability and Validity," *Journal of Public Administration Research and Theory* 6 (1996): 5–24.
29. John Brauer and Jed Emerson, "Saving the World and Nonprofit Staff, Too," *Foundation News & Commentary* 43, no. 1 (2002), accessed January 11, 2012, http://www.foundationnews.org/CME/article.cfm?ID=1726.
30. Victor H. Vroom, *Work and Motivation* (Hoboken, NJ: Wiley, 1964).
31. Rainey, *Understanding and Managing Public Organizations*.
32. Steven Kerr, "On the Folly of Rewarding A, While Hoping for B," *Academy of Management Executive* 9, no. 1 (1995): 7–14 (original article published 1975).
33. Rob Paton, *Managing and Measuring Social Enterprises* (Thousand Oaks, CA: Sage, 2003). Also see Ben Cairns, Margaret Harris, Romayne Hutchison, and Mike Tricker, "Improving Performance? The Adoption and Implementation of Quality Systems in U.K. Nonprofits," *Nonprofit Management & Leadership* 16, no. 1 (2005): 135–151.
34. Albert Bandura, *Social Learning Theory* (New York: General Learning Press, 1977).
35. Bernadette Sánchez and Joseph R. Ferrari, "Mentoring Relationships of Eldercare Staff in Australia: Influence on Service Motives, Sense of Community, and Caregiver Experiences," *Journal of Community Psychology* 33, no. 2 (2005): 245–252.
36. Key scholars contributing to this line of research are Edwin A. Locke, Gary P. Latham, and Craig C. Pinder. See, for example, Edwin A. Locke, "Toward a Theory of Task Motivation and Incentives," *Organizational Behavior and Human Performance* 3, no. 2 (1968): 157–189.
37. Rainey, *Understanding and Managing Public Organizations*.
38. Tschirhart et al., "Stipended Volunteers."
39. J. Stacy Adams, "Toward an Understanding of Equity," *Journal of Abnormal and Social Psychology* 67 (1963): 422–436.

40. Laura Leete, "Wage Equity and Employee Motivation in Nonprofit and For-Profit Organizations," *Journal of Economic Behavior & Organization* 43, no. 4 (2000): 423–446.
41. Deckop and Cirka, "The Risk and Reward of a Double-Edged Sword."
42. Anna Haley-Lock, "Variation in Part-Time Job Quality Within the Nonprofit Human Service Sector," *Nonprofit Management & Leadership* 19, no. 40 (2009): 421–442.
43. Light, "The Content of Their Character." Also see Carlo Borzaga and Ermanno Tortia, "Worker Motivations, Job Satisfaction and Loyalty in Public and Nonprofit Social Services," *Nonprofit and Voluntary Sector Quarterly* 35, no. 2 (2006): 225–248.
44. William A. Brown and Carlton F. Yoshioka, "Mission Attachment and Satisfaction as Factors in Employee Retention," *Nonprofit Management & Leadership* 14, no. 1 (2003): 5–18. Also see Waters and Bortree, "Building a Better Workplace for Teen Volunteers Through Inclusive Behaviors."
45. Tschirhart et al., "Is the Grass Greener?"

Chapter Thirteen

1. Case details are from Andy Goodman, *The Story of David Olds and the Nurse Home Visiting Program* (Princeton, NJ: Robert Wood Johnson Foundation, 2006); Nurse-Family Partnership, "About" (n.d.), accessed December 24, 2011, http://www.nursefamilypart nership.org/about/program-history; and David Olds, Perry Hill, Ruth O'Brien, David Racine, and Pat Moritz, "Taking Preventive Intervention to Scale: The Nurse-Family Partnership," *Cognitive and Behavioral Practice* 10, no. 4 (2003): 278–290.
2. Patricia Flynn and Virginia Hodgkinson, "Measuring the Contributions of the Nonprofit Sector," in *Measuring the Impact of the Nonprofit Sector*, ed. Patricia Flynn and Virginia Hodgkinson (New York: Kluwer Academic/Plenum, 2001), 3–16.
3. Susan Paddock, "Evaluation," in *Understanding Nonprofit Organizations: Governance, Leadership, and Management*, ed. J. Steven Ott (Boulder, CO: Westview, 2001).
4. Peter Rossi, Howard Freeman, and Sonia Wright, *Evaluation: A Systematic Approach* (Thousand Oaks, CA: Sage, 1979).
5. Robert Anthony and David Young, *Management Control in Nonprofit Organizations*, 6th ed. (Boston: McGraw-Hill/Irwin, 2003).
6. Merriam-Webster (online), definition of *accountability* (n.d.), accessed August 17, 2011, http://www.merriam-webster.com/dictionary/accountability.
7. Grover Starling, *Managing the Public Sector*, 3rd ed. (Chicago: Dorsey Press, 1986); and Merriam-Webster (online), definition of *accountability*.
8. Ronald E. Fry, "Accountability in Organizational Life: Problem or Opportunity for Nonprofits?" *Nonprofit Management & Leadership* 6, no. 2 (1995): 181–195.
9. Alnoor Ebrahim and Edward Weisband, *Global Accountabilities: Participation, Pluralism, and Public Ethics* (New York: Cambridge University Press, 2007).
10. Alnoor Ebrahim, "The Many Faces of Nonprofit Accountability," in *The Jossey-Bass Handbook of Nonprofit Leadership and Management*, 3rd ed., ed. David O. Renz and Associates (San Francisco: Jossey-Bass/Wiley, 2010), 101–122.
11. Kevin Kearns, *Managing for Accountability: Preserving the Public Trust in Public and Nonprofit Organizations* (San Francisco: Jossey-Bass/Wiley, 1996), 11.
12. Melissa M. Stone, Barbara Bigelow, and William Crittenden, "Research on Strategic Management in Nonprofit Organizations: Synthesis, Analysis, and Future Directions," *Administration & Society* 31, no. 3 (1999): 378–423.

13. United Way of America, *Measuring Program Outcomes: A Practical Approach* (Washington, DC: United Way of America, 1996).
14. Michael Hendricks, Margaret Plantz, and Kathleen Pritchard, "Measuring Outcomes of United Way–Funded Programs: Expectations and Reality," in *Nonprofits and Evaluation*, New Directions for Evaluation, no. 119, ed. Joanne G. Carman and Kimberly A. Fredericks (San Francisco: Jossey-Bass/Wiley, 2008).
15. Hendricks et al., "Measuring Outcomes of United Way–Funded Programs."
16. Stacey Hueftle-Stockdill, Michael Baizerman, and Donald W. Compton, "Toward a Definition of the ECB Process: A Conversation with the ECB Literature," in *The Art, Craft, and Science of Evaluation Capacity Building*, New Directions for Evaluation, no. 93, ed. Donald W. Compton, Michael Baizerman, and Stacey Hueftle-Stockdill (San Francisco: Jossey Bass/Wiley, 2002).
17. Boris Volkov and Jean King, "A Grounded Checklist for Implementing Evaluation Capacity Building in Organizations," paper presented at the Joint Meeting of the American Evaluation Association and the Canadian Evaluation Society, Toronto, October 2005.
18. Paddock, "Evaluation."
19. John Thomas, "Outcome Assessment and Program Evaluation," in *The Jossey-Bass Handbook of Nonprofit Leadership and Management*, 3rd ed., David O. Renz and Associates (San Francisco: Jossey-Bass/Wiley, 2010): 401–430.
20. Michael Quinn Patton, *Utilization-Focused Evaluation: The New Century Text*, 3rd ed. (Thousand Oaks, CA: Sage, 1997).
21. ActKnowledge and the Aspen Institute Roundtable on Community Change, *Guided Example: Project Superwomen* (2003), accessed September 5, 2010, http://www.theoryofchange.org/pdf/Superwomen_Example.pdf.
22. Argosy Foundation, *Research Brief: Nurse-Family Partnership* (Milwaukee, WI: Argosy Foundation, 2006), accessed August 10, 2011, http://www.argosyfnd.org/usr_doc/Nurse_Family_Brief.pdf.
23. Carol H. Weiss, *Evaluation Research: Methods of Assessing Program Effectiveness* (Upper Saddle River, NJ: Pearson Prentice Hall, 1972).
24. David Olds, Charles Henderson, Robert Chamberlin, and Robert Tatelbaum, "Preventing Child Abuse and Neglect: A Randomized Trial of Nurse Home Visitation," *Pediatrics* 78 (1986): 65–78.
25. David Olds, Peggy Hill, Ruth O'Brien, David Racine, and Pat Moritz, "Taking Preventive Intervention to Scale: The Nurse-Family Partnership," *Cognitive and Behavioral Sciences*, forthcoming.
26. The results of these follow-up studies are summarized at GiveWell, *Nurse-Family Partnership (NFP)—Full Review* (n.d.), accessed December 24, 2011, http://www.givewell.org/united-states/early-childhood/charities/NFP/full-review#FormalstudiesoftheNFPmodel. See also the Nurse-Family Partnership Web site at http://www.nursefamilypartnership.org.
27. For a more detailed discussion of outcome and process evaluation data, see Adele Harrell, Martha Burt, Harry Hatry, Shelli Rossman, Jeffrey Roth, and William Sabol, *Evaluation Strategies for Human Service Programs: A Guide for Policymakers and Providers* (Washington, DC: Urban Institute, 1996).
28. Olds et al., "Preventing Child Abuse and Neglect."
29. Mary Kopczynski and Kathleen Pritchard, "The Use of Evaluation by Nonprofit Organizations," in *Handbook of Practical Program Evaluation*, ed. Joseph Wholey, Harry Hatry, and Kathryn Newcomer (San Francisco: Jossey-Bass/Wiley, 2004), 649–669.

30. Salvatore Alaimo, "Nonprofits and Evaluation: Managing Expectations from the Leader's Perspective," in *Nonprofits and Evaluation*, New Directions for Evaluation, no. 119, ed. Joanne G. Carman and Kimberly A. Fredericks (San Francisco: Jossey-Bass/Wiley, 2008).
31. Joanne Carman and Kimberly Fredericks, "Nonprofits and Evaluation: Empirical Evidence from the Field," in *Nonprofits and Evaluation*, New Directions for Evaluation, no. 119, ed. Joanne G. Carman and Kimberly A. Fredericks (San Francisco: Jossey-Bass/Wiley, 2008).
32. Margaret Plantz, Martha Greenway, and Michael Hendricks, "Outcome Measurement: Showing Results in the Nonprofit Sector," in *Using Measurement to Improve Public and Nonprofit Programs*, New Directions for Evaluation, no. 75, ed. Kathryn Newcomer (San Francisco: Jossey-Bass/Wiley, 1997).
33. Kopczynski and Pritchard, "The Use of Evaluation by Nonprofit Organizations."
34. Alaimo, "Nonprofits and Evaluation."
35. Georgiana Hernandez and Mary Visher, *Creating a Culture of Inquiry: Changing Methods—and Minds—on the Use of Evaluation in Nonprofit Organizations; A Look at WOW: Working On Workforce Development Project* (San Francisco: The James Irwin Foundation, 2001).
36. Plantz et al., "Outcome Measurement."

Chapter Fourteen

1. Case details are from a series of articles titled "Big Green," by David B. Ottaway and Joe Stephens, published on various dates beginning in 2001 in *The Washington Post*, accessed February 14, 2011, http://www.washingtonpost.com/wp-dyn/nation/specials/natureconservancy.
2. Max Stephenson Jr. and Elisabeth Chaves, "The Nature Conservancy, the Press, and Accountability," *Nonprofit and Voluntary Sector Quarterly* 35, no. 3 (2006): 345–366.
3. The Nature Conservancy, "Setting the Record Straight Regarding *The Washington Post* 'Big Green' Series," *Newsroom* (n.d.), accessed February 14, 2011, http://www.nature.org/pressroom/links/art10505.html.
4. Eric Kong and Mark Farrell, "The Role of Image and Reputation as Intangible Resources in Non-Profit Organizations: A Relationship Management Perspective," *Proceedings of the 7th International Conference on Intellectual Capital, Knowledge Management & Organizational Learning*, Hong Kong Polytechnic University, Hong Kong, China. November 11–12, 2010.
5. Nha Nguyen and Gaston Leblanc, "Corporate Image and Corporate Reputation in Customers' Retention Decisions in Services," *Journal of Retailing and Consumer Services* 8, no. 4 (2001): 227–236.
6. Paul Herbig and John Milewicz, "The Relationship of Reputation and Credibility to Brand Success," *Journal of Consumer Marketing* 10, no. 3 (1993): 18–24.
7. Donald Lange, Peggy Lee, and Ye Dai, "Organizational Reputation: A Review," *Journal of Management* 37, no. 1 (2011): 153–184.
8. Ian Fillis, "Image, Reputation and Identity Issues in the Arts and Crafts Organisation," *Corporate Reputation Review* 6, no. 3 (2003): 239–251; Roger Bennett and Helen Gabriel, "Image and Reputational Characteristics of U.K. Charitable Organisations: An Empirical Study," *Corporate Reputation Review* 6, no. 3 (2003): 276–289.

9. Edmund R. Gray and John M. T. Balmer, "Managing Corporate Image and Corporate Reputation," *Long Range Planning* 31, no. 5 (1998): 695–702.
10. John Baxter, "Corporate Reputation Management," *Ezine Articles* (n.d.), accessed January 12, 2011, http://ezinearticles.com/?Corporate-Reputation-Management&id=4773569.
11. Janel Radtke, *Strategic Communications for Nonprofit Organizations: Seven Steps to Creating a Successful Plan* (Hoboken, NJ: Wiley, 1998).
12. Kathy Bonk, Emily Tynes, Henry Griggs, and Phil Sparks, *Strategic Communications for Nonprofits: A Step-by-Step Guide to Working with the Media* (San Francisco: Jossey-Bass/Wiley, 2008).
13. Public Relations Society of America, "What Is Public Relations?" (n.d.), accessed December 24, 2011, http://www.prsa.org/aboutprsa/publicrelationsdefined.
14. Philip Kotler, *Marketing for Nonprofit Organizations*, 2nd ed. (Upper Saddle River, NJ: Pearson Prentice Hall, 1982), 47.
15. This list is quoted from Public Relations Society of America, "What Is Public Relations?"
16. Scott M. Cutlip, Allen H. Center, and Glen M. Broom, *Effective Public Relations*, 8th ed. (Upper Saddle River, NJ: Pearson Prentice Hall, 1999).
17. Smith, Bucklin & Associates, "Using Public Relations Tools to Reach a Broader Audience," in *The Complete Guide to Nonprofit Management*, 2nd ed. (Hoboken, NJ: Wiley, 2000).
18. Eileen Wirth, "Strategic Media Relations," in *The Nonprofit Handbook: Management*, 3rd ed., ed. Tracy Connors (Hoboken, NJ: Wiley, 2001), 266.
19. Janet A. Weiss and Mary Tschirhart, "Public Information Campaigns as Policy Instruments," *Journal of Policy Analysis and Management* 13, no. 1 (1994): 82–119.
20. See Lori Mcgehee, "What Is the Best Media to Get Your Message Across?" *Rich Tips* 2, no. 28 (2004), accessed December 10, 2010, http://richardmale.com/?cat=20&paged=2; and Wirth, "Strategic Media Relations."
21. To post a PSA on the Clear Channel Web site, visit http//publicservice.clearchannel.com.
22. Ben Rigby, *Mobilizing Generation 2.0: A Practical Guide to Using Web 2.0 Technologies to Recruit, Organize, and Engage Youth* (San Francisco: Jossey-Bass/Wiley, 2008).
23. The Web sites are, for YouTube for nonprofits, http://www.youtube.com/user/nonprofits; for the *NonProfit Times*, http://www.nptimes.com; for *The Chronicle of Philanthropy*, http://www.philanthropy.com; and for *Philanthropy Journal*, http://www.philanthropyjournal.org.
24. Sharon S. Brehm and Jack W. Brehm, *Psychological Reactance: A Theory of Freedom and Control* (Maryland Heights, MO: Academic Press/Elsevier, 1981).
25. Some of these examples come from Kathy Fitzpatrick and Carolyn Bronstein, *Ethics in Public Relations: Responsible Advocacy* (Thousand Oaks, CA: Sage, 2006).
26. American Patriot Friends Network, "If You Donated to the Red Cross . . ." (November 13, 2001), accessed December 24, 2011, http://www.apfn.org/apfn/WTC_red-cross.htm.
27. Paula DiPerna, *Media, Charity, and Philanthropy in the Aftermath of September 11, 2001* (New York: The Century Foundation, 2003); this publication is also available through the Foundation Center.
28. Melanie Herman and Barbara Oliver, *Vital Signs; Anticipating, Preventing and Surviving a Crisis in a Nonprofit* (Washington, DC: Nonprofit Risk Management Center, 2001), 6.
29. Matthew Hale, "Superficial Friends: A Content Analysis of Nonprofit and Philanthropy Coverage in Nine Major Newspapers," *Nonprofit and Voluntary Sector Quarterly* 36, no. 3 (2007): 465–486.

30. Melanie Herman, "Risk Management," in *The Jossey-Bass Handbook of Nonprofit Leadership and Management*, 3rd ed., ed. David O. Renz and Associates (San Francisco: Jossey-Bass/Wiley, 2010), 642–666.
31. Larry Lauer, "How to Handle a Crisis," *Nonprofit World* 12, no. 1 (1994): 34–40.
32. Herman and Oliver, *Vital Signs*.
33. Lauer, "How to Handle a Crisis."
34. See, for example, Richard Thompson, "Contingency and Emergency Public Affairs," in *The Nonprofit Handbook: Management*, 3rd ed., ed. Tracy Connors (Hoboken, NJ: Wiley, 2001), 251–266; and Lauer, "How to Handle a Crisis"; Herman and Oliver, *Vital Signs*.
35. Lauer, "How to Handle a Crisis."
36. Colorado Nonprofit Association, *Crisis Communication Plan: Nonprofit Toolkit* (n.d.), accessed January 10, 2011, http://www.coloradononprofits.org/crisiscomm.pdf.
37. J. Craig Jenkins, "Nonprofit Organizations and Political Advocacy in the Nonprofit Sector," in *The Nonprofit Sector: A Research Handbook*, 2nd ed., ed. Walter W. Powell and Richard Steinberg (New Haven, CT: Yale University Press, 2006), 307–332.
38. Bob Smucker, "Nonprofit Lobbying," in *The Jossey-Bass Handbook of Nonprofit Leadership & Management*, 2nd ed., ed. Robert D. Herman & Associates (San Francisco: Jossey-Bass/Wiley, 2005), 230. Also see the exempt organizations' continuing professional education (EO CPE) document by Judith E. Kindell and John Francis Reilly, *Lobbying Issues* (1997), accessed December 24, 2011, http://www.irs.gov/pub/irs-tege/eotopicp97.pdf, for a review of the legislation and IRS codes affecting lobbying up to 1997.
39. Smucker, "Nonprofit Lobbying."
40. Internal Revenue Service, "Charities & Non-Profits: Political and Lobbying Activities" (February 11, 2011), accessed December 24, 2011, http://www.irs.gov/charities/charitable/article/0,,id=120703,00.html.
41. See a watchdog group's coverage at OMB Watch, "NAACP IRS Audit" (February 23, 2005), accessed December 24, 2011, http://www.ombwatch.org/node/2281.
42. For useful lobbying resources, including descriptions of laws related to lobbying by nonprofits, see the Center for Lobbying in the Public Interest, *The Law: IRS Rules* (2008), accessed December 24, 2011, http://www.clpi.org/the-law/irs-rules. For the U.S. government's position on political and lobbying activities, as well as other resources for nonprofits, see Internal Revenue Service, *Tax Information for Charities & Other Non-Profits* (n.d.), accessed December 24, 2011, http://www.irs.gov/charities/index.html. For articles and analysis on the lobbying rights of nonprofits, see OMB Watch, *Nonprofit Lobbying Rights* (n.d.), accessed December 24, 2011, http://www.ombwatch.org/Nonprofit_Lobbying_Rights.
43. Michael J. Worth, *Nonprofit Management: Principles and Practices* (Thousand Oaks, CA: Sage, 2009).
44. Internal Revenue Service, *Tax-Exempt Status for Your Organization*, Publication 557 (revised October 2011), accessed December 24, 2011, http://www.irs.gov/pub/irs-pdf/p557.pdf.
45. For ideas on how to use the Web, see Rigby, *Mobilizing Generation 2.0*.
46. Steven Rathgeb Smith and Kirsten A. Gronbjerg, "Scope and Theory of Government-Nonprofit Relations," in *The Nonprofit Sector: A Research Handbook*, 2nd ed., ed. Walter W. Powell and Richard Steinberg (New Haven, CT: Yale University Press, 2006), 221–242.
47. Jenkins, "Nonprofit Organizations and Political Advocacy in the Nonprofit Sector."

48. John D. McCarthy, "Pro-Life and Pro-Choice Mobilization," in *Social Movements in an Organizational Society*, ed. Mayer N. Zald and John D. McCarthy (New Brunswick, NJ: Transaction, 1987), 46–69.
49. Barry Hessenius, *Hardball Lobbying for Nonprofits* (New York: Palgrave MacMillan, 2007).
50. Katya Andresen, *Robin Hood Marketing: Stealing Corporate Savvy to Sell Just Causes* (San Francisco: Jossey-Bass/Wiley, 2006).
51. Saul Alinsky, *Rules for Radicals* (New York: Random House, 1971).
52. Jenkins, "Nonprofit Organizations and Political Advocacy in the Nonprofit Sector."
53. Smucker, "Nonprofit Lobbying."
54. Much of this advice is adapted from Smucker, "Nonprofit Lobbying." Some additional ideas are taken from Kristen Wolf, *Now Hear This: The Nine Laws of Successful Advocacy Communications* (Washington, DC: Fenton Communications, 2001).

Chapter Fifteen

1. Case details are from the following Cancer Research Institute sources: *CRI Fact Sheet* (2009), http://www.cancerresearch.org/fact-sheet.html; *Pressroom* (n.d.), http://www.cancerresearch.org/Pressroom.aspx?id=2646 ; and *Cancer Vaccine Collaborative: A Global Partnership for Clinical Development of Therapeutic Cancer Vaccines* (2010), http://www.cancerresearch.org/programs/research/Cancer-Vaccine-Collaborative.html; all accessed October 5, 2010; and also from Ludwig Institute for Cancer Research, *Success Stories* (n.d.), accessed October 5, 2010, http://www.licr.org/index.php/Success_Stories.
2. Thomas McLaughlin, *Nonprofit Mergers and Alliances: A Strategic Planning Guide* (Hoboken, NJ: Wiley, 1998).
3. Darlyne Bailey and Kelly McNally Koney, *Strategic Alliances Among Health and Human Service Organizations* (Thousand Oaks, CA: Sage, 2000).
4. David Campbell, Barbara Jacobus, and John Yankey, "Creating and Managing Strategic Alliances," in *Effectively Managing Nonprofit Organizations*, ed. Richard Edwards and John Yankey (Washington, DC: NASW Press, 2006), 391–406.
5. Robert D. Herman, "Preparing for the Future of Nonprofit Management," in *The Jossey-Bass Handbook of Nonprofit Leadership and Management*, ed. Robert D. Herman & Associates (San Francisco: Jossey-Bass/Wiley, 1994), 616–625.
6. Ian MacMillan, "Competitive Strategies for Not-for-Profit Agencies," in *Advances in Strategic Management*, vol. 1, ed. Robert Lamb (Greenwich, CT: JAI Press, 1983), 61–81.
7. Jessica Sowa, "The Collaboration Decision in Nonprofit Organizations: Views from the Front Line," *Nonprofit and Voluntary Sector Quarterly* 38, no. 6 (2009): 1003–1025.
8. James Austin, *The Collaboration Challenge: How Nonprofits and Businesses Succeed Through Strategic Alliances* (San Francisco: Jossey-Bass/Wiley, 2000).
9. Deborah Askanase, "Nonprofit Collaboration: Doesn't It Make the Pie Bigger?" *Community Organizer 2.0*, blog (February 16, 2010), accessed December 27, 2011, http://www.communityorganizer20.com/2010/02/16/nonprofit-collaboration-doesnt-it-make-the-pie-bigger.
10. Jane Arsenault, *Forging Nonprofit Alliances* (San Francisco: Jossey-Bass/Wiley, 1998).

11. David La Piana, *The Nonprofit Mergers Workbook: The Leader's Guide to Considering, Negotiating, and Executing a Merger* (St. Paul, MN: Amherst H. Wilder Foundation, 2000).
12. La Piana, *The Nonprofit Mergers Workbook*.
13. Alexander Cortez, William Foster, and Katie Smith Milway, "Nonprofit M&A: More Than a Tool for Tough Times" (February 25, 2009), accessed December 27, 2011, http://www.bridgespan.org/Nonprofit-M-and-A.aspx.
14. Cortez et al., "Nonprofit M&A."
15. John Bryson, Barbara Crosby, and Melissa Stone, "The Design and Implementation of Cross-Sector Collaborations: Propositions from the Literature," *Public Administration Review*, 66, suppl. s1 (2006): 44.
16. H. Brinton Milward and Keith G. Provan, *A Manager's Guide to Choosing and Using Collaborative Networks* (Washington, DC: IBM Center for the Business of Government, 2006), accessed December 27, 2011, http://www.businessofgovernment.org/report/managers-guide-choosing-and-using-collaborative-networks.
17. Robert Putnam, *Bowling Alone* (New York: Touchstone, 2000).
18. Joseph Galaskiewicz and Michelle Sinclair Colman, "Collaboration Between Corporations and Nonprofit Organizations," in *The Nonprofit Sector: A Research Handbook*, 2nd ed., ed. Walter W. Powell and Richard Steinberg (New Haven, CT: Yale University Press, 2006), 180–204.
19. KaBOOM! Web page, accessed October 2, 2011, http://kaboom.org.
20. Global Environmental Management Initiative and Environmental Defense Fund, *Guide to Successful Corporate-NGO Partnerships* (2008), accessed October 3, 2011, http://www.gemi.org/resources/GEMI-EDF%20Guide.pdf.
21. Austin, *The Collaboration Challenge*.
22. Ida Berger, Peggy Cunningham, and Minette Drumwright, "Social Alliances: Company/Nonprofit Collaboration," *California Management Review* 47, no, 1 (2004): 58–89.
23. The various models are discussed and outlined in John Yankey and Carol Willen, "Collaborations and Strategic Alliances," in *The Jossey-Bass Handbook of Nonprofit Leadership and Management*, 3rd ed., ed. David O. Renz and Associates (San Francisco: Jossey-Bass/Wiley, 2010), 375–400. James Austin, in *The Collaboration Challenge*, identifies the stages as connection making, ensuring strategic fit, generating value, and relationship management. David La Piana, in *Real Collaboration: A Guide for Grantmakers* (New York: Ford Foundation, 2001), presents a framework that includes inspiration, formalization, operation, and institutionalization or termination. John Yankey, Barbara Jacobus, and Kelly McNally Koney, in *Merging Nonprofit Organizations: The Art and Science of the Deal* (Cleveland, OH: Mandel Center for Nonprofit Organizations, 2001), discuss decision making, planning, implementation, and reviewing or evaluating. Suzanne Feeney, in "Governance Framework for Collaborations and Mergers," in *The Nonprofit Handbook: Management*, 3rd ed., ed. Tracy Connors (Hoboken, NJ: Wiley, 2001), 108–127, breaks the stages down into exploration, decision making, initiation and design, implementation, and monitoring.
24. Arsenault, *Forging Nonprofit Alliances*.
25. Yankey et al., *Merging Nonprofit Organizations*.
26. Yankey and Willen, "Collaborations and Strategic Alliances."
27. Amelia Kohm and David La Piana, *Strategic Restructuring for Nonprofit Organizations: Mergers, Integrations, and Alliances* (New York: Praeger, 2003).
28. Bailey and Koney, *Strategic Alliances Among Health and Human Services Organizations*.

29. Feeney, "Governance Framework for Collaborations and Mergers."
30. Paul Mattessich, Marta Murray-Close, and Barbara Monsey, *Collaboration: What Makes It Work?* 2nd ed. (Saint Paul, MN: Amherst H. Wilder Foundation, 2001).
31. See Yankey and Willen, "Collaborations and Strategic Alliances"; and Michael J. Worth, *Nonprofit Management: Principles and Practices* (Thousand Oaks, CA: Sage, 2009).
32. McLaughlin, *Nonprofit Mergers and Alliances.*
33. Gerald Bubis and Steven Windmueller, *From Predictability to Chaos? How Jewish Leaders Reinvented Their National Communal System* (Baltimore, MD.: Baltimore Hebrew University Center for Jewish Studies, 2005). See also D. Cohen, "Merger of Jewish Groups Fails to Meet Expectations, Report Finds," *Chronicle of Philanthropy*, February 17, 2005.
34. William T. Mallon, "The Alchemists: A Case Study of a Failed Merger in Academic Medicine," in *Academic Medicine, Management Series: Strategic Alliances in Academic Medicine* (Washington, DC: Association of American Medical Colleges, 2006), 26–37.

Chapter Sixteen

1. Case details are from Jerry Hauser, "Organizational Lessons for Nonprofits," *McKinsey Quarterly*, June 2003, accessed August 20, 2011, https://www.mckinseyquarterly.com/Nonprofit/Performance/Organizational_lessons_for_nonprofits_1314.
2. Charles Kahn, *The Art and Thought of Heraclitus: Fragments with Translation and Commentary* (New York: Cambridge University Press, 1979).
3. "How Companies Approach Innovation: A McKinsey Global Survey," *McKinsey Quarterly*, October 2007, accessed January 18, 2012, https://www.mckinseyquarterly.com/How_companies_approach_innovation_A_McKinsey_Global_Survey_2069.
4. Jane Wei-Skillern, James Austin, Herman Leonard, and Howard Stevenson, *Entrepreneurship in the Social Sector* (Thousand Oaks, CA: Sage, 2007).
5. Noelle Barton, Maria DiMento, Holly Hall, Peter Panepento, Suzanne Perry, Caroline Preston, et al., "2010: Daunting Challenges Face the Nonprofit World," *Chronicle of Philanthropy*, December 10, 2009.
6. Lester Salamon (ed.), *The State of Nonprofit America* (Washington, DC: Brookings Institution Press, 2002).
7. Richard L. Daft, *Organizational Theory and Design*, 10th ed. (Mason, OH: South-Western/Cengage Learning, 2010).
8. Andrew H. Van de Ven and Marshall Scott Poole, "Explaining Development and Change in Organizations," *Academy of Management Review* 20, no. 5 (1995): 510–540.
9. Warner Burke, *Organization Change: Theory and Practice*, 2nd ed. (Thousand Oaks, CA: Sage, 2008).
10. Larry E. Greiner, "Evolution and Revolution as Organizations Grow," *Harvard Business Review*, July–August 1972, 37–46. See also Michael Morris, Donald Kuratko, and Jeffrey Covin, *Corporate Entrepreneurship & Innovation* (Mason, OH: South-Western/Cengage Learning, 2008).
11. Richard Hall, *Organizations: Structures, Processes, and Outcomes*, 9th ed. (Upper Saddle River, NJ: Pearson Prentice Hall, 2005).
12. Patrick Dawson, *Understanding Organizational Change: The Contemporary Experience of People at Work* (Thousand Oaks, CA: Sage, 2003).

13. Rajesh Tandon, "Organization Development in Nongovernment Organizations," in *Handbook of Organization Development*, ed. Thomas Cummings (Thousand Oaks, CA: Sage, 2008), 615–628.
14. Harold J. Leavitt, "Applied Organizational Change in Industry: Structural, Technical, and Human Approaches," in *New Perspectives in Organization Research*, ed. William W. Cooper, Harold J. Leavitt, and Maynard W. Shelly (Hoboken, NJ: Wiley, 1964), 55–71.
15. Tandon, "Organization Development in Nongovernment Organizations."
16. Daft, *Organizational Theory and Design*.
17. Indianapolis Metropolitan High School, "About Us" (n.d.), accessed August 12, 2011, http://www.indianapolismet.org/mod/aboutUs.
18. Burke, *Organization Change*.
19. David Wilson, *A Strategy of Change: Concepts and Controversies in the Management of Change* (New York: Routledge, 1992).
20. Stephen Jay Gould, *Ever Since Darwin* (New York: Norton, 1977).
21. March of Dimes, "Mission" (2011), accessed September 2, 2011, http://www.marchofdimes.com/mission/mission.html.
22. Dawson, *Understanding Organizational Change*.
23. Tony Eccles, *Succeeding with Change: Implementing Action-Driven Strategies* (New York: McGraw-Hill, 1994).
24. Jennifer George and Gareth Jones, *Organizational Behavior*, 3rd ed. (Upper Saddle River, NJ: Pearson Prentice Hall, 2002); Wilson, *A Strategy of Change*.
25. Jacquelyn Wolf, "Managing Change in Nonprofit Organizations," in *The Nonprofit Organization: Essential Readings*, ed. David Gies, J. Steven Ott, and Jay Shafritz (Pacific Grove, CA: Brooks/Cole, 1990), 241–257.
26. Kate Cooney, "The Institutional and Technical Structuring of Nonprofit Hybrids: Organizations Caught Between Two Fields?" *Voluntas* 17 (2006): 143–161.
27. Burke, *Organization Change*.
28. Wolf, "Managing Change in Nonprofit Organizations."
29. Kurt Lewin, *Field Theory in Social Science* (New York: HarperCollins, 1951).
30. Wilson, *A Strategy of Change*.
31. David Jamieson and Christopher Worley, "The Practice of Organizational Development," in *Handbook of Organizational Development*, ed. Thomas Cummings (Thousand Oaks, CA: Sage, 2008), 99–122.
32. Michael Hitt, Chet Miller, and Adrienne Colella, *Organizational Behavior: A Strategic Approach* (Hoboken, NJ: Wiley, 2006), 540–546; George and Jones, *Organizational Behavior*; Wilson, *A Strategy of Change*.
33. Tandon, "Organization Development in Nongovernment Organizations."
34. David Renz, "Reframing Governance," *Nonprofit Quarterly* 17, no. 4 (2011): 50–53.
35. Carl Sussman, *Building Adaptive Capacity: The Quest for Improved Organizational Performance* (Boston: Management Consulting Services, 2003), 1–18, accessed January 18, 2012, http://www.systemsinsync.com/pdfs/Building_Adaptive_Capacity.pdf.
36. Thomas Davenport and Laurence Prusak, *Working Knowledge: How Organizations Manage What They Know* (Boston: Harvard Business Press, 2000).

37. Paul Light, "The Spiral of Sustainable Excellence," in *Sustaining Nonprofit Performance* (Washington, DC: Brookings Institution Press, 2004), 136–176.
38. Ralph H. Kilmann and Teresa Joyce Covin, *Corporate Transformations: Revitalizing Organizations for a Competitive World* (San Francisco: Jossey-Bass/Wiley, 1988).
39. Felice Perlmutter and Burton Gummer, "Managing Organizational Transformations," in *The Jossey-Bass Handbook of Nonprofit Leadership and Management*, ed. Robert D. Herman & Associates (San Francisco: Jossey-Bass/Wiley, 1994), 227–246.
40. Daft, *Organizational Theory and Design*.
41. John Kimberly, "Managerial Innovation," in *Handbook of Organizational Design*, vol. 1, ed. Paul Nystrom and William Starbuck (New York: Oxford University Press, 1981), 84–104.
42. Morris et al., *Corporate Entrepreneurship & Innovation*.
43. Drew Boyd, "Innovation for the Non-Profit Sector," *Innovation Excellence*, blog (January 23, 2011), accessed December 27, 2011, http://www.business-strategy-innovation.com/wordpress/2011/01/innovation-for-the-non-profit-sector.
44. Gerald Zaltman, Robert Duncan, and Jonny Holbek, *Innovations and Organizations* (Hoboken, NJ: Wiley Interscience, 1973).
45. Marshall H. Becker, "Sociometric Location and Innovativeness: Reformulation and Extension of the Diffusion Model," *American Sociological Review* 35, no. 2 (1970): 267–282.
46. Richard Daft and Selwin Becker, *Innovation in Organizations: Innovation Adoption in School Organizations* (New York: Elsevier, 1978); Constance Holden, "Innovation—Japan Races Ahead as U.S. Falters," *Science* 210 (1980): 751–754.
47. Kenneth McNeil and Edmond Minihan, "Regulation of Medical Devices and Organizational Behavior in Hospitals," *Administrative Science Quarterly* 22 (1977): 475–490.
48. James Goes and Seung Ho Park, "Interorganizational Linkages and Innovation: The Case of Hospital Services," *Academy of Management Journal* 40 (1977): 673–696; Gautam Ahuja, "Collaboration Networks, Structural Holes, and Innovation: A Longitudinal Study," *Administrative Science Quarterly* 17 (2000): 425–455.
49. Peter F. Drucker, *Innovation and Entrepreneurship* (New York: Harper Business, 1985).
50. Arthur C. Brooks, *Social Entrepreneurship: A Modern Approach to Social Value Creation* (Upper Saddle River, NJ: Pearson Prentice Hall, 2009).
51. Gregory Dees, *Responding to Market Failure*, Harvard Business School Case 9-396-344, 1999.
52. James E. Austin, Roberto Gutierrez, Enrique Ogliastri, and Ezequiel Reficco, *Effective Management of Social Enterprises: Lessons from Business and Civil Society Organizations in Iberoamerica* (Cambridge, MA: Harvard University Press, 2006).
53. Morris et al., *Corporate Entrepreneurship & Innovation*.
54. Morris et al., *Corporate Entrepreneurship & Innovation*, 42.
55. Gregory Dees, "Mastering the Art of Innovation," in *Enterprising Nonprofits: A Toolkit for Social Entrepreneurs*, ed. Gregory Dees, Jed Emerson, and Peter Economy (Hoboken, NJ: Wiley, 2001), 161–198.
56. Paul Light, *Sustaining Innovation: Creating Nonprofit and Government Organizations That Innovate Naturally* (San Francisco: Jossey-Bass/Wiley, 1998), 99–124.

Chapter Seventeen

1. Peter Frumkin, *On Being Nonprofit: A Conceptual and Policy Primer* (Cambridge, MA: Harvard University Press, 2002).
2. See Peter M. Senge, "The Leader's New Work" (SoL: Society for Organizational Learning, n.d.), accessed December 21, 2011, http://www.solonline.org/res/kr/newwork.html. Also see Peter M. Senge, *The Fifth Discipline: The Art and Practice of the Learning Organization* (New York: Doubleday, 2005).
3. National Intelligence Council (United States) and Institute for Security Studies (European Union), *Global Governance 2025: At a Critical Juncture* (September 2010), accessed December 21, 2011, http://www.dni.gov/nic/PDF_2025/2025_Global_Governance.pdf.
4. Zachary Sniderman, "What Does the Social Good Ecosystem Look Like?" infographic (May 18, 2011), accessed December 21, 2011, http://mashable.com/2011/05/18/social-good-ecosystem-infographic.
5. Frances Kunreuther, Helen Kim, and Robby Rodriguez, *Working Across Generations: Defining the Future of Nonprofit Leadership* (San Francisco: Jossey-Bass/Wiley, 2008).
6. For a listing of nonprofit management education programs see Roseanne M. Mirabella, *Nonprofit Management Education: Current Offerings in University-Based Programs* (Seton Hall University, 2009), http://academic.shu.edu/npo.

INDEX

Page references followed by *fig* indicate an illustrated figure; followed by *t* indicate a table; and followed by *e* indicate an exhibit.

A

Abilities inventory, 257
Abzug, R., 219, 290
Accountability: change driven by nonprofit's, 391; debate over regulatory enforcement of, 29; definition of, 303; four core components of, 303–304; Habitat for Humanity International (HFHI), 422; managing program evaluation and, 302–304; organizational ethic of, 27–28; three fundamental questions about program, 304
Accounting: GAAP (generally accepted accounting principles) of, 148–150, 161–162, 163; internal controls for, 150–153; tracing accounts, 146–147
Accounting cycle, 147–148
Accounting for Contributions, 148
Accounting Standards Codification (ASC), 148
Acid-test ratio, 165
ACORN, 152–153
Ad hoc committees, 221
Adaptive capacity model of change, 403–404
Addams, J., 119, 234–235
Administration consolidation, 367
Advance ruling, 52
Advisory groups, 221
Advocates: description of nonprofit's, 352; designing and delivering advocacy message, 353–354; engaging, 352–353
Affiliate organization, 57
Aggressive competition orientation, 92, 92*t*
Aggressive divestment orientation, 92, 92*t*
Aggressive growth orientation, 92, 92*t*
Ahlstrand, B., 87, 105, 107

469

AIDS Action Committee of Massachusetts, 120
AIDS/HIV epidemic, 360
Alaimo, S., 324
Alcoholics Anonymous (AA), 42
Alderfer, C., 284, 287
Alderfer's ERG theory, 287–288
Alinsky, S., 352
Allison, M., 250
Alternative coverage, 91, 359
American Bar Association, 220
American Cancer Society: founding of, 35; franchise relationships of, 57–58
American Heart Association (AHA), 168, 179, 181, 189, 335; public relations "Liberty Fun" 9/11 crisis faced by, 339–340. *See also* Go Red For Women
American Institute of Philanthropy, 150
American Medical Association (AMA), 122
American Quilt Memorial, 149
American Red Cross: branding by, 185; Clara Barton as founder of the, 235; community preparedness planning partnership with, 372; differentiated marketing used by, 184; disaster relief and human services provided by, 407; donor lists shared by, 120; founding of, 35; franchise relationships of, 57; hypothetical strategic planning process for, 94–104; identification of strategic issues by, 100, 102*e*; online donations to, 336; SWOT analysis of, 96*e*, 99*e*, 102*e*. *See also* International Red Cross
Americans with Disabilities Act (ADA), 276
AmeriCorps VISTA, 257, 263, 289, 295
Amherst H. Wilder Foundation, 379
Analyzers, 90
Anderson, A., 313
Anderson, B., 120
Andresen, K., 352
Ansoff, H. I., 86, 182

Answerability, 303
Aramony, W., 244, 245
Arizona's Children Association (AzCA), 368–370, 376, 378
Arsenault, J., 364
The Art of War (Sun Tzu), 86
ASAE: The Center for Association Leadership, 421
Asset transfer merger, 368
Assets: current ratio of, 165; permanently restricted, 148; temporarily restricted, 148; unrestricted, 148; unrestricted net assets ratio, 165
Associated Press, 149, 336
Association of Certified Fraud Examiners, 151
Association of Fundraising Professionals (AFP), 126, 215
Auditing, 161–162
Austin, J., 38, 39, 315, 363, 364

B

B corporations, 10, 422
Baby Boomer retirements, 251, 420
Bailey, D., 358
Bair, A. M., 126
Balanced approach: evaluating nonprofit's, 20–21; triangle of organizational foci for, 21*fig*
Balanced scorecards, evaluation function of, 20
Banking relations, 157
Baptist Foundation of Arizona (BFA): evaluating internal processes of, 16–17; evaluating resource acquisition by, 16; evaluating stakeholder satisfaction of, 18–19; story of, 11–12
Barber, P., 420–421
Barnes Foundation, 206
Barton, C., 35, 235
Basic program theory, 305

The Beehive Collective, 132
Behavior: Alderfer's ERG theory on, 287–288; equity theory on, 295–296; expectancy theory on, 291–292; goal-setting theory on, 294–295; Herzberg's two-factor theory on, 288–290; McClelland's learned needs theory on, 290–291; operant conditioning and behavior modification, 292–293; public service motivation (PSM) theory on, 291; social learning theory on, 293–294
Behavioral complexity theory, 241
Bekkers, R., 285
Ben & Jerry's, 374
Benefits, 275–276
Benzing, C., 144
Better Business Bureau's Wise Giving Alliance, 150, 161
Big Brothers Big Sisters: Edmonton & Area (BBBSE): assessment of current HR capacity of, 258; examining HR capacity of, 257; HR capacity-building decisions of, 261; story of, 225–226
"Big Green" series (*The Washington Post*), 328
Blanchard, K. H., 25, 237
Block, S., 248
Board committees, 220–221
Board Composition Analysis Grid, 217*e*
Boards: activities during collaboration, 379; advisory groups of the, 221; bylaws of, 220; committees of, 220–221; determining composition of, 216–219; managing conflict within the, 221–224*e*; officers of the, 220; orientation, training, self-assessments, and reports of, 221. *See also* Governing boards
BoardSource, 231
Bohr, N., 420
Bolman, L., 240
Bond, J., 346

Bonds, 158
Borrowing: issues to consider when, 157–158; types of, 158
Bortree, D., 288
Bowman, W., 261
Boy Scouts of America: controversy over moral code of, 23; franchise relationships of, 57; geographical structure of, 71; marketing segment used by, 182; serving needs of youth, 286
Boy Scouts of America et al. v. Dale, 23
Boys and Girls Clubs, 286
Boys Town, 125
Bradshaw, P., 213, 215
Branding, 185–187
Brauer, J., 291
The Bridgespan Group, 251, 368, 370
Bron Afon Community Housing, 219
Brooks, A., 41
Brown, E., 127
Brown, L. D., 248
Brown, W., 220
Bryson, B., 371
Bryson, J., 101, 103
Budget reserve policy, 145
Budgeting: description and nonprofit issues related to, 153–154; estimating and reviewing revenues and expenses, 154–157; example of monthly budget report, 156*e*; producing realistic budget, 154
Buffett, W., 131
Build strength orientation, 92*t*, 93
Build up best competitor orientation, 92*t*, 93
Bureaucracy, 65–66
Burke, W., 394, 397
Burning Man organization, 230
Burns, T., 68
Bush administration, 116
Bush, G. W., 346

Business case for nonprofit: business plan, 42–53; market potential assessment, 43; social value potential assessment, 43; sustainability potential assessment, 43

Business partnerships: four types of nonprofit and, 372–374; Nonprofit Shopping Mall, 410; philanthropic collaborations, 364, 372–373; *Plumstead* case on, 123; revenue source through, 121–124

Business plans: establishment process, 49–53; executive summary, 47–48; generic outline of the topic headings for, 43–45, 46*e*–47*e*; key objectives, 48–49; nonprofit vision and mission statements, 45; organizations that may qualify for tax exemptions, 51*e*

Business strategy: a brief history of, 86–87; contemporary, 87–88. *See also* Strategy

Businesses: funding provided by, 134; nonprofit partnerships with, 121–124, 372–374

Buying experience, 196–197

C

Campbell, D., 358
Cancer Research Institute (CRI), 356
Cancer Vaccine Collaborative (the Collaborative): collaboration benefits to, 362; collaboration negotiation forming the, 377; as integrative collaboration, 363*t*, 365; as joint venture corporation, 367; partnerships making up the, 356–357; story of, 356–357
CANDO (Chicago Association of Neighborhood Development Organizations): evaluating ability to take balanced approach, 20*fig*–21; evaluating goal accomplishment by, 13–15; evaluating growth, learning, and adaptation of, 18–20; evaluating stakeholder satisfaction of, 17–18; story of, 11
Cantillon, R., 36
Capital resources: description of, 15; as indicator of effectiveness, 15; social entrepreneurship model on, 37–38*fig*
Carman, J., 322
Carnegie, A., 128
Carver, J., 207, 208, 214
Case studies, 320
Cash flows: number of days of cash on hand, 165; statement of cash flows, 163
The Center for Civil Society Studies, 116
Center for Lobbying in the Public Interest, 353
Centrality-related power, 244
Centralized advocacy structures, 351–352
Centralized organizations, 64
CFRE (certified fundraising executive): Donor Bill of Rights followed by, 25, 26*e*; professionals with, 25
Chaffee, F., 370–371
Chait, R., 208, 211
Chambre, S., 248
Chandler, A., 86
Chang, C., 127
Change: examining degree of, 394–395; experienced by nonprofits, 385–386; managing the process of, 397–399; nonprofit elements that can go through, 392–394; process-driven, 387–390; resistance to, 395–397, 398–399; specific drivers of nonprofit, 390–392; Teach For America's experience with, 384–385
Change drivers: external, 390–391; internal triggers, 391–392
Change models: adaptive capacity, 403–404; development spiral, 389, 404–407, 405*fig*; innovation, 410–416; Lewin's force field model, 400–401*fig*; nonprofit transformation, 407–409; organizational development (OD), 400–403
Charismatic leaders, 246–247, 408–409
Charitable trust, 50

Charity: description of, 128; organizational ethic of, 27–28. *See also* Philanthropy
Charity Navigator, 150
Charity Navigator survey (2004), 120
Charles M. Bair Family Museum, 126
Chicago Lighthouse, 364
Chief financial officer (CFO), 145
Chronicle of Philanthropy, 131, 144, 337, 386
Church of Scientology, 55
Ciconte, B. L., 131
Cirka, C., 289, 296
Citizens United v. *Federal Election Commission,* 346
Civil society organizations: demographics of U.S. volunteers in, 9; popular term for nonprofits, 7. *See also* Nonprofit sector
Clary, E. G., 287
Classen, J., 208
Clean Air Partners Membership Strategy (2008), 121, 122*e*
Clear Channel Communications, 336
Cleveland Foundation, 133
Clinton, H., 346
Coaching, 273–274
Coe, C. K., 140, 156
Coercive isomorphism, 78
Collaboration: Cancer Vaccine Collaborative (the Collaborative) example of, 356–357, 362; challenges facing, 374–375; developing process for, 375–378; domain influence issue of, 361; environmental validity issue of, 361; governing during, 378–379; operational efficiency issue of, 360; as organizational life cycle stage, 387; resource interdependence issue of, 360; social responsibility issue of, 358–360; strategic enhancement issue of, 361–362; successful, 379–382
Collaboration continuum, 363*t*–365
Collaboration process: evaluating the collaboration, 378; forming the collaboration, 377; identifying potential partners, 376–377; initial planning, 375–376
Collaborative relationships: collaboration continuum, 363*t*–365; cross-sector collaborations, 371–374; defining types of, 362–374; mergers, 368–371; partnership matrix, 365–367
Collaborative success: challenges to, 381–382; factors promoting, 379–381
Collegiate School (later Yale University), 55
Colman, M., 372, 374
Combined Federal Campaign, 134
Comcast Corporation, 126
Commercial collaborations, 373
Commissioner, Plumstead Theatre Society v., 123
Commitment to perform, 283
Committed line, 158
Common Cause, 353
Community capacity-building networks, 372
Community Education and Programs, Inc. (CEAP), 141, 150
Community organizations, 69
Community-based resources: description of, 15; as indicator of effectiveness, 15
Companion organizations, 55
CompassPoint Nonprofit Services, 240
Compensation, 274–276
Competition: innovation and perceived advantage for, 411; pricing tied to, 195
Competitive position, 91, 359
Complexity: geographical, 64; horizontal, 64; information process, 74; vertical, 64
Compliance, 304
Concentrated marketing, 184
Conflict: change and organizational, 389–390; handling government board, 224*e*; as structural deficiency, 79
Conflict of interest policy, 142–144
Conflict resolution, 224*e*
Constituency/representative governance, 214

Contextual elements: description of, 38; social entrepreneurship framework on, 38fig-39
Conti-Brown, P., 124
Contingent workers, 257
Corporate integrations, 367
Cost leadership positioning, 89
Costs: of collaboration, 382; innovation, 410–411. *See also* Expenses
Counseling, 273
Courtney, R., 107, 108
Covin, J., 413
Covin, T., 407
Crazy Horse Memorial, 117
Crisis management: American Red Cross "Liberty Fund" for 9/11 victims, 339–340; public relations process during, 340–346
Criticality-related power, 244
Crosby, J., 371
Cross-sector collaborations: description of, 371; nonprofit and for-profit collaborations, 121–124, 372–374; nonprofit and government collaborations, 371–372; pros and cons of, 374–375
Crowdsourcing, 267
Cultural Competence Learning Initiative (CompassPoint Nonprofit Services), 240
Culture: changes to people and organizational, 393–394; collaboration and incompatible, 381; national, 77; organizational, 78, 381
Cummings, S., 105, 108
Cycle of involvement: stage 1: initial involvement, 263–269; stage 2: development, 269–274; stage 3: maintenance, 274–277; stage 4: separation, 277–278; volunteer employees and, 262e

D

Daft, R., 392
Dale, Boy Scouts of America et al. v., 23
Darfur Is Dying (video game), 336
Daring to Lead study (2006), 251, 289
David, J., 280, 281
Davis, G., 63
Dawson, P., 390, 395
Deal, T., 240
Decentralized advocacy organizations, 351, 352
Decision making: framing moral, 24; self-assessment needed prior to merger, 369; as structural deficiency, 79
Deckop, J., 289, 296
Dees, G., 413
Dees, J. G., 120
Defenders, 90
Definitive ruling, 52
Delaware Association of Nonprofit Organizations, 323
Delegate governance, 215–216
Dell Computer, 184
Demographic shifts, 259
Detroit Zoo, 27
Development spiral, 389, 404–407, 405fig
Differentiated marketing, 184
Differentiation positioning, 89–90
DiMaggio, P., 78
DiPerna, P., 339
Distribution channels, 196–197
Divisional structure, 71
Document retention policy, 146
Domain influence, 361
Dominant coalition, 77
Donations: accounting of gifts by donor wishes, 148–149; debate over government grants "crowding out," 127; honoring donors' intentions for their, 126; pass-through contribution, 149; revenue source of, 126
Donor Bill of Rights, 25, 26e, 126
Donor lists, 119–120
Donor types: breakdown of giving by, 129fig; businesses, 134; federated

funders, 134; foundations, 132–133; giving groups, 132; individuals, 130–131
Donors: accounting of gifts by, 148–149; duty of obedience and adherence to wishes of, 205–206; nonprofit change driven by preferences of, 391; pyramid of giving, 131*fig*; types of, 129*fig*–134
Douglas, S., 151
Dowling School, 414
Drucker, P., 41
Duncan, R., 410
Duty of care, 204
Duty of loyalty, 204–205
Duty of obedience, 205–206
Dynamism, 403

E

Earned income: aligning missions with, 118–119; considerations for payments for, 118; description of, 118; donor list sales for, 119–120; UBIT (unrelated business income tax) payments due to, 119, 123
Ebrahim, A., 304
Eccles, T., 395
Economic conditions factor, 259
Edelman (PR firm), 335
Effort-related power, 243–244
Ego-clashes, 382
Egyptian demonstrations (2011), 194
Electronic format for promotion, 193
Eli Lilly and Company Foundation, 115
Elmira study, 318
Emergent cellular governance, 214
Emergent strategy: definition of, 104–105; as strategic challenge, 104–107
Emerson, E., 264
Emerson, J., 120, 291
EmployAlliance, 364
Employees. *See* Staff
Endowment campaigns, 124
Endowments: investment recommendations for, 125; as revenue source, 124; "underwater," 125
Enforcement, 304
Enron scandal, 142
Entrepreneurial corporate spin-off, 54–55
Entrepreneurial/corporate governance, 214
Entrepreneurship: diverse definitions of, 36; social, 36–42, 421
Environment: definition of, 63; HR capacity service demands and natural, 260; information process linked to, 74–75; providing safe and productive work, 276; resistance to change due to demanding, 396; situational analysis of external and internal, 95–100; structural deficiency of failed response to changed, 78–79
Environmental Defense Fund (EDF), 374
Environmental Protection Agency (EPA), 328
Environmental scanning, 98
Environmental validity: collaboration and, 360–361; key factors to consider for, 361; legitimacy perceived as resource in, 361
Equity theory, 295–296
ERG theory, 287–288
Ethical codes: encouraging moral action in keeping with, 24; honoring donors' intentions, 126; Public Relations Society of America (PRSA), 338*e*
Ethical issues: building moral awareness of, 24; government relations and related, 351; overview of nonprofits and, 21–30; personal, 22–25; public relations communication, 337–339. *See also* Organizational ethics
Ethnography, 321
European Union's Institute for Security Studies, 420
Evaluation: of the collaboration, 378; nonprofit organizational, 13–21; program, 302–325

Evaluation and Program Implementation Division (OMB), 303
Evaluation Quarterly, 303
Evers-Williams, M., 201, 202, 212, 223
Evolutionary change, 394
Evolutionary transition, 394
Executive centrality, 231, 244
Executive director (ED): board roles and responsibilities versus, 207–210; founder, 247–248; job description for the Santropol Roulant, 232*e*; leadership responsibilities of the, 233–234; loss of legitimacy by, 242; overview of the, 230–231; phases of dynamics between board and, 209*t*; responsibilities of the, 231–232. *See also* Leadership
Executive governance, 216
Expanded reproduction, 394
Expectancy theory, 291–292
Expenses: budgeting, 153–157; estimating and reviewing, 154–157; GAAP on reporting, 149–150; monthly budget report on, 156*e*. *See also* Costs
Expert power, 243
External environmental analysis, 95–98
External relations OD interventions, 402–403
Extrinsic incentives, 288–290

F
Facebook, 193
FACTNet, 55
Fahrenheit 9/11 (film), 346
Fatt, N., 248
Federal Election Commission, 346
Federal Election Commission, Citizens United v., 346
Federated funders, 134
FedEx, 374
Feedback: how evaluation provides, 323; measuring employee performance and, 271–273

Feeney, S., 378
Felt conflict, 222
Financial Accounting Standards Board (FASB), 148
Financial analysis, 162–163
Financial indicators and ratios, 164–165
Financial literacy, 166
Financial management: accounting, 146–153; auditing and financial analysis, 161–166; banking relations, 157; borrowing, 157–158; budgeting, 153–157; financial risk management, 158–161; GAAP (generally accepted accounting principles) used in, 148–150, 161–162, 163; setting up policies for, 142–146
Financial policies: budget reserve policy, 145; conflict of interest policy, 142–144; document retention policy, 146; investment policy, 145–146; whistle-blower protection policy, 144–145
Financial resources: description of, 15; as indicator of effectiveness, 15
Financial risk management: issues to consider for, 158–159, 161; methods for reducing risk, 159*e*; types of insurance policies, 160*e*
Fiscal sponsorship, 52–53
Fitzpatrick, K., 228
501(c)(3) organizations: accountability of, 202; advocacy efforts by, 353; companion organizations established by, 55; funds raised from membership fees of, 120; government's position against political activities by, 346; regulations governing lobbying by, 347, 348–349; requirements for establishing, 52; tax status of, 50, 51*e*. *See also* Section 501(c)(3) tax status
501(c)(4) organizations: companion organizations established by, 55; political activities allowed by, 346; requirements for establishing, 52; tax status of, 50, 51*e*

501(c)(6) organizations: National Football League's, 57; political activities allowed by, 346
501(c)(7) organizations, 120
Flag of Honor Fund, 149
Flexibility-related power, 244
Flinn Foundation (Arizona): identification of strategic issues by, 100; industry analysis of, 97; mission drift of, 95; story of, 85; strategic planning by, 85–86
Focus groups, 320–321
For-profit and nonprofit partnerships: four types of, 372–374; Nonprofit Shopping Mall, 410; philanthropic collaborations, 363*t*, 364, 372–373; *Plumstead* case on, 123
For-profit businesses: funding provided by, 134; nonprofit partnerships with, 121–124, 372–374; revenue source through, 121–124
Force field analysis, 98
Force field model, 400–401*fig*
Ford, W. C., Sr., 57
Ford Foundation, 115
Form 5768, 348
Form 990, 143, 144, 148, 377
Formal organizations, 63
Formalization, 64
Foundation Center, 133, 323
Foundations: format of proposals submitted by, 133; three types of, 132–133
Founder executive directors, 247–248
Founder's syndrome, 34, 247
Franchise relationships, 57–58
Fraud: classifications of, 151; description and examples of, 150–151; of Hurricane Katrina Web site donations, 151; practices to reduce likelihood of, 152
Fredericks, K., 322
The Free Management Library, 323
Freevibe.com, 191
Freiwirth, J., 225
French, J., 242
Friends of the High Line: enabling individuals to pursue basic needs, 286; resources to perform provided by, 283; story of, 280–281
Frumkin, P., 124
Fuller, M., 55
Fuller Center for Housing, 55
Functional structure, 71
Fund development: principles of, 137–138; process of, 134–137
Fundraising efficiency ratio, 164

G

GAAP (generally accepted accounting principles), 148–150, 161–162, 163
Galaskiewicz, J., 219, 372
Gandhi, M., 233
Gardner, J., 247
Gates, B., 131
Gates, M., 131
Gateway capacity, 412
General Motors Corporation, 133
Generation Y, 420, 422
Geographical complexity, 64
Geographical structure, 72
Girl Scouts of the USA: court decision on eliminating local councils of, 58; earned income from cookie sales of the, 119; geographical structure of, 72; serving needs of youth, 286
Giving circle, 132
Giving groups, 132
Giving USA, 129, 131
GM Foundation, 133
Go Red For Women: concentrated marketing used by, 184; evaluations of, 179; marketing data collection and analysis approach by, 176–177; marketing objectives and strategy used by, 181; marketing planning process used by, 173–174; public relations campaign

for, 335; social marketing by, 189; story of, 168–169. *See also* American Heart Association (AHA)

Goal setting: change and organizational, 389; measureable, time bounded, and challenging criteria for, 14–15

Goals: ensuring stakeholder acceptance of, 15; evaluating CANDO accomplishment of their, 13; prioritizing your, 15; setting public relations, 333–334; specifying program, 314

Goal-setting theory, 294–295

Godsall, C., 228

Godsoe, B., 249

Goldman Sachs Foundation, 45

Goodwill Industries: charter school established by, 402; distribution channels of, 196; franchise relationships of, 57; geographical structure of, 72; products of, 187–188; strategic positioning of, 89

Goodwill Industries of Central Indiana, 393

Gould, S. J., 394–395

Governing board effectiveness: considerations and issues of, 210–211; determining board composition for, 216–219; determining board configuration by contingency, 213–215; four general types of association boards for, 215–216; six competencies contributing to, 211–212

Governing board responsibilities: ED (executive director) roles vs. board roles and, 207–208, 210; legally required board duties, 204–206; protection from liability, 206–207

Governing boards: collaboration role of, 378–379; description of nonprofit, 202; effectiveness of, 210–223; examining a broader conception of governance by, 225; five conflict-handling modes for, 224*e*; functions during collaboration, 379; NAACP, 201, 202;

phases of dynamics of ED and, 209*t*; responsibilities of nonprofit, 203–208, 210; symptoms of groupthink among members of, 223*e*. *See also* Boards

Government contracts, 115–117

Government grants: debate over donations being "crowded out" by, 127; nonprofit revenue through, 115–117

Government Performance and Results Act (1993), 304

Government relations: designing and delivering advocacy message, 353–354; engaging advocates, 352–353; lobbying regulations, 347–349; planning and implementing, 349–352

Government vouchers, 115–116

Government-nonprofit collaborations, 371–372

Graham, J., 421

Grassroots lobbying, 347

Grassroots organizations, 69

Gratuity, 144

Great Society (1960s), 302

Green Bay Packers, 57

Greenlee, J., 151

Greiner, L. E., 387, 404

Groupthink, 223*e*

GuideStar Nonprofit Services, 275

Gummer, B., 407–409

H

H-1B hires, 268

Haag, R., 120

Habitat for Humanity International (HFHI): accountability of, 422; board composition of, 218; educational material provided to clients by, 108; entrepreneurial corporate spin-off of, 54–55; founding of, 35; franchise relationships of, 57; ReStore of, 118

Haley-Lock, A., 275, 296

Hall, P., 77

Hammond, D., 233
Hammond, R., 280, 281
Hardison, A., 190
Harlem School for the Arts, 142
Harnett County Partnership for Children (HCPC): financial mismanagement accusations against, 150; need to change financial management systems, 142; story of, 141
Harrell, A., 318
Harvard University, 35, 55, 90, 125
Heifer International, geographical structure of, 72
Heimovics, R. D., 231, 241
Heraclitus, 385
Herman, R. D., 211, 231, 241
Hersey, P., 237
Herzberg, F., 284, 288, 289
Herzberg's two-factor theory, 288–290
Hesselbein, F., 238
Hessenius, B., 352
Hierarchical organizational chart, 66, 67e
Hierarchy of authority, 65
Hierarchy of needs (Maslow's), 285–286fig
High Line (Manhattan), story of, 280–281
Holbek, J., 410
Hold harmless clause, 159
Holland, T. P., 211, 213
Homes for Families, 225
hopeFound: story of, 140–141; SWOT analysis of, 140–141
Horizontal complexity, 64
Horizontal information linkages, 76
HR Council for the Nonprofit Sector, 233–234
Hull House, 235
Hull House Association, 119
Human dimension OD interventions, 402
Human resource (HR) capacity: assessing current, 257–258; definition of, 256–257; forecasting demand for services, 258–260; forecasting needs for, 260–261

Human resource management: cycle of involvement, 261–278; definition of, 257
Human resources: description of, 15; as indicator of effectiveness, 15. *See also* People
Humane Society of the United States: branding by, 185; distribution channels of, 196; undifferentiated (mass) marketing used by, 183
Hurricane Katrina, 151, 391
Hybrid boards, 215
Hygiene factors, 288

I

"I Have a Dream" speech (King), 233
Image: definition of, 329; as intangible nonprofit resource, 329–330; public relations to enhance, 331–339; risk and crisis management of, 339–344; strategic communication of, 330–331
Image research, 334
Inc. magazine, 119
Indian National Congress, 233
Industry analysis, 97
Influence strategies, 245–246
Informal organizations, 64
Information diffusion networks, 371–372
Information process: complexity, uncertainty, and interdependency of, 74–75; environment and strategy linked to, 75; horizontal linkages, 76–77; organizational structure and, 74–77; vertical linkages, 75–76
In-kind gift, 129
Inner-circle governance, 216
Innovation: building adaptive capacity role of, 403–404; characteristics affecting adoption, 410–412; description of, 410; environmental sources of, 412–413; management of, 413–416; resources available for, 415
Innovator organization, 34–35

Institute for Security Studies (European Union), 420
Institutional influences, 77–78
Institutional isomorphism, 78
Integrative collaborations, 363t, 365
Integrity, 27
Intended strategy, 106, 106fig
Interdependency: information process, 74; types of, 74–75
Interlocking boards, 368
Internal factors analysis, 98–100
Internal Revenue Service. See U.S. Internal Revenue Service (IRS)
International Red Cross, 35, 336. See also American Red Cross
Internet: program evaluation tools found on the, 323; as public relations outlet, 336
Intrapreneurship, 36
Intrinsic incentives, 288–290
Investment income: nonprofit revenue through, 124–125; recommendations for nonprofit, 125–126
Investment policy, 145–146
IRC Form 5768, 348
IRS. See U.S. Internal Revenue Service (IRS)
IRS Form 990, 143, 144, 148, 377
Issue impact analysis grid, 98
Iverson, J., 220

J
Jackson, J., 276
Jacob, J. G., 131
Jacobus, B., 358
Jamieson, D., 400
Janis, I., 223
Jeavons, T., 27, 32, 240
Job enrichment, 274
Job Path, 55
Job rotation, 274

John D. and Catherine T. MacArthur Foundation, 132
Johnson, J., 251
Joint programming, 367
Joint ventures: corporations, 367; nonprofit revenue sources through, 121–124; orientation toward, 92t, 93; *Plumstead* case on, 123
Jospin, D., 247
Junior League, 218
Jurkiewicz, C. L., 239
Justification, 303

K
KaBOOM!, 233, 373, 374
Kalegaonkar, A., 248
Kanter, R. M., 242
Kearns, K., 101, 304
Kennedy, J. F., 15
Kickback, 144
Kilmann, R., 407
King, J., 306
King, L., 190–191
King, M. L., Jr., 233, 235
Kitzi, J., 42
Knowledge resources: description of, 15; as indicator of effectiveness, 15
Kohm, A., 378
Koney, K., 358
Kopp, W., 34, 37, 384, 392
Kotter, J., 232
Kouzes, J., 233
Kruzich, J., 275
KSAs (knowledge, skills, and abilities), 266
Ku Klux Klan, 8
Kuratko, D., 413

L
La Piana, D., 363, 365, 368, 378
Laissez faire leadership, 236
Lampel, J., 87, 105, 107

Latent conflict, 222
Leaders: charismatic, 246–247, 408–409; laissez faire, 236; personal and positional sources of power by, 242–245; relationship-oriented, 236; strategies for influencing others, 245–246; task- and relationship-oriented, 235–236; "walking around" management by, 294
Leadership: charismatic, 246–247, 408–409; five basic principles of, 234–246; strong leaders and shared, 246–249; trait theories of, 234. *See also* Executive director (ED)
Leadership development: future opportunities for, 423; transitions of, 249–253
Leadership principles: effective leaders are not all the same, 234–235; effective leaders are self-aware and operate out of a strong value system, 237–240; effective leaders change their style to fit the situation, 235–237; effective leaders integrate and balance roles and perspectives, 240–241; effective leaders use power and influence wisely, 242–246
Leadership transitions, 392
Learned needs theory, 290–291
Learning Project, 384, 385
Leasing, 158
Leete, L., 275, 296
Legal cases: *Boy Scouts of America et al. v. Dale*, 23; *Citizens United v. Federal Election Commission*, 346; *Plumstead Theatre Society v. Commissioner*, 123; *Queen of Angels Hospital v. Younger*, 204; *Stern v. Lucy Webb Hayes National Training School for Deaconesses & Missionaries*, 205
Legislation: Americans with Disabilities Act (ADA), 276; Government Performance and Results Act (1993), 304; Lobby Law (1976), 347, 348; Lobbying Disclosure Act (1995), 347; Occupational Safety and Health Administration (OSHA) Act, 276; Public Law 94-142, 111; Revised Model Nonprofit Corporation Act, 220; Sarbanes-Oxley (SOX) Act, 142, 144, 146, 206; Title VII, 267
Legitimacy: accountability as source for, 304; based on being perceived as trustworthy, 329; challenges to nonprofit's, 10; change in nonprofit, 408; executive directors who have lost their, 242; funding tied to, 361; governing board's role in establishing, 202, 210; as resource, 361; strategic collaboration for credibility and, 373
Legitimate power, 242
Leonard, H., 315
Lewin, K., 400–401
Lewin's force field model, 400–401*fig*
Liabilities: acid-test ratio of, 165; current ratio of, 165
Light, P., 36, 389, 404–407, 405*t*, 414
Lightner, C., 238
Lilly Endowment, 115
Lindblom, C., 106
Line of credit, 158
Loans, 158
Lobby Law (1976), 347, 348
Lobbying: direct, 347; grassroots, 347; limitations on nonprofits engaged in, 347; what activities are permissible by nonprofits, 347–349
Lobbying Disclosure Act (1995), 347
Locus of control, 23
Logic models: applied to Project Superwomen, 312*e*–313*e*; evaluation use of, 310–311
Loseke, D., 261
Loudon, D. L., 96, 99
Lucy Webb Hayes National Training School for Deaconesses & Missionaries, Stern v., 205

Ludwig Institute for Cancer Research (LICR), 54, 356
Luther Theological Seminary, 414–415

M

MacArthur Foundation, 132
MacMillan, I., 91, 359
MacMillan's strategic orientation framework, 91–93
MADD (Mothers Against Drunk Driving), 238
Malcolm Baldrige National Quality Award, 17
Malik, S. D., 270, 272
Management services organizations, 367
Manifest conflict, 222
Manitou Girl Scout Council, 58
March of Dimes: changed mission of, 20, 395; goals of the, 14–19; recognition of opportunity by, 42
Marcus Aurelius, 125
Market segmentation: demographic criteria of, 182–183; description of, 182; geographical criteria of, 183; product or service criteria of, 183; psychographic criteria of, 183; strategic targeting of, 183–184
Marketing: branding, 185–187; distinctive aspects of nonprofit, 170–171; distribution channels, 196–197; general philosophies on nonprofits and, 169–170; identifying offerings and markets, 181–182e; managing offerings, 187–197; objectives and strategy of, 181; positioning, 184–185; pricing and, 194–195; promotion component of, 191–194; segmenting markets, 182–184; social, 189–191
Marketing audit: description of, 177–178; five areas to focus on, 178–179; portfolio analysis included in, 180; on product life cycle, 179–180*fig*
Marketing mix (four Ps), 187
Marketing orientation, 172–173
Marketing planning process: data collection and analysis, 176–177; interpretation and reporting of findings, 177; marketing information and research, 174–175; overview of, 173–174*fig*; problem identification and research objectives, 175–176; research plan formulation, 176
Markets: segmented, 182–184; targeting, 183–184
Martin, P., 186
Maslow, A. H., 285–286
Maslow's hierarchy of needs, 285–286*fig*
Mass customization, 184
Massey, T. K., Jr., 239
Mathis, R., 276
Matrix structure, 72–73
Mattessich, P., 379
McClelland, D., 284
McClelland's learned needs theory, 290–291
McCormick, S., 328
McKinsey & Company, 386
Mechanistic structure: comparing organic and, 68*t*; description of, 68
MediaLink, 336
Medicaid, 115
Medicare, 115
Membership fees, 120–121
Memo of understanding, 377
Mentoring, 273–274; role model, 293–294
Mergers: complexity of negotiation in, 370–371; description of, 368; different options for, 368–369; potential partner assessment prior to, 369–370; self-assessment needed prior to deciding on, 369
Metropolitan Opera, 230
Migliore, R. H., 96, 99
Miles, R., 90, 91
Millennials: branding approach for, 186–187; social media connections of, 194

Mills, K., 151
Milward, H. B., 371, 372
Mimetic isomorphism, 78
Mintzberg, H., 87, 88, 105, 106
Mission: aligning earned income with, 118–119; change driven by the, 20, 390–391; changing focus of the, 408; collaboration and incompatible, 381; drifting away from primary, 20; executive directors' responsibility for the, 238; HR capacity and realization of, 259; network connections to accomplish, 403; spin-offs to expand, 55. *See also* Nonprofit organizations; Vision
Mission drift, 20
Mission-driven spin-off, 55
Model Cities, 303
Monsey, B., 379
Moore, M., 346
Moral awareness, 24
Moral decision making, 24
Morris, M., 413
Mosdut Shuva Israel, 142
Motivation: as influence on performance, 282*e*; intrinsic and extrinsic, 288–290; Maslow's hierarchy of needs, 285–286*fig*. *See also* Volunteers
Motivation theories: Alderfer's ERG theory, 287–288; applications to nonprofit workplaces, 284–285; equity theory, 295–296; expectancy theory, 291–292; goal-setting theory, 294–295; Herzberg's two-factor theory, 288–290; McClelland's learned needs theory, 290–291; operant conditioning and behavior modification, 292–293; public service motivation (PSM) theory, 291; social learning theory, 293–294
Motivators, 288
Mount Sinai Hospital and School of Medicine, 144
Muddling through, notion of, 106

Murray-Close, M., 379
Mutual benefit, 50
MySpace, 193

N

NAACP (National Association for the Advancement of Colored People): civil rights mission of, 212; companion organization established by, 55; constituency/representative governance used by, 214; governance effectiveness competencies of the, 212; governing board of, 202; government inquiry on political activities by, 346; power dynamics of the board chair, board, and ED of the, 208; story of, 201; subsidiary of, 56
National Alliance on Mental Illness (NAMI), 175
National Association of Manufacturers, 215
National Association of Schools of Public Affairs and Administration (NASPAA), 3–4, 423
National Association to Protect Children, 116
National Center for Charitable Statistics (NCCS), 113
National Center for Nonprofit Boards, 210
National Children's Facilities Network, 403
National culture, 77
National Football League, 57
National Institutes of Health, 372
National Trust for Historic Preservation, 45
National Youth Anti-Drug Media Campaign, 191, 194
Natural environment, 260
The Nature Conservancy: crisis management following bad press on, 339–340; image and reputation of, 329–330; land-selling practices of, 347; public perception of business partnerships by, 123; story of, 327; strategic response to media attacks

by, 328–329; *Washington Post* critiques of, 327–329, 330
Needs: Alderfer's ERG theory on, 287–288; Maslow's hierarchy of, 285–286*fig*
Network connections, 403
New nonprofit organizations: establishment process, 49–53; making a business case for, 42–49; social entrepreneurship framework for, 36–42; starting from an existing organization, 53–58
New York City Criminal Justice Agency, 55
New York Public Interest Research Group, 144
The New York Times, 153
9/11 charities, 149
Non-distribution constraint, 206
Nonexperimental designs, 319
Nongovernmental organizations (NGOs), 7
Nonprofit Academic Centers Council (NACC), 4, 423
Nonprofit career competencies, 3–4
Nonprofit corporation, 50
Nonprofit FAQ (Barber), 420
Nonprofit Finance Fund, 140
Non-Profit Management Education Section (NASPAA), 3–4
Nonprofit organization evaluation: goal accomplishment criteria for, 14–15; growth, learning, and adaptation criteria for, 20; internal processes criteria for, 16–17; multiple dimensions for, 13–21; resource acquisition criteria for, 15–16; stakeholder satisfaction criteria for, 18–19*fig*; taking a balanced approach to, 20–21*fig*
Nonprofit organization types: charitable trust, 50; mutual benefit, 50; nonprofit corporation, 50; private foundations, 8, 52; public benefit, 50; public charities, 7, 52, 113*fig*–114*fig*; unincorporated association, 50

Nonprofit organizations: challenge of understanding current reality, 419; competency and curriculum guidelines developed for, 3–4; ethics for, 21–30, 126, 337–339, 338*e*, 351; founding of, 34–35; imagining the future of the, 419–423; lobbying by, 347–349; making a business case for, 42–49; multiple dimensions for evaluating the effectiveness of, 13–21; the nature of, 6–7; social entrepreneurship framework for, 37–42; stakeholder's view of the, 31*t*; stewardship mandate of, 3; widespread societal influence of, 12. *See also* Mission
Nonprofit Risk Management Center, 339
Nonprofit sector: challenge of understanding current reality of the, 419; description of the, 7; diversity in the, 7–9; drivers of the, 259–260; imagining the future of the, 419–423; leading and managing in the, 9–10; multiple functions of the, 8–9; study on resilience of the, 259; volunteers working in the, 9–10. *See also* Civil society organizations
Nonprofit Shopping Mall, 410
NonProfit Times, 337
Nonprofits in Washington (Barber), 420–421
Normative isomorphism, 78
Northern Clay Center, 335
Norton, E., 280
NPower Basic business plan: executive summary of, 47–48; key objectives of, 48–49; outline of (2005), 45, 46*e*–47*e*
Nurse-Family Partnership National Service Office, 302
Nurse-Family Partnership (NFP) program: basic elements of the program, 305*fig*; collecting data on the, 314–316, 318; determining evaluation approach of the, 309; evaluation goals for the, 308; goals of the, 314; purpose of evaluation

of, 307; story of, 301–302; theories of change and logic models applied to evaluation of the, 310–311

O

Oakes Children's Center: diversified funding base developed by, 111–112; fund development process taken by, 135–136; government contracts and grants sought by, 116; revenue portfolio of the, 127; story of, 111–112
Objective scientist approach, 308–309
Occupational Safety and Health Administration (OSHA) Act, 276
O'Donnell-Tormey, J., 357
Offering and Market Opportunity Matrix, 182*e*
Office of Management and Budget, 303
Olds, D., 301, 308
Omaha Sun, 125
O'Neill, L., 255, 256, 258, 263, 264
Online integration model to promote behavioral change, 190*fig*–191
Ono, N., 204
Openness ethic, 27
Operant conditioning and behavior modification, 292–293
Operational efficiency, 360
Opportunity: recognition of an entrepreneurship, 41–42; social entrepreneurship framework on, 38*fig*, 39
Oral Roberts University, 142
Orderly divestment orientation, 92*t*, 93
Oregon Organic Coalition, 69, 70*e*
Organic structure: comparing mechanistic and, 68*t*; description of, 68–69
Organizational conflict: change and, 389–390; handling government board, 224*e*; as structural deficiency, 79
Organizational crisis: definition of, 339–340; public relations during, 339–346

Organizational culture: changes to people and, 393–394; collaboration and incompatible, 381; organizational structure influenced by, 78
Organizational development (OD) model, 400–403
Organizational ethics: attributes included for, 27; building trust through application of, 27–28; description of, 27. *See also* Ethical issues
Organizational evolution, 389
Organizational life cycles, 387–389
Organizational structure: bureaucratic, 65–66; deficiency in, 78–79; description of, 62–63; dimensions of, 64–65; divisional, 71; elements of, 63*fig*–64; functional, 69, 71; geographical, 72; hierarchical, 66–67*e*; information processing influence on, 74–77; matrix, 72–73; mechanistic, 68*t*; organic, 68*t*–69, 70*e*; political, cultural, and institutional influences on, 77–78; reorganization of SCS into Our Piece of the Pie, 60–62; virtual network, 73
Organizational structure dimensions: centralization, 64; complexity, 64; formalization, 64; hierarchy of authority, 65; professionalism, 65; specialization, 65; standardization, 65
Osmond, M., 335
Ospina, S., 249
Oster, S., 57, 97
Ostrower, F., 208
Our Piece of the Pie: founding of, 60; linking strategy and information process in, 75; reorganization of Southend Community Services into, 61*fig*–62
Outright mergers, 368

P

Paddock, S., 302
Paid advertising, 192

Panel on the Nonprofit Sector, 161
Parent-subsidiary relationships, 367
Partnership matrix, 365–367
Partnership on Nonprofit Ventures, 45
Pass-through contribution, 149
Payton, R., 128
Peace Corps, 257, 264
Peale, N. V., 25
People: organizational contributions of, 64; social entrepreneurship model on, 37–38*fig*. *See also* Human resources
Perceived conflict stage, 222
Performance: change driven by pressure to improve, 392; influences on, 281–284*t*; measuring employee, 271–273; structural deficiency due to declining, 79; theories of motivation for, 284–296
Perlmutter, F., 407–409
Permanently restricted assets, 148
Perry, J., 291
Personal ethics: goals of nonprofit training on, 24; nonprofit issue of, 23
PEST analysis, 96, 178
Philanthropic collaborations, 363*t*, 364, 372–373
Philanthropy: origins and description of, 128; types of donor gifts of, 129*fig*–134; types of gifts, 129. *See also* Charity
Philanthropy Journal, 275, 337
The Phoenix Group, 414
Planned Parenthood, 120, 318
Plumstead Theatre Society v. *Commissioner*, 123
Points of Light, 153
Police Assessment Resource Center, 55
Policy governance, 214
Political collaborations, 374
Political influences, 77–78
Pollack, T. H., 113, 114
Poole, M., 387
Pooled interdependence, 74
Population shifts, 259

Porter, M., 89, 97, 181
Portfolio analysis, 180
Positioning, 184–185
Posner, B., 233
Powell, W., 78
Power: how leaders effectively use, 242–245; legitimate, 242; personal and positional sources of, 242–245
PR Newswire, 336
Pricing: complexities of nonprofit, 194; strategies for, 194–195; user demand and, 195
Private foundations: tax status of, 52; U.S. Internal Revenue Code category of, 8
Problem solving networks, 372
Process-driven change: organizational conflict, 389–390; organizational evolution, 389; organizational goal setting, 389; organizational life cycles, 387–389
Product life cycle, 179–180*fig*
Products: convenience goods, 196; description of, 187–188; innovation of new, 410; as market segmentation criteria, 183; nonprofit change to, 393; pricing tied to cost of producing, 195
Professional ethics: attributes of, 27; description of, 25–26
Professionalism, 65
Program administration failure, 310
Program attractiveness, 91, 359
Program efficiency ratio, 164
Program evaluation: accountability management and, 302–304; challenges to practice of, 322–325; objective scientist approach to, 308–309; online resources for, 323; process of, 305–322; understanding basic program theory for, 305; utilization-focused, 309
Program evaluation process: analyzing data and presenting results, 321–322; collecting data, 314–321; determining

the evaluation approach, 308–309; preparing for, 306–308; specifying program goals, 314; understanding theories of change and logic models, 309–313*e*

Program resources: description of, 15; as indicator of effectiveness, 15

Promotion: description of, 191–192; tools used to deliver, 192–194

Promotional mix, 192

Prospectors, 90

Protection from liability duty, 206–207

Provan, K., 371, 372

Psychological contract, 268–269

Public benefit, 50

Public charities: limited lobbying allowed by, 348–349; number of expenses (2008) of reporting, 114*fig*; revenue sources (2008) for reporting, 113*fig*; Section 501(c)(3) tax status of, 7; tax status of, 52

Public Law 94-142, 111

Public relations: assessing internal and external factors affecting, 333; communication outlet and delivering messages, 336–337; description of, 331–332; developing messages, 334–335; ethical issues of, 337–339; evaluating effectiveness and ethics of communication, 337; identifying and researching target audiences, 334; origins of, 331; setting goals, objectives, and strategies for, 333–334

Public Relations Society of America (PRSA), 331, 337–338*e*

Public service announcement (PSA), 192, 336

Public service motivation (PSM) theory, 291

Public-serving organizations, 8

Punctuated equilibrium model of change, 394–395

Pyramid of giving, 131*fig*

Q

Quaqua Society, 54

Quasi-experimental designs, 319

Queen of Angels Hospital v. *Younger*, 204

Quinn, J., 106

Quinn, R., 238

R

Rabinowitz, J., 229, 232, 235, 236

Raven, B., 242

Reactors, 90

Ready to Lead? study (2008), 289

Realized strategy, 106, 106*fig*

Reciprocal interdependence, 75

Reckford, J., 422

Recognition/rewards, 275–276

Reel Grrls, 126

Referent power, 243

Reichers, A. E., 272

Relationship-oriented leadership, 236

Relevance-related power, 245

Renz, D., 211, 225

Reproducer, 34

Reputation: definition of, 329; as intangible nonprofit resource, 329–330; public relations to enhance, 331–339; risk and crisis management of, 339–344; strategic communication of, 330–331

Request for Proposal (RFP), 377

Resistance to change: description of issues involved in, 395–396; nonprofit factors that contribute to, 395–397; techniques for dealing with specific reasons for, 398

Resource acquisition: danger of complacency regarding, 113; Oakes Children's Center's diversified funding for, 111–112; revenue portfolios, 127; sources and concerns of, 113*fig*–126

Resource interdependence, 360

Resource types: capital, 15, 37–38*fig*; community-based, 15; financial, 15;

human, 15, 37–38*fig*; knowledge, 15; program, 15
Resources: available for innovation, 415; collaboration and costs of, 382; collaboration and interdependence of, 360; devoted to evaluation, 306; evaluating nonprofit's acquisition of, 15–16; legitimacy perceived as, 361; nonprofit mandate for stewardship of, 3; performance influenced by, 283; recommendations for influencing high performance, 284*t*
ReStore (Habitat for Humanity), 118
Restructuring-driven spin-off, 54
Reuters, 336
Revenue portfolios, 127
Revenue sources: donations, 126; earned income, 118–120; government contracts, grants, and vouchers, 115–117, 127; HR capacity demands and changes in, 260; investment income, 124–126; membership fees, 120–121; partnerships with business, 121–124; reported by public charities (2008), 113*fig*–114, 113*fig*
Revenues: days in accounts receivable ratio, 165; estimating and reviewing, 154–155, 157; monthly budget report on, 156*e*
Revised Model Nonprofit Corporation Act, 220
Revolutionary change, 394
Revolutionary transformation, 394
Reward power, 243
Reichers, A., 270
Risk: four options for responding to identified, 341; image and reputation, 339–344; innovation, 411
Risk management: definition of, 340; financial, 158–159*e*, 160*e*, 161; public-relations process during, 340–346
Robert Wood Johnson Foundation (RWJF), 233
Robert's Rules of Order, 220

Roeger, K. L., 113, 114
Roosevelt, F. D., 42
Rosenberg, S., 248
RSVP, 257
Ryan, W., 208

S
Sagawa, S., 247
Sahlman, W. A., 37
Salamon, L., 9, 386
Sales promotion, 192–193
Salvation Army, branding by, 185
Santropol Roulant: high turnover experience at, 277; internal leadership development at, 252; job description for the executive director of, 232*e*; nine core principles of engagement, 239*e*; relevance-related power of executive director of, 245; shared leadership approach taken by, 249; story of, 228–229; transactional and transformational leadership styles used by, 237
Sarbanes-Oxley (SOX) Act, 142, 144, 146, 206–207
Sargeant, A., 130, 181, 182
Satellite governance, 215
Scenario analysis, 98
Schall, E., 249
Schumpeter, J., 36
Schwartz, B., 190
Scott, W. R., 63
Section 501(c)(3) tax status, 7, 8. *See also* 501(c)(3) organizations
Segmentation. *See* Market segmentation
Self-dealing prohibition, 206
Sell-out orientation, 92*t*, 93
Senge, P., 419
Sequential interdependence, 74–75
Service implementation networks, 371
Service network, 260
Services: convenience, 196; description of, 188–189; innovation of new, 410;

as market segmentation criteria, 183; nonprofit change to, 393; organizational ethic of commitment to, 27; pricing tied to cost of producing, 195
Sesame Street (PBS TV show), 121
Sesame Workshop, 121
Shakespeare, W., 419
Share Our Strength, recognition of opportunity by, 42
Shrader, A., 238
Simple collaborations, 363*t*, 364
Skinner, B. F., 292
Slivinski, A., 127
Smart Roofs, 55
Smith, D. H., 8
Smucker, B., 353
Snow, C., 90, 91
Social entrepreneurship: continued expansion of, 421; description of, 36–37; framework of, 37–42; process of, 40–41; recognition of opportunity for, 41–42; special issues of, 40
Social entrepreneurship framework: context, 38*fig*–39; on opportunity, 38*fig*, 39, 41–42; on people and capital, 37–38*fig*; social value proposition, 38*fig*, 39
Social investing, 373
Social learning theory, 293–294
Social marketing, 189–191
Social media promotion, 193–194
Social responsibility: definition of, 358; how collaboration may impact, 359–360; key factors to consider for, 358–359
Social returns, 302
Social value proposition: social entrepreneurship framework on, 38*fig*, 39; Teach For America's, 39
Social Ventures Partners, 132
Socialization of workers, 270–271*fig*
Societal ethics: debate over regulatory enforcement of, 29–30; legal environment supporting, 28–29; watchdog groups setting nonprofit, 28
Soul of the agency orientation, 92*t*, 93
Southend Community Services (SCS): divisional structure of, 71; linking strategy and information process in, 75; reorganization of, 61*fig*–62; story of, 60
Southern Christian Leadership Conference, 233, 235
Specialization: definition of, 65; differentiation positioning through, 89–90
Spin-offs: description of, 53–54; entrepreneurial corporate, 54–55; mission-driven, 55; restructuring-driven, 54
St. Vincent Hospital, 45
Staff: attracting candidates, 264–267; Baby Boomer retirements affecting, 251, 420; career competencies of, 3–4; compensation, benefits, recognition, and rewards, 275–276; cycle of involvement by, 261–278; determining rationale for new, 263–264; establishing written and psychological contracts, 268–269; facilitating a safe and productive work environment, 276; Generation Y, 420, 422; maintaining records on, 276–277; measuring performance, development, and feedback for, 271–273; providing learning opportunities for, 273–274; renegotiating position of, 277–278; resistance to change by, 396–397; screening and selecting, 267–268; separation of, 277; socialization of, 270–271*fig*. *See also* Volunteers
Stakeholder mapping: description and function of, 19; example of simple, 19*fig*
Stakeholders: ensuring goal acceptance by, 15; evaluating nonprofit's ability to satisfy their, 18–19; getting evaluation buy-in from, 307; view of the nonprofit by, 31*t*

Stalker, G. M., 68
Standardization, 65
Standby letter, 158
Standing committees, 221
Statement of activities, 163
Statement of cash flows, 163
Statement of financial position, 162
Statement of functional analysis, 163
Stern v. *Lucy Webb Hayes National Training School for Deaconesses & Missionaries*, 205
Stevens, D., 364
Stevens, R. E., 96, 99
Stevenson, H., 38, 39, 315
Stone, M., 208, 371
Strategic collaborations, 373
Strategic enhancement: collaboration and, 361–362; key factors to consider for, 362
Strategic issues: definition of, 100; identification of, 100–101; moving to strategies from, 103
Strategic orientations: MacMillan's framework for nonprofits, 91–93; positioning, 89–91
Strategic philanthropy, 373
Strategic planning: American Red Cross hypothetical, 94–104; challenges to, 104–107; combining perspectives for, 107–109; general model of, 93*fig*; nonprofits and, 88–89; process of, 93–104
Strategic planning process: identification of strategic issues, 100–101; preparing to plan, 94–95; situational analysis of external and internal environments, 95–100
Strategic plans: adopting and implementing, 104; periodic review and reassessment of, 104; process of developing the, 93–104
Strategic positioning: cost leadership, 89; defender, prospector, analyzer, and reactor roles in, 90–91; differentiation, 89–90

Strategies for Change: Logical Incrementalism (Quinn), 106
Strategy: definition of, 63, 86; emergent, 104–107; information process linked to, 74–75; moving from strategic issues to, 103; nonprofit change to, 392–393; nonprofit transformations affecting, 409; OD interventions related to, 402; pragmatic approach to, 108–109; public relations, 333–334. *See also* Business strategy
Structural contingency theory, 213
Structural deficiency: decision making as, 79; declining employee performance, 79; lack of response to environmental changes, 79; too much conflict, 79
Subsidiaries, 56
Sun Tzu, 86
Sunbeam Corporation, 122
Support corporation, 56
Sussman, C., 403–404
Sustainable South Bronx, 55
SWOT analysis: of American Red Cross, 96*e*, 99*e*; description of, 95, 419; establishing strategic issues using, 101, 103; of hopeFound, 140–141; identification of strategic issues using, 100–101, 102*e*; producing realistic budget using input from, 154

T

Target audiences: government relations and related, 350; identifying and researching public relations, 334; public relations objectives related to, 331
Targeting markets, 183–184
Task-oriented leadership, 235–236
Taylor, B. E., 208, 211
TEACH!, 384, 385
Teach For America: change experienced by, 384–385, 392; contextual elements of, 38*fig*–39; founding of, 33; as innovator

organization, 34–35; organizational life cycle of, 388–389; people and capital resources of, 37–38*fig*; rapid growth problem experienced by, 406; social value proposition of, 39; story of, 384–385

Technology: definition of, 63, 74; HR capacity demands and shifts in, 260; nonprofit change to, 393, 408; organization structure and information processing, 74–77

Technostructural OD interventions, 402

Temporarily restricted assets, 148

Ten Thousand Villages, 119

Theories of change: adaptive capacity, 403–404; applied to Project Superwomen, 312*e*–313*e*; development spiral, 389, 404–407, 405*t*; evaluation application of, 309–311; innovation, 410–416; Lewin's force field model, 400–401*fig*; nonprofit transformation, 407–409; organizational development (OD), 400–403

Theory failure, 310

Thomas, J., 308

Thomas, K. W., 222, 224

Time magazine, 244

Title holding company, 56

Title VII, 267

Tolbert, P., 77

Training: performance influenced by, 283; recommendations for influencing high-performance, 284*t*

Training employees, 274

Trait theories of leadership, 234

Transactional collaborations, 363*t*, 364–365

Transactional leadership style, 237

Transformational leadership style, 237

Transparency: evaluation and accountability, 303; organizational ethic of, 27

Tschirhart, M., 295, 335

Tuckman, H., 127

Turf wars, 382

Twitter, 193

Two-factor theory, 288–290

U

UBIT (unrelated business income tax) payments, 119, 123

Uncertainty, 74

Uncommitted line, 158

"Underwater endowments," 125

Undifferentiated (mass) marketing, 183

Unincorporated association, 50

United Way of America (UWA): branding by, 185; as federated funders, 134; financial management problems of, 151–152, 244–245; franchise relationships of, 57; GAAP requirements on expenses and, 150; geographical structure of, 72; mission statement of, 45; operational efficiency pressure on, 360; outcome measurement initiative launched by, 304; resource acquisition by, 16

United Way of Central Carolinas, 268

United Way of King County, Washington, 216

University of Wisconsin–Extension, 323

Unrestricted assets, 148

Unrestricted net assets ratio, 165

Urban Institute, 114

Urban League, mission statement of, 45

Urban Life Ministries, 149

Urban Ministries of Durham, 336

U.S. Bank, 126

U.S. Department of Education, 115

U.S. Department of Health and Human Services, 115

U.S. Department of Labor, 60

U.S. Internal Revenue Code: organization tax status options under the, 51*e*; private foundations under the, 8; public-serving organizations under the, 8; tax-exempt status under the, 7, 50–53

U.S. Internal Revenue Service (IRS): employee classification by the, 268; 501(c)(3) tax status granted by, 50, 51*e*, 52, 120, 202, 346, 347, 348–349, 353; 501(c)(4) tax status granted by, 50, 51*e*, 55, 346; 501(c)(6) status granted by, 57, 346; 501(c)(7) status granted by, 120; Form 990 required by, 143, 144, 148, 377; Form 5768 of, 348; non-distribution constraint regulation of, 329; tax-exempt status granted by the, 7, 50–53; twenty-five types of nonprofits recognized by, 8; UBIT payment to, 119, 123
U.S. National Intelligence Council, 420
Utilization-focused evaluation, 309

V

Values: change in societal, 409; clarifying moral intent by promoting, 24; collaboration and incompatible, 381; personal ethics, 24; professional ethics, 25–26
Van de Ven, A., 387
The Vanguard Group, 124
Vera Institute of Justice, 55
Vertical complexity, 64
Vertical information linkages, 75–76
Visibility-related power, 245
Vision: better world, 418–419; collaboration and incompatible, 381; drifting away from mission and, 20. *See also* Mission
Volkov, B., 306
Volunteer Functions Inventory (VFI), 287
Volunteers: assessing needs fulfillment of, 287; community and grassroots organizations, 69; cycle of involvement by, 261–278; demographics of U.S. nonprofit, 9; resistance to change by, 396–397; Volunteer Functions Inventory (VFI), 287. *See also* Motivation; Staff

Von Furstenberg, D., 280
Von Schnurbein, G., 216
Vroom, V., 291

W

Walker Art Center, 415
"Walking around" management, 294
The Walmart Foundation, 115
Wanous, J. P., 270, 272
War on Poverty, 303
The Washington Post, 327–329, 330
Waters, R., 288
Webb, N., 290
Weber, M., 65, 68
Wei-Skillern, J., 38, 39, 315
Weiss, C., 314
Weiss, J., 335
Welch, P., 124
Whistle-blower protection policy, 144–145
Wikimedia Foundation, Inc., 66, 71
Wilder Foundation, 379
William and Flora Hewlett Foundation, 115
Williamson, S., 96, 99
Wilson, D., 394
Wing, K. T., 113, 114
Wise Giving Alliance, 150
Wise, L., 291
Wolf, J., 396, 398
Women's Action to Gain Economic Security, 55
WomenVenture, 416
Wood, M. M., 208, 209, 248
Work: definition of, 63; formal organizational structure of, 63; informal organizational structure of, 64
Workers. *See* Staff
World Bank, 193
World Wildlife Fund (WWF): ethical conduct guidelines of, 25; initial attitude toward for-profit businesses by, 327; recognition of opportunity by, 42

Worley, C., 400
Worth, M., 231

Y
Yale School of Management, 45
Yale University, 54–55, 124
Yankey, J., 358
YWCA, 218
Young, D., 36

Young Adult Institute, 268
Younger, Queen of Angels Hospital v., 204
Youth Opportunities grant, 60
YouTube, 193

Z
Z. Smith Reynolds Foundation, 218
Zaltman, G., 410